MEXICAN CINEMA

MEXICAN CINEMA

EDITED BY PAULO ANTONIO PARANAGUÁ

Translated by Ana M. López

BRITISH FILM INSTITUTE

bfi

BFI PUBLISHING

IMCINE

Produced in association with the
Consejo Nacional Para la Cultura y las Artes de México

First published in 1995 by the
BRITISH FILM INSTITUTE
21 Stephen Street
London W1P 2LN

In association with
IMCINE, Tepic 40, Col. Roma Sur, 06760 Mexico DF, Mexico
Copyright © British Film Institute and IMCINE 1995

This is a revised and enlarged version of *Le Cinéma mexicain*
original copyright © Editions du Centre Pompidou, Paris 1992
No. d'éditeur: 832; ISBN 2-85850-669-8
Copyright © Editorial material and selection Paulo Antonio Paranaguá 1995
Copyright © Translation Ana López 1995
Translation of *All the People Came and Did Not Fit Onto the Screen: Notes on the Cinema Audience in Mexico* and the *Preface* copyright © John King 1995
Stills courtesy of IMCINE, UNAM's Filmoteca, the BFI's Stills, Posters and Design Collection, Paulo Antonio Paranaguá

The British Film Institute exists to promote appreciation, protection and development of moving image culture in and throughout the whole of the United Kingdom. Its activities include the National Film and Television Archive; the National Film Theatre; the London Film Festival; the Museum of the Moving Image; the production and distribution of film and video; funding and support for regional activities; Library and Information Services; Stills, Posters and Designs; Research; Publishing and Education; and the monthly *Sight and Sound* magazine.

British Library Cataloguing in Publication Data
A catalogue record for this book is available from the British Library

ISBN 0-85170-515-4 hbk
       0-85170-516-2 pbk

Design: Design & Art (London)
Printed in Great Britain by The Trinity Press, Worcester

Contents

Acknowledgments

The original French edition of this book, revised and enlarged for its English publication, was produced under the aegis of the Centre Pompidou and Jean-Loup Passek to accompany an extensive retrospective of Mexican cinema at the Centre from October 1992 to February 1993. We are extremely grateful for the generous assistance provided by IMCINE and its director Ignacio Durán Loera as well as his successor Jorge Alberto Lozoya, and the director of the Filmoteca de la UNAM, Iván Trujillo Bolio, and the Cineteca Nacional.

In addition, for the English version, the help of Professor John King has been invaluable. We are also deeply indebted to the following for their unfailing support: Omar Chanona Burguete of IMCINE and Guadalupe Ferrer Andrade, the Muestra de Cine Mexicano at Guadalajara, the Mexican Ministry of Foreign Affairs, the Mexican Embassies in Paris and London, the Centre Culturel du Mexique in Paris, the Vitae Foundation in São Paulo, Mario Aguiñaga Ortuño, Salvador Alvarez Hermosillo, Francisco and Pablo Barbachano Herrero, Nelson Carro, Marc Cheymol, Miguel Angel Echegaray, Jesús Fernández Perera, María del Carmen Figueroa, María del Rosario Freixas, Emilio García Riera, Francisco Gaytán Fernández, Suzette Glénadel and the team of the Cinéma du réel in Paris, Véronique Godard, Guadalupe Gómez Rojas, Alma González Figueroa, Philippe Jacquier, Paul Leduc, Erasto Xiqui D'Leo, Abel Montaño Hernández, Carlos Narro Robles, Marie-Christine de Navacelle, Francisco Osornio Vargas, Jorge Pellicer, Gillian and Tomás Pérez Turrent, José Antonio Ramírez Castillo, Federico Serrano, Chantal Steinberg, Teresa Toledo, François Tomas, Alvaro Uribe, Jorge Antonio Valencia López and Eduardo de la Vega Alfaro.

In London, Paul Willemen, Edward Buscombe, Roma Gibson, Dawn King, Sue Bobbermein and John Smoker of the BFI deserve my warmest appreciation.

Preface to the English Edition

Ignacio Durán Loera

Cinema, the art form of our century, took root in Mexico from the earliest times and in almost one hundred years of its history, its creativity and enterprise have made it one of the most representative of Mexico's cultural treasures.

In these years, the number of cinema screens greatly increased throughout the country and became the space where cineastes, producers, artists, creators, technicians and many others gave life to genres, narrative and creative ideas and innumerable films, many of them classics and part of the universal film heritage.

The 'Retrospective of Mexican Cinema' that was held at the Georges Pompidou Artistic and Cultural Centre provided the opportunity of contributing to the study of this cinematographic tradition and its social and cultural context that we, in Mexico, have already begun. The retrospective ran for three months between October 1992 and February 1993 in the Beaubourg, and screened 140 of the most representative titles of Mexican film history, from the first views taken at the end of the 19th and beginning of the 20th century right up to the most recent films produced until 1992. This allowed for the reconsideration of directors, eras, genres, influences and new tendencies in recent production. It also offered the possibility of analysing in depth the significance and the development of Mexican cinema throughout its history and today.

This, the most complete study to date of Mexican cinema, grew out of this reflection. It brought together the most distinguished critics of Mexican cinema and was published originally in French. Now in an expanded English edition, without of course exhausting the many different possibilities opened up by the work, it offers an intelligent and critical account of Mexican cinema throughout its history, an individual and a collective endeavour aimed at those who wish either to begin or to extend their study of Mexican history and society in the field of film production, in this year of the centenary of world cinema and on the eve of the centenary of Mexican cinema, in 1996.

As in few other countries, cinema became rapidly assimilated in Mexico and bore witness to the most important events in the century, from the views of daily life in the early years to the columns of the Revolutionary armies that led the armed movement in the 1910s. For the first time, and on many occasions, cinema documented the armed struggles and the political events that would give birth to modern Mexico.

Its presence also provoked a debate about how society would be affected by the new invention, which was unusually successful in getting right inside its new audience, and which began to initiate change in the multiplicity and diversity of its cultures. Mexico was transformed by and in the cinema: the Mexico reflected on the screen and the one which, every night, was made up of uproarious audiences who learned about the existence of other Mexicans, of other nations and other realities, broadening their horizons in a way that society must do if it is to grow and extend beyond itself. Thus cinema unleashed imagination and creative potential which would stimulate intellectual debate in the country and eventually lead to works that would become essential statements about the different lives of Mexicans in the 20th century.

The first films produced in Mexico were documentaries, as were the first films made about Mexico. The latter would be shown all over the world, and Mexico, in turn, would assimilate influences from outside, helping to consolidate an industrial sector which, in its time, showed great strength, conquered markets and sustained levels of production that made it the third largest industry in the country. It was enriched by the return of a great number of Mexicans who found their first jobs in Hollywood, before, during and after the so-called Hispanic cinema period in the early 30s. Hollywood, the mecca of cinema, was also the training ground for the Rodríguez brothers, who developed their own sound invention there, and later in Mexico and gave voice to the first Mexican talkie, *Santa*, directed by Antonio Moreno in 1931. Hollywood also displayed the splendours of Dolores del Río and gave Emilio, 'el Indio' Fernández, Alejandro Galindo and many others their first work in cinema.

From Hollywood and from other parts of the world arrived Eisenstein, Paul Strand, Fred Zinnemann, Buñuel and many others who tapped into the creativity of Mexico, as can be seen in their subsequent work, even to this day.

Mexican cinema shares a similar development to

many other national cinemas. Innumerable crises and periods of enormous creative and financial vitality occurred throughout its history. However, then as now, there have always been new generations, new voices expressed on the screen who have found many different ways of ensuring its continuity.

We have produced our own versions of film genres like the *comedia ranchera* or melodrama, the rumba movies or frontier films. Also unique aesthetic works emerged, such as those imagined by 'el Indio' Fernández and Gabriel Figueroa, Ismael Rodríguez, Roberto Gavaldón, Buñuel, Jorge Fons, Arturo Ripstein, Felipe Cazals, Alfonso Arau and Paul Leduc.

The work of contemporary women directors and of the new directors, most of whom have made one or two films, like Carlos Carrera, Fernando Sariñana and Francisco Athié, give Mexican cinema its own distinctive style and narrative voice despite its proximity to the USA and its shared border. This distinctive character, which continues today in the work and the imagination of the new directors, allows us to be optimistic that it will also continue in the future. Times have changed and Mexican cinema today is striving to adapt to the new realities of the audiovisual product, especially film, in the world today. It is a difficult task, of course, but one which is not new to Mexican creators, who have always had things to say on the screen and who will doubtless continue to say them.

For these reasons the Mexican Film Institute of the National Council for Culture and the Arts was very pleased to accept the proposal of the British Film Institute to co-edit this volume. I would like to thank the following for their work on this project: Ed Buscombe and Paul Willemen for their interest and generosity, John King for his enthusiasm and Paulo Antonio Paranaguá for his careful and constant participation right from the outset of this adventure, in 1990.

Ten Reasons to Love or Hate Mexican Cinema

Paulo Antonio Paranaguá

Allow me to use the first person to emphasise the particular importance of this volume. Although I am Brazilian by birth, Mexican cinema interests me, not because of Latin American solidarity (which is all too often reduced to a kind of sacrosanct rhetoric to commemorate the dead), but for a series of reasons listed below that stir up the whole spectrum of emotions, ranging from delight to depression.

1. *Undoubtedly for the first time in Latin America, if not in the world, Mexico witnessed the birth of a contemporary political cinema directly linked to major national social upheavals.* This cinema was neither a sequel to 1968 nor a weak descendant of the thundering manifestos for a 'third cinema', an aesthetics of violence or an imperfect cinema. It was, in fact, the birth of the documentary initiated by the Revolution of 1910. Reference books on literary history recognise the existence of the Mexican Revolution novel as a genre (Mariano Azuela, Martín Luis Guzmán). Why should film history be generally unaware of the documentaries of this same Revolution? Because of contempt for the documentary? The documentary, after all, came first. One cannot write the history of world cinema by focusing only on the pre-eminence of fiction films in the industries of the hegemonic film-producing nations within the international distribution system. The minimal attention paid to documentaries and the alibi of presenting information parenthetically with which historians reduce the significance of the documentary have led to long-lasting paradoxes. A few lines have thus always been duly dedicated to the short films shot during the Spanish Republic, but the documentary explosion following June 1936, due mainly to the anarchists, communists and nationalists (notably in Catalonia), has been systematically ignored. Was cinema the only domain in which Franco's version of history successfully imposed itself? Referring to a totally analogous phenomenon, the principal historian of Mexican silent cinema, Aurelio de los Reyes, writes without hesitation in 1977:

> This first Mexican cinema constituted Mexico's principal contribution to world cinema. As time went by, this cinema has become doubly important. Firstly, because it showed images of the Revolution that no literary practice could match. Secondly, because its faithfulness to the geographic and chronological sequence of events and its desire to record 'historical events' was a local vernacular form of presenting newsreels ...

In fact, during its initial nomadic phase, travelling camera operators carried the cinema all over Mexico. These projectionist-operators thus acquired important experience (decentralisation had not yet become fashionable). In 1910, on the eve of the armed insurrection against the dictatorship, production and exhibition were nationally controlled. The foreign presence was limited to a few distributors and to technological dependence. The film business enjoyed its first boom in 1906 with the opening of the first real movie theatres. The Mexican Revolution caused business to thrive (thirty-three new theatres opened in 1911). The many peasants who arrived in Mexico City constituted enthusiastic new audiences eager to recognise themselves on the screen. *Revolución orozquista* (*Orozco's Revolution,* 1912), and its alternating montage of the troops of Huerta and Orozco, revealed the Alva brothers' concern with objectivity (they had followed Francisco Madero everywhere). Aurelio de los Reyes considers the period of the Madero regime to be the 'golden age' of Mexican cinema (although this term is normally reserved for the apogee of the film industry in the 40s).

Imbued with a moralist, paternalistic and messianic spirit, the new regime eventually inhibited this kind of cinema. Instead of filming symbolic exits from factories or churches, it focused on social upheavals and aroused the passions of the public. Censorship was established in 1913 and the Revolution had disappeared from the picture by 1916. Henceforth it would reappear only in the evocations of the past at the time of the assassinations of Emiliano Zapata (1919) and Pancho Villa (1923). It is quite paradoxical that the principal leaders of this regime, a direct product of the Revolution, were conservative, whereas the dictatorship of Porfirio Díaz, enlightened by French influences, had leaned towards liberalism. The images recorded by Salvador

1

Andrea Palma and Domingo Soler in *La mujer del puerto* (Arcady Boytler and Rafael J. Sevilla, 1933)

Toscano Barragán have been gathered in *Memorias de un mexicano* (1950), those of Jesús H. Abitia in *Epopeyas de la Revolución mexicana* (1963). It is hardly necessary to state that the organising principles of these compilations are quite different from the original intentions of the pioneers.

2. *In its preindustrial phase, the Mexican cinema exhibited both remarkable creativity and lucidity.* In the traditional film-making countries, the First World War generated changes that transformed the cinema into a big industry. In Latin America, on the other hand, the artisan or handicraft period lasted throughout the silent era and even somewhat beyond. It was during this stage that Latin American film fiction had its first successes. In Brazil, Humberto Mauro started filming at Cataguases (Minas Gerais) with rather more ingenuity than equipment, and the same was true for the production of Mario Peixoto's

only masterpiece, *Limite* (1929). In Argentina, José Agustín Ferreyra brought the populist mythology of the tango, which he was instrumental in shaping, to the screen with a great deal of imagination and improvisation and the participation of the incomparable Libertad Lamarque, just as the industry took off in Buenos Aires after the coming of sound.

In Mexico, Fernando de Fuentes captured the events of the Revolution of 1910 with undeniable lucidity and a critical eye in *El compadre Mendoza* (1933) and *¡Vámonos con Pancho Villa!* (1935). His view was quite different from the saccharine sweetness and truculence which were to follow. *El compadre Mendoza* was the first step in the direction of the anti-epic, with soldiers who dragged their guns and a protagonist who masked his weakness with the phrase: 'I am the enemy of all romanticism and little sighs.' We may interpret this as a fundamentally class-based opportunism, since the film deals with a property-owner who cannot decide whether to participate in the peasant revolt or to comply with the ruling powers. The *mise en scène* felicitously unites strange and unorthodox camera movements, surprising camera angles and framings, rapid associational transitions (dancing feet, the feet of troops interrupting the party, the feet of a hanged man). Two excellent supporting roles, that of the lawyer and the mute servant, contribute to the density of the film. *El compadre Mendoza* summarises the conflict of contemporary society through the drama of its main characters without in any way limiting the breadth of its vision.

¡Vámonos con Pancho Villa! certainly mobilized the support of Lázaro Cárdenas's army, but the camera lingers more on individual faces and characters than on the mass of extras, who at first seem slightly awkward. The characterisation of Villa does not contribute to any personality cult because the film's resolutely egalitarian humour does not spare him: when we first see him in the film, proceeding towards the populist division, one can distinguish a chamber-pot among the hats held out to catch gifts ... The on-screen Villa seemingly has no policy other than to send his men to be slaughtered, and his sense of justice seems as variable and petty as his moods. In short, in the context of all the rhetoric of a revolution which had not yet been fully institutionalised and was in the midst of a full Cardenista civic upheaval, these two films shock because of their caustic vision. They do not participate in the wave of nostalgia for the old regime of Porfirio Díaz, which would eventually unfurl across the screens almost as a separate genre.

As for the novelists, they were still at the descriptive stages and we had to wait ten or twenty years to find similarly stimulating interpretations of the founding events of contemporary Mexico by writers of the calibre of Agustín Yáñez, Juan Rulfo, José Revueltas and Carlos Fuentes. At the time of *El compadre Mendoza,* only the painter José Clemente Orozco seemed to share this irreverence while espousing the libertarian and egalitarian aspirations of the insurgent peasants and workers.

Soon after the sound revolution, Sergei M. Eisenstein, already haunted by the crushing power of Stalin, thought that everything was possible and could be reinvented in the still effervescent Mexico. In fact, the truncated experience of *¡Que Viva México!* (1931) would shatter his illusions and fascinate Mexicans for a long time to come. About this time, Arcady Boytler, a Russian who would never

again leave Mexico, was navigating a course between vice and virtue, chance and fate, woman and sin with *La mujer del puerto* (1933), an unashamedly heterogenous film making all existing and conceivable models into examples of heterodoxy.

Like Humberto Mauro's masterpiece of the same year, *Ganga bruta,* it straddled the silent and sound eras. In *La mujer del puerto,* there are two films and an epilogue. The first story, the drama of a young woman who is seduced and abandoned, immediately imposes a stylistic eclecticism. The bucolic and lyrical first love scene is followed by a rather more sordid sequence set in an undertaker's establishment. The young woman remains as pure, white and luminous as in the preceding shots, but when she finds her dying father wandering in and out of the shadows, she curses. Visually, we are always reminded of silent cinema, but the film is already able to combine styles to the degree of cutting from the mourners' grief to the seductive image of maskers on their way to a ball. Similarly, the tone is melodramatic when the heroine discovers her fiancé with another woman, but slides into mockery (the gossips who prey on her) and subsequently into excess: the father as a murderer (we see him in close-up, advancing with hammer in hand) who ends up dead. The beauty of the matches and superimpositions unifies the text and accounts for the surprises. The carnival is filmed as a documentary. When the maskers meet and take over the funeral procession, the counterpoint intensifies the drama: finally, when the maskers drop their disguises and a passage is cleared for the dead Don Antonio, his daughter Rosario appears veiled in the indigenous style.

The second part of *La mujer del puerto* is of comparable length and begins at sea, on the bridge of a ship, with an Argentine sailor singing a song. The entry into the port of Veracruz also has a rather documentary feel to it. The Argentinian goes to Nicanor's cabaret with a group of sailors – an American, a Cuban, a Frenchman and a German – all of them stereotypes. The representation of the cabaret pushes the film's penchant for detail even further and reveals a fondness for faces and close-ups. We hear and discover the most elegant *cabaretera.* Languid and beautiful, she is dressed, posed and illuminated like Marlene Dietrich: 'I sell pleasure to the men who come from the sea and leave at dawn. Why should I love?', she sings. Only a spectator trained in physiognomy could recognise her as Andrea Palma, the same actress who starred in the first part of the film. Arcady Boytler proceeds by accumulation rather than exclusion, from the Jazz parody scene to the melodramatic climax, when incest is revealed: Rosario and the Argentinian are brother and sister who have been raised apart. In between these two moments, there are such noteworthy scenes as the play of shadows in the corridor leading to the bedrooms at Nicanor's and, most of all, the cut-in to a woman's nude torso in the middle of the main characters' love scene. The resolution takes place off-camera, after Rosario runs across the jetty, her face stricken by tragedy.

Some critics have claimed, with hindsight, that *La mujer del puerto* presages the *cabaretera* films that became fashionable ten years later. In fact, it is more likely that the brothel melodramas were based upon *Santa,* an adaptation of the moralising, naturalist novel by Federico Gamboa that had already been adapted for the screen twice (by Luis G. Peredo in 1918 and by Antonio Moreno in 1931). Although prostitutes proliferated in the early sound cinema, they were all very different. This critical assessment concealed the originality of Boytler's film without contributing to our understanding, because this film's differences from the cabaret melodramas are more numerous and revealing than its similarities.

In this preindustrial stage, each film tended to constitute an independent entity, even if it was inspired by a model or aspired to become one. Just as was the case much later, when one could finally talk about an auteur cinema, directors produced prototypes and their repetition of formulae did not necessarily compromise the creativity of their work. We can find proof of this by looking at the diversity of several films. Juan Bustillo Oro explored a certain expressionism and symbolism in an enduringly peculiar film, *Dos monjes* (1934), and its two juxtaposed narrative perspectives. Fred Zinnemann, Emilio Gómez Muriel and their cameraman Paul Strand sowed the seeds of a social cinema with *Redes* (1934), but they found little support. Eisenstein's influence was not yet thoroughly entrenched, despite the fact that the photogenic representation of rural indigenous life inaugurated by Carlos Navarro in *Janitzio* (1934) found a certain following.

Nevertheless, experimentation, audacity and diversity most definitely were at play in the early Mexican sound cinema. Conversely, the rapid expansion of the industry following the unprecedented success of *Allá en el Rancho Grande* (1936) took place under the banner of uniformity and conformity. Mass production and the predominance of genres numbed the erratic impulse for innovation. The director of this latter film and

the inventor of the *comedia ranchera* (rural, peasant comedy), the much-vaunted national genre par excellence, was the very same Fernando de Fuentes of *El compadre Mendoza.* Thus de Fuentes made his mark with both the very best and the very worst of Mexican cinema (which means that later auteurs' politics miss the point of what was going on in peripheral, dependent or emergent film-making).

3. *The figures of the mother and the whore haunt the dreams of Latin Americans with a Mexican accent.* The Spanish-language films made in Joinville, Hollywood and New York in the early sound period, with their standardised language and accents, were short-lived. The artificial, hybrid character of these quickies assembled in cosmopolitan production centres provoked the same reaction all over the Spanish-speaking world. The rejection was so complete that the films were immediately put back into their boxes and thrown away, making this Hispanic production episode of the 30s a pivotal and much misunderstood period in film history.

However, the Mexican family melodrama and its fanatically devoted wives and mothers touched the Oedipus in every Latin American. An irrepressible crescendo was reached by Juan Orol's *Madre querida* (1935), Gabriel Soria's *Mater nostra* (1936), Rolando Aguilar's *Madres del mundo* (1936) and a host of others which made Sara García the perfect incarnation of the Latin mother. Long before the radio soap operas and the proliferation of *telenovelas,* the cinema was reproducing and transfiguring a sentimentality rooted in the private sphere and giving it a friendly wink of solidarity. Departing from the practice of the Spanish-language films concocted in the USA, the Mexican films' stress on folklore, on local specificities and differences earned them a following beyond the national frontiers. The success of *Allá en el Rancho Grande* in the countries north and south of Mexico did not derive from a pre-existing fashion, as was the case with the tango and Argentine film. In fact, it was the *comedia ranchera* that popularised Mexican songs in the region.

However, the paradoxically popular hold of the regionally specific, one could even say the local, was much more widespread. For instance, Tin Tan's work is clearly much more cinematic than that of Cantinflas. His referential universe always brought him back to the cinema itself. Throughout his career, Tin Tan made parodies and established a dialogue with well-known stories and figures (Zorro, Sinbad, Sleeping Beauty, the Count of Monte Cristo, the Three Musketeers, Robinson Crusoe, La Violetera).

Ninón Sevilla and Rodolfo Acosta in *Sensualidad* (Alberto Gout, 1950)

As we know, parody is the colonised's weapon: the paradigmatic, intertextual relationship of a subjugated culture to powerful models that are mocked while simultaneously reinforcing them by acknowledging their superiority and universality. In Gilberto Martínez Solares's *El rey del del barrio* (1949), Tin Tan plays with the gangster genre, the *cabaretera* films and family melodrama. He disguises himself as an archetypical Galician, Frenchman and Italian. Visual and situational gags predominate. Simply shouting 'police' provokes a disaster at the pool-hall, and freak-show women crow like roosters. Compared to Cantinflas, Tin Tan (and his mischievous, big-mouthed grin) was the more accomplished comedian, endowed with a more inventive and dynamic personality. In contrast, Cantinflas's comedic style was more static and typical of radio. He used puns and finely elaborated or improvised dialogue, often peppered with sexual innuendos. In *Ahí está el detalle* (Juan Bustillo Oro, 1940), Cantinflas distinguished himself from the wealthy men at the trial that closes the film by his fast, jerky speech much more than by his *peladito* (tramp) attire. Almost aphasic, his speech pattern is a sign of extreme poverty and dispossession, as the most extreme poverty is alienation from language. His obstinacy, however, wins through: when Cantinflas takes the stand, judge and lawyers end up imitating his speech. Nevertheless, despite the difficulty of understanding his peculiar way of talking, Cantinflas gained more public acclaim than Tin Tan, personifying the Mexican *pícaro* for spectators throughout Latin America.

The romantic, suave and lascivious world of the bolero also had its cinematic equivalent. Music, the greatest creation of the Latin American spirit, was translated into images. If there is an evident nostalgia in the term 'golden age' when it is applied to the Mexican film industry, perhaps we can trace its secret catalyst to the industry's musical and lyrical repertory, and its imprint on the public's memory. This repertory was all the more powerful because of its links to other Caribbean and Central American countries.

At the same time as it nationalised the oil industry, Mexico did the same, so to speak, with the principal Hollywood genres, adding its own characteristics to the product. Melodrama, picaresque comedy, musical comedy and urban or suburban drama were certainly all born abroad, but they found their own, undeniably Mexican, generic forms. No other Latin American film industry succeeded in creating such distinctive myths. Bound to the star system, Mexico also produced personalities who undermined its own archetypes. The most flagrant example is that of María Félix, a woman whose personality was so strong that she was able to appropriate generic mechanisms and to turn traditional roles upside down.

One particular post-war genre appears as the swamp-flower of this already decadent era: the *cabaretera* film. Ninón Sevilla was the most appealing *cabaretera,* especially when directed by Alberto Gout in intrigue-laden screenplays devised by the Spanish-born Alvaro Custodio. However, Ninón was not a typical *rumbera.* She was a blonde tropical dancer who stood out in a universe where brunettes, *mulatas,* or other 'exotics' such as Tongolele predominated. Suggestive and aggressive to the men who manipulated her, Ninón's behaviour challenged the prevailing morals and customs. In any case, the mother and the whore were finally united at the private altar of the worshippers of the Virgin of Guadalupe and contributed to shaping the libido of a large audience.

Thus, Caribbean rhythms flew down to Brazil with more authenticity than the Hollywood couple of Dolores del Río and Fred Astaire (*Flying Down to Rio,* Thornton Freeland, 1933). The exuberant María Antonieta Pons (like Ninón Sevilla, of Cuban origin) seduced the colonised intellectual played by Oscarito in the memorable *chanchada* (a farcical Brazilian comedy), *Carnaval Atlantida* (José Carlos Burle, 1952). Forty years later, the Mexican influence in Brazil through Televisa's *telenovelas* is less pervasive, although they have been able to shake TV Globo's powerful hold on the Brazilian mass audience. These troublesome characters affected spectators much more than the pious images produced by the 'serious' Mexican cinema of Emilio Fernández and Gabriel Figueroa that was celebrated in Europe. While paying homage to the undeniable personality and value of these individuals who worked in an ungrateful environment, we are allowed to prefer their few incursions into the delightfully ambiguous debauchery of the metropolis over their edifying rural dramas, crowded with limpid clouds and tortured ideas. We are presented with the two extremes of the Mexican cinema: the Oedipus complex and the Eisenstein syndrome.

4. *Luis Buñuel stopped at Mexico, completely by chance, he claims in his autobiography,* My Last Breath. An objective chance, as the surrealists would have it (after all, André Breton, Antonin Artaud and Benjamin Péret had all stopped there too). Buñuel was not the only Spanish intellectual of the 1927 generation to find a safe haven in Alfonso Reyes's homeland and to help open channels of communication between the two Hispanic cultures on either side of the Atlantic. His was not, however, the happiest of visits. While diplomats often praise Mexican hospitality, good manners barely mask a very real xenophobia which is the flip-side of nationalist excess. (Emilio Fernández even went so far as to protest against the growing Jewish influence in the Mexican film industry.) Buñuel was criticised for *Los olvidados* (1950) before winning the Cannes film festival's approval. In the regressive atmosphere of the 50s, only Buñuel and his fellow Spanish-born Mexican immigrant, Luis Alcoriza, seem to have kept their heads above water, swimming against a very strong current. Other immigrants from the Spanish Republic founded intelligent film criticism and historiography in Mexico.

A markedly Eurocentric or otherwise biased criticism tends to see Mexico as a long parenthesis in the creative career of Don Luis, untroubled by the fact that he chose to live, work and die there. Sometimes Buñuel himself contributed to this impression, as he did in his autobiography. Admittedly, Jean-Claude Carrière held the pen while Buñuel spoke in an entirely different voice (for evidence of this one need only look at the interviews with Tomás Pérez Turrent and José de la Colina or Max Aub). Mexico aroused conflicting emotions in this old surrealist who had been weathered by the defeats and tragedies of the century. He evidently held on to all the rebellious instincts he had learned in Spain and France, while his integration in Mexico, albeit troubled and bearing the marks of both acceptance and rejection, is nevertheless visible in his works. A distanced position was already fully in evidence in many of his French films from *L'Age d'or*

(1930) onwards, as it was in the vision of Spain he presents in *Las Hurdes* (1932), but the best example of this simultaneously acute and distanced viewpoint remains *Los olvidados*. Despite his personal touches, Buñuel offers the first authentic picture of Mexico City, its seedy districts and shanty towns. Urban melodrama had already run through the whole gamut of representational styles, from the *cabaretera* films to those which seem more or less to have been inspired by neo-realism (such as the films of Ismael Rodríguez and Alejandro Galindo). Nevertheless it was Buñuel, no lover of Italy's post-war cinema, who unveiled the real face of the city with the sharpness and candour of a genuine discoverer.

During the era of industrial, assembly-line production in Mexico, even the great directors could not ignore the question of genre. That Luis Buñuel had a long-term, though ambivalent, relationship with the conventions used on Mexican screens was evident from his first cinematic effort, *Gran casino* (1946), starring the inevitable Libertad Lamarque and Jorge Negrete, both formidable singers. This ambivalence reveals the tension beneath his integration into the industry and into society as a whole. His incomplete allegiance to the genres in fashion is evident in the way he undermined convention with small touches, subtle shifts, humour, by exaggerating certain features, deploying explosive characters, unusual details and final pirouettes. Thus, *La hija del engaño* (*Daughter of Deceit*, 1951) dynamites the melodrama from within with irony and excess. *Susana: carne y demonio* (1950) may be considered an anti-*comedia ranchera*, a film dedicated to the deconstruction of the ranch and the family, the two most basic staples of the Mexican cinema. With Buñuel's characteristically economical editing, desire is written all over Fernando Soler's face when he first sees Susana, although he quickly tries to cover it up. He transposes this desire to his own wife by kissing her ardently, while we are shown the cut-in of Susana's leg. The foreman (appropriately named Jesús) valiantly resists temptation, but desire soon equalises them all, transforming them into voyeurs peeping at Susana's shadow through the window, and upsetting the status quo by revealing the struggles and repressive maternal sadism implicit in these apparently trouble-free personal relationships. Both the dialogue and the images (with or without sombreros) imply a reversal of stereotypes. Fernando Soler, the bourgeois Guadalupe (the name of the patron saint of Mexico and a fitting companion for Jesús), suffers after kissing, while Susana is delighted and amused by the strife between father and son.

Born into a famous acting dynasty, Soler had already played a host of circumspect characters who were well known to audiences. In *Susana,* he became a free-falling archetype.

Similarly, Arturo de Córdova was used against type in *El* (1952). As if the Mexican star system had been thought up by Pedro Camacho, the screenwriter in Mario Vargas Llosa's *Aunt Julia and the Screenwriter,* de Córdova had been the epitome of the mature, respectable and seductive man. But for the protagonist of *El*, desire is necessarily dirty, the opposite of his servant's feelings. Furthermore, his desire gradually diminishes as he goes through stages that take him from bigotry to fetishism, from jealousy to possession and on to obsession, ending up with masturbation (on the stairs of his crazily decorated house) and alienation. As for his poor victim, she receives neither support nor consolation from her mother or the church (the tried and trusted values of Mexican cinema). Venturing even further into this simultaneously sanctimonious and secular country, Buñuel again takes up the crusade (introduced in the epilogue to *L'Age d'or*) against Catholicism, noble sentimentality, Christian charity and the spirit of sacrifice (*Nazarín, Viridiana, Simón del desierto*) before taking on all dogmas in *La Voie lactée.*

Subida al cielo (1952) is set in a village on the Guerrero hillside, prefiguring tropical Macondo, where all Mexican clichés are gathered and viewed kindly, though in a mocking light (not forgetting the Spanish chicken-vendor, a subtle dig at the origins of the director and of Manuel Altolaguirre, the producer and writer of the film and a poet of the 1927 generation). The characters' wedding night is interrupted by the dying mother who wants to make her last wishes known. This typically Buñuelian case of interrupted desire is motivated by the mother: a capricious, negative and intrusive figure, the antithesis of the omnipresent maternal screen stereotype. And Buñuel creates another mother figure, this time serenaded by the bus driver on her birthday (echoing the *mañanitas* or dawn serenades which feature in any *comedia ranchera* worthy of the name) to the great displeasure of her son, who is otherwise eager to satisfy his mother's every wish. A political candidate cannot but make a speech about the glory of mothers throughout the ages, before mistaking his supporters for a counter-demonstration (Mexico being a unique one-party regime). During a waking-dream sequence, the idolised mother is contrasted to the maternity monument erected in Mexico City (insistently invoked in Emilio

Fernández's *Victimas del pecado* (1950)). The insipid fiancée is confused with Lilia Prado whose *décolleté* is reminiscent of Rosita Quintana's in *Susana*. Moreover, both exhibit charmingly firm thighs, possibly maintained with milk as in *The Young One* (1960). But while Susana uses her breasts and shoulders to seduce, in *Subida al cielo* we see rather more of touchingly rounded buttocks. In Buñuel's work the flesh is decidedly never sad. The refreshingly liberated, spontaneous women and ridiculous, narrow-minded mothers who inhabit his Mexican films gain a unique dimension when analysed in relation to the typical female characters in the parish of Our Lady Of Guadalupe. In short, they exist in counterpoint to the figures inscribed in the genres and in the popular imagination of an entire era.

Far from being a parenthesis, during which his surrealism had to be hidden or doled out in small doses in a few dreamlike scenes (a parenthesis containing undeniable masterpieces such as *Los olvidados, El, Nazarín, El ángel exterminador* and *Simón del desierto*), Buñuel's Mexican period was an example of an indomitable personality in permanent confrontation with social and aesthetic conventions. Moreover, is it really accidental that the name Luis Buñuel became synonymous with surrealism in Latin America because of his Mexican films as much as, if not more so, than through *Un Chien andalou* and *L'Age d'or*?

5. *Mexican cinema is the most pitiful victim of the industrial mirage darkening a Latin America which grew up in the shadow of Hollywood.* Aesthetic imitation is a recurring temptation in the Third World and despite the *indigenismo* trend that followed after independence, Mexico is no exception. Just as Maximilian's empire failed to halt the French influence, punitive measures and military interventions have had no effect on the steadily growing Mexican fascination with the USA. Cinema has been simultaneously a vehicle for this penetration and one of the issues at stake in the battle. The rejection of Hollywood's images of Mexicans was one of the principal factors that led to the establishment of a local industry. However, although an excess of identification motivated screen self-representations, nationalism and imitation are inextricably woven together.

After a while, the crisis provoked by television in the established industries freed a number of European critics to focus on the new national cinemas like entomologists studying a rare species or the fruit of a new experiment in cross-breeding. The search for one's own cinematic language effectively presided over the birth of movements like Cinema Novo in Brazil, whose national breakthrough implied a specific demarcation from foreign hegemonic models. This aesthetic struggle was sometimes accompanied by a critique of the industrial production system (such was the case with Glauber Rocha in the 60s), although this line of questioning was soon abandoned. However, aesthetic forms and production models are closely linked as, for example, Italian neo-realism and the French New Wave demonstrated. There never was any irresistibly compelling technical reason for organising the mass production of films in big Hollywood-type studios, neither in the 30s nor today. One must not confuse the minimum technical needs (infrastructure, laboratories, sound recording and filming equipment, props, recording studios and even sound stages) with a specific production method. In Argentina and Mexico, it was always assumed that very little was possible unless one disposed of Hollywood's resources. The same was true in Brazil, as illustrated by the quickly aborted Vera Cruz experiment (although there, it was more like an attempt to relocate Cinecittà, personnel and all).

The Mexican industry used and abused several genres in record time: the *comedia ranchera* and the family melodrama; later, the picaresque comedy, the religious drama, adaptations of literary classics and the urban drama. This surfeit of production doubled the number of films released after the Second World War, when the decadence of the industry was already firmly established. The list of studios which opened one after the other is long: even without mentioning the more temporary establishments and limiting ourselves to the sound period, there were México Films (1932), Clasa (1935), Azteca (1937), Churubusco (1944), Cuauhtémoc (1945, which became Studio América in 1957), Tepeyac (1946) and San Angel Inn (1951). The capital had as many as fifty-eight sound stages. This was not only a symptom of a forward push, but also of an attitude very much at odds with the times. To be more precise: production leaned towards *El conde de Montecristo* (Chano Urueta, 1942) rather than towards Buñuel's *Los olvidados*.

Another persistent myth sees industrialisation as a guarantee of national autonomy. The Mexican film industry did not plunge into serious industrialisation in opposition to Hollywood, but rather with its blessing, interested protection and active participation. The first boom followed *Allá en el*

Rancho Grande (21 films in 1933, 57 in 1938) and benefited from the sudden decrease in Spanish fiction film production during the Civil War. The crisis was temporarily checked. The Second World War gave another burst of energy to the Mexican industry (70 films in 1943, 82 in 1945). This conflict also provoked a certain propagandistic tone in Hollywood and caused difficulties within the traditional European film-producing nations. The Spanish-speaking market was, therefore, for the taking. The USA backed Mexico's efforts, which seemed closer (despite its nationalist tendencies) than Franco's Spain, where cinema was rapidly taking off, or neutral Argentina, its only serious rival. Churubusco was built thanks to RKO's 50 per cent stake, while the American William Jenkins consolidated his exhibition monopoly. Even growing state participation in the industry did not check this tendency towards amicable co-operation: while the Banco Cinematográfico (founded in 1942, it became an official national institution in 1947) was set up with government and private funds, the latter were provided primarily by the Marine Midland Trust and the Bank of America. At the peak of his success, Cantinflas made profits for Columbia Pictures. Poor Mexico, so far from God and so close to Hollywood.

6. *Mexico has promoted the concept of state participation in the film industry more than any other Latin American country, except Cuba.* This state participation was geared to save what was there, rather than to shape production culturally or socially. Certainly, during General Lázaro Cárdenas's government (a brief return to the origins of the Mexican Revolution), support for the production of *Redes* and *¡Vámonos con Pancho Villa!* came from the very top, but there was no follow-up. The Clasa company produced barely one film before the state was called upon to come and rescue it from bankruptcy. If a governmental decree made the exhibition of at least one domestic feature film in all theatres obligatory after 1939 (so as to combat the market's preference for imports), censorship regulations included prior censorship of scripts (introduced in 1941) and some highly placed civil servant did not hesitate to declare that films like *El compadre Mendoza* could not be tolerated now. Film-making was placed under the control of the Ministry of the Interior as if it were some common police matter.

The growing intervention of the state after the war vainly attempted to halt the collapse of the industry. Around 1954, the Banco Nacional Cinematográfico (BNC) was in charge of both national and overseas distribution. It took over the laboratories and the Churubusco-Azteca studios in 1959 and, in 1960, the chain of theatres owned by Compañía Operadora de Teatros (COTSA), which controlled 321 screens in Mexico City alone. Eventually, the BNC was financing over half the films produced (70 per cent in 1965 and in 1970). In short, cinema had become a state industry when its collapse was almost complete. The nationalisation demanded by the left had benefited the right: the losses had been debited to the national purse. Other Latin American countries do not seem to have taken heed of this experience. Throughout the 70s and the 80s, many Latin American governments assumed a leading role within their national industries, oscillating between vigilant censorship and invasive protectionism.

7. *The Mexicans were the first to attempt to break the distribution blockage.* Distribution, the Achilles heel of the Argentine industry and the Vera Cruz studios (Lima Barreto's *O Cangaceiro* of 1953 also benefited Columbia Pictures), has been the Gordian knot which film industries dominated by foreign productions could not unravel. Even *Allá en el Rancho Grande* was distributed by United Artists. In the domain of the culture industries, one did not yet speak of unequal exchange and unilateral flow. Such notions have now earned UNESCO an undeserved reputation as a subversive organisation and provoked the wrath of the USA.

As early as 1945, Mexican producers had founded the Pelmex distribution company and were already attempting to preserve their foreign market. At one time, Pelmex undoubtedly was the principal distributor in Latin America, operating in roughly twenty countries through a dozen branches, and with a stake in exhibition in order to get the better of the Hollywood multinationals. For example, its former theatres in Brazil became the basis for the circuit of the now-defunct Brazilian Cinema Co-operative founded by Cinema Novo veterans in 1980. Contrary to popular belief, Latin America was never a natural market for any industry other than Hollywood's. From the start, the market had been shaped, expanded and consolidated to serve imports. The golden era when there was a good relationship between exhibition and production, more harmonious than when they both were under the same control, scarcely lasted longer than the primitive and unstable nomadic phase of the industry. Although Mexican producers created Películas Nacionales in 1947 to control domestic distribution, they did not contest Jenkins's monopoly, and they paid for this dearly. Individuals like the indomitable writer José Revueltas and the old nationalist film-maker Miguel Contreras Torres were the lone critical voices in an environment in which the methods of Jenkins's gangsters (comparable to those of the government-controlled unions) barely raised eyebrows. Exhibition is the last defensive bastion of the foreign interests in dependent film markets.

8. *Attempts to renew the industry from the 60s onwards generated both hope and despair.* Mexico is not only the country of the frozen Revolution, but also that of stifled renovations. Unlike Argentina, Brazil and Cuba, Mexico's film industry did not experience a lasting revitalisation in the 60s, that phenomenal decade in which new waves seemed to be taking off simultaneously in Paris, Tokyo, Prague and New York. In an earlier period, neo-realism failed to make the kind of impact in Mexico that it had achieved elsewhere in Latin America, despite the presence of Cesare Zavattini in Mexico and the numerous projects envisaged by the independent producer Manuel Barbachano Ponce. Perhaps this was because of the industry's sluggishness: in the mid-50s, when the neo-realist influence was felt in Brazil and Argentina, national industrial production was in shambles. In Mexico, on the other hand, the traditional industry was still churning out movies despite the deadly stagnation caused by twenty years of the closed-door policy followed since 1946. However, a different conception of cinema did emerge, outside the industry, where a developing film culture joined forces with a growing political consciousness. Cuba and the French New Wave were not far away.

The timid efforts to open a space within the existing system (such as the first Experimental Cinema Competition organised by one of the trade unions in 1965) had failed. For a decade (1966–76), Mexico tried to adopt the tone of the New Latin American Cinema. The progressive nationalisation of the film industry had led to a false and dangerous cultural and economic situation. The new generations had to take the hazardous path of so-called independent productions enabled by universities, the new film schools and actors' and technicians' co-operatives. Trapped in a deceptive microcosm and evolving out of step with the rest of Latin America, Mexican film-makers could not find their own voice and were unable to consolidate their position. At the same time, because they had broken with the traditional producers, they were subject to the hostility of powerful sectors

determined to dismantle the framework built before and during Echeverría's government.

In any event, efforts to revitalise the cinema in the 60s and 70s were primarily thematic. Questions of a different cinematic language and of formal innovation were hardly ever posed as they had been in Brazil, Cuba and Argentina. It was as if the cinematic past, no matter how hollow, weighed too heavily in the present. The new Mexican film-makers explored other subjects, invented other characters and obviously distanced themselves from the old genres, but rarely did they construct their stories differently. The exceptions to this rule were Alejandro Jodorowsky and his friend Rafael Corkidi, but they moved very much in the margins of the industry. In some cases, there was evidence that Luis Buñuel was no longer regarded as an isolated, alien figure. Many had begun to assimilate his lessons, which helped to strengthen the anti-naturalist trend and the resistance to neo-realism.

A case in point is a film-maker who preceded this generation, Luis Alcoriza, especially because he had no qualms about working within the industry. His most personal films search elsewhere rather than differently. In *Tiburoneros* (1962) and *Tarahumara* (1964), we see the coast and the sierra, the shark-fishers and the Indians, counterposing, without excessive Manicheism, two types of liberated life in touch with nature against contemporary society. In a sense, his view is tinged by nostalgia. However, his commitment to the Indian, a true Mexican archetype, does not repeat the aesthetic idealism characteristic of the indigenist trend from Emilio Fernández's *María Candelaria* (1943) and *La perla* (1945) to Roberto Gavaldón's *Macario* (1959) via Benito Alazraki's *Raíces* (1953). Parenthetically, we should note that a new approach to indigenous communities would emerge within the documentary, notably in the works of Nicolás Echevarría and Paul Leduc.

Without doubt, the cinephile generation of the journal *Nuevo Cine* (1961) did try to find its own voice. Their film manifesto, Jomí Miguel García Ascot's *En el balcón vacío* (*On the Empty Balcony*, 1961), was a contemporary of the New Wave and Antonioni and feels like Saura *avant la lettre*, mainly because of its mournful tone and its memory of the Spanish Civil War as seen through the eyes of little girl who could be Ana Torrent's sister, as well as its deliberately subjective style. Similarly, Rubén Gámez's *La fórmula secreta* (1964), the winner of the first Experimental Cinema Competition, is reminiscent of surrealism, of Manuel Alvarez Bravo's photography and of Juan Rulfo, which are rare

El imperio de la fortuna (Arturo Ripstein, 1985)

allusions indeed. Nevertheless, this 'leap year' director gifted with a singular vision had to wait another twenty-five years before he could make his next feature, *Tequila* (1992). *Familiaridades* (1969) revealed Felipe Cazals's experimental streak. But the follow-ups to all these efforts were more than problematic. On the other hand, there is no shortage of revamped subjects and characters. These can be found in Alberto Isaac's *En este pueblo no hay ladrones* (*There Are No Thieves in This Town,* 1964) or *Los días del amor* (*The Days of Love,* 1971), in Jaime Humberto Hermosillo's *La pasión según Berenice* (1975) or *Las apariencias engañan* (1977), in Arturo Ripstein's *El castillo de la pureza* (1972), *El Santo Oficio* (1973), *El lugar sin límites* (1977) or *Cadena perpetua* (1978), in Felipe Cazals's *El apando* (1975) or *Las poquianchis* (1976). An exception is Cazals's *Canoa* (1975), which offers an original, albeit documentary-inspired, narrative.

José Estrada's *Los indolentes* (1977) has an almost unique setting, as magnificent as Manuel Fontanals's sets for *El castillo de la pureza* and as fantastic as the setting of *El.* The director, as much a voyeur as his hero, depicts the world with the help of numerous inserts and with an attention to detail worthy of Alejo Carpentier.

He veers towards the abstract in his accumulation of isolated details, fetish objects (a bed for the image of the Holy Virgin), associated images (incense and billiards, maternal masturbation and her son taking breakfast) and bestiality. One can see Buñuel's influence here just as clearly as in Jorge Fons's sketch in *Fe, esperanza y caridad* (1972), but that is to their credit. The little old lady who inaugurates all the dramas made by Fons is, of course, played by Sara García. Although *Cadena perpetua* consciously borrows from the thriller genre, Ripstein is also indebted to Buñuel.

Even such a beacon of this generation's work as Paul Leduc's *Reed, México insurgente* (1971), owes its initial impact to its historical point of view (the human side of the Revolution) and to its production methods rather than to its representational style or its narrative structure. We almost have to wait until *Frida, naturaleza viva* (1984) finally to perceive the primacy of *mise en scène* in Leduc's work. *Frida* is a doubly important milestone: because of its own success and because, having become more aware of their aesthetic choices, film-makers began to exhibit personal touches. Ariel Zúñiga's *El diablo y la dama o El itinerario del odio* (*The Devil and the Lady* or *The Itinerary of Hate,* 1983) successfully reworked the *cabaretera* film with marked modernist touches. In some instances, it was a question of the film-makers becoming more mature, as in Ripstein's case (*La mujer del puerto,* 1991) or in Nicolás Echevarría's long-deferred first feature, *Cabeza de Vaca* (1990). In other cases we are dealing with young film-makers trained in film schools and able to resist the seductive sirens' chant of imitation and fashion: Dana Rotberg's *Angel de fuego* (1992), Carlos Carrera's *La mujer de Benjamín* (1990) or María Novaro's *Danzón* (1991).

Surprisingly, to the degree that it is possible to find a common denominator between old and new film-makers, they seem to share a similar attitude towards tradition. In *Latino Bar* (1990), Leduc adapts and reinterprets *Santa,* Federico Gamboa's often filmed naturalist novel. Ripstein also revisited the classics. Juan Rulfo's *El gallo de oro,* filmed by Roberto Gavaldón (1964), becomes Ripstein's *El imperio de la fortuna* (1985). He also remade Arcady Boytler's *La mujer del puerto,* playing hide and seek with melodrama. María Novaro evokes dance and Veracruz, two heavily connotative motifs, and Carrera's film is reminiscent, perhaps unconsciously, of Buñuel's *The Young One.* In short, film-makers from both contingents established a fruitful dialogue with the past without neglecting the essential: a renewal of its form. This renewal thus coincided with a revitalisation of their ancient roots.

9. *Film research, criticism and historiography were affected by national events.* The *Nuevo Cine* group, even if they did not successfully transform film production to the extent they had hoped, were at least able to establish a different critical approach to the cinema. Their magazine was fairly short-lived, but they found other areas in which to exercise their influence. Thanks to them, in particular, the introduction of film studies at university level

fortunately did not result in the hegemony of pseudo-scientific work and theoretical abstraction fashionable in the northern hemisphere. Stimulating work on the past and the present of their respective cinemas was produced in Mexico City, Guadalajara, São Paulo and Rio de Janeiro. Technical and academic training also found a place at these institutions (the shock treatment Argentine universities experienced after 1966 explains the delay in Buenos Aires).

In Mexico, the work of Emilio García Riera and his successors, Jorge Ayala Blanco's first writings, Aurelio de los Reyes's research, and the studies by Carlos Monsiváis and Tomás Pérez Turrent were as decisive as those of Paulo Emilio Salles Gomes, Jean-Claude Bernardet, Maria Rita Galvão, Ismail Xavier or José Carlos Avellar in Brazil. They broadened cinematic analysis and its conceptual framework which, until then, had been based on the theories of the directors themselves (notably Glauber Rocha, Fernando Solanas and Octavio Getino, Jorge Sanjinés and Julio García Espinosa). The ground-breaking critics who appeared in the 60s were no longer isolated: they were joined by other enthusiasts of the new generations, able to multiply the discoveries and perspectives, broaden the methodological realms, enliven new specialised journals, and establish a much-needed debate about works, genres, film-makers and mythologies. These historians, essayists and critics forced a rediscovery of Mexican cinema, its re-inscription as one of the richest stores of images produced in Latin America: nearly 5,000 films (more than the combined production of all other Latin American countries) whose psycho-analytical, ideological, sociological, iconographic, semiotic and historical interpretation still has much to teach us about our tame imaginary and our collective unconscious.

Of course, still many shadowy areas await clarification and study to enhance our enjoyment of Mexican cinema. There is no doubt that Mexican cinema's bibliography is already one of the largest in Latin America (even excluding works about Buñuel), but the subject is far from exhausted. Students searching for a topic for a thesis, researchers and simple cinephiles are still in luck. But only on condition, of course, that access to these films is not prevented ...

10. *Hope is always allowed, for it is cyclically reborn in Mexico as elsewhere in Latin America.* The evolution of Mexican cinema has avoided the implacable succession of presidential mandates for a long time.

In fact, we can sketch the following periodisation:

1896–1916: primitive nomadism and Revolutionary documentaries
1917–1930: period of imitation of foreign fiction cinema
1931–1936: artisan and experimental sound period
1937–1946: industrial apogee with fixed codes and genres
1947–1964: industrial decadence and the regressive repetition of old formulae
1965–1976: attempts at renewal, the timid appearance of an auteur cinema and the resurgence of nationalism
1977: dismantlement of the film industry

The fire at the Cineteca Nacional in Mexico City in 1982 was not only a tragic disaster, it also symbolically crowned Margarita López Portillo's cinematic reign. Things could not have been worse. Since then, many young directors have been able to make their first features, while experienced film-makers have rediscovered more personal routes. Significantly, the young student population and the middle class seem to have re-bonded with the national cinema they had previously, and quite understandably, rejected. The Mexican Cinema Festival organised by the Guadalajara university since 1986 was a first sign, confirmed by the subsequent success of several of the films shown there. Without audiences, any cinematic renewal is stillborn. It is symptomatic of the roadblocks still in place that this renewed encounter with the most demanding sector of the public occurred with Jorge Fons's *Rojo amanecer* (1989), the first film openly to tackle the subject of the 1968 student massacre at Tlatelolco (or the Plaza of Three Cultures) in Mexico City. With self-censorship and without freedom of expression, renewal is not possible.

However, the question we can still legitimately ask is whether Mexican cinema has entered a new phase or whether these recent events are simply isolated incidents without a future. The dismantling of the old industrial system has continued, legitimately, because of the industry's need to disentangle itself from the state. Neo-liberal ideas are also circulating south of the Rio Grande, which is not surprising given that these days the presidents are educated at Harvard. After all, the previous stagnation of the industry and the subsequent artificiality of state-controlled production do not make us mourn the sale of studios which almost no Mexican film-makers used anymore, or of theatres which never showed domestic films (or which were lamentably ill-equipped and uncomfortable).

Other means of support, other organisations providing incentives and promotion, new production formulae (as well as new forms of distribution and exhibition) must undoubtedly take over. The problem is that no one can guarantee their creation or continuity. While Canada tried to protect its cultural industries during the free-trade agreement discussions with the USA, Mexico did not seem to want to follow this course. The foundation of a huge single North American market is a defeat: for many Mexicans, it implies a direct confrontation of their cultural identity with Anglo-Saxon imperialism. Five hundred years after the Conquest, a new war of images has begun. There is a very real danger that Mexican films will be consigned to museums, alongside Meso-American artefacts, despite their considerable interest and artistic merit. Will Mexico have any other choice but to watch its film industry disappear under the lengthening shadow of Hollywood and the power of the local Televisa conglomerate? Cultural politics aside, this question also has symbolic value. To what extent will the Mexican cinematic tradition and its 5,000 films continue to have an effect on the collective imagination? Will this past remain present on the small screen, as it has until now, to the point of transforming old Mexican films into a living cinema? Will future generations choose to prolong or deny this tradition? It does not matter which, as long as they still desire to establish a dialogue with it, to express themselves with cameras, and to produce their own images. Love it or hate it, Mexican cinema has no worse enemy than indifference.

Mexico and its Cinema

Alexander Pineda and Paulo Antonio Paranaguá

1895

General Porfirio Díaz has been in power for nineteen years since his *coup d'état;* favouritism and corruption are rife. He opened the nation to foreign capital, created a vast railroad network, regulated the ports and valorised its mineral wealth. Industrial development is spectacular, but so are social inequalities: in the mines and the haciendas, production is assured by a mass of semi-enslaved workers. Mexico has 12,632,000 inhabitants.

José Guadalupe Posada introduces a zinc engraving technique and produces almost 20,000 prints. Publication of the photographically illustrated newspaper *El Mundo Ilustrado*. Introduction of the *danzón,* originally from Cuba. The composer Julián Carrillo begins to use micro-intervals in musical composition. Production of Vicente A. Galicia's *zarzuela, El vice-almirante.*

The Edison Kinetoscope comes to Mexico City (17 January) and to Guadalajara (30 May).

1896

Porfirio Díaz is re-elected to a fourth presidential term. The telephone network, installed in Mexico City in 1882, expands to the provincial cities. The mining industry is electrified: the first motors are installed in the Santa Ana mines.

Publication of the newspaper *El Tiempo Ilustrado* and closure of the liberal papers *El Siglo XIX* and *El Monitor Republicano*. José Guadalupe Posada begins to design his famous *calaveras* (skulls) in the illustrations of the *Calendario del Padre Cobos*. Federico Gamboa publishes the novel *Suprema ley*. Production of the first Mexican *zarzuela, Verbena de Guadalupe*, based on the Spanish *Verbena de la Paloma*. Musicians praise the polka recently imported from Europe: Salvador Molet composes 'Las bicicletas' and Jacinto Osorio 'Las mandolinistas'.

Gabriel Veyre and C.F. Bon. Bernard introduce the Cinématographe Lumière to Mexico. The first public screening takes place in Mexico City on 14 August. It is presented in Guadalajara from 20 October. Veyre and Bon. Bernard shoot the first documentaries: *Le Président* [Porfirio Díaz] *prenant congé de ses ministres, Transport de la cloche de l'Indépendance, Ruraux au galop, Le Président en promenade, Exercice à la baïonette, Lassage d'un cheval sauvage, Repas d'Indiens, Lassage d'un boeuf, Danse mexicaine, Lassage des boeufs pour le labour, Marché indien sur le canal de la Viga, Cavalier sur un cheval rétif, Baignade des chevaux, Bal espagnol dans la rue.* Screenings of Edison's Vitascope in Mexico City and in Guadalajara (27 September).

1897

Creation of the Confederation of Railway Workers of the Mexican Republic, the base for future labour unions.

Introduction of the phonograph. The landscape painter José María Velasco paints *El Citlaltepetl*. Posada publishes his engraving *Algo podrido en el Estado de Dinamarca* in the newspaper *El Popular*.

First projectionist-exhibitors appear in various locations: at the Guerrero theatre in Puebla, Churrich presents *Corrida entera de toros por la cuadrilla de Ponciano Díaz, Verbena del Carmen el la ciudad de Puebla,* and *Pelea de gallos en Guadalajara;* in Mexico City, Ignacio Aguirre presents *Riña de hombres en el Zócalo* and *Rurales mexicanos al galope;* In San Luis Potosí, Henri Moulinié presents *Llegada del presidente Díaz a su palacio en el castillo de Chapultepec acompañado de sus ministros.* Screenings also in Orizaba, Mérida (at the Peón Contreras theatre), San Juan Bautista (in the state of Tabasco, at the Merino theatre), Tepic, Guanajuato and in the state of Sonora. In Guadalajara, screenings in the Principal theatre, then in the city's most luxurious Degollado theatre.

1898

French people originally from the Low Alps, the Barcelonnettes, make their fortune in business and textiles. The first automobiles arrive in Veracruz.

Publication of the *Revista Moderna* featuring modernist writers, composers, painters and sculptors.

In Mexico City, Salvador Toscano shows *Norte en Veracruz, El Zócalo, La Alameda, Corridas de toros en las plazas mexicanas, Escenas de la Alameda;* in Celaya he shows *Pelea de gallos, Charros mexicanos lazando un potro, Llegada del Tlacotalpan a Veracruz, Corrida de toros por Guerritas.* In Veracruz, there are screenings at the Principal theatre, in Mexico City at the Nacional theatre, in Monterrey at the Juárez theatre. Sessions are also organised in Tehuantepec.

Edison cameramen film in Mexico.

1899

Socialist ideas circulate in the Yucatán peninsula in an ephemeral newspaper published by the Spaniard José Zaldívar. Establishment of Patricio Milmo e Hijos, a banking and investment house with interests in mining and railroads.

Mexico adopts the *zarzuela:* the poet Amado Nervo writes the sentimental operetta *Consuelo;* the Principal theatre presents *La cuarta plana,* in which the future star Esperanza Iris makes her mark; Rafael Medina stages *Los de abajo,* a comedy of manners tinged with political satire (the title was later recycled by the novelist Mariano Azuela).

Guillermo Becerril shows *Maniobras militares en San Lázaro el 4 de abril* in Mexico City and in Tepic. In Mexico City, Salvador Toscano films and presents scenes from a production of *Don Juan Tenorio;* in San Luis Potosí, he shows, among other titles, *Rosario Soler en Sevillanas* and *Luisa Obregón y su esposo en Canarios de Café.* Carlos Mongrand exhibits *Entrada de una boda a una iglesia* and *Salida de empleados de una fábrica* in Matehuala.

1900

Population: 13,607,000 inhabitants, with 345,000 in Mexico City. While the Yaqui Indians continue the armed struggle for their lands in the north, the government begins a military campaign against the indigenous peoples of the states of Yucatán and (present-day) Quintana Roo. The brothers Ricardo and Enrique Flores Magón establish the anarchist weekly *Regeneración.* Congress re-elects Porfirio Díaz to a new presidential term. Introduction of electric streetcars.

Premiere of Ricardo Castro's opera *Atzimba.* Demolition of the ancient national theatre; the Italian architect Adamo Boari will undertake the construction of a new one, the Palacio de Bellas Artes, which will not be finished for another thirty-four years. Opening of the Renacimiento theatre starring Virginia Fábregas. Great success of the Spanish *zarzuela Cara de Dios.* Ernesto Icaza paints *La suerte de varas,* featuring the bullfighter Ponciano Díaz in the ancient bullrings of Mexico City.

Salvador Toscano makes *Saliendo de la catedral de Puebla.* The Becerril brothers produce *En las chinampas, Desfile de carros alegóricos, Riña en una canoa, Carpinteros en el taller, Segadores en el campo* and *Baile familiar;* in Toluca, they present *Vistas de Tenango del Valle.* Carlos Mongrand films and organises screenings in Veracruz, Jalapa and

Guanajuato: *Suertes de toros ejecutadas por Antonio Fuentes, Bailes por la señora Soler, Vistas de Veracruz, Retrato del general Mucio Martínez, Jardín del Cantador de Guanajuato, Jardín de la Unión en Guanajuato.* Mexico City has 22 film projection sites, but precarious installations force most exhibitors to close their locales or to go on the road.

1901

Oil prospecting begins. Progress in the sugar industry, the most industrialised of the agricultural sector. The fall of Chan Santa Cruz ends fifty years of quasi-independence for Yucatán. Tetabiate, the chief of the Yaquis, dies in battle. In San Luis Potosí, opponents of Porfirio Díaz organise the anti-reelectionist club Ponciano Arriaga. Birth of the Confederación Nacional Liberal.

Triumphal tour of the Italian transformist Fregoli. María and Teresa Conesa make their debut as chorus girls with the group La Aurora Infantil. Opera and the Spanish *zarzuela* continue in fashion among the elites, but pieces by Mexican authors begin to attract popular audiences to the Principal, María Guerrero and Manuel Briceño theatres. Miguel Lerdo de Tejada creates a typical orchestra. Carlos Curti composes the polka 'El diablito'.

In Colima, the Becerril brothers present *Los bufos de Cyutlán.* In Orizaba, screening of *La llegada del general Porfirio Díaz al Palacio Nacional* (Francisco Sotarriba) and of films with musical accompaniment. In Mexico City Salvador Toscano shows the films he brought back from Paris at the Orrin circus. Other exhibition sites open towards the end of the year.

1902

Inauguration of the central post office in Mexico City, the work of Italian architect Adamo Boari. Second congress of the Clubes Liberales at San Luis Potosí. The daily *El Hijo del Ahuizote,* directed by the brothers Flores Magón, begins a campaign against Porfirio Díaz.

The production of the play *Guadalupe,* Marcelino Dávalos's fierce critique of Porfirian society, causes a scandal in Mexico City. First work by José F. Elizondo, *La gran avenida,* a parody of the *zarzuela, La gran vía.* Creation of the Sociedad de Autores Mexicanos. The painter José María Velasco continues his series of landscapes with *Vista de Querétaro.* Publication of Rafael Delgado's novel *Los parientes ricos.* Alberto M. Alvarado composes the waltzes 'Rio Rosa' and 'Recuerdo'.

The nomadism of the pioneers reaches new heights: Carlos Mongrand presents *El señor general*

Díaz y su esposa paseando a caballo en el bosque de Chapultepec in Aguascalientes, Zacatecas (at the Calderón theatre), Guanajuato (Principal theatre) and Guadalajara (Degollado theatre). Films are screened in Chihuahua at the theatre de los Héroes.

1903

First automobile race in Mexico. The metallurgical industry is born with the installation of La Fundidora de Hierro y Acero de Monterrey, the first blast furnace in Latin America (with French businessman Léon Signoret as principal stockholder). Construction begins at the Necaxa dam. The Flores Magón brothers reorganise the Círculo Liberal.

Publication of the novel *Santa* by Federico Gamboa, the 'Mexican Zola'. Inauguration of the Juárez theatre of Guanajuato, designed by the architect Antonio Rivas Mercado. The Principal theatre presents Aurelio González Carrasco's *La sargenta* featuring a popular female character who is the precursor of the famous *Adelita*. Julio Ruelas illustrates the *Revista Moderna*.

Carlos Mongrand films *El coronel Ahumada llegando en su coche al palacio de gobierno de Guadalajara, Los charros mexicanos* and *Time is Money*, a comedy. The Becerril brothers film *El carnaval de Mazatlán*. *Jarabe tapatío* is presented in Pachuca (Hidalgo).

1904

President Porfirio Díaz is re-elected for the sixth time. Massive deportation of Yaqui Indians to the large aloe (*henequén*) plantations of Yucatán. The church encourages the creation of co-operative Catholic workers' groups. Establishment of the Gran Liga Mexicana de Obreros Ferroviarios.

José F. Elizondo writes the first great success of the Mexican popular theatre or *género chico*: the *zarzuela, Chin chun chan,* featuring the comedian Anastasio 'Tacho' Otero, a precursor of Cantinflas. Wilhelm Kahlo photographs the most important buildings and monuments built during the Porfirio Díaz regime, intending to publish them as a book.

Carlos Mongrand makes a first attempt at fiction film by invoking historical figures: *Cuauhtémoc y Benito Juárez, Hernán Cortés, Hidalgo y Morelos.* Toscano and Barreiro film *Fiestas del 16 de septiembre en Tehuacán.* Agustín Jiménez and Enrique Rosas shoot *Vistas de Orizaba y alrededores* and *La Cervecera Moctezuma de Orizaba.* In Mexico City, the tobacco company El Buen Tono organises open-air screenings on the Alameda Central.

1905

Successful aloe production brings prosperity to Mérida (Yucatán), where mansions are built with marble imported from Europe. Discovery of important petroleum deposits. The electricity generator at Necaxa begins service. First Congreso de Trabajadores. The Flores Magón brothers devote themselves to the organisation of the Partido Liberal.

Julián Carrillo takes over the direction of the Mexican conservatory. The Hidalgo theatre presents a lyrical drama about the French exped-ition to Mexico entitled *Patria y honra o la intervención francesa.* Publication of the magazine *Arte y Letras.* Amado Nervo publishes his poems *Los jardines interiores.* Catholic church officials ban the *mojigangas,* popular masquerades organised around Easter.

Nomadic filming and exhibition is still the norm: Carlos Mongrand films *Plaza de Armas de Chihuahua, De Guadalupe a Zacatecas en un tren en marcha, Ceremonia al pie del monumento del mártir de la patria Melchor Ocampo en Morelia, Paseo en coche por la plaza principal, calle de San Francisco y calle del palacio del gobierno de Guadalajara.* Various current events test the agility of the cameramen: Salvador Toscano records *La inundación de Guanajuato,* presented in Puebla. Enrique Rosas challenges him with *Vistas al día siguiente de la inundación de Guanajuato,* screened at León and Orizaba. Gonzalo T. Cervantes films *Grupo de señoritas de las principales familias de Orizaba* and *12 vistas tomadas 6 horas después de la catástrofe del ferrocarril mexicano en el puente de Metlac.* Augusto Venier films *Salida de misa de 12 de la catedral de Hermosillo.* The brothers Jorge, Carlos and Alfonso Stahl inaugurate the Salón Verdi in Guadalajara.

1906

British and North American companies begin and control petroleum exploitation. Creation of the anarchist-influenced Gran Círculo de Trabajadores Libres. The strike organised by the miners of Green Consolidated Copper in Cananea (Sonora) is violently repressed by the army: 23 dead. Distribution in St Louis (Missouri) of the Programa del Partido Liberal and of a manifesto inviting the people to rise against the dictatorship. 800 cars circulate in Mexico City.

A show of young painters includes works by Diego Rivera, Gerardo Murillo (Dr Atl), Francisco de la Torre and Ponce de León. A group of intellectuals, including Alfonso Reyes, Antonio Caso, José Vasconcelos and Pedro Henríquez Ureña, organises literary soirées in Mexico City. The poet Amado Nervo writes *Almas que pasan*. Publication of the magazine *Savia Moderna*. In Guanajuato, Romualdo García masters the photographic portrait.

Enrique Rosas's *Fiestas presidenciales en Mérida* is c.3,000m long. Salvador Toscano's *Viaje a Yucatán* combines two newsreels about Porfirio Díaz with editing to improve narration. Jorge and Carlos Stahl present *Acróbatas en el circo Orrin* in Tepic. The brothers Salvador, Guillermo, Eduardo and Carlos Alva film *Kermesse del Carmen* in Mexico City. Antonio Gómez Castellanos shoots *Vistas de Zacatecas*. The consolidation of the film business reduces nomadism. Mexico City has over thirty exhibition sites and, at last, permanent cinemas: the Academia Metropolitana holds 600 spectators and La Boite seats 400. The smaller sites are called Paris, Majestic, Salón Mexicano, Salón High Life, Salón Art Nouveau, Salón de Moda, Salón Rubiar, Salón Verde, Pabellón Morisco, Arcadia, Salón Variedades, San Francisco, Apolo, Sala Pathé (the French company's subsidiary in Mexico), Spectatorium, Salón Rojo, Montecarlo, Music Hall, Artístico and Moulin Blanc. Toscano (Orrin circus) and Rosas (Riva Palacio theatre) continue their rivalry.

1907

The army massacres textile workers striking in Rio Blanco (Veracruz): 200 dead. The textile industry is the most developed in the nation.

Establishment of the Museo de Tecnología e Industria. The golden age of the Mexican popular theatre begins. The María Guerrero theatre organises a successful contest for Mexican *zarzuela* authors, staging a new production each week. Two plays denouncing the misery and exploitation of the peasants draw audiences: *En la hacienda* by Federico Carlos Kegel with music by Roberto Contreras and *Rebelión* by Lorenzo Rosado and Arturo Cosgaya. Inauguration of the Teatro Lírico. Federico Gamboa writes the play *La venganza de la gleba*. The *tiple* (star soprano) María Conesa debuts at the Principal theatre. Death of the indigenous painter Hermenegildo Bustos, first great Mexican portraitist. Diego Rivera obtains a scholarship and leaves for Europe. Rebirth of the *Revista Azul*.

The actor and director Felipe de Jesús Haro and The American Amusement Co. take on the challenge of narrative fiction film: the comedy *Aventuras de Tip Top en Chapultepec* and especially the historical film *El grito de Dolores* (seven sequences). New cameramen-exhibitors: Julio Kemenydy (Salón Rojo, Mexico City), the firm of Jorge A. Alcalde and

Enrique Echániz Brust (Mexico City), the company of Juan C. Aguilar and Bretón (Orizaba). Manuel Noriega stars in *El San Lunes del valedor* filmed at Orizaba. The Principal theatre programmes a film season.

1908

The army suppresses armed uprisings organised by the Partido Liberal in Coahuila and Chihuahua. Francisco Madero publishes *La sucesión presidencial de 1910,* against the re-election of Don Porfirio.

The anti-clerical musical review *México festivo* by Carlos Fernández Ortega provokes negative reactions in Catholic circles. Opening of the first cabaret, Sylvain. José María Velasco continues to paint the valley of Mexico City. Mariano Azuela publishes his novel *Los fracasados.* The song 'Corrido de Madero' is launched.

Juan C. Vasallo films *Accidente en el kilómetro 253 del ferrocarril México–Veracruz.* Success of documentaries about bullfighting: the torero Rodolfo Gaona is especially honoured. First attempts to develop industrial distribution and exhibition: the Unión Cinemato-gráfica. Max Linder is the most popular movie star in Mexico City.

1909

Francisco Madero creates the Partido Anti-Reeleccionista and assumes control of the opposition to President Díaz. Appearance of two Porfirian newspapers, *El Reeleccionista* and *El Debate.* 97% of arable land is in the hands of 1% of the rural population. US nationals hold all technical and management posts of the national railway company (20,000km).

Alfonso Reyes, the 'Latin American Montaigne', establishes the Ateneo de la Juventud, the first cultural society and a forum for conferences and debates frequented, among others, by José Vasconcelos, Alfonso Caso and Alfonso Cravioto. Julián Carrillo writes the opera *Matilda*. Publication of two song collections from Yucatán: *El ruiseñor yucateco* and *Chan Cil,* the latter with forty piano scores. The Guerrero theatre presents José F. Elizondo's musical review *La onda fría.* Mariano Azuela publishes his novel *Mala yerba.*

The Alva brothers cover the meeting between the Mexican and US presidents: *La entrevista Díaz–Taft* (c.1,000m). Gustavo Silva makes documentaries for the Ministry of Public Instruction and Fine Arts: *El viaje del presidente a Manzanillo, Viaje de Justo Sierra a Palenque, Incendio del pozo petrolero de Dos Bocas, Ver. Expedición técnica de los alumnos de la escuela de ingeniería a Necaxa.* Enrique Rosas experiments with fiction: *El Rosario de Amozoc* and *Don Juan Tenorio.* Jacobo Granat buys the Salón Rojo and turns it into a movie theatre that would become the most prestigious in Mexico City for over twenty years. The fire at the Flores movie theatre in Acapulco causes numerous deaths.

1910

Mexico has 15,160,369 inhabitants. Centennial of Father Hidalgo's Grito de Dolores (Independence Cry). The Convención Anti-Reeleccionista names Francisco Madero as its presidential candidate. Because his campaign is successful, General Díaz imprisons Madero in San Luis Potosí on charges of armed conspiracy. Freed after the re-election of Don Porfirio, Madero publishes (in Texas) the San Luis de Potosí Plan announcing the insurrection. The Revolution begins in November in the state of Chihuahua, led by Pascual Orozco and the cattle thief Francisco 'Pancho' Villa.

Artists led by Gerardo Murillo (Dr Atl) boycott the centennial celebrations for their excessive Europeanism and organise a counter-exhibition of modern Mexican paintings. Establishment of the Artistic Circle where the muralist movement is already simmering. Inauguration of the Universidad Nacional and the Escuela de Altos Estudios. The Russian Lydia de Rostow dances at the Principal theatre. Leopoldo Beristáin's typically Mexican comic characters gain popularity. Song: 'Corrido del levantamiento de Madero'. Waltz: 'Sobre las olas' by Juventino Rosas. Federico Gamboa's novel *La llaga.* Poetry: Amado Nervo's *Juana de Asbaje.*

Many operators compete to cover the centennial celebrations, the apotheosis and swan-song of the Porfirio Díaz regime: the brothers Alva, Salvador Toscano and Antonio F. Ocañas, maybe Guillermo Becerril. Twenty movie theatres open for the occasion. The Unión Cinematográfica S.A. reconstructs *El suplicio de Cuauhtémoc,* presented at the Cine Club in Mexico City. José Cava rejoins the cameramen-exhibitors and shows his films at the Palatino theatre in Mexico City.

1911

The Revolutionary flame spreads throughout the country. Francisco Madero joins the rebels at Chihuahua. In the state of Morelos, the uprising is led by the peasant leader, Emiliano Zapata. After the takeover of Villa Juárez by Pascual Orozco and Pancho Villa, Porfirio Díaz resigns and goes into exile. Madero makes a triumphal entry into Mexico City, becomes president of the Republic and forms a moderate government with only two ministers who had participated directly in the Revolution. Zapata initiates an agrarian reform programme, the Ayala Plan.

Political parodies take over the theatres: musical reviews like *El tenorio maderista* and *La presi alegre* put national political figures on stage. Lauro D. Uranga becomes one of the better musical review composers with *Héroe del día, La onda fría* and *Rosario de Amozoc.* The academy San Carlos (fine arts school), paralysed by an artists' strike, closes. Alfonso Reyes publishes his *Cuestiones estéticas.*

Film-makers change sides and vie to offer the most complete documentaries of the events of the Revolution: the Alva brothers' *Insurrección de México* in three parts programmed on successive days; their *Asalto y toma de Ciudad Juárez* and *El viaje del señor don Francisco Madero de Ciudad Juárez a la ciudad de México* reached 1,500m. *Los acontecimientos de Ciudad Juárez* ran for two hours.

Other titles include *Viaje del señor Madero al sur del país* (Alva) and *Los últimos sucesos sangrientos de Puebla y la llegada de Madero a esa ciudad* (Guillermo Becerril).

The success of the Revolutionary films did not diminish the appeal of films about corridas, other current events or annual reviews such as *Hojeando el año de 1910* and *Hojeando 1911.* Pedro J. Vázquez plays the title role in *Colón.*

The film business grows in Mexico City: forty cinemas able to seat more than 25,000 spectators. The Salón Allende, with a 6m high screen, seated 1,500 people.

1912

Orozco and Zapata accuse Madero of treason for hesitating to implement agrarian reform, and refuse to lay down their weapons. Pancho Villa fights alongside General Victoriano Huerta's federal troops. After defying the general's authority, Villa is imprisoned for insubordination and pillaging. He escapes and crosses the US border. The press multiplies its attacks on the government. Adoption of a special tax on crude oil. Foundation of the Casa del Obrero Mundial, influenced by Kropotkin, Bakunin and Elisée Reclus.

Opening of the Café Tacuba in Mexico City. The governor of Mexico City censors the musical review *El chanchullo* and jails the entire company of the Apolo theatre. The cinema inspires a popular musical review, *Películas ABC. Chin chun chan* is still on stage. Mimí Derba debuts at the Lírico theatre.

María Conesa stars at the Principal theatre. Agustín Victor Casasola opens a photographic press agency. Establishment of the Universidad Popular Mexicana, which functioned for a decade.

Given the political instability, *Revolución orozquista o La Revolución en Chihuahua* (Alva, 1,500m) reveals a concern for impartiality, using parallel editing to alternate footage shot from the point of view of each of the adversaries, the rebels led by Pascual Orozco and the federal armies under Victoriano Huerta. *Revolución en Veracruz* (Enrique Rosas, 1,000m) is shown at the Principal theatre, Mexico City's popular meeting place.

The short-lived *La Revista Nacional* was intended to be the first regular Mexican newsreel.

1913

An uprising by a battalion commanded by Félix Díaz, nephew of Don Porfirio, unleashes the *Decena Trágica* (tragic ten days): more than 2,000 die in the capital city alone. Betrayed by Huerta, Madero is deposed and imprisoned. Huerta assumes power with the support of bankers, businessmen and the US ambassador. Madero and Vice-president Pino Suárez are executed, initiating a period of terror marked by the assassination of numerous Maderista partisans and deputies. Parliament is disbanded. The Casa del Obrero Mundial speaks against the usurper and organises the first May 1st demonstration. Zapata refuses Huerta's advances and continues to fight. Venustiano Carranza, governor of Coahuila, decides to fight Huerta with a constitutional army: he forms a parallel government in Piedras Negras, authorising the land redistribution. Alvaro Obregón takes charge of the constitutionalists in the state of Sonora, Pancho Villa in Chihuahua.

José F. Elizondo writes the musical reviews *El tenorio Sam, Las musas del país* and *El país de la metralla,* the latter evoking the events of the *Decena Trágica,* angering the dictator Huerta. The author goes into exile to escape persecution while Rafael Gascón, the composer, commits suicide shortly after. Manuel M. Ponce proposes to safeguard popular music. Julián Carrillo writes the opera *Ossian.* José Guadalupe Posada depicts the *Decena Trágica* in illustrations. The Fine Arts School reopens, headed by Alfredo Ramos Martínez; at Santa Anita he establishes an open school influenced by the Barbizons.

The Alva brothers film *Aniversario del fallecimiento de la suegra de Enhart,* a small sketch in the French style starring the fashionable comedians Alegría and Enhart.

Several film-makers offer their version of the events in the capital: *La decena trágica en México o Revolución felicista, La revolución felicista o los sucesos de la decena roja, Decena trágica.* Many US cameramen also film Revolutionary events. Cinemas still programme *El señor general don Porfirio Díaz en París.*

First decree instituting political and moral censorship under the pretext of protecting morality. French films (Pathé, Eclair) control the market.

1914

Obregón and Villa control the north and move towards Mexico City. Zapata heads the army liberating the south. US marines land in Veracruz. Once Zapata circles Cuernavaca, Villa and Felipe Angeles attack the federal army at Zacatecas. Obregón seizes Guadalajara. After the escape of Victoriano Huerta (July), the constitutional armies of Obregón and Carranza arrive in Mexico City. A struggle for power begins among the victors. Villa and Zapata join forces against Carranza. The Aguascalientes convention gathers the representatives of the constitutionalist armies and names General Eulalio Gutiérrez provisional president. Carranza establishes a parallel government in Veracruz, which US forces had just evacuated. Villa and Zapata have a historic meeting in Xochimilco (December) followed by their triumphal entry into Mexico City.

The songs 'Adelita' and 'La cucaracha', hymns of the Revolutionary armies, are sung throughout the country. Current events inspire the 'Corrido del peligro de intervención americana' and the 'Corrido de la toma de Zacatecas'. The María Guerrero theatre presents the *zarzuela, María Pistolas.* Classical music seeks to develop an authentic national style, as in Manuel M. Ponce's *Balada mexicana* for piano and orchestra, and his successful song 'Estrellita'. US writer John Reed follows Pancho Villa's campaign. Jack London accompanies the invasion by the marines as a Collier's correspondent. Agustín V. Casasola photographs the meeting at Xochimilco and the arrival of the Villista and Zapatista armies in Mexico City.

Current events are recorded in documentary style espousing the point of view of those locally in power: *La invasión norteamericana o Los sucesos de Veracruz* (1,000m); *Marcha del ejército constitucionalista por diversas poblaciones de la República y sus entradas a Guadalajara y México y el viaje del señor Carranza hasta su llegada a esta ciudad; Entrada de los generales Villa y Zapata a la ciudad de México el domingo 6 de diciembre de 1914; Sangre hermana.* The US company Mutual Film signs an exclusive contract with Pancho Villa, who looks after his image.

In Mérida, Carlos Martínez de Arredondo and Manuel Cirerol Sansoles direct the fiction films *En tiempos mayas* and *La voz de su raza;* in Hermosillo (Sonora), Abitia films *Los amores de Novelti.*

1915

In Veracruz, Carranza promulgates the first agrarian reform law. With the support of the Casa del Obrero Mundial, Obregón organises battalions of workers in the capital. Villa re-enters Chihuahua and Zapata retrenches in Morelos. Harassed by Obregón, Villa is driven back to the far north where he unleashes a railway war, capturing entire trains to transport his troops. Carranza regains Mexico City and is recognised by the USA. The various caudillos give themselves the right to issue currency; the country is in chaos. A hunger uprising breaks out in the capital and stores are pillaged, while the black market in gold and silver thrives. Death of Porfirio Díaz in Paris.

The first Revolutionary novel, Mariano Azuela's *Los de abajo,* is published in serial form in an El Paso (Texas) newspaper. Diego Rivera paints *Zapatista Landscape* under the influence of cubism. Two musical reviews by José María Romo play for months: *Su Majestad el Hambre,* about the hunger uprising, and *El país de los cartones,* a parody about the financial chaos. Staged in a number of theatres in Mexico City (Apolo, Briceño, María Guerrero, Díaz de León and Lírico), the latter had successful runs in Monterrey, Guadalajara, San Luis Potosí, Chihuahua, Tampico, Orizaba and Mérida. Pablo Prida becomes known with a *sicalíptica* (pornographic) play, *Los efectos del vacilón.* Mimí Derba and María Conesa remain extremely popular. Opening of the Juan Ruiz de Alarcón theatre.

Historia completa de la Revolución de 1910–1915 by Enrique Echániz Brust and Salvador Toscano is 8,000m long and lasts three hours.

Film criticism starts in the weekly *España,* edited in Madrid by José Ortega y Gasset, with Federico de Onís writing under the name El Espectador, and, later, Alfonso Reyes and Martín Luis Guzmán sharing the pseudonym Fósforo.

1916

Inflation takes off. Urban strikes multiply and the countryside remains agitated. In the north, Villa's rebels set upon passenger trains. In Morelos, Zapata rules. Villa's attack on the small town of Columbus in New Mexico provokes reprisals by the USA in the form of a punitive expedition commanded by General Pershing. Carranza sends General Pablo González to take the state of Morelos from the Zapatistas. Zapata derails the Mexico–Cuernavaca train: 400 dead. A convention meets in Querétaro to draft a new constitution. The first workers' congress meets in Veracruz. A three-day general strike in Mexico City is suppressed by the Carranza government. Prosperity in Tampico, thanks to the oil industry.

Publication of the daily *El Universal.* Newspapers proliferate in the capital, including *El Pueblo, El Demócrata, El Nacional, Boletín de Guerra, Le Courrier du Mexique* (in French), *El Tribunal, Revista de Revistas* and *Acción Mundial* (edited by the painter Gerardo Murillo). The bookstore Biblios organises the first show of José Clemente Orozco's paintings. First strikes by theatre workers. Lupe Rivas Cacho debuts at the Principal theatre. The success of the oil industry inspires the *zarzuela, El oro negro.* Pablo Prida writes the musical review *La ciudad triste y desconfiada,* a parody of a Benavente play. The poet Ramón López Velarde writes *La sangre devota.*

Patriotic fiction: in Yucatán, Manuel Cirerol Sansores and Carlos Martínez de Arredondo produce *1810 o ¡Los libertadores de México!,* the first fiction feature. Felipe de Jesús Haro's *Fatal orgullo* remains incomplete. María Conesa appears in *El pobre Valbuena* by Manuel Noriega, based on Carlos Arniches's work.

With the support of Carranza and his ministers, the production company Queretana organises a script competition narrating the Revolution from the perspective of those in power.

Documentary: Enrique Echániz Brust recalls pre-Revolutionary pageantry in his *México en 1910 o Sea la celebración del Primer Centenario de la Independencia* (8,000m); Enrique Rosas concentrated on more topical information, as in his *Documentación histórica nacional, 1915–1916,* but the Revolution disappears from the screen.

1917

Adoption of a constitution with a positivist and communitarian spirit and a strong anti-clerical tone. The church is forbidden to participate in education, in civil government and to own land. The new charter foresees a series of social measures such as an eight-hour work day, a minimum wage, union rights and the prohibition of child labour; the subsoil becomes the property of the state; monopolies are banned; the new constitution authorises a socialist, secular, free and obligatory education. National

El automovíl gris (Enrique Rosas, Joaquín Coss and Juan Canals de Homes, 1919)

elections are organised (except in Morelos, still insurgent). Venustiano Carranza becomes president of the Republic.

Publication of the newspaper *Excélsior*. Creation of the Directorate of Archaeological and Ethnographic Studies (shortly thereafter becoming the anthropology directorate). Carlos Chávez composes the piano sonata, *Exágonos*. The Principal theatre stages Guz Aguila's play *El diez por ciento,* the first to capitalise upon the popularity of the cinema. Mariano Azuela publishes his novel *Los caciques*. Alfonso Reyes publishes the essay *Visión de Anáhuac*.

Fiction film production increases. Characteristic of the predominant mimeticism is Ezequiel Carrasco's *La luz, tríptico de la vida moderna* plagiarising Piero Fosco's *Il fuoco* (Italy, 1915). Azteca Films (Mimí Derba, Enrique Rosas and General Pablo González) produces Joaquín Coss's *En defensa propia, Alma de sacrificio* and *En la sombra; La tigresa* (perhaps directed by Derba herself) and Eduardo Arozamena's *La soñadora*. Manuel Cirerol Sansores and Carlos Martínez de Arredondo direct *El amor que triunfa*. Manuel de la Bandera organises an Academy of Cinematographic Art; with his students, he shoots *Triste crepúsculo* and *La obsesión*.

The documentary is definitely put to rest. Alvarez, Arrondo y Cia. produce the newsreel *Semana gráfica*.

The newspaper *El Universal* entrusts a regular cinema column to Hipólito Seijas, the pseudonym of Rafael Pérez Taylor.

1918

Zapata is harassed by the federal troops of General Pablo González. Organisation of the Confederación Regional Obrera Mexicana (CROM), headed by Luis Napoleón Morones. Creation of the National Agrarian Party under the auspices of President Carranza.

Mariano Azuela publishes his novel *Las moscas*. The author Pablo Prida is expelled from the country because of his play *La ciudad de los camiones*. Dancer Anna Pavlova performs in Mexico City. Opening of the Esperanza Iris theatre.

The fiction cinema is in search of its voice. Producer Germán Camus and director Luis G. Peredo shoot *Santa,* based on Federico Gamboa's novel, the prototype of the golden-hearted prostitute melodrama, followed by *Caridad*. Luis Lezama directs *Tabaré,* based on Juan Zorrilla de San Martín's work, within the indigenist tradition. Carlos E. González and José Manuel Ramos make *Tepeyac,* invoking the Virgin of Guadalupe cult. Lupe Rivas Cacho, a well-known star, stars in Domingo de

Mezzi's *La muerte civil.*

The imitation of foreign models continues: for instance, Santiago J. Sierra's *Maciste turista*. Newsreels close to those in power include the *Revista Universal* and *Actualidades de México*.

Jacobo Granat, the owner of the Salón Rojo, controls eight theatres, increased to nineteen a year later.

1919

Trapped by General González, Emiliano Zapata is assassinated in Chinameca. Pancho Villa takes up arms again. General Alvaro Obregón announces his candidacy to the presidency. CROM holds its first annual convention in Zacatecas and organises the Mexican workers' party. The organisation of the Partido Comunista Mexicano (PCM) begins.

The approaching presidential election means that political themes are back in vogue in musical reviews. The most sought-after authors are Carlos M. Ortega, Pablo Prida and Guz Aguila. In Monterrey, the engineer Constantino de Tárnava sets up the first experimental radio station: Tárnava Notre-Dame (TND). The RCA company produces the first *ranchera* (country) music record, including such songs as 'Paloma blanca', 'A la orilla de un palmar', 'Juan soldado' and 'Perjura'. The thirteen-year-old singer Lucha Reyes makes her first public appearance. At the Principal theatre, great success of the play *Del rancho a la capital* which popularised the songs 'Las cuatro milpas' and 'La norteña'. José López Portillo y Rojas publishes his novel *Fuertes y débiles*. Poetry: Ramón López Velarde's *Zozobra*.

Consolidation of melodrama: Rafael Bermúdez Zataraín's *María*, based on Jorge Isaacs's work; Francisco de Lavillete's *Dos corazones* with Mimí Derba; Carlos E. González and José Manuel Ramos's *Confesión trágica*.

A contemporary event generates two film versions: Ernesto Vollrath's *La banda del automóvil o La dama enlutada,* produced by Camus, and especially Enrique Rosas, Joaquín Coss and Juan Canals de Homes's *El automóvil gris* produced by Azteca. Carlos Martínez de Arredondo also uses the serial formula in *Venganza de bestia o Xandaroff,* filmed in Mérida. *El rompecabezas de Juanillo* by Juan Arthenak is a comedy.

With his script *Tlahuicole,* the anthropologist Manuel Gamio tries to propose an alternative to films such as Manuel de la Bandera's *Cuauhtémoc* (1918). Newsreels: *Emiliano Zapata en vida y muerte* by Enrique Rosas. The *Cine Revista Semanal México* becomes the leading newsreel.

Institutionalisation of censorship, the sisters

Adriana and Dolores Elhers playing an important role. Creation of the Union of Confederated Film Workers.

International Pictures, Fox and Universal open subsidiaries in Mexico City.

Carlos Noriega Hope (writing under the name Silvestre Bonnard) takes charge of the film column in *El Universal*, which becomes a Hollywood mouthpiece.

1920

President Carranza promotes the candidacy of one of his followers. With the support of Pancho Villa and most of the army, Alvaro Obregón releases the Agua Prieta Plan, calling for an uprising. In a few weeks, power relations change; Carranza escapes from Mexico City and is assassinated on the road to Veracruz. Congress names Adolfo de la Huerta interim president. The Mexican workers' party backs General Obregón's candidacy. Villa stops fighting. Obregón is elected president. The Revolution is officially over. Its toll: a million dead.

Opening of the Salón Mexico, the temple of *danzón*. Beginning of the golden age of songs, prominently featured in musical reviews, one of them being inspired by Federico Gamboa's *Santa*.

A decree by President Huerta reduces the tax on national entertainment to 2%, while foreign entertainers are taxed at 10%. On stage, various political sketches, including Guz Aguila's *El jardín de Obregón* starring Celia Montalván who popularizes the song 'Mi querido capitán'. The success of the oil industry inspires the review *El tesoro del Panuco*.

The poet Amado Nervo publishes *La amada inmóvil*.

Federico Gamboa inspires and co-produces Luis G. Peredo's *La llaga*. Leopoldo Beristáin stars in José Manuel Ramos's *Viaje redondo,* based on an idea by Noriega Hope.

The War and Marine Ministry continues to produce edifying fictions: *Cuando la patria lo mande* by Juan Canals de Homes; *Juan soldado* by Enrique Castilla; *El honor militar, El precio de la gloria* and *El blockhouse de alta luz* by Lt.-Col. Fernando Orozco y Berra. Another military man, Miguel Contreras Torres, debuts as actor and producer in José Manuel Ramos's *El Zarco*, based on Ignacio Manuel Altamirano's work. Other films include Enrique Castilla's *Partida ganada* and *Don Juan Manuel;* Jesús H. Abitia's *Los encapuchados en Mazatlán;* Alfredo B. Cuéllar's *El escándalo* and producer Germán Camus *Alas abiertas,* directed by Luis Lezama.

1921

New census: 14,800,000 Mexicans. Alvaro Obregón begins to put the institutions of modern Mexico in place. Creation of the Ministry of Education (Secretaría de Educación Pública) headed by José Vasconcelos; start of a literacy campaign focused on teaching Spanish to the Indians. José Vasconcelos opens a vast library network, creates a publishing house and starts the muralist movement by inviting artists to celebrate the Revolution on the walls of public buildings. Organisation of the Confederación General de Trabajadores (CGT), with the powerful textile industry as its nucleus.

The radio station in Monterrey begins to broadcast regularly with a fixed schedule. Carlos Chávez composes the ballet *El fuego nuevo,* borrowing from Aztec music. First popular art show organised by the painter Gerardo Murillo (Dr Atl). Manuel Maples Arce begins a literary movement, stridentism, with its own journal, *Actual.* Salvador Quevedo's novel, *En tierra de sangre y broma;* Alfonso Reyes's essay, *El cazador;* Carlos Pellicer's poetry volume, *Colores en el mar y otros poemas.* Photography: *Album histórico-gráfico* by Agustín V. Casasola.

Germán Camus produces with some regularity thanks to his Mexico City studio: *Hasta después de la muerte* (made in 1920 with Emma Padilla), *Carmen, En la hacienda* (a rural *zarzuela* by Federico Carlos Kegel), *Amnesia* (based on Amado Nervo), all directed by Ernesto Vollrath. Jorge and Carlos Stahl begin to produce fiction films: *El crimen del otro, Malditas sean las mujeres, La dama de las camelias.* Miguel Contreras Torres films *El caporal,* a sort of Mexican Western and, in association with Guillermo Calles ('el Indio'), *De raza azteca.* Other films: Ernesto Vollrath's *La parcela,* Jesús H. Abitia's *Carnaval trágico,* Enrique J. Vallejo's *Mitad y mitad* and, in Guadalajara, María Cantoni's *La bastarda.*

1922

Organisation of the National Catholic Labour Confederation. Bloody encounter in Guadalajara between Catholic unions and the unions favoured by those in power.

The muralist movement begins with Diego Rivera's *La creación* at the National Preparatory School. David Alfaro Siqueiros establishes the Union of Workers, Technicians, Painters and Sculptors. Its declaration of principles denounces dependence on European art and extols a national aesthetic. Actors organise themselves into an association that later became the Asociación Nacional de Actores (ANDA). The public hails Roberto Soto as the best comic actor. Publication of the literary magazine *Falange.*

Anthropologist Manuel Gamio publishes three volumes of interdisciplinary studies of the population of the Teotihuacán valley.

Jesús H. Abitia builds the Chapultepec studio. Outlines of a nationalist trend in fiction: Miguel Contreras Torres's *El hombre sin patria;* Eduardo Martorell and Gómez's *Fulguración de raza;* Enrique Castilla's *I;* Rafael Trujillo's *La puñalada.* Other films include Rafael Trujillo's *Luz de redención;* Froylán Torres's *Amor;* Adolfo Quezada's *Llamas de rebelión;* Manuel Sánchez Valtierra's *Fanny o el robo de veinte millones;* Alberto Bell's *El último sueño;* Carlos Noriega Hope's *La gran noticia* and Pedro J. Vázquez's *Bolcheviquismo.*

Institutional documentaries: *Revista cinematográfica de la SEP* (Ministry of Education); *Fiestas de Chalma* (Miguel O. de Mendizábal and Ramón Díaz Ordaz).

Conflict between Hollywood and the authorities, who are unhappy with the image of Mexico in US films. Paramount and United Artists set up agencies in Mexico City.

1923

Assassination of Pancho Villa in Parral, Chihuahua. The USA recognises the government of Alvaro Obregón and renews diplomatic relations with Mexico. The first commercial radio stations air in the capital: the CYL, founded by the businessman Raúl Azcárraga, and CYB, part of the tobacco company El Buen Tono. La Casa de la Radio, created by the daily *El Universal* follows. Inauguration of the Great Radio-electric fair. Defence minister Plutarco Elías Calles and finance minister Adolfo de la Huerta announce their candidacy to the presidency. President Obregón backs General Calles. Angered, de la Huerta heads an armed uprising. An international feminist convention meets in Mexico City.

Diego Rivera begins a series of murals at the Secretaría de Educación Pública. Publication of *El Machete,* the mouthpiece of the Union of Workers, Technicians, Painters and Sculptors. It publishes a manifesto signed by Rivera, Orozco and Siqueiros exalting monumental art as a public service and insisting upon the political function of painting. Music: 'Corrido de la muerte de Pancho Villa'; introduction of the foxtrot, celebrated in the Arbeu theatre production *Tenga su fox* and by composer Belisario de Jesús Abreu's 'Tristeza de Pierrot' and 'Canción del recuerdo'. Ricardo Palmerín composes 'Peregrina'. Delia Magaña debuts at the Ideal theatre. Publications: *Mexican Life* (magazine); *El minutero*

(poems by Ramón López Velarde); *Así era …México* (photographs by Hugo Brehme).

Miguel Contreras Torres initiates new themes with *Almas tropicales,* shot in Veracruz, and *Oro, sangre y sol,* with Rodolfo Gaona and other bullfighting celebrities; Francisco García Urbizu films *Sacrificio por amor* in Zamora, Michoacán; Angel E. Alvarez and José Ortiz direct *El secreto de un pecado* in Puebla; the actress Adela Sequeyro 'Perlita' debuts in *El hijo de la loca* by José S. Ortiz; Gustavo Sáenz de Sicilia directs *Atavismo;* Manuel Gamio shoots *La población del Valle de Teotihuacán.* Another documentary is *Vida, hechos y hazañas de Francisco Villa, de 1910 a 1923.*

1924

The rebellion headed by Adolfo de la Huerta is stifled. Plutarco Elías Calles, a rabid anti-clericalist, is elected president of the Republic. Luis Napoleón Morones, the director of the Confederación Regional Obrera Mexicana (CROM), is named Minister of Industry, Commerce and Labour. A new tax on revenues, called income tax, triggers waves of protests. Mexico is the first Latin American country to establish diplomatic relations with the Soviet Union.

Emilio Pacheco composes the first Mexican bolero, 'Presentimiento'. The theatre pays tribute to radio in the musical review *Los efectos de la radio* and continues its political parodies with *El candidato en gira, La doctrina Monroe* and *El último impuesto.* The *tiple* Celia Padilla debuts at the Lírico theatre. The Regis theatre, a future cinema, opens. Carlos Gustavo Villenave authors close to 200 musical reviews. Roberto Montenegro paints the mural *Fiesta de la Santa Cruz* in the ancient convent of Saint Peter and Saint Paul. Publication of the *Manifesto estridentista* calling for complete creative freedom. Poetry: *Del cuartel y del claustro* and *Libro de Dios* by Alfredo R. Placencia; Carlos Pellicer's *Piedra de sacrificios, Seis, Siete poemas;* Manuel Maples Arce's *Urbe.*

Gustavo Sáenz de Sicilia films *Un drama en la aristocracia* and, in collaboration with Miguel Contreras Torres, *Aguiluchos mexicanos.* José S. Ortiz films *No matarás* in San Luis Potosí.

The film business flourishes: Monterrey (80,000 inhabitants) has eleven cinemas totalling 21,000 seats. Henceforth, 90% of the market will be controlled by Hollywood.

1925

Morones, the head of the CROM, starts a dispute when he attempts to impose a religious schism. Bloody incidents occur in Mexico City when unionists invade a church. The Catholics represented by the League in Defence of Religious Freedom react strongly. Institutionalisation of agrarian reform policies. Creation of the Banco Central Mexicano and the Banco Nacional de Crédito Agrícola. Creation in Yucatán of the co-operative of aloe producers.

Eleven radio stations broadcast throughout the country, seven in Mexico City and four in the provinces (Mazatlán, Monterrey, Oaxaca and Mérida). The anthropology department is removed from the Ministry of Agriculture and Development and placed under the Ministry of Education; archaeological studies lose their social dimension. In Teotihuacán, at the Nature theatre, Rubén M. Campos stages anthropologist Manuel Gamio's *Tlahuicole*. Expedition in the Mayan country by archaeologist Franz Blom and linguist Olivier La Farge. Lupe Vélez debuts at the Principal theatre in the light comedy *No la tapes*. Marco Antonio Jiménez writes the song 'Adiós Mariquita linda' and Emilio D. Uranga writes 'La negra noche'. José Vasconcelos publishes the essay *La raza cósmica;* poetry: *Canciones para cantar en las barcas* by José Gorostiza; *XX poemas* by Salvador Novo.

Disappearance of fiction films, with isolated exceptions in the provinces: Gabriel García Moreno's *El buitre* in Orizaba; Francisco García Urbizu's *Traviesa juventud* in Michoacán; Alejandro Peniche Sierra's *La verdad de la vida* in Mérida. The North American William P.S. Earle films *Tras las bambalinas del Bataclán* at the Iris theatre in Mexico City. The Mexican actor Ramón Novarro becomes a Hollywood star in Fred Niblo's *Ben Hur.*

After a strike, the Confederated Cinematographic Employees Union (UECC) signs its first collective agreement.

Jaime Torres Bodet writes film criticism for the *Revista de Revistas* under the pseudonym Celulóide.

1926

The Calles Law imposes new measures upon the church (such as the registration of priests with the Ministry of the Interior) and provokes a break between the church and state. The bishops announce the suspension of all religious services. Despite their calls for passive resistance, the Catholic peasantry rises: the Cristeros or Christian rebellion starts in Jalisco, Colima, Guanajuato and Michoacán, spreading throughout the entire central Mexican plateau. Organisation of the National Peasant League in sixteen states. Managua accuses Mexico in the League of Nations because of Mexico's support for Augusto César Sandino's Nicaraguan revolutionary movement.

The painter José Clemente Orozco begins a series of murals entitled *La trinidad revolucionaria* at the National Preparatory School. A commercial establishment hosts the first solo exhibition by Rufino Tamayo. Carlos Chávez composes the ballet *Los cuatro soles.* Agustín Lara writes his first song, 'La prisionera'. Doctor Alfonso Ortiz Tirado debuts as a singer. Belisario de Jesús García composes 'Tango Encantador' and 'Tango negro'. Publication of *Máscaras mexicanas,* Roberto Montenegro's book about the ritual masks used in popular celebrations.

Modest revival of production, though still influenced by Hollywood. Celia Montalván stars in William P.S. Earle's *El milagro de la Guadalupana,* a religious melodrama with intertitles written by Federico Gamboa. Miguel Contreras Torres directs *El relicario* in Spain and in the USA. Guillermo Calles shoots *El indio yaqui* in the state of Sonora and in Hollywood. Manuel R. Ojeda and Basilio Zubiaur direct a historical drama, *El Cristo de oro.* Eduardo Urriola films *La banda del cinco de oros* and *Del rancho a la capital* with actors from the film academy of Artistas Unidos Mexicanos, which he founded with Manuel Arvide.

1927

General Alvaro Obregón fights to win a new presidential mandate: his two opponents in the elections, Arnulfo Gómez and Francisco Serrano, are assassinated. The Cristeros multiply their terrorist acts, including a spectacular attack on the Mexico–Guadalajara train and an attempt to assassinate Obregón; thousands of families seek a better future in the cities. Bloody repression of a CGT-directed railway workers' strike.

The Lírico theatre organises a public contest for the best songs heard on the radio. The first prize is awarded to Guty Cárdenas for the song 'Nunca'; Agustín Lara wins second prize for the bolero 'Imposible'; the trio Garnica-Ascencio make their first appearance in the contest. The song 'Allá en el Rancho Grande' becomes popular. Success of *Las cuatro milpas,* a musical review about the misadventures of a peasant family newly arrived to the capital. At the Principal theatre, Carlos Rivelles's Spanish troupe presents Luigi Pirandello's *Sei personaggi in cerca d'autore* (1921). Poetry: *Hora y veinte* (Carlos Pellicer); *Poemas interdictos* (Manuel Maples Arce). Francisco Goitia paints *Tata Jesucristo.*

Manuel R. Ojeda organises another film school and directs another historical drama, *Conspiración.* Juan Bustillo Oro makes his directorial debut with the comedy *Yo soy tu padre.* In Orizaba, Gabriel García Moreno shoots *El tren fantasma* and *El puño de hierro.* Guillermo Calles films *Raza de bronce* in Baja California. Miguel Contreras Torres shoots *El león de la Sierra Morena* in Spain. Eduardo Urriola makes his last film, *Una catástrofe en el mar.*

Dolores del Río becomes a Hollywood headliner with Raoul Walsh's *The Loves of Carmen,* and, later, Edwin Carewe's *Resurrection* (1931).

1928

The Cristeros attack the port of Manzanillo. Plutarco Elías Calles's mandate ends. Re-elected as president, General Obregón is assassinated sixteen days later by a Catholic student. Emilio Portes Gil becomes interim president, but General Calles has more power and imposes his will as Jefe Máximo for a long period known as the Maximato. Organisation of the Confederación Sindical Unitaria de México (CSUM) under communist influence. Split within CROM: its leader, Luis Morones, is charged with corruption. Founding of the Partido Nacional Revolucionario (PNR, National Revolutionary Party, the future PRI) which dominates Mexican politics from 1929 onwards.

Publication of the newspaper *La Prensa.* The journal *Contemporáneos* gathers a group of intellectuals, poets, critics and playwrights, including Salvador Novo, Jorge Cuesta, Xavier Villaurrutia, Gilberto Owen, Jaime Torres Bodet and Carlos Pellicer. Publication of Martín Luis Guzmán's *El águila y la serpiente,* a novel about the Revolution. Carlos Chávez directs the Mexican conservatory and organises the symphonic orchestra. Opening of the Politeama theatre, a temple to popular music. Tenor Pedro Vargas releases his first record and makes his stage debut in the opera *Cavalleria rusticana.* The theatre promotes cinema: the play *Por el objetivo* invites playwrights to participate in a screenplay competition. The actors' union splits off from CROM and ridicules its leader in the play *El desmoronamiento de Morones.* First Mexican Photography Salon with Manuel Alvarez Bravo and the Italian Tina Modotti. Essay: *Cuestiones gongorianas* (Alfonso Reyes). Poetry: *La feria* by José Juan Tablada.

Cándida Beltrán Rendón is simultaneously director, producer, writer and principal actress of *El secreto de la abuela,* also starring Catalina Bárcena and members of the troupe of the Spaniard Gregorio Martínez Sierra, who subsequently goes to Hollywood. Manuel R. Ojeda directs *El coloso de mármol* glorifying the regime. In the provinces:

Guillermo Calles shoots *Sol de gloria* in Nayarit and California; Angel E. Alvarez shoots *Vicio* in Puebla; Oriel Lester Adams shoots *El caballero misterioso* in Hermosillo (Sonora) for a production company based in Mazatlán (Sinaloa).

Lupe Vélez follows in Dolores del Río's footsteps and succeeds in Hollywood.

1929

An accord between the church and President Emilio Portes Gil ends the Cristero Rebellion (150,000 killed). The authorities develop the PNR and nominate Pascual Ortiz Rubio to the presidency to block José Vasconcelos. A movement advocating a return to the sources of the Revolution is mobilised around the old education minister. The election of Ortiz Rubio begins the hegemonic system of the official party that henceforth will characterise Mexican politics. The Mexican Communist Party becomes clandestine. Cuban communist leader Julio Antonio Mella is assassinated in Mexico City. Affected by the crisis, the USA repatriates 300,000 Mexicans. Strike for autonomy at the Universidad Nacional in Mexico City.

The authors of the play *El desmoronamiento de Morones* (Carlos G. Villenave, Juan Díaz del Moral and Rodolfo Sandoval) are expelled from the country by the war minister. María Izquierdo shows at the Modern Art Gallery in Mexico City. Manuel M. Ponce composes *Chapultepec,* three symphonic sketches. Martín Luis Guzmán publishes the novel *La sombra del caudillo.*

Lloyd Bacon's *The Singing Fool* (1928) definitively announces the coming of sound. Last gasps of the silent cinema: Gustavo Sáenz de Sicilia's *La boda de Rosario,* Luis Lezama's *Los hijos del destino;* Charles Amador's *Terrible pesadilla.*

First attempts at sound cinema: Guillermo Calles's *Dios y ley,* shot in California (USA); Miguel Contreras Torres's *El águila y el nopal.*

Hollywood releases its productions for Spanish-speaking markets: Cliff Wheeler's *Sombras habaneras,* produced in New York by and starring René Cardona; Andrew L. Stone's *Sombras de gloria* with José Bohr; Cyril Gardner and A. Washington Pezet's *El cuerpo del delito* (USA: Frank Tuttle's *The Benson Murder Case*) for Paramount with Ramón Pereda and Antonio Moreno; James Tinling's *El precio de un beso* (USA: *One Mad Kiss*) at Fox with José Mojica.

1930

Mexico has 16,553,000 inhabitants. Investiture of Pascual Ortiz Rubio, always under the thumb of strongman general Plutarco Elías Calles. The textile industry continues to develop, 60% controlled by French capital.

Foundation of the French school in Mexico City. A new radio station established by Raúl Azcárraga, XEW (Voz de América Latina), is the first to broadcast nationally. Diego Rivera finishes the mural *Historia de México, de la conquista al futuro* at the Palacio Nacional. Premiere of Carlos Chávez's ballet *Los cuatro soles*. Hosted by Agustín Lara for XEW, the show *La onda azul* beats all audience records. Miguel Lerdo de Tejada directs the Típica de Policía orchestra. Singer Lucha Reyes obtains a contract in the USA. Two musical reviews about political corruption: *La fuga del oro* and *Las plagas de México*.

136 of the 830 movie houses are equipped for sound. Of the 225 films released, 200 are North American.

New experiments with sound: Salvador Pruneda's *Abismos o Náufragos de la vida;* Raphael J. Sevilla's *Más fuerte que el deber;* Miguel Contreras Torres's *Soñadores de la gloria* shot in Hollywood, Spain and Morocco.

The Hollywood Spanish-language cinema functions as the training ground for future collaborators of the Mexican industry: Ramón Novarro's *Sevilla de mis amores* aka *La sevillana* (USA: Charles Brabin's *Call of the Flesh*); George J. Crone's *Así es la vida* (USA: *What a Man*) with José Bohr; William McGann's *El hombre malo* (USA: Clarence Badger's *The Bad Man*) with Antonio Moreno; George Melford's *La voluntad del muerto* (USA: Rupert Julian's *The Cat Creeps*) with Antonio Moreno and Lupita Tovar; Melford's *Oriente y occidente* (USA: Monta Bell's *East is West*) with Lupe Vélez.

A trade publication: *Mundo Cinematográfico*.

1931

General Lázaro Cárdenas resigns the governorship of the state of Michoacán, takes over the direction of the PNR and becomes Minister of the Interior. Conflicts between President Ortiz Rubio and General Calles: the Jefe Máximo imposes his will and obtains the resignation of the president. Adoption of the first federal labour law. The official party gets its own radio station: Radio Nacional de México.

Manuel Alvarez Bravo takes his famous photograph *Parábola óptica*. Octavio Paz founds the journal *Barandal*. Novels: *Vámonos con Pancho Villa* (Rafael F. Muñoz); *Campamento* (Gregorio López y Fuentes). Poetry: *Proserpina rescatada* (Jaime Torres Bodet). Silvestre Revueltas composes the symphonic poem *Ventanas* and a score for voice and orchestra, *Dúo para pato y canario*. Two musical reviews address the Indian question: *Upa Yapa* and *Raza de Bronce*. The Iris theatre presents *El corrido de la Revolución* by Juan Bustillo Oro and Mauricio Magdaleno. Entries for the Imperial theatre's waltz competition include Alfonso Esparza Oteo's 'Intimo secreto', Jorge del Moral's 'Divina mujer', Agustín Lara's 'Cortesana' and Espinosa de los Monteros's 'Ann Harding'.

Antonio Moreno's *Santa* is the first successful sound film: the archetypes of Federico Gamboa are re-enacted by Lupita Tovar, Carlos Orellana and Juan José Martínez Casado, enhanced by Alex Phillips's cinematography and Agustín Lara's music.

Other titles: Alberto Méndez Bernal's *Contrabando;* the Germán Camus production *Así es México*.

Eisenstein shoots the earthquake in Oaxaca (16 January) and *¡Que viva México!*

At Paramount's Joinville studios, Fernando Soler appears in *¿Cuándo te suicidas?* by Manuel Romero. Other Spanish-language films from Hollywood: George Melford's *Drácula* (USA: Tod Browning's film) with Carlos Villarías and Lupita Tovar; David Selman's *Resurrección* aka *El principe y la aldeana* (USA: *Resurrection*) with Lupe Vélez; Lewis Seiler's *Hay que casar al príncipe* (a remake of Howard Hawks's *Paid to Love,* 1927) with José Mojica; George Melford's *Don Juan diplomático* (USA: Malcolm St Clair's *The Boudoir Diplomat,* 1930) with Celia Montalván.

Creation of the first Mexican film society.

1932

Abelardo Rodríguez is inaugurated to fill the vacancy created by the resignation of Pascual Ortiz Rubio.

The communist writer José Revueltas is imprisoned in the Islas Marías. First solo exhibition of photographer Manuel Alvarez Bravo at the Posada gallery in Mexico City. At the Detroit Arts Institute, Diego Rivera paints the *Mural in Detroit*. Silvestre Revueltas composes two symphonic poems, *Colorines* and *Alcancías*. Carlos Chávez composes the choral work *Tierra Mojada* and the *Sinfonía de Antígona* for the presentation of Cocteau's *Antigone* at the Orientación theatre. Singer María Antonia Peregrino aka Toña la Negra makes her debut at the Lírico theatre. Production of *El Periquillo Sarmiento*, based on the novel by Joaquín Fernández de Lizardi. The Imperial theatre presents *La ciudad sin luces,* a parody of Charles Chaplin's *City Lights* (1931). Mariano Azuela's novel *La luciérnaga*.

Jorge Stahl builds the México Films studio. The year's six features are shot in the studios of Nacional Productora (the old Chapultepec studios): Antonio

Redes (Fred Zinnemann and Emilio Gómez, 1934)

Moreno's *Aguilas frente al sol;* Miguel Contreras Torres's *Revolución;* John H. Auer's *Una vida por otra;* Miguel Zacarías's. *Sobre las olas;* Arcady Boytler's *Mano a mano;* Fernando de Fuentes's *El anónimo.*

Spanish-language Hollywood: James Tinling's *El caballero de la noche* (a remake of John G. Blystone's *Dick Turpin,* 1925) and Lewis Seiler's *Mi último amor* (USA: Chandler Sprague's *Their Mad Moment),* both with José Mojica.

Publications: *El Cine Gráfico* (weekly); *El Exhibidor* (trade paper).

1933

Establishment of a minimum wage. Creation of the National Mortgage Bank for urban and public works, and to finance infrastructural construction. Always under the influence of Plutarco Elías Calles, the government begins to expropriate the clergy. The CROM breaks up: the leftist unions regroup in a new organisation, the Confederación General de Obreros y Campesinos de Mexico (CGOC) headed by Vicente Lombardo Toledano. The government grants autonomy to the Universidad de México. Lázaro Cárdenas is nominated to the presidency. The city of Tampico is devastated by a tornado.

Octavio Paz publishes his first poetry anthology, *Luna silvestre,* and establishes the journal *Cuadernos del Valle de México.* Leopoldo Méndez and Pablo O'Higgins create the League of Revolutionary Writers and Artists (LEAR). Rufino Tamayo paints *La música* at the old Mexican conservatory.

First year with a significant number of sound films: 21 features. Two works stand out: the Russian director Arcady Boytler's *La mujer del puerto,* introducing the actress Andrea Palma, and Fernando de Fuentes's *El compadre Mendoza,* an exceptionally lucid film about the Revolution. De Fuentes also makes *El prisionero trece* with an ending imposed by the censors, *La Calandria* and *El Tigre de Yautepec.* Other titles: Raphael J. Sevilla's *Almas encontradas;* José Bohr's *La sangre manda;* Ramón Peón's *La Llorona, Sagrario* and *Tiburón;* Chano Urueta's *Profanación* and *Enemigos.*

1934

Lázaro Cárdenas's election inaugurates a period of prosperity and social mobility and ends the Maximato, for the new president does not pay allegiance to General Calles. Creation of a bank for development, la Nacional Financiera.

A young seventeen-year-old man, Guillermo González Camarena, brings an iconoscope from the USA and builds an electronic television camera. Inauguration of the Palacio de Bellas Artes with paintings and murals by Rivera and Orozco. Birth of the publishing house Fondo de Cultura Económica. Samuel Ramos's essay *El perfil del hombre y la cultura en México* sets the trend for essays about national cultural identity. Pablo O'Higgins paints the mural series *La explotación del campesino y del obrero* at the Abelardo Rodríguez market (Mexico City). Salvador Novo publishes *Poemas proletarios.* Carlos Chávez composes the *Sinfonía proletaria* for chorus and orchestra and the choral work *El sol.* Publication of Manuel Alvarez Bravo's photograph *Obrero en huelga asesinado.* At the Garibaldi theatre: *El quejido del proletariado* by Juan D. del Moral. The Orientación theatre produces Alfonso Reyes's *Ifigenia cruel.* The Lírico theatre pays homage to Diego Rivera in Carlos M. Ortega and Francisco Benítez's play *El último fresco,* with sets designed by the painter himself.

Juárez y Maximiliano by Miguel Contreras Torres has an exclusive six-week run. Other directors also command attention: Gabriel Soria's *Chucho el Roto,* Raphael J. Sevilla's *Corazón bandolero* and Fernando de Fuentes's *Cruz Diablo* and *El fantasma del convento.* Juan Bustillo Oro combines two narrative points of view and an expressionist style in *Dos monjes.*

A social and nationalist trend begins with *Redes* by Fred Zinnemann and Emilio Gómez Muriel, produced by the Ministry of Education, shot by Paul Strand and scored by Silvestre Revueltas; the current continues in Carlos Novarro's *Janitzio* and in Adolfo Best Maugard's short film *Humanidad.* Other films: *¿Quién mató a Eva?* by José Bohr; *Mujeres sin alma* by Ramón Peón; *Bohemios* by Rafael E. Portas; *El primo Basilio* by Carlos de Nájera; *Rebelión* by Manuel Gómez.

Salvador Pruneda makes the animated cartoon *Don Catarino.*

1935

New president Lázaro Cárdenas takes on the mission of modernising Mexico and begins an ambitious agrarian reform programme. The newly organised National Committee in Defence of the Proletariat backs Cárdenas in power struggles with General Calles.

Inés and Carolina Amor open the Galería de Arte Mexicano. The Palacio de Bellas Artes shows the photographs of Henri Cartier-Bresson and Manuel Alvarez Bravo. Travelling shows introduce the comedians Mario Moreno 'Cantinflas' and Shillinsky. Joaquín Pardavé organises a political theatre company (*El peso murió, Camisas rojas* and *Educación socialista*). Roberto Soto presents *Los hijos de Pancho Villa, México político, Calles y más Calles, Santa política* and *Resurrección de Lázaro* on the Lírico stage. Rodolfo Usigli writes *Tres comedias impolíticas,* a biting critique of Calles. Silvestre Revueltas composes the ballet *El renacuajo paseador* and *Homenaje a García Lorca* for piano and orchestra; Carlos Chávez composes *Obertura republicana* and Manuel M. Ponce his *Poema elegíaco* for chamber orchestra. Agustín Lara signs the bolero 'Noche de Ronda'. José Vasconcelos publishes his autobiographical novel *Ulises Criollo;* Gregorio López y Fuentes publishes the novel *El indio.*

CLASA (Cinematográfica Latinoamericana S.A.) builds the best studios in Mexico. There, Fernando de Fuentes directs *¡Vámonos con Pancho Villa!,* an acute analysis of the Revolution despite its censored ending. The government rescues CLASA from bankruptcy and promotes the proliferation of ephemeral production co-operatives. Juan Orol's *Madre querida* stimulates the family melodrama.

Other films: Juan Bustillo Oro's *Monja, casada, virgen y mártir* and Gabriel Soria's *Martín Garatuza* are based on novels by General Vicente Riva Palacio; Arcady Boytler's *El tesoro de Pancho Villa;* José Bohr's *Sueño de amor* and *Luponini de Chicago;* F. de Fuentes's *La familia Dressel;* Ramón Peón's *Sor Juana Inés de la Cruz* and *Silencio sublime;* Juan Bustillo Oro's *El misterio del rostro pálido;* Raphael J. Sevilla's *María Elena;* Pedro Armendáriz was noticed in Miguel Zacarías's *Rosario,* while Arturo de Córdova debuts in Arcady Boytler's *Celos.*

In France, Celia Montalván appears in Jean Renoir's *Toni.* In Hollywood, the majors abandon Spanish-language production.

Mexico City has 37 movie houses. Slight diversification: of the 269 films released, 196 are from the USA, 20 from Germany, 12 from France and 11 from Great Britain; only 22 are Mexican.

1936

Former president Plutarco Elías Calles is expelled to the USA. The agrarian reform plan is accelerated when the Lázaro Cárdenas government expands land distribution to the poorest peasants. In Yucatán, 80% of the aloe plantations pass into the hands of agricultural workers. Regulation of the *ejido,* lands assigned to peasant groups. Vicente Lombardo Toledano establishes the Workers' University and participates with Fidel Velásquez in the creation of the Confederación de Trabajadores Mexicanos (CTM).

The success of the muralist movement continues: Orozco works at the Universidad de Guadalajara, and Rivera on the murals *La dictadura* and *México folklórico y turístico* at the Palacio de Bellas Artes; Francisco Goitia paints *Camino a la tumba.* Abel Quezada publishes his first comic strips, *Idolo rojo* and *Máximo Tops.* Opening of the Folies Bergère theatre. Cantinflas is a success in the play about land distribution, *San Lázaro el milagroso.* Rodolfo Usigli writes the comedy *Estado de secreto.* Agustín Lara scores the musical reviews *El rival* and *El robador de estrellas;* Gonzalo Curiel writes the song 'Vereda tropical'. Carlos Chávez composes *Sinfonía india.* Literature: José Rubén Romero's *Mi caballo, mi perro y mi rifle,* a novel based on the Revolution; *La tormenta* by José Vasconcelos; *Cuentos de todos colores* by Dr Atl.

Antonin Artaud visits the Tarahumara Indians and praises the paintings of María Izquierdo.

The international success of *Allá en el Rancho Grande* by Fernando de Fuentes wards off the crisis. Mexico becomes the premier Spanish-language film producer. Henceforth, local colour will be unabashedly displayed as part of a new formula combining folkloric nationalism and narrative mimeticism within the codes established by Hollywood.

A second *ranchero* (rural) melodrama consolidates the genre: *¡Ora Ponciano!* by Gabriel Soria. Cantinflas makes his cinematic debut in Miguel Contreras Torres's *No te engañes corazón.* The PNR finances the rural drama *Judas* by Manuel R. Ojeda.

First colour featurette, *Novillero* by Boris Maicon. Other films: F. de Fuentes's *Las mujeres mandan;* Gabriel Soria's *Mater nostra;* Rolando Aguilar's *Madres del mundo;* José Bohr's *Marihuana;* Miguel Zacarías's *El baúl macabro;* Juan Bustillo Oro's *Malditas sean las mujeres;* Raphael J. Sevilla's *Irma la mala; Suprema ley* by Rafael E. Portas, based on Federico Gamboa's novel, and Roberto O'Quigley's *Cielito lindo.*

1937

Nationalisation of the railways. President Lázaro Cárdenas offers protection and political asylum to Spanish Republicans. The first exiles, the 'children of Morelos', disembark in Veracruz in June: 500 orphans transported by the carrier *Mexique.* Leon Trotsky arrives in Mexico, where he will also benefit from Cárdenas's asylum. Organisation of agricultural co-operatives. Organisation of the Unión Nacional Sinarquista (fascist). General strike in the oil industry. Foundation of the Instituto Nacional Politécnico. XEW begins short-wave transmissions.

José Clemente Orozco paints *Hidalgo* in the Palacio del Gobierno in Guadalajara. Establishment of the National Engraving Workshop by Luis Arenas, Leopoldo Méndez and Pablo O'Higgins. The Folies Bergère presents Alfredo Robledo's *Balance de la Revolución* with Cantinflas headlined in the poster. The magician Fu-Man-Chu appears successfully at the Abreu theatre. Jorge Negrete makes his stage debut in a parody entitled *México Fu-Man-Chu.* Pedro Infante makes his first public singing appearance in Sinaloa. Pepe Guízar writes the song 'Guadalajara'. Gonzalo Curiel organises the orchestra Escuadrón del Ritmo. Production of the plays *El gesticulador* by Rodolfo Usigli and *El ausente* by Xavier Villaurrutia. Poetry: Octavio Paz's *Raíz del hómbre* and *Bajo tu clara sombra;* Carlos Pellicer's *Hora de junio.* Novel: *El resplandor* by Mauricio Magdaleno.

Industrial expansion and the beginning of Mexican cinema's golden age as 38 features are produced. Mexico City has a new studio, Azteca.

Ranchera comedies and melodramas are fashionable: Fernando de Fuentes's *Bajo el cielo de México; La Adelita* by Guillermo Hernández Gómez; Ramón Pereda's *Las cuatro milpas;* Rafael E. Portas's *Adiós Nicanor;* Chano Urueta's *Jalisco nunca pierde; Amapola del camino* and *Huapango* by Juan Bustillo Oro; *¡Así es mi tierra!* by Arcady Boytler; *A a orilla de un palmar* by Raphael J. Sevilla, and last but not least, the parody with children *Allá en el Rancho Chico* by René Cardona.

Fernando de Fuentes brings Lupe Vélez back to Mexico for *La Zandunga.* Jorge Negrete, prototype for the macho singing *charro,* makes his debut in *La madrina del diablo* by Ramón Peón. Adela Sequeyro 'Perlita' goes behind the camera: *La mujer de nadie.* A cursed work: *La mancha de la sangre* by Adolfo Best Maugard. Other films: A. Boytler's *Aguila o sol;* J. Bustillo Oro's *La honradez es un estorbo;* Rolando Aguilar's *Noches de gloria.*

Xavier Villaurrutia writes film criticism for the magazine *Hoy.*

1938

The Cárdenas government nationalises the oil industry. Washington quickly responds with economic reprisals and freezes Mexico's reserves. A large popular mobilisation supports the reorganisation of refineries under workers' control. Saturnino Cedillo, governor of San Luis Potosí, begins an anti-Cárdenas rebellion with the support of oil capitalists. The PNR becomes the Partido de la Revolución Mexicana (PRM). Land reform continues, mainly in the state of Michoacán and in Morelos's sugar plantations. Organisation of the Confederación Nacional Campesino, the official peasants' union.

Foundation of the Casa de España, a centre for research and animated debates among the exiled Spanish Republicans (the future Colegio de México). Creation of the Instituto Nacional de Antropología e Historia (INAH). In Mexico City, André Breton and Leon Trotsky write *Manifeste pour un art révolutionnaire indépendant*. Octavio Paz founds the journal *Taller*. Novels: *Tribulaciones de una familia decente* by Mariano Azuela, *La vida inútil de Pito Pérez* by José Rubén Romero. Frida Kahlo finishes her *Autorretrato con marco integrado y pájaros*. Rivera paints a portrait of Dolores del Río. Juan O'Gorman paints murals in the Mexico City airport. Silvestre Revueltas composes *Siete canciones para García Lorca* for voice and piano and the symphonic poem *Sensemayá*. Appearance of the weekly *Radiolandia*.

57 features are produced. Alejandro Galindo's *Mientras México duerme* is the first of a series of films about the underworld; a search for urban *costumbrismo*, such as *La casa del ogro* by Fernando de Fuentes; *Juntos, pero no revueltos* by Fernando A. Rivero. Galindo's *Refugiados en Madrid* makes reference to the war in Spain.

The 19th century and the Porfiriato return: *Perjura* by Raphael J. Sevilla; *María* by Chano Urueta. Comedy is in full bloom: for instance *Los millones de Chaflán* by Rolando Aguilar; *Los enredos de papá* by Miguel Zacarías. Populist films include *El indio* by Armando Vargas de la Maza and *Hambre* by Fernando A. Palacios. However, folkloric films predominate: for example *Nobleza ranchera* by Alfredo del Diestro; Chano Urueta's *Hombres de mar*; Raúl de Anda's *La tierra del mariachi*; Martin de Lucenay's *La Valentina*; Antonio Helú's *La india bonita*; Carlos Véjar's *Rosa de Xochimilco*; Fernando A. Rivero's *Aquí llegó el valentón*; *Juan Soldado* by Louis Gasnier. The melodrama is always a sure bet: for instance *Una luz en mi camino* by José Bohr. José Mojica is *El capitán aventurero* for Arcady Boytler. Publication of the weekly *Cinema Reporter*.

1939

Organisation of the Partido de Acción Nacional (PAN), linked to the Catholic church and other conservative forces. Creation of the Banco Nacional de Comercio Exterior and the Banco Nacional de Crédito Ejidal (agricultural credits). President Cárdenas pushes through a constitutional amendment stipulating that the federal government has exclusive oil-exploitation rights. Saturnino Cedillo's rebellion is suppressed and he is executed. Thousands of Spanish refugees are given the right to naturalisation.

Appearance of the daily *Novedades*. The CTM publishes the newspaper *El Popular*. Orozco paints murals at the Cabañas hospice in Guadalajara. Frida Kahlo finishes *Las dos Fridas*. In Paris, a Mexican art show is held at the Renou et Colle gallery, introduced by André Breton. Foundation of the Spanish Republican Centre and the Hispanic-Mexican Institute Ruiz de Alarcón. The Spanish refugee Rafael Giménez Siles creates the publishing house EDIAPSA (Editora y Distribuidora Iberoamericana de Publicaciones, S.A.). José Gorostiza publishes the poem *Muerte sin fin*. Silvestre Revueltas composes the ballet *La coronela*. Alberto Domínguez composes the songs 'Perfidia' and 'Frenesí'. On stage, Cantinflas and Roberto Soto are the public's favourite comedians.

A decrease in production (38 feature-length films) as Argentina overtakes Mexico. A presidential decree forces theatres to programme at least one national film per month. RKO decides to invest in the Mexican industry (*Perfidia* and *Odio* by William Rowland). Formation of the Sindicato de Trabajadores de la Industria Cinematográfica (STIC, Union of Film Industry Workers).

The comedy *En tiempos de don Porfirio* by Juan Bustillo Oro cultivates nostalgia for the *ancien régime*. Melodrama eclectically increases its range, tackling *indigenismo* in Chano Urueta's *La noche de los mayas*, colonial history in Raphael J. Sevilla's *El secreto de la monja*, national literature in Chano Urueta's *Los de abajo*, based on Mariano Azuela's novel, and foreign literature in *Corazón de niño* by Alejandro Galindo, based on Edmond D'Amicis's work. Other films: *Con los dorados de Villa* by Raúl de Anda; *Café Concordia* by Alberto Gout; *Papacito lindo* by Fernando de Fuentes.

In Hollywood, Lupe Vélez becomes the 'Mexican Spitfire'.

1940

Mexico has 19,654,000 inhabitants. Leon Trotsky is assassinated in his house in Coyoacán. In Vichy, an accord is signed whereby Mexico agrees to accept all Spanish refugees currently on French soil. Development of a vast railway network. First Inter-American Indigenist Congress. In December, having distributed 18 million hectares among the peasantry during his term, Lázaro Cárdenas hands over the presidency to General Manuel Avila Camacho. La Casa de España becomes El Colegio de México, a prestigious higher-education centre.

International surrealist exposition at the Galería de Arte Mexicano. *XX Centuries of Mexican Art* at the Museum of Modern Art in New York. Frida Kahlo paints *La mesa herida*. During the electoral campaign, political theatre proliferates. The writer Manuel Castro Padilla is murdered outside the Lírico theatre after attending the opening of his play *Lo que nos espera*. A musician of Spanish origin, Rodolfo Halffter, creates the modern ballet company La Paloma Azul and successfully stages *La coronela* by Silvestre Revueltas with choreography by Waldeen. Novel: *Memorias de Pancho Villa* by Martín Luis Guzmán.

Mexican production further decreases to 29 films, while Spain recuperates rapidly from the war and Argentina maintains its pre-eminent position in the Spanish-speaking market. Two box-office successes: *Ahí está el detalle* by Juan Bustillo Oro with Cantinflas, and *El Charro Negro* by Raúl de Anda with the director/producer as a new mythic hero.

Other films: *Pobre Diablo* and *El zorro de Jalisco* by José Benavides Jr; *Allá en el trópico, Creo en Dios* and *El jefe máximo* by Fernando de Fuentes; *Mala yerba* by Gabriel Soria; *La torre de los suplicios* by Raphael J. Sevilla.

Mexico City has forty movie theatres, only twelve of which are first-run cinemas.

1941

The adoption of an industrial law is a sign of the Avila Camacho administration's interest in industrial development. The metallurgical and electrical sectors are especially favoured. Federal labour laws are regularised, establishing terms of prior notice for strikes.

José Clemente Orozco paints *La Justicia* and *La Violencia* in the Supreme Court building. María Izquierdo finishes painting *Adornos*. A burlesque company opens the Apolo theatre. Manuel M. Ponce writes *Concierto del sur* for guitar and orchestra, played for the first time by Andrés Segovia. Agustín Lara composes the bolero 'Solamente una vez'. Jesús Silva Herzog publishes the journal *Cuadernos Americanos*. Novel: *Los muros de agua* by José

Revueltas. Poetry: *Recinto y otras imágenes* by Carlos Pellicer. Production of Xavier Villaurrutia's play *La hiedra*. Creation of the bilingual publisher Quetzal, partly financed by French capital and directed by the Spaniard B. Costa-Amic. Foundation of the Colegio Madrid to receive the children of Spanish refugees.

Directorial debuts by Emilio Fernández (*La isla de la pasión*) and Julio Bracho (*¡Ay, qué tiempos, señor don Simón!*). Comedias rancheras do well at the box-office, such as *¡Ay, Jalisco, no te rajes!* by Joselito Rodríguez. Cantinflas does well also: *Ni sangre ni arena* by Alejandro Galindo and *El gendarme desconocido* by Miguel M. Delgado. Palillo attempts to compete with *Lo que el viento trajo* by José Benavides Jr. Other comedies: Fernando Soler's *El barbero prodigioso*; Fernando de Fuentes's *La gallina clueca*. Melodrama continues to flourish with *Cuando los hijos se van* by Juan Bustillo Oro; *La epopeya del camino* by Francisco Elías; *Flor de Fango* by Juan J. Ortega; *Seda, sangre, y sol* by Fernando A. Rivero.

Mexico pays tribute to wartime pan-Americanism with the super-production *Simón Bolívar* by Manuel Contreras Torres and the musical comedy *La liga de las canciones* by Chano Urueta, whose *El conde de Montecristo* also initiates a series of literary adaptations.

US director Herbert Kline films *The Forgotten Village*. There is a record number of US imports: 218 out of 296 films released. Argentina provided 30 feature films, Mexico 22 (the decrease in production slows down, 37 Mexican films are produced during the year). Establishment of four production houses: Jesús Grovas, Filmex (Simón Wishnak–Gregorio Wallerstein), Films Mundiales (Agustín J. Fink), Posa Films (Santiago Reachi–Jacques Gelman).

A presidential decree creates a Censorship Department under the Ministry of the Interior to vet scripts.

1942

Mexico declares war against the Axis nations after a German submarine sinks the tanker *Potrero del Llano*. Adoption of obligatory military service. 300,000 Mexican workers are sent to the USA to replace the enlisted manpower. Creation of the Mexican Social Security Institute. Foundation of the Escuela Normal Superior.

Birth of Radio Mil and the Radio Continental networks. Orozco writes a series of autobiographical articles for the newspaper *Excélsior*. Antonio Ruiz creates the Ministry of Education's school of painting and sculpture. Rivera begins the construction of the

Anahuacalli pyramid to house his pre-Colombian art collection. Juan O'Gorman paints *Ciudad de México*. Miguel Covarrubias and Wolfgang Paalen begin the journal *Dyn* and publish Paalen's essay *Adieu au surréalisme*. Leonora Carrington moves to Mexico, where Benjamin Péret also lives. The Manuel Avila Camacho government orders the temporary closure of the Salón Colonial and censors the musical review *Los barberos de don Manuel*. Víctor Cordero composes the corrido 'Juan Charrasqueado'. Carlos Chávez writes the ballet *La hija de Colquide*. Essays: Edmundo O'Gorman's *Los fundamentos de la historia de América*; Alfonso Reyes's *Ultima Tule*.

Because of the war, Hollywood's imports decrease (163 out of a total of 233) and national production increases (47 features; Argentina continues ahead of Mexico with 56).

María Félix debuts in Miguel Zacarías's *El peñón de las ánimas*; Ismael Rodríguez's directorial debut with *¡Qué lindo es Michoacán!* Julio Bracho directs the new literary super-production *Historia de un gran amor* based on Alarcón's work. Cantinflas makes the parodic *Los tres mosqueteros* for Miguel M. Delgado. Other comedies include *El baisano Jalil* by Joaquín Pardavé; *Yo bailé con don Porfirio* by Gilberto Martínez Solares; *El circo* by M.M. Delgado. Melodramas: *El ángel negro* by Juan Bustillo Oro; *Soy puro mexicano* by Emilio Fernández; *Noche de ronda* by Ernesto Cortázar.

First colour feature: *Así se quiere en Jalisco* by Fernando de Fuentes.

A religious comeback: *Jesús de Nazareth* by José Díaz Morales; *La virgen morena* by Gabriel Soria; *La virgen que forjó una patria* by Julio Bracho, with Ramón Novarro.

Creation of the Banco Cinematográfico S.A. Appearance of the magazine *México Cinema*.

1943

The size of the *ejido* increases from 4 to 6 hectares. The government imposes strict price controls and creates CONASUPO to organise food distribution. Establishment of the Confederación Nacional de Organizaciones Populares (CNOP), representing small and medium businesses.

Publication of the journal *El Hijo Pródigo* (which includes the first Spanish translation of Lautréamont's work). Rodolfo Usigli writes *Corona de sombra*, a historical drama about the ephemeral empire of Maximilian. Novel: José Revueltas's *El luto humano*; Max Aub's *Campo cerrado*. José Clemente Orozco designs the sets for the dance season of the Ballet de México. Pedro Infante releases his first

record. Inauguration of the first *Salón Libre 20 de Noviembre* by painters, engravers and sculptors. The painter Gerardo Murillo (Dr Atl) begins a series of canvasses of Mexican volcanos.

Marked increase in national production (70 features). Mexico leads all Spanish-speaking countries. The STIC has 7,000 members.

The best of the year: *María Candelaria* by the team of Emilio Fernández and Gabriel Figueroa; *Distinto amanecer* by Julio Bracho. *Flor silvestre* (also by Fernández) heralded Dolores del Río's return to her country. María Félix is a hit in *Doña Bárbara* by Fernando de Fuentes (six-week run).

US director Norman Foster makes the third version of *Santa*. Literary scavenging continues: Tolstoy's *Resurrección* by Gilberto Martínez Solares; Victor Hugo's *Los miserables* by Fernando A. Rivero; Alexandre Dumas's *El hombre de la máscara de hierro* by Marco Aurelio Galindo; A. Dumas fils's *La dama de las camelias* by Gabriel Soria; Jules Verne's *Miguel Strogoff* by Miguel M. Delgado; Émile Zola's *Naná* by Celestino Gorostiza; Maupassant's *La fuga* by Norman Foster; Cantinflas's parodic *Romeo y Julieta* by Miguel M. Delgado.

Other films: Alejandro Galindo's *Tribunal de justicia*; Juan Bustillo Oro's *México de mis recuerdos*; Miguel Contreras Torres's *La vida inútil de Pito Pérez*; Gilberto Martínez Solares's *Internado para señoritas* and *El globo de Cantolla*; Julio Bracho's *La corte de Faraón*, the last three films starring Mapy Cortés. Chano Urueta's *Ave sin nido* was inspired by a popular radio serial.

Publication of the magazine *Diario Fílmico Mexicano*.

1944

Minister of Education Jaime Torres Bodet begins a literacy campaign. Adoption of a social security law.

Inauguration of the Instituto Francés de America Latina (IFAL) under the auspices of liberated France. Opening of the National History Museum at the Chapultepec castle. Philosopher Leopoldo Zea defends his doctoral theses about the rise and fall of positivism in Mexico. Alfonso Reyes publishes the essays *Tentativas y orientaciones* and *Norte y sur*. Theatre: Xavier Villaurrutia's *El hierro candente*. Poetry: Alí Chumacero's *Páramo de sueños*; short story: *Dios en la tierra* by José Revueltas. The Avila Camacho government creates a national award for science and arts. Singer Lucha Reyes commits suicide. Influenced by Cantinflas, the famous Folies Bergère transforms its musical shows into variety theatre, giving priority to sketches, improvisation and circus-like numbers.

Construction of Churubusco, the country's principal studios, in partnership with RKO (50%), headed by radio magnate Emilio Azcárraga.

Roberto Gavaldón's directorial debut, *La barraca*, based on Vicente Blasco Ibáñez, is a quasi-Spanish exile film. Emilio Fernández and his team continue with *Las abandonadas* (which had censorship problems) and *Bugambilia*. Other films: Julio Bracho's *Crepúsculo;* Antonio Momplet's *Amok;* Miguel Zacarías's *Me he de comer esa tuna;* Gilberto Martínez Solares's *Un beso en la noche;* Juan Bustillo Oro's *Cuando quiere un mexicano;* Norman Foster's *La hora de la verdad;* Ismael Rodríguez's *Escándalo de estrellas;* René Cardona's *El museo del crimen;* Juan Orol's *Los misterios del hampa.*

1945

The Virgin of Guadalupe, patron of Mexico, is declared empress of the Americas by Pope Pious XII. A constitutional amendment allows the church to re-enter the field of education and to develop a vast confessional network. Meeting in Chapultepec of an inter-American conference on peace and war-related problems.

The Palacio de Bellas Artes pays homage to nineteenth-century painter Juan Cordero with a show of his entire *oeuvre*. Orozco paints murals at the Hospital de Jesús. Rivera paints the canvas *Mujer con lirios;* Siqueiros works on *Nueva Democracia*. The gallery Decoración organises the first engraving salon. Architect Luis Barragán designs the Jardines del Pedregal. Francisco Monterde publishes the historical work *Moctezuma, el de la silla de oro*. Max Aub writes the novel *Campo de sangre*. Foundation of the Sociedad de Autores y Compositores Musicales. Rodolfo Halffter writes the ballet *Elena la traicionera*. Chucho Navarro invents and introduces the *requinto,* a new small guitar which became very popular in Mexican music. Miguel Aceves Mejía makes his first record of *canciones rancheras*.

Hollywood imports drop to their lowest level: 86 out of 152 films released. Mexico produces 82 features. The principal films of the year include Alejandro Galindo's *Campeón sin corona* and Emilio Fernández's *La perla*.

Other films: Julio Bracho's *El monje blanco* and *Cantaclaro;* Fernando de Fuentes's *La selva de fuego;* Miguel Zacarías's *Flor de durazno;* Juan Bustillo Oro's *Canaima;* Ismael Rodríguez's *Como lloran los valientes;* Roberto Gavaldón's *El socio;* E. Fernández's *Pepita Jiménez;* Antonio Momplet's *Vértigo;* José Díaz Morales's *Pervertida; El hijo desobediente* by Humberto Gómez Landero, featuring the comedian Tin Tan.

The 'creative' talent breaks off from the STIC and forms the Sindicato de Trabajadores de la Producción Cinematográfica (STPC), headed by Cantinflas, Negrete, Figueroa, Galindo and Gavaldón. A governmental arbiter establishes the limits: distribution, exhibition and newsreels remain within the STIC; feature films go to the STPC. Películas Mexicanas S.A. (Pelmex) takes over Latin American distribution. Mexico City has one more studio (Cuauhtémoc) and a magazine (*Cine Continental*).

1946

The party in power reorganises, takes the name Partido Revolucionario Institucional (PRI), and elects its candidate Miguel Alemán to the presidency. The army opens fire on demonstrators in León (Guanajuato): fifty dead. Constitutional reforms favour new *latifundios* (large estates). Privatisation of Radio Nacional de Mexico, formerly the property of the official party.

Guillermo González Camarena operates the first experimental television transmitter which airs musical programmes on Saturdays. Choreographer Martha Graham stages Carlos Chávez's ballet *La hija de Colquide*. Chávez composes 'Canto a la tierra'. Rodolfo Halffter edits the journal *Nuestra Música* and rules the Ediciones Mexicanas de Música. Revival of the musical comedy *Chin chun chan*. Rosita Fornés and Manuel Medel's company open the Tívoli theatre. Celia Montalván's troupe is much in demand. Roberto Montenegro founds the Museo de Artes Populares in Toluca. Rufino Tamayo paints *Mujeres alcanzando la luna*. Poetry: Xavier Villaurrutia's *Nostalgia de la muerte*.

International recognition for Emilio Fernández as *María Candelaria* goes to Cannes while *Enamorada* has a seven-week run. Roberto Gavaldón gives a masterpiece to melodrama with *La otra*. Ismael Rodríguez prefers action: *Los tres García* and *Vuelven los García*.

Other films include Gilberto Martínez Solares's *Su última aventura;* Fernando de Fuentes's *La devoradora;* Julio Bracho's *La mujer de todos;* Antonio Momplet's *A media luz;* R. Gavaldón's *La vida íntima de Marco Antonio y Cleopatra* with the Argentine actor Luis Sandrini.

Among the foreigners attracted to the Mexican industry, there is Luis Buñuel with *Gran casino*.

Merging of Clasa and Films Mundiales. Inauguration of the Tepeyac studio. 288 million pesos ($144 million) are invested in the cinema. The Mexican Academy of Cinematographic Arts and Sciences inaugurates the Ariel awards. There are 1,245 theatres in the nation, with c.100 in Mexico City.

1947

Women obtain the right to vote in municipal elections. President Miguel Alemán asks Guillermo Gómez Camarena and writer Salvador Novo to study the US and British television systems. Eventually, the government decides to emulate the US system of private and commercial television. Massacre in Tuxtla-Gutiérrez (Chiapas). Agrarian politics changes and favours big landowners.

Publication of the daily *Ovaciones* which emphasises sports and brief news items. Creation of the Instituto Nacional de Bellas Artes (INBA), headed by Carlos Chávez, who also founds the Academy of Mexican Dance. Rivera paints the mural *Sueño de una noche dominical en la Alameda Central*. Leonora Carrington paints *La casa de enfrente*. The Popular engraving workshop publishes *Estampas de la Revolución mexicana*. A new radio station appears, La Voz de México and boycotts many songs deemed immoral, such as 'La última noche', 'Diez minutos más', 'Tú ya no soplas', 'Aventurera', 'Pervertida' and 'Pecadora'. Inspired by his wife of two years, María Félix, Agustín Lara composes the waltz 'María bonita'. First Mexican book fair. Agustín Yáñez publishes the novel *Al filo del agua*. Poetry: Manuel Maples Arce's *Memorial de la sangre*. Essay: Francisco Monterde's *Moctezuma II, señor del Anáhuac;* Emilio Abreu Gómez's *Quetzalcóatl, sueño y vigilia*. Theatre: *Invitación a la muerte* by Xavier Villaurrutia; *La huella* by Agustín Lazo.

Production decrease: 58 features compared to 72 the previous year. The México Films studios close. While *La perla* receives awards at Venice, Emilio Fernández films *Río Escondido*. The year's most successful film is Ismael Rodríguez's *Nosotros los pobres,* prototype for the suburban/working-class melodrama starring Pedro Infante.

Films about *cabareteras* and prostitutes take off, especially when starring María Antonieta Pons (*Angel o demonio* by Victor Urruchúa; *La sin ventura* by Tito Davison; *La bien pagada* by Alberto Gout), Emilia Guiú (*Pecadora* by José Díaz Morales) or Meche Barba (*Cortesana* by A. Gout).

Other films: *La diosa arrodillada* by Roberto Gavaldón; *El ladrón* by Julio Bracho; *Soledad* by Miguel Zacarías; *Maria la O* by Adolfo Fernández Bustamante.

The Banco Cinematográfico (with the state as majority shareholder) and independent producers set up Películas Nacionales to oversee domestic distribution.

1948

An economic crisis strikes the nation. The currency is devaluated by almost 100%; the dollar's value increases from 4.85 to 8.75 pesos. Decrease in agricultural and mineral production. Vicente Lombardo Toledano breaks off with the official union, the Confederación de Trabajadores Mexicanos (HCTM) and creates the Partido Popular Socialista (PPS).

Complete show of Rufino Tamayo's work at the Palacio de Bellas Artes. José Clemente Orozco paints the mural *Juárez, el clero, y los imperialistas* at the Chapultepec castle. Poetry: Carlos Pellicer's *Subordinaciones;* Alí Chumacero's *Imágenes desterradas*.

Essay: Alfonso Reyes's *Letras de la Nueva España*. The Trio Los Panchos makes its first Mexico City appearance at the cabaret El Patio. The dancer Yolanda Montes 'Tongolele' triumphs at the Tívoli. The musical review *El cuarto poder* causes the temporary closing of the Lírico theatre. First performance of Gonzalo Curiel's *Concierto para piano y orquesta en ré bémol*.

Cantinflas is very successful with Miguel M. Delgado's *El supersabio,* which has a twelve-week run. Hollywood regains its position in distribution: 203 films out of 369. Exhibition flourishes with the appearance of several new theatres in Mexico City. Annual attendance passes the 130 million mark. Nevertheless, a crisis is visible, with production (81 feature films) becoming increasingly more formulaic. The best is always the work of Emilio Fernández (*Pueblerina, Salón México, Maclovia*). Alejandro Galindo continues to explore the urban milieu (*¡Esquina … bajan!; Hay lugar para dos; Una familia de tantas*).

The cabaret consecrates *rumbera* Ninón Sevilla and musician Agustín Lara, as well as the singers Pedro Vargas and Toña la Negra (*Revancha* by Alberto Gout). Comedian Tin Tan hits his stride with Gilberto Martínez Solares's *Calabacitas tiernas*. Other titles include *Los tres huastecos* and *Ustedes los ricos* by Ismael Rodríguez; Roberto Gavaldón's *Han matado a Tongolele;* Matilde Landeta's *Lola Casanova;* Julio Bracho's *Rosenda;* Miguel Zacarías's *La vorágine;* the colour remake of *Allá en el Rancho Grande* by Fernando de Fuentes. On the fringes of the industry, José Ignacio Retes films *Noches de angustia*.

Creation of the film society of the Instituto Francés de América Latina (IFAL).

1949

Establishment of the Instituto Nacional Indigenista. Creation of the Compañía de Importación–Exportación de México, S.A. (CEIMSA). Oil

María Félix in *Maclovia* (Emilio Fernández, 1948)

remains the principal source of revenues.

The Cuban Dámaso Pérez Prado introduces the mambo, a rhythm that would define an entire musical epoch. Creation of the Salón de la Plástica Mexicana. Complete show of the work of Diego Rivera at the Palacio de Bellas Artes. Establishment of El Ateneo Español de México, a space for conferences and debates. Juan Grijalbo, a Spanish refugee, opens the publishing house bearing his name. José Revueltas publishes the novel *Los días terrenales.* Within the indigenist tradition, Ramón Rubín writes *El callado dolor de los tzotziles.* Poetry: Jaime Torres Bodet's *Sonetos.* The newspaper *Novedades* begins to publish the special section 'México en la cultura'.

New legislation regulating the film industry is adopted but is unable to stop the decline of the industry or to ease censorship: instead of favouring new talent, it protects those working within existing structures. Mexico produces 108 features, including Emilio Fernández's *La malquerida;* Alberto Gout's *Aventurera;* Gilberto Martínez Solares's *El rey del barrio; La oveja negra* and *No desearás la mujer de tu hijo* by Ismael Rodríguez; *Cuatro contra el mundo* and *Confidencias de un ruletero* by Alejandro Galindo; Luis Buñuel's *El gran calavera;* Roberto Gavaldón's *La casa chica; Doña Diabla* and *El embajador* by Tito Davison; *Perdida* by Fernando A. Rivero; *San Felipe de Jesús* and *La posesión* by Julio Bracho; *La Negra Angustias* by Matilde Landeta; *Vino el remolino y nos alevantó* by Juan Bustillo Oro.

The writer José Revueltas attacks William Jenkins's exhibition monopoly and is disowned by his union, the STPC.

1950

Population: 25,791,000, of which 3 million live in

Mexico City. Illiteracy remains at 44%. There are 1.8 million radio receivers in Mexico. Rómulo O'Farril opens Canal 4, the first commercial television station in Latin America. The economy develops fast; for the first time industrial production exceeds the combined output of the agricultural and mining sectors.

Creation of the Instituto Mexicano del Café. Octavio Paz publishes *El laberinto de la soledad,* a fundamental essay about Mexican identity. Leopoldo Zea organises the philosophical group Hiperión, which will concentrate on researching *mexicanidad.* The Unión Nacional de Autores's first annual theatre season begins with the play *Saber morir* by Wilberto Cantón. Diego Rivera designs sets for *El cuadrante de la soledad* at the Abreu theatre. Production of Emilio Carballido's comedy *Rosalba y los llaveros.* Canal 4 airs *Teatro de la televisión.* André Breton presents the first Parisian exhibition of Rufino Tamayo. Opening of the Galería Popular José Guadalupe Posada. Mathias Goeritz opens the galleries Clardecor (Mexico City) and Arquitac (Guadalajara). Festival of Mexican culture in Havana; exhibition of Mexican engravings in Tokyo. Javier Solís, one of the great names of the *canción ranchera,* releases his first record. Rubén Méndez writes the songs 'Cartas a Eufemia' and 'Pénjamo'. Xavier Villaurrutia commits suicide.

With *Los olvidados,* Luis Buñuel demonstrates an anti-mainstream personality able to play ironically with the conventions of the Mexican industry (cf. *Susana*). 125 features produced, including Roberto Gavaldón's *Rosauro Castro, En la palma de tu mano* and *Deseada;* Albert Gout's *Sensualidad;* Fernando Méndez's *El Suavecito; El gavilán pollero* by Rogelio A. González; Fernando de Fuentes's *Crimen y castigo* and *Por la puerta falsa;* Alejandro Galindo's *Capitán de rurales* and *Doña Perfecta; El hombre sin rostro* by Juan Bustillo Oro; Carmen Toscano de Moreno Sánchez's *Memorias de un mexicano;* Emilio Fernández's *Víctimas del pecado;* Tito Davison's *La mujer que yo amé;* Gilberto Martínez Solares's *¡Ay amor . . . cómo me has puesto!, La marca del Zorrillo* and *Simbad el mareado; Sobre las olas* by Ismael Rodríguez; *Pecado* by Luis César Amadori.

Fashionable rhythms invade the screen: Chano Urueta's *Al son del mambo;* Ramón Pereda's *La reina del mambo.*

Miguel Contreras Torres begins his campaign against the Jenkins monopoly. Merger of the Churubusco and Azteca studios.

1951

Construction of low-income housing. Mexico satisfies its agricultural needs and is able to export rice, sugar and bananas. 27% of all foreign investments are from the USA.

Emilio Azcárraga Vidaurreta starts the second television network, Canal 2; the first sports broadcast is a baseball game. The radio serial *El derecho de nacer* by Félix B. Caignet breaks all audience records and is filmed by Zacarías Gómez Urquiza as an utterly formulaic but successful melodrama. First great classical dance season in Mexico City: the dancer José Limón completes four choreographies, among them Silvestre Revueltas's *Redes.* Leonard Bernstein is invited by the National Symphonic Orchestra for a series of concerts. The songs 'Yo, Ella' and 'Cuatro caminos' by José Alfredo Jiménez mark a turning-point for the *canción ranchera.* The Instituto Nacional de Bellas Artes produces *Los empeños de una casa* to celebrate the tricentennial of Sister Juana Inés de la Cruz's birth. Poetry: Octavio Paz's *¿Aguila o sol?* Novel: Max Aub's *Campo abierto.* Theatre: Sergio Magaña's *Los signos del zodíaco.* Essay: Alfonso Reyes's *Ancorajes.*

Symptoms of the industry's sclerosis multiply (cf. the film of *El derecho de nacer* and the decrease in production to 101 features); even established directors lose their touch: Emilio Fernández's *La bien amada* and *Acapulco,* Alejandro Galindo's *Dicen que soy comunista,* Julio Bracho's *Paraíso robado* and *La ausente,* Alberto Gout's *No niego mi pasado* and *Mujeres sacrificadas,* Roberto Gavaldón's *La noche avanza.* Henceforth, hack film-makers will reign as cheap quickies, *churros* and potboilers become the norm. Jorge Stahl opens a new studio, San Angel Inn. Comedies contribute a breath of fresh air: Gilberto Martínez Solares's *El revoltoso* with Tin Tan; Ismael Rodríguez's *A toda máquina (ATM)* with Pedro Infante and Luis Aguilar. The warm reception of *Los olvidados* in Cannes reinvigorates Buñuel's career. He also directs *La hija del engaño, Una mujer sin amor* and *Subida al cielo.*

1952

Inauguration of the Ciudad Universitaria. Construction of the Ciudad Juárez–Mexico–Ciudad Cuauhtémoc road. 5.3 million hectares will have been distributed to peasants by the end of President Miguel Alemán's term. Vicente Lombardo Toledano fights for the presidency in the name of the Partido Popular. The PRI candidate, Adolfo Ruiz Cortínes, is elected president.

A third commercial television network appears:

Canal 5, owned by Guillermo González Camarena. Canal 2 gets new headquarters, Televicentro, with ultra-modern equipment. The radio station Voz de México transmits the Olympic Games from Helsinki. First television serial: *Los ángeles de la calle* by Félix B. Caignet, adapted by Brígida Alexander. Mathias Goeritz builds the Museo Experimental del Eco attempting to introduce 'emotional architecture'. Architect Luis Barragán begins the construction of the Tlalpan chapel. Creation of the Orquestra de Cámara de Bellas Artes. Igor Stravinski is invited by the National Symphonic Orchestra. Rodolfo Halffter composes *Obertura festiva*. In popular music, José Alfredo Jiménez continues his success with the *rancheras*, 'Corazón' and 'Serenata sin luna'. Rufino Tamayo paints two murals in the Palacio de Bellas Artes and the canvas *Homenaje a la raza india*. The work of the indigenous painter Hermenegildo Bustos is shown in Paris and Stockholm. Anthropologist Ricardo Pozas publishes *Juan Pérez Jolote*. Leopoldo Zea begins the collection *Mexico y la mexicanidad*; Zea also publishes the essay *Conciencia y posibilidad del mexicano*. Theatre: Celestino Gorostiza's *El color de nuestra piel*; Rodolfo Usigli's *Jano es una muchacha*. Essay: Alfonso Reyes's *La X en la frente*. Short story: *Confabulario* by Juan José Arreola.

Luis Buñuel once again overcomes industrial constraints in *El, Robinson Crusoe* and *El bruto*. The STPC participates in the production of *El rebozo de Soledad* by Roberto Gavaldón. 98 films are produced, including Ismael Rodríguez's *Dos tipos de cuidado,* reuniting Jorge Negrete and Pedro Infante; Rogelio A. González's *Tal para cual*; Gilberto Martínez Solares's *El bello durmiente* and *Me traes de un ala,* always with Tin Tan; Alberto Gout's *Aventura en Río,* with Ninón Sevilla for the last time.

René Cardona's *El Enmascarado de Plata* inaugurates the prolific genre of masked wrestler movies.

Creation of the film society Progreso. Manuel Barbachano Ponce begins the company Teleproducciones and rejuvenates the newsreel with *Tele-Revista* and *Cine-Verdad*.

1953

President Adolfo Ruiz Cortines and US president Dwight D. Eisenhower inaugurate the Falcon dam over the Rio Bravo.

Radio Joya begins FM transmissions. Juan Rulfo publishes the short story *El llano en llamas*. Philosopher Leopoldo Zea writes *América como conciencia*. Publication of the journal *Artes de México* and of the magazine *¡Siempre!* Opening of the Insurgentes theatre, with a façade decorated by

Diego Rivera which features a triumphant Cantinflas and other historical characters. The opening programme is the musical review *Yo Colón,* a violent parody of the government and Cantinflas's last stage appearance. Rivera paints his last murals at the Hospital de la Raza. Rufino Tamayo wins the grand prize in painting at the São Paulo biennial. First one-man show of José Luis Cuevas's work in Mexico City. Show in honour of Frida Kahlo at the Contemporary Art Gallery. Mathias Goeritz inaugurates the Museo del Eco. The Instituto Nacional de Bellas Artes publishes Jesús Bal y Gay's *Polifonía sagrada de los siglos XVI y XVII*. José Alfredo Jiménez writes the songs 'Jinete' and 'Paloma Querida'.

83 feature films are produced. Eduardo Garduño, director of the Banco Nacional Cinematográfico, proposes a plan to renovate the industry and restructure the market, but his suggested 50% domestic film quota is never enforced.

Benito Alazraki's *Raíces* marks the debut of Manuel Barbachano Ponce as independent producer. Emilio Fernández directs four films: *La rosa blanca, Reportaje, El rapto* and most notably, *La red;* Alejandro Galindo directs *Espaldas mojadas* and *Los Fernández de Peralvillo;* Roberto Gavaldón makes *El niño y la niebla* and *Camelia;* Luis Buñuel directs *Abismos de pasión* and *La ilusión viaja en tranvía*.

French director Yves Allégret shoots *Les Orgueilleux* in Mexico.

1954

Currency devaluation (the US dollar is at 12.5 pesos). The government announces an austerity plan to decrease public spending and deal with inflation. Establishment of the Partido Auténtico de la Revolución Mexicana (PARM).

Creation of television Channel 7 in Puebla. First cable television service in Nogales (Sonora). The painters José Luis Cuevas, Alberto Gironella, Pedro Coronel and Enrique Echeverría write a manifesto denouncing the privileges of the muralists within the official salons. Leopoldo Méndez produces engravings for the film *La rebelión de los colgados*. Playwright Emilio Carballido receives the *El Nacional* prize for his play *Las palabras cruzadas,* later re-titled *La danza que sueña la tortuga*. The Instituto de Bellas Artes sponsors theatre festivals, first organised at regional level, later nationally. Rodolfo Halffter composes *Tres piezas* for orchestra and strings. Tomás Méndez Sosa writes the song 'Cucurrucucú paloma'. Poetry: Octavio Paz's *Semillas para un himno;* Jaime Torres Bodet's *Fronteras*. Publication of Carlos Fuentes's first book, a short-story anthology entitled *Los días enmascarados.*

Mexico produces 118 features, but only 22 are distributed during the year. While William Jenkins consolidates his exhibition monopoly, production is undercapitalised.

Noteworthy films include Rogelio A. González's *La vida no vale nada;* Emilio Fernández and Alfredo B. Crevenna's *La rebelión de los colgados;* Tulio Demicheli's *Un extraño en la escalera;* Luis Buñuel's *El río y la muerte;* Emilio Gómez Muriel's *El joven Juárez;* Julio Bracho's *María la voz;* Alejandro Galindo's *¡Y mañana serán mujeres!;* Ismael Rodríguez's *Los paquetes de Paquita* and *Maldita ciudad;* Roberto Gavaldón's *Sombra verde;* Alberto Gout's *La sospechosa;* Fernando Méndez's *Los tres Villalobos;* Gilberto Martínez Solares's *El vizconde de Montecristo.*

1955

Women participate in legislative elections for the first time.

Merger of television channels 2, 4 and 5 into Telesistema Mexicano S.A. Establishment of Bloque de Unidad Obrera to represent most of the country's labour unions. Juan Rulfo publishes his only novel *Pedro Páramo,* introducing 'magical realism' to Latin American literature. Publication of the *Revista Mexicana de Literatura,* edited by Carlos Fuentes. The essayist Alfonso Reyes begins to edit his complete works. First French translation of *Livres de Chilam Balam* by Benjamin Péret. Painter José Luis Cuevas exhibits in Paris. Remedios Varo paints *Ruptura.* Establishment of the cultural association Jardín del Arte. Creation of the university theatre group Teatro en Copa under the direction of Héctor Azar. Cuco Sánchez composes 'Puñalada trapera', one of the most representative titles of the *ranchera* genre.

Of the 89 films produced, 19 are in colour and 5 in CinemaScope, with a tendency towards high budgets.

Luis Buñuel directs *Ensayo de un crimen* and *Cela s'appelle l'aurore* (the latter in France). Roberto Gavaldón directs a super-production, *La escondida.* Other titles include Gilberto Martínez Solares's *Lo que le pasó a Sansón;* Rogelio A. González's *El inocente,* Iñigo de Martino's *Chilam Balam;* Alfredo B. Crevenna's *Talpa,* based on Juan Rulfo's work; R. González's *Escuela de vagabundos* (a successful eighteen-week run).

Short film: *También ellos tienen ilusiones* by Adolfo Garnica and Luis Magos Guzmán.

Organisation of the first Federation of Mexican Film Societies. Cesare Zavattini unsuccessfully attempts to collaborate with the Manuel Barbachano Ponce team.

1956

Economic indicators signal a slight improvement. President Adolfo Ruiz Cortines participates in the meeting of American chiefs of state in Panama.

Octavio Paz publishes *El arco y la lira,* reflections on the poetic experience. Carlos Pellicer writes *Práctica de vuelo* (religious poems) and Alí Chumacero *Palabras en reposo.* First individual show of Remedios Varo's work at the Diana gallery. Abel Quezada is hired as illustrator by the daily *Excélsior,* where he will publish his famous cartoon strips *El charro Matías, El tapado* and *Don Gastón Billetes.* Cuco Sánchez composes two successful songs, 'Paloma negra' and 'Huapango torero'.

Of the 98 features produced, 45 are in colour. Manuel Barbachano Ponce produces Carlos Velo's *¡Torero!* Luis Buñuel again works with French producers for *La Mort en ce jardin.*

Other titles: Emilio Fernández's *Una cita de amor;* Fernando Méndez's *Ladrón de cadáveres;* Alfonso Corona Blake's *El camino de la vida;* Alejandro Galindo's *Hora y media de balazos;* Ismael Rodríguez's *Tizoc;* Gilberto Martínez Solares's *Los tres mosqueteros . . . y medio;* Fernando Cortés's *Refifí entre las mujeres.*

José Díaz Morales's *Juventud desenfrenada* inaugurates a series of moralising juvenile melodramas. Cantinflas goes *Around the World in 80 Days* for Michael Anderson's Hollywood production.

Establishment of new university film societies.

1957

The PRI nominates Adolfo López Mateos, labour minister during the Ruiz Cortines government, to the presidency. A violent earthquake unsettles the capital.

Publication of *Piedra de sol,* one of Octavio Paz's greatest works. Philosopher Leopoldo Zea publishes *América Latina en su historia,* an analysis of Latin American identity and the relationship between the West and the Third World. Novel: Rosario Castellanos's *Balún Canán.* Theatre: Emilio Carballido's *Felicidad.* Mathias Goeritz and Luis Barragán build the towers of the Ciudad Satelite, symbols of Mexico's modernity. Rufino Tamayo paints the mural *Prometeo* at the Universidad de Puerto Rico. José Luis Cuevas publishes a manifesto against the muralists entitled *La cortina de nopal.* The Proteo gallery gathers independent artists, while Inés Amor's Mexican Art gallery represents the traditional Mexican school. The IFAL opens its gallery space. Canal 4 airs the first *telenovela, Senda prohibida* by Fernanda Villeli. Joaquín Gutiérrez Heraz organises

Raíces (Benito Alazraki, 1953)

the group Nueva Música. Lucho Gatica records 'Voy a apagar la luz' composed by Armando Manzanero.

Pedro Infante's fatal accident is a national disaster. While the Tepeyac and Clasa studios disappear, the Cuauhtémoc studio is renovated and renamed Studio América. Producers and the STIC make compilation features inexpensively with the pretext of making shorts.

Noteworthy films of the year include Fernando Méndez's *El vampiro* and *El ataúd del vampiro;* Alfonso Corona Blake's *La torre de marfil;* Roberto Gavaldón's *Flor de mayo;* Fernando Cortés's *Las mil y una noches;* Benito Alazraki's *Rebelde sin casa;* Ismael Rodríguez's *Así era Pancho Villa.*

A new generation of critics emerges: Emilio García Riera, Eduardo Lizalde, Carlos Fuentes, José de la Colina and Jomí García Ascot. *Séptimo Arte* is published by the Universidad Iberoamericana.

1958

The PRI candidate, Adolfo López Mateos, is elected president with 90% of the votes. The Mexican Communist Party candidate wins fewer than 10,000 votes and suffers a crushing defeat.

Carlos Fuentes publishes his first novel, *La región más transparente,* a magisterial invocation of the Mexican metropolis. Poetry: Octavio Paz's *La estación violenta.* Miguel Salas Anzures establishes the Museo de Arte Moderno and organises the first Mexican inter-American biennial. Inauguration of the Frida Kahlo museum. Remedios Varo paints *El alquimista o la ciencia inútil.* Pedro Coronel finishes the canvas *Cabeza de mujer del viento.* Under the auspices of INBA, Mexico City hosts the first Pan-American theatre festival. Opening of the Teatro Arcos-Caracol, later the home of university productions. Telesistema Mexicano acquires video-transmission equipment and exports *telenovelas* to the USA and Latin

America. The first exported *telenovela* is *Gutierritos*. Introduction of the cha-cha-cha.

Mexico beats its own record: 136 features, although some are 'false' features, that is to say, compilation films. Always looking for creative freedom, Luis Buñuel directs *Nazarín,* produced by Manuel Barbachano Ponce. Another independent production, Giovanni Korporaal's *El brazo fuerte* was not shown until 1974 due to censorship problems.

Hugo Butler, a victim of McCarthyism in the USA, directs *Los pequeños gigantes* under the pseudonym Hugo Mozo.

Other titles include Ismael Rodríguez's *La cucaracha* (23-week run); Roberto Gavaldón's *Miércoles de ceniza;* Benito Alazraki's *Café Colón;* Mauricio de la Serna's *Las señoritas Vivanco;* Alejandro Galindo's *México nunca duerme* and *La vida de Agustín Lara.*

The first *Reseña* (film festival) happens in Mexico City before moving permanently to Acapulco.

The Azteca studio closes its doors.

1959

The López Mateos presidency begins with the army's repression of a railway workers' strike and the incarceration of labour leaders. In the last national rural uprising, the peasants led by Rubén Jamarillo take over the territories of Guarín and Michapa in Morelos. Reactivation of agrarian reform.

Establishment of a national public television channel, Channel 11, under the direction of the Instituto Politécnico Nacional. Telesistema installs transmitters in twenty states. The magazine *¡Siempre!* begins to publish the supplement 'La cultura en México'. Creation of the Fondo Editorial de la Plástica Mexicana dedicated to Mexican art. Rufino Tamayo paints a new version of his *Prometheus* in the conference rooms of UNESCO in Paris. Leonora Carrington paints *Reflexión del oráculo* and *¿Quién sois, blanco rostro?* Alvaro Carrillo composes the bolero 'Sabor a mí'. Novels: *La creación* by Agustín Yáñez; *Las buenas conciencias* by Carlos Fuentes. Short story: *Benzulul* by Eraclio Zepeda. Poetry: *Delante de la luz cantan los pájaros* by Marco Antonio Montes de Oca.

Of the 114 features produced, 20% are cheaply produced serials. Chili-Western production (Fernando Méndez's *Venganza apache*) overtakes melodramas (Alfonso Corona Blake's *Yo pecador* has a 25-week run). The best film of the year is Roberto Gavaldón's *Macario* (sixteen-week run).

Manuel Barbachano Ponce begins co-production: Julio García Espinosa's *Cuba baila;* Juan Antonio

Bardem's *Sonatas.* Luis Buñuel attempts to extend his creative freedom thanks to foreign productions: *La fièvre monte à El Pao* aka *Los ambiciosos.* Notable titles include Rogelio A. González's *El esqueleto de la señora Morales* and Benito Alazraki's *El toro negro.*

On the margins of the industry: the short film *Perfecto Luna* by Archibaldo Burns is based on Elena Garro's idea; the ethnographic documentary *Carnaval chamula* by José Báez Esponda.

The Universidad Nacional Autónoma de México (UNAM) establishes a Departamento de actividades cinematográficas.

1960

Nationalisation of the electricity industry. Confrontations between peasants and state forces in Guerrero indicate that rural unrest continues. David Alfaro Siqueiros and the journalist Filomeno Mata are charged with subversion and imprisoned. Creation of the National Institute for the Protection of Childhood, in an attempt to deal with one of the planet's highest population growth rates (3.5%; 34,923,000 inhabitants). 350,000 emigrate legally to the USA.

Publication of the magazine *Política* (left) with the collaboration of Carlos Fuentes, Víctor Flores Olea and Enrique González Pedrero. Adoption of radio and television legislation (650,000 sets in the country). Establishment of the publishing house ERA. Poetry: Octavio Paz's *Libertad bajo palabra.* Essay: *Al yunque* by Alfonso Reyes; *Breve historia de la Revolución mexicana* by Jesús Silva Herzog. Photography: *Historia gráfica de la Revolución mexicana* by Gustavo Casasola. Over 100,000 copies of C. Wright Mill's *Listen, Yankee* are printed. Opening of the Museo Universitario de Ciencias y Artes at UNAM. Mathias Goeritz and José Luis Cuevas organise an ephemeral neo-dadaist movement, Los Hartos; their show, *Mensajes metacromáticos,* scandalises Mexico City.

Another record year: 442 films released (192 US, 109 Mexican, 33 French, 25 British, 25 Italian, 22 German, 14 Spanish). The state acquires the Jenkins exhibition circuit and the Churubusco studio. UNAM will henceforth have a film archive.

Luis Alcoriza makes his directorial debut with *Los jóvenes.* Luis Buñuel directs *The Young One* aka *La joven.* Julio Bracho's *La sombra del caudillo* is based on Martín Luis Guzmán's novel and remains censored for the next thirty years.

Other films include Roberto Gavaldón's *El siete de copas;* Servando González's *Yanco;* Gilberto Gazcón's *La cárcel de Cananea;* Emilio Gómez Muriel's

Simitrio; Gilberto Martínez Solares's *El violetero;* Miguel Zacarías's *Juana Gallo.*

Short films: *El despojo* by Antonio Reynoso and Rafael Corkidi from an idea by Juan Rulfo; *Carnaval en la Huateca* by Roberto Williams; *Sueño de plata* by Adolfo Garnica.

1961

Failed conspiracy against president López Mateos. Influenced by the Cuban revolution, organisation of the National Liberation Movement (MLN).

The 5% tax imposed in 1960 on radio and television stations is reduced to 1.25%; Emilio Azcárraga Vidaurreta sets up a television station in San Antonio, Texas.

The painters Arnold Belkin and Francisco Icaza publish their manifesto, *Nueva presencia,* critiquing academicism and social realism while rejecting abstractionism. Alberto Gironella paints *La reina negra;* Remedios Varo paints *Mujer saliendo del psicoanalista.* Mexico's folkloric ballet is awarded first prize at a theatre festival in Paris. France opens an archaeological and ethnographic mission in Mexico. Félix Candela receives the Auguste Perret Prize from the International Architects' Association. The publication of Oscar Lewis's anthropological narrative *The Children of Sánchez* sparks an intense debate.

Film societies flourish. The production crisis gets worse: 71 features are made (114 the previous year). Spain becomes the leading Hispanic film country.

Jomí García Ascot's *En el balcón vacío* becomes the manifesto for a new 'auteurist' cinema, defended by the critics of the journal *Nuevo Cine* (José de la Colina, Salvador Elizondo, J.M. García Ascot, Emilio García Riera, Carlos Monsiváis, Gabriel Ramírez and Luis Vicens, soon joined by José Luis González de León, Rafael Corkidi, Paul Leduc, Manuel Michel, Eduardo Lizalde, Manuel González Casanova, Tomás Pérez Turrent, José Báez Esponda, Fernando Macotela, Juan Manuel Torres, Jorge Ayala Blanco, Salomón Láiter and Ludwik Margules; support is given by Luis Alcoriza, Carlos Fuentes and José Luis Cuevas). The group's totem figure, Buñuel, returns from Spain to film *Viridiana.*

Roberto Gavaldón's *Rosa Blanca* will remain banned for eleven years.

Other films: Luis Alcoriza's *Tlayucan;* Ismael Rodríguez's *Los hermanos del Hierro* and *Ánimas Trujano.*

1962

Assassination of peasant leader Rubén Jaramillo and his family. Jaramillo participated in the Revolution alongside Zapata, and led agrarian struggles in the state of Morelos for half a century. Visit of US president John F. Kennedy. Mexico refuses to vote in favour of sanctions against Cuba at a meeting of the Organisation of American States (OEA).

Publication of the daily *El Día* (left). Carlos Fuentes publishes his novel *La muerte de Artemio Cruz,* a vigorous and iconoclastic reinterpretation of the Mexican Revolution. Poetry: Octavio Paz's *Salamandra;* Carlos Pellicer's *Material Poético.* Short story: *Los muros enemigos* by Juan Vicente Melo. The publishing house Joaquín Mortiz is set up.

The Instituto Nacional de Bellas Artes creates the Ballet Clásico de México (later the Compañia Nacional de Danza) and the group Temporada de Oro del Teatro Mexicano, which stages Sergio Magaña's *Los signos del Zodíaco.*

Telenovelas: Penumbra and *La herencia* (directed by Julio Bracho).

Studio América's low-budget films represent almost a third of the 81 features produced. Luis Buñuel is faithful to his surrealist tendencies with *El ángel exterminador.* Luis Alcoriza directs a paean to freedom, *Tiburoneros.*

The success of Federico Curiel's *Santo contra el cérebro diabólico* leads to a proliferation of filmic masked wrestlers.

Other films: Roberto Gavaldón's *Días de otoño;* Emilio Fernández's *Paloma herida;* Roberto Rodríguez's *La bandida;* Sergio Véjar's *Los signos del zodíaco.*

Short films: *Magueyes* by Rubén Gámez; *El ron* by Salomón Láiter.

UNAM begins to publish the monograph series *Cuadernos de Cine.*

1963

Signing of the El Chamizal treaty by which the USA agree to return the El Chamizal border region to Mexico. Creation of the Independent Peasant Central (left). Guerrilla groups are organised after the violent repression of a peasant uprising in Chihuahua. Organisation of the People's Electoral Front (left). President López Mateos goes on a European tour.

The Ministerio de Comunicación y Transporte begins the construction of a national telecommunications network. Mexico has close to 1 million television sets. Channel 3 of Mérida (Yucatán), locally financed and in association with Telesistema Mexicano, goes on the air.

Under the direction of Celestino Gorostiza, INBA promotes theatre activities: two tents with the capacity to hold 2,500 spectators are placed at the disposal of the Teatro Popular de Bellas Artes; youth theatre seasons are organised and four marionette companies tour the public schools of Mexico City. Creation of the Compañía de Teatro Universitario. Their first production is *Divinas palabras* by Valle Inclán and receives a prize at the International University Theatre Festival in Nancy (France). Influenced by Ionesco, Héctor Azar writes the play *Apasionata y Olimpia.* Elena Garro publishes *Los recuerdos del porvenir,* an evocation of the persecution of Catholics during the Maximato. José Emilio Pacheco publishes *Los elementos de la noche.* Opening of UNAM's cultural centre Casa del Lago. The industrial conglomerate Condumex establishes the Centro de Estudios sobre la Historia de México.

Establishment of the Centro Universitario de Estudios Cinematográficos (CUEC), the first real film school, at the UNAM. 83 films are produced, including *Epopeyas de la Revolución mexicana* by Gustavo Carrero, based on Jesús H. Abitia's newsreels; Ismael Rodríguez's *El hombre de papel* and *Así era Pedro Infante;* Luis Alcoriza's *Amor y sexo;* Tito Davison's *Cri Cri el grillito cantor;* Miguel Zacarías's *La vida de Pedro Infante.*

Luis Buñuel begins a new career in France with *Le Journal d'une femme de chambre.*

1964

Installation of the first *maquiladoras,* factories for the assembly of US products, in the northern border region. Official visit by General de Gaulle. Investiture of President Gustavo Díaz Ordaz, who begins a thorough agrarian reform programme: priority is given to agriculture and cattle-breeding.

Opening of the Museo Nacional de Antropología e Historia, the work of architect Pedro Ramírez Vázquez. At the museum, Rufino Tamayo paints *Serpiente y jaguar.* The Museo de Arte Moderno de México opens in the Chapultepec forest. Remedios Varo retrospective at the Palacio de Bellas Artes. Boom in experimental theatre. The most representative figures are Alejandro Jodorowsky, Juan José Gurrola and Rafael López Miarnau. The INBA's school of dramatic arts presents *King Lear* directed by Seki Sano. The play *Juan Pérez Jolote,* based on Ricardo Pozas's story, is staged at the Hidalgo theatre. Novel: José Revueltas's *Los errores; Los albañiles* by Vicente Leñero. Short stories: *Cantar de ciegos* by Carlos Fuentes; *La semana de colores* by Elena Garro. Essay: *Las literaturas precolombinas de México* by Víctor Flores Olea. Cuco Sánchez releases his famous song 'Anillo de compromiso'.

Production increases: 109 features, most of them outside the studios. Luis Buñuel directs his last Mexican film, *Simón del desierto.*

Alberto Isaac debuts with *En este pueblo no hay ladrones.* Luis Alcoriza shoots *Tarahumara;* Roberto Gavaldón directs *El gallo de oro* based on Juan Rulfo's work. Notable films include Servando González's *Viento negro;* L. Alcoriza's *El gángster;* Alfonso Corona Blake's *Yo, el valiente;* Gilberto Martínez Solares's *Tintansón Crusoe.*

Short films: *Pulquería La Rosita* by Esther Morales, a CUEC production; *Los primos hermanos* by Julián Pastor; *Todos hemos soñado* by Ricardo Carretero; *Morir un poco* by Mariano Sánchez Ventura.

Cantinflas is more popular than ever: *El padrecito* by Miguel M. Delgado has a 58-week run.

The technical sector of the STPC organises the first experimental cinema competition.

1965

Mexico hosts a conference on the denuclearisation of Latin America to discuss banning nuclear arms in the continent. The government condemns US interventions in the Dominican Republic. Thirty well-known leftists are accused of subversive activities and arrested. Establishment of the Banco Nacional Agropecuario. Serious floods in western Mexico.

Publication of the dailies *El Sol de México* and *El Heraldo de México* (right). First intercontinental television transmissions through the satellite Pájaro Madrugador. Gustavo Sanz publishes the novel *Gazapo,* part of the literary movement 'la onda', characterised by irreverence, slang, anglicisms, neologisms and linguistic puns. Salvador Elizondo publishes *Farabeuf o la crónica de un instante.* Essays: *Caudrivio* and *Los signos en rotación* by Octavio Paz; *La democracia en México* by Pablo González Casanova. Theatre: *Yo también hablo de la rosa* by Emilio Carballido. The painter Alberto Gironella participates in the international surrealist exposition, *L'Ecart Absolu* in Paris. The Salón Esso, organised by Standard Oil, promotes abstract art and awards the works of Lilia Carrillo and Fernando García Ponce. Javier Solís records two hits: 'Sombras' and 'Cuando calienta el sol'.

The jury of the experimental cinema contest hails Rubén Gámez's *La fórmula secreta,* a mid-length feature indebted to Juan Rulfo's imaginative universe, Manuel Alvarez Bravo's photography and surrealism. *En este pueblo no hay ladrones* by Alberto Isaac also received an award. Other participants included the compilation film *Amor, amor, amor,* produced by Manuel Barbachano Ponce and consisting of the following films: Juan José Gurrola's *Tajimara,* Juan

Ibáñez's *Un alma pura,* José Luis Ibáñez's *Las dos Elenas,* Miguel Barbachano Ponce's *Lola de mi vida* and *La Sunamita* by Héctor Mendoza. There was also the compilation film *El viento distante,* which included *En el parque hondo* by Salomón Láiter, *Tarde de agosto* by Manuel Michel and *Encuentro* by Sergio Véjar; *Amelia* by Juan Guerrero, *El día comenzó ayer* by Icaro Cisneros, *Mis manos* by Julio Cahero, *El juicio de Arcadio* by Carlos Enrique Taboada, *Llanto por Juan Indio* by Rogelio González Garza, *Una próxima luna* by Carlos Nakatani, *La tierna infancia* by Felipe Palomino and *Los tres farsantes* by Antonio Fernández. The existence of a new generation is further confirmed by Arturo Ripstein's *Tiempo de morir* and Jaime Humberto Hermosillo's short film *Homesick.*

The Instituto Nacional de Bellas Artes commissions Manuel Michel to produce a television programme; he favours films about the arts, such as Felipe Cazals's *Cartas de Mariana Alcoforado* (1966), *¡Qué se callen!, Leonora Carrington o el sortilegio irónico.*

UNAM produces Juan José Gurrola's *Cuevas, Gironella* and *Vicente Rojo.*

1966

Inauguration of the Aztec stadium in Mexico City (105,000 seats) and of the Infiernillo dam. The student movement stirs the city of Morelia (Michoacán), marking the beginning of a long period of student unrest. Bloody confrontation between the armed forces and peasants at San Martín Atarco: fourteen deaths. Arrest of Victor Rico Galán, a Spanish writer accused of training guerrilla groups. The Confederation of Chambers of Commerce evokes the need to control population growth. Mexico opposes US moves to organise a unified Latin American military force.

Debut of colour television broadcasts on Canal 4. Mexico becomes an associate of the international consortium Intelsat. On television: *Maximiliano y Carlota,* the first of a wave of historical serials. Publication of José Agustín's novel *De perfil,* one of the most representative works of 'la onda'. Fernando del Paso publishes his first novel, *José Trigo.* Juan Vicente Melo writes the tale *El festín de la araña.* Octavio Paz publishes *Viento entero* (poetry collection). Publication of José Emilio Pacheco's *El reposo del fuego.* Establishment of the publishing house Siglo XXI. Father Lemercier founds the Emmaüs psychoanalytic centre in Cuernavaca.

The greater part of the 100 features produced are in colour; henceforth, this will continue to be the case. The traditional genres give way to youth themes, violence and sex, but always overdetermined by moral conformism and under the meddling surveillance of the censors.

Members of the new generation make their feature debuts: Juan Ibáñez's *Los caifanes,* written in collaboration with Carlos Fuentes; José Bolaños's *La soldadera.* Carlos Velo films Juan Rulfo's *Pedro Páramo,* a Barbachano Ponce production.

Other films include Alberto Mariscal's *El silencioso;* Emilio Fernández's *Un dorado de Pancho Villa;* Arturo Ripstein and Luis Alcoriza's *Juego peligroso.* Short films: *Remedios Varo* by Jomí García Ascot; *Número 45* by Leobardo López Aretche. A second version of the melodrama *El derecho de nacer,* directed by Tito Davison, reaches the screen.

1967

Student unrest in various cities throughout the country. Guerrilla groups appear in the state of Guerrero. Fidel Velásquez is elected leader of the Confederación de Trabajadores Mexicanos (HCTM) for the fourth time. Washington returns the area of Chamizal (177 hectares) to Mexico. Construction begins on the Mexico City subway system. Hurricane Beulah causes flooding in the eastern part of the country, especially in the cotton plantations of the Río Bravo.

Carlos Fuentes publishes the novels *Cambio de piel* and *Zona sagrada.* Homero Aridjis writes his poem-novel *Perséfone.* Sergio Pitol publishes the short story *No hay tal lugar.* José Emilio Pacheco writes the novel *Morirás lejos.* Fernando Benítez publishes his study of *Los indios de México.* Posthumous show of the work of Wolfgang Paalen at the Palacio Nacional de Bellas Artes. Siqueiros is awarded the Lenin prize by the Soviet government. Historical *telenovela: La tormenta* by Miguel Sabido and Eduardo Lizalde.

STPC organises the second experimental cinema contest: the only outstanding film is Archibaldo Burns's *Juego de mentiras.* Alejandro Jodorowsky has more impact with his first film *Fando y Lis.* Other features (91 this year): Alberto Isaac's *Las visitaciones del diablo;* Sergio Véjar's *Cuatro contra el crimen;* Carlos Velo's *Cinco de chocolate y uno de fresa,* scripted by José Agustín; Carlos Enrique Taboada's *Hasta el viento tiene miedo.*

Short films: Marcela Fernández Violante's *Azul,* Leobardo López Aretche's *Catarsis* and *SOS* and Manuel González Casanova's *Tamayo.*

Paul Leduc, Rafael Castanedo, Alexis Grivas and Bertha Navarro organise the group Cine 70.

Tiempo de morir (Arturo Ripstein, 1965)

1968

Student unrest spreads: there is trouble in Mérida (Yucatán), in Villahermosa (Tabasco), later in Veracruz, until it reaches the capital in July. Classes are suspended at UNAM and the strike spreads to all the universities in the country. Anti-government demonstrations multiply. On 2 October, the tragedy of the Plaza de Tlatelolco (or the Plaza de las Tres Culturas) as the army opens fire upon student demonstrators, killing 200 and wounding hundreds. Ten days later, President Díaz Ordaz opens the Olympic Games in Mexico City. Finalisation of the treaty of Tlatelolco concerning the denuclearisation of Latin America. Mexico has been the principal mover behind this accord. The Mexican Communist Party condemns the soviet intervention in Czechoslovakia.

Establishment of two new television channels: Channel 8 and Channel 13. An educational programme (high-school level) begins to air on television. The Tlatelolco massacre makes waves in intellectual circles: Octavio Paz resigns his ambassadorial post in New Delhi; José Revueltas finds himself in Lecumberri prison again; Elena Garro goes into exile. Motivated by the Olympic Games, the government organises an art series called *Olimpíada Cultural,* which includes a *Sun Exhibition* and the *Ruta de la Amistad.* Conceived by Mathias Goeritz and realised by nineteen artists from different countries, this latter show consisted of a 'road' of monumental statues installed on the 17km stretch between UNAM and the Olympic Village. On the margins of the official celebrations, artists organise the first *Salón Independiente.* In the USA, Carlos Castaneda publishes *The Teachings of Don Juan: A Yaqui Way of Knowledge.* The series *Leyenda de México* introduces colour to the *telenovela*. Other *telenovelas: Los caudillos* by Miguel Sabido and Eduardo Lizalde, *Chucho el roto, Rubí* and *El derecho de nacer*.

110 features. The San Angel Inn studio will henceforth be occupied by television. Mauricio Wallerstein and Fernando Pérez Gavilán's Cinematográfica Marte bets on the new generation: *Trampas de amor* by Tito Novaro, Manuel Michel and Jorge Fons. *La manzana de la discordia* is Felipe Cazals's first feature film.

Birth of a militant cinema: *Comunicados del Consejo Nacional de Huelga* by Paul Leduc and Rafael Castanedo; *El grito* by Leobardo López Aretche, produced by CUEC; *1968: Homenaje a José Revueltas* by Oscar Menéndez. Other titles: Luis Alcoriza's *El oficio más antiguo del mundo;* Alberto Isaac's *Olimpíada en México;* Arturo Ripstein's *Los recuerdos del porvenir;* Alberto Mariscal's *Todo por nada;* Emilio Gómez Muriel's *Santa; El libro de piedra* by Carlos Enrique Taboada. Essay: *La aventura del cine mexicano* by Jorge Ayala Blanco.

1969

Line no. 1 of the Mexico City subway system begins service. The presidents Gustavo Díaz Ordaz and Richard Nixon inaugurate the Amistad dam over the Río Grande. Reinforcement of border controls to curb the drug traffic.

Establishment of the news agency Notimex. First steps towards the establishment of a public television system: the Ministry of Education takes over Channel 11, formerly used by the Instituto Politécnico, and announces the creation of a federal network with 37 regional channels. Birth of Cablevisión, a cable television provider in the capital. Elena Poniatowska publishes *Hasta no verte, Jesús mío.* José Revueltas uses his experiences in the Lecumberri prison to describe the penal world in *El apando.* Novels: *Cumpleaños* by Carlos Fuentes; *La obediencia nocturna* by Juan Vicente Melo. Poetry: *Ladera este* by Octavio Paz.

89 features were produced. The group Cine Independiente de México (Rafael Castanedo, Tomás Pérez Turrent, Pedro Miret, Tony Kuhn, Alexis Grivas, Jorge Fons, Paul Leduc and others) produces Felipe Cazals's *Familiaridades* and Arturo Ripstein's *La hora de los niños.* Cinematográfica Marte produces *Patsy mi amor* by Manuel Michel, *Paraíso* by Luis Alcoriza, *Siempre hay una primera vez* by José Estrada, Guillermo Murray and Mauricio Wallerstein, *El sabor de la venganza* by Alberto Mariscal.

First features: Alfonso Arau's *El aguila descalza;* Jorge Fons's *El quelite;* Raúl Kamffer's *Mictlán, la*

casa de los que ya no son; Federico Weingartshofer's *Quizá siempre sí me muera,* the latter two produced by CUEC.

Other titles: Alejandro Jodorowsky's *El Topo;* Juan Ibáñez's *La generala.* Documentary: *Los adelantados* by Gustavo Alatriste; *Sur* by Gabriel Retes, in super-8.

Publication: *Historia documental del cine mexicano* by Emilio García Riera.

1970

Population: 50,694,000, with 9 million in Mexico City. Mexico organises the soccer World Cup. The trials of the instigators of the student riots of 1968 end: 68 people are condemned to between three and seventeen years in prison. Luis Echeverría Alvarez, the PRI candidate, wins the presidential elections.

Jacobo Zabludovsky begins the television news programme *24 Horas* for Telesistema. Carlos Monsiváis publishes a collection of essays, *Días de guardar,* about the student movement and the counter-culture. Octavio Paz publishes *Posdata.* Carlos Fuentes writes the play *El tuerto es rey* and the essay *Casa con dos puertas.* Poetry: *No me preguntes cómo pasa el tiempo* by José Emilio Pacheco. Essay: *Estética y marxismo* by Adolfo Sánchez Vasquez; *Lo efímero y lo eterno del arte popular mexicano* by Leopoldo Méndez and Marianne Yampolsky. Photography: *Las ventanas* by José Luis Neyra; *Fotoimágenes* by Pedro Meyer. Public television broadcasts *Tiempo de cine.* Telenovelas: *Renzo el gitano, Yesenia* and *La Constitución.* Adoption of a federal law protecting the cultural heritage of the nation.

Alfredo Joskowicz's first feature (*Crates*) is produced by CUEC. One of the film-makers of the new generation, Felipe Cazals, turns to super-productions: *Emiliano Zapata.* Among the 93 feature films of the year: Alberto Bojórquez's *Los meses y los días;* Salomón Láiter's *Las puertas del paraíso;* Gonzalo Martínez, Juan Manuel Torres and Jorge Fons's *Tú, yo, nosotros;* José Estrada *Para servir a usted;* Mauricio Wallerstein's *Las reglas del juego;* Toni Sbert's *Sin salida;* Julián Pastor's *La justicia tiene doce años;* Alberto Mariscal's *Los marcados;* Carlos Enrique Taboada's *El arte de engañar* and *El negocio del odio;* José Bolaños's *Arde baby arde; Ya sé quien eres, te he estado observando* by José Agustín.

First experimental super-8 film contest, won by Enrique Escalona's *El padre o Why.*

Militant cinema: *México, la revolución congelada* by Raymundo Gleyzer; *Dos de octubre: aquí México* by Oscar Menéndez.

Publication of the magazine *Cine Club.*

1971

Mexico has 190,000 university students. 45% of the population is urban. Two million peasants are destitute. Industrial and financial activities are in the hands of a dozen groups. 70% of all commercial trade is with the USA. Contradictions of the new political openness: while president Echeverría wants to erase the scars of 1968 and frees the imprisoned student leaders, a paramilitary group attacks student demonstrators in Mexico City, killing ten and wounding hundreds while government forces look on complacently. Eighteen-year-olds win the right to vote.

Establishment of the Organisation of Ibero-American Television (OTI) to exchange programmes by satellite among Latin America, Spain and Portugal. Elena Poniatowska publishes *La noche de Tlatelolco* about the 1968 executions. Adolfo Gilly writes *La revolución interrumpida,* an interpretative historical essay written in prison. Pablo O'Higgins's exhibition at the Palacio de Bellas Artes. The members of Arte Colectivo en Acción paint murals in the Morelos neighbourhood in Mexico City. Musician Mario Lavista organises the composers' group Quanta. President Luis Echeverría attempts to mend the relationship between intellectuals and the state.

87 feature films are produced. Rodolfo Echeverría (the brother of the president) is in charge of the Banco Nacional de Cinematografía and proposes a plan to restructure the industry.

The most significant film of the new independent cinema: *Reed: México insurgente* by Paul Leduc is in production. Marco Polo, a new company, produces Jaime Humberto Hermosillo's first feature, *La verdadera vocación de Magdalena,* Jorge Fons's *Los cachorros* and Sergio Olhovich's debut, *Muñeca reina.* CUEC produces Alfredo Joskowicz's *El cambio* and Carlos González Morantes's *Tómalo como quieras.*

Other titles of the year: Alberto Isaac's *Los días del amor;* Luis Alcoriza's *Mecánica nacional* and *El muro del silencio;* Mauricio Wallerstein's *Fin de fiesta;* Rafael Corkidi's *Angeles y querubines;* Juan López Moctezuma's *La mansión de la locura;* Felipe Cazals's *El jardín de tía Isabel;* José Estrada's *Cayó de la gloria el diablo* and José Luis Ibáñez's *Las cautivas.*

Documentary: Eduardo Maldonado's *Testimonio de un grupo;* Gustavo Alatriste's *QRR (Quien resulte responsable);* Marcela Fernández Violante's *Frida Kahlo.*

A national independent super-8 cinema competition includes *Victor Ibarra Cruz* by Eduardo Carrasco Zanini. An international film festival in Mexico City, the Muestra.

1972

Luis Echeverría's presidency is characterised by a revival of third-worldist discourses. At the United Nations, Mexico supports the drafting of a charter for the economic rights and duties of nation-states. Echeverría makes an official visit to Chile during the Popular Unity government.

Birth of Televisa, thanks to a merger of the principal private television channels. The state purchases Canal 13. *Telenovela: El Carruaje,* about Benito Juárez's campaign against Maximilian's empire. Alberto Gironella has a painting show at the Palacio de Bellas Artes. In Paris, José Luis Cuevas produces a series of lithographs entitled *La Rue des Mauvais Garçons.* Photography: *El paisaje de México* by Enrique Bostelmann. Creation of the Centro Nacional de Conservación y Restauración del Patrimonio Artístico. First international Cervantino festival in Guanajuato. Armando Ramírez publishes *Chin Chin el Teporocho,* a chronicle based on the Tepito neighbourhood. Roca, a new editorial house, is created from a split within Grijalbo.

89 features are produced. Arturo Ripstein re-establishes his position with *El castillo de la pureza.* The new generation of film-makers continues to set the trend: Gonzalo Martínez's debut, *El principio;* Alberto Bojórquez, Luis Alcoriza and Jorge Fons's *Fe, esperanza y caridad;* Alberto Isaac's *El rincón de las vírgenes;* Alejandro Jodorowsky's *La montaña sagrada;* Jaime Humberto Hermosillo's *El señor de Osanto;* Felipe Cazals's *Aquellos años* and José Estrada's *El profeta Mimí.*

Establishment of a marginal (read 'militant') film co-operative led by Paco Ignacio Taibo II, Enrique Escalona, Gabriel Retes and Jesús Dávila. Aligned with the new labour movements, the co-operative produces *Comunicados de Insurgencia Obrera* in super-8. Other documentaries: Eduardo Maldonado's *Reflexiones;* Francisco Gaytán's *Viva la raza;* Roberto G. Rivera's *Los marginados* and Juan José Gurrola's *Robarte el arte.*

Isela Vega embodies the new sex symbol.

1973

Foreign investment in Mexican businesses is limited to 49% of a company's capital. A demographic law seeks to restrict the birth-rate and plans immigration controls. Establishment of two leftist organisations: the Partido Socialista de Trabajadores (PST) and the Movimiento de Acción y de Unidad Socialista (MAUS). Bloody confrontation between students and the army in Puebla. Mexico welcomes more than a thousand Chileans fleeing from the Pinochet dictatorship.

José Agustín writes the novel *Se está haciendo tarde (Final en laguna)*. The Palacio de Bellas Artes exhibits the work of the nineteenth-century painter Juan Cordero. Juan Soriano paints *Apolo y las musas*. In France, the Comédie de Saint-Etienne tours with Emilio Carballido's play *Yo también hablo de la rosa*. Televisa programmes the *telenovela, Cartas sin destino* based on *Cyrano de Bergerac*.

Production decreases to 69 features. The distance between the newcomers and the old guard increases: on the one hand, Arturo Ripstein's *El Santo Oficio*; Alfonso Arau's *Calzonzín inspector*; Archibaldo Burns's *Juan Pérez Jolote*; Sergio Olhovich's *Encuentro de un hombre solo*; Raúl Kamffer's *El perro y la calentura* and *Los años duros* by Gabriel Retes in super-8; on the other side: Emilio Fernández's *La choca* and Alejandro Galindo's *Ante el cadáver de un líder*.

Documentary: Felipe Cazals's *Los que viven donde sopla el viento suave*; Carlos Ortíz Tejada's *Contra la razón y por la fuerza*.

Eduardo Maldonado, Francisco Bojórquez and Raúl Zaragoza establish the group Cine Testimonio and produce *Atencingo, cacicazgo y corrupción*. A short-film production centre is created within Churubusco. The so-called *paquete* system of production is established (the crew invests part of their wages into the film against profit participation).

1974

The guerrilla movement is crushed. Uprising and assassination of Efraín Calderón, student leader and labour union adviser. His death is attributed to the police of the state of Yucatán. Establishment of the Partido de la Democracia Mexicana (right) and Partido Mexicano de los Trabajadores (left). Creation of two new states: Quintana Roo and Baja California Sur.

Radio Mezquital goes on the air to serve the Otomi Indians. Eraclio Zepeda wins the national fiction award for the novel *Asalto nocturno*. José Revueltas publishes the short-story collection *Material de los sueños*. Inauguration of the Carrillo Gil museum in Mexico City. The Alfa corporation begins its art collection. Francisco Toledo paints *El coyote y el conejo*.

The decline in production continues: 65 features. Inauguration of the Cineteca Nacional foreseen by the 1949 cinema law.

Establishment of the production company Conacine, a subsidiary of the Banco Cinematográfico. Raúl Araiza, José Estrada, Jaime Humberto Hermosillo, Alberto Isaac, Gonzalo Martínez, Sergio Olhovich and Julián Pastor establish the production company Directores Asociados, S.A. (DASA) to take advantage of state production credits.

Notable titles: J.H. Hermosillo's *El cumpleaños del perro*; Marcela Fernández Violante's *De todos modos Juan te llamas*, a UNAM production; Alberto Isaac's *Tívoli*; Luis Alcoriza's *Presagio*; J. Pastor's *La venida del rey Olmos*; Rafael Corkidi's *Auandar Anapu*; Ariel Zúñiga's *Apuntes*; Alfredo Gurrola's *Descenso del país de la noche*; Alberto Bojórquez's *La lucha con la pantera*; *Más negro que la noche* by Carlos Enrique Taboada; *La casa del sur* by Sergio Olhovich.

Los tres reyes magos by Adolfo Torres Portillo and Fernando Ruiz is the first feature-length animation.

Militant cinema: *Chihuahua: un pueblo en lucha* by Trinidad Langarica, Angel Madrigal and Abel Sánchez; *Los albañiles* and *Explotados y explotadores* by Taller de Cine Octubre, whose publication is the magazine *Octubre*.

1975

President Luis Echeverría makes an official visit to Cuba. Establishment of the Partido Popular Mexicano (PPM, left). Creation of the Unión Agrícola Nacional (UAN), an organisation representing private producers. Organisation of the Congreso Nacional de Pueblos Indígenas (CNPI).

Named ambassador to Paris, Carlos Fuentes publishes the novel *Terra nostra*, illustrated by Alberto Gironella. Octavio Paz publishes *El mono gramático*. Philosopher Leopoldo Zea writes *Dialéctica de la conciencia americana*. Establishment of the National Council for Culture and Leisure for Workers (CONACURT). A presidential decree authorises artists to pay their estate taxes through donations of their works. Painter Daniel Manrique organises the group Arte-Acá in the popular lower-class neighbourhood Tepito. In collaboration with the Ministry of Education, Televisa airs the *telenovela, Ven conmigo*, inaugurating a series of educational serials.

The decrease in production continues: 59 features. The state purchases the América studio and creates the production companies Conacite Uno and Conacite Dos, also inaugurating the Centro de Capacitación Cinematográfica (CCC), the second cinema school after CUEC. The Banco Nacional Cinematográfico cuts credits to traditional producers. The Echeverría administration has invested 1 million pesos in the cinema. The nationalised sector controls 375 theatres.

In top form are Felipe Cazals with *Canoa* and *El apando*; Jaime Humberto Hermosillo with *La pasión según Berenice*.

Other titles: José Estrada's *Recodo de purgatorio* and *Maten al león;* Julián Pastor's *El esperado amor desesperado;* Arturo Ripstein's *Foxtrot;* Miguel Littín's *Actas de Marusia;* Luis Alcoriza's *Las fuerzas vivas;* Rafael Baledón's *Renuncia por motivos de salud;* Gabriel Retes's *Chin Chin el teporocho;* Sergio Olhovich's *Coronación;* Gonzalo Martínez's *Longitud de guerra; Alucarda* by Juan López Moctezuma.

Documentary: Eduardo Maldonado's *Una y otra vez; Valle de México* by Rubén Gámez. The Frente Nacional de Cinematografistas welcomes the changes but defends artistic production against all forms of censorship (the manifesto is signed by Leduc, Araiza, Cazals, Estrada, Fons, Hermosillo, Isaac, Martínez, Olhovich, Pastor, Torres and Láiter).

1976

The Mexican peso is devalued by 100%. In accordance with the IMF, Mexico begins an economic adjustment plan. José López Portillo, the only candidate (designated by the PRI), is elected president with 95% of the vote. Creation of the Partido Revolucionario de los Trabajadores (PRT). Closing of the Centre for International Research in Cuernavaca.

Publication of the weekly *Proceso* (left), the result of a split within the newspaper *Excélsior.* The Televisa network grows with the establishment of Televisa-Europa in Spain and Sistema Univisión in the USA. Inauguration of the Fundación Cultural Televisa. Luis Alcoriza directs a television series based upon his film *Mecánica nacional.* Octavio Paz edits the journal *Vuelta.* Carlos Monsiváis publishes *Amor perdido* about popular culture myths. Leopoldo Zea issues *Filosofía de la historia americana.* Publication of the magazine *Jardín del Arte.* The painters Santiago Rebolledo and Javier Macotela create the group Suma, devoted to muralism and new technologies. Creation of the Centres for Artistic Education (CEDART).

The traditional producers withdraw: the state produces 36 of the 56 features of the year. To the vulgar commercial trend represented by Miguel M. Delgado's *Las ficheras,* one may contrast Felipe Cazals's *Las poquianchis; Matinée* by Jaime Humberto Hermosillo; *Los albañiles* by Jorge Fons; *Pafnucio Santo* by Rafael Corkidi; *Pedro Páramo* by José Bolaños; *El viaje* by Jomí García Ascot; *La casta divina* by Julián Pastor; *Lo mejor de Teresa* by Alberto Bojórquez; *Caminando pasos . . . caminando* by Federico Weingartshofer; *Cananea* by Marcela Fernández Violante; *Cascabel* by Raúl Araiza; *Raíces de sangre* by Jesús Salvador Treviño; *Cuartelazo* by Alberto Isaac; *La mujer perfecta* and *El mar* by Juan

Manuel Torres; *Nuevo mundo* by Gabriel Retes; *Xoxontla, tierra que arde* by Alberto Mariscal.

The documentary remains a fruitful terrain: *Etnocidio: notas sobre el Mezquital* by Paul Leduc; *Lecumberri: El palacio negro by* Arturo Ripstein.

1977

Political reforms open the way for parliamentary representation for the opposition and introduces the principle of proportional representation for 200 of the 500 seats. The remaining 300 seats are provided for by the traditional majority system that ensures the control of the Federal Chamber of Deputies by PRI. Enforcement of a family-planning programme to control demographic growth.

The *telenovela, Acompáñame,* encourages family planning. Publication of the daily *Unomásuno* (left) which sparks the modernisation of the written press. Fernando del Paso publishes the novel *Palinuro de México.* President López Portillo names his wife Carmen director of the Cervantino festival and increases its budget. Rufino Tamayo paints a mural at the Mexico City Alfa corporate headquarters. Establishment of an arts workshop, Taller de Investigación Plástica (TIP), in Morelia. David Alfaro Siqueiros writes his autobiography, *Me llamaban el Coronelazo.* First auction of Mexican art at Sotheby's (New York).

Margarita López Portillo (the president's sister) takes charge of the new Directorate of Radio, Television and Cinema (RTC) under the Ministry of the Interior. The authorities renew their relationships with traditional producers and distributors. The company Conacite Uno disappears. Because of the previous administration's legacy, the state produces 45 out of the 77 features of the year.

Notable titles: José Estrada's *Los indolentes;* Jaime Humberto Hermosillo's *Naufragio;* Arturo Ripstein's *El lugar sin límites* and *La viuda negra* (the latter banned for six years); Miguel Littín's *¡El recurso al método!;* Felipe Cazals's *La güera Rodríguez;* Gonzalo Martínez's *El jardín de los cerezos;* Julián Pastor's *Los pequeños privilegios;* Sergio Olhovich's *Llovizna;* Carlos Enrique Taboada's *La guerra santa;* Fernando Vallejo's *Crónica roja;* Rafael Montero's *Adiós, David;* Rafael Corkidi's *Deseos;* Juan Ibáñez's *Divinas palabras.*

Documentary: *Jornaleros* by Eduardo Maldonado; *La luz del hombre* by Tony Kuhn; *El tiempo del desprecio* by Margarita Suzan; *La experiencia viva* by Gonzalo Infante; *Cuaderno veneciano* by Ludwik Margules.

1978

The oil boom entices agricultural workers into the

industry. 1,850,000 Mexican would-be immigrants are expelled by the USA. About 800,000 cross the frontier illegally each year hoping to find work north of the Rio Grande. Suspected of belonging to the guerrilla organisation Unión del Pueblo, the rector and 45 professors of the Benito Juárez university are arrested (Oaxaca).

Televisa exports 24,000 programme hours per year to Latin America and is seen in 16 million US homes. Discovery in the very centre of Mexico City of the ruins of the Templo Mayor, the high place of Aztec civilisation. Publication of the monthly magazine *Nexos.* Carlos Monsiváis publishes *A ustedes les consta,* an anthology of journalistic chronicles. Vicente Leñero writes *Los periodistas.* María Luisa Puga publishes the novel *Las posibilidades del odio.* First Latin American photography colloquium. Mexican photographers include Graciela Iturbide, Héctor García, Nacho López, Lázaro Blanco, Pablo Ortíz Monasterio, Marianne Yampolsky, Lourdes Grobet, Pedro Meyer and Víctor Flores Olea. The trio Los Panchos records its last album, *Hasta siempre con Los Panchos.* Opening of the Alfa cultural centre.

Production increases to 107 features; only 35 with the participation of the state. Televisa establishes its own film production company, Televicine (*El chanfle* by Enrique Segoviano).

Certain films stand out: Arturo Ripstein's *Cadena perpetua* and *La tía Alejandra;* Jaime Humberto Hermosillo's *Amor libre;* Raúl Araiza's *En la trampa;* Ariel Zúñiga's *Anacrusa;* Alfredo Joskowicz's *Constelaciones;* Felipe Cazals's *El año de la peste;* Raúl Kamffer's *¡Ora sí tenemos que ganar!;* José Estrada's *¿Angela Morante, crimen o suicidio?;* Julián Pastor's *Estás ruinas que ves;* Alfredo Gurrola's *La sucesión;* Diego López's *Niebla;* Servando González's *Las grandes aguas;* Rafael Castanedo's *Cuentos de príncipe y princesas.*

Documentary: *María Sabina, mujer espíritu* by Nicolás Echevarría; *Estudio para un retrato* and *Puebla hoy* by Paul Leduc; *Jubileo* by R. Castanedo; *El desempleo* by María Elena Velasco; *Iztacalco, campamento 2 de octubre* by Alejandra Islas, José Luis González and Jorge Prior.

Militant feminism: *Cosas de mujeres* by Rosa Marta Fernández; *Vicios en la cocina* by Beatriz Mira; *La vida toda* by Carolina Fernández.

Animation: *Los supersabios* by Anuar Badín.

Establishment of a independent distributor: Zafra.

1979

In Puebla, Pope John Paul II opens the third general assembly of the Latin American Episcopal Confederation (CELAM). Over 95% of the Mexican population is Catholic. Amnesty for political prisoners. Mexico breaks off diplomatic relations with Somoza's Nicaragua. The US announcement of the construction of a 13km wall along the Mexican frontier to curb illegal immigration causes a wave of Chicano protests. Establishment of the Sistema Mexicano de Alimentación (SAM) to alleviate the brutal decrease in agricultural production.

Elimination of taxes on the revenues of private radio and television corporations. Twenty million radio receivers. Publication of the magazine *TV y Novelas,* devoted to *telenovelas. Telenovela* of the year: *Vamos juntos.* The playwright Emilio Carballido writes the intimist play *Orinoco.* Elena Poniatowska publishes the collection of stories *De noche vienes.* Maria Luisa Puga publishes the novel *Inmóvil sol secreto.* Abel Quezada paints *Marta Yolanda en las ventanas del mundo.* Lázaro Blanco outlines the *Imagen histórica de la fotografía en México.*

Production continues to increase: 113 features, 15 of them publicly funded. The Banco Cinematográfico and Conacine are wound down. Gabriel García Márquez's work is filmed: Jaime Humberto Hermosillo's *María de mi corazón* and Miguel Littin's *La viuda de Montiel.* Also the release of Jaime Humberto Hermosillo's *Las apariencias engañan.*

Other titles: Arturo Ripstein's *La seducción;* Alberto Bojórquez's *Retrato de una mujer casada;* Alfredo Gurrola's *Llámenme Mike;* Raúl Araiza's *Fuego en el mar;* Marcela Fernández Violante's *Misterio;* Archibaldo Burns's *Oficio de tinieblas;* Alfonso Arau's *Mojado Power;* Federico Weingartshofer's *Bajo el mismo sol y sobre la misma tierra;* Douglas Sánchez's *Cualquier cosa;* Gerardo Pardo's *Max Domino;* José Estrada's *¡Pum!;* Julián Pastor's *Morir de madrugada.*

The documentary remains politicised: Jorge Fons's *Así es Vietnam;* Bertha Navarro's *Nicaragua: los que harán la libertad;* Carlos Cruz and Carlos Mendoza's *Chapopote (Historia de petróleo, derroche y mugre);* Ramón Aupart's *Tatlácatl;* Oscar Menéndez's *Primer cuadro.*

Feminist films: Rosa Marta Fernández's *Rompiendo el silencio;* Gloria Ribé's *Monse;* Dora Guerra's *Hacer un guión.*

Indigenist cinema: Raúl Kamffer's *Parto solar 5.*

1980

Population: 66,846,833, 14.5 million of them in Mexico City. More than 10 million are illiterate. In the countryside, 90% of the children have fewer than six years schooling. There are 8 million television receivers. The installation of *maquiladoras* continues along the northern border; 1 million would-be Mexican emigrants are turned back by the US authorities. Mexico produces 2.2 million barrels of oil per day.

Inter-American indigenist conference in Mérida (Yucatán). Elena Poniatowska publishes *Fuerte es el silencio* (stories). Daniel Leyva writes the novel *¿ABCDErio o ABCDamo?* and two poetry collections, *Talabra* and *El león de los diez caracoles*. Novel: *Inmaculada o los placeres de la inocencia* by Juan García Ponce. Short story: *La noche navegable* by Juan Villoro; *El caguamo* by Eraclio Zepeda. Publication of a book of Juan Rulfo's photographs, *Inframundo*. Abel Quezada wins the national journalism award.

107 features (7 with state participation), including Raúl Araiza's *Lagunilla mi barrio;* Mario Hernández's *¡Que viva Tepito!;* Raúl Zermeño, Luis Mandoki and Alejandro Tavera's *Mundo mágico;* Marcela Fernández Violante's *En el país de los pies ligeros;* Ramón Cervantes's *Todos los espejos llevan mi nombre,* a CUEC production. Featurettes include *¿Y si platicamos de agosto?* by Marysa Sistach.

Documentaries: *Poetas campesinos* by Nicolás Echevarría; *Historias prohibidas de Pulgarcito* by Paul Leduc; *La indignidad y la intolerancia serán derrotadas* by Alberto Cortés and Alejandra Islas; *El chahuistle* by Carlos Cruz and Carlos Mendoza; *Mujer, así es la vida* by Taller de Cine Octubre.

Feminist films: *Historias de vida* by Adriana Contreras; *Espontánea belleza* by Lilian Liberman.

1981

Twenty-two chiefs of state meet in Cancun and attempt to re-establish a North–South dialogue. Mexico multiplies its exports by a factor of sixteen because of the oil boom. Exceptional corn harvest: 15 million tons. The country also imports 6.6 million tons of other food products. Foreign debt passes the $53 billion mark. Arrival of the first large waves of Guatemalan refugees.

Publication of the economic daily *El Financiero*. In Mexico City, opening of the Rufino Tamayo contemporary art museum to house the painter's personal collection. Abel Quezada paints *La dama de La Coupole* and works as illustrator for *The New Yorker*. Carlos Aguirre has a sculpture show in the Museo de Arte Moderno. Birth of the journal *Balletomanía*. Organisation of the theatre group Contigo America directed by Blas Braidot. Publication of Jose Emilio Pacheco's novel *Batallas en el desierto*. Short story: *El cuento de nunca acabar* by

Alvaro Uribe; *Nocturno de Bujara* by Sergio Pitol; *Textos extraños* by Guillermo Samperio. Poetry: . . . *fresca de risa* by José Luis Rivas. Photography: *Los pueblos del viento* by Pablo Ortiz Monasterio.

The state invests in *Campanas rojas* by Sergei Bondartchuk and participates in only 5 of the 97 feature films produced.

Beyond the box-office success of *El mil usos* by Roberto G. Rivera, notable titles include: Ariel Zúñiga's *Uno entre muchos o una anécdota subterránea;* Miguel Littin's *Alsino y el cóndor;* Alberto Isaac's *Tiempo de lobos;* Luis Alcoriza's *Han violado a una mujer;* Paul Leduc's *Complot petrolero;* Mario Hernández's *Noches de carnaval;* Jorge Prior's *Café Tacuba;* Gustavo Montiel's *Entre paréntesis;* José Buil's *Adiós, adiós, ídolo mío.*

Documentaries: *El niño Fidencio, taumaturgo de Espinazo* by Nicolás Echevarría; *Patricio* by José Luis García Agraz.

Feminist films: *Es primera vez* by Beatriz Mira; *No es por gusto* by María del Carmen Lara and María Eugenia Tamés.

1982

Nationalisation of the banking industry. Mexico announces its inability to meet its foreign debt obligations and stops making payments, initiating an international debt crisis. Inflation is close to 100%. Between $20 and $30 billion leave Mexico for the USA. Land distribution to peasants is suspended. The PRI candidate, Miguel de la Madrid, is elected president of the Republic with 65% of the votes. Alfonso García Robles, a former foreign affairs minister and the force behind the Tlatelolco treaty, wins the Nobel Peace prize. Eruption of the Chiconal volcano.

Twenty million Mexicans own a television set. Publication of the weekly *Punto*. Luis Reyes de la Maza's *telenovela, Toda una vida,* pays homage to the *zarzuela*. Remake of the *telenovela, El derecho de nacer*. Octavio Paz publishes his essay *Sor Juana Inés de la Cruz o los trampas de la fé*. Carlos Fuentes publishes *Orquideas a la luz de la luna,* a Mexican comedy about the myths of María Félix and Dolores del Río. Carlos Monsiváis publishes *Celia Montalván, te brindas voluptuosa e impudente*. Eraclio Zepeda publishes his collection of stories *Andando el tiempo*. The novels *Ciudades desiertas* by José Agustín and *Juegos florales* by Sergio Pitol are published. Poetry: Elsa Cross's *Bacantes;* Marco Antonio Montes de Oca's *Migraciones y visperas;* José Luis Rivas's *Tierra nativa*. Lola Alvarez Bravo publishes his portrait-book, *Escritores y artistas de México*. Rufino Tamayo makes the huge stained-

María Rojo and Héctor Bonilla in *María de mi corazón* (Jaime Humberto Hermosillo, 1979)

glass window, *El universo,* in Monterrey.

Fire at the Cineteca Nacional. New official avatar: Carlos Saura's *Antonieta.* The state participates in only 3 of the 87 features.

The troubled production sector includes: Ruy Guerra's *Eréndira;* Alejandro Pelayo's *La víspera;* Jaime Humberto Hermosillo's *Confidencias;* Felipe Cazals's *Bajo la metralla;* Gonzalo Martínez's *El hombre de la mandolina;* Claudio Isaac's *El día que murió Pedro Infante;* Alfredo Gurrola's *La fuga del Rojo;* Alfredo Joskowicz's *El caballito volador.*

Animation: *Crónicas del Caribe* by Paco López and Emilio Watanabe.

Documentary: *La tierra de los tepehuas* by Alberto Cortés; *Laguna de dos tiempos* by Eduardo Maldonado; *Charrotitlán* by Carlos Cruz and Carlos Mendoza; *¡Los encontraremos!* by Salvador Díaz Sánchez.

1983

President Miguel de la Madrid announces the social and economic modernisation of Mexico. Fleeing from wars, 150,000 Salvadoreans and 250,000 Guatemalans seek refuge in Mexico. 8% unemployment.

Establishment of the Instituto Mexicano de Televisión (IMEVISION) to take charge of the public networks. The literary Xavier Villaurrutia prize is awarded to María Luisa Puga's novel *Pánico o peligro.* Héctor Aguilar Camín publishes a short story collection, *La decadencia del dragón.* Complete Frida Kahlo exhibition at the Museo de Arte Moderno. *Telenovela: El maleficio.*

Creation of the Instituto Mexicano de la Cinematografía (IMCINE) with Alberto Isaac in charge. The Churubusco studios are increasingly occupied by foreign producers (David Lynch's *Dune,* John Huston's *Under the Volcano,* Richard Fleischer's *Conan the Destroyer*).

Mexico produces 91 features, including: Ariel Zúñiga's *El diablo y la dama;* José Luis García Agraz's *Nocaut;* Jaime Humberto Hermosillo's *El corazón de la noche;* Luis Mandoki's *Motel;* Gerardo Pardo's *De veras me atrapaste;* José Estrada's *Mexicano, tú puedes;* Raúl Araiza's *Toña Machetes* and Jaime Casillas's *Memoriales perdidos.* At the box-office, Raúl Fernández's *Lola la trailera* triumphs.

Feminist films: *Conozco a las tres* by Marysa Sistach; *Mi vida no termina aquí* by María Eugenia Tamés; *Querida Carmen* by María Novaro.

Emilio García Riera publishes the journal *Dicine.* Publication of *Cine y sociedad en México* by Aurelio de los Reyes.

1984

Explosion in Mexico City of a natural-gas bottling factory of the national petroleum company, Pemex: 500 dead, 2,000 wounded. Creation of the National Agricultural Council to represent private producers within the Ministry of Agriculture.

Publication of the daily *La Jornada* (left). 33% of all homes have a television set. 76% of all homes are equipped with a radio. Sergio Pitol writes *El desfile del amor.* Héctor Aguilar Camín publishes the essay *Saldos de la Revolución.* Héctor Mendoza stages *La verdad sospechosa,* based on the novel by Juan Ruiz de Alarcón. In the tradition of political parody, the play *Agarren a López por pillo* denounces the corruption of the López Portillo government. Exhibition of Abel Quezada's journalistic work at the Rufino Tamayo museum. *Telenovelas: La traición; La pasión de Isabela; Eclipse.*

Decrease in production: 68 features. The success of *El día de los albañiles* by Gilberto and Adolfo Martínez Solares consolidates the *sexycomedia,* the trendy new sub-genre.

Against the current, Paul Leduc's *Frida, naturaleza viva* provides evidence of artistic ambition. Equally notable titles: Jaime Humberto Hermosillo's *Doña Herlinda y su hijo;* Raúl Busteros's *Redondo;* Juan Antonio de la Riva's *Vidas errantes;* Gerardo Lara's featurette *Diamante;* Carlos Enrique Taboada's *Veneno para las hadas.*

Documentary: *Juchitlán, el lugar de las flores* by Salvador Díaz Flores.

Feminist cinema: *¿Y por que no?* by María Eugenia Tamés; *Desde el cristal con que se mira* by María del Carmen Lara; *Lugares comunes* by Lilian Liberman.

Rafael Corkidi begins to work in video (*Figuras de la pasión*).

La vida de Pedro Infante appears as a weekly cartoon strip.

1985

On 19 September, a violent earthquake devastates Mexico City, causing over 20,000 deaths and leaving hundreds of thousands homeless. Organisation of the One Hundred Group to protect the environment, headed by the writer Homero Aridjis. A diplomatic incident between Mexico and the USA is provoked by the disappearance of the Drug Enforcement agent Enrique Camarena in Guadalajara. He had just completed a detailed report on the compromising relationships between high-ranking police officers, army officers, government officials and drug traffickers.

Launching of two telecommunication satellites of

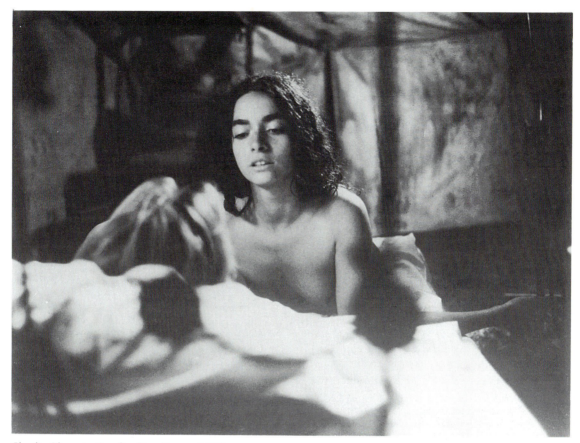

Claudia Ohana in *Erendira* (Ruy Guerra, 1982)

the Morelos system. Alejandro Pelayo directs the serial *Los que hicieron nuestro cine* for television. Novel: *Gringo viejo* by Carlos Fuentes; *1492 vida y tiempos de Juan Cabezón de Castilla* by Homero Aridjis; *Arráncame la vida* by Angeles Mastretta. Short story: *Albercas* by Juan Villoro. Poetry: *Relación de travesía* by Eraclio Zepeda. The Museo de Arte Moderno exhibits the works of Abel Quezada. Essay: *La música de México* by Julio Estrada.

Production goes up to 89 films. Alberto Isaac resigns as director of IMCINE shortly before the third experimental cinema competition, which includes *Amor a la vuelta de la esquina* by Alberto Cortés, *Crónica de familia* by Diego López and *Calacán* by Luis Kelly.

Felipe Cazals's *Los motivos de Luz* deals with the same events as the documentary *Elvira Luz Cruz, pena máxima* by Dana Rotberg and Ana Diez Díaz. *¿Como ves?* by Paul Leduc falls between genres. *El imperio de la fortuna* is the first Arturo Ripstein film based on a screenplay by Paz Alicia Garciadiego (adapted from Juan Rulfo). Other features: Luis Alcoriza's *Lo que importa es vivir* and Mario Hernández's *Astucia.*

Documentary: *El eterno retorno: Testimonio de los indios kikapu* by Rafael Montero.

Video: *Las lupitas* and *Retablos* by Rafael Corkidi. UNAM publishes the magazine *Pantalla.*

1986

A member of PRI is elected governor of the state of Chihuahua under questionable circumstances. A new democratic tendency appears within the PRI, headed by Cuauhtémoc Cárdenas, former governor of Michoacán and son of former president Lázaro Cárdenas. Allegiance to GATT marks the end of forty years of protectionism. Foreign debt reaches the $100 billion mark. Inflation grows beyond the historical barrier of 100%. With 17 million inhabitants, Mexico City is the most populous city in the world.

Mexico hosts the soccer World Cup sponsored by Televisa. The Azcárraga group, owners of Televisa, diversifies its activities, investing in car dealerships, hotel chains, videocassette and dish antenna factories. Televisa controls 4 national television stations, 6 cable stations, 7 transmitters, 2 telecommunication satellites, 13 AM stations, 2 FM networks, a film production and distribution company, 8 theatres, a record producer, a newspaper with a 200,000 daily run, as well as several entertainment magazines. Spanish International Network airs Spanish-language programming in the USA. The popular *telenovela, Los ricos también lloran,* starring Verónica Castro is exported throughout Latin America and Europe. Opening of the Museum of Mexican Photography. The Museum of Modern Art in Paris organises a large retrospective of the photographer Manuel Alvarez Bravo. Novels: *Morir en el Golfo* by Héctor Aguilar Camín; *Cerca del fuego* by José Agustín. Short story: *Gente de la ciudad* by Guillermo Samperio. Theatre: *Rosa de dos aromas* by Emilio Carballido. Publication of *Zurda,* an alternative culture magazine.

Jaime Humberto Hermosillo and the Universidad de Guadalajara organise the first Muestra de Cine Mexicano, designed to showcase the best films produced as well as to promote relations among cinema professionals and the student population of Mexico's second largest city.

76 features produced, including Felipe Cazals's *El tres de copas* and *Las inocentes,* the latter on video.

Documentary: *Ulama* by Roberto Rochín.

Feminist cinema: *No les pedimos un viaje a la luna* by María Eugenia Tamés and María del Carmen Lara.

Publication of the magazine *Intolerancia.*

1987

Cuauhtémoc Cárdenas announces his candidacy to the presidency representing the left wing of the PRI, with a platform advocating the democratisation of the party and a refusal of the IMF's dictates. He is expelled from the PRI. Mexico feels the sting of the Wall Street crash: brutal retrenchment of foreign investments, massive flight of capital and currency devaluation. In response, the government adopts draconian measures, the Economic Solidarity Pact, and imposes harsh price controls. Inflation rate: 150%. Half of the active population is either unemployed or underemployed.

Carlos Fuentes publishes *Cristóbal Nonato,* a Rabelaisian work about contemporary Mexico. The publishing house Fondo de Cultura Económica begins the series *México en la obra de Octavio Paz.* Novels: *Noticias del imperio* by Fernando del Paso; *Los nombres del aire* by Alberto Ruy Sánchez. Short story: *Amor del bueno, juegos de los puntos de vista* by José Agustín. Poetry: *Canto malabar* by Elena Cross; *Obra poética* by Homero Aridjis; *Pedir el fuego* by Marco Antonio Montes de Oca; *La transparencia del deseo* by José Luis Rivas. Manuel Felguérez paints *Camino de luz.* Televisa airs the historical serial *Senda de Gloria.*

88 features are produced. Emilio García Riera is the director of the new Centro de Investigación y Enseñanza Cinematográficas (CIEC) of the University of Guadalajara, and undertakes a vast publishing project. Organisation of the Fundación de Cineastas Mexicanos, a branch of the Fundación del Nuevo Cine Latinoamericano headed by Gabriel García Márquez in Havana.

The censor refuses a certificate to *¿Nos traicionará el presidente?* by Fernando Pérez Gavilán.

UNAM produces Mitl Valdés's *Los confines* and Marcela Fernández Violante's *Nocturno amor que te vas.* Other notable titles: Alejandro Pelayo's *Días difíciles;* Felipe Cazals's *La furia de un dios;* Alberto Isaac's *Mariana, Mariana.*

Documentary: *Xochimilco* by Eduardo Maldonado. Animation: *Tlacuilo* by Enrique Escalona.

1988

Three candidates dispute the presidency: Carlos Salinas de Gortiari for the PRI, Cuauhtémoc Cárdenas for a left coalition and Manuel Clouthier for the Partido de Acción Nacional (PAN, right). For the first time in sixty years, the official party is in trouble. After an electoral process described by the newspaper *El Universal* as 'the largest electoral fraud in history', Salinas is named the winner by the Federal Chamber of Deputies. Cárdenas organises the Partido de la Revolución Democrática (PRD). Fire at an enormous Pemex motor-fuel warehouse in Chihuahua. The US press accuses the Minister of Defence, General Juan Arévalo, of receiving $10 million from drug dealers.

Publication of the daily *El Economista.* First performance in Teotihuacan of the Nahuatl symphony *Cantos Aztecas,* with an arrangement by Lalo Schifrin and sung by the tenor Plácido Domingo. Carlos Monsiváis publishes *Escenas de pudor y liviandad,* chronicles about the entertainment world. Elena Poniatowska writes *Nada, nadie,* a testimony about the 1985 earthquake, and the novel *La flor de lis.* The magazine *Artes de México*

Ofelia Medina in *Frida, naturaleza viva* (Paul Leduc, 1984)

reappears, henceforth under the direction of Alberto Ruy Sánchez. Publication of *Alfil*, the cultural magazine of the IFAL. Novel: *Ayer es nunca jamás* by Vilma Fuentes. Short story: *No hay censura* by José Agustín; *La linterna de los muertos* by Alvaro Uribe. Essay: *Discurso sobre la marginación y la barbarie* and *¿Por qué América Latina?* by Leopoldo Zea.

Production again decreases, to 74 features. Of the 356 films released, 184 are from the USA. The Fondo de Fomento a la Calidad Cinematográfica becomes the most dynamic institution.

Emergence of a new generation: *Historias de ciudad* by María Novaro, Gerardo Lara, Rafael Montero and Ramón Cervantes; *El secreto de Romelia* by Busi Cortés; *El camino largo a Tijuana* by Luis Estrada.

In animation, young film-maker Carlos Carrera makes *Malayerba nunca muerde* and *Amada*.

Arturo Ripstein directs *Mentiras piadosas;* Jaime Humberto Hermosillo shoots *El verano de la señora*

Forbes for Spanish television. Other titles: *Esperanza* by Sergio Olhovich; *El jinete de la divina providencia* by Oscar Blancarte; *Ciudad al desnudo* by Gabriel Retes.

1989

Anti-pollution plan for Mexico City: private cars are forbidden to circulate on one day per week. Renegotiation of foreign debt: Mexico is the test case for the Brady Plan. President Salinas announces a privatisation plan and eliminates the 49% limit for foreign investments in Mexican companies. The informal economy develops at the rate of 6.9% per year, while the official economy grows only by 2%. Mexico is the fourth largest oil exporter. For the first time, the PRI recognises an electoral defeat in a gubernatorial race, conceding to PAN (right) in the state of Baja-California. After years of mutual indifference, the Salinas government sets out to charm intellectuals in order to promote its own legitimacy.

Creation of the Consejo Nacional para la Cultura y las Artes headed by Víctor Flores Olea. Organisation of the first Mexico City theatre festival. Laura Esquivel publishes a bestseller, the novel *Como agua para chocolate*. María Luisa Puga publishes another novel, *Antonia*. The television serial *Carrusel* is wildly successful.

Mexico produces 100 features. IMCINE is henceforth under the new Consejo Nacional para la Cultura y las Artes.

Jaime Humberto Hermosillo experiments in order to sit out the crisis: *La tarea (El aprendiz de pornógrafo)* and *Intimidades en un cuarto de baño*. Paul Leduc shoots *Barroco* thanks to a co-production agreement with Spain and Cuba. Alejandro Jodorowsky's comeback, *Santa Sangre,* is an Italian production. First features by a number of women directors: *Lola* by María Novaro; *Intimidad* by Dana Rotberg; *Los pasos de Ana* by Marysa Sistach. Other films: *Morir en el Golfo* by Alejandro Pelayo; *Goitia: un Dios para si mismo* by Diego López; *Maten a Chinto* by Alberto Isaac; *Una moneda en el aire* by Ariel Zúñiga.

1990

Population: 81,140,922; 18.7 million in Mexico City. Over half of the population (50 million) is urban. The government announces the privatisation of all the banks nationalised in 1982 and the sale of the two principal metallurgical industries. France-Télécom takes control of 5% of Telmex, the telephone company. Foreign investment record ($4 billion) and an important move to repatriate capital ($3 billion). A report published by the humanitarian organisation Americas Watch denounces institutionalised violence and the authorities' tolerance of police and army corruption and torture. Carlos Salinas de Gortari and George Bush begin to talk about a free-trade agreement.

Octavio Paz wins the Nobel prize for literature. The Centre for Contemporary Art and Culture organises an exhibition presenting its notion of fine art, *The Privileges of Vision*. Mexico is honoured by the Metropolitan Museum (New York) and the Grand Palais (Paris) with exhibitions of pre-Colombian art. The Museo de Arte Moderno presents the paintings of Fernando del Paso. On stage: *Rosa de dos aromas* by Emilio Carballido. Jesusa Rodríguez stages José Antonio Guzmán's opera *Ambrosio o la fábula del mal amor,* based on Mathew G. Lewis's *The Monk*. Novels: *La campaña* by Carlos Fuentes; *Mujeres de ojos grandes* by Angeles Mastretta; *Cuaderno imaginario* by Guillermo Samperio; *Charras* by Hernán Lara Zavala; *Notas sin música* by Juan Vicente Melo; *Todo México* by Elena Poniatowska is an interview book.

The state begins to wind down its cinema commitments and closes five companies (among them, Conacine and Conacite Dos). Production falls to 52 features. *Rojo amanecer* (1989), the first film to deal with the student massacre at Tlatelolco in 1968, is approved by the censors. Also approved by the censors is a film that had been banned for thirty years, Julio Bracho's *La sombra del caudillo*. At the box-office, only *La risa en vacaciones* by René Cardona Jr competes with US imports.

Film-makers from various generations establish a dialogue with the Mexican film heritage: José Buil's *La leyenda de una máscara,* Paul Leduc's *Latino Bar,* produced in Venezuela; Arturo Ripstein's *La mujer del puerto,* María Novaro's *Danzón* and Carlos Carrera's *La mujer de Benjamín* soon follow.

Other films: Juan Mora Catlett's *Retorno a Aztlán;* Juan Antonio de la Riva's *Pueblo de madera*.

First Video Biennial in Mexico City. Publication of the film journal *Nitrato de Plata*.

1991

Opening of negotiations between Mexico and the USA to establish a North American common market. Privatisation of 23 companies (eight of them large banks). Approval of a free-trade agreement with Chile. The border city of Tijuana has 650 *maquiladoras:* 600 of them are US-owned. Cholera reaches Mexico. While the Protestant churches are growing within the predominantly Catholic country (90%), the PRI sponsors a constitutional amendment in order to normalise relations with the Vatican which had been interrupted since 1861. The first Ibero-American summit takes place in Guadalajara.

After a loud intellectual outcry against the privatisation of television channels 7 and 22, the government announces the transformation of Channel 22 into a cultural channel. A Televisa programme dedicated to María Félix beats all audience records. The IFAL exhibits the engravings of José Luis Cuevas in Paris. First performance of Héctor Quintana's 'Trio' for violin, cello and piano. The National Symphonic Orchestra pays homage to Carlos Chávez with a series of concerts of his works. Popular music: the rock group Magneto makes waves with the record 'Vuela, vuela'. Novel: *La guerra de Galio* by Héctor Aguilar Camín. Short story: *El registro de los sueños* by Víctor Flores Olea. Essay: *Salidas del laberinto* by Claudio Jamnitz. Poetry: *En las pupilas del que regresa* by Francisco Hernández.

Production decreases to the lowest level since the 1930s: 34 features. The magazine *Dicine* awards its first annual prize to Nicolás Echevarría's *Cabeza de Vaca* and names Arturo Ripstein best director of the 80s. Jorge Fons's *Rojo amanecer* and a new 35mm version of Jaime Humberto Hermosillo's *La tarea* contribute to a reconciliation between young middle-class audiences and national cinema. With Alfonso Arau's *Como agua para chocolate,* the new generation moves into commercial production.

1992

Mexico, the USA and Canada sign the North American Free Trade Agreement (NAFTA). Pollution in Mexico City reaches a new high: the authorities decide to reinforce measures designed to limit cars and industrial activity. The USA and Mexico announce a programme to improve the environment of the border areas, polluted by over 8 million tons of toxic waste generated by US industries. A violent natural-gas explosion in a residential district in Guadalajara causes close to 200 deaths (official figures contested by the press). The government announces a restructuring of Pemex, held responsible for the catastrophe. 92-year-old Fidel Velásquez is re-elected to head the powerful CTM which he had directed since 1936. Controversial election of PRI governors in the states of Michoacán and Durango; in exchange for the ratification of these elections, the PRI accepts the victory of the PAN (National Action Party) in the state of Chihuahua.

Privatisation of two television channels: Channel 13 and Channel 7. Their sale marks the disappearance of national public television.

Diego Rivera's painting *Mujer con lirios* is auctioned for $2.8 million by Sotheby's in New York. There is a wave of interest in Frida Kahlo's work in Europe and in the USA.

Inauguration of the Museo de Guadalajara on the city's 450th anniversary. Winter colloquium organised by the magazine *Nexos,* the University of México and the Consejo Nacional para la Cultura y las Artes. Víctor Flores Olea resigns from the Consejo after criticisms from the rival group *Vuelta* (Octavio Paz's journal). Elena Poniatowska evokes the heroic era of the Mexican Revolution and the life of the Italian communist photographer Tina Modotti in her novel *Tinísima,* written instead of an unfilmed script commissioned by Gabriel Figueroa. Paco Ignacio Taibo II publishes a bestseller: *La lejanía del tesoro.* Essay: Carlos Fuentes's *El espejo enterrado.* The Frankfurt Book Fair pays homage to Mexico.

Two resolutely personal works: Dana Rotberg's *Angel de fuego* and Rubén Gámez's *Tequila.* The new generation moves into commercial production: Alfonso Cuarón's *Solo con tu pareja;* Alberto Cortés's *Ciudad de ciegos;* Marysa Sistach's *Anoche soñé contigo;* Carlos García Agraz's *Mi querido Tom Mix;* Luis Estrada's *Bandidos.* Other films: Carlos Carrera's *La vida conyugal,* Gabriel Retes's *El bulto;* Alejandro Pelayo's *Miroslava;* Felipe Cazals's *Kino;* Jaime Humberto Hermosillo's *Encuentro inesperado* and *La tarea prohibida.*

Revised and brought up to date: *Historia documental del cine mexicano* by Emilio García Riera.

The privatisation of the state-controlled exhibition circuit (COTSA) and the sale of the Churubusco studio give cause for concern. The Centre George Pompidou in Paris organises the most important retrospective of Mexican cinema to date. Octavio Paz writes the preface of a photo-album of María Félix, published under the auspices of the president of the Republic.

1993

The new peso comes into force (worth 1,000 old pesos). Gun battle at Guadalajara airport leaves seven people dead, including Cardinal Posadas. Crackdown on drug traffickers and their accomplices in the police force. Pope John Paul II makes first papal visit to Mexico and addresses the Indian communities in Yucatán. The NAFTA Agreement with the USA includes measures for the protection of workers and the environment; a free-trade agreement is concluded between the G3 (Mexico, Colombia, Venezuela) and five Central American countries. Friction between Mexico and Washington over illegal immigrants in Texas. Twenty-five years after the event, a group of intellectuals (Elena Poniatowska, Carlos Monsiváis, Carlos Montemayor, José Agustín, Jorge Castañeda, Lorenzo Meyer and others) set up a commission of enquiry into the massacre of the students on the Tlatelolco Square in 1968, a blood bath still to be elucidated, while the number of casualties remains a state secret. More than 250 PRD militants are assassinated under the Salinas presidency. The president personally asks the leading industrialists to finance the PRI's election campaign. The government hopes to reap the benefits from their Pronasol (National Solidarity Programme).

Televisión Azteca has two privatised channels (13 and 7) providing competition, for the first time, for Televisa. The journalist Miguel Angel Granados is censured for conducting an interview with Cuauhtémoc Cárdenas, the presidential candidate of the PRD.

Evangelina Sosa in *Angel de fuego* (Dana Rotberg, 1992)

The government allocates a series of lifelong stipends to some sixty eminent 'creative' intellectuals, including Octavio Paz, Carlos Monsiváis, Carlos Fuentes, Gabriel García Márquez, Elen Poniatowska and Arturo Ripstein. Some younger intellectuals benefit from three-year grants. The whole scheme costs nearly $8 million. Fuentes and García Márquez donate their stipend to a university chair in the name of Julio Cortázar. Fuentes publishes *El naranjo,* partly based on the Hollywood actor Steve Cochran. The militant ecologist Homero Aridjis publishes the novel *La leyenda de los soles.* Enrique Krauze, a historian and biographer close to Octavio Paz, has tremendous success with his *Siglo de caudillos.* Jorge Castañeda writes an essay about the dilemmas faced by the Latin American left, *La utopía desarmada.* The irreverent Gloria Trevi replaces the rock singer Alejandra Guzmán (Silvia Pinal's daughter) in the affections of Mexican youth. Pedro Almodóvar sponsors the comeback of the singer Chavela Vargas.

274 films are released, of which 166 are from the USA and about 47 from Mexico. Alfonso Arau's *Como agua para chocolate* makes almost $20 million in the USA.

Arturo Ripstein and his scenarist Paz Alicia Garcíadiego are on top form with the melodrama *Principio y fin,* based on a novel by Naguib Mahfouz. It paints a disabused portrait of the Mexican family and its oppressive *mater familias.* Paul Leduc mixes music, dance and politics in *Dollar mambo.* The young Guillermo del Toro makes a notable debut with the fantasy film *Cronos.* Other first features include Francisco Athié's *Lolo,* Guita Schyfter's *Novia que te vea,* Gerardo Lara's *Un año perdido,* Eva López Sánchez's *Dama de noche* and Ernesto Rímoch's documentary *La línea.*

The big box-office draws are still La India María (*Se equivocó la cigüeña*) and Gloria Trevi (*Zapatos viejos*).

Distribution and exhibition are disturbed by the split of COTSA into three separate circuits: COTSA, Cadena Real and Grupo Intercine.

1994

On the first day of the year, the Zapatista National Liberation Army (RZLN) in the state of Chiapas rebels. This peasant guerrilla army invokes the name of the Revolutionary peasant leader and selects the coming into force of the NAFTA agreement as the moment for its eruption onto the national social and political stage. After a violent, repressive campaign, the government accepts a cease-fire and starts negotiations, but no peace agreement is reached. Splits among the ruling elite deepen: the PRI presidential candidate, Luis Donaldo Colosio, is assassinated; so is the official ruling party's general secretary, Francisco Ruiz Massieu. The results of the national elections, under international supervision, are challenged in some states, notably in Chiapas. Mexico is the first developing country admitted into the OECD, but the national debt rises to $122 billion. The new president, Ernesto Zedillo (PRI), devalues the peso and triggers an economic crisis with international repercussions.

Carlos Fuentes, Laura Esquivel, Paco Ignacio Taibo II, Lorenzo Meyer, Enrique Krauze and other intellectuals and political personalities set up the Grupo San Angel. They advocate democratisation.

The news broadcast by Televisa is contested in the streets of Mexico. Finding itself in difficulties, Televisa associates itself with Telmex (the Mexican telephone business), which was privatised in 1990. TV Azteca signs an agreement with the US network NBC. *El vuelo del aguila* is a television serial with a megabudget made by Enrique Alonso about the life of Porfirio Díaz. The singer Gloria Trevi, the new sex symbol for teenagers, is hired by Columbia Pictures for *El Mariachi II* by Roberto Rodríguez. Another popular singer, Emmanuel, publishes a book of poems, *Palabras calladas*. Astrid Hadad y sus Tarzanes makes cover versions of the old hits by Lucha Reyes in her show *Heavy Nopal*. Katy Jurado proposes a boycott of Arnold Schwarzenegger and Frank Sinatra because of their support for a campaign to deprive illegal immigrants in California of access to education and health services. Mexico hosts the first international meeting of writers in indigenous languages.

Publication of Carlos Fuentes's *Nuevo tiempo mexicano*, Bárbara Jacobs's *Vida con mi amigo*, Héctor Aguilar Camín's *Subversiones silenciosas*, Carmen Boullosa's *Duerme* and Daniel Sada's *Una de dos.*

In Cannes, the Golden Palm is awarded to Carlos Carrera's animated film *El héroe*. Arturo Ripstein's modern and flamboyant melodrama about the fraught relationship between Lucha Reyes and her mother, *La reina de la noche,* confirms his international standing. María Novaro's *El jardín del Edén* (co-produced by Canada) benefits from a larger budget than her previous films. Jorge Fons makes a come-back with *El callejón de los milagros.*

Other films: Gabriel Retes's *Bienvenido – Welcome,* Luis Esatrada's *Ambar,* José Luis García Agraz's *Desiertos mares,* Fernando Sariñana's *Hasta morir,* Roberto Sneider's *Dos crimenes* and Mitl Valdés's *Los vuelcos del corazón.*

García Agraz starts a remake of *Salon México* produced by Televicine (part of the Televisa group). John Frankenheimer shoots *The Burning Season* in Mexico.

The family of the still widely cherished idol Pedro Infante sets up a cultural centre, providing information about the star's life over the telephone.

The Silent Cinema

Aurelio de los Reyes

First Period: 1896–1914
1896–1900

The first public film screening in Mexico took place on Friday 14 August 1896 in the mezzanine of the Droguería Plateros, 9 Plateros Street, in the heart of Mexico City.[1] The programme consisted of *Arrivée d'un train en gare, Montagnes russes, Partie d'ecarté, Repas de bébé, Sortie des usines Lumière à Lyon, L'Arroseur arrosé, Démolition d'un mur* and *Baignade en mer.* Nothing in the production of these films could be considered Mexican. Even the projectionists, two employees of the Lumière brothers, were French, but the site where the screening took place and the audience were quite Mexican. Some days later, the same Lumière cameramen, C.F. Bon. Bernard and Gabriel Veyre, organised a screening of the first films shot in Mexico at the Chapultepec castle for General Díaz: *Grupo en movimiento del General Díaz y de algunas personas de su familia (Moving Group of General Díaz and Some Members of his Family), Escena de los baños Pane (Scene at the Pane Baths), Escena en el Colegio Militar (Scene at the Military School), Escena en el canal de la Viga (Scene at the Viga Canal)* and *El General Díaz paseando por el bosque de Chapultepec (General Díaz Taking a Walk in the Chapultepec Forest).* Subsequently, Bernard and Veyre travelled to Guadalajara to exhibit the cinématographe (Edison's Vitascope had preceded them there). The last Guadalajara screening of the cinématographe was advertised for 29 December 1896. Meanwhile, screenings continued in Mexico City with the two camera-projectors Bernard and Veyre had brought with them. Their last Mexico City screening was on 9 January 1897. The next morning they left for Havana.

In October 1896, Edison's agents opened at another site more appropriate for the Kinetophone. As in the French case, the producers and the equipment were foreign, but the locale and the public were Mexican. Sessions were held daily for over a

year. The French filmed approximately thirty-two films with Mexican themes, while the North Americans in Guadalajara showed only one, *El lazador Mexicano (The Mexican Lasso Thrower),* which had been filmed at Edison's Black Maria in West Orange, New Jersey. According to the archives, the French had brought along all they needed to shoot and develop their films. When they left, they sold one of the camera-projectors to Ignacio Aguirre, who continued to hold public screenings in Mexico City. However, Aguirre remained dependent on the foreigners, for the public had already seen the 'views' he had purchased with the equipment, and he had no access to either film stock or processing chemicals to make new films.

In March 1897, another Mexican company, owned by Guillermo Becerril, began cinematographic activities in Guadalajara with a Vitascope. Becerril's programming included no Mexican scenes but contained shots of the *Laboratorio Edison,* a lynching in the USA, a street in Cairo and a stable fire, among others. Neither Aguirre nor Becerril owned their exhibition sites and had made temporary arrangements with the property-owners. The cinematographic phenomenon was not disseminated from the capital city to the periphery. Mexican journalists had chronicled the first screenings in Mexico City and Guadalajara, but cinema only really began to spread when curious individuals from provincial cities ordered projectors from manufacturers through advertisements in *La Nature* (France) and in the *Scientific American* (USA). Cinema was also popularised by world travellers arriving by ship or train, such as Carlos Mongrand, John C. Hull and others.

In July 1897, a Mr William Taylor Casanova, resident of San Juan Bautista (Tabasco), imported a projector from New York. In Puebla, a Frenchman, Churrich, once again showed Mexican themes with *El presidente Díaz y sus ministros (President Díaz and his Ministers),* and reinitiated Mexican film production with a view of the Carmen festival and a Ponciano Díaz bullfight. The growing curiosity about cinema led to the rapid appearance of Mexican producers in the more prominent cities of the interior. By March 1898, the cinématographe was an instrument for the transmission of culture as well as for entertainment: it disseminated other ways of life and amusements, such as boxing, rejected by some sectors of society but accepted by the majority.

The Aristógrafo, a national invention which produced a three-dimensional impression, was announced in April 1898. Using glasses invented by

Adrián Lavie, the films were seen in relief, but the images were projected at such speed that retinal persistence of vision made them appear still. The public admired *The Venice Bridge of Sighs, Fachada principal de la Escuela de Ingenieros (Principal Façade of the Engineering School), The Lion's Patio of the Alhambra in Granada, Duelo a muerte en el bosque de Chapultepec (Duel to the Death in the Chapultepec Forest), Paisaje agreste en el valle de México (Rural Landscape in the Mexico Valley)* and *The Medici Venus in the Florence Museum.*

Exhibition activities grew with new companies appearing quickly: in 1899, the Mexico City council received twenty-five applications to open cinematographs in various neighbourhoods. Almost all the companies owned tents, which were installed in various plazas. There were twenty-two of these in Mexico City by January 1900. However, the number of exhibition sites and the erratic supply of films made it difficult to sustain varied programming.

With the exception of the Edison agency, there were no film distributors. Each *empresario* had his personal inventory of films, most often purchased along with the equipment: some had purchased lots of 100 films, others had eighty-six, and the same films were exploited by various businessmen. These meagre film inventories were soon exhausted and the public, who favoured French films, became very familiar with the repertoire. Competition and the constant demand for novelty led exhibitors to write to producers directly or to travel to the USA or Europe in search of new views. Given the scarcity of new films and the precariousness of the exhibition sites, twenty of the twenty-two Mexico City exhibitors closed down in 1900 after the press, alarmed by scandals and audience complaints, had started a campaign against them. The exhibitors had attempted to alternate film and live acts, with mixed results: since their shows were inexpensive, they hired amateur actors who got into fights with the audience and generated much mayhem. Harassed by the press, the exhibitors were forced to go on the road.

To increase their repertoire, exhibitors resorted to filming the places they visited. The films they produced were short, since they travelled only with basic equipment. Although meagre, this production was constant. Formally, the national films were no different from foreign productions, only the topics were Mexican: the *zócalo* (central plaza), the *alameda* (boulevard) and bullfights in Mexican plazas. Occasionally, they filmed the local congregation leaving church after mass so that the participants could watch themselves on film the next day. Fiction

films did begin to arrive in Mexico, such as a version of *Vie et Passion du Christ* (presumably instalments of Pathé's sixteen-part epic made between 1896 and 1900) and Méliès's *Neptune et Amphitrite* and *Le Diable au couvent* (both made in 1899). Similarly, newsreels of, for instance, *The Transvaal War,* arrived, but the scarcity of local resources made fictional production impossible. Material conditions allowed exhibitors to film only the most salient events of the places they travelled through. Alternatively, and to ensure success, they would film the local townspeople. At this stage, Mexican cinema existed only as a programming supplement.

1900–1906

The period between 1900 and 1906 is characterised by the itinerant nature of cinema as the exhibitors criss-crossed the nation. Most of the companies were small and family based. Some exhibitors even travelled with wives and children. However, other companies were more complex, with two or three partners, equipment and employees travelling throughout the country. These larger concerns were able to schedule simultaneous screenings in different cities and to exchange films between locations to offer greater programming variety. Thus, there were two types of exhibitors, the majors and the minors. The former had more resources, a sharp business sense and good reputations: Carlos Mongrand, Enrique Rosas, Salvador Toscano, Juan C. Aguilar, Guillermo Becerril and their colleagues formed part of this sector. They were adventurers who travelled from city to city without routes or schedules, trusting only to their luck and learning on the road. Some of them exhibited films by Ferdinand Zecca, Georges Méliès, Edwin Porter and others. Again, to attract more audiences, they also continued to film the people of the towns where they stopped:

> We would advertise that the following Sunday we would be at the door of the church to film views of the congregation leaving the twelve o'clock mass and recommended that all those wishing to appear in the film should be properly attired. This would cause much excitement among the townspeople. At the stated time, they would crowd together, jostle for close-ups and gesticulate wildly in front of the camera. Needless to say, all the improvised actors would attend the show on the night of the premiere. There was much enthusiasm when they recognised themselves or their friends and relatives on the screen! In Orizaba, we also filmed workers as they left the

Moctezuma brewery with the same result: not one worker missed the premiere.[2]

These productions filmed daily life, people taking walks, marriages and popular customs. While other nations developed the language of cinema and produced fiction films without neglecting newsreels, Mexico seemed permanently bound to the Lumière-style documentary tradition and to the observation of moving, proto-cinematic phenomena.

In addition to its itinerant character, another cultural factor played a role in determining the nature of film production: from the moment cinema arrived in Mexico, intellectuals linked it to the illustrated press and, following the positivist spirit of the era, to science. In that context, fiction cinema was rejected because of its potential to dupe the public: the cinema was a science and as such should show truths. Moreover, most camera operators had studied at the Preparatory School, the bastion of Mexican positivism.

Mexican films were characterised by their simplicity and lack of narrative pretensions. However, some of the films of the Guanajuato floods evidence a desire to go beyond the simple one-take model. A set of eight 'moving scenes taken after the catastrophe' was entitled *Guanajuato* and consisted of *Plaza del Baratillo, Calle de la Compañía, Cuatro aspectos de la calle de Cantaranas, Barrio del Hinojo, Ruinas de la calle de la cruz Verde* and a *Panorama of the Guanajuato sierra*. The director seems to have been inspired by a series of views chronicling the meeting between President Félix Faure and Czar Nicolas II, as well as scenes of the Russo–Japanese War that had been widely distributed in Mexico City. Like the films that inspired them, the exhibitor had the option of showing the Guanajuato views either as a set or individually, since there were no connections between them that might develop a central thesis or lead the spectator to any conclusions. Individually or as a group, they offered spectators nothing but a cinematographic spectacle based on movement, which may be the reason why they were exhibited in combination with nineteen stills. The director's only desire was to illustrate the catastrophe.

However, *Viaje a Yucatán* (1906), a film about one of Porfirio Díaz's journeys, exceeds these parameters. Salvador Toscano was given three months' advance notice of the president's plans and he organised a tour of the south-east to coincide with the trip. His intention was to reconstruct as far as possible Díaz's itinerary, from his departure from Mexico City for Yucatán to his return home. The structure of the scenes is reminiscent of the primitive narrative structure of Méliès's films, such as *Cendrillon* (1899) or *Jeanne d'Arc* (1900). Toscano constructed a linear chronology of the trip, which served as the narrative thread organising the brief story from beginning to end. The newspaper *El Imparcial* emphasised that the views gave an accurate idea of the festivities. The individual scenes were: *Salida del señor general Díaz de México; Bahía de Veracruz y muelle; El cañonero Bravo; En el puerto de Progreso; El general Díaz desembarca en Progreso; El presidente en Mérida; Vista panorámica de Mérida; El general Díaz visita el Instituto; La señora Romero Rubio de Díaz visita la catedral y el obispado; El lago de la colonia de San Cosme; El general Díaz sale de Mérida* and *El presidente se despide de Yucatán.* Engineer Toscano produced two versions of the trip: a series of fifty-one still images and one of twelve moving-image shots. The first was a minutely detailed account of the trip, while the second was a synthesis (determined perhaps by the scarcity of film stock) from which he had excised material of secondary importance. As in the Méliès films, each of the moving images had its place in the narrative.

Although based upon the Méliès precedent, the Toscano film initiated the process whereby the Mexican newsreel began to distinguish itself from foreign models. Montage played an important role in both sets of views illustrating the trip.[3] The Mexican cinema was beginning to assume its own characteristics; unconsciously, a national style was being created that would culminate in 1919 with Enrique Rosas's *El automóvil gris*.

A number of new distribution companies opened to satisfy the demand for novelty in 1906, and began to centralise the haphazard cinema business. The itinerant entrepreneurs were the first to suffer the consequences of these changes: they were forced to settle down in permanent locales or to travel to the more remote areas of the country as motion picture salons appeared in Aguascalientes, Orizaba, San Luis Potosí and Zacatecas.

Some of the new Mexico City distributors were owned by Mexicans like Jorge Alcalde who bought films in Europe and the USA, either reselling or renting them to exhibitors. Others were producers' agencies: the Mexican National Phonograph company was Edison's distributor, and the Pathé company was managed by a Frenchman. Internationally, production companies had an indiscriminate sales policy. Not even the agencies had exclusive territorial rights, which gave rise to complicated, prolonged and scandalous suits. As a

The Alva brothers (c.1909-10)

countermeasure, Pathé decided to open agencies in various parts of the world to discipline the film market and prevent the theft of its films.

1907–1911

By 1907 cinema had become so popular a form of entertainment in the capital city that distributors had opened 34 movie salons. Film chronicles, sporadically published before then, began appearing more regularly. In March 1907, the Sala Pathé exhibited 'a film of the festivities in the Isthmus celebrating the inauguration of the Tehuantepec railroad with the participation of the president of the Republic'. All who had enjoyed the privilege of accompanying the president came to see themselves. In May, the Mexican scene *Combate de flores (Flower Battle)* was included in the programme. This film 'faithfully shows the more salient and poetic details of the shimmering festivities of the month', and was described as 'a most accomplished film of the 5 May military parade'. On 28 May, the same businessman responsible for the *Combate de flores* showed films which may have been Mexican: *Pelea de gallos (Cockfights), Bueyes pasando un río (Oxen Crossing a River), San Rafael, Caretas y muecas (Masks and Grimaces), Perro ladrón (Thieving Dog), Tribulaciones de un bombero (Adventures of a Fireman), El asesino and Aplastado por un automóvil (Flattened by an Automobile),* the latter imitating the cartoon techniques popularised by the weekly *El Mundo Ilustrado*. In June, he filmed *Matrimonio aristocrático*. Despite the growing number of movie houses, there was little production in Mexico City. Perhaps the costs were too high, or the market and profit potential were too small since producers were limited to showing films only in their own theatres.

In January 1907, American Amusement, Lillo, García & Co. opened what was perhaps the first workshop or film studio. They made documentaries of daily life in Mexico City and two fiction films: *El grito de Dolores* (*Dolores's Cry*, Felipe de Jesús Haro, 1907) and *Aventuras de Tip Top* (director unknown, 1907). *Día de campo en Xochimilco* (*A Country Day in Xochimilco*, director unknown, 1908) was admired for 'the precision and stability of the figures and the clarity with which even minor details are reproduced'. A second film following the style initiated by engineer Toscano premiered on January 1909: *El viaje del presidente a Manzanillo* (*The President's Trip to Manzanillo*). It began with the departure of a train from the Buenavista station and illustrated 'the most beautiful parts of the road to Colima and the reception of the train in that city, in Manzanillo, and in Guadalajara'. Cameraman Gustavo Silva was hired especially for this occasion.

The most ambitious Mexican film of this time, *La entrevista Díaz–Taft* (*The Díaz–Taft Meeting*), was made in October. Once again, the Alva brothers, Eduardo, Guillermo and Salvador, continued the style of *Viaje al Yucatán* and followed the geographical and chronological sequence of the events. The film was approximately 850m long and lasted a little over thirty minutes. However, *La entrevista Díaz–Taft* went a step further towards the development of a specific newsreel style. While respecting the spatio-temporal sequence of the events, the film-makers had also intended to narrate two parallel stories, a technique undoubtedly borrowed from the narrative cinema. Although circumstances prevented them from filming the events in Mexico and in the USA that led to the meeting, another step towards the development of a national style had been taken.[4]

In September 1910, during the centennial celebrations, twenty-seven movie houses were opened: twenty of them had an average of 250 seats, the other seven averaged over 500 each. It is useful to review the state of the cinema in Mexico at the end of the Porfiriato: most of the companies handling distribution, production and exhibition were owned by Mexicans; some of the distribution companies were owned by foreigners, but the others were exclusively Mexican. The movie houses were Mexican-owned, their numbers and seating capacity increasing steadily. The final assessment is therefore positive: we can say that 95% of the capital invested was national and that a specific cinematographic style had begun to emerge. Nevertheless, as in the earliest days, we were unable to produce film stock or equipment. We bore the burden of the original sin of our dependence.

There was as yet no government censorship. Film exhibition was authentically free. Of course, 'men only' screenings had taken place, but the press and society had eliminated them without the need for censorship measures. The authorities did nothing to stop them, since the Díaz regime was liberal in spirit and the local authorities responsible for regulating and overseeing movie shows were the last bastions of this liberal ideology, despite the changes in the higher echelons of the administration. The Mexico City authorities limited themselves to collecting taxes, granting licences and ensuring compliance with the minimum hygiene and safety requirements, and with other exhibition norms such as the implementation of the advertised schedules without substitutions or changes, the prevention of overcrowding, and so on. An inspector was charged with overseeing the films' morality, but there was no prior censorship. Censorship was left in the hands of society.

From a global perspective, the Porfirian cinema can be divided into two groups. The first includes the documentary films that captured the people on their Sunday walks and leaving church, those featuring well-known individuals, those filmed from the last car of a moving train or from a moving car, and so on. The second group focused on extraordinary current events, a Porfirio Díaz trip or the consequences of a catastrophe, and were informative in nature. The films in this second group can be further subdivided into two categories: those that reported on predictable events such as a presidential trip and for which cameramen prepared in advance, and those that filmed unpredictable occurrences such a cold front in Veracruz, the floods in Guanajuato or railroad accidents.

There were, however, two catastrophes with profound national consequences that the cameramen ignored: the miners' strike in Cananea and the textile workers' strike in Río Blanco. The Cananea strike was quite unexpected. At first, newspapers paid little attention to it; their coverage began only when US forces intervened to help suppress the strikers. In this case, perhaps distance and communication problems made the trip too difficult for cameramen, but this was not true for the Guanajuato floods. Because of its proximity and better railroad connections, Enrique Rosas and Salvador Toscano were able to travel there to witness the disastrous consequences of one of the city's worst floods.

From a cinematographic perspective, the events at Río Blanco were of uncertain interest. Although the violence of the strike could not be predicted, the newspapers had amply described the severity of the situation at least a month prior to the outbreak of violence. Nevertheless, the cameramen did not film any part of the events, either before or after the violence, and avoided these and other disagreeable aspects of reality: the images of poor neighbourhoods and even the images of workers leaving factories disappeared from national productions. Instead, the cameramen attempted to spread images of progress, banking on the belief that films do not lie since they are 'authentic and exact copies of reality'. Was there any better way of convincing the people that Mexico was on the right track? Like the rest of society, the cameramen indulged in escapism.

Despite these limitations, a special method of organising the images of current events had been developed, especially in the feature-length and more ambitious films. These films were not yet newsreels. In fact, the Pathé Journal began only in 1909 and newsreel production in the USA only in 1911. The Mexican films constituted, therefore, a unique local representational form.

1911–1913
El Diario of 26 May 1911 noted:

> The overwhelming enthusiasm of the *maderistas*[5] [after General Díaz's resignation] was evidenced yesterday at dawn. Since the earliest hour, the people, students, and artisans took to the streets in peaceful demonstrations … and the representatives of the Revolution made a wonderful gesture to the poor demonstrators. They bought out the tickets for the Lírico and María Guerrero theatres and the Salto del Agua movie houses and handed them out to the demonstrators as they marched by the Avenida Juárez.

On 30 May 1911, the Palatino theatre showed *La vista de la revuelta (The View of the Uprising)*, filmed during the events that took place in the north of the Republic and featuring preliminary peace negotiations. It also featured the group of government leaders on the day the accord was signed, Madero, Vázquez Gómez, Orozco, Villa and various newspapermen: 'The figures are extremely clear and we see the revolutionary leaders perfectly; the public is very enthusiastic and applauds energetically.' On 11 June, the owner of the Palatino began a national tour to exhibit the film.

In *Asalto y toma de Ciudad Juárez (Assault and Capture of Ciudad Juárez)*, the third part of *Insurrección en México (Insurrection in Mexico)*, the

cameramen added a new structural element: 'an apotheosis' in which 'the people were excited to delirium', acclaimed Pascual Orozco, the hero of the battle, in El Diario of 30 May 1911. In view of the popularity of Méliès's films in Mexico, the apotheosis in question may well have been borrowed from the theatrical special-effects techniques that he employed in his more ambitious narrative films. Besides, the cinematographer-exhibitors were very familiar with the structure of Méliès's films, as is evidenced by the descriptive booklets included with their film purchases (these were often reproduced as programme brochures handed out to spectators as they entered the theatre, or used for newspaper advertisements).

The Salón Rojo premiered *El viaje del señor don Francisco Madero de Ciudad Juárez a esta capital*, a film about Madero's journey to Mexico City, and another film about his trip to Cuernavaca to meet with Emiliano Zapata. These films so pleased the public that they were exhibited over a long period. On 18 June, forty-one screening venues were open, thirty-three of them exhibiting movies or alternating between movies and variety shows. The average capacity increased to 250, while individual cinemas could seat 135, 890 or even 1,200 spectators. There were fourteen more movie houses than the year before, which helps to explain the growth of cinema during the Revolutionary period. Contingents of Revolutionary peasants had arrived in the capital anxious to experience and enjoy the sinful attractions of the big city. Programmes featuring the Revolution proved popular and thus cameramen produced many of them.

In this period of intense activity, the Alva brothers mastered the techniques and aesthetics of the documentary, and the armed struggle became their favourite subject for several years. On 5 July 1911, the Palacio cinema premiered *Viaje del señor Madero al sur del país*, and at José Cava's Palatino cinema audiences were shown *Los sucesos sangrientos de Puebla (The Bloody Events at Puebla)*, documenting the fight between peasant troops loyal to Madero and the troops of the old federal army. In August 1912, the Alva brothers premiered their most ambitious film, *Revolución orozquista*, a 1,500m film shot in the camps of the rebel and federal forces during the battle between General Huerta and the leader Pascual Orozco. The cinematographers were often verbally insulted and their lives were endangered when they were caught in a cross-fire that seriously damaged their equipment. With two sides to the Revolution, it was logical to show both: thus the public would be able to appreciate the totality of the events and would not be duped. The cameramen did not favour either side and limited themselves to observing events: they would attempt to show the public 'the truth'. In this way, the national style built upon following the close chronological sequence of events reached its apex. It was difficult to improve upon the intention and execution of *Revolución orozquista*. The film told two parallel stories that converged in the final battle. However, the Alva brothers chose only to show the preparations for battle and a few scenes of the fighting, and did not feature the defeated side, concluding instead with an 'apotheosis' of the government's forces. Despite this glorification, it was difficult to tell where the authors' sympathies lay, for they restricted themselves to the presentation of what they saw and did not try to justify the actions of either side. This is clearly a symptom of the objectivity and impartiality that positivism required of the historian. It appears that the authors felt that the events could speak for themselves.

La Revista Nacional (National Magazine), the first newsreel produced in Mexico, was released in September 1912. Sponsored by the distributors Navascúes and Camus, it was inspired by, among others, the Pathé and Gaumont newsreels. The producers intended to produce it bimonthly, but apparently the first issue was also their last. It showed the exhumation of the cadaver of the journalist Sánchez Santos; the Olympic Games; the 16 September parade; triumphal arches on the San Francisco Avenue; Covadonga festivities; a melée in the Chamber of Deputies and the Xochimilco regatta. By comparison with the monumental events represented in *Revolución orozquista, Viaje del señor Madero al sur del país, Viaje de Madero a Cuernavaca* and *Los sucesos sangrientos de Puebla,* its contents were meagre, and it is no surprise that the *Revista Nacional* did not go beyond its first issue. Shortly thereafter, the movie houses exhibited a film of Justo Sierra's funeral. It began with the arrival of his remains at Veracruz on the steamboat *Spain* and ended with the burial: 'The film is the work of Mexicans and its presentation of national characteristics and remarkable details lends honour to the nascent film industry.'

In November, the Principal theatre once again closed its doors to comedic variety shows and opened them to cinema. Enrique Rosas, recently returned from Havana, began showing his programmes: on his way to Mexico City, he had stopped in Veracruz and filmed Díaz's uprising against Madero. His film premiered with the title *Revolución en Veracruz*.

For better or worse, Mexican cinema at this time set out to inform. It had developed its own mode of representation and carefully documented, unhindered, the major national events with complete freedom. The period of Madero's regime may be described as the 'golden age' for Mexican cinema. The cinema documented real events and informed the public, even though the producers had no political agenda. The relationship between the public and the topics addressed by the films was harmonious: the cameramen filmed the activities and lives of everyday people, and these same people went to the movies to see themselves or to admire their favourite political leaders.

From 1911 on, the Mexico City authorities began to intervene energetically. In late September and early October, city council members appointed extra inspectors to visit movie houses. Until then, there had been only two inspectors, and they had found it difficult to control the cinemas and the owners' abuses: confusion, overcrowding, filthy toilets and other irregularities were the norm. The Mexico City authorities agreed to sponsor a much-needed corps of inspectors whose salaries would be paid by the exhibitors. Each company had to pay 25 or 30 pesos to underwrite the inspectors' payroll. At this time, there were forty active exhibitors who had invested approximately 1 million pesos in the business (the exchange rate was 2 pesos to the dollar). The head of the Entertainment Commission wanted to impose pre-censorship because, in his opinion, some films taught thievery and contained immoral scenes. His moralist attitude was no isolated eccentricity; on the contrary, it was a characteristic of Maderismo. When, on entering Mexico City, government representatives had distributed movie and variety theatre tickets among the 'poor demonstrators', this was entirely congruent with the moral paternalism of the director of Public Entertainment. Maderismo was imbued with a moralist, paternalist and messianic frenzy, and pretended that its aim was to 'regenerate the fallen' and 'save the lower classes'. In line with this spirit, censorship was imposed. Although Porfirian society had also been a moralistic one, it never stressed a need to improve the lower classes' morals. Now, however, the official political agenda and public taste had changed, and this included City Hall, which henceforth intended to regulate cinema by prohibiting those films it deemed damaging to public morals. It was obvious that their censorship would be moral rather than political.

Victoriano Huerta's *coup d'état* against Madero in February 1913 forestalled the move to introduce pre-censorship legislation. However, the initiative set precedents and left significant traces. Madero and Vice-president José María Pino Suárez were assassinated and General Huerta came to power. Desiring peace and 'order' above all, Huerta was nostalgic for the old Porfirian order. The film industry was not affected by the coup: new and bigger movie houses continued to open and, on the whole, the prevailing conditions favoured Mexican cinema. The documentary, which at this time was synonymous with Mexican cinema, reached maturity. The film industry and its capital investments continued to be in Mexican hands.

Although Mexico did not have access to the technology for manufacturing film stock or equipment, Indalecio Noriega Colombres, a Spaniard living in Guanajuato, patented the prototype of an apparatus to synchronise the cinematograph to a phonograph. Known as the Sincrophonograph, the invention consisted of 'two needles moving over a quadrant: one linked to the phonograph the other following the cinématographe'. Apparently, the system adapted already existing foreign equipment, but the novelty of Noriega's ingenious invention lay in the fact that the phonograph and projector operated simultaneously, thereby improving synchronicity between sound and image.

1913–1914

Eight days after the so-called *Decena Trágica*, the ten days of violent conflict in Mexico City, a film documenting the events of the coup was exhibited, as if the coup itself had not altered the nature of everyday life. Three films by different directors were exhibited simultaneously to audiences who were curious and hungry for information. In May 1913, the Salón Rojo premiered *Aniversario del fallecimiento de la suegra de Enhart (The Anniversary of the Death of Enhart's Mother-in-Law)*, one of the few Mexican fiction films of this period that we know of. Directed by the Alva brothers, the film imitated the then fashionable films of Max Linder. The Alva brothers took advantage of the popularity of Alegría and Enhart, two Lírico theatre comedians, and created a narrative around them filmed 'in the French style'. The story of the film was simple: Enhart's wife wakes him from a nap and asks him to accompany her to lay flowers on his mother-in-law's grave. Various incidents occur on their way to the cemetery. He gets drunk in front of the grave, digs up his mother-in-law's remains and lies down in the grave. A scandal ensues and he is imprisoned, but since he is supposed to perform in the theatre that evening, the police commissioner agrees to set him

free. With this fiction film, the Alva brothers seemed to indicate that they were more interested in entertaining than in informing the public. *Aniversario del fallecimiento de la suegra de Enhart* is, in fact, the first of three significant changes that took place in the cinema during the Huerta regime. The others were the establishment of censorship and the appearance of Porfirian nostalgia.

Aniversario del fallecimiento was exhibited on 6 May 1913; a month later, according to *El Diario* of 3 June, a *Revista Semanal* (by Gaumont) was exhibited which, after some scenes of the Balkan war and other European events, announced that a future newsreel would report on US preparations for a military intervention in Mexico and showed images of US troops on the frontier. Immediately, the primarily urban public showed its disapproval and the film was withdrawn.

Although in this case a foreign film made reference to national political matters, the Revolutionary documentary often awakened similar violent reactions in audiences. For example, as Martín Luiz Guzmán recounts in *El aguila y la serpiente*, at one point, *convencionista* soldiers objected to the images of Venustiano Carranza and shot at the screen. Not surprisingly, a few days after the newsreel incident, the first moral and political censorship decree was passed. It prohibited 'views representing crimes, if they do not include punishment of the guilty parties', views which 'directly or indirectly ... insult an authority or person, morality or good manners, provoke a crime or offence, or in any way disturb the public order'. Importers were now forced to show films to a government inspector before they could be exhibited. This change in the cinematic sphere seems consonant with the statement Huerta offered to the press soon after assuming power: 'I would look favourably upon the press if it would discuss scientific matters and issues related to material improvements and administrative matters rather than debate political problems.'

Given all this and the radicalisation of the parties involved in the armed conflict, cameramen began to define their positions. Two years after *Revolución orozquista*, impartiality had become impossible. In *Sangre hermana (Sister Blood)*, 'the public will marvel at the sight of real zapatista fighters; it will appreciate the courage of our [federal] soldiers; it will witness towns set on fire, trains blown up by dynamite, executed zapatistas, and all the horrors of the

Revolution in the south.' Clearly, spectators were offered very tendentious information. The directors of *Sangre hermana* were neither interested in understanding or analysing the events, nor in presenting the reasons for the armed conflict in such a way that the public could arrive at its own conclusions.

The newspapers of the time demonstrated a nostalgia for a distant 'golden age', bemoaning that the much-desired restoration had not yet begun. The good manners that certain social sectors associated with Don Porfirio contrasted with the brutal Huerta government. For example, Huerta needed a strong military force to control the nation, which he built by signing up men through raffles, often held as people came out of popular amusements such as movies, bullfights or theatres. Time and again, Don Porfirio was invited to return, to rejoin Mexican society and the army. The newspapers frequently published his declarations and his pictures, kept track of his trips, and organised events in his honour:

El señor general don Porfirio Díaz en París (General Don Porfirio Díaz in Paris). We have no doubt that this film will satisfy public expectations and attain the success it deserves, for the camera has captured fascinating scenes of the life in the City of Light of our aged and illustrious ex-president and his virtuous wife and other relatives. In this film we can appreciate the exceptional vigour of this great expatriate who, despite all political issues, has had the courage to offer his life and the services of his glorious sword to defend the independence of his fatherland.[6]

Despite such nostalgia, a Porfirian peace would not return and the system was unable to reconstitute itself after its demise. Conditions were deteriorating and the uprising spread throughout the nation: Maytorena in Sonora, Carranza in Coahuila, Villa in the north, while Zapata and Morelos pretended that such setbacks were impossible.

The most important cinematic consequences of the Huerta regime were the appearance of moral and political censorship and the subsequent redirection of the early Mexican cinema. Initially Mexican cinema had aspired to document reality with a promising, zealous objectivity. However, the responses it evoked gave rise to direct state control, and this unconsciously political and simple cinema that attempted to show 'the truth' of events was, therefore, slowly abandoned. It took only two years for it to develop into Mexican fiction cinema.

Arguably, this early Mexican cinema constituted Mexico's principal contribution to world cinema. In retrospect, it has become doubly important: first, because it showed images of the Revolution that no literary equivalent could match; secondly, because its faithfulness to the geographic and chronological sequence of events and its desire to record historical events constituted a local vernacular form of the representation of contemporary happenings. What is surprising is that this practice was unrelated to newsreels in the style of Gaumont, Pathé or Selig, but was, rather, the norm for national production and, therefore, a unique phenomenon in the international history of the cinema. The itinerant nature, technical limitations, scarce funds and artisanal nature of the nascent industry, together with other cultural forces, determined the appearance of this first Mexican cinema, which only later became dangerous when it concerned itself with political matters. It graduated from documenting popular everyday experience such as exits from churches and factories, to recording the Revolutionary events of interest to audiences. This was, apparently, its mistake and the cause of its demise.

In another sector, in 1913, Pedro Requena y Abreu patented a projector of still and moving images. This was an original apparatus, not a modification of existing technology, but, as usual, it went unnoticed and we do not even know if it was demonstrated in public. The movie houses and the distribution and production companies continued to be in the hands of Mexicans. US investors were not visible yet, although there surely must have been one or two foreigners in the distribution or exhibition sectors.

Second Period: 1916–1930
1916–1920

The exhibition of Revolutionary documentaries dwindled, and by 1916 they had disappeared from the theatres to reappear later only in exceptional circumstances. When Zapata and Villa were assassinated (respectively 1919 and 1923), summaries of the important events of their lives were shown, but the events had a different significance since they were now of historical rather than contemporary interest. In 1916, it was firmly believed that the Mexican film industry was about to take off and that it was necessary to build a solid foundation for it. The belief was that as its future members prepared and improved themselves, the industry would become large and prosperous. Manuel de la Bandera opened a film school to prepare new actors, a clear indication that people

El automovíl gris (Enrique Rosas, Joaquín Coss and Juan Canals de Homes, 1919)

now wanted to make and see narrative films. Cinema, and the individuals involved in its production, changed. Before, film-makers were pragmatists who had learned their craft by documenting people and events in order to attract audiences. Now film-makers trained themselves to make fictional narratives. National producers had never before dealt with narrative, a term that had been used exclusively to refer to foreign fiction films. Similarly, no one considered actors in terms of 'cinematographic mimicry', for the films reproduced the everyday life of ordinary people, walking, working, in battle or amusing themselves. These people did not need to pretend in front of the camera. Now a different conception of cinema made its way. The 'views' had lost their appeal and the desire was for *films d'art* based on foreign models.

The Mexican views were denied the possibility of developing the language of cinema in their own terms. *Aniversario del fallecimiento de la suegra de Enhart* had been an exception. A newspaper announced that Mimí Derba was developing 'matters of national interest that will illustrate the real customs of the Mexican people and that will stimulate the public and orient it toward the social practices required by our civilisation'. This announcement referred to the fact that US films about Mexico had provoked public and (occasional) governmental protests. Few US films represented dignified Mexicans: for the most part, Mexicans were portrayed as wild men, drunkards, grotesquely attired bandits, all caricatures. The early Mexican cinema had been forgotten. The documentary was now ignored in favour of *films d'art*.

The first film that attempted to adopt this style, *La luz* (*The Light*, Ezequiel Carrasco, 1917), was received as 'an inept plagiarism of Piero Fosco's *Il Fuoco*, without the dramatic and artistic intensity of the original. *Il Fuoco* featured Pina Menichelli ... and the resemblance [between Emma Padilla and Pina Menichelli] is forced, and, at best, limited to Emma's obsessive imitation of Pina's attitudes, movements, gestures, and manners.' The situation could not be clearer: the first Mexican narrative film was modelled on the Italian cinema, and thus began the process of attempting to base the Mexican cinema on other film-making practices. This was not surprising, given that Italian *films d'art* were very popular with audiences. Between 1896 and 1913, audiences had preferred French films, but between 1913 and 1920 the public leaned towards Italian cinema and its family melodramas, tormented passions, love triangles and stories of incest set among the upper or upper-middle class.

Italian cinema introduced not only melodrama but also the cult of stars. Previously, the stars had been the events themselves or the leaders of the Revolution. Many of the events featured in the first Mexican cinema had been dramatic in and of themselves. *La luz* attempted to incorporate Mexican cinema's documentary experience: the difference between *Il fuoco* and *La luz,* besides technical ineptitude, seems to reside in 'the photographer's ability to show that Mexico could and should feature its beautiful landscapes on the screen'. Finally, *La luz* was also a curious allegory of the thinking that would prevail in national production: although inspired by a foreign archetype, it adopted a typically Mexican *mise en scène*. Outside of the country, this latter trait would come to be regarded as characteristic of Mexican cinema. This combination became a basic aspect of Mexican cinema, allowing it to develop while preserving some of its characteristics.

The first film produced by Mimí Derba's company, *En defensa propia* (*In Self-Defence,* Joaquín Coss, 1917), was exhibited a month after *La luz.* According to the newspaper announcement of this project, the expectation was that it would deal with themes of national and historical significance. Actually, the film turned out to be a typical middle-class domestic melodrama modelled on the Italian examples: an orphan employed as the nanny of the daughter of a rich young widower grows to love the child and marries the widower. The conflict of the film emerged out of a classic love triangle, in this case unconsummated because the husband realised that the 'other woman' was insincere. The novelty here was the theme: it was the first film to deal with family relations, foreshadowing the motherhood motif that would proliferate in the sound cinema.

La tigresa (*The Tigress,* Mimí Derba, 1917) was also said to be based on *Il fuoco*. Italian cinema may have had such an impact because of the similarities between the Italian and Mexican situations at this time: war in Italy and revolution in Mexico. In Italy, cinema provided an escape from a painful reality. In Mexico, this cinema was also consumed in order to forget the problems inherent in the Revolution: national unrest, lack of urban safety, shortages of basic products and currency, speculation, black markets, and so on. It is not surprising that La tigresa exclaims: 'I would like to live an extraordinary novel'. Neither is it a coincidence that another Mimí Derba film was entitled *La soñadora* (*The Dreamer,* Eduardo Arozamena, 1917). Dreams and fantasies are also central to *La obsesión* (Manuel de la Bandera, 1917), a film based on a script by its star, María Luisa Ross. The plot revolves around an artist who cannot find the right inspiration for his sculptures. He ultimately discovers it in the corpse of his young girlfriend who has committed suicide because of his infidelities. It is clearly an unrealistic, fantastic story: who could sculpt when contemplating the corpse of a lover whose death you have caused?

Such Mexican films were based on stories written specifically for the cinema. However, literature was also a frequent source of inspiration. Several adaptations were produced in 1918: Federico Gamboa's *Santa* (Luis G. Peredo); José Zorrilla de San Martín's *Tabaré* (Luis Lezama); José Velarde's *Confesión trágica* (Carlos E. González and José Manuel Ramos). Others followed in 1919: Jorge Isaacs's *María* (Rafael Bermúdez Zataraín) and Federico Gamboa's *La llaga* (*The Wound,* Luis G. Peredo). Stories dealing with impossible loves predominated. It seems that the public liked to cry and suffer. As mentioned earlier, *En defensa propia* had introduced the mother motif that would be fully developed by the sound cinema, and *Santa* contained the seeds of a second perennial motif, that of the good prostitute. *Tepeyac* (José Manuel Ramos, 1918) and *Confesión trágica* featured religious themes; *Cuauhtémoc* (Manuel de la Bandera, 1919) and *Tabaré* introduced historical themes. Rural themes were absent. Only two films dealt with the countryside, *Viaje redondo* (*Round Trip,* José Manuel Ramos, 1920) and *Partida ganada* (*The Winning Round,* Enrique Castilla, 1920), but we don't know how they addressed the issue. The images that we have been able to find suggest that the films dealt with *costumbrista* topics: *Viaje redondo* is possibly the first film to be based on the so-called Mexican theatrical genre derived from the Spanish *género chico,* while *Partida ganada* seems to deal with the *fiestas pueblerinas*. In-depth treatments of rural issues would become one of the taboos of the Mexican cinema.

Undoubtedly the most important film of this period, Enrique Rosas's *El automóvil gris* (1919), was both the swan-song of the first Mexican cinema and a symptom of what was to follow. Based on real events and organised in a series of tableaux, it told of a gang who used a car as well as the military uniforms belonging to the Carranza faction to rob houses with impunity. Rosas's representation of the various house robberies follows their historical sequence and chronology, thus adapting the style introduced by Salvador Toscano for *Viaje a Yucatán* and developed further by the Alva brothers in *Revolución orozquista*. Like *Aniversario del fallecimiento de la suegra de Enhart*, this film was shot on location and we can see how the city had changed in seven years. In the earlier film we see people walking in the streets of a clean, well-maintained city. In the latter, however, the effects of the long struggle have transformed the city: it is dirty, in ruins, and, with the exception of the Avenida Juárez, empty. The visibility of these changes is clear evidence of Rosas's drive towards realism. Some of the gang members were arrested and executed to appease the public: Rosas included footage showing the actual execution to underline what he understood as 'cine-truth'. *El automóvil gris* is the last film to have a documentary feel in the style of the first Mexican cinema, but its modification of the events and its melodramatic elements, included to meet the expectations of the public and in response to the influence of the Italian cinema, also served as a model for the development of Mexican sound cinema. Rosas's narrative also reveals the influence of US cinema: his use of a peep-hole recalls Griffith's *Intolerance* of 1916, already shown in Mexico, and the twelve-episode structure is in the style of US serials.

Around 1919, the US cinema had intensified its efforts to usurp the popularity of the Italian cinema in Mexico. Thus *El automóvil gris* is significant three times over: it represents the last gasp of the first Mexican cinema, it announces what Mexican cinema will be like in the future, and it embodies the influence of both Italian and US film-making.

Censorship was re-established on 1 October 1919. The ninth article of the decree affirmed that the censorship council would ban only those films offensive to 'public morals in their content or intertitles' and those that 'present criminal behaviour in detail or convey a sense of the supremacy of criminals, either because of their intelligence, prowess, or any other reason that may inspire sympathy for the characters or their immoral behaviour'. This implies that censorship would be moral rather than political. However, Rosas had to be extremely careful with his film, for the story was intimately linked to contemporary politics because of rumours identifying some gang leaders as government officials. Rosas's characterisations indicate that he obeyed the censorship measures. The scene of the real execution added at the end was in the spirit of the censorship decree, claiming that 'the police are always vigilant', without betraying his cine-truth ideals. For all these reasons, *El automóvil gris* was the most important film of the period 1917–20.

Film newsreels were well established before the Revolutionary documentaries disappeared. These were the topics addressed by the second issue of *Revista Mexico:* 'Ceremonies at the French Pantheon for those Mexicans who died in France; French celebrations at the Eliseo Tívoli; Inauguration of the vegetable and flower show of the Cayoacán Forestry Department; Fashion; Agriculture; Civic ceremonies honouring the anniversary of the death of the illustrious Don Benito Juárez'. Surprisingly, we can conclude that both newsreels and narrative films avoided all topics dealing with reality and political information. Reality had become Mexican cinema's central and most significant taboo. And, during this time, 'the real' included the Revolution, agrarian problems, poverty, illiteracy and speculation.

The pioneers aspired to develop a national industry that would have its own characteristics. This in many ways they achieved, for the films produced between 1917 and 1920 already contained the seeds of the sound cinema's themes, archetypes and attitudes. In exhibition, the number of movie theatres had been constant since 1911. However, their capacity increased markedly at this stage: the new Olimpia theatre alone could seat 4,000. Exhibition consortia began to appear which combined a distribution company with a chain of movie theatres. This time not all investors were Mexican, as US citizens began to invest in these chains through their Mexican representatives. For obvious reasons, the US cinematic penetration began in the north. Juan de la Cruz Alarcón, the owner and manager of various movie theatres along the USA–Mexico border was also the principal stockholder of the International Pictures Co. based in El Paso, Texas. It was said that he used the support of four of the better production houses to begin an intense campaign with US films. De la Cruz Alarcón was of the opinion that the first thing that needs to be done if the cinema is to influence the ideas of the people ... is to present carefully selected good films with good titles. ...Given that the cinema is a form of education, and given that we are all in agreement that this is what Mexico needs, I don't think it unjustified to use the cinema as an educational instrument.

On October 1919, International Films, Fox Film and Universal Film set up offices in Mexico City. After the Revolution, Mexico swapped European influence for the far more aggressive US pressure. In cinema, the US influence was not limited to film exhibition or production, but went much deeper than expected. The national inventors were also productive between 1917 and 1920, undoubtedly because the optimistic assessments of the future potential of a Mexican film industry were contagious. Indalecio Noriega Colombres renewed the 1911 patent for the Sincrophonograph; Leandro Girón Alvarez patented a cinema projector; Juan Ortega González patented an invention for film repair and reels; Salvador A. Contreras invented an apparatus to sell candy automatically in theatres and cinemas; Daniel Sada recorded another invention to synchronise images and sound, a 'graphonetic apparatus adapted to film'; Jesús Herrera y Gutiérrez invented 3-D glasses; Miguel de J. Bernal patented 'an invention addressing the simultaneous reproduction of movements and sounds via a cinematographic apparatus combined with a phonograph'; in *Empalme Sonora*, Ricardo Larroque invented a machine to project film titles in any language; Felipe Sierra y Domínguez patented 'an invention referring to a system to produce a real image in relief of cinematographic views without a screen'; and Luis G. Alcorta patented 'an invention for a film made with dolls, letters, and other figures and the process to produce it'. The list is endless. Suffice it to add that among the many patents recorded were some for solar-powered projectors, theatre seats, screens and other cinema implements. Among the cited inventions, Noriega Colombres's Sincrophonograph was built upon equipment already patented in other nations, but Leandro Girón Alvarez's projector and Luis G. Alcorta's system were apparently original. The proliferation of national inventions went hand in hand with the euphoria to establish a Mexican cinema industry, but the efforts of these 'little geniuses' went for nought since none of their inventions was taken up. Mexican cinema inherited what appears to be an authentic original sin: dependence upon foreign technology.

The balance of the 1917–20 period for the national cinema was negative: there was censorship, production was based on foreign models, US capital was prominent, national inventions were wasted and the realistic or critical representation of reality had become the first taboo in Mexican cinema.

1920–1924

During this period, the USA consolidated its cinematic presence in Mexico and the national industry was unable to combat this new aggressive influence. The USA had its advocates: the magazine *Cine Mundial,* edited in New York, and *El Universal Ilustrado,* a weekly edited in Mexico City, whose writers argued that the national cinema had to assimilate US technical expertise and admire US stars. First published in 1916, *Cine Mundial* was aimed at the Spanish-speaking international market. Its intentions were clear from the start: to promote the position of US cinema in the 'natural' Latin American market at a time when the First World War had lowered European production. Of course, by this time the USA had developed and perfected its film language and it had now become impossible to develop one's own voice totally independently. Perhaps this would have been acceptable had the US cinema transmitted only technological and syntactical innovations, but the film business also disseminated other ways of life and social organisation. The trade in films went hand in hand with an unavoidable promotion of consumption and of products such as cosmetics, silk stockings, plastic surgery, fashion, hair styles, toothpaste, and so on. Mexico exchanged its Europeanisation for Americanisation. The slogan 'America for the Americans' was being fully realised.

El Universal Ilustrado established a contest for the most popular movie actress: Bertini came out in first place and Mabel Normand in second. US cinema demystified old fetishes and made kissing a commonplace:

The value of the kiss has suffered a terrible decline. Less than five years ago, our more prudish ladies complained because actresses 'really' kissed actors and even offered graphic lessons on the art of kissing which, after Astarté, had no didactic value whatsoever. [Now] the kiss has suffered a visible decline: it has little importance and the same status in affairs of the heart as timid hand-holding.[8]

Production took place in the shadows of US influence. One of the first films produced in the

1920s, *El caporal* (*The Chief*, scripted by Miguel Contreras Torres, 1921), was set in the countryside. The date on the script, January 1920, indicates that it was planned during the Carranza regime, which helps to explain why the film avoids the problems of land ownership. Instead, it is a comedy of Mexican manners much influenced by the US Western genre (even though, as if in response to the US cinema's misrepresentation of Mexicans, one of the film's villains is North American). The influence of the Western is also evident in the structure of the narrative, the inclusion of duels and the characterisation of villains who are defeated by the ability, intelligence, courage, cunning and fists of the heros.

The story of *En la hacienda* (*In the Hacienda*, Ernesto Vollrath, 1921) serves as a pretext for the presentation of the Mexican lifestyle. It is a love story complete with jealousies, revenge and intrigue, while also avoiding the problems of land ownership. Instead, like Fernando de Fuentes's later film, *Allá en el Rancho Grande* (*Over on the Big Ranch*, 1936), *En la hacienda* ultimately favours the preservation of the great agricultural estates. Other films of this period that were set in the countryside included: *La parcela* (*The Plot*, 1922), an adaptation of José López Portillo's novel directed by Vollrath; and *De raza azteca* (*About the Aztec Race*, 1921) directed by Miguel Contreras Torres and Guillermo Calles. And middle-class or bourgeois settings formed the background for films such as Vollrath's *Carmen* (1921), an adaptation of Pedro Castera's novella, and *La dama de las camelias* (*The Lady of the Camelias*, 1921), a free adaptation from Alexandre Dumas's novel. Mexican cinema's main themes were gradually being defined, eventually setting the agenda for its sound cinema.

Atavismo (*Atavism*, 1923) was a singular film: 'As its title indicates, it was based on the horrors of hereditary degeneration.' The film's central theme concerned the fatal consequences of alcoholism. Most telling is the pessimism of its social reading and its biological determinism. Its director, Gustavo Sáenz de Sicilia, the founder of the Mexican Fascist Party, saturated the film with his ideology.[9]

Adolfo de la Huerta, appointed interim president after the assassination of Carranza (and who governed only during the six-month period before the election of Alfaro Obregón in 1920), abolished censorship, but Obregón re-established it in Mexico City. Although this might seem to indicate that censorship was only practised in the federal district, in fact Mexico City communicated its findings on banned films to all state and municipal governments and its censorship was *de facto* national.

The Obregón regime was characterised by its interest in education. José Vasconcelos was its central promoter: his interest in visual education led him to foster the muralist movement. The cinema also had a place in the government's projects. The state sponsored films through the ministries of War and Marines, Education, and Agriculture and Development. Consequently, the new documentary had a pedagogical mission. The armed Revolution was far away. Among the three ministries, Education sponsored the greatest number of films and Agriculture the most interesting ones. The former documented its various activities and produced its own newsreel. The latter produced scientific and educational films through its various agencies. Among the most interesting were the ethnographic films produced by the archaeologist Manuel Gamio in the Teotihuacán Valley. His most ambitious film was perhaps *La población del valle de Teotihuacán* (*The Population of the Teotihuacán Valley*, 1923). Some of his films were exhibited with musical accompaniment recorded on discs.

The National History, Ethnography and Archaeology Museum produced *Fiestas de Chalma* (Miguel de Mendizábal and others) in 1922. This was an interdisciplinary film-essay produced by the ethnographer de Mendizábal in collaboration with cinematographer Ramón Díaz Ordaz, documenting the annual religious festivities frequented by large groups of Indians. They also benefited from the collaboration of musicologist Francisco Domínguez, the historian Enrique Juan Palacios and the ethnologist Canuto Flores. Another notable production of the Ministry of Agriculture and Development was the documentary about the total solar eclipse of 1921, which was filmed with a special camera. Inspired by the US Department of Agriculture's films, the Ministry also attempted to produce scientific films based on laboratory research of the Mexican flora and fauna. Unfortunately, Adolfo de la Huerta's 1923 rebellion over the presidential succession interrupted the work of the Ministry of Agriculture. The war forced the government to trim budgets and the cinematographic departments of both ministries were the first to be cut.

By 1924, the national narrative film was at its lowest ebb since 1917. The optimists who wanted to develop a national cinema felt defeated; they blamed the limited size of the national market, the investors' lack of courage, the deficient technical abilities of national cinematographers and, above all, the state. Several accused Vasconcelos directly for not promoting the national cinema. They were partly right, although the real problem was that the government never curtailed US cinema's formidable competition. Vasconcelos saw the cinema as an educational tool, but he neither sponsored nor stimulated producers to develop narrative films. With the state blocking only those films that denigrated the Mexican nation, US films inundated the national market, and the national cinema had to declare itself unable to compete. The discouragement was, to some degree, justified, for the state did not even attempt to encourage the development of a narrative cinema parallel to the pictorial movement and the educational documentary.

For their part, the inventors continued their activities. In fact, the apparatuses they patented seem to indicate that they were attempting to build a national industry from the ground up by inventing technology to liberate the national cinema from its 'original sin' of dependence. Felipe Sierra patented an apparatus for solar projection based on mirrors; Carlos M. Arredondo invented 'a strip to develop, fix, wash, wind or tint cinematographic film easily and economically'; Juan Ortega González developed 'a camera to record, on a single film strip, stereophonic films'; a Mr Andrade patented a system that apparently would have revolutionised sound techniques: 'an apparatus to record voice on film and to combine the movement of the figures on film with the phonograph', in other words, an optical sound system and not simply a combination of the phonograph and motion-picture technology. Finally, José García Garibay, Federico Bouvi and A. García patented 'a cinematographic apparatus to record and project stereoscopically'. With time, the inventors perfected their techniques: instead of modifying existing equipment, they invented new and original mechanisms. Of course, we cannot tell how successful these apparatuses were nor why they were never utilised.

Meanwhile, US investment reached the movie house real-estate market. The Granat brothers Olimpia circuit, the largest in the country, was purchased by North Americans in a rather shady deal. Apparently, the programme outlined in 1916 by *Cine Mundial* had been realised: cinematographically speaking, 'Mexico belonged to the North Americans'.

1925–1930

Little can be said of the Maximato period, so-called because General Plutarco Elías Calles, General Obregón's presidential successor, governed the nation through third parties and was called the *Jefe Máximo*. Few changes took place in relation to the Obregón period. On the contrary, the invasion of US films continued. The themes of *El Cristo de oro* (*The Golden Christ*, Manuel R. Ojeda and Basilio Zubiaur, 1926) and *El coloso de mármol* (*The Marble Colossus*, Manuel R. Ojeda, 1928) are typical of the films of the period. The title *El Cristo de oro* alludes to the Cristero Rebellion of 1927–9, even though the film never refers to it:

> The action took place in the 17th century and featured a story filled with romance, intrigue, and sacrifices. The anguish of old Mexico was transcribed with the flavour of its mysteries. This was the era in which justice frightened the criminals of New Spain. An intense drama, full of human details.[10]

The Cristeros joined the list of Mexican cinema's list of taboo subjects, which by now included the Revolution, the countryside and labour problems. The tendency to turn away from real problems begun in the Carranza period continued. Thus, unsurprisingly, *El Cristo de oro* was exhibited without difficulties, since it presented a nostalgic vision of the remote past.

The events of *El coloso de mármol* took place in 1927. The film dealt with a conspiracy against the government and, although never mentioned, obviously referred to the Cristeros. It was, therefore, an official propaganda film. The settings were the Calles prison, 'a marvellous and eloquent representation of progress' and the Palacio de Bellas Artes, from which the film derived its title. In fact, the film is an advertisement for the efforts of the Obregón and Calles governments to promote culture, education, irrigation and the cultural integration of the Indians. A question arises: Was this kind of film attempting to compete with US productions? If so, the failure of Mexican film pioneers to develop a national industry is understandable.

Some films were produced in the provinces because film production was not yet centralised. In the most important cities – Guadalajara, Monterrey, Mérida, Puebla and San Luis Potosí – local cameramen first recorded local events and later, especially those who were also exhibitors, attempted to produce narrative films. In Mérida, the first narrative feature, *1810 o los libertadores de México* (*1810 or the Mexican Liberators*, Carlos Martínez de Arredondo), was produced in 1916. In Guadalajara,

María Cantoni appeared in and financed *La bastarda* (1921). Believing that to know the provinces was to know Mexico, José Ortiz Ramos directed and photographed films in Tampico, San Luis Potosí and Aguascalientes. The sense of defeat also reached the inventors: in this period the only registered patents were for advertising systems, probably used to promote the consumption of US products in movie houses, and for modifications to existing foreign systems. The sound cinema widened the gulf between foreign technology and the Mexican inventors. It also contributed to the consolidation of production since sound production demanded a far more skilled labour force.

With the advent of sound cinema, Mexico was experiencing a high level of cinematic North Americanisation against which national productions had to compete. The national sound cinema began as a subsidiary of US cinema and faced a gigantic challenge. To what degree was it successful? What was the response to North Americanisation? How was it faced? Between 1896 and 1930, the cinema contributed to the radical transformation of Mexico. From its beginnings as a scientific curiosity, cinema became a mass entertainment that contributed to the dissemination of other modes of life, customs and ways of thinking. It was a new and powerful tool of acculturation. When cinema arrived in Mexico, women still wore long dresses. By 1930, they were dressed in short skirts, transparent stockings and they were wearing bras; they copied the make-up and hairstyles of US actresses and used slimming devices or plastic surgery in order to look like them. To a large degree, the cinema was responsible for this change in public taste.

Notes

1. The first screening that we know of took place privately, on Thursday 6 August 1896, for General Díaz and his family and friends in the Chapultepec palace. Detailed references to newspapers and other reports cited in this essay can be found in Aurelio de los Reyes's contribution to David Ramón and María Luisa Amador, *80 años de cine en México* (Mexico City: UNAM, 1977), pp. 89–92.

2. José María Sánchez García, 'Historia del cine mexicano' in *Cinema Reporter* (Mexico City), 28 July 1951, p. 18.

3. For further details, see Aurelio de los Reyes, *Cine y sociedad en México, 1896–1930*, vol. 1, *Vivir de sueños, 1896–1920* (Mexico City: UNAM, 1983).

4. Ibid., and by the same author, *Medio siglo de cine mexicano (1896–1947)* (Mexico City: Trillas, 1987).

5. The Maderistas were followers of Francisco I. Madero, the instigator of the Mexican Revolution. He governed between November 1911 and February 1913, when he was defeated by a *coup d'état* led by General Victoriano Huerta.

6. 'Espectáculos' in *El Independiente* (Mexico City), 23 August 1913, p. 6.

7. Some narrative films were produced earlier, most notably those with historical themes such as *El grito de Dolores* and *Colón*. Others were simply experiments (*El San Lunes del Valedor, Aventuras de Tip Top*).

8. 'El amor, el beso, y el cine' in *El Universal Ilustrado* (Mexico City), 19 August 1920, p. 20.

9. José María Sánchez García, 'Historia del cine mexicano' in *Cinema Reporter* (Mexico City), 25 April 1952, p. 20.

10. Ibid., 9 January 1954, p. 37.

Origins, Development and Crisis of the Sound Cinema (1929–64)

Eduardo de la Vega Alfaro

First Sound Films (1929–31)*

In the late 20s and early 30s, Mexico underwent a significant political transformation. The governments led by Emilio Portes Gil (November 1928–September 1930), Pascual Ortiz Rubio (September 1930–September 1932) and Abelardo Rodríguez (September 1932–November 1934) make up what is known as the Maximato callista. This was a period sustained by the political power of Plutarco Elías Calles, the last caudillo of the faction that won the armed struggle initiated in 1910. Taking advantage of his position as the 'national political strongman', Calles limited the power of the president and controlled for his own personal gain three key sectors of the political infrastructure: the Partido Nacional Revolucionario (which under various names has continued in power as the hegemonic party and the principal extension of the state), the Chamber of Deputies and the various presidential cabinets. But, despite all the efforts of the Jefe Máximo, it was impossible to ignore the demands of farmers and workers. The new presidential regime of December 1934 began a series of reforms and reorganisations that would determine the modern history of the country.

If for these and other reasons the decade of the 20s was of great political and social significance, it was no less important for the development of a national cinema. In fact, in the late 20s, national cinema languished under the pressure of Hollywood competition and the disorganisation and ineptitude of its practitioners. Mexican silent cinema had failed almost completely by 1929–30 (only two films were produced in each of these two years). It appeared as if José Vasconcelos, the minister of Public Education (1921–4) who promoted the work of the great muralists José Clemente Orozco, Diego Rivera, David Alfaro Siqueiros and others, had been right when he had argued that cinema was a 'typically North American' cultural product, impossible to develop as a national form: 'In 1930, the prospects for a national industry were dismal: cinema had failed as a medium for nationalist propaganda, while producers and exhibitors had not been able to establish themselves as a real 'cinematic bourgeoisie'.'[1]

While Mexican cinema suffered its own peculiar difficulties, another crisis gripped the most powerful industry in the world in the USA. Threatened by bankruptcy because of fierce domestic competition, Warner Bros. began a series of experiments that would revolutionise the industry: sound cinema. Sound was not that much of a novelty, since experiments had been made from the earliest days of the cinema, but the Hollywood magnates, afraid of losing their vast international markets because of language barriers, had resisted the innovation. The unexpected but tremendous success of Warners' sound films such as *The Jazz Singer* (Alan Crosland, 1927), triggered a radical change in commercial strategies and concerns. Hollywood businessmen decided to produce sound films in other languages in order to maintain their control of the European, Latin American and Asian markets. For the Spanish-language markets, Hollywood produced the so-called 'Hispanic films', a series of hybrid, low-quality films unable to provide their audiences with valid cultural models. The rapid and resounding failure of this 'Hispanic' cinema created a favourable conjuncture for those who dreamed of developing national industries in Mexico, Argentina, Brazil and Spain, the giants of the Ibero-American world and the only nations able to undertake such an enterprise.

However, the only way to develop film industries in these countries was to compete with Hollywood on its own terms. Thus, from 1929 on (also the date that marked the beginning of the 'Hispanic' cinema), Mexico began to produce sound films, either with sound-on-disc or synchronised with rudimentary methods. In addition to a series of sound shorts and sound newsreels, such as the ones directed by Gabriel Soria (1903–71) for the newspaper *Excélsior,* the national filmographies list the production of eight mid-length and feature films of an experimental nature: Guillermo Calles's *Dios y ley* (*God and the Law,* 1929), Miguel Contreras Torres's *El águila y el nopal* (*The Eagle and the Nopal,* 1929) and *Soñadores de la gloria* (*Dreamers of Glory,* 1930), Raphael J. Sevilla's *Más fuerte que el deber* (*Stronger than Duty,* 1930), Salvador Pruneda's *Abismos o náufragos de la vida* (*Abysses or Shipwrecked from Life,* 1930), Joselito Rodríguez's *Sangre mexicana* (*Mexican Blood,* 1930), Angel E. Alvarez's *Alas de gloria* (*Wings of Glory,*

Emilio Fernández in *Janitzio* (Carlos Novarro, 1934)

1930) and Frank Wells and Alberto Méndez Bernal's *Contrabando* (1932). Several of these films were produced either in Hollywood or with equipment rented from US producers.

One might assume that these films would have been more successful than their 'Hispanic' counterparts because they respected national and linguistic traditions. That they were not was due to the sound systems they used, which created more problems than they solved. However, a group of exhibitors and journalists who felt an urgent need to develop a national industry (Juan de la Cruz Alarcón, Carlos Noriega Hope, Gustavo Sáenz de Sicilia, Eduardo de la Barra and Miguel Angel Frias) decided

to sponsor film with optical sound using a system patented by two Mexican engineers living in Los Angeles, the brothers Joselito and Roberto Rodríguez Ruelas, producers of the already cited *Sangre mexicana*. Their method also had the advantage of being lighter than other similar inventions. In 1931 they produced a new version of *Santa*, already filmed by Luis G. Peredo in 1918. The box-office success of Antonio Moreno's melodramatic adaptation of the 'Mexican Zola', Federico Gamboa's homonymous novel about a prostitute with a heart of gold, established a basis for the development of the much-desired national film industry. *Santa* also included Agustín Lara's music and thus incorporated the first romantic musical successes promoted by the national record and radio industries. From this moment on, the relationship between cinema and radio would remain very productive, contributing to each other's growth and, along with comic books, establishing the bases for a great cultural industry.

Eisenstein's Mexican Adventure (1930–2)

The production of *Santa* started in November 1931, four months after the beginning of a national campaign led by a group of deputies to 'raise the consciousness of Mexicans to consume only Mexican-made products'. This campaign was a short-lived effort to establish protectionist barriers, which facilitated the production of *Santa* and its subsequent success. Finally, the state had decided to support, even if only indirectly, the birth of a Mexican film industry.

At the time of the implementation of this protectionist policy, Sergei Eisenstein, one of the greatest film-makers of all time, was filming on national territory a film of great aesthetic ambition to which he dedicated all his talent, sensibility and hopes. According to Eisenstein's original project, the film was to have been entitled *¡Que viva México!* and would have taken the form of a sort of 'cinematographic mural' and a 'filmic symphony' synthesising Mexican history, art, customs and landscape. Eisenstein had arrived in Mexico on December 1930, after a frustrated attempt to film an adaptation of Theodore Dreiser's famous novel *An American Tragedy* for Paramount. Interested in Mexican politics and culture since his early days as a militant bolshevik, Eisenstein was able to set up a project that would improve his standing in his native land. With the financial support of the leftist US writer Upton Sinclair, and after overcoming a series of terrible customs problems and rejection from a sector of the Mexican government, the famous director of *Battleship Potemkin* began shooting *¡Que viva México!* in February 1931. For a series of reasons that are not to the point here,[2] Eisenstein's Mexican film was never finished and Sinclair, in an attempt to recuperate his investment, either sold or used the rushes, which have appeared in various forms, all of them ignoring Eisenstein's aesthetic intentions.

The undeniable influence of Eisenstein's unfinished film on Mexican cinema has given rise to various polemics. For some, his legacy was harmful because it led to a perfectly anti-cinematic hieraticism and folkloricism with markedly touristic overtones. For others, Eisenstein was the authentic 'father' of Mexican cinematic art, the artist who

enabled the development of a national aesthetic. Whatever the case may be, it nevertheless appears that his enormous talent allowed him to develop cinematographic versions of some of the visual characteristics of the muralist, engraving and photography movements that were cultivated in Mexico in the 20s as part of the 'national culture' project. In this sense, Eisenstein did not invent the aesthetics of Mexican cinema, as some have argued, but he did nudge it in directions that sooner or later Mexican film-makers would have had to discover anyway. His contribution was as a harbinger of things to come. He was a masterful teacher rather than a 'creative father', without diminishing the implicit beauty of his filmic images, his ability and talent, or the extraordinary visual sense of his cameramen Edouard Tissé. We must also note that because of Eisenstein's international prestige, the first apocryphal versions of *¡Que viva México! (Thunder Over Mexico, Eisenstein in Mexico)* familiarised the world with the cinematic image of a country of moving visual beauty whose traditions and customs were worthwhile subjects for the 'seventh art'. Eisenstein returned to the USSR in May 1932, and it is said that he never got over the tragedy of his unfinished Mexican film, a work with which he had planned to equal or surpass the visual and stylistic achievements of D.W. Griffith's monumental *Intolerance* (1916).

The Preindustrial Sound Cinema (1932–7)

By 1932, Mexican cinema already possessed two essential requirements for the industrial development of film production: a trustworthy sound system and a well-defined national aesthetic. The six films made that year were produced with the Rod-ríguez brothers' invention, and one of them, *Mano a mano (Hand to Hand),* clearly demonstrates the direct influence of Eisen-stein's interest in folklore and landscape. The reason for this was simple: the film was directed by Arcady Boytler Rososky (1895–1965), a Russian emigré who had befriended Eisenstein and had even acted in one of the episodes of *¡Que viva México!*[3] Before arriving in Mexico, Boytler had made films in Germany, Chile and in New York, where he had worked for Empire Films, a producer of 'Hispanic' shorts.

In spite of the economic success of *Santa* and the laudable films of 1932, cinema barely managed to infiltrate the domestic market. What was needed were themes and genres that could deliver the domestic audiences and would also conquer the great Spanish-speaking market, which had unanimously rejected the Hollywood Spanish-language films once their novelty had worn off. Given that the businessmen of the cinematic mecca were not willing to abandon the production of 'Hispanic' films, even though they were in crisis, the incipient Mexican film bourgeoisie had sufficient time to experiment and to find a type of cinema to conquer the foreign market. This was the only way to develop a national film industry. The generic experimentation of the period 1933–7 was aesthetically and commercially successful.

Without a doubt, such experimentation would have been impossible in the socially unstable climate of the 20s. However, despite the effects of the US economic crisis in Mexico and profound governmental contradictions, the 30s can be considered as the last stage of the process of national reconstruction. The much-desired institutionalisation of a presidential regime and the control of social forces by the state itself were phenomena that firmly established political stability and, therefore, capitalist development. Within this socio-political context, national film producers were able to compete freely. This led to an increase in the volume of production and allowed various film-makers to direct some of the most important films of Mexican cinema's history. Through-out this period, the most diverse attitudes co-existed. From the beginning, some took on the role of simple businessmen, and the box-office success of their films reinforced their vision of the cinema as pure enter-tainment. The most not-able example of this tendency was that of the Spanish-Mexican Juan Orol García (1897–1988), producer and director of the films *Sagrario* (*Sanctuary*, 1933), *Madre querida* (1935) and *El calvario de una esposa* (*The Calvary of a Wife*, 1936), terrifying melodramas about conjugal infidelities, orphaned children and female subjugation, in which we can easily trace the influence of the *radio-novelas* of the period. *Madre querida* was also a popular success in Central America and the Caribbean.

At the opposite end of the spectrum, we find the avant-garde playwright Juan Bustillo Oro (1904–89) and his films *Dos monjes* (*Two Monks*, 1934), an ambitious expressionist essay; *Monja y casada, virgen y mártir* (*Nun and Married, Virgin and Martyr*, 1935), an adaptation of the homonymous novel by the writer/historian Vicente Riva Palacio; and *El misterio del rostro pálido* (*The Mystery of Pale-Face*, 1935), a curious romantic horror film also filmed in a style inspired by the German expressionists (Wiene, Pabst, Murnau).

A third tendency was represented by the series of films which benefited directly or indirectly from state support. The state moved into production to promote quality cinema with a marked social content to echo the demands and principles of the new revolutionary forces proposed by Lázaro Cárdenas (president from 1934 to 1940). This state support was given to works such as *Redes* (*Nets,* Fred Zinnemann and Emilio Gómez Muriel, 1934), *Rebelión* (Manuel Gómez, 1934), *¡Vámonos con Pancho Villa!* (Fernando de Fuentes, 1935) and a good number of documentaries and newsreels exalting the popular politics and economic progress of the Cárdenas regime.

The fourth tendency was represented by films in which directors managed to articulate commercial and aesthetic demands with extraordinary results: *La mujer del puerto* (*The Woman of the Port,* 1933), a brilliant brothel melodrama by Arcady Boytler; Gabriel Soria's *Chucho el Roto* (1934), the exegesis of the life of a nineteenth-century bandit; Carlos Navarro's *Janitzio* (1934), an indigenista anthropological film much influenced by Eisenstein's and Robert Flaherty's aesthetics (starring Emilio Fernández Romo, who would become one of the principal figures of the national cinema in the next decade); Fernando de Fuentes's *El fantasma del convento* (*The Convent Ghost,* 1934), a good example of horror cinema; Miguel Zacarías's *El baúl macabro* (*The Macabre Trunk,* 1936), a mixed-genre film combining comedy, horror and the detective genre; and Adolfo Best Maugard's *La mancha de sangre* (*The Bloodstain,* 1937), a new brothel melodrama praised for its realism by the muralist Diego Rivera.

José Bohr Elzer (born in 1901) was somewhat on the margin of these trends, but participated actively in the creative enthusiasm of the period. A former Latin star of the 'Hispanic' Hollywood cinema, this Chilean-born film-maker became part of national cinema with a trilogy of delirious, but well-made gangster-detective films often included among the best works of the period: *¿Quién mató a Eva?* (*Who Killed Eva?,* 1934), *Luponini de Chicago (Luponini–The Chicago Terror)* and *Marihuana–El monstruo verde,* shot, respectively, in 1935 and 1936.

The conjuncture also allowed for the debut of Adela Sequeyro 'Perlita' (born in 1901), a theatre and silent-film actress who became the first female Mexican sound film director with *La mujer de nadie* (*Nobody's Woman,* 1937). The recent discovery of this film, which was believed lost, revealed her acute cinematic sense and her ability to incorporate the industrial melodrama in order to create an exceptional female character for Mexican cinema of this period. It is a shame that Adela Sequeyro was only able to direct one other film, *Diablillos del arrabal* (*Little Suburban Devils*, 1938).

Among film auteurs, none was more exceptional than Fernando de Fuentes Carrau (1894–1958), without a doubt the most gifted film-maker of the early Mexican sound cinema. A poet, political essayist and manager of a famous movie house in Mexico City, de Fuentes made his cinematic debut as assistant director on *Santa* and as dialogue coach for John H. Auer's *Una vida por otra* (*A Life for Another*, 1932). With his first production, *El anónimo* (*The Anonymous One*, 1932), he embarked on a remarkable career, which included three films set during the Mexican Revolution: *El prisionero trece* (*Prisoner Number 13*, 1933), *El compadre Mendoza* (1933) and *¡Vámonos con Pancho Villa!* (1935), a trilogy that offered a critical analysis of a historical moment of great contemporary significance. At first glance, these films are classical tragedies, with characters living in extreme circumstances playing out an inexorable destiny. But de Fuentes's films also provide a realistic and allegorical view of the series of betrayals and corruptions that gave the armed movement of 1910–17 historical meaning. It is especially significant that *¡Vámonos con Pancho Villa!* was censored by Lázaro Cárdenas himself, who found the massacre at the ranch in the final scene too cruel and bloody.

In the first stage of his career, de Fuentes was also noted as a good director of genre films, a reputation established by his impeccable adaptation of a *costumbrista* novel by Rafael Delgado, *La calandria* (*The Lark*, 1933); his horror film *El fantasma del convento* (1934); his *Cruz Diablo* (1934), an excellent swashbuckler set in the colonial period; his magisterial portraits of the urban middle class in *La familia Dressel* (1935) and of the rural mind set in *Las mujeres mandan* (*Women Command*, 1936). Neither the great films by de Fuentes nor any other director would have been possible without the creative participation of four cinematographers whose style dominated the period: Alex Phillips, Jack Lauron Draper, Ross Fisher and Agustín Jiménez constituted the first generation of cinematographic artists who set the stage for all later achievements.

As Aurelio de los Reyes pointed out, correctly,[4] the period 1933–7 also witnessed the development of two aesthetic tendencies which could be called antagonistic, even though they were both ramifications of so-called cinematic nationalism. On the one hand, the liberal nationalism promoted by the Lázaro Cárdenas regime was represented by films such as *Redes, Rebelión, Janitzio* and *¡Vámonos con*

Pancho Villa! Most of these were strongly influenced by Eisenstein and were also open to the musical tendencies of authors like Manuel Castro Pasilla, Silvestre Revueltas, Manuel M. Ponce and Carlos Chávez. It is often said that the financial failure of *¡Vámonos con Pancho Villa!*, Mexican cinema's first great epic, also determined the failure of the politics promoted by a liberal and self-critical nationalism.

This liberal nationalism tried to counterbalance the conservative and reactionary ideas of silent films such as *Partida ganada* (*The Winning Round*, 1920), *En la hacienda* (*At the Hacienda*, 1921), *Viaje redondo* (*Round Trip*, 1920)), *La parcela* (*The Parcel*, 1922), *El caporal* (*The Chief*, 1921), and so on. Similar ideas had also surfaced in sound cinema and were evidenced in the exaltation of the agrarian world of the Porfirian period, 'putting aside the social changes brought about by the Revolution and defending the established order'.[5] Somewhat inevitably, the conservative nationalism of films like *Mano a mano* (1932) made an overwhelming reappearance in 1936, with three folkloric films clearly derived from the popular genre theatre, *costumbrista* novels and painting and especially from popular music radio programmes: Roberto O'Quigley's *Cielito lindo* (*Beautiful Little Sky*), Fernando de Fuentes's *Allá en el Rancho Grande* and Gabriel Soria's *¡Ora Ponciano!* (*Now Ponciano!*). These films were produced the very same year that the Cárdenas government initiated an agrarian reform that included, among other elements, the redistribution of *latifundios*. The colossal success of de Fuentes's film in the Spanish-speaking markets finally allowed for the emergence of an industrial Mexican cinema. The film's plot revised that of the silent film, *En la hacienda* (a landowner and his foreman fight for the love of a young ranchera) and added music and other national folkloric elements such as cock fights, dances, horse races and singing duels. Paradoxically, de Fuentes was able to seduce the Latin American and Spanish mass audiences, who found in *Allá en el Rancho Grande* and its many sequels elements of cultural identification that the 'Hispanic' films had been unable to propose. In sum, Mexican cinema was able to become an industry based upon radical and theatrical antecedents and to the detriment of a state-sponsored cinema inspired by first-class cinematic and artistic antecedents. This contradiction would determine the new paths taken by the national cinema.

Birth, Peak and Consolidation of the Film Industry (1938–53)

In the period 1931–7, the developing sound cinema integrated the most diverse artistic and technical personnel. A significant minority (Miguel Contreras Torres, Guillermo 'Indio' Calles, Manuel R. Ojeada, Juan Bustillo Oro, Adela Sequeyro and Rafael Bermúdez Zataraín) had had silent-film experience. Others (David Kirkland, John H. Auer, Robert Curwood, Roberto O'Quigley, Alex Phillips, Jack Lauron Draper and Ross Fisher) were foreigners with extensive Hollywood experience. Another small group (Fernando de Fuentes, Juan Orol, Agustín Jiménez and Luis Márquez) had prior experience in newspapers, radio or photography. But the majority of the directors of the period (Ramón Peón, Arcady Boytler, José Bohr, Gabriel Soria, Chano Urueta, Raphael J. Sevilla and Miguel Zacarías) and others who made their mark somewhat later (Alejandro Galindo, Alberto Gout, Fernando Méndez, Raúl de Anda, Gilberto Martínez Solares, René Cardona and Emilio Fernández) came up through the ranks of the industry as supporting actors or technicians (assistant directors, make-up artists, translators, still photographers) for the small or medium companies that emerged in Hollywood or New York after the coming of sound.

Any analysis of the development of the film industry in Mexico as a mass medium and spectacle must take into account a symptomatic event: on 25 June 1934, the growing Mexican film bourgeoisie organised itself under the banner Asociación de Productores de Películas (Association of Film Producers). At first, this organisation consisted of the same group of enthusiasts who had witnessed the birth and irregular early development of Mexican sound cinema. On February 1936, some months before *Allá en el Rancho Grande* went into production, Mexican film businessmen reorganised as the Asociación de Productores Cinematografistas de México, a corporate organisation that already indicated the maturity and class beliefs of its members. The extraordinary success of de Fuentes's film did not take them by surprise: they immediately invested large sums to finance a good number of films that, given the favourable reaction of foreign markets, would simply repeat the formula of *Allá en el Rancho Grande*. De Fuentes himself immediately directed two sequels: *Bajo el cielo de México (Under the Mexican Sky)* and *La Zandunga* (both in 1937). The latter film marked the national debut of the famous Mexican actress Lupe Vélez, already a well-established Hollywood actress. It set an important

precedent for other Mexican actors who had become famous in the cinematic mecca (José Mojica, Ramón Novarro, Dolores del Río) to become part of a national industry that was already able to recognise and promote their prestige. This was the basis for the development of the star system without which no film industry can survive.

In an apparently irreversible first push, 57 features were produced in 1938 and the Mexican film industry was officially born, surpassing the production of Argentina and Spain, which were expanding their industries. However, it is important to highlight a fact that has often been ignored by national film historians: the industrial transformation of Mexican cinema involved, on the one hand, the definitive defeat of the Hollywood's 'Hispanic' cinema and, on the other, the constant supremacy over the other Spanish-language producers. But the other US-produced cinema never lost its hegemony over Latin American or Mexican screens. For example, as Jorge Ayala Blanco and María Luisa Amador have noted, of the 3,081 feature films premiered in the capital in the 30s, 2,338 (76%) were from the USA, 544 (17.5%) were from other foreign nations and only 199 (6.5%) were Mexican.[6] In this sense, we can say that Mexican cinema, like that of other underdeveloped nations, has never been a serious threat to the very powerful US industry.

True to its character as an industry of a dependent capitalist nation, the Mexican film industry experienced its first crisis as early as 1939 due to its disorganised and voracious development and to the market's saturation by countless *comedias rancheras*. A quick review of the titles produced in 1937 and 1938 indicates an extraordinarily high percentage of folkloric films set in a countryside unaffected by social changes. Among all these films, we must note Arcady Boytler's *¡Así es mi tierra!* (*That's How my Country Is!*, 1937), a brilliant parody of the Eisensteinian cinema and the one that marked the debut of Mario Moreno 'Cantinflas', who soon thereafter achieved tremendous popularity throughout Latin America.

The last two years of the Lázaro Cárdenas government and the first year of his successor's, Manuel Avila Camacho, were marked by a dramatic drop in production (to 38, 29 and 37 films, respectively). Although not quite a sign of an imminent death, these decreases did indicate the precariousness and irregularity of the situation. That the Argentine cinema recuperated its vitality in this same period was also of great concern to national film producers. This crisis coincided with the sudden deterioration of the Mexican economy due to the expropriation of oil holdings decreed by Cárdenas in March 1938. According to historians Héctor Aguilar Camín and Lorenzo Meyer, Cárdenas's decree 'not only affected oil revenues, but international reprisals also resulted in decreased mineral sales and created a climate of mistrust that practically stopped all private sector investments'.[7] However, in the film industry, this crisis was considered a temporary phenomenon during which there were signs of progress: first, the foundation in 1941 of the new Sindicato de Trabajadores de la Industria Cinematográfica de la Republica Mexicana (STIC), an organisation affiliated to the powerful Confederación de Trabajadores de México (CTM); secondly, the production between 1938 and 1939 of a series of reactionary films that longed for the Mexican *belle époque* of the Porfirian period, such as Raphael J. Sevilla's *Perjura (Perjury)*, Alberto Gout's *Café Concordia* and, above all, Juan Bustillo Oro's *En tiempos de don Porfirio (In the Time of Don Porfirio)*. These were very popular among the conservative middle classes, nostalgic for the dictatorship.

Another symptom of progress was the 1940 production of Raúl de Anda's *El Charro Negro (The Black Charro)*, Bustillo Oro's *Ahí está el detalle (There's the Detail)* and Fernando de Fuentes's *El jefe máximo*, which also attracted a public increasingly identified with the aims of the national cinema. The first one managed to produce an authentic film hero derived from legends and Mexican comic books; the second film transformed one of it protagonists, Cantinflas, into the first great idol of the national cinema; and the third was an excellent farce which articulated a veiled critique of the corruption of the party in power.

Finally, in 1941, two film-makers representative of a new generation made their cinematic debut: Julio Bracho Pérez (1909–78) and Emilio Fernández (1914– 86). They gave the industry its most decisive impetus. Bracho began his career with a good Porfirian film, *¡Ay qué tiempos señor don Simón! (Oh What Times Don Simon!)*, while with *La isla de la pasión – Clipperton (The Island of Passion – Clipperton)*, Fernández directed his first contribution to wartime nationalism.

The beginning of Manuel Avila Camacho's presidential term also marked the beginning of a long period, approximately 1940–68, commonly referred to as the Mexican miracle. This was a period of combined political stability and economic development unmatched anywhere else in Latin America. In its first period, 1941–5, the Mexican

Pedro Armendáriz and Dolores del Río in *Bugambilia* (Emilio Fernández, 1944)

miracle was characterised by a singular fact: the pact established between Mexico and the USA, especially given the history of conflicts between the two nations since 1910 and their intensification after the oil expropriations of 1938. Of course, this alliance was the result of a specific conjuncture: the Second World War. The Mexico–USA pact was supposedly beneficial to both parties: in exchange for military co-operation, inexpensive labour and guaranteed sales of raw materials, Mexico received numerous loans and technological aid to invigorate its shaky economy and to reposition itself in the Latin American, European and even US markets. This was translated into a process of accelerated industrialisation which substantially changed the face of the nation. A predominantly agricultural economy was transformed into a manufacturing one, and an agrarian society began to make the qualitative leap into a typically urban one.

If, ultimately, the war favoured capitalist development in the country, it also favoured the national film industry. From 1942 (the year of the creation of the Banco Cinematográfico, a loan-granting organisation created by the state to consolidate the development of the industry) until 1945, the industry lived through a great period of artistic and commercial creativity. During this same

Rosanna Pdestá in *La Red* (Emilio Fernández, 1953)

period, Hollywood obviously concentrated on the production of war-related films to promote the Allied cause. As part of the programme to aid Mexican industrial development, Hollywood interests granted technological help and raw materials to the national industry and, on several occasions, made direct production investments. All this allowed Mexican cinema to diversify its production beyond *comedias rancheras,* lachrymose melodramas, Revolutionary and Porfirian nostalgia films and everyday dramas. After the US pact, the Mexican industry attempted to abate US hegemony by quickly producing substitutes of the successful Hollywood genres (biographies of celebrities, literary adaptations, musical comedies) and managed to produce higher-budget and higher-quality films than in previous periods. With practically guaranteed markets and the solid backing of US producers (a support that had been denied for political reasons to the Spanish and

Argentine film industries), the Mexican film industry became the fifth largest sector of the national economy. According to Jorge Ayala Blanco, this allowed the national cinema to function imperialistically in most Spanish-speaking countries of the continent which lacked a film industry of their own. In other words, it proposed aesthetic tastes and values to the great semi-literate masses, it created and reversed social and individual myths, it opened and exploited markets as it wished.[8]

During this period production exceeded 70 films per year, which was a sign of the prosperity of the industry; in contrast, from 1945 on, Argentine production decreased to fewer than 30 films per year. This fulfilled the prediction peremptorily made by *Variety* on 19 May 1943: 'The US has made up its mind to knock Argentina down from its position as the most important Spanish-language producer and to install Mexico in its place'.[9] Statistics elaborated by

Gaizca de Usabel complete this picture: in 1942, Cuba, a small Caribbean country with little national production, imported 47 Mexican films against 35 Argentine; the following year, import figures increased to 43 Mexican and 42 Argentine; in 1944, Cuban distributors imported 68 Mexican films to 27 Argentine; in 1945, 56 Mexican films to 25 Argentine.[10] These same statistics confirm the fact that Hollywood maintained itself above the competition between Mexico and Argentina: in the same years, Cuba imported, respectively, 380, 340, 342 and 300 US films.

Under these circumstances, the Mexican film industry enjoyed the luxury of producing films for the vast, impoverished sectors of Latin America and of supporting the careers of a number of individuals who had already proven their creative skills in directing, acting, cinematography, script writing, art decorations, and so on. Certain names recur: Julio Bracho, Emilio Fernández, Alejandro Galindo Amezcua (born in 1906), Roberto Gavaldón Leyva (1909–86), Gabriel Figueroa, Alex Phillips, Mauricio Magdaleno, José Revueltas, Pedro Armendáriz, Dolores del Río, Andrea Palma, María Félix, Jorge Negrete, Arturo de Córdova, David Silva, Jorge Fernández, Gunther Gerszo and others.

The first name on this list, Julio Bracho, came from one of Mexican society's most elite groups. He was a personal friend of poets like Xavier Villaurrutia and trained as a scenic director in experimental and avant-garde theatre productions. After participating in the pre-production of *Redes,* writing some scripts and debuting with *¡Ay qué tiempos señor don Simón!* in 1941, Bracho signed a series of films that made him the best director of a refined cinema with intellectual aspirations: *Historia de un gran amor* (*Story of a Great Love,* 1942), *La virgin que forjó una patria* (*The Virgin Who Forged a Nation,* 1942), *Distinto amanecer* (*A Different Dawn,* 1943) and *Crepúsculo* (*Twilight,* 1944). The third of these films was a landmark in so far as it attempted to analyse the process of urbanisation and its inevitable social consequences in terms of prostitution, marginalisation, labour union corruption and moral disenchantment. Excellently acted by Pedro Armendáriz and Andrea Palma, *Distinto amanecer* is above all a police drama conveying allegorical intentions. Starring Arturo de Córdova, *Crepúsculo* narrates the private life of a university professor tormented by moral and psychological problems that eventually push him to suicide. In both films, Bracho attempts to provide the filmic testimony of a generation and a sector of society which, in the late

20s, had blindly followed José Vasconcelos's struggles to democratise the nation and had fallen into a profound existential crisis when the movement failed. Bracho received support from critics, who even compared him to the Orson Welles of *Citizen Kane.*

On the other hand, it was the team Fernández–Figueroa–Magdaleno which used the opportunity to redirect the national aesthetic, elevating its quality and rigour to levels comparable only to the genius of Eisenstein–Tissé. In their films of this period (*Flor silvestre* and *María Candelaria,* both 1943, *Las abandonadas* and *Bugambilia,* both 1944, and all starring Pedro Armendáriz and Dolores del Río), the team expressed a lyricism and a vision that would be appreciated at various international festivals, especially the European ones. The long-cherished aspirations of Mexican film-makers had finally been achieved: to impose upon the world a filmic image of our nation and its history in which we could legitimately take pride. After the success of the Fernández–Figueroa films, Europeans began to refer to a Mexican film-making movement. But soon, this appraisal proved to lack a serious or rigorous analytical base. However, as Alejandro Rozado has argued,[11] there is no doubt that the cinematic work of 'el Indio' Fernández and Figueroa is to be valued for its representation of the struggle between tradition and modernity, the principal feature of Mexican culture in the 40s.

The impetus provided by Bracho and Fernández's work was extended in 1943 by the Fernando de Fuentes's films featuring María Félix, the first female star to emerge from the Mexican industry itself, with *Doña Bárbara,* based on the Venezuelan novel by Rómulo Gallegos, and *La mujer sin alma.* The Bracho–Fernández impetus also worked through in the films of Miguel Zacarías Nagain (born in 1908) with the singer Jorge Negrete (*El peñón de las ánimas, The Rock of the Souls,* 1942; *Una carta de amor, A Love Letter,* 1943), into the films of Roberto Gavaldón (*La barraca,* 1944) and Alejandro Galindo (*Campeón sin corona,* 1945). *La barraca* was Gavaldón's debut, a successful adaptation of Vicente Blasco Ibáñez's novel of the same title. Influenced by the work of Samuel Ramos (*El perfil del hombre y la cultura de México*), Galindo's film was a psycho-social analysis of the inhabitants of marginal Mexico City neighbourhoods, which established a solid precedent for the urban films that were to emerge after the end of the war.

After overcoming the crisis caused by market saturation, the national film industry began to make new plans in 1942. To some degree motivated by the extraordinary wartime context, generic diversity provided a balanced series of topics, some of which emerged as an immediate response to the war itself. In exchange for the support given to the Mexican industry, Hollywood producers demanded the production of films promoting the ideology of pan-Americanism and the Allied cause. This resulted in the production of a series of films with illustrative titles: Chano Urueta's *La liga de las canciones* (*The League of Songs*, 1942), Ramón Pereda's *Canto a las Américas* (*Song to the Americas*, 1942) and René Cardona's *Hotel de verano* (*Summer Hotel*, 1943). All these musical comedies featured a collection of Latin American performers representing their respective nations. Another group of films promoted the Allied cause via anti-Nazi or anti-Japanese topics: Herbert Kline's *Cinco fueron escogidos* (*Five Were Chosen*, 1941), Emilio Fernández's *Soy puro mexicano* (*I Am Pure Mexican*, 1942), Rolando Aguilar's *Espionaje en el Golfo* (*Espionage in the Gulf*, 1942), José Benavides Jr's *Tres hermanos* (*Three Brothers*, 1943), Fernando A. Palacios's *Cadetes de la naval* (*Naval Cadets*, 1944), Roberto Gavaldón's *Corazones de México* (*Mexican Hearts*, 1945) and Jaime Salvador's *Escuadrón 201* (1945).

On the other hand, a good portion of the films systematically adapted novels and plays written by prestigious European and South American writers. In addition to the two already cited (based on works by Blasco Ibáñez and Rómulo Gallegos), over 65 adaptations were produced of the work of French authors such as Alexandre Dumas (Chano Urueta's *El conde de Montecristo*, 1941), Paul Fèval (Jaime Salvador's *El jorobado o Enrique Lagardere*, 1943), Alexandre Dumas fils (Gabriel Soria's *La dama de las camelias*, 1943), Jules Verne (Miguel M. Delgado's *Miguel Strogoff*, 1943) and Emile Zola (Celestino Gorostiza's *Naná*, 1943); of Spanish authors such as Pedro Antonio de Alarcón (Bracho's *Historia de un gran amor*, a version of *El niño de la bola*), Benito Pérez Galdos (José Díaz Morales's *El adulterio*, 1943, a version of *El abuelo*) and Juan Valera (Emilio Fernández's *Pepita Jiménez*, 1945); of British authors such as William Shakespeare (*Romeo y Julieta* by Miguel M. Delgado, a parody starring Cantinflas) and Oscar Wilde (*El abanico de Lady Windermere*, Juan J. Ortega, 1943); of the Russian authors Leon Tolstoy (*Resurrección*, Gilberto Martínez Solares, 1943); of the Italian author Emilio Salgari (*El corsario negro*, Chano Urueta, 1944), and the Austrian author Stefan Zweig (*Amok*, Antonio Momplet, 1944). All these films were super-productions intended to give the national industry a cosmopolitan flavour by way of adaptations for

which, thanks to the war, no copyright fees had to be paid.

All indicators seemed to signal a prosperous and healthy film industry and in 1942, the Asociación de Productores de Películas joined forces with distributors and exhibitors to form the Cámara Nacional de la Industria Cinematográfica Mexicana, an organisation that consolidated the interests of the powerful within the capitalist structure of the film business. In 1945, however, a serious disagreement within the old STIC led to the creation of the Sindicato de Trabajadores de la Producción Cinematográfica (STPC) to represent the industry's creative workers: directors, writers, musicians, actors and technicians (cinematographers, sound men, set designers, make-up artists, editors, and so on). The new union was headed by prestigious names such as Gabriel Figueroa, Jorge Negrete and Cantinflas, but was rejected by the CTM.

The situation developed in a predictable way. Prosperity was followed by a period of scarcity and setbacks in the years immediately after the war. This period was characterised by decreases in production: 72 films in 1946 and 57 in 1947. This was the logical consequence of the overwhelming renaissance of the Hollywood cinema and the consequent withdrawal of the support of US producers. The post-war film crisis coincided with the first two years of the Miguel Alemán Valdés *sexenio*. In addition to being the first government headed by a civilian (henceforth soldiers would remain within the armed forces), the Alemán regime attempted a second Mexican miracle: modernisation and accelerated technological development, which involved new and ever more acute forms of dependence on the USA. However, precisely in the worst year of this new critical phase, the national cinema discovered a formula for survival and consolidation: the production of low-budget films based on urban–suburban themes to match the demands of an increasingly urban public that was making the cities (especially Mexico) grow as a result of industrialisation.

Two film-makers, Alejandro Galindo and Ismael Rodríguez Ruelas (born in 1917) were influenced by Italian neo-realism and US liberal realism (better known as film noir). With solid antecedents such as *Mientras México duerme* (*While Mexico Sleeps*, 1938), *Virgen de medianoche o El imperio del hampa* (*Midnight Virgin or Mysteries of the Underworld*, 1941) and *Campeón sin corona*, Galindo directed two films starring David Silva about the personal life and labour union struggles of an urban bus driver: *¡Esquina ... bajan!* and *Hay lugar para dos*, both in

Tlayucan (Luis Alcoriza, 1962)

1948. Rodríguez also made two films, *Nosotros los pobres* (1947) and *Ustedes los ricos* (1948), starring Pedro Infante, an actor with natural grace and charisma, discovered by Rodríguez in films like *Cuando lloran los valientes* (*How the Courageous Cry,* 1945) and *Los tres García* (*The Three Garcias,* 1946). In the most extreme melodramatic style, Infante portrayed a humble carpenter living with his family in a *vecindad,* a marginal urban conglomerate in the poorest zone of the city. The unexpected but delirious box-office success of these films, especially those of Ismael Rodriguez, redirected Mexican cinema towards a primarily commercial practice dedicated to satisfying the demands of the great urban masses for whom the cinema had become the primary form of entertainment. Mediated by melodramatic or comedic formulas, urban poverty became good business and urban films energised production: between 1948 and 1952, production

reaches an average of 102 feature films per year. This production is perceived as a simple extension of the so-called 'golden age' of Mexican cinema, in other words, the period corresponding to the Second World War.

The situation, however, was deceptive. Nothing illustrates this better than the case of Emilio Fernández, the great lyrical, nationalist film-maker. After *La perla* (1945), *Enamorada* (1946), *Río Escondido* (1947) and *Maclovia* (1948) – almost all starring the diva María Felix – 'el Indio' Fernández made a series of films from *Salón México* (1948) to *El rapto* (1953, Jorge Negrete's last film), including *Pueblerina* (1948), *La malquerida* (1949), *Víctimas del pecado* (1950), *Acapulco* (1951), *El mar y tú* (1951), *La red* (1953), and so on, all on comparatively low budgets. Thus 'el Indio's' reputation began to wane, his decline reflecting upon Mexican cinema's international prestige, which soon became an object of nostalgia.

The Mexican industry re-established itself by way of a generic cinema for popular consumption. The most typical genre of the Alemán period was the *cabaretera,* the brothel-cabaret melodrama with antecedents in films of the 30s *(Santa, La mujer del puerto, La mancha de sangre),* in serial literature and in the lyrics of Agustín Lara's songs. After the unexpected success of the tropical-cabaret melodrama *Humo en los ojos (Smoke in the Eyes)* directed by Alberto Gout Abrego (1913–66) in 1946 with David Silva and Mercedes Barba, a large number of films repeated the well-nigh infallible formula of the fallen woman who becomes a prostitute, singer or rumbera, and who Lara himself or his imitators and interpreters describe as 'perverted, treacherous, hypocritical, lost, suburban, thieving, sinner, courtesan, flirtatious', along with other assorted moralising terms. Among the many *cabaretera* films, we should highlight the importance of the trilogy produced by Pedro Calderón (producer), Alberto Gout (director), Alex Phillips (cinematographer) and the Spanish scriptwriter Alvaro Custodio featuring the Cuban rumbera, Ninón Sevilla: *Aventurera* (1949), *Sensualidad* (1950) and *No niego mi pasado* (*I Do Not Deny My Past,* 1951). With these films, Gout and Custodio were able to take advantage of the genre's conventions to produce profoundly subversive works that even garnered the attention of the French press. But this was the exception to the rule.

The other successful genres of the period were also derived from the urban film model: comedies and family melodramas. Gilberto Martínez Solares (born in 1906) stands out in the comedy genre. After making respectable films such as *Internado para señoritas (Boarding School for Girls)* and *El globo de Cantolla (Cantolla's Balloon),* both in 1943, he became the director of Germán Valdés 'Tin Tan', an excellent and vigorous comedian originally from the popular theatre: *Calabacitas tiernas (Tender Pumpkins,* 1948), *El rey del barrio (The King of the Neighbourhood,* 1949), *El revoltoso (The Trouble-Maker,* 1951) and the entertaining parodies *La marca del Zorrillo (The Mark of the Little Zorro,* 1950), *Simbad el mareado (Sinbad the Seasick,* 1950), *El ceniciento (Snow White,* 1951) and *El bello durmiente* (*Sleeping Beauty,* 1952).

The family melodrama's boom followed from the successful Juan Bustillo Oro's *Cuando los hijos se van* (*When the Children Leave,* 1941) and was sustained by films such as Rolando Aguilar's *El cuarto mandamiento (The Fourth Commandment,* 1948),

Martínez Solares's *La familia Pérez* (1948) and Miguel Zacarías's *El dolor de los hijos* (*The Pain of the Children,* 1948). An exceptional contribution to this genre deserves to be singled out: Alejandro Galindo's 1948 film, *Una familia de tantas (A Family Among Many),* starring Fernando Soler (another great actor of the period), David Silva and Martha Roth. With this film Galindo gave dignity to an otherwise profoundly reactionary genre and anticipated the narrative virtues of *Doña Perfecta* (1950), a lucid adaptation of the homonymous Benito Pérez Galdos novel in which the film-maker describes the ideological struggle between conservatives and liberals.

In the realm of auteur cinema, the sombre Roberto Gavaldón collaborated with the cinematographers Alex Phillips and Gabriel Figueroa and the leftist writer José Revueltas, achieving critical and popular success with films like *La otra* (1946), *La diosa arrodillada (The Kneeling Goddess,* 1947), *Deseada (Desired,* 1950), *Rosauro Castro* (1950), *La noche avanza* (*Night Advances,* 1951) and *El rebozo de Soledad (Soledad's Shawl,* 1952). Gavaldón was known as a quality film-maker, and with *Deseada, Rosauro Castro* and *El rebozo de Soledad* he was able to improve the level of the national aesthetic. In this period he was considered the successor to Emilio Fernández.

There are other examples which, although exceptional films, belong nevertheless to the same contextual framework, such as the work of Matilde Landeta (born in 1910), Mexican sound cinema's second woman film-maker. After working as continuity girl and assistant director, she enjoyed a brief directing career making melodramas with unusually strong and well-defined female characters: *Lola Casanova* (1948), *La Negra Angustias (Angustias the Black,* 1949), and *Trotacalles (Streetwalker,* 1951). The example of Luis Buñuel (1900–83) is, undoubtedly, even more interesting. Settled in Mexico since 1946, he was able to enter the Mexican industry and after two films that can be described as conventional (*Gran casino* in 1946 and *El gran calavera* in 1949), he directed *Los olvidados* in 1950, his first great Mexican masterpiece and a film which brutally demystifies the conventions of the urban cinema through poetry and 'estrangement'. In the words of Emilio García Riera, *Los olvidados* is 'the national cinema's first film of genius'.

The Mexican film industry's consolidation would reach its apex in 1954, when 118 features were made. At the time, this was the highest level of production achieved by any Spanish-language industry. Previously, the state had taken some measures to support, regulate and control cinema's industrial structures. In 1945, it had created Películas Mexicanas S.A. to take charge of distribution in Latin America, Europe and the southern USA. In 1947 the Banco Cinematográfico became the Banco Nacional Cinematográfico (BNC), a loan-granting agency funded primarily by the state to protect, promote and remodel the production sector. That same year, the mixed-capital distributor Películas Nacionales S.A. was created to handle domestic distribution. Finally, in 1949, the still-active Ley de la Industria Cinematográfica (Film Industry Law) was promulgated. 1949 was also the first year of the Dirección General de Cinematografía, a sub-agency of the Secretaría de Gobernación (Ministry of the Interior) assigned the task of censoring, supervising and preserving the national cinema through a Cineteca, which, for bureaucratic reasons, would not come into existence until twenty-six years later!

When the Ley de la Industria Cinematográfica was promulgated, it was noticed that some of its articles prohibited the development of monopolies: the measure was, at the very least, anachronistic, since precisely in 1949, the monopoly headed by US magnate William Jenkins, in association with the Mexicans Manuel Espinoza Yglesias, Manuel Alarcón and Maximino Avila Camacho (brother of the ex-president), controlled 80% of the national exhibition sector. Developed during the Manuel Avila Camacho *sexenio,* this monopoly sought in the 50s to subjugate the production sector to its own interests. In 1952, the last year of the Miguel Alemán *sexenio,* the submission to the interests of the monopoly was a fact: several of the more powerful producers (Gregorio Wallerstein, Raúl de Anda) combined with Jenkins to provide him with films designed exclusively for the domestic market, since the foreign markets by this time were irredeemably lost. Thus the stage was set for one of Mexican cinema's worst eras.

The Ghost of Crisis (1955–64)
What historians have called 'the prolonged structural crisis of Mexican cinema' coincides with the governments of Adolfo Ruiz Cortínez (1952–8) and Adolfo López Mateos (1958–64). Both regimes were framed by the third and last period of the Mexican miracle, or the era of stabilising development: an economic strategy begun in 1954 designed to prevent the devaluation of Mexican currency against the US dollar and to halt the inflationary process begun in 1948. This strategy was successful in so far as the

price index increased only by 50% over the next decade. The situation helped the film industry to maintain the appearance of stability between 1955 and 1960. Production increased to an average of more than 90 features per year, while the industry was in fact really undergoing a severe crisis which affected primarily the quality of its films.

In good part generated by the nefarious Jenkins monopoly, the film crisis was exacerbated by competition from television: here, as elsewhere in the world, the new medium gradually seduced middle-class audiences away from cinema. To further complicate the scenario, production and direction were increasingly concentrated in the hands of a few. In fact, Federico Heuer's statistics in *La industria cinematográfica mexicana* indicate that of the 867 films produced between 1954 and 1964 by 100 production companies, 435 – that is 50% – were financed by 15 of these companies.[12] A series of facts compiled by Emilio García Riera in his *Historia del cine mexicano* demonstrate that while between 1951 and 1955, 705 of the films produced were directed by 23 of the 58 active directors, in the period 1956–60, 66% of all films were directed by 20 of the 67 active film-makers. The situation became worse still in 1961–5: 56% of all films were directed by only 14 of the 86 active film-makers.[13] The conclusion is simple: by far the largest part of Mexican cinema produced in the 50s and early 60s was financed by a few companies and filmed by a few directors. And to further consolidate this sort of monopoly, the sons of René Cardona, Raúl de Anda, Miguel Zacarías, Valentín Gazcón, Gregorio Wallerstein, and so on, became part of the industry as producers and directors in the 60s. In other words, the film industry began to revolve almost exclusively around a number of family-based companies.

The state responded weakly to this crisis with the sadly famous Plan Garduño decreed in 1953, which pretended to limit the Jenkins monopoly by producing a better cinema capable of generating its own star system. In response, the principal members of the film bourgeoisie began to produce films in colour and CinemaScope, or began making risqué films with 'artistic' nudity. Satisfied with their privileges and indifferent to the crisis, the other producers limited themselves to the production of genre films that could recoup their low budgets in the popular domestic market. *Ranchero* dramas proliferated, featuring one or two stars, as did films with masked wrestlers (creating their own cult following), urban comedies, religious and juvenile melodramas, edifying biographies, new versions of the Mexican Revolution, literary adaptations, fantasy/horror films, which aspired to compete with Hammer films, and Westerns of the lowest possible quality.

Two of the more prolific film-makers of the period were able to take advantage of the growth of this type of cinema to produce works with a degree of relevance. The first is Fernando Méndez García (1908–66), the director of *El suavecito* (*The Soft One,* 1950), a classic of the frustrated Mexican 'Black Series'. He made some good urban comedies such as *Fierecilla* (*Little Beast,* 1950) and *La hija del ministro* (*The Minister's Daughter,* 1951), but achieved greater success with his Westerns *Los tres Villalobos* (*The Three Villalobos*) and *La venganza de Villalobos* (*Villalobos's Revenge*), both in 1954, and especially with his horror films: *Ladrón de cadáveres* (*Corpse Thief,* 1956), *El vampiro* (1957, a much-praised film in France) and *Misterios de ultratumba* (*Mysteries from Beyond the Grave,* 1958). After a splendid debut with a *comedia ranchera,* the second film-maker, Rogelio A. González (1920–84), also made a series of successful urban comedies: *El mil amores* (*The Thousand Loves*), *Escuela de vagabundos* (*School of Vagabonds*), *El inocente* and *Escuela de rateros* (*School of Thieves*), all in 1954–6. These comedies enshrined the mythic fame of their protagonist, Pedro Infante, shortly before his death in an automobile accident. González's career peaked with *El esqueleto de la señora Morales* (*Mrs Morales's Skeleton,* 1959), a good example of macabre humour.

While directors like Méndez and González produced their best work, most film-makers of the 1935–45 generation continued their decline. After *Espaldas mojadas* (*Wetbacks,* 1953), a film that was censored because of its anti-US theme, and *Los Fernández de Peralvillo* (*The Fernandez's from Peralvillo,* 1953), a family melodrama criticising the social ambitions of the urban middle class, Alejandro Galindo concentrated on family films. Emilio Fernández was able to match his past achievements only with *Una cita de amor* (*A Love Date,* 1956), a remarkable romantic melodrama set in the director's beloved countryside. Roberto Gavaldón, the specialist in quality films to meet the demands of festivals, barely managed to sustain the prestige of the national cinema with films like *La escondida* (1955), *Macario* (1959) and *Rosa Blanca* (1961). After a series of frustrating films, Julio Bracho finally directed a good adaptation of Martín Luiz Guzmán's homonymous novel *La sombra del caudillo* (*The Caudillo's Shadow*) in 1960. But the film was censored for thirty years because of its veiled critique

of the genesis of post-Revolutionary *caudillismo* and state corruption.

Pressured by the industry's critical situation in 1960, the state purchased most of the theatres of the Jenkins monopoly and created the Compañía Operadora de Teatros (COTSA), a mixed-capital corporation. But this measure did not halt the industrial crisis, which entered its most acute phase in 1961, characterised by a severe decrease in normal production (films produced by members of the STPC) and an increase in the number of series filmed in the Estudios América. These series had been produced since the late 1950s and were extraordinarily inexpensive genre films.

Paradoxically, during this period of acute crisis, we find two extreme cases of auteur cinema. First, there is Luis Alcoriza de la Vega (born in 1921) who, despite being a Spanish immigrant, must be considered as a film-maker formed within the Mexican industry. After working as an actor and writing scripts in the 40s and 50s, Alcoriza made his directing debut in 1960 with *Los jóvenes (Youth),* describing the world of urban adolescents with sobriety and maturity. Later he directed a trilogy of particular quality, *Tlayucan* (1961), set in the provinces and directed with great sarcasm and irony; *Tiburoneros* (*Shark Fishermen,* 1962), a beautiful elegiac poem to freedom; and *Tarahumara* (1964), a demonstration of the complexity of the indigenous world denouncing its exploitation and marginalisation by white men.

Luis Buñuel operated on another level. After making a number of masterful films in the 50s (*El,* 1952; *Ensayo de un crimen,* 1955, and *Nazarín,* 1958), he began the last phase of his Mexican period with *Viridiana* in 1961. Buñuel, producer Gustavo Alatriste and the great actress Silvia Pinal (perhaps the last of the great Mexican divas) were successful and internationally acclaimed. In this last stage, the Buñuel–Alatriste–Pinal team produced *El ángel exterminador* (1962) and *Simón del desierto* (1964), but the production difficulties encountered during the filming of the latter provoked the cinematic exile of this great Spanish-Mexican film-maker.

Alcoriza and Buñuel were not the only representatives of a cinematic counter-current against the stilted and increasingly scorned Mexican industry. On the margins of this industry, which ignored all artistic tendencies, we begin to see the appearance of more intelligent cinematic forms. Thus an independent movement with solid antecedents dating back to the 40s began to gain strength in the 50s with José Ignacio Retes's *Noches de angustia* (*Nights of*

Anguish, 1948) and Alfredo Pacheco's *Tu pecado es mío* (*Your Sin is Mine,* 1949). The best examples of this experimental and marginal practice, Benito Alazraki's *Raíces* (*Roots,* 1953), Carlos Velo's *¡Torero!* (1956) and Giovanni Korporaal's *El brazo fuerte* (*The Strong Arm,* 1958), are usually associated with Manuel Barbachano Ponce, a producer born in Yucatán. Barbachano Ponce had put together an excellent technical team for the production of quality newsreels such as *Tele-Revista* and *Cine-Verdad* with a top-notch team. He had also produced Buñuel's *Nazarín.* He was able to direct the ambitions of an important group of film enthusiasts who were unable to gain access to the increasingly closed industry and who needed the cinema to express their artistic sensibilities. The international prizes awarded to *Raíces, ¡Torero!* and other independent films confirmed the importance of this type of cinema and the quality of its directors.

In the 60s, Manuel Barbachano Ponce's solitary and somewhat foolhardy position found an echo in the desires of a group of film critics and aspiring film-makers trained in the pages of serious cultural publications and the film society of the Instituto Frances de América Latina (IFAL). Influenced by the French New Wave (Truffaut, Godard, Resnais, and so on), the group constituted by Jomí García Ascot, Emilio García Riera, José de la Colina, Salvador Elizondo, Gabriel Ramírez, Carlos Monsiváis, Julio Pliego, Eduardo Lizalde, Luis Vicens and others called itself Nuevo Cine. They established a specialised journal and began a devastating critique of our *cinéma de papa.* Under the direction of Jomí García Ascot (1927–86) some members of the group also independently produced a film manifesto: *En el balcón vacío* (*On the Empty Balcony,* 1961–2), an excellent example of a poetic cinema in which personal memory serves as a lacerating and vibrant testimony of historical events.

The intense film society movement at the Universidad Nacional Autónoma de Mexico (UNAM) laid the foundation for the establishment of the Centro Universitario de Estudios Cinematográficos (CUEC) in 1963. Directed by Manuel González Casanova, the CUEC was the first official film school in the country. Many of the first generations of CUEC students made their mark soon thereafter as practitioners of what came to be called the New Mexican Cinema.

The crisis finally produced reactions within the industry itself. In August 1964, the year in which Roberto Gavaldón directed *El gallo de oro (The Golden Cock),* the most significant film of the nationalist cinema of the 60s, the technical sector of the STPC headed by Jorge Durán Chávez organised the first experimental film competition. Responding to the critical demands for a renovation of the industry's technical and artistic personnel, the contest promised to open the industry's doors to the winners. The hope was that the new perspectives thus produced would, in theory, help overcome the Mexican film industry's profound crisis.

Notes

* This essay was developed in the Centro de Investigación y Enseñanza Cinematográficas de la Universidad de Guadalajara.

1. The concept of a cinema bourgeoisie is derived from the work of the French scholar Jesús González Requena, 'Burguesia cinematográfica y aparato' in *La mirada: textos sobre cine* (Barcelona), no.1, April 1971, pp. 13–21. The concept is not used pejoratively, but as an analytical category to define the groups with economic and political power within the film industry.

2. A detailed account of these events can be found in Harry M. Geduld and Ronald Gottesman (eds.), *Sergei Eisenstein and Upton Sinclair: The Making* and *Unmaking of* ¡Que viva Mexico! (Bloomington, Indiana: Indiana University Press, 1970).

3. According to the original plans, Eisenstein's film would have consisted of a prologue, an epilogue and four episodes or stories: *Zandunga, Fiesta, Maguey* and *Soldadera.*

4. See Aurelio de los Reyes, *Medio siglo de cine mexicano (1986–1947)* (Mexico City: Trillas, 1987), pp. 197 sqq.

5. Ibid., pp. 187 sqq.

6. Jorge Ayala Blanco and María Luisa Amador, *Cartelera cinematográfica 1930–1939* (Mexico City: UNAM, 1980).

7. Héctor Aguilar Camín and Lorenzo Meyer, *A la sombra de la Revolución* (Mexico City: Cal y Arena, 1989).

8. Jorge Ayala Blanco, *La condición del cine mexicano* (Mexico City: Posada, 1986), p. 508.

9. Cited by José Luis Ortiz Garza, *México en guerra: La historia secreta de los negocios entre empresarios mexicanos de la comunicación, los nazis y EUA* (Mexico City: Planeta, 1989), p. 174.

10. Gaizca de Usabel, *The High Noon of American Films in Latin America,* a PhD dissertation for the University of Wisconsin, 1975, reprinted (Ann Arbor, Michigan: UMI Research Press, 1982), cited by José Luis Ortiz Garza, *Mexico en guerra,* p. 175.

11. Alejandro Rozado, *Cine y realidad social en México: Una lectura de la obra de Emilio Fernández* (Guadalajara: CIEC/Universidad de Guadalajara, 1991), p. 108.

12. Federico Heuer, *La industria cinematográfica mexicana* (Mexico City: Policromía, 1964).

13. Emilio García Riera, *Historia del cine mexicano* (Mexico City: SEP, 1986).

Crises and Renovations
(1965–91)

Tomás Pérez Turrent

We have been talking about 'crisis' since the late 30s. In other words, from the period immediately after the consolidation of the film industry. The term reappeared in the late 40s and in the early 60s. Since then, Mexican cinema has lived in a permanent state of crisis.

After the Second World War, a privileged period in which Mexican cinema benefited from favourable wartime conditions because of US technical and economic aid and produced the most important Spanish-language cinema, the crisis became an essential component of all its developments. This crisis has been economic, political, artistic, industrial and technical. Producers and most directors refused to take risks and were content to repeat formulas. The production, distribution and exhibition systems became dysfunctional. The only thing that interested producers was making the least expensive product with the least possible effort.

Thus, without realising it, Mexican cinema lost the audiences it had won in the 30s through its ability to reflect the historical and cultural reality of the nation, the values, dreams, myths and desires of a society which the cinema itself had shaped and given a national, even a pan-continental identity. This privileged relationship between cinema and the audience continued until the mid-50s. When the national industry restricted itself to the repetition of formulas, this link was lost, and cinema no longer reflected the development of Mexican society. The high and middle sectors of society lost interest in the national cinema. Thanks to subtitles, many audiences now turned to foreign films, and the middle and elite classes were beginning to identify with the cultural values and ideas of the English-language cinema, especially Hollywood's. Juan Antonio Bardem's famous pentagram about the state of the Spanish cinema, presented at a colloquium in Salamanca on 10 May 1955, could have been used to describe the Mexican cinema in 1965. He described the Spanish cinema as:

- Politically inefficient
- Socially false
- Intellectually insignificant
- Aesthetically null
- Industrially unstable.[1]

Obviously, the conditions of Mexican cinema were different, but the need for change was the same, and the Salamanca conclusions were equally relevant in 1965. In Mexico it was also necessary to produce a cinema to 'reflect the situation of humanity ..., its conflicts and reality in past eras and especially in the present'. The Salamanca conclusions about the state–cinema relationship and the need to provide financial support for 'a cinema of artistic quality and national interest' were also applicable. Similarly, Mexican cinema also had to challenge censorship. In 1965, the nation was no longer in the same social and political situation that had existed in 1931 (the period of post-Revolutionary stabilisation) or 1945 (the beginning of industrial development and the birth of an industrial bourgeoisie). Many things had happened. On the one hand, the urban middle class had been consolidated and had become influential; on the other, there were signs of unrest among peasants (always struggling for land) and in the growing workers' sector that had been stimulated by industrial development (in good part composed of peasants and the sons of peasants who had emigrated to the cities). It was difficult to control them through the corporatism of the official labour unions. There were also significant new socio-economic sectors: bureaucrats, intellectuals and an ebullient youth. In the 50s, important protest movements organised by railroad workers and teachers were bloodily repressed with arrests and imprisonments. In the 60s, unrest among oil workers worried the official unions. We cannot lose sight of the fact that the student movement of 1968 would erupt only three years later: that is to say, in 1965 things were already simmering.

Everything was changing except cinema: always the same genres transformed into formulas, exploited until the point of exhaustion and without any enrichment or evolution; the same stereotypes and characters; the same inconsistent narrative, figurative and representational systems that were servile, underdeveloped copies of Hollywood cinema. The only thing that had changed was the music. From the *corrido ranchero* and the romantic bolero, we switched to the mambo, later the cha cha cha, and eventually, in the late 50s, to a style of rock which became known as 'a go go' music in the following decade.[2]

The paralysis of the film labour union completed this scenario. The union was conceived as a self-contained system to defend privileges and fought off any attempts at renovation, including those by its own personnel. The same directors, cinemato-graphers, sound recordists and screenwriters divided up the work among themselves, and in a difficult economic context,[3] the doors to the industry were closed even more firmly. It was evident that new people would have had the ability to bring to the cinema the desires and needs of the new social groups, including those of students. Thus by 1965, the break between Mexican cinema and a large part of its potential public was complete. However, a new generation of critics was emerging. They had a different mentality and saw cinema as a specific phenomenon with multiple aesthetic, sociological, political and cultural consequences. Although there were illustrious critical antecedents – writers and poets who had ventured into criticism, such as Alfonso Reyes, Xavier Villaurrutia, Jaime Torres Bodet, and even Carlos Fuentes – film criticism had been used primarily to promote stars and to voice the interests of the industry. Despite some exceptions, the idea of a film culture did not exist.

Towards an Auteur Cinema

The young critics were influenced by foreign, especially French, critical practices and, above all, by *Cahiers du Cinéma* (and to a lesser degree by *Positif*). From the early 60s onwards, critics began to take a stand in the pages of the cultural supplements of the principal newspapers, fighting to promote a film culture. In 1961, they created the group Nuevo Cine[4] and published seven issues of a magazine with the same name. Their magazine, albeit ephemeral, had a determining influence upon the developing film culture and on cineastes and cinephiles.

Most of the members of Nuevo Cine had leftist political tendencies, but they were able to conciliate theories associated with the right with their own political positions. The theoretical positions of the group and the magazine were grounded on *mise en scène* (as evidence of cinematic writing) and auteurism. The group was criticised for holding idealist and utopian positions, and for having theories which were out of step with reality. Nuevo Cine's ideas were put into practice in the first and only film made by the group, *En el balcón vacío* (*On the Empty Balcony*, 1961), an independent 16mm film directed by Jomí García Ascot. But Nuevo Cine would also influence, directly or indirectly, all subsequent efforts to revitalise the national cinema.

Parallel to Nuevo Cine, there was also an important university film society movement, which included some Nuevo Cine members and other kindred individuals. This movement reinforced and expanded the experiences of the Cine Club de México (sponsored by IFAL, the Instituto Francés de America Latina) which had been directed by García Ascot and in 1961 was headed by José Luis González de León (a member of the group and a graduate of the French film school, IDHEC). This helped to create a new audience, still minoritarian, but with different kinds of demands. The Filmoteca de la UNAM (Universidad Nacional Autónoma de Mexico) was founded in 1960. It was the first official film archive and is today the most important one in Latin America (all prior efforts to establish a national film archive had failed). This same university inaugurated the first film school in the country in 1963: CUEC (Centro Universitario de Estudios Cinematográficos).

The ferment created by Nuevo Cine and the film society movement emerged at a time when reforms had become an urgent necessity in the face of the prolonged cinema crisis. In 1964, the STPC (Sindicato de Trabajadores de la Producción Cinematográfica)[5] announced the establishment of the first experimental film competition (which took place in 1965). This was a landmark in the history of the Mexican cinema: the significance of the competition was much greater than its immediate results.

Forty projects entered the competition and the participants sought all types of financing: personal funds, friends, occasional partners, team production, even some independent producers like Manuel Barbachano Ponce. Only twelve of these films featuring eighteen new directors were actually completed (two of them were compilation films: one had five episodes, the other three). The competition had met one of its principal goals: 'to renovate the artistic and technical structure of the national industry'. But it also had another important mission: if the national cinema was to reconquer the market and the audiences it had lost in Mexico and throughout Latin America, it was necessary to change its approach fundamentally. It was essential to win over the enormous post-1945 urban middle class that had turned its back upon the national cinema. To do so, it was necessary to address its particular problems, aspirations, myths and values.

All those who had been unable to cross the hurdles erected by the exclusionist labour unions – writers, directors and would-be directors, actors, cinematographers, and so on – had an opportunity to

Presagio (Luis Alcoriza, 1974)

demonstrate that their declarations, manifestos and violent critiques of the 'real' Mexican cinema were well founded.

Until then, the national cinema had been made by individuals trained in the field. Film-makers built their careers by slowly climbing through the ranks of the industry according to rigid labour union regulations. Culturally, the films they made were incapable of reflecting or appealing to the lost audiences. There was a need for new practitioners – the young intelligentsia emerging out of the universities, writers, painters, more or less avant-garde theatre directors – who would be able to register the changes and the cultural, sociological and psychological effervescence of the new Mexican society, who would choose to chart different paths and find new themes.

This was the background of most of the participants in the competition. There were also several members of the union, individuals who were part of the industry but who, for one reason or another, had not been able to move into film directing. The interests and background of these new – and not so new – film-makers was clearly evidenced. On the one hand, there were those who had already gained a foothold within the film industry – Julio Cahero *(Mis manos; My Hands)*, Carlos Enrique Taboada *(El juicio de Arcadio; Arcadio's Trial)*, Rogelio González Garza *(Llanto por Juan Indio; Cry for Juan Indio)*, Felipe Palomino *(La tierna infancia; Tender Childhood)*, and in television, Antonio Fernández *(Los tres farsantes; The Three Phonies)* – and who insisted upon the traditional forms of Mexican cinema. On the other hand, there were those who aspired to 'modernity' and proposed a cosmopolitan, imitative, Europeanised cinema that rejected underdevelopment and social contradictions. This cinema was addressed to the bourgeoisie, which to some extent shared the aspirations of the intellectuals. Examples are: *Amor, amor, amor (Love, Love, Love)*, a compilation film by Juan José Gurrola, Juan Ibáñez, Héctor Mendoza, José Luis Ibáñez and Miguel Barbachano Ponce;[6] *Amelia* by Juan Guerrero; *Una próxima luna (A Nearby Moon)* by Carlos Nakatani and, if we add nostalgia to modernity, *El viento distante (The Distant Wind)*, another compilation film, by Salomón Láiter, Manuel Michel and Sergio Véjar. Another member of the union, who was also one of the competition's organisers, Icaro Cisneros, slipped over into the group of 'intellectuals' with a confused version of the French New Wave and Chabrol's *Les Cousins* (1959) in *El día comenzó ayer (The Day Began Yesterday)*. In between these two tendencies, and with the added influence of the independent US cinema, was Alberto Isaac's *En este pueblo no hay ladrones* (*In This Town There Are No Thieves*, 1964). Rubén Gámez's *La fórmula secreta* (*The Secret Formula*, 1964) was a unique film: the only mid-length feature (54 mins) and the only film really to propose new narrative and figurative strategies.

The awarded films in the 1965 competition were, in order: *La fórmula secreta, En este pueblo no hay ladrones, Amor, amor, amor* and *El viento distante*. It was believed that, beyond the awards and the immediate results of the competition, the event itself represented a new start. At the very least, prestigious names in national and Latin American letters had been incorporated into the cinema: Inés Arredondo, Carlos Fuentes, Gabriel García Márquez, Juan García Ponce, Sergio Magaña, José Emilio Pacheco and Juan Rulfo.

The road seemed clear, but we would have to wait a while longer for changes. Among the contestants, only a few became a permanent part of the industry: Alberto Isaac, one of the winners; Carlos Enrique Taboada, who had written scripts but had only worked for television; Icaro Cisnero and Sergio Véjar were already inside. Some joined the industry sporadically: Juan Ibáñez, Salomón Láiter, Manuel Michel and José Luis Ibáñez. Juan Guerrero made two mediocre films before his premature death. Others continued their careers in different media: Juan José Gurrola in the theatre, Carlos Nakatani in painting. Rubén Gámez, the first prizewinner, was unable to make a second film until 1991.

The second experimental film competition took place in 1967. The results were quantitatively weaker. Only seven films were completed and they reflected the flaws of the existing industrial cinema: artisanal primitivism, boundless cosmopolitan pretensions,

attempts at political denunciation neutralised by dullness. Only one valuable film was produced: Archibaldo Burns's *Juego de mentiras (Game of Lies)*, an analysis *à la* Genet of the relationship between an (Indian) domestic servant and her mistress (of European descent), which focused on themes of revenge, the master–slave relationship and interracial conflict.

The conditions for the competition appeared designed to discourage potential participants. The organisers manipulated the rules so that the jury declared no first prizewinner and gave Burns the second-place award. This meant that Burns did not have the right to be admitted into the industry's union. Subsequently, Burns filmed only one other feature film outside the industry, *Juan Pérez Jolote* (1973), an interesting mixture of documentary and fiction, and two unimportant industrial films.

In 1965, Arturo Ripstein, the son of the well-known producer Alfredo Ripstein and therefore well connected to the industry, made his directorial debut on the margins of the competition with the film *Tiempo de morir*, scripted by Gabriel García Márquez in collaboration with Carlos Fuentes. Ripstein had assisted Buñuel on *El ángel exterminador* (1962) and *Simón del desierto* (1964) and had worked as assistant to director to Rogelio González and Chano Urueta.[7] Ripstein was the youngest film-maker to start directing features in Mexican cinema: born in December 1943, he was barely twenty-one when he made *Tiempo de morir*. Obviously, he was able to take advantage of his connections within the industry. Almost immediately he made his second film, *H.O.* (1966), a Brazilian–Mexican co-production consisting of two episodes (the second one was directed by Luis Alcoriza) and later, the ambitious but failed film, *Los recuerdos del porvenir* (*Memories of the Future*, 1968).

The rhetoric of 'new values' allowed several important new film careers to take off. Alejandro Jodorowsky made his debut in 1967–8 with *Fando y Lis,* an adaptation of Arrabal's play, which had caused a scandal among the straightlaced during the Acapulco festival of 1968 (the film was not commercially exhibited until 1972). Chilean by birth and cosmopolitan by vocation, Jodorowsky was a unique character, used to causing scandals with his theatre work, comics, happenings and television appearances (where he once smashed a piano on camera).

Felipe Cazals, who had finished his studies at IDHEC in 1965, made his debut in 1968 with a film produced outside the industry: *La manzana de* la discordia (The Apple of Discord). Cazals, Arturo Ripstein (who had given up on the industrial cinema because of production problems during his last film) and several young cinematographers, editors and writers founded the group Cine Independiente de México and created a new production alternative. The group was able to complete a number of shorts and two black and white features in 1969: Felipe Cazals's brilliant comedy, Familiaridades (Familiarities) and Arturo Ripstein's La hora de los niños (The Children's Hour), an interesting albeit irritating formal experiment with camera distance.

Another interesting experience provoked by the need for change was Cinematografía Marte, a company founded by Fernando Pérez Gavilán and Mauricio Wallerstein. Mauricio was the son of Gregorio Wallerstein, a powerful and influential producer linked to the Jenkins exhibition monopoly and, until the 80s, considered the 'czar of cinematographic production'. Without compromising himself, Gregorio Wallerstein wagered on change and delegated the responsibility to his son and Pérez Gavilán, who has since headed various Wallerstein production companies.

Cinematografía Marte began its activities in 1966 with Los caifanes (The Scoundrels) by Juan Ibáñez (scripted by Ibáñez himself and Carlos Fuentes). An ambitious film, it was occasionally pedantic but presented an interesting record of Mexico City life and was a popular success. From this film on, Marte sponsored the debut of a number of new directors, some of them survivors of the 1965 competition: Manuel Michel's Patsy mi amor (Patsy My Love, 1969), Tito Novaro and Jorge Fons's Trampas de amor (Love Traps, 1968), Salomón Láiter's Las puertas del paraíso (The Doors of Paradise, 1970), Mauricio Wallerstein's Las reglas del juego (The Rules of the Game, 1970), Tony Sbert's Sin salida (Dead End, 1970), José Estrada's Para servir a usted (At Your Service, 1970), Julián Pastor's La justicia tiene doce años (Justice is Twelve Years Old, 1970). Undercapitalised, Cinematográfica Marte ended its activities in 1971 with José Estrada's Cayó de la gloria el diablo (The Devil Fell From Grace). Maurico Wallerstein moved to Venezuela to continue his work as a producer and director.

The belief that the new film-makers were going to rescue the industry enabled some of them to make their debut films within and outside the industry in the late 60s. José Bolaños directed the chaotic but rich La soldadera (1966). 1969 was distinguished by opera primas, as the industry twice opened its doors. Comedian Alfonso Arau rescued the visual gag in El águila descalza (The Barefoot Eagle). Also working within the comedy genre, Jorge Fons finished his first feature film, El quelite, a parody of the traditional charro film. Gustavo Alatriste, the producer of Buñuel's last Mexican films, directed Los adelantados, an accomplished example of cinéma vérité with a minimal team, which addressed the conditions of Yucatán peasants dependent on henequén (aloe) production. Jaime Humberto Hermosillo filmed in 16mm and without a budget, Los nuestros (Ours), already broaching some of the themes characteristic of his future work. Raúl Kampffer touched upon pre-Hispanic myths in Mictlan, la casa de los que ya no son, and painter Gelsen Glass sought recourse in the visual and cinemato-graphic avant-garde for Anticlimax. Leobardo López Aretche assumed responsibility for a film that was not only independent but also clandestine and militant (so much so that he paid for it with a jail sentence): El grito (The Shout), the best available record of the 1968 student movement.

Meanwhile, the established industry did not think it was necessary to change, and continued its usual activities as if nothing had happened. It had already allowed for the industrial debut of Alberto Isaac with Las visitaciones del diablo (The Devil's Visits, 1967) and allowed some new craftsmen such as Alberto Mariscal into their ranks. Mariscal generated an exaggerated enthusiasm with some of his rural melodramas (Crisol; Hearth, 1965; El caudillo, 1966) and Westerns. He did direct the most successful examples of the Chili-Westerns: El silencioso (The Silent One, 1966), Todo por nada (All for Nothing, 1968), El sabor de la venganza (The Taste of Revenge, 1969) and El tunco Maclovio (Maclovio the Pig, 1969).

However, the vast majority of the films produced in this period corresponded precisely to the most conventional criteria. In this rigid environment, few of the veteran film-makers distinguished themselves. The veteran director Juan Bustillo Oro made his last film, Los valses venían de Viena y los niños de Paris (Waltzes Came from Vienna and Children from Paris, 1965); Carlos Velo directed the ambitious and equally unsuccessful Pedro Páramo (1966). Reduced to silence by the producers (he was considered a 'difficult and expensive' director), Emilio 'el Indio' Fernández was forced to survive as an actor, but managed to direct Un dorado de Pancho Villa (Pancho Villa's Soldier) in 1966. This melodrama repeated situations and characters from his previous films and thus continued the kind of revision of his own work that would preoccupy him until the end of his career.

In 1968 he directed *El crepúsculo de un dios (The Twilight of a God)*, a complete failure that seemed to indicate that the producers who had frozen him out might have been right. Roberto Gavaldón directed the interesting but minor work *Las figuras de arena (Sand Figures,* 1969) and gave full play to his irony in *La vida inútil de Pito Pérez (The Useless Life of Pito Pérez,* 1969), a confrontation ('the only one that really counts') between life and death.[8]

By the late 60s, Mexican cinema had perfected its routine. The established producers had found the means to survive despite the crisis: films which would (allegedly) recoup their costs immediately and which were totally or partly financed by the Banco Nacional Cinematográfico (BNC, a state organism created in 1942) with no other guarantee than the negatives of their prior films. In this context, the only exceptions besides the already cited examples, were Buñuel's last Mexican film, the unfinished *Simón del desierto* and Luis Alcoriza's *Tarahumara* (1965) and *Paraíso (Paradise,* 1969).

At the end of the 60s, it was clear that economically and structurally Mexican cinema was in bad shape. Artistically and cinematically, things were even worse. The era of the great popular figures was long gone. In fact, only one popular idol was successfully circulated in this decade: El Santo and his genre. In the Santo genre, masked wrestlers modelled on Superman and other Anglo-Saxon prototypes found time – in between wrestling bouts – to defend the Good and to fight crazy scientists as well as Dracula, Frankenstein, the wolf man, the mummy, and so on. The last year of the decade produced two films emblematic of the genre: Julián Soler's *Santo contra Blue Demon en la Atlántida (Santo Against Blue Demon in Atlantis)* and Gilberto Martínez Solares's *Santo y Blue Demon contra los monstruos (Santo and Blue Demon Against the Monsters).*

The Chili-Western replaced the *charro* cinema. It combined the prototypes, conventions and characters of the classic Western with the conventions of the Spaghetti-Western and the Paella-Western: the traditions of the mythic universe of the West were taken to their extreme through stylisation (violence, character traits, the role of women, and so on) of the European Western. The disappearance of the *charro* also implied the disappearance of the *comedia ranchera,* the only uniquely national genre (other than the 'mexmelodrama'). It was replaced by the urban comedy. This was a logical development, since the middle and upper classes had cosmopolitan pretensions: like them, the country had overcome its

rural origins and had become urban and (semi) industrialised. Films dealing with the young fit well within this trend:[9] musical comedies, romantic comedies, moralising films full of reproaches. To be young was to be disoriented, a 'go-go' dancer, perverse, overexcited, long-haired (like the Beatles), weirdly dressed and dedicated to sex, drugs, abortion and rock 'n' roll. To blame for the excesses of the young were either their rich and indifferent parents or their own intrinsic evil (the legacy of melodrama). In fact, the real problem was the fear that the relaxation of social mores would lead to the splintering of the traditional Mexican family structure and its values. This cinematic trend which, according to chroniclers of the period, began as an imitation of Hollywood films like *Rebel Without a Cause* (Nicholas Ray, 1955), was still going strong in the following decade. However, the films, even when ostensibly more open, always approached the problem of youth from an adult perspective and reworked the point of view so well represented by *Los perversos (The Perverse Ones,* 1965) by Gilberto Martínez Solares: 'This is a real-life story. About difficult boys and easy girls in the crazy world of the young', said an off-screen narrator while a group of youths sped by on their motorcycles.

Meanwhile, a sizeable portion of the real youth demanded – and was assassinated in the streets and plazas for doing so – an urgent and much-needed change in the life of the country. However, the cinema was still not able to capture, feel or intuit what lay behind this rebellion 'without a cause'. There was not, and could not be, a Godard able to make a Mexican *Masculin féminin* in 1966.

The 1968 student movement left its mark on the history of contemporary Mexico, making it clear that change was inevitable and that it was essential to restructure the political, social, cultural and economic life of the nation, even if only so that, according to the well-known formula, things could remain the same. The film industry faced the same challenge.

The Echeverría Period: The State Cinema

On 1 December 1970, Luis Echeverría became president of the nation and inaugurated a new regime with a reformist calling. Perhaps 'calling' is not the right term, but the fact was that reforms were desperately needed and called for by the real conditions of the country. Things could not remain the same after the events of 1968, when Echeverría had been minister of Gobernación, the equivalent of the US State Department. It was easy to prove that the developmentalist policies that had been in force since the 40s had failed. There was an incipient democratic and independent labour movement, which challenged, even if it did not ultimately threaten, the corporatism and narrowness of official unionism, one of the pillars of the system. It was necessary to renovate, reform and revitalise certain structures to avoid the collapse of the entire edifice. Nevertheless, the dominant private sector felt that the proposed reforms, which ultimately aimed to preserve this very same class, cut back its exaggerated privileges, and undertook a policy of economic sabotage.

Previous governments (Adolfo López Mateos, 1958–64; Gustavo Díaz Ordaz, 1964–70) had adopted an attitude towards cinema characterised by 'complicity by omission'. Governmental involvement in cinema was greater each time: financing through the BNC, purchase of the principal studios in 1960, nationalisation of the principal exhibition chains (Operadora de Teatros and Cadena de Oro), control, at least in appearance, of the domestic and international distribution of national productions (although the established producers retained a majority of the stock). State intervention softened the crisis, assured the survival of cinema through the control of its central cortex, and guaranteed its ideological hegemony. But cinema as an aesthetic and cultural product was relegated to a secondary place.

From the beginning, the new government demonstrated an interest in cinema and, as in other fields, renovations were imperative. The president's brother, Rodolfo Echeverría, an actor and long-time union leader, was named director of the BNC, given the power of a real cinema minister and charged with dealing with the problems of the market. Since the traditional cinema had become a cultural product unable to meet new social demands, the first task was to win over the huge urban middle class that now preferred the Hollywood cinema (and, perhaps among the elites, the European cinemas). Once again, to appeal to this sector it was necessary to represent it on the screen, but the old directors did not seem able to register the changes, and the cultural and sociological effervescence of Mexican society. The state sided with the post-1965 directors and other newcomers. But for this stake to be successful, they needed to open new routes, find new themes and topics, reduce censorship and fight against self-censorship (its unavoidable corollary). From the start the renovation was determined by economic and humane factors.

The dominant private sector viewed all reforms with suspicion, and the film industry proved no

exception. In response to the first measures, which attempted to restructure the industrial system, to control it more tightly, and to demand higher-quality products, the producers began to withdraw from the field. State control grew and when the absence of producers caused an alarming drop in production,[10] the state took matters into its own hands assuming control of production, first through the Churubusco studios (1972–3) and later through its own production companies (Conacine, 1974; Conacite Uno and Conacite Dos, 1975). The new companies generated new forms of production and co-production: the state as sole producer or as co-producer with workers, film-makers' groups like DASA (Directores Asociados, S.A.), new private producers and foreign companies and organisations; the so-called *paquete* (packaged) films which were produced in a collaboration between the state and technicians, workers and actors, who invested between 2 and 20% of their salaries (according to salary level) in the productions. In April 1975 the BNC modified its regulations for granting production credits: henceforth, such funds were reserved exclusively for state-produced or co-produced films. This did not cancel out the potential for private production: established producers could continue to produce, but using their own resources and without recourse to state aid. The last step was the state's purchase of the América studios in 1975. In the four previous years, private producers had sought refuge there, taking advantage of its markedly lower production costs and the few demands of its union. The cinema had been nationalised, said the optimists. In fact, it had become a state institution.

Since the early days of the regime, the BNC had struggled to place the national cinema in the best movie theatres of the nation, but these screens were devoted to foreign films, especially from the USA. This was true even within the state-owned exhibition chains in the year they were purchased. Access to theatres was crucial in order for the national cinema to achieve a broad cultural impact. On the other hand, creatively ambitious projects, new themes and new topics were given priority. Censorship, until then one of the most severe in the world, was (relatively) relaxed. Film-makers became promoters of their projects, counting upon an economic and creative freedom that, although relative, had been unprecedented in the medium.

These material changes offered film-makers new opportunities. The favourable conjunctures in the 30s and during the Second World War had been completely different. One must question whether they were able to live up to this political and economic conjuncture and the conflicts of their own contradictions. At first glance, one may conclude that the film-makers were always behind the times and thus bolstered the traditions of paternalism and self-censorship. To the calls for openness and creative freedom for film-makers, they responded with scepticism instead of testing the limits of this openness and creative freedom.

Although at first glance this is undoubtedly true, an in-depth look reveals other nuances. Things were neither that simple nor that clear-cut. In the first years, although the state's intention was to change the cinema, it did not know how to proceed. State production dabbled here and there: political cinema, social cinema, quality cinema, cinema to educate and raise consciousness. Soon there emerged a platform that was more or less theoretically defined with the idea of an auteur cinema previously defended by Nuevo Cine. This coincided broadly with the interests and ambitions of the film-makers who were, for the most part, children of the bourgeoisie or the educated petty bourgeoisie, individuals with experience in the theatre (José Estrada, for example) or literature (Juan Manuel Torres), or film-school graduates from Mexican schools (Jorge Fons, Alberto Bojórquez, Jaime Humberto Hermosillo) or foreign schools like IDHEC in France (Felipe Cazals, Paul Leduc), the Lodz school in Poland (Juan Manuel Torres), or the Moscow school (Sergio Olhovich, Gonzalo Martínez). The idea of an auteur cinema allowed for individual struggles, the re-vindication of freedom and creative imagination. However, with the exception of Leduc, no one assumed a political position, in the best sense of the term, and no one questioned the function of cinema and the film-maker in a specific social context. The objective of individual struggle was to re-establish the myth of the Artist-God. This was, however, a combative position against what were the real conditions of cinema at the time, and played an important role in a paral-ysed medium buried under conformity and rigidity: the cinema could and should be a medium for personal expression.

Between 1971 and 1973, several films were produced which are interesting as examples of auteurist film-making. In *El castillo de la pureza* (*The Castle of Purity,* 1972), for example, Arturo Ripstein further develops various techniques – especially the use of time – he had already experimented with during his independent phase.[11] The film contributed to his development of the theme of a closed and suffocating world where man, like God, attempts to create a world in his image and, as Christian Zimmer pointed out, developed a magisterial political metaphor about fascism (daily and familiar).[12] Later he directed *El Santo Oficio* (*The Holy Office,* 1973) without achieving the same results. Other films of interest included Alberto Isaac's *Los días del amor* (*The Days of Love,* 1971); José Estrada's *Cayó de la gloria el diablo* (*The Devil Fell From Glory,* 1971) and *El profeta Mimí* (*The Prophet Mimí,* 1972); Jaime Humberto Hermosillo's *El señor de Osanto* (*The Gentleman from Osanto,* 1972) and Gonzalo Martínez's first film, *El principio* (*The Beginning,* 1972).

However, the first film that really proposed a different kind of cinema emerged outside the commercial circuit and was made in 16mm black and white with a minimal budget: Paul Leduc's *Reed: México insurgente* (1970–1). It tells the story of an awakening of political consciousness in the form of a semi-documentary and presents an unusual look at the Mexican Revolution, in which the immediate, daily, lived and fresh truth of that period appears as a process, confused and imprecise, rather than as history, rhetoric or folklore. The film was acquired by the state, who paid to legalise it with the unions and to blow it up to 35mm, and featured it widely in festivals and touring retrospectives of Mexican cinema between 1972 and 1975.

The period of hesitations and guesswork continued, oscillating between efforts to produce an auteur cinema and various approaches to the critical analysis of Mexican reality. It is evident that a majority of the film-makers did not believe in the 'opening' and were resigned to accept whatever the paternal state would grant; they adapted to the conjuncture instead of pushing beyond it.

We often have the sense that the state did everything during the Echeverría years. This, however, overlooks one important fact: the presence of new producers and new production companies from different sectors who were not part of the recognised labour union association. This was the case with Alfa Centauri, created around Felipe Cazals. He had moved from independent film-making with minimal budgets (*La manzana de la discordia, Familiarid-ades*) to the multimillion dollar super-production *Emiliano Zapata* (1970), a stylistic exercise domin-ated by a sometimes emptily virtuoso perform-ance from the actor Antonio Aguilar. In 1971, already in association with Alfa Centauri, he directed *El jardín de tía Isabel* (*Aunt Isabel's Garden*), an uneven, rich, confusing and exuberant film about the early years of the Conquest in the 16th century.

Following the desires of the government, Alfa Centauri and Marco Polo (another of the new production companies) produced *Aquellos años* (*Those Years,* 1972), another historical super-production dealing with Benito Juárez's struggles during the French intervention and Maximilian's empire, and featuring characters who resembled national monuments. Given his limited possibilities, Cazals devoted himself to calligraphy and playfulness (long sequence shots with an always moving camera). The company would still produce another film, again with Cazals, the documentary *Los que viven donde sopla el viento suave* (*Those Who Live Where the Light Wind Blows,* 1973) about the Seris Indians of northern Mexico.

The activity of the company Producciones Marco Polo, founded by the industrialist Marco y Leopoldo Silva, was somewhat broader. Marco Polo began in 1970 with *Tú, yo, nosotros* (*You, Me, We,* 1970), a compilation of three stories directed by Gonzalo Martínez, Juan Manuel Torres and Jorge Fons. It followed this in 1971 with Jorge Fons's *Los cachorros* (*The Dogs*), Sergio Olhovich's debut *Muñeca reina* (*Doll Queen*) and Jaime Humberto Hermosillo's first commercial film, *La verdadera vocación de Magdalena* (*Magdalena's True Vocation*). After co-producing *Aquellos años, El Santo Oficio,* Olhovich's *Encuentro de un hombre solo* (*Meeting With a Solitary Man,* 1973) and *La casa del sur* (*The House of the South,* 1974), the company declined and finally disappeared.

Producciones Escorpión suffered a similar fate. It began on the right foot with *Mecánica nacional* (*National Mechanic,* 1971), an aggressive satire by Luis Alcoriza (who followed the Italian model and used comedy as a tool to uncover social ills) and *El muro del silencio* (*The Wall of Silence,* 1971), also by Alcoriza. These films were followed by a three-episode compilation film about the theological virtues, *Fe, esperanza y caridad* (*Faith, Hope and Charity,* Alberto Bojórquez, Luis Alcoriza and Jorge Fons, 1972). The company ended its activities with *Presagio* (*The Omen,* 1974) and *Las fuerzas vivas* (*The Living Strengths,* 1975), both by Alcoriza, when it was already operating under the name Unifilms.

The Escorpión experiment was a failure because of the conditions of the industry. The new producers were prominent in other fields and had approached the cinema with curiosity, but with very concrete opportunistic interests (it was rumoured that, among other things, helping the industry headed by the president's brother would result in easier contract negotiations elsewhere, tax concessions, and so on).[13]

The fact is that all the films they produced were economic disasters. No matter how rich, no matter how advantageous film production activity might have been to other business deals, no matter how much social status might have been earned, no one persists in businesses without profit potential.

Certainly, by 1973 many theatres that had been off-limits to domestic films had opened their doors. But several factors determined that this would not have the desired effect. On the one hand, the low admission prices: between 2 and 15 pesos (US$0.16 to 1.24) in 1972, from 3 to 20 pesos in 1973, 1974 and 1975, and from 6 to 25 pesos (from US$0.30 to 1.25) when the national currency was being devalued in the wake of an inflationary spiral.[14] Cinematic entertainment in Mexico was, and continues to be, the least expensive in the world.

There were other problems that are still important today: the distribution of box-office pesos. The largest chunk was (and still is) taken by the exhibitors (42.5%); they are followed by federal taxes (17.5% plus an additional municipal tax in the provinces) and distributors (between 25 and 30%). In other words, the producer only receives between 11 and 16 cents of each peso. If one deducts the costs of producing copies and advertising expenses, what remains is closer to 7 to 10 cents of each peso. Furthermore, the new producers did not have a share in the distribution companies (Películas Nacionales S.A. and Pelimex) primarily controlled by the Asociación de Productores.

This was really the central problem, which could not be resolved in this period. If the Asociación de Productores had withdrawn gradually from production and exhibition under state control, they would have been taken over by the Hollywood cinema. In fact, the members of the Asociación controlled and manipulated distribution and therefore had a number of exhibition prerogatives. In 1975, when most of the institutions still in the private sector were nationalised (América studios, Créditos del BNC, Pelimex), there was something left over for the private producers: Películas Nacionales, the principal institution in domestic exhibition. The state had acquired all of Pelimex, the company that handled the distribution of the national cinema abroad. At this time, the company was bankrupt, exhausted by corruption and poor management (it had been controlled by the state bureaucracy since the 1954 Plan Garduño, the first decisive state intervention in the cinema), and had little or no international visibility. Películas Nacionales was privately held until its recent (1991) bankruptcy. The state cinema pyramid was not able to, did not want to, and did not know how to create its own distributor or to acquire Películas Nacionales as it had acquired Pelimex. This was the missing link.[15]

These were good years for independent cinema, that is the cinema produced outside the established sector. A number of films were made alongside *Reed: México insurgente:* CUEC produced *El cambio* (*The Change,* Alfredo Joskowicz, 1971), *Quizá siempre si me muera* (*Maybe Always If I Die,* Federico Weingartshofer, 1971), *Tómalo como quieras* (Carlos González Morantes, 1972) and, elsewhere, *Los meses y los días* (*The Months and the Days,* Alberto Bojórquez, 1971), *Los marginados* (*The Marginals,* Roberto G. Rivera, 1972), *El perro y la calentura* (*The Dog and the Heat,* Raúl Kampffer, 1973) and *Apuntes* (*Notes,* Ariel Zúñiga, 1974).

The first super-8 competition was held in 1971. Even before the awards were announced, the event gave rise to a number of other competitions for this format; groups and co-operatives were established, and a good number of films were produced in all genres and forms (including a feature, Gabriel Retes's *Los años duros* (*The Hard Years,* 1973)). This was an alternative route that produced a great cinematic effervescence. Among those concentrating on super-8 production, there were those who attempted to develop a new aesthetic appropriate to the medium, and those who simply produced a mini-cinema. Several ended up within the industry (Gabriel Retes, Alfredo Gurrola, Diego López).

Another group typical of this period, but which worked exclusively at the América studios was formed around the strong personality of Alejandro Jodorowsky, producer Roberto Viskin and the companies Pániza, Prisma and Cineproducciones. Jodorowsky make his delirious Western *El topo* (1970) and *La montaña sagrada* (1972) in co-production with the US company Abkco. His cinematographer, Rafael Corkidi, directed *Angeles y querubines* (*Angels and Cherubs,* 1971), a unique vampire story of great visual beauty, and *Aundar Anapu* (1974); Juan López Moctezuma directed *La mansión de la locura* (*The House of Madness,* 1971) and *Mary, Mary, Bloody Mary* (1974). *Pubertinaje* (1972) featured the debut of theatre director Pablo Leder and music critic José Antonio Alcaraz. In contrast, the unfinished *Apolinar* (1971–4), by the talented theatrical director Julio Castillo, was a complete failure.

Another unusual case was that of José Bolaños's second film, *Arde, baby, arde* (*Burn, Baby, Burn),* a necrophiliac Western completed in 1971 and shown at the Venice film festival. Bolaños took notice of the critics and not only re-edited the film, but also re-shot several sequences. The new version was exhibited in 1974. Bolaños seems to have specialised in this type of project. In 1977 he finished *La casa de la media luna* (*The House of the Half-Moon),* a second adaptation of Juan Rulfo's *Pedro Páramo.* The film was shown at the San Sebastian festival and in Mexico City with little success. Since 1981, Bolaños has been re-editing the film and adding previously excised footage to produce a new four-hour version.

1975 was the year of state cinema, not only because by then the state had established almost complete control over cinema, but also because of the appearance of several films which reflected a more coherently cinematic project and a better understanding of the relations between cinema, politics and audiences. Several film-makers seem to have decided to test the limits of the so-called 'opening' and to take advantage of the conjuncture. Furthermore, the *paquete* production system contributed several original projects. It enabled Felipe Cazals's trilogy of *Canoa* (1975), *El apando* (*Solitary,* 1975) and *Las poquianchis* (1976) as well as Jaime Humberto Hermosillo's *La pasión según Berenice* (1975), the veteran film-maker Rafael Baledón's *Renuncia por motivos de salud* (*Resignation for Health Reasons,* 1975), Jorge Fons's *Los albañiles* (*The Bricklayers,* 1976), Alberto Isaac's *Cuartelazo* (*Mutiny,* 1976), Gabriel Retes's professional debut with *Chin Chin el teporocho* (1975), Alberto Bojórquez's *Lo mejor de Teresa* (*Teresa's Best,* 1976) and exiled Chilean film-maker Miguel Littín's co-production *Actas de Marusia* (1975). Experienced television director Raúl Araiza made his film debut with the interesting *Cascabel* (*Rattle,* 1976). In documentary production, Arturo Ripstein made *Lucumberri* (1976), focusing on the sinister prison in Mexico City, and Paul Leduc, always on the margins of the official industry, finished his impressive *Etnocidio* (1976). On the other hand, the veteran film-makers seemed to have been forgotten. Alejandro Galindo became part of the *paquete* cinema with his failed *Ante el cadáver de un líder* (*In Front of a Leader's Corpse,* 1973).

After the failure of his ambitious biography of the painter José Clemente Orozco (*En busca de un muro; In Search of a Wall,* 1973), Julio Bracho made *Espejismo de la ciudad* (*Mirage of the City,* 1975) and persisted with a 40s moralising vision of country–city relations. Roberto Gavaldón had to resign himself to directing *La playa vacía* (*The Empty Beach,* 1976) in Spain, *El hombre de los hongos* (*The Mushroom Man,*

Enrique Lucero in *Canoa* (Felipe Cazals, 1975)

1975) in Mexico and a *paquete* film, *Las cenizas de un diputado* (*The Ashes of a Deputy,* 1976), which served as a bitter summation of his film work. In 1973, after five years of silence, Emilio 'el Indio' Fernández made his most personal, and naive, film since the 50s: *La choca (The Prey).*

The Breakdown
1 December 1976 marked the beginning of José López Portillo's presidential mandate, as well as a new stage in the history of the Mexican cinema. By this time, cinema had been to all intents and purposes nationalised. Efforts had been made to clean up the industry and to strengthen the role of the state within it.[16] In addition to controlling production, distribution (except for Películas Nacionales), exhibition, promotion and the studios, the state had also inaugurated the Cineteca Nacional in 1974 and placed it under the Dirección General de

Cinematografía of the Secretaria de Gobernación (Ministry of the Interior). Thus the same institution that was in charge of censorship was also entrusted with the protection of film culture. The reason: a clause of the Ley Cinematográfica of 1949–52 granted the Dirección General de Cinematografía the right and duty to create a national film archive.

In 1975, the state had created a second film school in Mexico City on the grounds of the Churubusco studios: the Centro de Capacitación Cinematográfica (CCC), with Luis Buñuel as president and under the direction of film-maker Carlos Velo. Velo was followed by Alfredo Joskowicz (1977–82), Eduardo Maldonado (1983–90) and Gustavo Montiel (since 1990). The state thus guaranteed the training of future film-makers.[17] Nevertheless, from a political, social, aesthetic and cinematographic point of view, what was accomplished in this period?

This was a time of great activity, an important characteristic of the era. However, a genuinely national cultural cinema was not consolidated, and no one established a good foundation for a healthy film economy nor for the development of a new aesthetic. No one addressed the question of a national film school, the development of specific aesthetic principles (most of the films of this period were derived from the Hollywood model), or created any significant personal films. It was impossible magically to fill the vacuum left after so many years of neglect. However, there was optimism about the future. On the one hand, the state had assumed a number of responsibilities after years of dissimulation and ambiguity; on the other, there were some potential points of departure: *Reed: México insurgente, El castillo de la pureza, Canoa,* (a key film because of its narrative form and its treatment of a political theme) and *La pasión según Berenice,* which offered an acute analysis of the myths and behaviour of the provincial middle classes. These directions needed to be explored further.

In spite of changes and reforms, the basic structure of the system was still intact. Distribution remained in the hands of private producers who had gone into retirement. It was believed that the changes were irreversible, but it only took the new administration a few months to destroy everything the previous one had accomplished. Its activities began in the middle of an economic crisis, some months after the first currency devaluation in three decades,[18] at a time of enormous inflation. The International Monetary Fund and other international financial institutions recommended (or demanded) that the state reduce its public investments. The effects were felt immediately in cinema. In 1976, the state had financed 36 of the 52 commercial features produced (the lowest annual production figure since the 40s). Under the new administration, in 1977, the state backed 45 of the 74 films produced (although many of these were inherited from the previous administration). The figures decreased: in 1978 the state participated in 35 films, 15 in 1979, 7 in 1980, 5 in 1981 and 3 in 1982. The activity of private producers increased accordingly: 29 films in 1977, 55 in 1978, 73 in 1979, 90 in 1980, 67 in 1981 and 92 in 1982.[19] The traditional producers restarted their activities as if nothing had happened. A new player appeared in 1978: Televicine, a subsidiary of the great television conglomerate Televisa. Televicine was the company that produced most films between 1978 and 1982.

One of the state production companies, Conacite Uno, was closed down in 1978. The *paquete* films, which had been central during the previous administration, disappeared completely in 1977. To replace them, several groups attempted to produce co-operatively, but they failed because of the lack of support and the difficult rules of the game of distribution and exhibition. Furthermore, because of the difficulty of changing the 1976 regulations, the BNC was liquidated in 1978. The only valid yardstick was box-office profit. Private producers – publicly maligned in previous years – were deemed to know its secrets and they took advantage of the situation.

The auteur cinema and the so-called critical approach to reality were put back into the closet. Family cinema was the new watchword of the cinema authorities, headed by the little-known writer and sister of the president, Margarita López Portillo (the brother was substituted by a sister, which seems to indicate that those in power think of cinema as a family affair). Power was no longer centred on the liquidated BNC, but around a kind of Ministerio de Comunicación (Ministry of Communication) created especially for the sister: RTC (Dirección de Radio, Televisión y Cinematografía). The producers and artistic and intellectual post-holders displaced by previous administrations mounted a counter-offensive. Thus, to the previous administration's obsession with culture and education, the response was that these areas were now to be the responsibility of the Ministry of Education and the universities. 'Criticism' and 'messages' were derided because cinema was a business and its only function was to entertain: 'The only good films are those that turn a profit' was repeated over and over again.

In 1977, the commitments of the previous administration were finally completed and several significant films appeared: Arturo Ripstein's *El lugar sin límites (The Place Without Limits),* Carlos Enrique Taboada's *La guerra santa (The Holy War),* José Estrada's *Los indolentes (The Indolents),* Julián Pastor's *Los pequeños privilegios (Little Privileges),* Jaime Humberto Hermosillo's *Naufragio (Shipwreck)* and Miguel Littín's *El recurso al método (Reasons of State).* In the following years, when Margarita López Portillo and RTC decided to pursue a 'cultural' cinema, there were still some interesting productions, such as Arturo Ripstein's *Cadena perpetua (Life Sentence,* 1978), Alfredo Gurrola's *Llámenme Mike (Call Me Mike,* 1979), Nicholas Echevarría's *El niño Fidencio (The Child Fidencio,* 1981), Felipe Cazals's *Bajo la metralla (Under Fire,* 1982) and some ambitious films such as Alberto Mariscal's *Bloody Marlene* (1977), Antonio Eceiza's *El complot mongol (The*

Mongolian Plot, 1977), Jaime Humberto Hermosillo's *Amor libre* (*Free Love,* 1978), Felipe Cazals's *El año de la peste* (*The Plague Year,* 1978), Alfredo Gurrola's *La sucesión* (*The Succession,* 1978), Sergio Olhovich's *El infierno de todos tan temido* (*Everyone's Much Feared Destiny,* 1979), Archibaldo Burns's *Oficio de tinieblas* (*Vocation of Gloom,* 1979), Arturo Ripstein's *La tía Alejandra* (*Aunt Alejandra,* 1978).

This meant that the state held on to the 'cultural' cinema (with which it satisfied its desire for personal and state-wide prestige), the worst of auteur cinema and, despite everything, the films that still aspired towards personal expression and searched for or approximated reality. This small space allowed for the production of films such as *El lugar sin límites,* with its analysis of power, machismo and paternalism, and of *Cadena perpetua* and its exploration of the victim–executioner relationship in the context of the dominant social structure. Private producers dominated the larger domain of family cinema and profitable cinema.

A foreigner newly arrived in Mexico might well have believed that the state's production was being sabotaged by its distribution and exhibition. Films took a long time to arrive at the theatres, there was no publicity, and box-office failure was thus guaranteed. Consequently, costs were not recouped, and this was used to justify cuts in production finance. *Cadena perpetua* was made in 1978 and premiered in 1981, *Llámenme Mike* (1979) did not come out until 1982, *El infierno de todos tan temido* (1979) was held back until 1982, *El recurso al método* (1977) premiered in 1982, and so on.

Film-makers with aesthetic ambitions had two choices: to abandon them and make potboilers instead, or to make films outside the industry, for instance in 16mm. Jaime Humberto Hermosillo opted for the latter (*Las apariencias engañan,* 1977; *María de mi corazón,* 1979; *Confidencias,* 1982). Alfredo Joskowicz directed *Constelaciones* (1978) about the life of Sor Juana Inés de la Cruz. Miguel Littin made *La viuda de Montiel* (1979) with a co-operative at the Universidad de Veracruz and in co-production with Cuba and Venezuela. Gabriel Retes directed *Bandera rota* (*Broken Flag,* 1979). Alberto Isaac made *Tiempo de lobos* (*Time of Wolves,* 1981). Others who had never worked within the system continued on their independent journey: Ariel Zúñiga's interesting *Anacrusa* (1978) and *Uno entre muchos* (*One Among Many,* 1981), Raúl Kamffer's *¡Ora sí tenemos que ganar!* (*Now We Have to Win!,* 1978), Paul Leduc's *Puebla hoy* (*Puebla Today,* 1978), a compilation of three shorts, and Douglas Sánchez's

Godardian CUEC thesis film *Cualquier cosa* (*Anything,* 1979). But given the state of distribution and the exhibitors' overt prejudices against Mexican films, neither the films produced by the state nor those made outside the system by known or unknown film-makers had any impact. Thus they had little chance of recouping their investments. These were individual and solitary ventures, without importance for the film business and with little significance for cultural struggles.

The traditional private producers had a free hand and once again became the vortex of an industrial film culture governed by the profit motive. The formulas for success returned, that is to say, the genres of the past were dressed in new clothes, old contents dusted off for representation, decorated by elements superficially signifying modernity. This practice was not only typical of the old producers, it was also faithfully followed by Televicine, the new powerful player in the field. This company had all the advantages of economic power, its own technical and artistic personnel and the political influence to guarantee, among other things, timely exhibition even in the worst moments. Televisa had defined the rules of the game for television for over twenty-five years, created an audience, shaped its perception and conditioned its taste. The easiest thing for Televicine was to repeat that which had assured Televisa's success in the past: the same characters, forms, genres, and so on.

However, with a few exceptions, the majority of its films have been failures. The exceptions in this period were Enrique Segoviano's *El chanfle* (1978) featuring Roberto Gómez Bolaños 'Chespirito', a television comic who had been very successful in Mexico and Latin America, and Raúl Araiza's *Lagunilla mi barrio* (*Lagunilla My Neighbourhood,* 1980), a film repeating the formula of the urban neighbourhood genre. The rest were comedies, melodramas and derivations of the *telenovelas,* a very influential television genre created by Televisa. These films were utter economic failures, including Gómez Bolaños's subsequent films for theatrical release. In the case of the melodramas, the traditional themes of fatality and the struggles of Good versus Evil were drowned by puritanism and prudery; although the public accepted this in television, they rejected it in the cinema.

Producer/director René Cardona Jr, a cunning follower of commercial trends, came closer to what the urban middle-class public, accustomed to Hollywood, wanted to see in the cinema: disasters, as in his *Ciclón* (*Hurricane,* 1977); monsters, as in

María Rojo and Ana Ofelia Murguía in *Naufragio* (Jaime Humberto Hermosillo, 1977)

Tiburones (*Sharks,* 1977); or sensational events such as *Guyana* (1979), a recreation of the group suicide by Jim Jones's sect. The most popular and characteristic genre of this period, however, was the *fichera*[20] film, a new variant of the *cabareteral* prostitute genre. It is symptomatic that the success of this type of film has always coincided with periods in which there is talk of abundance, but which are in fact characterised by wealth, waste and corruption: the regimes of Miguel Alemán (1946–52) and José López Portillo (1976–82). In the particular period under discussion here, the first films of this genre actually emerged just before the Portillo *sexenio,* with the great success of Miguel M. Delgado's *Bellas de noche* (*Beauties of the Night,* 1974) and his *Las ficheras* (1976).

There was, however, an evident generic shift and a change in tone. Although the films were still couched in melodramatic terms (the heroes and heroines were motivated by the desire for a decent life), the development of the narratives came close to the comedic and/or farcical. The apparently non-puritanical attitude and amorality were explained in the following terms: the world of cabarets, brothels and prostitution is a happy one, without contradictions or conflicts; the public is invited to participate in a gratifying and non-irritating space-time. The relative liberalisation of the previous period allowed for the abundant use of nudity, obscenities and scatological language, a positive representation of homosexuality, transvestism, and so on. The genre's success produced a chain reaction: all the variants of even the slightest plot elements were quickly developed, and producers plagiarised each other constantly. Even the state production companies made *fichera* films, such as Miguel M. Delgado's *Oye Salomé* (*Listen Salome,* 1978), temporarily forgetting their brief to produce family-entertainment films. Of course, its *fichera* films had less nudity, the language was not so vulgar and there were no homosexuals. Of the more than 100 films made in six years, not one was of the slightest interest, except as a symptom or as matter for sociological study. True, *El lugar sin límites* was produced during this period, but, even though it shared the space of the brothel with the *ficheras,* its approach and themes were diametrically different. In this genre, in which men dress like women and vice versa, and in which whores pretend to be artists and artists whores, there was one character who symbolised the period's cinema and culture in general: 'La Corcholata', an alcoholic woman, disguised as a whore, who smiled through thick and thin and functioned as a paradigm of optimism.

Other genres were developed as well, but less prolifically. The urban neighbourhood cinema had had its moment of glory in the 40s and 50s with the works of Alejandro Galindo and Ismael Rodríguez. The genre was linked to a specific idea of urban life and of the type of human relations it made possible. However, Mexico City had undergone a complete transformation since 1963–4 and the neighbourhoods to which the films referred no longer existed. The resurgence of this genre can be explained not only by the search for a successful box-office formula, but also by the growing nostalgia for the lost city.

Mario Hernández's Italian-inspired hit comedy *¡Que viva Tepito!* (*Viva Tepito!,* 1980) attempted to renovate stereotypical characters, places and themes such as poverty, promiscuousness, male friendship and solidarity by combining comedy and melodrama, and taking advantage of the power these themes continued to exercise over the popular unconscious, while avoiding the burdens of social perspicacity. This kind of cinema did not live up to its initial promise and the genre was quickly exhausted. The *mojados* (wetback) melodramas had a longer life.[21] The serious problems posed by the massive exodus of urban and rural workers to the USA became the stuff of conventional, optimistic melodramas in which *mojados* and *mojadas* seemed to have no other desire than to become successful singers.

Nevertheless, production figures for this period are surprising. During the Echeverría regime, when the new values reigned, 28 new film-makers made their first features (21 within the established industry). In the López Portillo period, 45 film-makers made their first features (38 within the industry). Some of the more significant debuts included Nicolás Echevarría's *María Sabina* (1978),

Diego López's Niebla (*Fog,* 1978), Jorge Prior's *Café Tacuba* (1981), José Luis García Agraz's *Nocaut* (*Knockout,* 1983) and Alejandro Pelayo's *La víspera* (*The Day Before,* 1982). All these films were produced outside the industry. José Luis Urquieta and Alfredo Gurrola also seemed promising. Few others managed to make a second film, and worked only occasionally.

Two particular events summarise this period: the fire and destruction of the Cineteca Nacional and the repression of a group of film-makers and functionaries. In response to the unrest and protests of film-makers and unions, on 26 July 1979 a group of armed agents forcibly entered the Churubusco studios and arrested film-makers, production personnel, company directors (those of Conacine and Churubusco) and even secretaries for their timid opposition to the current film policies. They were accused of multimillon dollar fraud, imprisoned, tortured and tried. Some were released on bail, others, such as Carlos Velo and Churubusco director Bosco Arochi, spent one or two years in prison. This was an attempt to teach the industry a lesson and to overcome opposition, but the ridiculous outcome of the action precluded further similar operations.

Almost three years later, on 24 March 1982, a fire destroyed the Cineteca Nacional, 200 negatives, about 4,000 positives, a library with thousands of books, scripts, photo-graphs, posters and other documents, two theatres and, most tragically, an undetermined number of human lives: at the time of the fire, 600 spectators watching Wadja's *Promised Land* were trapped in the theatre. This was not simply an unfortunate accident nor an act of sabotage (as many speculated at first). Against all international standards, inflammable nitrate material had been kept in a place frequented by the public. The vaults were located beneath the theatres and the offices, the ventilation system was malfunctioning and failed to maintain a stable temperature of 10 degrees Celsius (it is estimated that the vault temperature at the time of the fire was close to 35 degrees). This tragedy serves as a great metaphor for this period's *tabula rasa* film policies.

There were a significant number of directorial debuts during the new administration inaugurated on 1 December 1982 and headed by president Miguel de la Madrid. In this *sexenio,* 46 new film-makers made their debut, 41 of them within the industry. There was also something new in the administration: the creation, in 1983, of the Instituto Mexicano de la Cinematografía (IMCINE) directed by film-maker Alberto Isaac. But the new institute did not

Cabeza de vaca (Nicolás Echevarría, 1991)

presuppose the disappearance of the Dirección de Radio, Televisión y Cinematografía (RTC), created six years earlier. Despite the efforts of those concerned with cinema and culture, Isaac was not able to position IMCINE under the control of the Ministerio de Educación (Cultura). Administratively, it remained alongside the RTC within Gobernación (Interior). Isaac's hands were tied and he could accomplish little. One bright light was his organisation of the third experimental film competition, 1985–6. Given the restrictions imposed upon him, Isaac resigned in 1985 and was replaced by the professional politician Soto Izquierdo, whose goal was to keep the institute going for the three remaining years of the *sexenio* without actually doing anything. The third competition went ahead, and they produced and co-produced a number of films, such as the demagogical mammoth Servando González's *El último túnel* (*The Last Tunnel,* 1987), which consumed the entire budget for two years and prevented the production of other films like Nicolás Echevarría's *Cabeza de Vaca.*

During these six years Mexico produced 91 films in 1983, 68 in 1984, 89 in 1985, 76 in 1986, 88 in

1987 and 74 in 1988. These figures are questionable because of the appearance of a new player – video. Some works were recorded directly on video; others were filmed on 35mm or 16mm outside all institutional and union structures, destined exclusively for video distribution. After 1984, more and more former film producers turned to the exploitation of these new hens which could lay golden eggs: home video and the growing US Spanish-language market. But this market was exhausted by 1990 because of the extraordinarily low quality of the productions (videos made in a week to ten days), cheap scripts quickly written and a total absence of production values. The producers merely repeated what they had done previously.

Independent Production and New Support Systems
Although it was already evident that the state wanted to liquidate its commitment to cinema, it continued to produce through IMCINE, Conacine and, by 1987–8, the barely functioning Conacite. The few films produced or co-produced were, by and large, ambitious: *Vidas errantes* (1984), Juan Antonio de la Riva's first feature (he was also the first Centro de Capacitación Cinematográfica (CCC) graduate to join the industry); José Estrada's *Mexicano, tú puedes* (1983); Carlos Enrique Taboada's *Veneno para las hadas* (*Poison for the Fairies,* 1984); Arturo Ripstein's *El imperio de la fortuna* (*The Empire of Fortune,* 1986); Luis Alcoriza's *Lo que importa es vivir* (*What Matters is to Live,* 1986); Alberto Isaac's *Mariana, Mariana* (1986); Felipe Cazals's *El tres de copas* (*The Three of Spades,* 1986); Alejandro Pelayo's *Días difíciles* (*Difficult Days,* 1987); Sergio Olhovich's *Esperanza* (*Hope,* 1988) and Oscar Blancarte's *El jinete de la divina providencia* (*The Horseman of Divine Providence,* 1988). The third competition contained the notable films *Crónica de familia* (*Family Chronicle,* Diego López, 1985) and *Amor a la vuelta de la esquina* (*Love Around the Corner,* Alberto Cortes, 1985).

The difference now was that, for the first time, film-makers were in charge of their own projects and often functioned as co-producers (as was the case with *Vidas errantes, Días difíciles, El tres de copas, El jinete de la divina providencia* and the third competition films). Furthermore, since the possibility of state support was less likely than ever, various projects were produced independently, managed by the film-makers or by new producers and production groups: the CCC graduate Gerardo Pardo's *De veras me atrapaste* (*You Really Caught Me,* 1983); Ariel Zúñiga's *El diablo y la dama* (*The Devil and the Lady,* 1983); Paul

Cabeza de vaca (Nicolás Echevarría, 1991)

Leduc's *Frida* (1984); Jaime Casillas's *Memoriales perdidos* (*Lost Memorials,* 1983); Luis Mandoki's *Motel* (1983); Jaime Hum-berto Hermosillo's *Doña Herlinda y su hijo* (1984); Raúl Busteros's *Redondo* (1984); Paul Leduc's *¿Cómo ves?* (1985); Felipe Cazals's *Los motivos de Luz* (1985); Roberto Rochín's *Ulama* (1986); Mitl Valdez's *Los confines* (1987); Luis Estrada's *El camino largo a Tijuana* (*The Long Road to Tijuana,* 1988) and Arturo Ripstein's *Mentiras piadosas* (*Kind Lies,* 1988).

Often the film-makers or working groups sought the help of the Fondo de Fomento a la Calidad Cinematográfica, an organisation which, with the participation of IMCINE, had clout with the exhibition chains and private producers. The Fondo, combined with minor funding sources, enabled the production of films such as Busi Cortés's *El secreto de Romelia* (*Romelia's Secret,* 1988), which inaugurated the CCC's project to produce its graduates' opera

primas. The Fondo is the most important recently created film organisation for the future of the national cinema.

On their side, the traditional private producers persisted with old habits, despite the economic crisis, constant inflation and the increase in production budgets. At the start of the new presidential term, the formulas were the same as they had been before: *ficheras,* urban neighbourhoods, *mojados.* Little by little, the *fichera* films and the films about urban neighbourhoods were joined together into a new sub-genre which the producers themselves call the *sexycomedia,* attempting to adapt the style of minor 70s Italian comedies. From the *fichera* films, it inherited the transvestism, the cabaret, the brothel, sexual allusions, obscenity and scatology; from the urban neighbourhood films it adopted popular characters and their picturesque speech, especially the *albures* (sexual puns).

The *sexycomedia* was for a long time also a genre for the representation of various types of workers' groups: bricklayers in the veteran Gilberto Martínez Solares and his son Adolfo's *El día de los albañiles* (*The Day of the Bricklayers,* 1983), which, as the biggest box-office success of 1984, spawned two sequels; car mechanics in Raúl Ramírez's *Los mecánicos ardientes* (*The Ardent Mechanics,* 1985), and Victor Manuel Castro's *El Mofles y los mecánicos* (*El Mofles and the Mechanics,* 1985); taxi drivers, milk-delivery men, lunch-counter servers, taco street vendors, thieves, and so on. Other *sexycomedias* were merely pretexts for stringing *albures* together. The *fichera* films and the *sexycomedias* (*albures* and workers) had their own hero: Victor Manuel Castro. This former actor, dancer and popular comedian made his film debut in 1980 and became the champion of the decade, making thirty films between 1980 and 1989.

The other important films, from a quantitative and sometimes popular point of view, were in the action genre, set either in the world of *narcotráfico* (drug traffic) (c.50 films), or in the world of northern *pistoleros* (gunfighters) and their folklore. A new heroine followed in the footsteps of US television characters like Wonder Woman: Raúl Fernández's *Lola, la trailera* (*Lola, the Truck Driver,* 1983) starred the beautiful but limited Rosa Gloria Chagoyán driving an enormous articulated lorry while battling bandits and drug smugglers, protecting the virtuous and performing dangerous gags. Soon after, she appeared in two sequels and played other successful characters. National versions of karate, kung fu and ninja fighters took the place of the masked wrestlers, although Santo had enough time to pass the baton, via Alfredo Crevenna's *Santo en la furia de los karatecas* (*Santo in a Karate Fury,* 1983), to his son, who continued the good fight in Pérez Grovas's *El hijo del Santo en frontera sin ley* (*Santo's Son in the Lawless Frontier,* 1984). The *comedia ranchera* reappeared through the filter of Aristophanes's *Lysistrata* in Mario Hernández's *Viva el chubasco* (*Viva the Shower,* 1983).

The films dealing with drug trafficking, policemen, gunmen and folkloric groups were made in Monterrey, breaking the centralised monopoly of Mexico City. Humberto Martínez Mijares moved his entire family to make films in Durango. The 1985 earthquake was exploited by Eduardo Carrasco Zanini in *Derrumbe* (*Collapse,* 1986), in Francisco Guerrero's *Trágico terremoto en México* (*Tragic Earthquake in Mexico,* 1987) and even by the *sexycomedia* in Martínez Solares's *El día de los albañiles 3* (*The Day of the Bricklayers 3,* 1987), causing waves of righteous indignation. Mexico City was treated differently than in the urban neighbourhood films and the *sexycomedia* in Gabriel Retes's pessimistic and sordid *Ciudad al desnudo* (*Naked City,* 1988), while that same year Rafael Montero caused chills among the middle class with the first film of, and about, the crisis: *El costo de la vida* (*The Cost of Life*).

On 1 December 1988, Carlos Salinas de Gortiari was inaugurated as president after a tight electoral race. The voters manifested a serious disaffection with the official ruling party, in power under various names (PNR, PRM and finally PRI) since 1929. Various non-official sources maintained that it had even lost the elections. At the start of his term of office, the new president badly needed some form of legitimacy in the face of an acute economic crisis, galloping inflation (held in check for a year with an artificial straitjacket called the 'Pact for stability and economic growth', which basically meant cutting wages) and a foreign debt which was among the highest in the world and practically impossible to repay. This caused dissatisfaction throughout most sectors of society.

The new government's economic strategies were based on the principle that it was necessary to reduce the role of the state and to modernise the economy by dismantling protectionist barriers and adopting a market economy. By 1991, banking had been re-privatised (it had been nationalised in 1982 by López Portillo) as had been other state industries considered non-strategic. Naturally, this last category included the film industry. Of Echeverría's state cinema there were few traces left: the production companies Conacine and Conacite were liquidated; in 1992, América studios and the theatres of the exhibition chain Operadora de Teatros were up for sale; before the end of this administration the Churubusco-Azteca studios will probably also have been sold.

In general, the situation has not been good for cinema. Between 1989 and 1991, 992 movie theatres were closed and 10,082 video clubs had opened.[22] Most of the closed cinemas were located in the provinces, and many had exhibited primarily Mexican films. 100 films were produced in 1989 (74 in the previous year); by 1990 production decreased to 52 and by 1991 to 34. The state co-produced more or less the same number of films as in previous years (9) and the Fondo de Fomento a la Calidad Cinematográfica participated in 6 more.

The collapse of the traditional private production system was vertical. The distributor Películas

Nacionales, which dealt primarily with this kind of film, had to suspend settling its debts and finally was forced into bankruptcy. Many small producers who worked under the shadow of the powerful Gregorio Wallerstein no longer received his financial backing. Confusion reigned: the so-called US Hispanic market fell by 80 or 90% and further weakened the Mexican industry. The most successful film of 1990 was René Cardona Jr's *La risa en vacaciones 2 (Laughter on Vacation 2),* a Televicine production heavily promoted on television. While this success was easy to understand, more difficult to account for was the success of films like *La tarea, Danzón, Cabeza de Vaca, La mujer de Benjamín* and even 'difficult' films like *Retorno a Aztlán (Return to Aztlán)* and *Ciudad de ciegos (City of the Blind)* produced according to other criteria.

Some of the traditional producers have continued to insist upon their formulas, the *sexycomedias, albures* and, most recently, films centred on popular music groups. Others have declared that they are ready to produce quality films because of the success of the abovementioned titles and especially because one of them – actor, producer and director Valentín Trujillo – was a majority shareholder in the production of Jorge Fons's *Rojo amanecer (Red Dawn,* 1990), the first film to tackle the 1968 Tlatelolco massacre, one of the biggest box-office successes of the last fifteen years and a critical success abroad (it was awarded the Silver Shell at the San Sebastian film festival).

What we already knew in the 70s has now been confirmed: there is not one, but two Mexican cinemas. One is the traditionally produced film, the other is represented by IMCINE. There are producers who have always distinguished themselves (like Manuel Barbachano Ponce) and new producers who speak the same language as the new generation of film-makers. An important change occurred within IMCINE: it became part of the cultural sector and was directly accountable to the Consejo Nacional para la Cultura y las Artes. IMCINE began by producing two films through state companies: José Buil's first feature, *La leyenda de un máscara (The Legend of a Mask,* 1991), an ironic reflection on national heroes and myths, which was the last film produced by Conacite before its disappearance, and Juan Antonio de la Riva's loving yet bitter provincial tale, *Pueblo de madera (Town of Wood,* 1990), co-produced by Conacite and Televisión Española.

La leyenda de una máscara was the last film completely produced by IMCINE. Since then it has only co-produced. This is how the inertia that favoured the paternalist state has been broken and the initiative now placed in the hands of film-makers or producers who are close to them, who must develop their ability to deal and to take charge of the future of their films. The era in which the state put up all the money and decided the career of a film is over. Now things happen as in other parts of the real world: the film-maker or the producer has to search for financing from diverse national and international sources. The cinema is no longer totally in the hands of bureaucrats (although they are still influential).

An exemplary case is that of *Cabeza de Vaca* (1991), Nicolás Echevarría's noteworthy first fiction film, which broke formally and narratively with the stereotypical stories of historical films. This film should have been produced in 1985–6 by the previous IMCINE administration. The shoot was prepared, costumes were made, expenses were incurred, and a series of important resources were wasted. Days before shooting was scheduled to begin, the production was cancelled for mysterious reasons. Later, it became known that all the resources of the company had been invested in the production of *El último túnel.* The then director of the state company (the sole producer) was able to abandon the project because it did not suit his interests. This time, IMCINE was only one of twelve co-producers, among them the film-maker himself, who shared duties and responsibilities.

Unlike other, previously important Latin American film countries where production has been almost annihilated by economic crises and neo-liberal politics, 1990–1 were among the best years for Mexican cinema with the release of films including *La leyenda de una máscara, Pueblo de madera; Lola* (1989) and *Danzón* by María Novaro; *La tarea* (1990) and *Intimidades en un cuarto de baño (Intimacies in a Bathroom)* by Jaime Humberto Hermosillo; Carlos Carrera's first feature, *La mujer de Benjamín;* Luis Estrada's *Bandidos;* Juan Mora's *Retorno a Aztlán;* Alberto Cortés's *Ciudad de ciegos* and *Cabeza de Vaca* have found an audience (*Bandidos* may have been the exception) and, in general, they were well received by critics. The same happened at a number of festivals, which welcomed *Rojo amanecer* (exhibited in Mexico the previous year), Dana Rotberg's *Intimidad,* Marysa Sistach's *Los pasos de Ana (Ana's Steps)* and Alfonso Cuarón's *Solo con tu pareja (Only With Your Mate).*

Mexican cinema is going through a stimulating period, as much for its diversity as for its cinematographic qualities. The arrival of new film-makers, film-school graduates, has been important,

Ofelia Medina in *Frida, naturaleza viva* (Paul Leduc, 1984)

as has the emergence of scriptwriters, cinemato-graphers, sound engineers and set designers. What is also noteworthy is that in an environment where only three women were able to become directors in over fifty years of sound cinema, four young women have made their cinematic debuts in a three-year period: Busi Cortés, María Novaro, Marysa Sistach and Dana Rotberg. Similarly, pioneer film-maker Matilde Landeta, whose last film was made in 1951, has been able to make a new feature forty years later: *Nocturno a Rosario (Nocturne for Rosario)*.

As in the previous periods, there have been a good number of new film-makers: fifteen. The difference is that now we can no longer sharply distinguish between those who work for the industry and those who are independent. With the relaxation of the labour union regulations, such distinctions are finished. Similarly, one should not believe that IMCINE is behind all the energy. There are films

produced exclusively by Barbachano Ponce, such as *La tarea* and *Anoche soñé contigo (Yesterday Night I Dreamed of You)*; films produced by co-operatives and working groups, such as *Intimidades en un cuarto de baño, El bulto (The Trick), Nocturno a Rosario*; films made by director-producers, such as *Tequila*, Rubén Gámez's comeback film. Moreover, it is not only the newcomers who make good films; the 'old-timers' are fully active: Jaime Humberto Hermosillo (*La tarea, Intimidades,* and so on), Arturo Ripstein's *La mujer del puerto*, Alfredo Joskowicz's *Playa azul (Blue Beach)* and Jorge Fons's *Rojo amanecer*.

Will this new enterprise be consolidated or will it remain a fine but short-lived moment, another false start? The mechanics and the practices of distribution and exhibition continue to be deficient. In these two areas, policy makers have been timid, and there is a need for a comprehensive study of the market and its multiple audiences. Advertising and promotion need

José Carlos Ruiz (right) in *Los albañiles* (Jorge Fons, 1976)

to become more aggressive (*La leyenda de una máscara,* for example, had a respectable run, but it should have been better). Furthermore, the most appropriate theatres are not always selected and, even when they are, defective projection systems and bad sound do not further the cause of the national cinema.

There is a tendency in Mexico to cut projects short. What will happen when sooner or later the state abandons cinema completely? It is no longer the only player in production, but its presence continues to be significant. Mexican (and Latin American) cinema is already suffering from the disappearance of Televisión Española, which played a fundamental role in the late 80s and early 90s. In the key areas of distribution and exhibition, things look even worse. The sale of the state exhibition chain would be a lethal blow. Will Mexican cinema, this Mexican cinema, be able to consolidate itself or will it be forced to attend its own funeral?

Notes

1. Diego Galán, *Cine español 1896–1983* (Madrid: Ministerio de Cultura, Difusión General de Cinematografía, 1984), pp. 160–1.
2. 'A go go' music referred to 60s rock-derived rhythms such as the twist.
3. Production dropped from 136 (1958), 114 (1959) and 144 films (1960) to 71 (1961), 80 (1962) and 83 (1963).
4. The founders of the group were, in January 1961, José de la Colina, Rafael Corkidi, Salvador Elizondo, Jomí García Ascot, Emilio García Riera, José Luis González de León, Heriberto Lafranchi, Carlos Monsiváis, Julio Pliego, Gabriel Ramírez, José María Sbert and Luis Vicens. Others joined later, such as Armando Bartra, Ismael García Llaca, Paul Leduc, Tomás Pérez Turrent and Juan Manuel Torres.
5. For a better understanding of the film unions, see the essay entitled 'The Studios' in this collection.

6. *Amor, amor, amor* consisted of five mid-length films of 32 mins to 48 mins each: *Una alma pura (A Pure Soul)* by Juan Ibáñez, *Tajimara* by Juan José Gurrola, *Las dos Elenas (The Two Elenas)* by José Luis Ibáñez, *Lola de mi vida (Lola of my Life)* by Miguel Barbachano Ponce and *La sumamita* by Héctor Mendoza.

7. *Arturo Ripstein habla de su cine (con Emilio García Riera)*, (Guadalajara: CIEC/Universidad de Guadalajara), 1988, p. 25.

8. Ariel Zúñiga, *Vasos comunicantes en la obra de Roberto Gavaldón* (Mexico City: El Equilibrista, 1990), p. 273. The most rigorous analysis to date of this director's work.

9. *IX censo general de población*, 1970; Resumen general, Mexico, DF: Dirección General de Estadística, 1972; this document establishes that 75.6% (34,213,821 of 48,225,238 inhabitants) of Mexico's population was under thirty years of age.

10. While 82 films were produced in 1971 and 82 in 1972, there were only 50 in 1973, 54 in 1974, 44 in 1975 and 32 in 1976. Data from *Cineinforme general, 1976* (Mexico City: Banco Nacional Cinematográfico, 26 November, 1976).

11. *Salón Independiente (Independent Salon)* by Rafael Castellanos, Felipe Cazals and Arturo Ripstein, 1970; *Crimen*, 1970; *La belleza*, 1970; *Exorcismo*, 1970; *Autobiografía*, 1971.

12. Christian Zimmer, *Cinéma et politique* (Paris: Cinéma 2000/Seghers, 1974), p. 320.

13. Such rumours were heard then and are still repeated by some of the protagonists today. There is no document that verifies these assertions.

14. *Cineinforme general*, 1976.

15. It is said that Rodolfo Echeverría wanted to purchase the distribution company from the producers. They asked for a high price and the director of the BNC agreed to pay it, but proposed to discount it from what the producers owed the bank. The representatives of these partners blanched, but Echeverría did not dare to carry out this threat. Shortly thereafter, Echeverría himself declared in an interview that he had not followed up on the purchase because the currency had just been devalued and the economic situation was too difficult.

16. Julio Labastida, *Proceso político y dependencia (1970–1976)*, mimeographed document cited by Paola Costa in *La 'apertura' cinematográfica, México 1970–1976* (Puebla: Universidad Autónoma de Puebla, 1988), p. 81.

17. At that time, the CUEC was carried away by leftist myths such as the demand for pervasive politicisation, poor cinema, 'third cinema', rejection of specialised training (the film-maker should be, if needed, director, scriptwriter, cinematographer, sound engineer, producer or whatever was necessary), ideological mobilisation, an excess of meetings and assemblies, and so on. The CCC provided more rigorous technical and professional training.

18. Parity with the US dollar, sustained since 1953, declined to 20.90 pesos per dollar.

19. Costa, *La 'apertura' cinematográfica*, p. 170; Moisés Viñas, Filmografía nacional, Filmoteca UNAM.

20. The term ficheras was applied to prostitutes who frequented second- and third-rate cabarets to dance with customers, receiving a commission for every drink they or their clients consumed. Each time a drink was served, they were given a *ficha* (a token) exchangeable for cash at closing time.

21. *Mojados* is a contraction of the term *espaldas mojadas* (wetbacks) used since the 40s to refer to the illegal Mexican workers who cross the US frontier at the Río Bravo.

22. Data from SOGEM (Sociedad General de Escritores de México).

PART 3: CURRENTS & STRUCTURES

Mythologies

Carlos Monsiváis

Since the 1930 production of the first sound film (*Más fuerte que el deber; Stronger Than Duty,* Raphael J. Sevilla) until the present day, the Mexican film industry has produced some masterpieces and hundreds of significant films; established the existence of a mythical period (the 'golden age' of Mexican cinema); lost its family audience and recaptured it in a different form through television; affirmed nationalism and deformed it to the point of caricature; swung from the morality of the confessional to immorality, and from machismo as the centre of the universe to machismo as a sign of marginality; venerated business and occasionally believed in art; been declared dead on innumerable occasions and heard ritual announcements of its resurrection. Meanwhile, this cinema has gathered a very important dossier about the beliefs and lifestyles of the nation throughout an entire century: its linguistic styles; its ideas of the beautiful, the vulgar and the touristic; its valued and degraded forms of popular culture; the integration and disintegration of traditional morality; and, above all, the privileged position of melodrama, implying a vision of the world through misfortune which is the filmic equivalent of maturity.

Of greater sociological than artistic significance, the film industry had an initial advantage: the confusion and terror invoked by the power of the new technology (the capitulation to the new medium's 'magic') was buttressed by the idealisation of the provinces and the countryside, the admiring condemnations of the city, the exaltation of the patriarchal regime, the transformation of social weaknesses into virtues, and the excessive defence of conservative values.

In Mexico as elsewhere, the US film industry has been the inevitable model. Although the star system, the cult of exceptional faces and personalities and the canonisation of principal figures, was a latecomer here, the industry desired, from the beginning and without pretences, to entertain, creating habits through the reiteration of types of behaviour ('Let's give the audience what it wants because, in the end, it always wants the same thing'). Everything was learned from Hollywood: the treatment of genres, the manipulative use of music, the formulas for emotional blackmail, the stylistic conventions, the hypocritical games with the censors, the advertising techniques, the use of suspense, the contempt for quality scripts, the improvisation by directors and actors.

The founding project of the Mexican cinema was the 'nationalisation' of Hollywood. Although imitation was unavoidable, differences between the two industries abound. For example, certain Hollywood genres were impossible to translate: the screwball comedy, the thriller and, in the last instance, the Western. The melodrama was more important in Mexico than in the USA because, traditionally, Mexican popular culture is premised on the perennial confusion between life and melodrama and the corresponding illusion that suffering, to be more authentic, must be shared publicly. In many cases, there were no Mexican equivalents for specific US environments and moods (for reasons of religion, economics, cultural infrastructure, and so on). The result: the Mexican film industry believed that mere imitation was suicidal (among other reasons because of the lack of financial resources). It was preferable to have intensely local faces, landscapes, and ways of speaking and being within Hollywood-derived cinematic structures. Once the familiar landscapes and sounds were recognised, the audience happily accepted the mechanics of emotional blackmail, the endlessly repeated formulas and the lack of resources which is a sign of poverty as well as an invitation to fantasy (in Mexico, the luxury of super-productions tends to be a figment of the imagination of those who are not distracted by on-screen cardboard castles and 'crowds' of fifteen people).

During the 'golden age' of Mexican cinema (c.1935–55), the public plagiarised the cinema as much as possible: its way of speaking and gesturing, humour, respect of institutions and its typical perception of duties and pleasures were derived from the cinema. In fact, this was a 'golden age' not for the cinema, but for the public, who, among other things, trusted that its idols would explain how to survive in a bewildering age of modernisation. At weekends, families went to the cinema to find and experience entertainment, family unity, honour, 'permissible' sexuality, the beauty of the landscape and customs, and respect for institutions. Devotees of comedies and melodramas were not seeking to 'dream', but to learn skills, to lose inhibitions, to suffer and be consoled in style, painlessly to envy the elites, happily to be resigned to poverty, to laugh at the stereotypes that ridiculed them, to understand how they belonged to the nation. In this school-in-the-dark the people were educated in suffering and relaxation.

Mythologies I: Rural Innocence

In 1936, Fernando de Fuentes's *Allá en el Rancho Grande* gave concrete form to what had already been intuited: the degree to which the country was no longer rural, the increased idealisation of the world of haciendas, ranches and small towns. *Allá en el Rancho Grande* idealised everything: the purity of the maidens, the character of the peasant farmer, the kindness of the hacienda-owners, the perpetual jollity of the fiestas, the advantages of living on the margins of modernity. And the characters, the songs, the *fiesta del rancho,* and the essential kindness of the non-urban were as successful in Mexico as they were in the rest of Latin America. The genre proliferated, generating two idols with a huge popular following, Jorge Negrete and Pedro Infante, and produced comedies and dramas that revolved around the idea of a paradise lost located in an indefinite time where men were strictly male and women definitely female.

Mythologies II: Atmospheres

Which were the mythical environments or ceremonial habits that might allow us to identify the box-office formulas and official limits of the 'golden age'? Here is my list of the principal ones:

- The Mexican *fiesta* filled with *charros* and *chinas poblanas* (folkloric types), mariachis and trios, and fierce women and fighting roosters.
- The fantasy *à la* Broadway where, for example, the Aztec past (thanks to excessive staging impervious to historical authenticity) was Americanised and became a choreographic modernisation of a folkloric dance.
- The cabaret, a moral hell and sensorial heaven, where the 'forbidden' was normalised and where, through vocal styles, slightly heterodox songs were transformed into hymns to dissipation, while tropical orchestras produced the libidinal sounds that would later become popular art.
- The dancehall, Athenian agora of Tenochtitlan, where dance provided a relevant social space for the working class.
- The (preferably rural) cantina was the limit of experience, one of the three locales for suffering (the others were the shadowy churches and the

bedrooms of abandon). In the cantina, the male character was forged and his psychic collapse plotted, fatal resolutions were made, and songs became edicts of self-destruction.
- Ancestral history which, once filmed, became a costume party peppered with primary-school speeches.
- The countryside (the idyllic landscape, the town), the great set design in which primitivism and purity were one and the same.
- The streets and the prostitutes, the site of desolation and sexual utopia in a morally repressive context.
- The brothel, where noble souls were sullied in order to sustain the longing for virginity.
- The *vecindad* (a communal ghetto building), the only form of communal life available to the poor. In order to be representable, it demanded genres featuring the equivalent of Greek choruses: the melodrama, where the neighbourhood equals fatality, and the comedy, where the impossibility of leaving the neighbourhood begins and ends the story.
- Xochimilco and the Tehuantepec isthmus, the lost paradises.
- Jalisco, the eloquent defence of male identity.
- The 'Mexican Gothic' moments: the secularisation of the supernatural which featured ghosts from the viceroyalty, Aztec mummies, wolf men, Huitzilopochtli priests and female vampires.
- The boxing ring, a metaphor of the struggle for life (or, better yet, vice versa).
- The chapel, the priest, the confessional: whispers to designate spirituality, a lowered gaze bestowing the privilege of pronouncing absolute prohibitions.

Mythologies III: The Cinema of the Mexican Revolution

Although, ideologically, the melodrama and its retinue of dangers threatening the real heroine (family unity) are the central national legacy, the most vigorous repertory of nationalist feelings has been evoked by the Revolution, the central national event of the 20th century. The Mexican Revolution genre produced definitions of the epic, archetypes of the male, scenarios of fatality, and a programmatic pictorialism. However, at first, the film-makers had critical intentions. Thus, for example, Fernando de Fuentes's *El compadre Mendoza* (1933) respectfully and lyrically adapted Mauricio Magdaleno's analysis of opportunism, representing it as the only victor of the Revolution. Furthermore, a team featuring Fred Zinnemann (director), Paul Strand (cinematographer), Silvestre Revueltas (music) and Emilio Gómez Muriel (assistant director) produced *Redes* (1934), a state-funded film which exalted physical work as epic class consciousness and the beauty of community sentiments.

The greatest film of the Revolutionary genre was Fernando de Fuentes's *¡Vámonos con Pancho Villa!* (1935), based on Rafael F. Muñoz's magnificent novel about the 'Lions of San Pablo', six peasants who joined the Northern Division only to die, tragically, one by one. In this world of battles and city sieges, prowess becomes a part of everyday life and the Lions, unknown heroes, died heroically in order to fit better into a common grave. Despite the music by the great composer Revueltas (who appears in the film playing the piano), the script by the poet Xavier Villaurrutia, the quality of the acting and the energy of the direction, *¡Vámonos con Pancho Villa!* disappeared from the cinematic horizon for over twenty years (the *Nuevo Cine* critics rediscovered it) and did not inspire any sequels.

Instead, the dominant trend was to metamorphosise the historical movement into a nationalist spectacle filled with trains, *soldaderas,* executions, horse cavalcades, canons, admirable deaths on the portals of Progress, and an indifference to bullets as a sign of faith in the supernatural power of reified historical figures. In dozens of films, this folk-show was headed by the social bandit Pancho Villa and la Coronela, the Revolutionary woman who was his stereotypical complement. The figure of Pancho Villa, the primitive hero, was exploited to the point of delirium. The typical films presented only one enemy (the troops of the dictator Victoriano Huerta), propagated the sermons of Revolutionary idealists, trivialised the specific causes that led to the armed uprising, and focused only on a brief period of the Revolution (1910–17), overlooking the fact that the civil war did not end until 1929. Neither the regime nor the producers were interested in an authentic representation of the Revolution. Its violence was impossible to represent visually. Thus, not even Emilio 'el Indio' Fernández's remarkable Revolutionary films *Flor silvestre* (*Wild Flower*, 1943), *Las abandonadas* (1944), *Enamorada* (1946), were exempt from the prevalent superficiality. The other film-makers used the 1910–17 period to take advantage of the box-office appeal of 'historical' settings and events. This folkloric farce climaxed with *La cucaracha* (*The Cockroach,* 1958) by Ismael Rodríguez, where the armed struggle served only as a pretext for the histrionic duels of the sacred monsters of the Mexican cinema: María Félix and Dolores del Río, Pedro Armendáriz and 'el Indio' Fernández. Later, a series of films featured María Félix as the only salvageable Revolutionary character (the woman with the psyche of a cacique): *La bandida* (1962), *La Valentina* (1965), *Juana Gallo* (1960), and *La generala* (*The Female General,* 1970).

Despite everything, there were important accounts of the Revolutionary phenomenon. For example, the following films shared a clear demystificatory impulse: Matilde Landeta's *La Negra Angustias* (*Angustias the Black,* 1949), Julio Bracho's *La sombra del caudillo* (*The Shadow of the Caudillo,* 1960), José Bolaños's *La soldadera* (1966), Paul Leduc's *Reed: México insurgente* (1971) and Carlos Enrique Taboada's *La guerra santa* (*The Holy War,* 1977). In *La Negra Angustias,* Landeta 'betrays' the source novel and, rather than end with the image of a defeated Revolutionary *coronela* serving her husband and master a meal, the *coronela* Angustias is shown throwing herself into the whirlwind of Revolutionary action. In *La sombra del caudillo,* based on Martín Luis Guzmán's exceptional novel, the Revolution is but a power struggle without ideals. In *La soldadera,* the armed struggle loses its folkloric qualities to display its quotidian side: dust, fatigue, treason, uncertainty, heroism without ideals, ideals that cannot be verbally communicated, the suicidal courage that is nothing but a lack of alternatives. In *Reed,* the adaptation of *Insurgent Mexico,* the Revolution is a man's voyage through a chaos where motives are shipwrecked and cruelty provides the only rationale. Lastly, *La guerra santa* examines, almost for the first time, the Cristero Rebellion (1926–9) led by Catholic bishops and its fanaticism, brutality and devastating faith.

Mythology IV: The Family Melodrama ('As soon as I said I loved her, the priest appeared to read the bans')

In the first half of the 20th century, morality was what the church, family, state and society accepted. Immorality was what lay outside their domain. The melodrama seemed to be an excellent vehicle for securing the hegemony of traditional values. However, the ghosts of disunity also circulated among the familiar melodramatic sets and sounds: honour, adultery, separation. Before the essential message of all cinema was clearly understood (that is to say, the irrefutable power of modern life), the film industry exalted the repression of instincts in favour of moral servitude (with one great exception: Arcady Boytler's *La mujer del puerto,* 1933, and its treatment of incest).

María Félix in *Enamorada* (Emilio Fernández, 1946)

In the cinema, the traditional moral values (religious dogmatism and patriarchal submission) lost one of their principal rhetorical tools: the physical proximity that was the key to its power in the theatre. The close-up exalts, the mid-length shot hierarchises. The camera can assume the point of view of an outraged mainstream society or of redemptory marginality. According to how a close-up of a distraught face is photographed, we can tell whether its subject will be condemned or pardoned. In this cinema, an arched eyebrow or a certain tone of voice communicated the desperate submission to God's will (the same as 'blind destiny' or patriarchal insolence).

The cinema established a pact with the spectator: I shall praise the convictions that you claim to have if you accept that all your actions must be measured according to the presence or absence of cinematographic intensity. After some years, the

convictions were diluted or relativised, images cancelled the theoretical certainties and what was applauded refuted what had been previously believed. What is more important: liturgy or practice? A procession is dazzling; the staging of the familiar orthodoxy is depressing. Neither the vertigo of editing nor the star system tolerated the preaching for very long, and any reprimand lasting longer than one minute became unacceptable. When transmitted technologically, the ancestral messages were modified: darkness hid the physical response of the spectators, the screen magnified the offerings of sin. In the 'golden age' of Mexican cinema, the reproachful litanies were gradually shortened and what for one generation had been 'catastrophes of the soul' (the unspeakable evil of prostitution, the tragedy of adultery and the shatter-ing loss of virginity) became humorous episodes for the next.

If you sell your body, reserve your soul. As the

appeal of women's weakness and fragility wore off, other traits proliferated: a panoply of desirable bodies and complimentary faces, the substitution of angelic behaviour for the pleasures of woman-as-object, women who already knew how to exercise control. The well-known slogans persisted (for a married woman, monogamy is the only guarantee of your existence; for a single woman, your honour is your only justification; for the prostitute, tragedy is your punishment and your only chance for glory; for the daughter, in your hymen I have deposited my honour and your future), but the ability to move audiences eroded quickly.

The renovated moral mythology was centred on the sinner, the prostitute, the *demi-mondaine,* the devourer; a new morality was presented through the aegis of 'the woman who has lost her scruples and her virginal fragrance'. The representation of the prostitute staged the potential of desire and affirmed the degraded institution that protects the family. 'Let's canonise the whores', was the famous statement made by the poet Jaime Sabines. From *Santa* (1931) to *Amor a la vuelta de la esquina* (*Love Around the Corner,* 1985) and throughout the century that preceded the condom, the film-prostitute volubly responded to the idealisms of popular culture. She was brutally attractive, vain, given to sacrifice, enamoured of revenge and, at party-time, able to perform all the variants of copulation. In a way, each choreographed shake of Ninón Sevilla's *rumbera* hips could be analysed through Eisenstein's theory of metonym: *pars pro toto,* the part for the whole. Like Eisenstein's example of the eyeglasses in *Battleship Potemkin,* the isolated object which stands in for the end of authoritarianism, each of Ninón Sevilla's movements stands in for all the couplings prohibited by the censors. In *Aventurera* (1949), *Sensualidad* (1950), *Aventura en Río* (1952), *Revancha* (*Revenge,* 1948) and *Víctimas del pecado* (*Victims of Sin,* 1950), Ninón was the vamp who could not be represented in the 20s and the apotheosis of the mistress, the lover who does not confer respectability but gives prestige: 'I would not introduce her to my mother, but I want all my friends to know'.

Mythology V: Dolores del Río and María Félix

The Mexican film industry imitated Hollywood as much as possible, except in the area of the representation of women. With few exceptions, machismo ignored the feminine point of view. Women were looked at with scorn, affection, veneration or lust, but until very recently, they were never able to look for themselves. Women were never

Ninón Sevilla in *Aventurera* (Alberto Gout, 1950)

on the other side of the camera, and spectators, consciously or unconsciously, mechanically integrated woman into the landscape and believed that she could not be individualised. The 'golden age' of Mexican cinema had few independent female characters equivalent to those played in Hollywood by Katherine Hepburn, Rosalind Russell, Joan Crawford, Ginger Rogers or Jean Arthur. In *La mujer del puerto* (Arcady Boytler, 1933), Andrea Palma was transformed into a tropical Marlene Dietrich through the 'surgery' of lights, shadows and make-up, but she was an ambiguous character because of her aloofness, her out-of-context glamour, and the aura of sin that surrounds her like a second skin. But at that time, the audience would not have accepted women with unpredictable reactions, preferring rather heroines with well-defined virtues, fragile paragons of virtue, happy when crying, sad because resisting seduction contradicts the female spirit.

The beautiful and intangible Dolores del Río was the victim *par excellence,* so dazzling that she had to be humiliated so as not to offend. In her Mexican filmography, Dolores lacked will-power: *Flor silvestre,*

121

Dolores del Río in *Las abandonadas* (Emilio Fernández, 1944)

María Candelaria (both 1943), *Bugambilia, Las abandonadas* (both 1944), *La selva de fuego* (1945), *La otra* (1946), *La malquerida, La casa chica, Deseada* (all 1949) and *La cucaracha* (1958). She was the supreme form, but the meaning of her existence lay in other hands. Only María Félix constructed her powerful aura by plumbing the mysteries of her femininity. Félix's attitude, her imperious tone that subjugated and belied the assigned roles, her categorical voice and enslaving gestures undercut the humiliations demanded by the scripts. María Félix's

character began her apogee in Fernando de Fuentes's *Doña Bárbara* (1943), based on the Rómulo Gallegos novel, when she took on the traits of the *cacique* and renounced feminine psychology. She became something unheard of: a woman who controlled her destiny. The process was so dynamic that spectators still remember Doña Bárbara, the mistress of the plains, and have forgotten all about Santos Lizardo, the presumed victorious bearer of civilisation so languidly represented by Julián Soler.

María Félix and Dolores del Río are persistent

myths because, first and last, they personified dazzling and enduring beauty. Del Río played a woman who enslaved without mercy only once in her career (*Doña Perfecta,* Alejandro Galindo, 1950). In all her other melodramas (such as *La otra,* 1946; *La casa chica,* 1949; *La selva de fuego,* 1945, and *El niño y la niebla,* 1953), she communicated only a sense of defeated dignity and subordinated desire. María Félix, on the other hand, imposed upon her characters the strength of her personality, the luxury and security conferred by beauty when it is used to exercise the desire to control.

Mythology VI: Cultural Nationalism (Where the Regions of the Country are Equivalent to Astrological Signs)

Perhaps Mexican cinema's most emphatic myth was cultural nationalism, or, in other words, the idea that we find in countless movies: Mexico is a unique country whose powerful characteristics totally shape the mentality of its children. According to this catalogue of virtues and obligatory defects, the Mexican man was alternatively and simultaneously brave, generous, cruel, rakish, romantic, obscene, able to make the greatest sacrifice, family-oriented, and a friend until death. The Mexican woman was obedient, seductive, resigned, servile, devoted to her family, and enslaved to her children.

Since the early days of sound cinema, the industry assumed the programmatic duty of making local colour and folkloricism its ideological axis (in this instance, it was faithful to the chauvinistic Hollywood model). Stylistically, cultural nationalism was well represented by the extraordinary films directed by Emilio 'el Indio' Fernández between 1943 and 1950. Fernández's magnificent cinematic sequences equated his supremely cherished notion of *mexicanidad* (Mexicanness) with the great artistic achievements of his lyrical impulses, Gabriel Figueroa's admirable cinematography, and great actors: Dolores del Río, María Félix, Pedro Armendáriz, Columba Domínguez, Roberto Cañedo and Carlos López Moctezuma. With hindsight, we can see that these 'atavistic feasts' transcended anachronisms and demagogy because of their social conviction, aesthetic vigour and their representations of habits, tastes, traditions, landscapes, faces and songs.

Among the great films of 'el Indio' Fernández, we must cite *Flor silvestre* and *María Candelaria* (both 1943), *Enamorada* (1946), *Las abandonadas* (1944), *Salón México* (1948), *Río Escondido* (1947), *Pueblerina* (1948), *Víctimas del pecado* and *Islas*

Marías (both 1950) and *La malquerida* (1949). Of these films, only *Salón México* and *Víctimas del pecado* were set in the city, among the lights and shadows of prostitution and crime (which is an extension of impotence). In the others, the setting is an atemporal time on the margins of the Revolution; *mexicanidad* was the redemptive destruction and the legendary origin of the vibrant images. Everything was a symbol and everything was also literal. But for these rather limited exceptions, cultural nationalism was from the start a fertile terrain for involuntary humour as well as an unparalleled stimulant for a marginal society devastated by poverty and disinformation.

Mythologies VII: Mario Moreno 'Cantinflas'

In the 30s, the comedian Mario Moreno 'Cantinflas' was a revelation. Everything about him was novel: the humour, the mimicry, his gentleness and the irreverence of the *peladito* (urban pariah), which appeared in films considered extraordinarily entertaining upon their release: *Ahí está el detalle* (1940), *El gendarme desconocido* (1941), *Ni sangre ni arena* (1941), *El signo de la muerte* (1939).

His first film audiences admired Cantinflas's way of being and style. He stalked those around him, baffled them with linguistic excess and confused them with an acoustic deluge. The nation united around his character: the bourgeoisie, the middle class and the popular classes were entertained by the new social practice of *cantinflismo:* the art of saying much without communicating. Cantinflas's facial and verbal contortions were both mimicry and labyrinth: the eyebrows questioned, the arms resigned themselves, and the body was led astray by the autonomous power of verbs, nouns and adjectives. Although nonsensical, Cantinflas's infinite verbosity revealed a tactic: the onslaught of absurdities liberated us from the prison house of language. Intellectuals associated Cantinflas with the parody of the demagogical 'Revolutionary' style and grudgingly admitted that a pariah could be amusing when he had no other choice but to amuse.

The transition from the theatre to the cinema gave Cantinflas an aura that allowed him to become a myth. This myth persists despite the subsequent development of his *pelado* character. The early Cantinflas (in shorts, *Aguila o so,* 1937; *El signo de la muerte,* 1939) was visibly ill at ease because he did not fully control the medium and occasionally alleviated his discomfort by presenting cleaned-up versions of theatrical sketches. In the popular theatre where Cantinflas had learned his craft, comedians used verbal excess to neutralise their incursions into the realms of the 'forbidden' and of sexual allusions. In the cinema, censorship eliminated the double or triple *entendres* and Cantinflas replaced them with prefabricated jokes. But his successful sequences, when the famous combination of raised eyebrows and maddening words worked, transformed Cantinflas into a conditioned reflex for audiences: they laughed as soon as he appeared on the screen. Itself somewhat uncomfortable with grammar and its mastery of Spanish, the audience wanted to identify with his liberalisation of the language: for a while, *cantinflismo* was the surest path to eloquence.

Mythologies VIII: Dividing the Representative Functions

The Mexican cinema audience was formed by the genres (the melodrama variants, the country comedy, the Revolutionary films, the urban comedy, nostalgia for the Porfirio Díaz regime, the *rumbera* films, the adventuress films) and sustained by its addiction to larger-than-life figures; archetypes; endless stereotypes; privileged bodies and faces; 'common everyday' features which could be a neighbour's, a relative's or one's own; and 'idols', who gave rise to lay adoration. Each idol played a specific role. Thus, for example, Pedro Armendáriz and Dolores del Río evoked the apogee of rural society; between severity and tears, Fernando Soler and Sara García embodied the ideal Father and Mother and became synonymous with the burdens and ruses of patriarchy and matriarchy. While 'nationalising' the Hollywood cinema, the singer/actor Jorge Negrete was entrusted with a musical nationalist character who offered audiences a complete repertoire of behaviour patterns. Arrogant, self-assured, always about to break into song (a *ranchera* aria) or into a fight, Negrete was The Singing *Charro*, a macho who expressed himself through chauvinism and haughtiness. Even the titles of Negrete's films suggest this mix of native pride and commercial promotion: *¡Ay Jalisco, no te rajes!* (*Hey Jalisco, Don't Quit Now!*, 1941), *Así se quiere en Jalisco* (*This is How we Love in Jalisco,* 1942), *No basta ser charro* (*Being Charro is Not Enough,* 1945), *Me he de comer esa tuna* (*I Must Eat that Prickly Pear,* 1944), *El ahijado de la muerte* (*The Godchild of Death,* 1946). Throughout Latin America, the *charro* character was considered an amusing invention that synthesised a way of life or, at the very least, the essence of a collective psyche. Negrete sang: 'I am Mexican/ My land is brave/ I give you my macho word that there is no land/ more beautiful or courageous than mine', and audiences

admired without reservation what was, in the last instance, essentially parodic.

Among the committed comedians, Joaquín Pardavé and Germán Valdés 'Tin Tan' have recently been elevated to the status of mythic figures. Pardavé began in vaudeville and was also a composer, scriptwriter and director: he is the perfect example of how Mexican cinema capitalized on theatrical traditions. Pardavé was a master of timing, and his scenic resourcefulness overcame the stiffness of directors who refused to move the camera. Tin Tan was the *pachuco,* the transcultured one who uses Spanglish without guilt, and the first truly cinematic comedian of the Mexican industry. Tin Tan and Pardavé were not critically appreciated in their lifetimes; they were considered of 'local' interest only in contrast to Cantinflas's 'universal' appeal (which fell flat in his two 'international' films, Michael Anderson's *Around the World in 80 Days,* 1955, and George Sidney's *Pepe,* 1960). However, despite the necessary national character of their comedy (so linguistically innovative in Tin Tan's case) and the unevenness of their filmographies, neither Tin Tan's nor Pardavé's style has aged. They are evidence of an ingenuity and talent that overcame the medium's own lack of a real sense of humour.

Mythologies IX: The Children of the *Arrabal* (Ghetto)

In 1947, Ismael Rodríguez's *Nosotros los pobres (We the Poor)* was a great popular celebration. In the theatre, the audience's tears and laughter (community acts) prolonged the events of the film, which had a year-long first run. The audience could forget its own economic woes with the discovery that so many shared its own misfortune. *Nosotros los pobres,* the most successful film in the history of Mexican cinema, was an out-of-control melodrama. It was centred on an equilibrium between a surplus of good intentions and the lack of money which led audiences to identify with the domestic roots of the tragi-comedy. The paradox of 'laughing through one's tears' was sustained by songs, extreme situations, the formation and separation of the classic couple, characters so monstrous that they smoked marijuana, heroes and heroines who courted bad luck, the existence of dignified poverty among the lumpen proletariat.

Nosotros los pobres was the pinnacle of the *arrabal* genre, produced by combining the neighbourhoods of survival and marginality. In the mythology of the Mexican cinema, the *arrabal* was the zone of reconciliation between heaven and hell, between extreme purity and degradation. To the public who had to be emotionally engaged in order not to be disappointed ('If you are not grieving, you are not watching me'), the central couple of Pepe el Toro and la Chorreada (Pedro Infante and Blanca Estela Pavón) represented a great utopia. They cried, sang duets, went from tragedy to tragedy as if moving from room to room, laughed at naive jokes, suffered mishaps that they later invoked with affection, and rejected desperation in order not to offend the Lord. 'Cleaned up' by the censors and rooted in visions of suffering, the plot of *Nosotros los pobres* was in and of itself a genre, defined by heavenly virtues and unspeakable evils. Its subterranean theme was the (fragmentary) assimilation into the large cities. Who could tire of learning about that? Who was not forced to encounter these people daily? Pedro Infante, the supreme myth of Mexican cinema, was the handsome young singer who best represented these multiple crossings: from the rural to the urban, from the machismo of the caudillo to a machismo able to cry, from the arrogant generosity of the social bandit to the sympathy of the humble carpenter. As the uninterrupted cult of Pedro Infante demonstrates, for the Mexican audience this actor-singer has been a bridge of understanding between the old and the new: his biography is the ideal of the collective.

In the 40s and 50s, the *arrabal* was the thematic axis linking the public with its inevitable destiny: modernity. And, in a way, the symbolic location of resignation, anachronism, and the escape towards Progress was the neighbourhood dwelling, the temple of urban poverty whose great drama was divided into complementary small episodes: the alcoholic who mistreats his wife; the paralysed woman who feels that she is too heavy a burden on her family; the young, flirtatious woman who drowns in misery and climbs out of her rut by using her body as a ladder; the good son who would give anything to avoid the psychological collapse of his father ... The everyday places alternated with a succession of deserted streets, overcrowded cabarets and boxing rings where the fighter triumphs hours before he gives himself up to alcohol and the fear of success. Director Alejandro Galindo was the great chronicler of this mythology in *Campeón sin corona* (*Champion Without a Crown*, 1945), *¡Esquina ... bajan!* (*Corner Stop! All Descend!*, 1948), *Los Fernández de Peralvillo* (*The Fernández's from Peralvillo*, 1953) and *Cuatro contra el mundo* (*Four Against the World*, 1949).

In the late 70s, the idyllic neighbourhood is as absurd a notion as the happy provinces. If the provinces, synonymous with the nation, were endlessly demystified (especially in the theatre), why not expose the sordid nature of urban poverty? Luis Buñuel hated the saccharine treatment of poor characters and *Los olvidados* (1950) was the artistic rendition of his claim. But the *arrabal* cinema was not interested in verisimilar psychology, the oneiric play of characters or, of course, an authentic moral dimension. The rules of the ghetto were the only thing that counted: the monopolisers of tears and suffering amused themselves with the endless economic and existential vicissitudes of those who, at least, physically resembled them.

Mythologies X: Exceptional Moments

How was Mexican cinema's canon established? While awaiting a detailed analysis, a provisional answer must take into account national and international critics (especially those of the 60s, much influenced by the auteur theory), audience preferences as manifested through attendance patterns (and, later, through television), and the collective memory that chooses, over and over again, in written or spoken form, a certain number of memorable films, directors, extraordinary sequences, actors, phrases, and so on. This canon has privileged the films of Luis Buñuel (*Los olvidados*, 1950; *El*, 1952; *La ilusión viaja en tranvía*, 1953; *Subida al cielo*, 1951; *Ensayo de un crimen*, 1955; *Viridiana*, 1961; *El ángel exterminador*, 1962); Emilio Fernández's nationalist paeans; Alejandro Galindo's urban chronicles; Roberto Gavaldón's melodramas combining delirium with austerity (*La barraca*, 1944; *Rosauro Castro*, 1950; *La noche avanza*, 1951); Fernando de Fuentes's first period; some isolated films by Alberto Gout, Fernando Méndez, Arcady Boytler. And the parade of comedians, dramatic actors, stellar figures, secondary actors ... and the great sequences of the cinematographers (Gabriel Figueroa, 'Jack' Draper, Alex Phillips) ... and scenic settings which are the visual legacy of the lost nation and a capital city disfigured to the point of macrocephaly.

All of this has intervened in the canon with mythological energy and problematised the position of the films made between 1964 and 1991, although there is a critical consensus that highlights a group of film-makers: Rubén Gámez (*La fórmula secreta*, 1964); Arturo Ripstein (*El lugar sin límites*, 1977; *Cadena perpetua*, 1978); Felipe Cazals (*Canoa*, 1975; *Las poquianchis*, 1976); Alberto Isaac (*El rincón de las vírgenes*, 1972); Jaime Humberto Hermosillo (*El cumpleaños del perro*, 1974; *Matinée*, 1976; *Doña Herlinda y su hijo*, 1984; *La tarea*, 1990); Jorge Fons (the *Caridad* episode in *Fe, esperanza y caridad*, 1972;

Allá en el Rancho Grande (Fernando de Fuentes, 1936)

Rojo amanecer, 1989) and, more recently, María Novaro, Alberto Cortés, Diego López, Dana Rotberg, Gabriel Retes ... The canon is slowly being renewed, while the old myths continue to exercise their power.

Mythology XI: The Availability of the Audience

Although the cinema has seduced audiences throughout the world, the Latin American variant of this appeal has been culturally determined by the high proportion of functional and complete illiteracy in the population. Given this order of things, the catalogue where everything is popular (because 'Mexico is a popular nation') is headed by the certainty of the box-office: 'The audience is like this and cannot nor should be any other way because we, directors, actors, scriptwriters, are also part of the audience.' For more than three decades, spectators accepted what was given so as not to be considered pretentious or traitors to their people. To do them photographic and dramatic justice, films were filled with tearful mothers overwhelmed by self-pity; prostitutes who simultaneously reached redemption and agony; priests who led their lives with the subtlety of traffic signals; severe patriarchs who served as God's ambassadors over the dessert table; policemen as good as sliced bread; gangsters who were once sergeants; families who suffered because no one told them in time about the separation of body and soul; the leading men, actors and comedians whose appeal was based on their resemblance to spectators; the Revolutionaries who dug their own graves without measuring. Unwillingly satirical, wilfully funny and sentimental, occasionally epic, surprisingly tragic, the repertory of three decades of Mexican cinema exhibited central myths and adjacent legends and sketched a portrait of a people: generous, prejudiced, and more emotional than rational; pious and fanatic; an enemy of bigotry and more liberal than it seemed; inhibited by the Lord and Master and all Lords in general; candid, as rebellious as possible, an enthusiast of the memorised joke, and always looking for amusement wherever it could be found.

Between 1935 and 1955 (as always, approximately) this cinema, more than any other cultural form, modernised tastes and prejudices and refashioned the idea of the nation by transforming nationalism into a big spectacle. With great grandiloquence and make-believe mourning, the cinema put to rest various inoperative (pre-modern) traditions and welcomed with laughter and verbal scoldings that which a selective and sectorial modernisation already demanded. Without any possible innocence and having lost faith in the possibility of an egalitarian encounter between audiences and the industry, some recent films have proven victorious against censorship, have introduced (or pretended to) more complex themes, have tried to identify how things are, have broken with the cycle of tradition and homophobia, have communicated feminist ideas. However, as we see it, they still have not reached the depth of that earlier cinema whose great mythologies always had a profound reason for being.

The Impact of *Rancho Grande*

Emilio García Riera

According to José María Sánchez García, 1936 was

> the year of the great crisis, when some even feared that the national cinema would disappear, because Spanish-speaking audiences, Mexican as well as foreign, were rejecting Mexican films. Many previously flourishing production companies folded and only a few poorly capitalised private companies remained afloat, hoping for better times. Then came the film that saved the industry from imminent ruin and proved that we were capable of producing quality cinema in Mexico: *Allá en el Rancho Grande*.[1]

The Franco uprising and the subsequent civil war reduced Spain's 1936 cinematographic production to nineteen films, many of which were never finished or premiered. In Argentina, fifteen films were made, only two more than in the previous year. As a result, Mexico recaptured first place in the production of Spanish-language films, even though it made only twenty-four films, just two more than in 1935, more than half of them being family melodramas. The small producers, impressed by the commercial success of Juan Orol's *Madre querida* (*Mother Dear,* 1935), inundated the screens with fanatically altruistic mothers and wives, fickle lovers and woebegone children, but only Orol, it seemed, possessed the formula for success: a combination of naivety, brashness and box-office intuition. In such a vale of tears, with mothers, children and movie producers joining together in one great sob, Fernando de Fuentes's ranch melodrama, *Allá en el Rancho Grande (Over on the Big Ranch),* demonstrated something that today seems obvious:

> what the public wanted from Mexican cinema were Mexican films, that is, the representation of a very characteristic national colour. If it took so long to arrive at this conclusion, it was, of course, because of the obligation to refute the denigrated and stereotyped Hollywood image of Mexico as a land of simple-minded, wild natives.

The enormous success of *Rancho Grande* derived precisely from the foreign markets, starting with the Spanish-speaking American audience, which was already accustomed to Hollywood's vision of the Mexican. The star of the film, tenor Tito Guízar, was a newcomer to his country's cinema but had already achieved a degree of fame in the USA. He had a virtuous image as a singing Latin lover and would always be more popular in the rest of America than in Mexico. *Rancho Grande* generated a good though unexceptional income in the domestic market. What was exceptional was its foreign earnings in what could be called the 'natural' markets of Mexican cinema. Thus *Rancho* guaranteed the foundations necessary for Mexican cinema to develop into a real industry, while becoming the first Mexican film to win an international prize: the award for cinematography granted to Gabriel Figueroa[2] at the 1938 Venice Festival held in Benito Mussolini's fascist Italy. Furthermore, in 1938 *Allá en el Rancho Grande* was the first completely Mexican film deemed worthy of subtitling in the USA, where it consequently reached an audience considerably larger than the Spanish-speakers. Before *Rancho Grande,* only *Redes* (*Nets,* a sort of co-production released in 1936) had been subtitled for a US release.

However, Fernando de Fuentes did not have any illusions. According to Hugo del Mar, the huge success of *Rancho Grande* did not stop the film-maker from believing that his *¡Vámonos con Pancho Villa!* (*Let's Go with Pancho Villa!,* 1935) was superior.[3] He knew that the folkloric aspects of *Rancho Grande* were merely embellishments of a standard melodramatic plot. His friend Juan Bustillo Oro must have spoken with full knowledge of the facts, when he wrote, many years later:

> Fernando de Fuentes took on a project with modest ambitions, *Allá en el Rancho Grande,* without suspecting that he was initiating the great expansion of our industry. He was virtually forced to do it, compelled by scarce resources, but he did so with the same enthusiasm that he put into all of his work. The plot was nothing new. It was basically the same as *En la hacienda (On the Ranch)* …, divested of that almost tragic air and lightened by our popular music and by the humorous touches at which Antonio Guzmán Aguilera was a master.[4]

Produced by Germán Camus and directed by

Lupe Vélez and Arturo de Córdova in *La zandunga* (Fernando de Fuentes, 1937)

Ernesto Vollrath, *En la hacienda* (1921) was based on a zarzuela (Spanish comedy/operetta) by the Jaliscan Federico Carlos Kegel who had used the very same name, *Rancho Grande,* as an alternative title for his piece. The film was apparently one of the few successful Mexican silent films. Its plot culminated with the attempted rape of a young indigenous woman (Elena Sánchez Valenzuela) by the ranch-owner's son (Luis Rosas), and the would-be rapist's justified death at the hands of the peon (Guillermo Hernández Gómez) who was engaged to the young woman. There is certainly a resemblance between this plot and that of *Rancho Grande,* but the storyline of Fernando de Fuentes's film was also similar to the less tragic *Nobleza baturra* (*Aragonian Gallantry,* 1935). This Spanish box-office hit directed by Florián Rey and starring Imperio Argentina had premiered in Mexico City in February 1936; that is, in time for the screenwriters of *Allá en el Rancho*

Grande to have been inspired by it. *Nobleza baturra* was the second version of another film directed by Joaquín Dicenta Jr in collaboration with Juan Vilá Vilamala in 1925. Dicenta, the author of the original play, wrote the script expressly for the cinema. The film, an apologia for rural life in Aragon, was one of the biggest successes of Spain's silent cinema. At the same time, Dicenta must have been inspired by Humberto Cairo's film *Nobleza gaucha* (*Gaucho Gallantry,* 1915), which was an enormous triumph for the Argentine silent cinema and had been shown in Spain. Both of the *Noblezas, gaucha* as well as *baturra,*[5] dealt with the same basic conflict as *Rancho Grande:* a rancher threatens the honour of a peasant girl loved by a young and noble gaucho, farmhand or foreman.

This unusual chain of sensational box-office hits manufactured by the far from vigorous film industries of the three principal Spanish-speaking countries could not have been accidental. Until then, these film industries had not known how to win public acclaim. I repeat, this confluence could not have been accidental because *En la hacienda,* as much as the *Noblezas* and *Rancho Grande,* resorted to the same thematic formula that combined the overthrow of the traditional right of *pernada* (which gave landowners sexual access to peasant women) with an emphasis on local colour. I imagine that this must have been very compelling for all those viewers who lived in rural areas or had rural family backgrounds and who comprised the majority of the population in Mexico, Argentina, Spain and the other Spanish-speaking countries at that time. However, de Fuentes himself, a man of urban culture and tastes, must have been surprised by the force of something that, from his perspective, had nothing to do with cinematographic art, but which changed the course of his career. The success of *Rancho Grande* encouraged the businessman de Fuentes, while the other de Fuentes, the admirer of Murnau, may have been discouraged by the economic failure of his favourite film, *¡Vámonos con Pancho Villa!*

Even before the premiere of *¡Vámonos con Pancho Villa!,* its production company Clasa (directed by Alberto R. Pani) was in the throes of reorganisation. In March 1936, Salvador Elizondo replaced the Frenchman Paul Castelain as manager of the company and the following month another film directed by Fernando de Fuentes went into production: *Las mujeres mandan (Women in Command).* President Lázaro Cárdenas, whose government decreed that same year that Mexican film producers would be exempted from the 6% revenue tax, attended the last day of filming of *Las mujeres mandan,* demonstrating his personal interest in the future of Clasa. However, the company's second picture was not commercially successful when it was finally released, like the first one, after considerable delay. Salvador Elizondo left Clasa soon after when he was named Mexican consul in Berlin. So there was a double contrast between de Fuentes's and Clasa's government-backed economic failure with the subsequent success of *Allá en el Rancho Grande,* which premiered in late 1936 and, by itself, could not change the gloomy panorama of Mexican production filled with exalted mothers and vituperous tramps.

1936 was barely noteworthy for Cantinflas's lacklustre debut, the proliferation of bullfighter-actors (Pepe Ortíz, Jesús Solórzano, Lorenzo Garza), José Bohr's *Marihuana* and for the governing Partido Nacionalista Revolucionario's attempt to participate

in film production, starting with *Judas.* Directed by Manuel R. Ojeda, *Judas* should have launched the production plans referred to by Marco Aurelio Galindo in *El Universal:* 'We have been assured that the PNR is prepared to contribute the sum of one million pesos for the development of the local film industry, and will float loans to co-operatives that make films with revolutionary themes.'[6] In effect, *Judas*'s message was revolutionary and agrarianist and, given the success of *Rancho Grande,* its box-office failure was as startling as that of *¡Vámonos con Pancho Villa!,* although much more understandable, since Ojeda was no de Fuentes. *Rancho Grande*'s plot, although set in the present, not only completely ignored the much-promoted agrarian reforms of the Cárdenas *sexenio,* but also professed openly reactionary sentiments. Thus, the official efforts to promote the cinema (the support of Clasa and the unsuccessful experience of the PNR) stumbled upon a public that yearned for idyllic, utopian ranches and which had given an enthusiastic reception to *Rancho Grande* ever since its première in the elegant Alameda theatre, opened in 1936 by magnate Emilio Azcárraga. The Alameda, whose main attraction was a ceiling that simulated a starry sky to make spectators feel they were outdoors, celebrated its recent opening with Gabriel Soria's *Mater nostra* in April of that year in its own way by catching fire soon after the première of *Allá en el Rancho Grande,* which had to be moved to the Balmori theatre. However, the damage was slight and the Alameda was soon functioning again.

Forty-six years later, another much more serious fire would destroy the Cineteca Nacional. Among the many materials lost in that fire were a number of films handed over by the Secretary of Public Education (SEP) only a few months earlier. The films had not yet been examined and we will never know which films these were. Perhaps this nitrate-based and hence very flammable material was part of what had been collected in the Filmoteca Nacional of the SEP established in 1936 (even earlier than the Cinémathèque française, commonly believed to be the oldest film archive in the world). The founder of that pioneering Filmoteca and apparently the victim of the same official negligence that led to the destruction of the Cineteca in 1982, was Elena Sánchez Valenzuela, the protagonist of the first *Santa* and other Mexican silent films, who had also been a film critic in the 30s for the newspaper *El Día* (unrelated to the present newspaper of the same name).

In January 1936 the Unión de Directores

Cinematográficos de México was founded with a provisional board consisting of Fernando de Fuentes (president), Gabriel Soria (secretary) and Juan Bustillo Oro. At first, the union had twenty-five members: the three mentioned above plus Arcady Boytler, Rafael E. Portas, Ramón Peón, Juan Orol, Guillermo Calles, Carlos Navarro, Raphael J. Sevilla, Miguel Contreras Torres, Boris Maicon, Miguel Zacarías, Rubén C. Navarro, Manuel R. Ojeda, José Bohr, Chano Urueta, Manuel Sánchez Valtierra, Carlos Amador, Adolfo Best Maugard, Alex Phillips, Roberto Curwood, Gustavo Sáenz de Sicilia, Rolando Aguilar and Roberto Montenegro.

1937

While the Spanish and the USA's Spanish-language cinemas practically disappeared from the market, the Mexican and Argentine cinemas made spectacular quantitative gains in 1937. Mexico produced 38 fiction features as compared to 25 the previous year, while Argentina produced 28 as compared to 15 in 1936. Thus began a fierce competition for the Latin American markets: from the start, Mexico would appropriate most of them. Mexican films proved to be much more to the liking of the Latin American masses than the Argentine ones, despite the fact that the latter were the product of a technically and industrially better-developed cinema which already boasted some very popular stars (especially Libertad Lamarque). But the Argentine films almost always seemed to be a European by-product, while the Mexican ones, in spite of their primitivism, perhaps because of it, enjoyed the prestige of authenticity granted by the presentation of even the most adulterated folklore.

The lesson of *Allá en el Rancho Grande* was clear: of the 38 Mexican films produced in 1937, over half were folkloric or nationalistic glorifications. The public continued to adore the selfless mothers and to vilify the unfaithful women, but both became more attractive when embellished with additional characteristics: humble origins, big peasant-style skirts and hair bows, and virile field workers as mates. Of these latter characters, Tito Guízar excited other Latin American audiences more intensely than Mexico's, who found Jorge Negrete, a 1937 newcomer, a much more convincing incarnation of the arrogant, gutsy, mustachioed macho.

However, Mexican cinema was quite justifiably anxious about its lack of celebrities. At the time, neither Cantinflas, Arturo de Córdova nor Pedro Armendáriz stood out from the morass of undistinguished actors. As far as the actresses were concerned, the prospects were even grimmer. Despite the fact that the popularity of Dolores del Río and Lupe Vélez had declined in Hollywood, the national cinema longed to attract the two most famous Mexican actresses of the time. Fernando de Fuentes was obliged to equal or surpass his success with *Rancho Grande* and, thanks to producer Pedro A. Calderón, apparently accomplished the task when he managed to get Lupe Vélez to return to her homeland to play the leading role in *La Zandunga*. Unfortunately, neither the movie nor its star achieved the sought-after success: Mexican cinema would have to wait a few more years to find the female stars it needed so badly.

A cinema without stars had to rely too heavily on motifs and genres to justify itself economically, which helps to explain the rush into the space opened up by *Rancho Grande*. Assuming innovation and intelligence to be poison at the box-office, Mexican producers became constipated and stingy: they wanted no risks and sought maximum profits at minimal effort. This attitude is *de rigueur* for all businessmen, but it was particularly virulent in a country that was just coming out of profound social, political and economic upheavals, still unable to see its future clearly. Among the conservative 1937 productions, perhaps only a peculiar film, Adolfo Best Maugard's *La mancha de sangre (The Bloodstain),* was exceptional for its boldness. Best Maugard paid dearly for it: he never directed another film and *La mancha de sangre* remained unreleased for six years. It was the first national film to be banned, despite the fact that its example yielded an abundant cinema of slums, cabarets and prostitutes throughout the next decade. Best Maugard was one of the seven directors to debut that year. Among the others (Ramón Pereda, Antonio Helú, Adela Sequeyro, Guillermo Hernández Gómez, René Cardona and Alejandro Galindo), only Galindo would stand out in the future as one of the most important and gifted Mexican directors. The case of the Veracruzan Adela Sequeyro should be noted as particularly interesting: she was the first female director of Mexican sound films and remained the only woman director in Mexican cinema for over forty years.

Notes

1. José María Sánchez García, *El Cine Gráfico anuario, 1945–46.*
2. *Allá en el Rancho Grande* was the first film that Figueroa shot unassisted.
3. Hugo del Mar, *Revista de Revistas* (Mexico City), 27 December 1936.

4. Juan Bustillo Oro, *Vida cinematográfica* (Mexico: Cineteca Nacional, 1984), p. 153.

5. Another Argentine version of *Nobleza gaucha* was made in 1937 by Sebastian M. Naón with Austín Irusta. Juan Orduña made another Spanish version of *Nobleza baturra* in 1964, in colour, with Irán Eory.

6. Marco Aurelio Galindo, *El Universal* (Mexico City), July 1936.

The Studios

Tomás Pérez Turrent

Mexican cinema was born under the sign of the documentary with the 'views' taken by the Lumière brothers' camera operators in 1896. For the first time, viewers saw and recognised images of their own reality and reflections of their customs and behaviours. The example of these cameramen was followed by the first Mexican operators, starting with Moulinié or Churrich's *Corrida de toros en Puebla con la cuadrilla de Ponciano Díaz* (*Bullfight in Puebla With the Ponciano Díaz Team*, 1897).

From the time of the first cinematic projections, artistic, intellectual and scientific circles demonstrated an interest in the medium. General Porfirio Díaz had been re-elected for the fifth time and had held power for twenty years. He had been a film enthusiast from the outset, as were the politicians around him (the positivists who called themselves 'the scientists'). These elite groups trusted in the cinema as a scientific instrument capable of reproducing visible reality undistorted. The faith in the cinema's truth was such that any reconstruction of events was rejected and considered a falsification. This is what happened with *Duelo de pistola en el bosque de Chapultepec* (*Duel in Chapultepec Forest*), produced in 1896 by the Lumière camera operators Bernard and Gabriel Veyra. Aurelio de los Reyes recounts that the film was considered a deception and a mockery:

> To simulate a duel, to feature individuals 'costumed' in the uniform of the respectable ranks of the police, and to do all this in order to take photographs that might be exhibited later … is a mockery of the police and of the law, a mockery of the most offensive kind, because those who see the show in theatres might be foreigners and people unfamiliar with the country who are under no obligation to know whether it is a simulation or a genuine duel.[1]

Consequently, the first Mexican fiction film was rejected in the name of the truth that the cinema was expected to guarantee. Under these circumstances the construction of film studios in Mexico was unthinkable, at least in the early days of cinema as commercial entertainment. The camera was supposed to register an immediate visual reality: it only needed to be set up in front of an event. Special places where reality could be altered, controlled or directed were unnecessary. Internationally, the urgent demand to control cinematographic material and its components (such as lighting) with an artistic, expressive sensibility and the desire to produce lavish spectacles, led to the construction of studios that made possible the production of 'views' under the best possible conditions, such as W.K.L. Dickson's Black Maria (1893) for the production of Kinetoscope films and Méliès's studio in Montreuil. In Mexico, the idea and the need for a studio would only appear later. The first antecedent – not really a studio – dates from January 1907 and was established by American Amusement, Lillo, García & Co. in Mexico City. It was a production office dedicated above all to making what today we would call documentaries. Nonetheless, it produced a fiction film, Felipe de Jesús Haro's *El grito de Dolores* (*Dolores's Cry*, 1907), an evocation of the onset of the struggles for independence in 1810 (in Mexico, the festivities for the first centennial of this heroic event were already being planned). The only existing report of the locale[2] describes an enclosed place similar to a warehouse in which there were a few precarious technical installations surrounded by gardens and uncultivated land. It had neither glass walls nor a glass roof to take advantage of the sunlight, as was the international norm at the time. Here, Felipe de Jesús Haro would also make *Aventuras de Tip Top en Chapultepec* (*Adventures of Tip Top in Chapultepec*) in 1907.

The Academia Cinematográfica, founded in 1906 in the Plaza Santos Degollado in the very heart of Mexico City, is also mentioned in the sources, but this was not a studio either, not even in the style of American Amusement. It was a display room and a photography workshop. From 1909 on it also served as a film laboratory. In April 1908 the Fábrica Nacional de Películas Enrique Rosas, Alva & Co. was founded. Rosas and the Alva brothers, important cameramen because of their work during the Mexican Revolution, were true pioneers, key people in the development of the national cinema during the silent period. The Fábrica produced and processed documentaries: social events, presidential trips, bullfights and disasters, such as the Guerrero theatre fire in Puebla.

It is commonly believed that at the beginning of the century, centralisation – that is, the dominance of Mexico City over the provincial cities, in the political, economic, cultural and artistic arenas – was absolute. In the cinema this was not so. Cinematic activities were actually quite diversified as a direct consequence of the nomadism of the late 1800s and early 1900s. The cameramen-operators travelled throughout the country with two missions: to document and to present events. When the time came to establish themselves, many of them did so in provincial cities and even founded studios in cities like Mérida[3] and Orizaba[4] in the late 10s. However, the activity of the travelling showmen, a phenomenon still awaiting a thorough study, declined with the outbreak of the Revolution.

Returning to the capital, the actress Mimí Derba and Enrique Rosas established a combined studio, laboratory, and production office in 1917, Azteca Films. It operated for almost a year in what is now the heart of downtown Mexico City (Balderas and Avenida Juarez). That same year, another pioneer, Manuel de la Bandera, founded Producciones Quetzal (233 Puebla Street), which was also a studio, laboratory and production office. Some interiors of the first Mexican version of *Santa* were filmed there, produced by Luis G. Peredo and starring Elena Sánchez Valenzuela. However, most of the film was shot on locations. In this film, the realist tradition that grew out of the documentaries of the Revolution rubbed shoulders with the melodramatic vocation that coloured the whole of Mexico's film history.

The existence of studios would be of great importance for the evolution of the new industry, especially when the cinema became fictional, that is to say, when it left the realm of science to become part of the culture industry. Thus it is not surprising that the evolution of the film studio paralleled the evolution of cinema itself. After early falterings, the first genuine film studios designed for the production of fiction films were finally built. Originally called Ediciones Camus S.A. (Revillagigedo and Victoria Streets, in downtown Mexico City), they consisted of a film stage, laboratories, dressing-rooms and warehouses. The studio was built by the impresario Germán Camus, a Spanish-born businessman who also distributed, exhibited and produced films. He had been the producer of *Santa* and *La banda del automóvil* (1919). While filming, he had realised the importance of being able to count on adequate, purpose-built facilities. In addition, the studios also became profitable, since the end of the Revolution

and the return of relative calm to the country had seen an increase in the production of fiction or narrative films.

Camus's studio opened in 1919 with the production of Ernesto Vollrath's *Hasta después de la muerte (Until Death Do Us Part)*, based on a story by the nineteenth-century Mexican writer Manuel J. Othón and adapted for the screen by the novelist, playwright and producer of several films, José Manuel Ramos. The cinematographer was Ezequiel Carrasco (also a laboratory technician), who would become an important figure in the early sound period. As there were no glass roofs, Carrasco introduced the use of spotlights. In his memoirs, film-maker Juan Bustillo Oro recalled what the existence of these studios meant to someone like him who dreamed of making movies one day: 'I vaguely glimpsed the possibility that in Mexico making movies would develop into a profession and for the first time I had hopes, albeit ill-defined, of devoting myself to it.'[5] Camus's experiment lasted for two years and produced six films: *Hasta después de la muerte* (1920), *En la hacienda* (both by Ernesto Vollrath, 1921), *Alas abiertas* (Luis Lezama, 1920), *Carmen* (Vollrath, 1921), *La parcela* (Vollrath, 1921), and *Amnesia* (Salvador Pruneda, 1921). All six films were shot by Carrasco, but the last two were no longer produced by Germán Camus. Unable to recover his investments in the previous films, he limited himself to renting the facilities. In November of 1921, financial insolvency forced Ediciones Camus to close its doors, although the company continued to produce intertitles for Mexican films and foreign films imported by Camus. By 1926, a repair shop operated in what had been the first 'formal' studio in Mexico.

Almost at the same time as Germán Camus's studio was closing, the Estudios Chapultepec (Escuela de Arte y Fotografía) was under construction, located on the Paseo de la Reforma, across from Chapultepec forest. At this time, the artisanal and preindustrial development of the Mexican cinema required ad hoc filming facilities. The studio was built by Jesús H. Abitia, another pioneer who had filmed the Revolution beside Madero and had been the chief cinematographer of the Sonora group headed by Calles, de la Huerta and Obregón. Abitia took advantage of his friendship with the latter, then president of the Republic, to acquire the property (at that time located on the outskirts of the city) at a very good price. The Chapultepec studio had a film stage, laboratory, dressing-rooms and administrative offices. The

Pedro Armendáriz and Maria Elena Marqués in *La Perla* (Emilio Fernández, 1945)

technical equipment was inherited from Ediciones Camus, as were the laboratory personnel, including Ezequiel Carrasco. Juan Bustillo Oro, who in 1927 filmed his first picture there, *Yo soy tu padre (I Am Your Father),* described the place in these terms:

a greenhouse through whose walls and glass roof the sun shone. … It was equipped with small curtains, movable by sections so as to measure the daylight in the style of the atelier that Georges Méliès had founded in the early days of the cinema. … One could see dilapidated electric spotlights, that Camus had discarded.[6]

Estudios Chapultepec opened in 1922 with Miguel Contreras Torres's *El hombre sin patria* and operated irregularly due to the intermittent nature of production, which meant that it was not possible to carry out any sort of technical renovation for many years. The arrival of US sound films and their prevalence by the late 20s – as well as the arrival of the first Spanish-language Hollywood films – complicated matters even more for the national production. After several failed attempts to produce sound films, Raphael J. Sevilla made *Más fuerte que el deber (Stronger than Duty)* in 1930 using the Wonder Voice-Vitaphone disc system. The film was exhibited in 1931 (the negative was burned in 1932 and all the copies disappeared soon after). *Más fuerte que el deber* was shot in Eduardo Baptista's studio, another ephemeral facility with poorer and even more limited equipment than Chapultepec, that had been built to compete with the latter. Baptista was a sound engineer attempting to take advantage of the talkie boom. Meanwhile, in 1931 Chapultepec was bought by a company headed by the film producer and director Gustavo Sáenz de Sicilia. The name of the company was Nacional Productora and its goal was to make sound films.

The Sound Film Studios

On 3 November 1931 the first sound film to be made with an optical system went into production at the Nacional Productora studios (formerly Chapultepec). It was another version of *Santa,* the second adaptation of Federico Gamboa's homonymous novel (four additional versions would be made, including most recently Paul Leduc's *Latino Bar* in 1990). This particular *Santa* was adapted by critic Carlos Noriega Hope, produced by Hollywood actor Antonio Moreno, shot by Alex Phillips (imported from Hollywood for this project), and starred Lupita Tovar, another Hollywood import. It kept the studios occupied for four weeks in addition to a week of exterior shooting.

The existence of Nacional Productora was inseparable from the early development of locally made sound films. In 1932, for example, six films were made, all of which used the studio's only film stage and studio laboratory. In subsequent years they were kept busy on a regular basis, even though from 1933 on they had to share the work with México Films, a new, more spacious and much better-equipped studio. That same year, Nacional Productora built an additional sound stage – not very large, without glass walls and roof – in order to compete with México Films.

Aside from the competition (Estudios Clasa also opened in 1935), Nacional Productora was overwhelmed by labour problems with the UTECM (Unión de Trabajadores de Estudios Cinematográficos de México). The situation deteriorated to such an extent that government intervention was required in 1934. In 1936, a fire forced the facilities to close, only to reopen in 1937 as the Estudios de la Universidad Cinematográfica. The last film shot there was *Los apuros de Narciso (Narciso's Hard Luck)* by Enrique Barrera, begun in November 1939, eight years after *Santa.* In 1940 the facilities were demolished, and four years later, the enormous and still-existing Chapultepec theatre would be built there. As a result, the site has a histor-ical connection to the cinema going back more than seventy years.

The México Films studio was constructed by the pioneer (impresario, photographer and laboratory technician) Jorge Stahl, whose family was of German origin. It was located on the streets of Fernando Montes de Oca, in the Condesa district (relatively close to Nacional Productora), which at that time marked the boundaries of Mexico City. Today the site is occupied by a supermarket. The studio had three sound stages, a laboratory, ten dressing-rooms, two bathrooms, and two editing rooms.[7] The first film shot there went into production on 18 May 1933: Miguel Contreras Torres's historic *Juárez y Maximiliano.* That year, of the 21 movies filmed in Mexico, eleven (including Arcady Boytler's milestone *La mujer del puerto*) were made there. Nacional Productora provided the interiors for another epoch-making film, Fernando de Fuentes's *El compadre Mendoza.*

As the labour problems afflicting Nacional Productora intensified, a new studio known as Industrial Cinematográfica S.A. was established to meet the growing production needs. Two of the 1933 films were shot there and that concluded their short-lived existence of four months. If we were to attempt to characterise the activities of the three remaining active studios, we could say that because of its better technical installations, México Films made the most ambitious films without generic specialisation (historical cinema, melodrama, and sweeping epic cinema like Fernando de Fuentes's outstanding adventure, *El Tigre de Yautepéc*). Nacional Productora specialised in melodrama and popular comedy (with the exception of *El compadre Mendoza*), while Industrial Cinematográfica handled the more inferior productions. Another short-lived studio appeared in 1934, the Empire, located in the exclusive Lomas de Chapultepec district and publicised profusely in the press: 'The best facilities and the best equipment'.[8] In reality, only one film was ever shot there: Miguel Contreras Torres's *¡Viva México!* The bulk of national production took place in the Nacional Productora studio and above all at México Films.

In contrast, the Estudios Clasa of the production company Cinematográfica Latinoamericana, S.A. were anything but ephemeral. Clasa was built in the middle of 1934, in a suburb to the south of the city, among what were then still the towns of Churubusco, Coyoacán and San Pablo Tepetlapa in the district in which today's surviving studios, Churubusco and América, are located. Clasa received assistance and financial support from the state (the government of Lázaro Cárdenas) and began its activities in January 1935 with Fernando de Fuentes's famous *¡Vámonos con Pancho Villa!,* the Mexican cinema's first super-production costing 1 million pesos (US$200,000). The government authorised a loan to the Clasa company in order for it to continue its activities while recouping its investment in the film. When the new Clasa studio began its operation, it was regarded as meeting all the technical and professional needs of film production in terms of equipment (cameras, sound, lights, stage machinery and supplies) and facilities (sound stages, laboratories, dressing-rooms and offices). It was said that Clasa was comparable to any Hollywood studio: 'For the first time in Mexico a studio had Mitchell cameras, sound recording equipment, a developing machine based on the gamma curve, back-projection equipment, and an optical printer.'[9] It is not surprising then that when it began to operate, Clasa supplanted México Films and reduced the activity of Nacional Productora. By 1937 (the year in which production soared to thirty-eight films, fifteen of them – generally the most ambitious, polished, and well made – were shot at Clasa, even though its facilities were more expensive to rent. As a producer, Clasa was regarded as the Mexican equivalent of Metro Goldwyn Mayer. Clasa's high rates, however, also allowed the other two studios to remain in business.

Studio construction fever continued. Another Mexican cinema pioneer, Gabriel García Moreno, opened a new studio in 1937, located in the south-eastern part of Mexico City (today the corner of Coyoacán and Universidad Avenues) in the same district as Clasa and where Churubusco and América had been previously located. The new studio, later to develop into Azteca, began to function in September 1937 with the filming of Alfredo Best Maugard's *La mancha de sangre (The Blood stain)*, not released until 1943 and, given its precarious means and formal and cinematic characteristics, classified as marginal cinema today.

1938 could be considered the first year in which the cinema truly operated as an industry, thanks to the success of Fernando de Fuentes's *Allá en el Rancho Grande* (1936). Although open to criticism for a number of reasons, the film did create the first specifically Mexican genre, the *comedia ranchera,* and was thus able to cross borders. This was the first year in which over fifty movies were made (57, to be precise). García Moreno's Azteca studio made three of them and, curiously, Nacional Productora, recently reopened under the name Universidad Cinematográfica, made 24, despite being the most deficient in equipment and facilities. The explanation is that their prices were lower than those of the other studios. For the first time, an industrial trend emerged, the consequences of which would be fatal for Mexican cinema: making the cheapest movies possible without regard to quality, not even from an industrial point of view, a tendency that would become more marked from the 50s onwards. The other 1938 films were divided almost equally between Clasa and México Films.

The enthusiasm of 1938 declined somewhat in 1939. The number of films produced dropped to 37 and in 1940 it went down to 29, triggering the first mentions of a crisis in the industry. Most of the European continent was at war and the immediate effect of this was fear: the Second World War affected all levels and social strata in the country. Nevertheless, in 1941 this situation led to the allocation of economic as well as technical assistance from the USA. Mexican cinema was the only reliable Spanish-speaking cinema, since Spain had just undergone a civil war and its victorious regime had been aided by Germany and Italy, the enemy, while Argentina was suspected of Nazi-fascist sympathies. Mexico had declared war on the Axis powers in 1941 and Argentina had adopted a neutral position.

US assistance helped Mexican cinema to broaden its markets. In 1941 the number of films produced rose to 37, in 1942 there were 47 and in 1943 and 1944 the increase was spectacular: 70 and 75 respectively. Clasa and Azteca studios controlled most of the production. They were the best-equipped and most expensive studios, but the bonanza experienced by Mexican cinema led the producers temporarily to disregard their usual stinginess. The so-called Universidad Cinematográfica finally closed its doors permanently and México Films stayed in business by making three or four films a year (those which Clasa or Azteca could not accommodate due to the saturation of the market). The industrial development of cinema revealed that the studio facilities were insufficient to sustain such production levels and that their efficiency was questionable. High salaries, inefficiency, defective services and legal entanglements were common, preventing any real improvement of production or any general expansion of the industry.[10]

In 1944, a group of capitalists seemed prepared to remedy the situation. Emilio Azcárraga, a prosperous radio producer and future founder of the Mexican television monopoly, and RKO Pictures, which was very interested in investing in Mexico, built Estudios Churubusco, said to be of Hollywood calibre and the most complete and best-equipped Latin American film studio. However, the initiative to build a new studio did not emerge from industrial calculation. The engineer Howard Randall, who had arrived in Mexico in 1935 as a concessionaire of RCA sound and was connected to Clasa, had influenced the construction of García Moreno's studio (later Azteca) which he also serviced. He then convinced another North American, Harry Wright, president of the

Ignacio López Tarso and Enrique Lucero in *Macario* (Roberto Gavaldón, 1959)

Country Club and owner of the adjacent land, to build a film studio to serve as a dyke on the Churubusco River to prevent the flooding of his property, thus increasing its value. Thus the idea to build the studio came from speculation in urban land values. Months later, Randall himself would use similar arguments to convince another North American named Gildred, also a substantial urban property-owner, to build another studio in the extreme north of the city, in Villa de Guadalupe: Estudios Tepeyac, famous above all for having served as the 'house' in Luis Buñuel's *Los olvidados* (1950).

The Churubusco studio was built on the Tlalpan highway and the Churubusco River (today sealed and converted into an expressway). The total surface area of the property was 180,000m². In order to build the studio, Emilio Azcárraga, PAMSA (Productores Asociados, S.A.) and RKO Pictures formed a new company (RKO president Peter N. Rathvon

participated in the negotiations). The contracts named Emilio Azcárraga president of the new company. Construction began in March 1944 and its mere announcement produced euphoria and awakened the megalomania of the people associated with film: Mexican cinema would now be able to compete with Hollywood. Once the studio was completed, producers claimed it would be possible to make up to 125 films[11] to supply the needs of the local market and the rest of Latin America as well, without taking into account the lack of movie theatres, the shortage of qualified technical personnel, and the wartime rationing of raw film stock (both negative and positive).

The first film shot at Churubusco was *Song of Mexico*, a US film produced by James A. Fitzpatrick of Republic Pictures, in November 1944. The filming took place at Clasa, in Acapulco, and later, for two weeks, at Churubusco, on the only sound stage that had been more or less completed (a floor had to be installed at the last minute). The real activities of the new studio would take several more months to get under way.

The following year, 1945, was characterised by the labour conflict that would lead to the creation of two unions: the STIC (Sindicato de Trabajadores de la Industria Cinematográfica), representing those who worked in distribution and exhibition, and the STPC (Sindicato de Trabajadores de la Producción Cinematográfica), comprised of actors, writers, directors, musicians and technicians. The STPC was headed by Gabriel Figueroa, Cantinflas and the popular actor Jorge Negrete. Previously, they had all been part of the STIC, but the production workers (the union elite) no longer wanted to be controlled by ticket-sellers, usherettes and janitors. The split was permanent and both factions were well defined. However, the government placed one stipulation on the new system: the STIC could produce films, but only newsreels and shorts. This decision would have important consequences in the late 50s.

The 1945 labour conflict was so bitter that it even interrupted work for two whole months. Then the STIC called a strike on the three operating studios (Azteca, Clasa and México Films) because it still had the allegiance of the laboratory workers, who held the collective contract. The members of the newly founded STPC prepared to defend their workplace: actors, producers and technicians formed armed patrols in the studios, even at Churubusco, which had not yet officially begun to operate. The conflict postponed the opening of Churubusco, whose first director was Charles B. Wooran, RKO's representative in Mexico. On 10 September 1945, one week after a presidential ruling determined the demarcations between the unions, the filming of Fernando A. Rivero's *La morena de mi copla (The Dark Lady of My Ballad)*, a 'folkloric-bullfighting melodrama',[12] crept onto the studio floor with little fanfare. This was followed by one of the first melodramas dealing with cabarets and prostitution, José Díaz Morales's *Pervertida (Depraved)* and by the first ambitious film undertaken at Churubusco: Emilio Fernández's *La perla,* co-produced by RKO in both its Spanish and English versions at an extraordinary cost (in Mexico) of 2¹/₂ million pesos (US$500,000).[13]

Churubusco began to make the super-productions in line with its own delusions of grandeur. The studio opened with twelve large sound stages, an electrical substation, two permanent and eight mobile emergency electrical plants, two projection rooms, a three-storey building for dressing-rooms, a recording studio, and (in 1946) a dubbing room, an RCA Victor sound system, mechanical and construction workshops, and a laboratory for both 35mm and 16mm, set up for colour as well as black and white.[14] In fact, the lab was not operational until 1947 and the first colour film was not developed until 1958. In 1947, they opened a large restaurant. Churubusco had the best-equipped studios in Mexico. RKO used the studio as a Trojan horse to penetrate the Spanish-language market, making movies in Spanish in Mexico with Mexican film stars. Directed by José (Joe) Noriega, RKO's chief editor in Hollywood, the Ramex company was founded specifically to meet this goal. Noriega set RKO's plan in motion by remaking Spanish versions of Hollywood films. RKO's advantage over other Mexican producers was that they had access to more resources. Ramex began in 1946 with three films and they added another one in 1947.

The strategy of remaking Hollywood movies in Spanish resulted in works that were as hybrid as they were artificial. The experience, reminiscent of the Hollywood Spanish-language films (1929–33), was a complete failure. When Ramex next produced such a film, in 1947, they used an original Spanish screenplay. In addition to *La perla*, RKO produced John Ford's *The Fugitive* in 1946 and went on to make two B movies in 1947 (Robert Florey's *Tarzan and the Mermaid* and Robert Wise's *Mystery in Mexico,* both released in 1948). Soon, RKO realised that they did not need to make films in Spanish in order to win back the Latin American market, which at that time was dominated by Mexican films. A few years later, Hollywood movies in English had penetrated the market directly without needing to be remade in Spanish or Portuguese, and were preferred by the upper classes and the burgeoning urban middle classes. Hollywood once again dominated the market.

In 1945 Churubusco made three films, and in 1946 they were responsible for 20 of the 72 films produced that year. The other 52 were divided among the rest of the studios: Azteca, Clasa and México Films. The new Estudios Tepeyac, in the extreme north of the city, made two films and a small studio called Cuauhtémoc made one. Tepeyac, built in 1945–6, opened on 8 July with Miguel M. Delgado's *Soy un prófugo (I Am a Fugitive,* 1946). The film starred Cantinflas and was backed by Columbia Pictures, which also had interests in Norman Foster's *El canto de la sirena (Song of the Siren).* Tepeyac's facilities were of the same calibre as

Churubusco's, although they lacked a lab. Cuauhtémoc had opened in 1945 producing only short films with its modest facilities of four sound stages (two of which were small), five dressing-rooms, one projection room, one sound room and two editing rooms.

The following year, 1947, production dropped to 58 films, making some studios redundant. The old México Films closed permanently after making one of the classics of the popular cinema, Ismael Rodríguez's *Nosotros los pobres,* with Pedro Infante, perhaps the greatest box-office success in the history of Mexican film. México Films had been in existence for fifteen years, but was overtaken by better-equipped competitors. Soon after, however, its owner, Jorge Stahl, would build a new studio. The other 'little studios' made three low-budget pictures, while the ambitious Tepeyac remained closed all year.

In the meantime, the STIC became a producer and, improvising a studio in Temixco in the state of Morelos, filmed *No te dejaré nunca* (*Never Will I Leave You,* Francisco Elías, 1947), a melodramatic detective story that took place in Paris and Guyana(!). 1948 was a troubled year full of conflicts between the film unions and the studio-owners of Azteca, Clasa, Churubusco and Tepeyac, who formed a united front, Churubusco and Tepeyac combining their interests. Nevertheless, 81 films were produced by the four studios. The greatest number went to Azteca and Churubusco, which also produced almost all of the US films made in Mexico. During the following years, Azteca and Churubusco dominated numerically, while fewer and fewer films were shot at Clasa. Despite the constant talk of crisis and loss of markets, these were years of quantitative expansion. In 1948, 1949, 1950 and 1951, the number of films produced was 81, 108, 125 and 101 respectively, but talk of the disappearance of some studios (Clasa) and the merger of others (such as Churubusco and Tepeyac) continued. At the same time, veteran Jorge Stahl built Estudios San Angel Inn in the south-western part of the city in 1949, the year in which the Cinematographic Law was voted which, with modifications made in 1952, is still in force. His studio would not begin operation until June 1951, with nine sound stages and all the necessary facilities except for a lab. By 1949 RKO's investment in Churubusco had declined (Charles B. Wooran, its trusted envoy, resigned from the directorship) and as of 1950 RKO liquidated even that remaining, minimal interest.

Then in 1950 the awaited merger took place between Churubusco and Azteca, from that time on

known as Estudios Churubusco-Azteca, S.A. However, the merger did not cause the immediate disappearance of Azteca, which would continue operating, although in a diminished capacity, until August 1958, when it closed permanently. Only the lab, known from then on as Filmolaboratorio, remained in service. By late 1951, Mexico City had a total of 58 sound stages[15] distributed among Azteca, Clasa, Churubusco, San Angel Inn, Tepeyac and the small Cuauhtémoc, which that year made only one movie. This was a considerable number when we consider that most films combined studio with location shooting. Despite the fact that the economic, cinematographic and artistic crisis was quite pronounced, the quantitative level of production between 1952 and 1956 remained at approximately 100 films, divided among the existing studios, with a preference for Churubusco and increasingly San Angel Inn. This apparent prosperity did not conceal the fact that all of the measures taken by the state to improve the conditions of Mexican cinema's production, distribution and exhibition failed, or that the powerful monopoly headed by the North American William Jenkins, with interests in all of the aforementioned sectors, particularly exhibition, increasingly dominated and overwhelmed the movie business. Nor was it possible to speak of prosperity when the quality, even in strictly industrial and professional terms, declined alarmingly as the industry's defects became fixed with the passage of time.

On 30 June 1957 Clasa shut down and in September of that same year Tepeyac made its last film, before being demolished in December. Clasa had lasted for twenty-two years and its role in the development of Mexican cinema had been very significant. Tepeyac's life had been only half as long, but it also had played an important role. The only remaining studios were Churubusco, San Angel Inn and Azteca, the latter taking the work that was unsuitable for the first two. As subsequent events revealed, the closing of Clasa and Tepeyac was due to the intervention of a series of interests connected with the Jenkins monopoly.

On the closure of Clasa, in which it had had a significant interest, the state bought Churubusco stock and became the principal stockholder, although it relinquished administrative control to the private company. It was said that the state acted in order to prevent Churubusco from falling into the hands of the Jenkins monopoly. According to film-maker Miguel Contreras Torres, this decision was made in order to favour Azcárraga.[16] Two studios closed but a

Domingo Soler in *La fé en Dios* (Raúl de Anda, 1949)

new one opened. The old Cuauhtémoc was remodelled and enlarged and became Estudios América, S.A., with Gregorio Wallerstein (Jenkins's production man) and the actor Víctor Parra being responsible for the reconstruction.[17] The studio opened on 21 March 1957 and was staffed with workers from the other union (STIC) who were asserting their legal right to participate in the production of shorts (38 minutes maximum duration). This restriction was quickly overcome by dividing feature-length films into episodes. As there were no labour demands, expenses decreased and the majority of the producers got what they had been dreaming of for years: cheap films made with minimal resources as quickly as possible (two to three weeks).

1958 saw the greatest number of films in the history of Mexican cinema: 136, reflecting the activities of the new studio and its particular form of production which led to the completion of twenty-two 'serials' of three or four chapters each. Of the rest, except for six co-productions filmed abroad and

three outside the industrial circuit, Churubusco made 58, San Angel Inn 35 and, in view of the demand, Azteca postponed its closure and made 12 more films before closing down. Despite the impressive numbers, however, the situation was not promising. Only one great film was made, Luis Buñuel's *Nazarín*. This kind of achievement was not repeated, but production remained at about 110 films per year until 1960 and averaged 90 films per year from 1961 to 1970. The number of films produced by América, always in the serial formula, grew. By the 70s the formal division between serials and fiction films was no longer necessary.

1960 was an important year because the government bought the Churubusco stock that was still privately held and acquired the theatres of Jenkins and his associates' well-known monopoly. The main studio and the principal exhibition chains were also nationalised, although it might be more correct to say that they were 'statified', that is to say, simply taken over by the state, an event that would prove of fundamental significance in the following

Redes (Fred Zinnemann and Emilio Gómez Muriel, 1934)

decade. In the 60s, América continued making fake features, compiled from shorts, and serials, while Churubusco and San Angel Inn took charge of the production of regular films. Since costs were definitively lower, producers increasingly chose América. If in 1960 the studios in the hands of the STPC made 90 films as opposed to 21 serials at América, in 1966, there were 57 regular films and 31 serials. This trend intensified in the 70s. For example, in 1975 Churubusco produced 23 Mexican films and 6 US ones; 21 were produced by the state alone or in co-production with groups of film-makers or private producers, while at América, which no longer had to make serials, 38 films were made. The traditional producers abandoned Churubusco.

By 1968 San Angel Inn had closed in bankruptcy, after film activities lasting for seventeen years. Their modern and efficient facilities, however, were not demolished, but rather redesigned for television production. They were first used by Channel 8 and, after a merger, by Televisa.

In the 70s, under the government of Luis Echeverría, the cinema became a state industry. Through the Banco Cinematográfico, the state managed the principal exhibition chains, Churubusco, two production companies and a cinema school. In addition, it bought América in 1975. Nevertheless, the usage of Churubusco began to decline. The traditional producers were not pleased by the industry's nationalisation. Since they had to keep making movies, even if only to protect the financial interests accumulated over the years, they preferred to work with América. Making movies there cost 30% less than at Churubusco. Starting in 1977 and throughout the 80s, the tendency towards denationalisation grew, although with few effects: for economic reasons, most production took place at América. For example, in 1985 Churubusco made 16 films (two US ones) and América made 60. This tendency continued, although it reverted in 1991: quantitatively, production figures were low, but most films were made at Churubusco-STPC. The crisis had exploded: the large, medium and small private producers had lost their capital. América-STIC was less active than in 1957, its first year of operations. The crisis was undeniable and the studios were in danger.

Now that the studios are threatened with extinction after more than 70 years, we may usefully ask what their contribution to Mexican cinema has been. It is evident that they were a crucial determinant in the early days of the industry (the preindustrial period 1920–36) as well as during its formalisation (after 1938) and consolidation. But did they have any relationship whatsoever to the aesthetic and cinematographic development of Mexican cinema? The answer is yes, although this may not be evident in the light of the differences between the products of the various studios. Nevertheless, two phases stand out. The first spans the period from 1933 (the first year of significant quantitative production gains) to 1957. During that period, films were made in one of several studios by the same people: producer, artistic teams, technicians and workers. The genres developed at the same time in the various studios. The differing styles were due mostly to the producers (the Clasa style was better defined and in general more polished than that of the others), the photographers (for example, Gabriel Figueroa and Alex Phillips), the artistic teams, the actors (María Félix, Jorge Negrete, Pedro Infante) and the workers.

The second stage (which resulted from the union split of 1949) began in 1957. There was a radical difference between what was done at Churubusco and San Angel Inn by members of the STPC and what was produced at América by members of the STIC. Speed and economy influenced the quality of the films, which mattered little to those who produced them. The visual differences were striking: América's cinematography was flat and lacked contrast, shading or value. The cinematographer, who had to work very quickly, limited himself to saturating shots with light: 'I don't want to see the flourishes but the actors who cost me a lot of money,' was the old adage of the typical producer. The same was true of the work of the set designers and sound and light technicians, as well as of the sensibilities of the rest of the staff.

Of course there were exceptions. Between 1968 and 1973 the Corkidi-Jodorowsky group made equally good if not better films, with the same or greater visual quality as Churubusco, with as much or more attention to detail than STPC. On his own, either as cinematographer or as director, Rafael Corkidi continued with this kind of work.

There were differences and nuances within these broad general trends. While it is true that from the 30s until 1957 the studios worked with the same people, each had its unique characteristics. For example, in the late 30s, Nacional Productora (later the Universidad Cinematográfica) was the equivalent of América in recent decades, while Clasa attended to quality. Churubusco would undertake the most ambitious films, even during the period when San Angel Inn was its only competitor. Thus each one of the studios had its own distinct style. Tepeyac is a case in point. Without abandoning other genres and types of cinema, they developed the prototype of the urban cinema. Ismael Rodríguez had always worked with México Films (Nosotros los pobres) and when it closed he moved to Tepeyac; there he made the sequel to the urban saga begun with Nosotros los pobres, Ustedes los ricos (You the Rich, 1948) and Pepe el toro (Pepe the Bull, 1952).

Mexico City, a large metropolis but not yet the colossus of the 80s, was transfigured on the Tepeyac sound stages. Also in 1948, when production had only just been regularised, two definitive titles in the representation of Mexico City appeared: Alejandro Galindo's ¡Esquina … bajan! and Hay lugar para dos (There's Room for Two), which combined modern and intimate sensibilities. This trend culminated in 1950 with Luis Buñuel's Los olvidados, an implacable analysis of the great city. On the other hand, due to what might be considered accidental circumstances, Buñuel made a good number of his Mexican films at Tepeyac. Ultramar Films, the company that produced much of his work, was connected to these studios (in fact, Buñuel's producer Oscar Dancigers was the manager from 1951 until its closure). But Tepeyac's desire to capture the city had always been visible throughout its eleven-year life. It is noteworthy that its last film, Quiero ser artista (I Want to Be an Artist, by Tito Davison, 1957), told the story of a postman who travels throughout the city and spends part of his time at the Tepeyac sound stages. A film about the city made it possible for this studio to appear on-screen for the first and only time. It was the ultimate testimonial.

Another consistent genre in Mexican film from the mid-40s to 1953 coincided with the government of Miguel Alemán (1946–52): the cabaretera melodrama peopled by tropical dancers, prostitutes, gigolos, gangsters, and so on. This was basically an urban genre that reflected the values, desires and fears of a society developing from the agricultural-pastoral stage into an urban and capitalist-based economy. Over 200 films were made in this genre and all of the studios participated, but Azteca and

Churubusco were the most prolific. All the actors (Ninón Sevilla, Leticia Palma, Emilia Guiú, Rosa Carmina, and so on), photographers, set designers and lighting and sound technicians (the best of whom tended to work at Churubusco), left their mark on the genre. The creation of an ambience was fundamental for the genre and it was inseparable from its black and white, chiaroscuro-filled, textured images. Logically, when colour became the norm, the genre disappeared.

Certain individuals were important to the style of each of the studios. Because they worked on sound stages, the set designers, sound and lighting technicians and the decorators were essential. It was not so much that the studio offered adequate spaces, but rather that there were men of taste and creativity to give shape to those spaces. In this realm no one surpassed Manuel Fontanals (one of the many important Spanish exiles who chose to live in Mexico) who worked primarily with Churubusco. By the late 60s, as studio filming dwindled and this know-how began to be lost. Fontanals's last work, the set design of *El castillo de la pureza* by Arturo Ripstein (1972) exemplified the best of his craft. The proof is that the set remained standing for three years, during which time it was used, with variations and additions, in several more films. Also important, obviously, were the people who were in charge of recording this style: cinematographers and their assistants, operators, lighting technicians and dolly operators, whose sensibilities led to the development of the particular styles of Churubusco, Apache and Puma.

Since the mid-80s there has been talk of the imminent sale of Churubusco-Azteca, which survive only because of their symbolic value. Certainly few contemporary films require a studio. This, however, did not deter the producer and film-maker Gustavo Alatriste from attempting to build a studio in Guadalajara during this time. The government of the state of Morelos also tried to build a studio in Cuernavaca, 80km from Mexico City.[18] If América and Churubusco are sold, their land will be used to build supermarkets, malls, housing or office buildings. In 1991, there was talk of selling América to a group of producers, but since 1989, the state has liquidated the production companies, put the exhibition chains up for sale, and even though it denies it, it would not be surprising if Churubusco were to be sold as well. If the cinema, the culture and the country itself are sold off, why should anyone bother to preserve the studios? At least, it is possible that cinema will outlive the studios.

Notes

1. Aurelio de los Reyes, 'Orígenes del cine en México (1896–1900)', *Cuadernos de cine*, no. 21 (Mexico City: Dirección de Difusión Cultural, UNAM, 1973) p. 72.

2. José María Sánchez García, 'Historia del cine mexicano', in *Cinema Reporter* (Mexico City), 12 January 1952, p. 12.

3. Gabriel Ramírez, *El cine yucateco* (Mexico City: Filmoteca UNAM, 1980).

4. Oral testimony by Juan Rodríguez Isla, gathered by Tomás Pérez Turrent in November 1984. Rodríguez Isla recalled that when he was a child there was a 'movie factory' across the street from his house in the city of Orizaba. His father and one of his brothers worked there.

5. Juan Bustillo Oro, *Vida cinematográfica* (Mexico City: Cineteca Nacional, 1984), p. 45.

6. Ibid., p. 54.

7. Emilio García Riera, *Historia documental del cine mexicano*, vol. 1, *1926–1940* (Mexico City: Era, 1969), p. 38.

8. Unsigned advertisement in *Ilustrado*, 6 April 1934, p. 24.

9. Emilio García Riera, *Cine mexicano*, p. 90.

10. Alfonso Pulido Islas, *La industria cinematográfica en México* (Mexico City: México Nuevo, 1939), p. 38.

11. Tomás Pérez Turrent, *La fábrica de sueños: Estudios Churubusco, 1945–1985* (Mexico City: IMCINE-Estudios Churubusco-Azteca, 1985), p. 25.

12. Emilio García Riera, *Historia documental del cine mexicano*, vol. 3, *1945–1948* (Mexico City: Era, 1971), p. 61.

13. Pérez Turrent, *Fábrica de sueños*, p. 32.

14. Ibid., pp. 32–3.

15. Ibid., p. 41.

16. Emilio García Riera, *Historia documental del cine mexicano*, vol. 6, *1955–1957* (Mexico City: Era, 1974), pp. 256–7.

17. Emilio García Riera cites the declarations of producer Miguel Contreras Torres, public enemy of the Jenkins monopoly. According to Contreras Torres, the Jenkins monopoly intended to gain a foothold in television (Azcárraga's domain) through producer Gregorio Wallerstein. Azcárraga hoped to sell Churubusco, ally himself with Jenkins and use América as a television studio.

18. Alatriste intended not only to build a studio, but rather a 'Cinema City' which would include living quarters. Above all, he was interested in attracting Hollywood productions. The government of the state of Morelos had the same intention. These projects remained sterile.

All the People Came and Did Not Fit Onto the Screen: Notes on the Cinema Audience in Mexico

Carlos Monsiváis

At the end of the 19th and the beginning of the 20th century, the technological revolution allowed the popular sectors to break out of their complete cultural isolation. For apart from traditional entertainments like games of chance, the circus, civic and religious festivals and musical theatre, the people were forced to get what little they could from a culture which was class-based. But anyone could go to the cinema, and this unexpected democratisation flew in the face of the exclusivity of 'high culture', whose representatives were either enthusiastic or worried by the phenomenon. In 1915, the poet Juan José Tablada opted for enthusiasm:

The landscape that amazes you, the gestures and smiles of the woman that captivates you are there; you will see them when you want and as often as you want. What a bewitching spell, what matchless seduction! The prodigious opium dream is within reach of all fortunes. There is the smiling and all powerful fairy for the baby who opens his eyes wide and believes in fairies. There are the landscapes that you have never seen, oh dreamer, who will never leave your own small corner. There is the woman idol, the Circe that you would never have met, oh poet, consumed by your desires and lavish dreams. Yours are the favours that magnates fight over. It is yours, calm down, savour your dream, let your soul bathe in its fascination, chain yourself to the radiant full moon of the phantasmagoric, the light that a dead star shines on this spectral land and chastely, since you can do nothing else, grow weary of realism. For cinema is the Zola of the impossible.

It is raining heavily and I'll have to change to go to the theatre; pay out five pesos for a stall seat at the opera. Bah! I'm a modern man and the city is beckoning me … I'll go to the cinema then! (Quoted in Luis Reyes de la Maza, *Salón Rojo* (Mexico City: UNAM, 1973).

The invention also provoked more bitter reactions. In 1906 the reporter Luis G. Urbina examined this dubious 'rebellion of the masses' and sensed that people who dreamed along with the marvels of the screen experienced some sort of collective feeling that calmed their instincts and brutishness. They were caressed, he thought, by the hand of illusion, an infantile illusion which made their spirits soar above the gross impurities of life. The bourgeois can smile at all this because they know about aesthetics. But the same is not true for those who, at their jobs, in the back of a workshop, in some corner of the factory, in their miasmatic, dingy little offices, do not know how to discuss or analyse their impressions, and cannot pay for their entertainments. They go to the Buen Tono cinema because it makes them feel, and entertains them with a calming childlike innocence, and later, when they go back to their broken-down dwellings, their imagination, like Aladdin's lamp, continues to light up the sadness of their existence with ephemeral pleasures.

Luis G. Urbina glimpsed what Ilya Ehrenburg would later develop in a famous book: cinema is a *dream factory*. He is already beginning to display hostility towards consumers of cultural rubbish and those who, without needing to, share their unfortunate predilections. His is the forerunner of the class criticism of the next fifty years:

I agree that the cinema entertains the curiosity of the multitude. … The popular masses, uncultured and infantile, in front of the screen full of photographs in movement, experience the enchantment of a child who is told fairy stories by his grandma. But I cannot understand how, night after night, a group of people who have the obligation to be civilised, are fascinated, in the Salón Rojo, the Pathé or the Monte Carlo, by the incessant reproduction of views in which aberrations, anachronisms and implausibilities are displayed *ad hoc* for a public of the lowest mental denominator, who lack even the most elementary notions of education.

The Canonisation of Technique

Three centuries as a colony and a century of battles to construct the nation provides a general but also precise explanation as to why modernity was incorporated only partially into Mexican society and for the interminable wonder at the 'marvels of civilisation' which reveals the extent of this cultural lag. The impact of technology is devastating. It increases a bitter admiration for North America, it

145

reaffirms the elite's appalled doubts about the future of the country and would help to cause a psychological split, which is illustrated in that curious thesis that would endure for half a century, that the USA has civilisation and Latin America has culture. Nobody is there to mediate the reactions to this scientific and technical leap forward, and workers faced by the telegraph feel the same alarm as the nuns in Puebla who, in 1890, denounced the Mother Superior of their convent for using 'an instrument of the devil' (the telephone), and as the public in a Mexico City dancehall in 1893 who, when presented with the invention of the phonograph, searched desperately for the hidden dwarf who was making the noises.

Silent cinema is the source of both inhibitions and enthusiasm. The spectators waver between supreme delight and terror when faced with these moving images which shelter them when they close their eyes or else cause them to run away when the train hurtles out of the screen towards the seats. In 1916, as Martín Luis Guzmán recounts in *El águila y la serpiente (The Eagle and the Serpent)*, at the Convention of Aguascalientes, the Revolutionaries watched a newsreel film, and their inability to distinguish between their own loyalties and phobias and what was happening on the screen led them to take action:

Carranza appeared, corpulent, solemn, hieratic, about to enter Saltillo in triumph. Another voice shouted: 'Viva Our Commander in Chief'. But instead of an enthusiastic cry from all assembled, chaos ensued. There were cries of 'viva' and 'death to', applause, blows, protests, hissing.

And straight after, as if the operator was doing it on purpose, there appeared, bathed in light, on his magnificent horse, the magnificent figure of Pancho Villa, legendary, dominating. The clamour from all sides drowned out the voices and only as a postscript to the volley of applause could one gradually hear above the noise: 'Viva the Northern Division'. 'Viva!' And applause erupted once again.

The same thing happened with all the others. For an hour or more the march past of the revolutionary leaders and their hosts went on, bathed in the light of the cinematograph and in the glory of their deeds.

We, however, did not see the end of the film because something happened unexpectedly which made us run away from our place behind the screen. Don Venustiano was, of course, the celebrity that appeared most often on the screen. His ever more frequent appearances had been becoming, as was to be expected, more and more irritating to the Conventionist audience. Fom hissing mixed with applause on the first occasions that he was seen, it moved to frank hissing; then to hissing bordering on whistling; then to open catcalls and finally to complete bedlam. In this way, in mounting stages, it ended up, when the scene of Carranza entering Mexico City on horseback was shown, in a sort of hellish uproar which culminated with two shots being fired.

Both projectiles hit the screen at the exact spot where the the chest of the Supreme Commander was outlined and ended up embedded in the wall, one half a metre above Lucio Blanco and the other, closer still, between Domínguez's head and mine.

The transition from silent cinema to the talkies helped to strengthen the conviction that what happens on the screen is a more real reality. It does not spurn us, but instead allows us instantaneous identification, it addresses us in the first instance, and makes us share its idea of the nation, family and society. And as a result of the fusion between the industry and its audience, the lack of distinction between the technological product and reality (which television will inherit), there is a confusion between characters and 'real life' people. Let me quote two examples, the first a classic in its way. To promote a film by Fernando de Fuentes, *Allá en el trópico* (1940), a group of actors were travelling around the country:

The group arrived in Puebla. Various artists were introduced, to great applause and acclaim. It came to the turn of Señora Roldán. ... And then the unexpected occurred. Instead of being greeted, like all the other artists, with ovations, Emma Roldán was received unanimously with whistles and angry cries: 'Old cow!' 'Get that witch out of here!' 'Down with the old crone'.

There was a tremendous confusion. The curtain had to be brought down. Señora Roldán came over faint and had to be revived with smelling salts. Until someone explained the reason for this angry reaction: for the public in Puebla, Emma Roldán would always, at all times, be Doña Angela, the old woman in the film *Allá en el Rancho Grande,* who tried to sell the sweet and innocent Crucita. That was why they all hated her, because they saw her as the despised character, not as the artist. (*El Universal*, 18 June 1940)

The second, more modest, example comes from the writer Mauricio Magdaleno:

I remember an incident with [Miguel] Inclán. I met him on a bus – we used to go on buses and suchlike. The gentleman alongside him moved away with a gesture of contempt and the lady behind gave him a dirty look. My seat was not occupied – then there was room on the buses – and he came to sit next to me. Everyone stared at him, because this was Inclán the villain, who killed children, the evil one in the pictures. (Mauricio Magdaleno, *Cuadernos de la Cineteca Nacional*, vol. 3, Mexico City: Cineteca Nacional, 1976).

The Celluloid Temples

It's just entertainment, they say, but everywhere cinema is an extraordinary agent of *secularisation*. This means, according to Weber, the 'demiraculisation of the world', reality as separate to the wonders of the divine order. As a generator of its own culture, cinema secularises, but only in order to plant miracles of its own in the psychic space of its spectators (marvels no longer computable to prayer or holy ornaments, but to murmurs in the dark and photos of the stars purchased at the exit to the show).

The initial astonishment at the technology is replaced by a link between entertainment and the exploration of the world, journeys through landscapes and lifestyles. Rather than the men, it is the women – first as divas, then as film stars – who become the vehicles of individual and collective identification, which will allow the new medium, especially in the provinces, to modernise local customs in an extraordinary fashion and offer, in their own way, a form of liberation. From the divas (especially the Italians, from Francesca Bertini to Giovana Terribili González), one could learn the eloquence of the passionate outburst and the imperious styles of fashion. From the stars (Clara Bow, Kay Francis, Greta Garbo, Marlene Dietrich, John Gilbert, Clark Gable, Gary Cooper, James Cagney, Spencer Tracey), one could imitate attitudes to life summed up in a gesture, ways of smoking, women's trousers that scorned gossip, little acts of cynicism and nihilism which are timid gestures of independence, the fashions that would become the universal language of elegance, urban sophistication and cultivated sincerity.

In its first decades, cinema takes charge of fashion, reorders sensual and sexual images, and invents – through close-up, make-up and careful camera angles – a feminine face that is the product of another, somewhat more egalitarian, conception of women. In a collectivity so overwhelmingly illiterate, cinema takes on the numerous responsibilities of oral culture, uses melodrama (a genre based on family morality) to filter heterodox views and is a guide to – a window on – a planet that is not exclusively political: how they dress in Paris, how daring and forward women are in North America, how the Chinese walk, what the family structures are in Asia.

This 'shock of recognition' of the films is complemented by the devotional policies of specialised magazines and the cinema sections in the newspapers. This universal fanaticism is consolidated by raising the cinema artists to an Olympus of news reports, by the plethora of publicity photos, brilliantly orchestrated fantasies ('Get to know the private lives of the famous film stars'), and the 'shamanist chants' of worship in the form of reviews of the Big Stars.

In Mexico, the idea of cinema as art does not even get a look in. It is a mass entertainment, offering an immediate link to the metropoli, a subliminal modernisation of rural and urban groups. The visits to the flea-pits or the cinemas in the villages, in city suburbs or city centres becomes a daily or Sunday ritual observed by fascinated children, adolescents, young single people and families. The surrender to the new medium is *almost* unconditional and *almost* explains the ideological resentment towards Hollywood. In particular, the right (priests, pious women, 'pro' groups, activists in ultramontane organisations), accused North American cinema of degrading tradition and subverting morality. The traditionalists lamented the disintegration – even in villages and small towns – of family gatherings, public innocence, children's games, 'feminine modesty' and 'honourable masculinity'.

In his autobiography, *Mis recuerdos: sinarquismo y colonia María Auxiliadora*, one of the founders of the Sinarquist National Union, Salvador Abascal, makes the point forcibly:

I did not have hobbies; my supreme entertainment was reading. I went to the cinema when I was just out of the seminary and I always came away with a deep feeling of unease, like a man who had wasted time as valuable as a treasure, with my soul empty, empty of something that it should have contained, stripped, robbed, desolate. When, many years later, I went back to the cinema, albeit infrequently, hoping to corroborate my first impressions, the effect was even more disastrous. The feminine images – for now, this industry of sensuality was fully developed – were a terrible temptation that took hold of all my feelings and fantasies until, one fine day, I swore never to return. I have kept to this vow and will continue to do so without effort, without being thus enslaved. In those years (the 1920s), I never went to the cinema in Morelia, to go to the cinema, I thought, was at best a miserable waste of time, although no voice was raised against this terrible corrupter of the mind and morals. It was not right that the senses and the soul should open up, with impunity, to all manner of lewdness and sensuality. Cinema is a drug which very soon enslaves and corrupts even the best prepared of men, the main drug that international Judaism has supplied us with to date. (Salvador Abascal, *Mis recuerdos: sinarquismo y colonia María Auxiliadora,* Mexico City: Tradición, 1980).

Abascal's ascetic fury intuits something: when faced with the electronic media, society as a whole, and much less traditional elements within society, did not know how to respond. The traditionalists are so ignorant of the phenomenon that they extend its appeal through censorship. Like the Hays Code in Hollywood, the League of Decency becomes a butt of parody and increases enormously the fascination for every banned film. In the medium and short term no good comes of intimidating theatre-owners, Sunday sermons or leafleting the spectators who go to 'inappropriate' films. Cinema shakes up urban and village morality and sets up models which are, to a great extent, independent of those proposed by the church and society. The weakness of the Mexican film industry in the silent era is not important: Hollywood cinema and, to a lesser extent, Italian cinema fills the gap to great advantage and coincides to some degree with the changes taking place in Mexico during the years of armed struggle and the demolition of the fortress of feudal mentality.

There is no point trying to resist. The right marks cinema down as a mortal enemy to no avail. And, without declaring itself to be against morality and, indeed, paying it all manner of lip service, an art (a technique) will become the culminating point of both false and true modernity, the great step forward that allows backward societies to feel that they are living in the 20th century, at the same moment as all other people on the earth. And if cinema brings ways of seeing the local, the national and the universal rapidly up to date, it does so through the *mystical feelings* of the spectators, who in the shadows construct a *sui generis* religion, which transfigures its followers and provides them with celestial visions. Part of this mystical impulse is a reaffirmation of the minimum certainties, a direct set of values: you, the spectator, understand what is happening around you, and you are important enough for the cinema to take you seriously, and you live in a devout, patriarchal, God-fearing society (at its own pace and with a certain humour), someone is watching over your property, and your language and behaviour are witty and fortunate, as your grandfather's and father's must have been before you.

At the other extreme, despite Lenin's enthusiastic endorsement of film, cinema does not have any impact on the left. This left vaguely believes in the Soviets (Eisenstein above all), makes fun of gringo cinema and has no awareness, even in the regime of President Cárdenas, of the importance of cinema in the ideological struggle.

Under Cover of the Shadows

At the end of the 19th century, cinema is a new tremor in a country that is still rural; in 1895, the Kinetoscope allows us to see, according to a note from the period, 'creatures as Christian as us, with souls like ours' and, under cover of the shadows, good society and common people come together, happy to frequent these new and exotic stories and sets. They are faithful to the cinema from the first moment and share another great attraction: the physical space, by its very nature anonymous and allowing behaviour that, in the light of day, would be condemned. A cabaret song puts it this way:

Vamos al cine, mamá (Let's go to the cinema, mama)
Mamá … matografo (Mama … matograph)
Que eso de la oscuridá (Because all that darkness)
me gusta una atrocidá (I really love)

According to the studies by José María Sánchez García, Luis Reyes de la Maza and Aurelio de los Reyes, and the research of Federico Dávalos and Esperanza Vásquez Bernal, among others, silent cinema is greeted with astonishment and censorship: the parish investigations into the screenings for 'men only', the systematic attempt by the Catholic church to control screenings in the provinces, together with the prohibitions and recommendations of the League of Decency. The best of Mexican film production still in existence is undoubtedly the documentary material of Salvador Toscano (brought together for the first time by his daughter Carmen in *Memorias de un mexicano,* 1950) and of Jesús H. Abitia (in *Epopeyas de la Revolución mexicana,* 1963), together with the feature *El automóvil gris* (1919) by Enrique Rosas, Joaquín Coss and Juan Canals de Homes, which is an extraordinary reconstruction of an important episode in the relationship between crime and power.

Hollywood dominates and national cinema tries to imitate it to attract its own following. Between 1906 and 1938, silent cinema is lavish in gestures of grief and joy, and teems with documentaries and historical reconstructions. The titles bear witness to this: *El precio de la gloria, La llaga, Confesión trágica, Venganza de bestia, La Virgen de Guadalupe, Cuauhtémoc, Tabaré, Santa, Barranca trágica, Alma de sacrificio, Amnesia (Dos almas en una)* … In smart locations like the Salón Rojo, the Good Families of the capital who had not managed to leave, and those who aspire to replace them, consider the Revolution a spectacle, they are roused by scenes of lavish weddings, they applaud the memory of the dictator Porfirio Díaz, they are terrified, without any risk to themselves, at the daring of the cameramen, they jeer at the peasant armies and draw moralistic conclusions from the 'views' of the Revolution. Take, for example, the publicity for a documentary on the Zapata army, *Sangre hermana,* released on 14 February 1914:

An unprecedented event. The first live shots taken in the revolutionary camp! Three thousand metres in six parts. *Sangre hermana,* a poem of grief and tears. Episodes of the Revolution. Its authenticity is verified by certificates from military authorities. From what they see on the screen, the public will be fascinated to know that at all times our brave cameraman has been in imminent danger. *Sangre hermana* does not contain scenes set in Rome, it does not involve preparations or lavish costumes costing millions of pesos; the scenes are real: they are shot at the very locations where the events take place. Its decor is the unrivalled beauty of the countryside. *Sangre hermana* rivals the best European films in terms of beauty and clarity. The public will be able to see with absolute clarity the horrors of *Zapatismo.* They will see our brave army marching to fight the Zapatistas; they will see the burned out villages and the terrible punishment that the guilty receive. *Sangre hermana* will be a topic of conversation for a long

time. It is an anguished cry, a sorrowful reproach of the Motherland. A faithful reflection of the horrors of the Revolution in the State of Morelos. (Quoted in Reyes de la Maza, *Salón Rojo*).

Never Was a Spectator of Myths So Well Served

The church looks after hopes beyond this world; earthly illusions are the domain of cinema, radio, the record industry and comics. A division of labour exists: the state controls the people's conduct (work and politics); religion is responsible for the final meaning of life (what happens to people when they die); the culture industry suggests to people *the best use of their time.* And cinema plays a decisive role in national integration, as a mediator between a victorious state and masses with no democratic tradition, formed by a sentimental education. (If there is no political life, let laughter and tears flow. If good society excludes us, then let the cinema, the radio and the cartoons recognise the different qualities of our lives. If there is no tradition of reading, let visual fancies abound.)

Cinema is useful to the lay state engaged in a process of imposing secularisation and confronting its last bloody resistance in the Cristeros War (1926–9), although the state does not realise it: it is useful in so far as it links the deepest convictions of the public to this process of change. The strong state is the master of revolutionary representation, of school education and of the different levels of interpreting politics, economics and society. It only leaves everyday life outside its control, to be taken up by anyone interested.

With the advent of sound cinema, a series of double-edged developments becomes manifest in the area of the electronic media:

- It modernises its listeners and promotes social anachronism at the same time (cinema is a school of comparative behaviour).
- It is a vehicle of cultural nationalism and of false cosmopolitanism.
- It invents an urban mentality and a rural morality.
- It encourages the disintegration of traditional values, subverts the moral message and adds a funereal tone to love of the past. (It praises what is being subverted or what has already died.) The traditional, it infers, is backward. Let us take, for example, the case of honour: in the era of the divas, it is disturbing; in the melodramas of the 40s, it is a form of collective catharsis; from the 60s, it is a source of amusement.
- It underscores the brutal sexism of Mexican society

and considers the function of women in a different way, by emphasising, through a series of close-ups, their sanctity or perversity, and by praising, of necessity, modern young people.

- It appeases the marginals in society with visions of opulence and makes them feel a nostalgia for something that they have never lived or possessed.
- It slowly introduces a spirit of tolerance by disseminating the customs of other places and it preaches intolerance.
- It strengthens and undermines a feeling of nationhood through a series of paradoxes: it praises the customs that are disappearing and it criticises the modernity that is being promoted. If the ostensible creed is reactionary and clerical, the visual translation is never quite so reactionary. No ideological pressure can neutralise images in an effective way.
- It praises local customs and introduces spectators imperceptibly to more complex ideas about the world and their country.

All this is accentuated when sound cinema spreads throughout the country. After Raphael J. Sevilla's melodrama *Más fuerte que el deber* (1930), cinema becomes the greatest social stimulus (outside employment, the home and the family) and takes up the mantle of cultural democratisation from poetry and popular theatre. The influence of national cinema soon spreads throughout Latin America. All over the continent, the Sunday scene is the same: one goes to the cinema to learn of the topics of conversation for the next week, to create the new family culture. Workers who a year earlier were peasants, are astonished at seeing things that they had never dreamed of and, shielded by their own inadequacies, they articulate fantasies in the form of demands: they want to possess the rumba dancer, marry the *ingénue,* imitate the ladies man, live out mild adventures, all without leaving the neighbourhood.

The country is industrialising and the cinema shows some of the (social and sexual) advantages of the anonymous urban condition. While 'high culture' is the preserve of one hundred thousand chosen ones in the city and in adjacent provincial circles, cinema and radio prepare the transition to fully urban life. In this process, the concept of entertainment allows for a deformation of reality (the countryside in *Allá en el Rancho Grande* is a fairy story; the rural population who go to see the movie several times know this, but it does not bother them), entertainment becomes a philosophy of life and the

epic of history is replaced by a smaller scale 'fantasy' epic, accompanied by the tears and laughter of Sunday evenings.

More for operative reasons than by intent, Mexican cinema, above all in the period 1939–55, makes great use of what is stored in the cultural memory of the people: expressions of love, forms of horror and catharsis, dishonour and excess, shared ideas about poverty and wealth, religious certainties, new forms of sexual appetite and hunger, songs, a sense of humour petrified in jokes and amusing, theatrical ways of evoking tradition. The cinema is not an altogether inexact encapsulation of the cultural life in the country and in Latin America, and its success is due to a great extent to the links between real situations, collective fantasies and the faithful reproduction of popular behaviour. In the decade of the 30s, amidst the strikes and the development of a trade union and socialist consciousness that would help secure popular loyalty to institutions, there is a convergence between the growth of a graphic industry (thanks, in part, to comics and sports papers), the growth of the cinema industry and the peak of the radiophonic industry. Without the intellectuals or the bureaucrats admitting or even suspecting it, in these conditions of growing urbanisation, a modest but implacable cultural revolution is replacing literature as the centre of mass veneration, promoting at the same time, and without contradiction, both literacy and functional illiteracy (let them read comics but nothing else) and opening up a tiny space for a new society, which is no longer rural, no longer dependent on the extremes of government dictates, that draws its inspiration both from old customs and from the demands of modernisation.

Between 1930 and 1950, the culture industry removes from collective experience a large number of customs drawn from the countryside and from rural and Hispanic culture, and cinema plays a major part in this pruning. It offers plots full of reprimands and moral exhortations so as to avoid too many problems with the dominant morality: it exalts the family, it meditates on honour, it prepares a sticky end for adultery and prostitution … and within its images it recognises, in a provocative way, the needs of an eager and repressed public.

Thanks to the newness of language and customs, cinema offers one certainty: that to persist in traditional ways is a form of living death. Movement becomes the theory of knowledge in a world shaken by wars and science. The modernisation of the public is partial and restricted, but undeniable, and can be seen in neighbourhood dance styles, a new sense of humour, the *look* of women and in the renewal of melodrama. To this end, the stories and characters of film are all important and they require an audience which has been formed by personal experience, on the margins of politics, history and society, and has been educated by the class system to accept as natural and just a contempt for its intelligence.

'Look How Difficult it is to Plant on the Terraces'
With hindsight, we can see the basic function of the electronic media at their first important moment of power: they mediate between the shock of industrialisation and the rural and popular urban experience which has not been prepared in any way for this giant change, a process that from the 40s modifies the idea of the nation. Civilisation is now technical and for that reason the school is seen as a guarantee of labour (from a government perspective, the illiteracy of the majority is seen as placing a great brake on the grandeur of the minority), and, in any case, a citizen is someone who once started primary school, occasionally voted for the official party, became a member of one of the unions and disappeared immediately afterwards. When the duties of the citizen are over, the culture industy appears.

Thanks to what they see on the screen, the spectators who have no theories that might help them to adjust quickly to the extraordinarily rapid changes happening all around them, recognise what they might once have glimpsed in a few poems: that what is most unique (their *private life*) is never the same as what actually happens to them. In such repressed communities, private life never corresponds to reality. In overcrowded conditions and in poverty, what is most private is the flow of fantasy, the relationship between what is lived and what is dreamed, individually and collectively, the string of tragicomic stories that make up genuine identity and privacy.

The illiterates or those who read the subtitles with difficulty do not entrust the representation of their most deeply felt experiences to subtitled North American movies. They go to these films to marvel at them, but they allow the national industry to supply them with what is irreplaceable: the *familiar turns of phrase,* the scenes of poverty, the faces-like-mirrors, the adventures of melodrama, the music which is stubbornly unsophisticated.

The first critic of the mass media, Gilbert Seldes, has remarked:

> If one believes that the cults and the idealisations of the people are isolated expressions of particularly stupid people, then one's focus will inevitably be satirical. But if one takes these cults and movements as abnormalities closely linked to normal life, as part of the uninterrupted existence of the nation, then one would need only to describe them and put them in their true perspective.

The ethics and aesthetics of Mexican cinema are based on a false obedience to the life of its spectators: what is considered beautiful and amusing must be similar to what has already been chosen and cultivated, the clichés, what is thought permissible in sex and violence. In an obvious way, the cinema will respect the opinions and prejudices of the audience. But initially in an involuntary way, these values will be subverted by the dictates of social change.

Melodrama: The Passion Machine

Gustavo García

The appearance of the cinematograph in 1895 and its rapid global diffusion permanently changed man's perception of the world and of his own self. He didn't know it then, but the cinematograph was destined to modify even the forms of behaviour, and people in the following century would, to a large degree, act according to what was shown on the screen. It is not too bold to assert that the 20th century was born with the cinema, although it is also true that the 19th century did not begin to disappear until the second decade of the following century when Europe and the USA were involved in the First World War and Mexico was in the midst of its own Revolution.

The cinema, the popular narrative medium *par excellence,* was aligned with the most uneducated and diverse audiences, for instance, immigrants in the USA, and must have inherited its affinity for the melodrama from the 19th century. The confusion that prevailed in the early years of cinema, when many vigorously debated whether the medium was better seen as a scientific instrument or as part of the fairground, produced a tangled skein of topics, representational forms and absurd experiments that took different forms in various nations and that had to be unravelled. The thread that was eventually pulled was popular narrative, whether in the form of rudimentary comic gags or powerful images charged with moral significance. The most popular among the Edison kinetoscopes were already those that captured the high points of boxing matches or *The Kiss.* The relationship between the film-maker (often an exhibitor-businessman as well) and the public produced a cinema of vicissitudes, indifferent to the incoherence of the actions or their comic, tragic or melodramatic resolutions. Examples proliferated throughout the world. Veyre and Bon. Bernard, the Lumière brothers' agents in Mexico, made a short film in 1897 called *Duelo en Chapultepec (Duel in Chapultepec)* which tried to pass as a documentary but was an obvious reconstruction: Porfirio Díaz's regime had prohibited duels and prosecuted them judicially, thus it would have been rather difficult to stage one at midday and in the presence of a film crew. In 1899, Salvador Toscano, the first Mexican cinematographer, exhibited *Don Juan Tenorio,* a condensed version lasting only a few minutes of a theatrical presentation of José Zorrilla's stage play.

The melodramatic sensibility was slow to develop in Mexican cinema: throughout the 19th century, Mexican dramaturgy had regularly followed the canons of French and Spanish melodrama without much imagination. In the last years of Porfirio Díaz's dictatorship, the most successful melodramas attempted to capture the lamentable conditions of a class-based racist society, deploring above all the subhuman conditions of a peasantry subjected to the semi-feudal power of the landowner. Melodramas such as *En la hacienda* (Federico Carlos Kegel, 1907) and *La venganza de la gleba* (*The Revenge of the Soil,* Federico Gamboa, 1906) belong to this genre. It was precisely Gamboa, a great fan of the French naturalists for whom visiting and corresponding with the Goncourt brothers took the dimensions of a mystical mission, who in 1903 published *Santa,* a novel that openly admitted its connection to Zola's *Nana. Santa* was the first major publishing success in the history of Mexican literature and its popularity would be long lasting. In addition to Mexicanising French naturalism (the story progressed from the idyllic village of Chimalistac, in the south of the Valley of Mexico, to a brothel in downtown Mexico City), *Santa* codified the central elements of subsequent Mexican melodramas: the opposition between a utopian province (the land of hard-working Christian people who respect mother and family and are in touch with Nature) and the city (a chaotic universe leading to vice, immorality, sensuality, venereal disease and death). In such stories, women were considered good in so far as they were virgins, and perverse if seduced; sexuality was a manifestation of evil and evil a form of knowledge (in the brothel, the only innocent soul is that of the pianist Hipólito, who is blind and, as a result, distanced from the sinful evidence surrounding him: he sees everything with his soul).

The first fiction films focused on comedy: in the Porfirian period, for instance, there were *El San Lunes del valedor* (*Saint Monday of the Comrade,* 1907), *Aventuras de Tip Top en Chapultepec* (*Tip Top's Adventures in Chapultepec,* 1907), and in 1913, during the Revolution, *Aniversario del fallecimiento de la suegra de Enhart* (*Anniversary of the Death of Enhart's Mother-in-law*). Nevertheless, the first efforts of the budding film industry of 1917 were marked by their interest in melodrama. There were obvious reasons for this: other than the documentaries about the Revolution, the most successful movies in Mexico were those featuring Italian divas and French or US melodramas. The Mexican public suffered as much over the fate of the combating armies as it did over the misfortunes of the Gish sisters or Francesca Bertini. *La luz* (*The Light*, E. Carrasco, 1917), openly adapted Piero Fosco's Italian film *Il fuoco* (1915), which had in turn been inspired by Gabriele D'Annunzio. The imitation tried to be so faithful to the original that the lead actress, Emma Padilla, was chosen because of her physical resemblance to Pina Menichelli. In that same year, Azteca Films produced five melodramas, either set in European mansions (*Confesión trágica* by José Manuel Ramos) or in Mexico City's insane asylum (Mimí Derba's *La tigresa*). Generally, women paid with their lives if they toyed with the affections of naive lovers (in some cases the gender roles could be reversed). The reality of Mexican life never appeared in the narratives.

In 1918, attempting to attract a more culturally sophisticated audience, Luis G. Peredo turned to literary adaptations and filmed the first version of *Santa*. However, it would be the second version of *Santa* (Antonio Moreno, 1931) which inaugurated Mexico's sound cinema, and its figuration of the moral and dramatic universe of the novel determined those of all the films that followed. Of course, the moral division between the country and the city had already been developed during the 20s. The successful cinematic version of the play *En la hacienda* (Ernesto Vollrath, 1921) anticipated the genre of the rural melodrama: the peasants Blas and Petrilla love each other, but Pepe, the ranch-owner's son, sends the young man to jail in order to seduce the girl. Blas kills Pepe and flees with Petrilla in search of a better life. Just as *Santa* defined the moral opposition between the provinces and the city, *En la hacienda* delineated the laws of the provincial melodrama: class difference was acknowledged as a basis for conflicts that never led to political reflection. *Patrón* and *peóns* occupied fixed, immutable positions: the *patrón* (or his son) can fall in love with a peasant woman, but a *peón* could never do the same with the *patrona* or a white woman without fatal consequences, as in *Tizoc* (Ismael Rodríguez, 1956), where the white María Félix's love for Tizoc (Pedro Infante) leads to her death from an Indian arrow and to the hero's suicide.

Santa engendered various characters faithful to the model: the young woman who has been seduced and

forced to leave her home town for the red-light district, where she flourishes as a prostitute only long enough to pay for her guilt; the pure, honest suitor, who is either an artist or handicapped (or both), who watches with indignation as his beloved gives herself to wealthy and decadent lovers. *Santa* was adapted twice more to the screen, by Norman Foster in 1943 and by Emilio Gómez Muriel in 1968, and also gave rise to a curious variation, *Hipólito, el de Santa* (*Santa's Hipólito* by Fernando de Fuentes, 1949), which continued the story of the blind pianist after the heroine's death.

Already in 1933, two years after the first sound version of *Santa*, the series produced its masterpiece, *La mujer del puerto*, directed by the Russian Arcady Boytler and based on Guy de Maupassant's short story. The basic story of a young woman who has been seduced, repudiated by society, and forced to become a prostitute, was supplemented by involuntary incest (Rosario beds her brother, a sailor who returns after several years at sea, and neither recognises the other). The possibility of subverting the conservative laws of the melodrama through the kinship taboos never caught on in Mexican cinema: Mexican culture challenges the cult of the macho with the cult of the mother as a supreme and untouchable authority. Thus it is surprising to find melodramas in which the mother is totally villainous. In *La familia Dressel* (Fernando de Fuentes, 1935), Frau Dressel (Rosita Arriaga), head of the immigrant merchant clan, does everything possible to tyrannise her daughter-in-law, the Mexican Magdalena (Consuelo Frank). In *Aventurera* (Alberto Gout, 1949), the extremely respectable provincial mother (Andrea Palma) is also a brothel and cabaret-owner in Ciudad Juárez where she prostitutes Elena (Ninón Sevilla), who (after complex plot twists) ends up as her daughter-in-law and mistress of the situation. In the powerful rural melodrama *Los hermanos del Hierro* (*The del Hierro Brothers*, Ismael Rodríguez, 1961), after a man dies in an ambush in front of his children, his widow brings them up to be obsessed with revenge: once grown, the sons are compulsive killers and the mother a desolate and tragic figure who waits only for news of her sons' deaths. In *La pasión según Berenice* (Jaime Humberto Hermosillo, 1976), the provincial Berenice (Martha Navarro) undergoes a slow process of sexual liberation that concludes when she burns her elderly mother to death in her own bed.

The melodrama is an emotion machine. Internationally, in between the primitive melodrama of the late 18th century and Harold Pinter's discreet

Pedro Armendáriz in *El rebozo de Soledad* (Roberto Gavaldón, 1952)

dramatic structures, authors learned how to exploit sentimentalism and manipulate spectators' reactions. We have witnessed the establishment, modification, parody and disappearance of tricks and characters, even if some reappear in the most unexpected places: the letter which, in Molièresque fashion, eliminates a character from the plot in Rohmer; Greenaway's villains, allies and condemned heroes, who are based on Elizabethan drama and the *commedia dell'arte*. A similar apprenticeship occurred in Mexican film melodrama: adaptations of local theatrical or novelistic melodramas followed the irrational imitations of Italian melodrama. In the 30s, the directors of the first sound films were all college graduates. Some had been involved in political activities (supporting the philosopher José

Vasconcelos in his 1927 presidential campaign); many had watched or made theatre and learned about film as spectators. Throughout the following decades, only the best Mexican film directors were able to overcome melodramatic conventions with their skill and honesty. Only three directors, Gilberto Martínez Solares, Juan Bustillo Oro and Ismael Rodríguez, were able to balance their comedic and melodramatic sensibilities. Martínez Solares concentrated on his comedic side and produced many of the best and zaniest comedies. He also forged a fantastic comedian, Tin Tan, who was comparable only to Groucho Marx. The other two directors will be discussed in more detail below.

Spaces

Throughout the world, melodrama obeys and makes use of recognisable, verisimilar physical spaces, imbued with cultural implications in order to save time in the definition of characters. In Mexican melodrama, the opposition between city and country is central. The country or a provincial setting consists of the following elements:

- The hacienda: a closed, feudal, authoritarian space, with internal laws; its harmony depends on the fact that everyone, from the *patrón* to the *peóns,* knows his place in the system. The *patrón* may be authoritarian but also paternalistic; the *peóns* work without complaining. The foreman mediates between the two classes; he is obedient and a good counsellor, even though he is sometimes the master's rival in love. The hacienda is economically and culturally self-sufficient, with areas dedicated to work (the corral, the stable, the barn, the farmland) and to leisure (the *peons'* houses, the manor hall).
- The village: this is the zone of dispersion, the *peón's* rather than the *hacendado's* territory. The village in turn is divided into the spaces of civil authority (the government building, the jail, the school) and those of religious authority (the church), the social meeting place (the bar), and the houses of the burgeoning middle class. The village may be tyrannically run by a political cacique (Emilio Fernández's *Río Escondido,* 1947; Roberto Gavaldón's *El rebozo de Soledad* aka *Soledad's Shawl,* 1952) who may not be a *hacendado,* but is at any rate an incarnation of the barbaric Mexican type. The cantina plays a double role as a space of entertainment and a place for meeting friends, but it is also the locus of violence, a space for meeting enemies.

The hero can enter the cantina and confront the group (when the collective stigmatises him, for example, after discovering that his girlfriend has been dishonoured (*Allá en el Rancho Grande,* Fernando de Fuentes, 1936)), or he can isolate himself at a corner table with a bottle of tequila to nurse his regrets.

- The countryside: this is more than just a space to work in, it is the epic site for settling accounts. Following the tradition of the Western, the hero and the villain can confront each other in the cantina or in the street, but from Rafael E. Portas's *Adiós Nicanor* (*Farewell Nicanor,* 1937) to Emilio Fernández's *Pueblerina* (*Townswoman,* 1948), a duel in a wide open space became the way justice was administered, simultaneously intimate and grandiose.

City spaces are equally typical and limited; melodramas take place within fixed settings that are skillfully blended or contrasted:

- The bourgeois mansion: though outlined in the films of the 30s, it acquired its definitive physical and moral characteristics during the following decade. There are historical reasons for this: the Revolution had eradicated the old governing class and it took a couple of decades for the new one to find its exclusive urban areas and its new posh neighbourhoods. During the 30s, Marxist discourse and politics supporting the workers and peasants were very intense, making the bourgeois millionaire a difficult character to develop. The 40s were radically different: the new ruling class wanted to claim responsibility for and display the new prosperity brought to Mexico by the Second World War. Although the bourgeois character was still not portrayed sympathetically, he was the incarnation of cosmopolitan Mexico. The bourgeois mansion was the space of insensitivity, commercial calculation and hard-hearted evil. Imitating the sets of fascist 'white telephone' films and Cedric Gibbons's work for Metro Goldwyn Mayer, these films resolved their dramas in marble vestibules the size of tennis courts and unending spiral staircases that led to bedrooms with mirrored walls and immense beds. On the ground floor were the dining-room (the family space) and the library (an intimate retreat). Luxury was an expression of dehu-manisation.
- The *vecindad:* since the 19th century, some old Spanish mansions were divided into small flats for

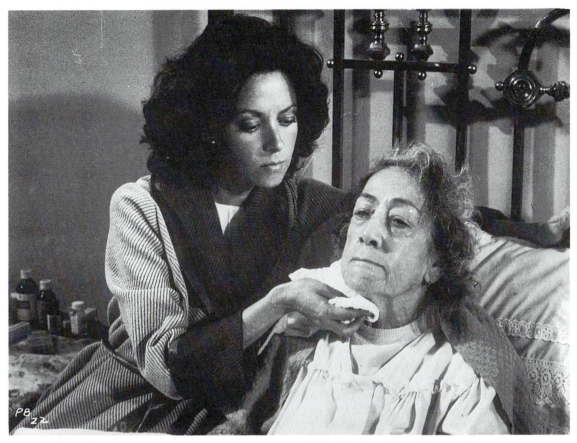

Emma Roldán and Martha Navarro in *La pasión segúnn Berenice* (Jaime Humberto Hermisillo, 1975)

the poor. The *vecindad* was such a mansion in ruins, parti-tioned and inhabited by a heterogeneous community. It was the space of solidarity, of the working people, of the poor but honourable; it was the space one left to climb the social ladder only to return, repentant, to one's roots and to the warmth that could not be found among the bourgeoisie. Already in *La mujer del puerto,* social pressure from the neighbours was a determining factor in Rosario/Andrea Palma's disgrace: her boyfriend and neighbour seduced her and when her elderly, ailing father climbs the stairs to demand retribution from the boyfriend, he falls and dies. Like a Greek chorus, the neighbouring women assess the general immorality of the misfortune and blame Rosario, who is then expelled from the community. The *vecindad* is most organically represented in Fernando de Fuentes's *La casa del ogro* (*The Ogre's*

House, 1938), in which an entire three-storey *vecindad* was reconstructed on the set to give it the same organic quality as the offices in Jean Renoir's *Le crime de Monsieur Lange* (1936). In this case, the inhabitants of each apartment are perfectly identifiable: the gossipy old maids, the reclusive homosexual, the juvenile delinquent, the flirtatious wife, the poor student, and so on. From the *vecindad* came the boxer Kid Terranova (David Silva) who became a world champion in Alejandro Galindo's *Campeón sin corona* (*Champion without a Crown,* 1945). In the style of Gorky, Ismael Rodríguez's *Nosotros los pobres* (1947) concentrates all the social pariahs in one *vecindad,* from the singing carpenter Pepe el Toro/Pedro Infante to the drunken beggar women La Guayaba and La Tostada (Amelia Wilhelmy and Delia Magaña).

• The cabaret: ever since *Santa,* the cabaret and the

brothel have been combined as two poles of the same space: in one, woman was exhibited as a public spectacle while in the other she suffered private humiliation.

But the leftist 30s were also strangely puritanical years: the cabaret and the brothel did not develop as cinematically dramatic spaces under the double sign of cosmopolitanism and decadence until the 40s. This space represented the nocturnal world in contrast to the daytime worlds of the bourgeois mansion and the *vecindad*; it was a world of unleashed sensuality, violence, and crime. Women danced half-naked to Afro-Caribbean rhythms, but were exploited by an unscrupulous *patrón* (who might also be a woman). As in *Santa,* in *La mujer del puerto* the young woman was expelled from the space of solidarity (the *vecindad*) and ended up in a brothel.

Gradually, melodrama began skilfully to combine all these spaces. In *Aventurera,* the heroine played by Ninón Sevilla escapes her mother's home and, of course, ends up in a cabaret run by a bourgeois woman whose mansion she subsequently acquires by marrying the madam's son (who is unaware of his mother's activities); in Emilio Fernández's *Salón México* (1948), the dancer and prostitute Mercedes/Marga López suffers the nightly exploitation of her pimp Paco/Rodolfo Acosta in order to keep her little sister (who thinks Mercedes is a constantly travelling executive), at a luxurious boarding school. Mercedes uses her wretched room in the *vecindad* to take care of the elegant clothes she wears, by day, to visit her sister's school. The three spaces are here intimately linked.

Directors

The 'golden age' of Mexican melodrama spanned the years from 1933, when its first indisputable masterpieces appeared, such as *La mujer del puerto* and Fernando de Fuentes's Revolutionary melodrama *El compadre Mendoza,* to 1964, when Roberto Gavaldón directed *El gallo de oro (The Golden Cock),* the last great provincial melodrama, scripted by Carlos Fuentes and Gabriel García Márquez from a plot by Juan Rulfo. The apprenticeship and mastery of the emotional machine of melodrama progressed from the irrational imitation of the silent period to the incorporation of diverse influences, ranging from the fascist melodrama to Hollywood's film noir by way of Jean Renoir and René Clair. But although these influences were significant for a young, still-evolving cinema, they also encountered a culture

which already possessed its own vigorous discourses. The Revolution had forged characters as well as an aesthetic: the figures of Emiliano Zapata and Francisco Villa, the fighting peasant troops, the trains packed with soldiers, the photographs and films of the newsreel cameramen, and the arrival of intellectuals from around the world (D.H. Lawrence, Edward Weston, Tina Modotti, Katherine Anne Porter, Hart Crane and Ben Traven in the 20s and, later, Antonin Artaud and André Breton, Leon Trotsky and Aaron Copeland, Graham Greene and Paul Morand) promoted aesthetic experimentation in all the arts, from muralism to music. That, in part, explains the rapid mastery achieved by the film-makers most inclined toward the melodramatic.

Fernando de Fuentes (1894–1958)

When the sound cinema appeared in Mexico, no other director introduced so many fundamental narrative options than de Fuentes. He had been a bureaucrat, a poet and the manager of a Mexico City cinema, and although his most famous film, *Allá en el Rancho Grande* (1936), leaned towards comedy, his principal idiom was melodrama. He was responsible for the most important fiction films about the Mexican Revolution: the triptych *El prisionero trece* (1933), *El compadre Mendoza* (1933) and *¡Vámonos con Pancho Villa!* (1935). The first film is a frank denunciation of the blind military authoritarianism that causes an official to order the execution of his own son. The second is the only film to show support for Emiliano Zapata's peasant movement, and reveals how the accommodating and immoral members of the old regime survived by stepping over the bodies of martyred Revolutionaries. The third film explicitly demolishes the figure of the Revolutionary caudillo by cataloguing the successive sacrifices of a group of soldiers until only the eldest remains, only to die at the hands of another Villista, in a conclusion censored at the time and only recently shown on television.

Although María Félix had made her debut two years earlier, it wasn't until de Fuentes directed her in *Doña Bárbara* (1943) that she defined the character she would continue playing throughout the rest of her career: a woman who, embittered by some masculine affront, ends up subjugating men. At times an expensive call girl, she was always a lonely and tragic figure, a *femme fatale* who challenged the country's prevailing machismo and the cinema itself. With de Fuentes, Félix made melodramas set in bourgeois mansions that emphasised the dehumanisation of internally ravaged characters: *La*

María Félix and María Elena Marqués in **Doña Barbara** (Fernando de Fuentes, 1943)

mujer sin alma (*Woman Without a Soul,* 1943) and *La devoradora* (*The Devourer,* 1946). In the latter she allowed herself the luxury of keeping the corpse of a lover who had committed suicide in her bedroom for an entire day, while she establishes an alibi and amuses herself with two other suitors in nightclubs. Towards the end of his career, de Fuentes successfully attempted a version of *Crimen y castigo* (*Crime and Punishment,* 1950), transposing Dostoyevsky's story to the Mexican *vecindades* and featuring a police inspector who persistently turns up like an obsessive presence, defying all logic. Unlike Emilio Fernández, who had an individual style somewhere between Eisenstein and Ford, de Fuentes did not have a distinctive style of his own. His films about the Revolution were more realistic and reminiscent of John Ford, while he evoked Clair and Renoir in his urban melodramas (*Las mujeres mandan,* 1936; *La casa del ogro*). His gaze was almost documentary

when filming everyday settings, be they the German community of *La familia Dressel,* Romania's King Carol during his Mexican exile in *El rey se divierte* (*The King Amuses Himself,* 1944), or simple, provincial life in which a father has difficulty shaving *(Las mujeres mandan).*

Roberto Gavaldón (1909–1986)

The undisputed master of melodrama. Although he lived in Hollywood in the early 30s, he was a waiter at the Roosevelt Hotel, and his only contact with the film industry was as a spectator and a friend of the community of Mexican actors who appeared in the Spanish-language versions of the first sound films. Back in Mexico, he learned film in ten years, during which he worked as an assistant director, a soundman, an editor, camera operator, and so on. While his first film, *La barraca* (*The Hut,* 1944, based on Vicente Blasco Ibáñez) is considered a

159

Pedro Infante in *Nosotros los pobres* (Ismael Rodríguez, 1947)

masterpiece of rural realism and a surprising reconstruction of a Spanish ambience, his subsequent films defined his narrative style (very similar to film noir, sometimes using even the same conventions) and his typical protagonists: anti-heroes living at the margins of society either because they choose to or are forced by circumstances. In the best cases, they were anti-heroes who initially belonged to the lower or upper middle class, like the chemical engineer who is madly in love with a model and thinks he has poisoned his wife in *La diosa arrodillada* (*The Kneeling Goddess,* 1947) or the phoney fortune-teller who tricks wealthy women and ends up fleeing with a corpse in his trunk and a lover who wants to murder him in *En la palma de tu mano* (*In the Palm of Your Hand,* 1950), and the successful jai alai player who uses his lovers to get rich until the most fragile of them murders him in his sleep in *La noche avanza* (*Night Advances,* 1951). His career also includes *La otra* (*The Other Woman,* 1946), with Dolores del Río, which merits special mention: the plot is identical, scene for scene, to Curtis Bernhardt's *A Stolen Life* (1946), although both films were adapted

from different literary sources and were filmed at the same time, with much more sensual and disquieting results in del Río's than in Bette Davis's version.

The tendency to place characters in precarious and paradoxical situations led Gavaldón to make rural melodramas such as *La escondida* (*The Hidden One,* 1955), in which a peasant woman (María Félix), who had been the mistress of a Porfirian politician, falls into the arms of a peasant who had become a Revolutionary colonel (Pedro Armendáriz), only to be consumed by the Revolution upon which they had both turned their backs. In *Macario* (1959), a starving peasant (Ignacio López Tarso) is protected by Death (Enrique Lucero) after he offers to share a turkey with her. Death grants him the gift of curing the hopelessly ill, although she does not grant him his own life. Echoes of Fritz Lang's *Der müde Tod* (1921) and Ingmar Bergman's *Det sjunde inseglet* (*The Seventh Seal,* 1956) are brilliantly reworked by a script that takes advantage of Ben Traven's short story and Gabriel Figueroa's exceptional photography. Finally, Gavaldón made *El gallo de oro* (1964), a melodrama touched by the fantastic, in which an incredibly lucky gamecock breeder ends up in the service of an hacendado gambler who uses his lover's presence as a talisman. In 1986, Arturo Ripstein produced a remake, *El imperio de la fortuna (The Empire of Fate),* which was impoverished by its realism: Gavaldón had followed cinematic conventions, with haciendas worthy of Orson Welles in their vastness, cinematic *charros* and a magical realism that followed Juan Rulfo's plot to the letter. No director filmed better on location or was as rigorous when staging interiors. Dozens of influences can be mentioned, especially those of great Hollywood film-makers, but he always demanded the highest quality in production regardless of the cost. His melodramas are perfect, spectacular, intense and ironic. The best Mexican film actors, Pedro Armendáriz, Dolores del Río, María Félix, Ignacio López Tarso, Pina Pellicer and many others, played their most complex roles in the films of Roberto Gavaldón.

Alejandro Galindo (born in 1906)

If Fernando de Fuentes was the most elegant film-maker and Roberto Gavaldón the most technically adept, Alejandro Galindo was the greatest realist. He received his training in Hollywood's studios writing Spanish-language dialogue and, if any foreign influence can be detected in his films, it is that of Warner Bros.' critical cinema of the 30s and of the films noirs of Archie Mayo, Michael Curtiz, Mervyn LeRoy, Lewis Seiler and Raoul Walsh. But what is central in Galindo is the need to document an immediate reality, to discover the germ of potential plots in everyday life. Already in his second film, *Refugiados en Madrid* (*Refugees in Madrid,* 1938), he had summed up the Spanish Civil War through the stories of a group of political refugees from different factions in the embassy of a Latin American country resembling Mexico. His masterpieces present critical ideas about being Mexican in fictions neatly inscribed within specific genres. *Campeón sin corona* (1945) was inspired by the recent defeat of the boxer 'Chango' Casanova. It presents, through the character of a boxer who starts out as an ice-cream vendor and becomes a world champion, the cultural obstacles that barred Mexicans from lasting success. *Una familia de tantas* (*One Family Among Many,* 1948) criticises the patriarchal family and the cultural immobility that subjects women to its authority, while parodying the family melodramas of Mexican cinema. In *Espaldas mojadas* (*Wetbacks,* 1953) he chronicles the inhuman living conditions of illegal Mexican workers in the USA, a problem that

became an international issue after the Second World War, and continues to grow to this day. In *La mente y el crimen* (*The Mind and Crime,* 1961), he reconstructs an actual crime in the places where the events occurred in order to make a pseudo-documentary about the criminal mind.

Galindo did not unnecessarily complicate his aesthetics: a firm believer in the virtues of studio filming, he exercised rigorous control over narratives that had to be, above all, verisimilar. His films featured for the first time 'street' Spanish, a lang-uage markedly different from the neutral Spanish spoken in conventional cinema. In his group scenes, dialogues take place in sonically chaotic backgrounds, commenting ironically on the usual purity of cinematic sound. Similarly, his comic touches demonstrated that reality always exceeds fiction.

Ismael Rodríguez (born in 1917)

Galindo's documentary precision contrasts with the baroque style of Ismael Rodríguez, the great film-maker of excess. His sets were always exaggerated, his actors overly dramatic, his characters victims of the greatest misfortunes. His melodramas shamelessly strove to manipulate the most elemental levels of emotion in the spectators. An example: in *Nosotros los pobres* (1948), a paralytic mother is beaten by a drug addict neighbour for money, the honest carpenter Pepe el Toro is falsely accused of murder. In prison he meets the real murderer whom he blinds with a stick to extract a confession, but months later the one-eyed man is released and seeks revenge. A lottery-ticket seller and friend of the hero recognises him and flees, losing his legs when he is run over by a streetcar. Pepe el Toro fights the one-eyed man on the roof of a building; the hoodlum falls to his death on the pavement. In the sequel, *Ustedes los ricos* (1948), the rich family of Pepe el Toro's dead wife takes his little daughter away from him, while the son of his new marriage burns to death in a fire. All this amid songs in which dozens of extras perform in a poverty-stricken neighbourhood street.

Rodríguez's imagination was boundless when it came to inventing conventions. He freely experimented with his favourite actor, Pedro Infante. In *Los tres huastecos* (*The Three Huastecans,* 1948), for example, Infante was made to play three different characters (a priest, a soldier and a gunman) who ultimately take on almost the same personality (that of a villain). Rodríguez also had Infante imitate Frank Sinatra's singing, even though he was playing a simple traffic cop in *A toda máquina* aka *ATM* (*At Full Speed,* 1951). In *Las mujeres de mi general* (*My*

Campeón sin corona (Alejandro Galindo, 1945)

General's Women, 1950), he incorporated some of Octavio Paz's theses from *El laberinto de la soledad (The Labyrinth of Solitude)* to tell the story of a Revolutionary general (Infante) who lacks real power and is destined to confront an entire army by himself when his laughter is confused with the noise of his machine gun, anticipating his own death. In *Los hermanos del Hierro* (1961), Rodríguez recasts the true story of a couple of northern *pistoleros* to describe how the mind of a killer is fostered in two boys trained by their mother to avenge their father's death. In *El hombre de papel* (*The Paper Man,* 1963), a poor trash-picker finds a thousand-peso bill in the street. He doesn't know how to spend it, although everyone, from fortune-tellers to prostitutes, counsels him. In his utter loneliness, he buys a ventriloquist's dummy thinking it alive; alone, his disillusionment only closes the circle of misery.

Given his excessiveness, Rodríguez, of course, made some errors: for example, hiring Toshiro Mifune to play the role of a southern farmer in *Animas Trujano* (1962) or Daniel Gélin and a Mexican cast to play Berliners in *El niño y el muro* (*The Boy and the Wall,* 1964), a melodrama that tried to denounce the absurdity of the Berlin Wall through the tragedy of a boy who loses his ball on the other side. Despite all this, Rodríguez always seemed to mistreat the cinema itself: he made a movie about the Mexican Revolution that was really a compendium of cinematic conventions, including the genre's legendary actors María Félix, Dolores del Río, Emilio Fernández and Pedro Armendáriz, in an absurd story, *La cucaracha* (*The Cockroach,* 1958). Rodríguez applied his intuition and lack of moderation to return melodrama to its roots, but without its original naivety.

The genre already had technical expertise, tradition and representational habits that could be relied upon. Mexican melodrama was a self-sufficient machine of effects and intentions that could either be hidden in enclosed spaces bearing no relation to reality or opened up to social contradictions. But it was a genre that was abandoned before it became exhausted, perhaps because of an excess of self-consciousness or because of a lack of faith in emotion.

Sorrows and Glories of Comedy

Rafael Medina de la Serna

Transplanted to Mexico in the era of General Porfirio Díaz, the cinematograph was naturalised as soon as the first public screening took place in August 1896. Shortly after, a number of enterprising Mexicans began to produce films with national themes because there was not enough foreign product to satisfy a public ever more eager for this new form of entertainment. Alongside the documentary recording of various events, the incipient Mexican cinema took its first steps towards fiction. The first comedies were probably produced in 1907 in the city of Orizaba: *Aventuras de Tip Top en Chapultepec* starring Tip Top, and *El San Lunes del valedor (St Monday of the Comrade)*. Like many early Mexican productions, both films appear to have been lost.

The public's preference for comedy was confirmed with *El aniversario del fallecimiento de la suegra de Enhart (The Anniversary of the Death of Enhart's Mother-in-law)*, the earliest Mexican comedy to be preserved, directed by the Alva brothers in 1913. *El aniversario del fallecimiento, El amor que triunfa (Triumphant Love)* by Manuel Cirerol Sansores (1917) and *Viaje redondo (Round Trip)* by José Manuel Ramos (1920), established three of the constants that characterised the development of Mexican film comedy during its so-called golden years. The first of these films featured Enhart and Alegría, two comedians from the popular variety theatre, a rich source for performers as well as for film scenes and themes. The second of these films was shot in Yucatán and aimed to extol the virtues of the city of Mérida. It inaugurated the folkloric style that would become the thematic mainstay of the early popular Mexican cinema geared towards folkloric and nationalistic glorification. *Viaje redondo* became the national cinema's first comedic success by introducing into the budding genre a character situation that would become a trademark of the national cinema: the naive provincial venturing into the big city. The role was played by Leopoldo Beristain, 'el Cuatezón', Mexican cinema's first real comedian.

From the Folkloric to Ranch Comedy

After the arrival of sound, Mexican cinema transferred successful musical revues from the music halls to the cinema. In *El águila y el nopal (The Eagle and the Prickly Pear*, 1929), director Manuel Contreras Torres elaborated the theme introduced in *Viaje redondo* and later recycled in *Del rancho a la capital (From the Ranch to the Capital*, Eduardo Urriola, 1926). In Contreras Torres's film, a rancher played by Roberto Soto discovers oil on his land and travels to the capital to arrange for the commercial exploitation of the precious hydrocarbon. The plot was enlivened by musical numbers and vernacular dialogue. This technique culminated in 1936 with Fernando de Fuentes's *Allá en el Rancho Grande*: a *comedia ranchera* and Mexican cinema's first blockbuster, which enabled the consolidation of the national film industry and established the first genuinely Mexican film genre, characterised by optimism, a profusion of popular songs, bucolic scenes of rural customs, simple humour, the mythification of provincial life and morality, and an explicitly reactionary ideological message.

The *comedia ranchera* was a parody, transplanted to the Mexican countryside, of the Spanish *sainete* (one-act farce) and the *zarzuela* (comedic operetta), but it was also a nostalgic reaction against the agrarian and cultural politics of President Lázaro Cárdenas's government. *Allá en el Rancho Grande* put an end to the isolation of Mexican cinema, opening up the Spanish-speaking markets to Mexican movies and increasing the popularity of actors, singers and comedians such as Carlos López 'Chaflán', who created the classic character of the picturesque ranchero (country clothes, thick moustache and drunkenly slurred speech) and became a star in two imitations of *El águila y el nopal*: Rolando Aguilar's *Los millones de Chaflán* (1938) and Manuel Contreras Torres's *Hasta que llovió en Sayula* (*Until It Rained in Sayula*, 1940).

Heir to Chaflán, Armando Soto la Marina, 'el Chicote', further developed the character of the comical ranchero and gallant lover in several *comedias rancheras* produced by Jesús Grovas, such as Miguel Zacarías's *Me he de comer esa tuna* (*I Will Have to Eat That Prickly Pear*, 1944), Juan Bustillo Oro's *No basta ser charro* (*It's Not Enough to Be a Cowboy*, 1945) and Fernando de Fuentes's *Hasta que perdió Jalisco* (*Until Jalisco Lost*, 1945). In these three typical *comedias rancheras* of the 40s, the gallant singing lover was played by Jorge Negrete, the heir to Tito Guízar's character in *Allá en el Rancho Grande*. Negrete had established himself as a popular idol in 1941 when he

Tin Tan in *Calabacitas tiernas* (Gilberto Martínez Solares, 1948)

played a bold, seductive, swaggering *charro* (cowboy) who broke into song at the slightest provocation in Joselito Rodríguez's fabulously successful *¡Ay Jalisco, no te rajes!* (*Oh Jalisco, Don't Quit Now!*, 1941). Negrete sustained his hegemony over the constellation of Mexican film stars until the appearance of Pedro Infante, the only actor who was able to compete successfully with the popular singing charro, and who became the national cinema's greatest popular figure. In contrast to Negrete's arrogance, Infante was identified with the contemporary, sympathetic popular archetype of the Mexican-style macho. In large part, Infante's film-musical reputation was due to the work of the Rodríguez brothers (Roberto, Joselito and Ismael), who directed his most famous movies. With Ismael Rodríguez's *Los tres García* (*The Three Garcías*, 1946), an ode to the virtues of the ranchero hero's machismo,[1] the *comedia ranchera* achieved one of its

major successes.

Ranchero machismo provided a deeply rooted archetype. Infante's macho character knew only the limits imposed by power (ecclesiastic and civil, in that order) and mother (incarnated with intrepid vitality by Sara García, Prudencia Grifell or Emma Roldán). Infante continued to seduce the public in movies like Ismael Rodríguez's *Los tres huastecos* (*Three From Huasteca*, 1948), in which he played the three title characters, or Roberto Rodríguez's *El seminarista* (*The Seminarian*, 1949), in which he appeared without his classic moustache, wearing a priest's cassock, only to give it all up to marry Silvia Pinal.

In order to boost the declining success of the 'old-fashioned' *comedia ranchera*, producers and screenwriters started putting two (or more) singing *charros* in the same film, trying to maximise the benefits of their combined popularity, a strategy that

Catinflas in *Ahí está el detalle* (Juan Bustillo Oro, 1940)

succeeded in revitalising the genre. Thus, Fernando de Fuentes combined Infante with Antonio Badú in *Los hijos de María Morales* (*The Sons of María Morales,* 1952), Roberto Rodríguez made Jorge Negrete compete with Luis Aguilar in *Tal para cual* (Two of a Kind, 1952), and Ismael Rodríguez himself teamed up with the greatest *comedia ranchera* idols, Negrete and Infante, in *Dos tipos de cuidado* (*Two Kinds of Care,* 1952), the film in which, according to Jorge Ayala Blanco,[2] the *comedia ranchera* lost its innocence and evolved into a comedy of errors of latent homosexuality. The equivocal relationship between two male protagonists climaxed in two very successful, 'urbanised' *comedias rancheras* directed by Ismael Rodríguez in 1951, *A toda máquina (ATM; At Full Speed)* and *¿Qué te ha dado esa mujer? (What Has That Woman Done to You?).* In these films, Infante and Luis Aguilar exchanged their horses for motorcycles, playing a pair of traffic cops who arrive at the 'radical' conclusion that 'no dame is worth as much as a buddy'.

In the mid-50s, the *comedia ranchera* lost its two principal stars and began to deteriorate. It was also put under stress by industrialisation and the urbanisation of national life. Given the need for renovation, the genre rather unsuccessfully deployed all sorts of popular singers like Manuel Capetillo in Gilberto Martínez Solares's *Contigo a la distancia* (*With You at a Distance,* 1954), Miguel Aceves Mejía in Adolfo Fernández Bustamante's *A los cuatro vientos* (*To the Four Winds,* 1954) and José Alfredo Jiménez, accompanied by the spirited singer Lola Beltrán, in Rafael Baledón's *Camino de Guanajuato* (*The Road from Guanajuato,* 1955).

However, only the northern comedian and singer Eulalio González 'Piporro' managed to give a final flourish to a genre that had lasted more than thirty years on the margins of the country's historical and social reality. His main 70s comedies were addressed primarily to an audience close to the US–Mexican border: Zacarías Gómez Urquiza's *El terror de la frontera* (*Border Terror*, 1962), Miguel M. Delgado's *El rey del tomate* (*The Tomato King*, 1962), Gilberto Martínez Solares's *Los tales por cuales* (*The Nobodies*, 1964) and *El pocho (The Half-Breed),* directed by Piporro himself in 1969.

Mexican-Style Musicals: From Porfirian Nostalgia to Juvenile Comedy

Mexican cinema learned to replace the conservatism of the *comedia ranchera* with an equally backward-looking, urban nostalgia for the Porfirian era. This was how the most reactionary sectors of the urban middle class demonstrated their ideals of decency and good manners, values which they felt were endangered by the populist Cárdenas government. An emblematic 1939 title ushered in the trend: *En tiempos de don Porfirio (In Don Porfirio's Day),* directed by Juan Bustillo Oro, the cycle's most ardent proponent. The film starred Joaquín Pardavé, a comical, inane, somewhat pathetic figure and a perfect example of the Porfirian lounge lizard.

Bustillo Oro's film established the sub-genre's basic clichés: a rigid but kind-hearted father (Fernando Soler, another archetypal figure), an aristocratic mother, a few maiden aunts and a tacky but decent daughter (the only three options available to 'respectable' Mexican women), a likeable singing suitor, usually poor but honourable, a comic character (the inevitable Pardavé), the guardianship of Don Porfirio Díaz (his presence in, or absence from, the film's plot was irrelevant), and the ever-present musical numbers that consisted of classic *zarzuelas* or light-hearted songs from the turn of the century.[3]

The formula was popular in the early 40s when a series of titles proclaimed their Porfirian affiliation: the film that launched Julio Bracho's 'prestigious' career, *¡Ay, qué tiempos, señor don Simón!* (*What a Time, Don Simón!,* 1941); Gilberto Martínez Solares's *Yo bailé con don Porfirio* (*I Danced with Don Porfirio*, 1942) and *El globo de Cantolla* (*Cantolla's Balloon*, 1943); Bustillo Oro's *México de mis recuerdos* (*The Mexico I Remember*, 1943); Ismael Rodríguez's *Amores de ayer* (*Loves of Yesteryear*, 1944); José Benavides's *La reina de la opereta* (*The Operetta Queen,* 1945). The clichés of the Porfirian farce were even applied to historical events that predated General Díaz's government, such as Emilio Gómez Muriel's *La Guerra de los Pasteles* (*The Cake War,* 1943), a comedy set during the 1838 French

intervention. The evocation of the Porfirian era was the pretext for the adaptation of the Hollywood musical, even though the Mexican industry was not used to that genre's typical choreographic and musical excesses. Nevertheless, the best things about films like *El globo de Cantolla* were the very commendable and likeable musical numbers.

Wartime pan-American solidarity was another theme typical of those films that attempted to imitate Hollywood's musical comedies: Chano Urueta's *La liga de las canciones* (*The League of Songs,* 1941) and Ramón Pareda's *Canto a Las Americas* (*Hymn for the Americas,* 1942). By the 50s, the Mexican middle-class musical was limited to the presentation of dance numbers and the repetition of fashionable rhythms within insignificant narratives: Chano Urueta's *Del can can al mambo* (*From the Can Can to the Mambo,* 1951) or Gilberto Martínez Solares's *Qué lindo cha cha cha* (*How Nice to Cha Cha Cha,* 1954). With the emergence of rock in the cinema, Mexican youth (as imagined by veteran producers, directors and screenwriters) moved into the forefront with films that took advantage of the (limited) popularity television and the recording industry had bestowed on young singers such as Julissa, Cesar Costa, Alberto Vázquez, Enrique Guzmán and Angélica María. These last two were idols of Mexican youth in the 70s and starred in what for Emilio García Riera[4] was the prototype of the juvenile musical comedy: Miguel M. Delgado's *Mi vida es una canción* (*My Life is a Song,* 1962). The inane juvenile rock-comedy did not improve much when the 'hip' young writer José Agustín, author of the novel *De perfil (In Profile),* wrote the script for the farce *Cinco de chocolate y uno de fresa* (*Five Chocolate and One Strawberry,* 1967) by Carlos Velo, a musical vehicle for Angélica María, who was being promoted by her publicists and by Agustín himself as America's sweetheart. Less fortunate still was Agustín's only directorial effort, *Ya sé quien eres – Te he estado observando* (*Now I Know Who You Are – I've Been Watching You,* 1970).

The Burlesque Comedy: Cantinflas, Tin Tan, Resortes and the Others

During the early sound period, Mexican cinema in general and comedy in particular, lacked authentic stars and was at a competitive disadvantage in its battle for the national audience with Hollywood. In the early 30s, the only comedic headliner was the Peruvian Leopoldo Ortín, the star of Juan José Segura's *El superloco (The Screwball)* in 1936. However, 1936 was also the year of the film debut of Mario Moreno 'Cantinflas', a comedian who came from the travelling tent-shows and variety theatres, as did the rest of his colleagues before the advent of television. He was featured in Miguel Contreras Torres's *No te engañes corazón* (*Don't Be Fooled My Heart*, 1936), followed by Arcady Boytler's *¡Así es mi tierra!* (*That's How My Land Is!* 1937) and *Aguila o sol* (*Eagle or Sun*, 1937), and Chano Urueta's *El signo de la muerte* (*The Mark of Death*, 1939). Cantinflas's early film career culminated with the spectacular success of Bustillo Oro's *Ahí está el detalle* (*There's the Detail*, 1940), which catapulted its star to fame throughout the Spanish-language cinema. In these early films, Mario Moreno played a *peladito*, an urban tramp, the Aztec equivalent of Chaplin's, challenging middle-class decency, hypocrisy and smugness with his incomprehensible speech and anarchic spirit. Cantinflas's success led him increasingly to mediate and mollify the class character of his comedy and of his world-view while attempting to preserve the trappings of his *peladito* character (a sparse moustache at the corners of his mouth, sagging pants and incoherent speech). Associated with Miguel M. Delgado (his director and chief 'yes man'), Cantinflas's creative decadence began while he reaped the economic fruits of his commercial popularity, exploited in films where he sought to parody professions, trades or popular behaviour while giving free reign to his moralising and grumbling temperament: *El gendarme desconocido* (*The Mysterious Gendarme*, 1941), *El circo* (*The Circus*, 1942, a notorious imitation of Chaplin's classic), *El bombero atómico* (*The Atomic Bomber*, 1950), *Si yo fuera diputado* (*If I Were Elected*, 1951).

Cantinflas's success in the Spanish-language markets convinced British producer Michael Todd to include the Mexican comedian in his extravagant production *Around the World in 80 Days*, directed by Michael Anderson in 1956. During the 60s, Mario Moreno completely abandoned his original popular character in order to associate himself with the most pedestrian and reactionary causes of films like *El padrecito* (*The Dear Little Priest*, 1964), *Su excelencia* (*Your Excellency*, 1966), *El profe* (*The Prof*, 1970), *El ministro y yo* (*The Minister and I*, 1975) or *El patrullero 777* (*Patrol 777*, 1977), again under the direction of Delgado.

The popularity of Cantinflas's *peladito* eclipsed other comic personalities, who were unable to achieve the same degree of success. Manuel Medel, Cantinflas's erstwhile collaborator, had his finest moment in Contreras Torres's *La vida inútil de Pito Pérez* (*Pito Pérez's Useless Life*, 1943), a film based on the homonymous novel by José Rubén Romero,

a Michoacán writer who recreated the *pícaro* figure of sixteenth- and seventeenth-century Spanish literature. But of all the national film comedians, Germán Valdés 'Tin Tan' was the most original and likeable. He emerged from the *teatro frívolo*, the popular theatre of the 30s, where he had developed a *pachuco* character, an elaborately zoot-suited Mexican-American wearing an enormous smile. Tin Tan made his film debut in 1943 playing a small role in René Cardona's *Hotel de verano* (*Summer Hotel*). Directed by Humberto Gómez Landero in five subsequent films, the comedian displayed an original style which was most fully developed, from 1948 onwards, in association with Gilberto Martínez Solares, beginning with a classic of Mexican comedy: *Calabacitas tiernas* (*Tender Pumpkins*), a curious musical fantasy with some surprisingly surrealist gags. Tin Tan starred in several parodies of classic tales, such as *La marca del Zorrillo* (*The Mark of the Little Zorro*, 1950), *Simbad el mareado* (*Sinbad the Seasick*, 1950), *El ceniciento* (*Cinderfellow*, 1951) and *Las mil y una noches* (*The Thousand and One Nights*, Fernando Cortés, 1957). However, Martínez Solares's *El rey del barrio* (*King of the Neighbourhood*, 1949) was his most successful film. Here, Germán Valdés abandoned his *pachuco* character to blend into Mexico City's slums, displaying a level of spontaneous humorous inventiveness that has remained unparalleled in Mexican comedy. In the 50s, Tin Tan froze the formulas that had made him the greatest national comedian and in 1969, physically diminished and in creative decadence, he made his directorial debut with *El capitán Mantarraya* (*Captain Mantarraya*), a lacklustre finale to a brilliant career.

None of the burlesque comedians matched Tin Tan's originality and humour. Antonio Espino 'Clavillazo', a disconcerting, hyperactive comedian who also emerged from the popular theatre, enjoyed some success during the 50s; Jesús Martínez 'Palillo', a specialist in political jokes from the travelling tent-shows, failed in the cinema; others, such as the team of Manolín and Schillinsky, the Yucatecan Daniel 'Chino' Herrera, or the Argentines Luis Sandrini and Nini Marshal 'Catita', enjoyed brief film careers, but few of their films were significant. The extraordinary dancer Adalberto Martínez 'Resortes' had better luck. He was associated with director Alejandro Galindo, the creator of acerbic popular urban comedies such as *¡Esquina ... bajan!* (*Corner Stop! All Descend!*) and its sequel, *Hay lugar para dos* (*There's Room for Two*), both made in 1948 and starring David Silva, as well as the beloved comedian Fernando Soto 'Mantequilla', the

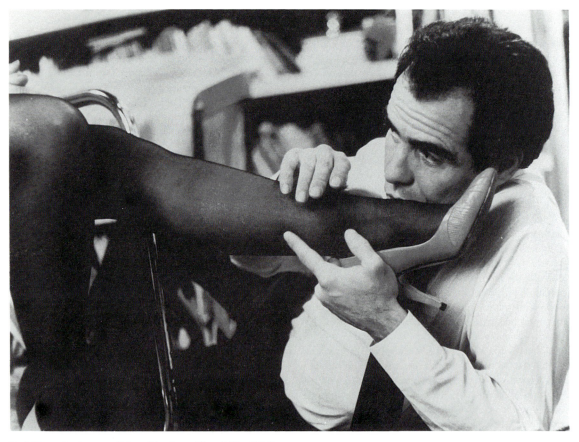

José Alonso in *La tarea* (Jaime Humberto Hermisillo, 1990)

incarnation of the classic urban *peladito*. Galindo's proven talent and 'Resortes' hyperkinetic comedic style resulted in entertaining populist films like *Confidencias de un ruletero* (*Confessions of a Roulette Player*, 1949), *Dicen que soy comunista* (*They Say I am a Communist*, 1951), *Policías y ladrones* (*Cops and Robbers*, 1956), *Echenme al gato* (*Throw Me to the Cat*, 1957) and *Ni hablar del peluquín* (*Out of the Question*, 1958). However, the popular comedian-dancer soon went into a decline, degenerating into a stereotype and following the pattern of most Mexican comedians who kept going long after their sell-by date.

From Television to Cinema

From the 50s onwards, television replaced the popular theatre as the principal source for cinema's comic talent. The electronic medium's strict control of content (contrasting with variety theatre's anarchic exuberance) and the influence of commercial sponsors help to explain why few comedians have been able to move successfully from the small screen to cinema. Neither the pitiful Mexican version of Abbott and Costello or the infantile fat man Gaspar Henaine 'Capulina' teamed with the vapid thin man Marco Antonio Campos 'Viruta' managed the transition. Neither did the demented humorous improvisations of Manuel 'Loco' Valdés (Tin Tan's brother), nor the biting routines of the Polivoces, the two mimics Enrique Cuenca and Eduardo Manzano. None brought glory to a genre that had already seen better days. The situation did not improve when the macro-company Televisa moved into film production with extensions of its television programmes crammed full of comedians like Guillermo Rivas, Leonorilda Ochoa and Sergio Ramos 'el Comanche', as in Fernando Cortés's *Los Beverly de Peralvillo* (*The Beverlys of Peralvillo*, 1971), derived from the US television series *The Beverly Hillbillies* (1962–71); or featuring the likes of Roberto Gómez Bolaños 'Chespirito', the king of 'white' humour (for the privately owned Mexican television network, this term meant not just a lack of mischievousness but, above all, a lack of humour itself), whose film *El chanfle* (1978) was spectacularly successful in Mexico and Latin America. This success turned to failure years later with the scatological comedy *Música de viento (Wind Music)*, which the comedian directed himself in 1990; or the clown Cepillín, whose film debut, *Milagro en el circo* (*Miracle at the Circus*, by Alejandro Galindo) flopped spectacularly in 1978, ending his career as swiftly as it had begun.

María Elena Velasco 'la India María' deserves a special mention: she was Mexican cinema's first successful female comedian and her films became real blockbusters. From her first appearance on the screen in Fernando Cortés's *Tonta, tonta pero no tanto* (*Dumb But Not That Dumb*, 1971), she was welcomed enthusiastically by the Mexican audience. In that film she introduced her comic persona: a coarse caricature of the unruly Indian woman transplanted to the big city as a domestic servant.

Héctor Suárez also began in television, but he was more versatile and had more talent than most of his television colleagues, and achieved considerable success with Roberto G. Rivera's *El mil usos* (*The Handyman*, 1981), a demographic warning which attempted to dissuade the marginal population of the rural areas from seeking their fortunes in the big city. The film turned out to be a curious and unexpected return to the founding theme of Mexican comedy as elaborated in *Viaje redondo, El águila y el nopal* and *Del rancho a la capital*.

From Picaresque Comedy to Sexual Puns

Sexual puns first appeared in Mexican comedy in the early 40s. At that time, a handful of films with a risqué edge tried to hook the public with representations of sexual misunderstandings, tuning in to the tastes and permissiveness of a middle class that felt repressed and lectured by President Avila Camacho's rule. Salvador Elizondo wrote: 'Mexican cinema, with a few shining exceptions, has been since its origins, a moralistic cinema, and what is worse, a judgmentally moralistic cinema ...'[5] In this context, films such as *Noches de recién casados* (*Newlywed Nights*, Carlos Orellana, 1941), *Las cinco noches de Adán* (*Adam's Five Nights*, Gilberto Martínez Solares, 1942), or *La corte de Faraón* (*Pharaoh's Court*, Julio Bracho, 1943), attempted to cause an authorised and, in any case, inoffensive hormonal uproar in the modern adult audience that admired Mapy Cortés,

the most celebrated female figure in light comedy.

However, during this decade the slum and brothel melodrama had a monopoly on sexual boldness, which returned to popular comedy in the 70s, where it made a contribution to the debates about sexuality but, unfortunately, did not improve the quality of Mexican comedy. As a comic ingredient, sexuality was used to motivate moral sermons and shame-filled stories. The 70s saw two kinds of erotic comedies. Firstly, those produced by a new group of directors with the participation of a young generation of actors (some from television, others from university theatres). These comedies tended to have thematic and artistic pretensions, such as Francisco del Villar's *Los cuervos están de luto* (*The Crows Are in Mourning*, 1965), Tito Novaro, Manuel Michel and Jorge Fons's *Trampas de amor* (*Snares of Love*, 1968) or Jorge Fons's *El quelite* (1969). All three films were less successful than had been expected. The second group of erotic comedies was produced by old-guard directors who dabbled in sexual matters in a superficially modern way without renouncing their petty-bourgeois moralising. The emblematic character of this type of comedy was the libertine and idle playboy incarnated by Mauricio Garcés, a comedian who did not lack humour and a certain congeniality, but who was eventually enslaved by his own caricature of an irresistible, middle-aged lover in vulgar and clumsily produced comedies such as José Díaz Morales's *Mujeres, mujeres, mujeres* (*Women, Women, Women*, 1967), Carlos Velo's *Don Juan 67* (1966) or René Cardona Jr's *El matrimonio es como el demonio* (*Marriage Is Hell*, 1967) and *Espérame en Siberia, vida mía* (*Wait for Me in Siberia, My Love*, 1969).

Searching for audacity along the most tortuous paths, a good number of private producers, headed by Guillermo Calderón, combined the risqué comedy with brothel films, generating the *fichera* sub-genre, beginning with Miguel M. Delgado's *Bellas de noche (Beauties of the Night)* and *Las ficheras*, both in 1974.[6] This type of cinema produced a new generation of comedians like Lalo el Mino, Alberto Rojas 'el Caballo', Pedro Weber 'Chatanuga', Manuel 'Flaco' Ibañez, Rafael Inclán, Luis de Alba, Raúl Padilla 'Chóforo', and so on. They were characterised by their florid language spiced with *albures* (sexual puns) and coarse language. In this way, the degradation of picaresque cinema resulted in a bastardised sub-genre. Redolent with rampant vulgarity, this genre has been laboriously milked for fifteen years by some directors, the architects of 'degree zero' comedy, such as René Cardona Jr, Gilberto Martínez Solares (who had directed the very decent comedy *El globo de Cantolla* in 1943), Julio Ruiz Llaneza, Javier Durán or Víctor Manuel 'el Gúero' Castro.

And Yet, There is Movement
The generation of young film-makers who became part of the industry in the 70s benefited from the state-production plans sponsored by the government of Luis Echeverría. Most of them tried their hand at comedy and brought to the genre an auteurist perspective, as in Jaime Humberto Hermosillo's *La verdadera vocación de Magdalena* (*Magdalena's True Calling,* 1971); Alberto Isaac's *El rincón de las vírgenes* (*The Virgins' Corner,* 1972) and *Tívoli* (1974); Juan Manuel Torres's *Diamantes, oro y amor* (*Diamonds, Gold and Love,* 1971); Julián Pastor's *La venida del rey Olmos (The Arrival of King Olmos)* and *El esperado amor desesperado (The Hoped-for Hopeless Love),* both in 1974; José Estrada's *Maten al león* (*Kill the Lion,* 1975); and Alfonso Arau's *El águila descalza* (*The Barefoot Eagle,* 1969) and *Calzonzín inspector* (*Underwear Inspector,* 1973). This auteurist approach to comedy, a genre which Mexican culture, all too solemn, continues to undervalue, persisted during the unfortunate 80s and was revitalised by the new generation of film-makers in the 90s. New directors with greater technical ability and renewed creative aspirations successfully worked in the comedy genre and have reconquered lost audiences, such as Dana Rotberg's *Intimidad* (1990), Carlos Carrera's *La mujer de Benjamín* (1990), Alfonso Cuarón's *Sólo con tu pareja* (*Only with Your Partner,*

1991) and Marysa Sistach's *Anoche soñé contigo* (*Last Night I Dreamed of You,* 1991). In this, they have been supported by film-makers from the previous generation, such as Hermosillo with *La tarea* (1990) or Arau with *Como agua para chocolate* (1991). Consequently, we may conclude that, despite the continued decline of Mexican comedians and the degenerative pressures of an excessively commercial system which spawns sequels and sub-genres, comedy has survived eighty-five years of sorrows and glories.

Notes
1. Regarding machismo in the *comedia ranchera,* Jorge Ayala Blanco wrote in *La aventura del cine mexicano* (Mexico City: Era, 1968), p. 68: 'Machismo … is a way of life in communities that are closed to time and space. In the comedia ranchera you either have a tremendously likeable macho or a character who has succumbed to the macho.'
2. Ibid., pp. 77–83.
3. Enrique Ames, in an article published in *Cine,* no. 21, December 1979, pp. 16–19, gives a label to these musical comedies nostalgic for the Porfirian era: the Ipiranga syndrome, after the name of the boat that carried the old dictator into exile.
4. Emilio García Riera, *Historia del cine mexicano* (Mexico City: SEP, Foro 2000, 1986).
5. Salvador Elizondo, 'Moral sexual y moraleja en el cine mexicano' in *Nuevo Cine,* no. 1, April 1961, pp. 5–11.
6. The term *ficheras* was applied to prostitutes who frequented second- and third-rate cabarets to dance with customers; each time a drink was served to them or to their clients, they were given a ficha or token exchangeable for cash at closing time.

The Labyrinths of History

Andrés de Luna

The discourse of history is always relative. Sometimes it seems enigmatic because the mere investigation of the past often reveals a series of potential mysteries. Archaeological ruins, archives, and documents of all kinds and from all sources are lucky finds for those attempting to pursue what is called historical work. However, we must be clear: we generally demand realism and verisimilitude when dealing with the representation of historical events. Ideally, this combination should produce a faithful image of historical events. But it would be absurd to impose upon painting, literature, theatre or film the rigour that only scientific practices can have. For any of the arts, history is an immense labyrinth that proposes themes and suggests re-enactments. However, each of the arts possesses its own expressive power and willingly provides a point of view on the important events that mark a country's fate. When the arts encounter historical reality, a logical link is established which must be freed from the illusion of there being any possible 'direct' correspondences, without falling into either the subjection of one to the other or an unbearable tyranny of one over the other.

The relationship between cinema and history is as exciting as it is broad and complex. Since its inception as a mass spectacle, cinema has used history as a source of thematic inspiration. Méliès managed to record a few incidents in his actuality films, such as the wedding of King Edward VII, that were reconstructed in his studio even before the historical events actually occurred. Although they are obvious examples, we should also recall that *Birth of a Nation* (David W. Griffith, 1915) and *Battleship Potemkin* (Sergei Eisenstein, 1925) were based on historical events and that many celebrated historical processes, such as the Roman Empire, the Middle Ages, the 'colonisation' of the Third World, the settling of the West, and so on, have played significant roles in the genesis of some cinematographic genres.[1]

It is a well-known fact that the Lumière brothers discovered some of the propagandistic abilities of this 'scientific novelty', as they called the cinematograph. They entered the realms of politics and history by recording images of some of the more relevant events of the turn of the century. European countries such as Belgium, Switzerland, Great Britain, Spain and Russia witnessed the production of the first documentary films, if one can give that label to those filmic exercises that constitute the prehistory of cinema. Despite their doubts about the acceptance and development of their technical innovation, the inventors trained a group of camera operators who devoted themselves to capturing all kinds of events on film: from a fire in France to the coronation of Czar Nicholas II. In 1896, Lumière operators like Promio, Mesguich, Doublier and others travelled far and wide in search of a present that could be included in the cinematic record of what later would become history.

It was about the same time that their emissaries Bernard and Gabriel Veyre arrived in a Mexico living under the Díaz dictatorship. The country was a vast territory that even included a concentration camp in the state of Oaxaca, housing some 15,000 prisoners. Don Porfirio, as the formerly victorious general was known, gained power in 1876 and had fully consolidated his control by 1877. From 1877 to 1889, his ambitions were focused on being constantly re-elected, although he allowed his friend Manuel González to take over the presidency for a four-year period (1880–4). It was well known that Díaz used González to prop up a government that could only collapse with the outbreak of the Revolution in 1911. But, without needing to provide further details of these stories, what is important for our purposes here is that the so-called Porfirian era gave our first national cinema a markedly propagandistic character.

The first screenings in the capital took place on 14 August 1896. Reactions were varied and Díaz himself was immediately associated with the Lumières' invention. The event led to the production of several shorts where one could see a *Grupo en movimiento del general Díaz y de algunas personas de su familia (Moving Scene of General Díaz and Some Members of his Family)* or else *El general Díaz paseando por el bosque de Chapultepec (General Díaz Strolling through the Chapultepec Woods,* Bernard or Veyre, 1896). The history registered by these naive documentary scenes demonstrated one of the virtues of the cinematograph: it served as a referential tool because the characters filmed 'live' were witnesses of an epoch. The ordinary acquires a new significance when it forges a 'document', defined by Michel Foucault in the following terms:

> The document, then, is no longer for history an inert material through which it tries to reconstitute what men have done or said, the events of which only the trace remains; history is now trying to define within the documentary material itself unities, totalities, series, relations. The document is not the fortunate tool of a history that is primarily and fundamentally memory.[2]

In turn-of-the-century Mexico, historical events were absorbed naturally and without obstacles, primarily because of the new forms of propaganda using modern techniques. This led to a more efficient dissemination of the sense of dailyness that was disappearing in this historical moment characterised by a multitude of deeply significant events.

The need to record the details of the chief executive's life became evident during Díaz's last re-election campaigns. The proof was the first national feature-length film, *Fiestas presidenciales en Mérida* (*Presidential Celebrations in Mérida*, Enrique Rosas, 1906), a documentary filmed in the south-eastern part of the country on the occasion of Díaz's visit to the provincial capital. The cinema would manage to establish independent traces that demonstrate just how political events are the key to understanding the complex history evidenced by the memory web of images. Thus, the film-makers carefully followed the president's agenda, since his itinerary was itself the noteworthy event. The spectators appropriated a chronicle that, through the alchemy of time, almost immediately became history.

Díaz appeared in a great number of films, but only a few sequences have survived. A pair of feature-length films announced the end of the epoch: *La entrevista de los presidentes Díaz–Taft en El Paso, Texas, el 16 de octubre de 1909* (*The Díaz–Taft Meeting in El Paso, Texas, 16 October, 1909*) and *El desfile histórico del Centenario* (*The Historic Centennial Parade*, 1910), both shot by the Alva brothers as part of their series *Fiestas del Centenario de la Independencia*. Years later, a cameraman crossed the ocean to record the last images of the old dictator, who had settled in Paris. We see him stubbornly waiting to be liberated by death.

Film documents are by no means innocent records. Discourse scholars have discovered 'that all verbal (and, obviously, visual) expression stylises and transforms, to a certain degree, the event which it

describes'.[3] The philosopher Ludwig Wittgenstein found that 'to discover an intention means to discover what happened from a particular point of view and with a specific purpose. It gives a specific version of the event.'[4] This implies that the historical discourses developed during the Díaz era and during the Mexican Revolution must be understood as contributions to the construction of the real.

The cinema is an echo box in which elements of the present combine with the extremely complex networks of the past. For example, the proximity of the Independence celebrations led film-maker Felipe de Jesús Haro to direct and star in *El grito de Dolores* (*The Cry of Dolores,* 1907), a short film recounting the uprising of the priest Miguel Hidalgo y Costilla. This national hero appeared on the screen again in *1810 o ¡Los libertadores de México!* (*1810 or Mexico's Liberators!,* Manuel Cirerol Sansores, 1916). Mexican silent cinema was characterised by a general tendency to summarise the history of the nation through an extremely select group of heroes and caudillos (military and political leaders). Of course, this view of events was incomplete and somewhat manipulative. Thus, we must accept as a given the propagandistic nature of the majority of the documentary films made during the fratricidal revolt of 1910–17 as well as those that followed until the founding of the Partido Nacional Revolucionario (PNR) in 1928 (which, with various name changes, continues in control of the nation to this day).

The Mexican Revolution was nebulous and difficult to decipher. The documentaries of the period showed what was visible: battlefields covered with corpses, battles where one can barely distinguish the faces of the combatants and, above all, images of the caudillos. Nevertheless, the cinematographic rhetoric astounded the public with its vitality, persuasiveness and unquestionable verisimilitude. Few other forms of discourse were accepted as quickly by the mass public. The short-film format imposed itself while armed conflict was at its most intense. A quintet of caudillos appeared repeatedly in the documentaries of Enrique Rosas, the Alva brothers, Salvador Toscano, Jesús H. Abitia, Eustasio Montoya, Ezequiel Carrasco, or those who have remained anonymous while risking their lives on the battlefield. These five caudillos were: Francisco I. Madero, a liberal who governed the nation from 1911 to 1913; Emiliano Zapata, one of the men most concerned with the nation's rural problems; Francisco Villa, the mythic Revolutionary who tried to eliminate injustices to impose a new order; Venustiano Carranza, the president who signed the

El compadre Mendoza (Fernando de Fuentes, 1933)

1917 Constitution; and Alvaro Obregón, an undefeated general who turned into a capricious and authoritarian leader. All were consecrated by the cinema and Villa even signed a contract with Mutual, a US production company, to have his battles filmed. This has been recounted by Raoul Walsh in his autobiographical book *Each Man in His Time* and by Kevin Brownlow in *The Parade's Gone By*, the latter revealing that cinematographer Charles Rocher spent several weeks in Villa's camps.[5] Luz Corral, one the general's several widows, also recounted that the Spanish producer Francisco Elías offered to reproduce the principal episodes of the life of this singularly vigorous man.

The first feature film to appear at the height of the conflict was *Revolución orozquista o La Revolución en Chihuahua* (*Orozquista Revolution or the Revolution in Chihuahua*, Alva brothers, 1912). In this film, Pascual Orozco's rebel forces confronted those of the traditional villain of Mexican history: Victoriano Huerta, who launched a *coup d'état* and assassinated President Madero and Vice-president José María Pino Suárez. This troubled period is known as *La Decena Trágica* (The Tragic Ten Days). Researcher Fernando del Moral González found some important sequences by an unknown camera operator which are believed to be the most complete record of that historical moment. In 1988, the same researcher restored a set of film reels that included *La batalla de Villaldama en Nuevo León* (*The Battle of Villaldama in Nuevo León*, Eustasio Montoya, 1915), as well as other material by the same cameraman.

Among the documentaries referring to the peasant struggle in the south of Mexico were *Sangre hermana* (*Kindred Blood*, Anonymous, 1914) and the shorts *Nueve hazañas de Emiliano Zapata* (*Nine Heroic Deeds of Emiliano Zapata*, Anonymous, 1918) or *Hazañas y muerte de Emiliano Zapata* (*Heroic Deeds and Death of Emiliano Zapata,* Anonymous, 1918), which historian Gabriel Ramírez believes to be the same film with two different titles. The documentaries about the Revolution disappeared gradually and, in 1916, the company Queretana Cinema S.A. attempted to organise a promotional contest to transform the armed movement into a topic for fiction films. Despite the apparent neutrality of this contest, it was obvious that there was a certain governmental interest in the project, but President Carranza's tactic failed.

In 1917 there was a definite attempt to polish the image of the chief executive, who used his influence to appear frequently in newsreels. Among the films shown at that time were *Las fiestas presidenciales* (*The Presidential Celebrations,* Anony-mous, 1917), *Patria nueva* (*New Fatherland,* General Jesús M. Garza, 1917) and *Reconstrucción nacional* (*National Reconstruction,* Anonymous, 1917). Political censorship predominated and no one dared to question the figure of Carranza.

The documentary turned into a simplistic and useless fragment caught in a vicious circle. For example, *Historia completa de la Revolución méxicana de 1910 a 1915* (*Complete History of the Mexican Revolution from 1910 to 1915*) by Enrique Echániz Brust and Salvador Toscano (1915) tried to summarise a complex historical event in only a few minutes, and used materials from various sources that neutralised each other politically. History was a headache for the producers of official culture. They went back to previous decades and even centuries, as far back as the Conquest itself. *Cuauhtémoc* by Manuel de la Bandera (1918) succinctly related biographical details of the last Aztec emperors.

1919 was a decisive year for a cinema interested in representing events of the recent past. At stake was the establishment of a paradigm or a conceptual model that would serve as the official version of events. The military men themselves produced the first films in which, according to the principles of the era, the civic spirit was mixed with the novelistic.

Fiction had to create the conditions for the spectator to lose critical distance and to be taken in by artifice, confusing the real with its proposed substitution. Thus were filmed *El honor militar* (*Military Honour*), *El blockhouse de alta luz* (*The Blockhouse of High Lights*) and *El precio de la gloria* (*The Price of Glory*), three 1919 films directed by Lt.-Col. Orozco y Berra and commissioned by the staff of the Secretaría de Guerra (War Ministry). Following the same principles, *Juan soldado* (*Johnny Soldier,* Enrique Castilla, 1920) also came to be

inscribed within this official framework. The critic Jorge Ayala Blanco has analysed the films dealing with the armed conflict between 1910 and 1917 and its consequences. He provides a crucial explanation of this period: 'For lack of a Mexican school of revolutionary cinema that could have expressed the needs of the working masses, cultural salvation came from above, from the ruling class: redemption through folklore.'[6]

The documentary appeared sporadically on national screens: *La rendición de Francisco Villa* (*The Surrender of Francisco Villa,* Anonymous, 1920); Cirerol Sansores and Santos Badía, film-makers settled in the Mexican south-east, made propagandistic shorts about General Obregón and other political and military figures such as Plutarco Elías Calles (founder of the Partido Nacional Revolucionario) and of the campaign of Ortiz Rubio, who became president in 1930. *Vida, hechos y hazañas de Francisco Villa* (*Life, Acts and Great Deeds of Francisco Villa,* Alva brothers, 1923, probably including some material by Sotelo) was also shown. Nostalgia was revived with an extremely short film: *Vida del general Porfirio Díaz en París* (*General Porfirio Díaz's Life in Paris,* Germán Camus, 1924). A melancholy homage restored those who had fallen by the wayside because of their abusive exercise of power: *Solemnes funerales de Obregón* (*The Solemn Funeral of Obregón,* Anonymous, 1927).

The sound cinema arrived in Mexico in 1931. At that time, history was a paradisiacal space, a kind of American Olympus that meekly accepted the official discourse. Censorship and self-censorship were the cornerstones of the recreations of the national past. The films that recounted Revolutionary events had (and would continue to have) a characteristic trait: dislocation without translation.[7] The events of the Revolution were complex and tangled. The Revolution had been a process in continuous flux without beginning or end. Film-makers avoided these complexities and instead produced films which highlighted hypothetical differences among similar elements, decontextualising the situations they represented. The uniforms might be familiar, the violence might seem verisimilar, the dead might keep silent, but everything led to the same impasse: an hollow representation. The historical was sifted for what was of interest: situations, characters and themes.

The phenomenon of 'dislocation' implies an improper use of a nation's memory. The opposite example is that of 'translation', which only occurred in exceptional situations. Translations restore the fullness of the problematic without implying a totalising historical impulse. Some concrete examples should clarify this point. The first sound feature with a Revolutionary theme was Miguel Contreras Torres's *La sombra de Pancho Villa o Revolución* (*The Shadow of Pancho Villa or Revolution,* 1932). The film was motivated by the desire to produce a translation. The plot simply offered a dramatisation of Villa's struggle against the Porfirio Díaz dictatorship. Important battles were represented, such as Villa's victory in the northern city of Zacatecas (which eradicated the power of the governmental army) and the crushing defeat of Villa's forces by General Obregón in Celaya. The historical modesty of the film is such that it shows General Villa only from the back and in a semi-documentary fashion. One of the masterpieces of the genre appeared in 1933: *El compadre Mendoza* by Fernando de Fuentes. It gives a detailed account of how a rancher betrays his close friend, a Zapatista, in order to preserve his wealth and become a part of the new Constitutionalist regime. These attempts to represent the Revolution have a certain depth: they are readings which give the revolt meaning and establish a perspective. Unfortunately, folklore would be more valued than the discourse of history. *Enemigos* (*Enemies,* by Chano Urueta, 1933) was an endless celebration of popular songs. The struggle of the southern peasants was presented as a simple and flat dislocation, a pretext which concluded with a flagrant misrepresentation.

Arcady Boytler, a Russian film-maker settled in Mexico, devised an enduring formula for film fiction that cancelled historical referentiality in *El tesoro de Pancho Villa* (*The Treasure of Pancho Villa,* 1935). The Revolution became a pretext for an endless stream of adventures which only required the figure of a general to set the plot mechanism going: he would always be ready to meet the challenges imposed upon him by the narrative. The national cinema would use this character in an endless series of comedies, entertainments and melodramas. As Jean Baudrillard has argued, 'the real has never interested anybody. It is the site of disillusionment par excellence, the site of the simulacrum …'[8]

Elsewhere, in *El coleccionador de ataúdes* (*The Coffin Collector*), a brief tale that formed part of the book *A orillas del Hudson* (*On the Banks of the Hudson,* 1920), Martín Luis Guzmán made a point that could be applied to the Mexican historical cinema. The writer recounts an anecdote that he once heard from Julio Torri, one of the masters of the short story, introducing us to immense rooms furnished with a complete repertory of coffins. To the same degree that some enjoy themselves with stamp or coin-collecting, the man in the story anxiously collects the coffins of the illustrious dead. After a few remarks, the anonymous character reflects on his proclivity and wonders, with knowing slyness: 'Do you think that a more eloquent or more profound trajectory of Mexican history has ever been written? Here we have a rich and clear version by merely turning our eyes towards these noble relics. Yes, Mexican history, one of the many rewards of my work, is the history of a country of dead men.'[9]

The historical process that flooded the Mexican cinema was linked to the closed universe of official doctrines. It produced innocuous films such as *Juárez y Maximiliano* (*Juárez and Maximiliano,* Miguel Contreras Torres, 1933), or its sequel, *La paloma* (*The Dove,* also by Contreras Torres, 1937); *Cristobal Colón* (*Cristopher Columbus,* José Díaz Morales, 1943), or the biography *Porfirio Díaz* by Raphael J. Sevilla and Rafael M. Saavedra (1944). Mexican cinema is filled with films alluding to historical figures or events. It is worth analysing how they create a historical discourse that erases obstacles and uses oversimplification to produce naive or clever lessons about the past of a Republic in crisis. The idea of the hero produced by these films from the silent era to the 30s resembles the one found in the museum filled with coffins. Films about the liberators Hidalgo, Morelos and Mina, the reform-minded president Benito Juárez or the 1910 revolt, confirmed that hybridity and indeterminacy were the essential characteristics of this celebratory cinema. Mexican heroes, in general, were portrayed with a false respect that dehumanised them and turned them into petrified statues. This was, for example, what occurred with José María Morelos y Pavón (1765–1815), a priest who joined the independence struggle and became an outstanding strategist. In *El padre Morelos* (*Father Morelos,* 1942) and *El rayo del sur* (*The Southern Ray,* 1943), both by Miguel Contreras Torres, the character is petrified and uninteresting because biographical verisimilitude required the presentation of incredibly boring facts.

A similar fate awaited Benito Juárez (1806–72), the man responsible for restoring the Republic after he defeated the invading forces and executed the European emperor Maximilian of Austria. Juárez was a skilful politician with signs of exceptional intelligence, but the cinematic Juárez only had a permanent anecdotal aura focused on the extreme poverty of his childhood and his rise to power as chief executive of the country. The so-called Benemérito (Meritorious or Worthy One) of the

Domingo Soler in *¡Vámenos con Pancho Villa!* (Fernando de Fuentes, 1935)

Americas was a man full of contradictions, but the films avoided these real conflicts and presented him only in the most heroic light. In *El joven Juárez* (*Young Mr Juárez,* Emilio Gómez Muriel, 1954), history consists of a series of references to the glorious past. One scene of this film is crucial to understanding the director's excesses: the brilliant lawyer's declaration of love to the woman who was to become the illustrious Doña Margarita Maza de Juárez. The action develops in front of a silent witness: the pre-Hispanic ruins of Mitla, a beautiful architectural example of Zapotec culture. We should remember that Juárez was from Oaxaca and that his roots were linked to this civilisation. Some time later, politicised writers like Carlos Fuentes and José Iturriaga wrote a script to commemorate the centennial of Don Benito's death. The film was called *Aquellos años* (*Those Years,* Felipe Cazals, 1972) and was an intellectual disaster, extraordinarily pretentious and unable to make the shift from dislocation to translation.

In a recent interview, film-maker Nicolás Echevarría has stated that Mexican history is a rich cinematographic field that has not been mined because of both self-censorship and real censorship:

'We must learn not to be afraid of our past, of interpreting it, or of unmasking its official aura. In the cinema it is difficult to deal with reality, because the medium is naturally close to the lie, to illusion; to approximate reality through the cinema is almost a contradiction.'[10]

Echevarría's argument is confirmed when we analyse the films that transgressed official discourses: *¡Vámonos con Pancho Villa!* (Fernando de Fuentes, 1935) and *La sombra del caudillo* (*The Shadow of the Caudillo,* Julio Bracho, 1960). These films were subject to different forms of censorship but with similarly acrimonious effects. *¡Vámonos con Pancho Villa!* ruptures the myth of a virtuous and messianic Revolution. We are shown the other side of the revolt and the disillusionment of a group of men who aspired to participate in a positive movement. Upon entering the battle, they realise that heroism is useless in such savage times. This film, one of the first great aesthetic achievements of Mexican cinema, was cut by ten minutes and its subversive charge diffused. It was not until 1982 that the final scenes could be viewed: Villa meets one of his lieutenants again, a man now living quietly with his family; in a burst of madness, General Villa murders the wife and daughter of his former comrade-in-arms, and as he tries to defend himself, the man falls victim to the shots of one of Villa's subordinates. The only survivor is a boy: with a newly developed paternalist spirit, Villa mounts him in his saddle and takes him away to train him to fight.

La sombra del caudillo was banned by the Secretaría de Gobernación (Ministry of the Interior) for thirty years. Despite all the critiques one may have, the film is interesting because it attempts to make sense of the political machinations which gave rise to the official party. In other words, historical reality overcomes all precautions and forces the locks that would cast Julio Bracho's film into the limbo of the past. It describes, step by step, the betrayals and excesses that characterised the post-Revolutionary period in Mexico. Consequently, Bracho's film was stigmatised by a state that was fully aware of its own illegitimacy. The ban was lifted in 1990 and finally the film could be viewed without restrictions or cuts.

In the context of historical events that were overlooked by the Revolutionary epic or the inflamed spirit of those who supported independence, one might mention the films about the 1968 student movement. The documentary that gathered the greatest number of testimonies was *El grito* (*The Cry,* Leobardo López Aretche, 1968). The extremist atmosphere of the period produced conflicts that ended tragically, as, for example, the one recreated in *Canoa* (Felipe Cazals, 1975). In the village after which the film is named, a group of workers were mistaken for political agitators and, incited by the parish priest, the villagers lynched them on the night of 14 September 1968. *Rojo amanecer* (*Red Dawn,* Jorge Fons, 1989) is a third example of this cinema. This chronicle alludes to the massacre of civilians in the Plaza de las Tres Culturas in Mexico City. The film is pathetically obvious and influenced by mainstream Mexican films of the 70s: the plot invariably leads to a final cathartic slaughter.

The pre-Hispanic period was forgotten by the national cinema. The only reminders have been *Retorno a Aztlán* (*Return to Aztlán,* Juan Mora, 1990) and *Cabeza de Vaca* by Nicolás Echevarría (1990), which both deal with topics where history is a point of dislocation, an avenue for the imaginary exercise

where legend and reality depend on the goodwill of directors and screenwriters. In Mexican cinema, history has followed a tortuous path fed by official discourses and censorship or has sometimes spread its wings and tried to fly above convention. Within this dual and hardly surprising territory, an endless number of films have been produced that acknowledge the power of memory and of oblivion. The obstacle lies in the repetition of clichés, the achievements in the search for those aspects that allude, indicate or propose a new meaning or perspective. That is the challenge.

Notes

1. Esteve Riambau and Joaquín Romaguera, *La historia y el cine* (Barcelona: Editorial Fontamara, 1983), p. 7.
2. Michel Foucault, *The Archaeology of Knowledge,* translated by A.M. Sheridan Smith (New York: Pantheon, 1972), p. 7.
3. Roman Jakobson, *Questions de poétique* (Paris: Editions du Seuil, 1973), p. 120.
4. Ludwig Wittgenstein, *Zettel* (Berkeley: University of California Press, 1970).
5. Raoul Walsh, *Each Man in His Time* (New York: Farrar, Strauss and Giroux, 1974) and Kevin Brownlow, The Parade's Gone By (Berkeley: University of California Press, 1968), pp. 224–6.
6. Jorge Ayala Blanco, 'Permanencia voluntaria' in Siempre, 16 April 1975.
7. Here, the author plays with the difference between traslación and traducción. In Spanish, the first term, literally 'translation', connotes displacement and decontextualisation. The second is the term commonly used for translation, although it is derived from *traductio* and could be literally translated as 'traduction', the repetition of a word with a changed meaning. I have translated *traslación* as 'dislocation' to preserve the author's sense of a relocation that uproots historical meaning and, following common usage, *traducción* as translation, a reinscription into a new signifying system. (Translator's note.)
8. Jean Baudrillard, *Oublier Foucault* (Paris: Editions Galilée, 1977), p. 73; translated in Peter Botsman (ed.), *Theoretical Strategies* (Sydney: Local Consumption, 1982).
9. Martín Luis Guzmán, *A orillas del Hudson* (México City: Compañía General de Ediciones), p. 142.
10. Raquel Peguero, 'Entrevista a Nicolás Echevarría' in *La Jornada,* 7 October 1991, p. 39.

177

Emilio Fernández: A Look Behind the Bars

Julia Tuñón

Emilio 'el Indio' Fernández (1904–86) was one of the most important directors of the Mexican cinema of the 40s and 50s; afterwards his influence declined. He had a clear personal style which, in his best period, was produced with the help of a top-quality technical team, in particular his favourite cinematographer, Gabriel Figueroa. 'El Indio' Fernández's films transcended frontiers and were well known internationally. They are considered representative of a hypothetical Mexican cinema school, which was, in fact, what he aspired to.

A Key Year

1934 is a key year for understanding Emilio Fernández. Amidst a general climate of cinematic experimentation, two films were produced which influenced him greatly: *Redes* (*Nets*, Fred Zinnemann, released in 1936) and *Janitzio* (Carlos Navarro, released in 1935). Both films dealt with the indigenous world, a topic that was closely linked to that historical moment when, on December 1934, Lázaro Cárdenas became president and revived some of the ideals of the 1910 Mexican Revolution.

In the 30s, *indigenismo* (Indianism) and nationalism flourished, popular education was re-conceived and promoted as an instrument for social change, and the official recognition of strikes and other social demands served to strengthen the state. The muralist movement begun in the previous decade was going strong and its principal artists had become important public figures. Painters, photographers, musicians and writers searched for Mexican themes and experimented to discover the most appropriate forms of expression. The Secretaría de Educación Pública (Ministry of Public Education) promoted cultural activities and united a generation of young restless intellectuals.

Nationalism marked almost all political and cultural activities of the period. It consisted of a panoply of ideas ranging from the most cosmopolitan to the traditionalism of landscape and folklore. The fashionable *indigenismo* of the period reveals a great paradox: the indigenous peoples considered most representative of *mexicanidad* (Mexicanness) were precisely the ones who had been excluded from the nation's development and marginalised into a separate sphere.

The cinema was not immune to the debates around it and was also searching to reach international screens: following a nineteenth-century model, it strove to reconcile a Mexican-based cinematic practice with universal aesthetic values.[1] The national landscape, customs and popular art forms were considered essential to achieve this goal, but, in fact, the national cinema continued to produce films about *charros y chinas,* the popular names for the cinematic stereotypes used to represent rural types. Formally, the cinema attempted to reclaim some *género chico* (popular theatre) traditions derived from the Parisian café-concert, such as the *zarzuela,* variety and *sainete,* which used popular types and jokes and interrupted narratives with songs.[2]

This is the climate that Sergei Eisenstein found when he arrived in Mexico. The famous Soviet filmmaker arrived in Mexico in 1930 and filmed isolated sequences with non-professional actors. Eisenstein assimilated some of the nationalist concerns of the Mexican intellectuals and his vision transformed them into *¡Que Viva México!* (1931), a film that would function as a stereotype for a certain strain of Mexican cinema.[3] He gave an original graphic dimension to elements such as the landscape, the maguey cactus and the Indian by combining them with the novelty of a critical analysis of the society around him.[4] Eisenstein's influence was important for some of those directors of the nascent Mexican industry, like Emilio Fernández, who were eager to develop their own formal styles.

'El Indio' had lived in Los Angeles and had had the opportunity to watch Eisenstein at work. His style fascinated him: 'This is what I learned: the pain of the people, the land, the strike, the struggle for freedom and social justice. It was wonderful!'[5] However, Eisenstein was not his only influence. The muralist movement also provided another aesthetic model, in particular the idea that an integrated artistic practice could reveal the essence and spirit of the people. Although the technology was foreign and Hollywood's stylistic influence all too evident,[6] these attempts to produce a national cinema were, to a large degree, successful.

Redes emerged in this context. Sponsored by the

Secretaría de Educación Pública directed by Narciso Bassols, it was shot in Veracruz using non-professional actors. The film sympathetically narrates the story of a fishermen's strike against speculators and attempts to raise public consciousness of social problems. Eisenstein's influence is quite evident in the privilege granted to the image over dialogue, and in the slow rhythm produced by an almost-still series of images. Silvestre Revueltas's music highlights the grandeur of the story. All the dramatic elements serve ideological ends: the death of a child is the pathetic element that pushes men to seek justice; they say 'it is not right, but we must know that it is not inevitable'.[7] Years later, a similar anecdote would unleash the barely contained conflicts of 'el Indio' Fernández's *Río Escondido* (1947).

Redes fits in with the kinds of issues that already troubled Emilio Fernández in Los Angeles, where Adolfo de la Huerta had told him:

No, Emilio, the Mexican Revolution is over, it triumphed, and what Mexico needs is peace. You are here now, in an incredible place of great importance for the world, for cinema, the cinematic mecca. The cinema is more powerful than a mauser, more powerful than a 30-30 rifle, a cannon, a plane, or a bomb. Since you are already here, learn to make movies and return to Mexico and teach them.[8]

Emilio Fernández returned to Mexico in 1933 and found a calm and ordered environment. He was fascinated by urban life: his memories of the north of the country, where he lived as a child, were rural. For him, Mexico had been its countryside.

Carlos Navarro's *Janitzio* was more commercial. The film followed the tradition of *indigenista* films such as *La india bonita* (*The Pretty Indian Girl*, Antonio Helú, 1938) and *La noche de los mayas* (*The Night of the Mayans*, Chano Urueta, 1939) which presented Indians in an idealised and romanticised fashion. *Janitzio* recounts a love story and the couple's problems with their society on an island that gives the film its title. In this society, women who have sexual contacts with white men are punished. The film's protagonist, Eréndira, has a sexual relationship with a white man to free her fiancé Zirahuén from prison. Zirahuén is played by Emilio Fernández in his first starring role. Besides the love story, the film also poses the problem of the marginalisation of Indians. It refers to the alternatives of adaptation or isolation. Narratively, the island is a perfect space for the representation of this dilemma: it is surrounded by water and simultaneously suggests the possibility of escape but also isolation. The figure of the island, literally and metaphorically, would often reappear in Emilio Fernández's films. The story presents a tense relationship between individuals and society: is love the exclusive property of one or the other? After Eréndira flees to Pázcuarro on the mainland, the community selects Zirahuén to bring her back to Janitzio to receive the prescribed punishment: she will be stoned to death by the community. The camera shows us the couple on the boat, with Zirahuén barely moving the oars: they are slow and silent, self-contained and in pain. The camera moves away until their figures are barely visible on the lake. The landscape takes over: the clouds, the immensity that mocks the couple's problems. Suddenly, the boat turns around and returns to the mainland: Zirahuén chooses their love over his social obligations. This is the film's climax, for it unravels an entire system of values. Respectfully, the camera records from afar, as if taking no sides.

Zirahuén's choice would become one of Fernández's leitmotivs. As a director, he would often repeat the story, sometimes literally, other times symbolically: in *Maclovia* (1948) he modifies it, allowing the couple to escape and save themselves. In *Janitzio*, Zirahuén's choice fails: Eréndira dies when her people stone her. When Zirahuén turns the canoe around, is he integrated into society or separated from himself? Was he individually marginalised although already part of a socially marginalised group? This tension reflects Emilio Fernández's own personal problem: he who looks from outside, who feels excluded. We do not know whether this was a result of his own Indian blood (his mother was Kikapú[9]), but he always defined himself in these terms.

This was particularly the case in the USA, where 'he felt like a fly in a glass of milk, totally out of place, desiring to return'. He would go to the frontier to stare across the bars of the fence: 'I was so nostalgic for Mexico that I would travel from the North to the frontier simply to see the desolation of the desert. I cried when I saw the Mexican side … I felt that I was missing half of my soul.'[10] Later, already in Mexico, he would stand behind the bars of the fence of his former school, the Colegio Militar [Military School]: 'Some afternoons like this, filled with nostalgia, I would go to the iron fence of the Colegio Militar and watch, from the outside, the six o'clock roll call.'[11] He was already part of the cinema world, but felt scorned because of his social origins: 'I knew perfectly well that they would never give me the chance to direct. It was very difficult. They were already here: the intellectuals, the college graduates, the sons of millionaires, etc.'[12]

Thus Emilio Fernández, the marginal, turned his gaze towards the ordinary world of the indigenous peoples to uplift it: he made it beautiful, honorific and dignified; threatened by such suffering that it was exempt from all wrongdoing. He constructed a paradise for his heroes where the dramas resulted from ruptures. Fernández offered his characters assimilation and tirelessly reconstructed the conflicts between individuals and society.

Emilio Fernández always remembered the year 1934. He remembered that he did not know which of the two films to participate in (although they were not in production simultaneously) and how ambivalent this made him feel. From his filmic style it would appear that he opted to fuse both films: to synthesise *Redes*'s aesthetic,[13] its narrative style and social message, with the commercial tone and love story of *Janitzio*. He thus developed a cinematic model that he repeated insatiably and that, in its time, represented Mexico to the world. It is not an exaggeration to say that it was his films that gave Mexico an edge in the export market, that they were the basis for the Mexican cinema school (which was really constituted by Fernández and his team). 'El Indio' himself founded his personal and filmic life upon this axis; he revolved around it endlessly: *'The individual with personality will always be the same.'*

Emilio Fernández's biography is complex and contradictory. His life was full of anecdotes, many of them surely invented. The man carefully created himself as a myth in the cinematic style, and, like cinematic myths, he became a stereotype. Like the two sides of a coin, his person and his films were symbiotically linked, inseparable. From this perspective, the anecdotes that surrounded him are significant: he was simultaneously described as delicate and rough, as intuitive and uncultured but with artistic talent. This was a man who was a product of the Revolution, proud of his indigenous roots, who privileged popular art in his films, home, parties and attire. In sum, a man who decanted and purified the people to arrive at their essence.

His cinematic style developed through a filmic instinct carefully filtered and controlled for aesthetic effects: 'I believe very much in the unconscious. My conscious doesn't solve any of my problems … I do everything by instinct. … There is something about me, I have this sensibility … if something moves me it must be good. I am a kind of barometer.'[14] The power of his films resides in the personal tension between his instincts and his aesthetic culture, between his desire for and the effects of assimilation.

Fernández participated in the Revolution as a child. In 1924 he was also part of the *delahuertista* rebellion and was forced to emigrate to the USA, where he worked at all sorts of jobs, including as a movie extra in Hollywood. He also found other Mexicans who formed a curious and restless group, and who would later influence this new industry without chimneys. Mexico welcomed with open arms those who could teach and practise the new techniques. When he returned to his country, 'el Indio' benefited from this climate. As already mentioned, he was the protagonist of *Janitzio* in 1934, and in 1937 he wrote the script for and starred in *Adios Nicanor* (*Goodbye Nicanor*, Rafael E. Portas), but he really wanted to become a director.

For years he carried around the script for *La isla de la pasión (The Island of Passion)* or *Clipperton*, which he eventually managed to direct in 1941. This film already demonstrates many of Fernández's typical themes. The story recounts the vicissitudes of a group of Mexicans abandoned on an island, located approximately a thousand kilometres from the Mexican coast, who passionately defend it from French invaders. Patriotism, the frustrated love of a couple, the subordination of individual rivalries for the high ideals of the nation, dialogues, and the power and beauty of nature are sketches of his later obsessions.

The next year he filmed *Soy puro mexicano (I am Pure Mexican)*, one of the few war films produced in Mexico during the Second World War. *Soy puro mexicano* is an espionage film set in the countryside, where Germans, Japanese and Italian conspire and where Lupe, a bandit from Jalisco, manages to spoil their plans. In this film, Fernández still had a free, almost playful, style that allowed him to celebrate his protagonist's pranks (for example, putting a bull in the living-room of the house where the spies meet). The film also already includes elements which he would later repeat tirelessly: a woman crying impotently on one side of the bars that imprison her mate, or a sad song that expresses what the impassive faces do not communicate.

In 1942, 'el Indio' became associated with Agustín Fink, a producer for Films Mundiales who wanted to bolster the national industry with better-quality films. Fink provided Fernández with the right environment for his kind of films and helped him to put together the technical team with which he would make the great films that brought international fame to Mexico. The team consisted of cinematographer

Gabriel Figueroa, writer Mauricio Magdaleno and, from *María Candelaria* (1943) on, editor Gloria Schoemann. His favourite actors, Pedro Armendáriz, Dolores del Río and, later, María Félix, became known as the faces of Mexico throughout the world: faces that were distinguished from the anonymous figures placed by Fernández in secondary positions (inspired by Eisenstein and *Redes*), the non-professional actors who served as a backdrop for the blinding beauty of the stars. This top-notch team enabled him to produce a personal cinema. The first film produced under these conditions was *Flor silvestre* (*Wild Flower,* 1943) the unhappy love story of a couple from different social classes who face the opposition of his wealthy hacienda-owning parents at a time of Revolutionary violence and confusion. This romance alludes to the conflictual encounter between tradition and the modern values implied by the desire for equality that José Luis discovers in Revolutionary ideas. This hacienda, we must note, is like an island, the stage for questioning and struggling over the individuality of love in a social context. *María Candelaria* also addresses this problem: an indigenous woman is scorned by her community because her mother was a prostitute. María Candelaria is involved in a series of misunderstandings that, as in the case of Eréndira in *Janitzio,* leads to her stoning. Her love for Lorenzo Rafael does not save her from social condemnation.

Fernández's films between 1944 and 1949 refined and perfected his personal style. In this period he directed *Las abandonadas* (*The Abandoned Ones,* 1944), *Bugambilia* (1944), *Pepita Jiménez* (1945), *La perla* (*The Pearl,* 1945), *Enamorada* (*A Woman in Love,* 1946), *The Fugitive* (co-directed with John Ford, 1946–7), *Río Escondido* (*Hidden River,* 1947), *Maclovia* (1948), *Salón México* (1948), *Pueblerina* (*Small Town Woman,* 1948), *The Torch* (aka *Del odio nació el amor,* the English-language version of *Enamorada,* 1949, released in Spain as *Una mujer rebelde*), *La malquerida* (*The Badly Loved One,* 1949), *Duelo en las montañas* (*Duel in the Mountains,* 1949). This is his basic filmography; even today these are the films cited as the Mexican quality cinema. In the words of Raymond Borde: 'During a whole era, Emilio Fernández was the very symbol of the Mexican cinema.'[15] This was the so-called 'golden age' of the Mexican cinema, the era in which national films were distributed throughout Latin America (because Hollywood could not provide these markets with enough films). Emilio Fernández's films benefited from this success but also, to a large degree, created it. *María Candelaria* won two prizes at

Cannes (1946)[16] and three in Locarno (1947), and the recognition that generated confidence. Fernández's films conferred signs of identity upon the national cinema: they defined the substance and form of what had to be said in order for the old world to recognise its values. While Europe was exhausted by the war, Mexico produced images that rehabilitated the idea of the natural benevolence of Indians and which probably contributed greatly to the appeal of this film.

It is interesting to note the effects produced by the awards. Before the films were sent to Cannes, many were sceptical and discussed the need for dignity and for improved production efforts. It was said that 'it is necessary for Mexico not to be content with honourable defeats in all the competitions it participates in'.[17] Various films were sent to Cannes, including Cantinflas's *Los tres mosqueteros* (*The Three Musketeers,* Miguel M. Delgado, 1942). Cantinflas himself headed the delegation accompanying the films. Soon it was widely known that the Cantinflas film had been soundly rejected, but that *María Candelaria* interested critics. In France, they said that the film 'offers an unknown Mexico (surprising customs and poetry) and is marvellously photographed'.[18] However, others expressed doubts: the critic for *Combat* indicated that 'it overused local colour in a bewildering imbecilic story'. Slowly, the cinema world began to take notice and the compliments circulated: 'The landscape is suffused with soul and this soul moves Mexicans, but it also moves foreigners who expect little or nothing from this revolutionary country whose history is tinged (sic) by savage blood and whose name always appears covered by a cloud of gunpowder.' Many commented that they had had faith in the film, but only 'up to the point that it allowed for the natural and habitual Mexican inferiority complex. … From now on we have to believe that the Mexican cinema is the best.'[19]

Surprise changed into pride and a formula was discovered. It now seems obvious that the temptation was large: 'We should not stop at self-congratulation but must continue to move forward in the direction established.'[20] Yes, the temptation was great. For Fernández it seems to have been murderous. The award paralysed him and forced him to follow a single path. His films were forged out of diverse aesthetic elements, out of his own history, and had been accorded value by other eyes. Furthermore, these were European awards about which there could be no suspicion since they were not associated with Hollywood interests. Emilio Fernández, a man who looked at the world from 'behind the bars' of the

Pedro Armendáriz and Dolores del Río in *María Candelaria* (Emilio Fernández, 1944)

fence, was overwhelmed: he was suddenly in the spotlight, passing from shadows to the bright light of stardom.

In 1940, Manuel Avila Camacho succeeded Lázaro Cárdenas to the presidency. This was the era when Mexico was able to take advantage of the world war to promote its own economic growth. Avila Camacho and his successors put aside the social issues and concerns of Cardenismo that had nourished Emilio Fernández. Although the context had changed and his messages were understood differently, the director continued to express the ideals of this period. Carlos Monsiváis has said that 'with Avila Camacho, the bourgeoisie abandoned their fear of socialism and allowed itself to be convinced by Emilio Fernández, in other words, the

Revolution has become an extension of postcards'.[21]

'El Indio' had jumped over the fence. He was no longer the marginal one; he was in the centre of the circle. This would only last a short, very short time. Later, under new circumstances, the need for other themes, styles and proposals became evident. To this were added the economic difficulties that began to affect the national industry and the appearance of other national cinemas able to supply international markets. The films of 'el Indio' would gradually be surpassed. He began to claim that there was a boycott against him. We return to that personal image from his youth: he was behind the bars of the fence again, but now he saw himself looking and, pitying his own marginalisation, complained constantly about his sacrifice. It is obvious that his themes, style and proposals remained anchored to the era in which the model crystallised. For Fernández, the cinema was not a road but a goal, and the monumental prizes he won, by affirming his and Mexico's success, both satisfied and paralysed him.

Between 1950 and 1956, the director made seventeen films:[22] his obsessions appeared in film after film and repeated the stereotypes of his earlier successes. Between 1957 and 1960 he did not direct. In 1961, *Pueblito (Small Town)* began a period of low-quality, scant productivity. In *La choca* (1973) and *Zona roja* (*Red Zone,* 1975), he oscillated between repetition and the desire to adapt to new commercial demands for nudity and explicit eroticism that went against his principles (he did not even like to show on-screen kisses). After these films he not only repeated ideas, shots, dialogues and themes, but even entire films. His last films were *México norte* (1977), a remake of *Pueblerina,* and *Erótica* (1978), a remake of *La red* (*The Net,* 1953).

A first conclusion: Fernández's filmography is characterised by its single-mindedness. We can look at it as if it were one single film. We know that each film is unique, but Emilio Fernández liked to repeat himself. His films cohere as a group, sharing themes, preoccupations, and stylistic traces even when they introduce novelties such as the urban settings of *Salón México* and *Víctimas del pecado* (*Victims of Sin,* 1950) or the comic vein of *Enamorada.* When he began to have difficulty finding financial backers and accepted commissioned work,[23] his films escaped from the auteurist mould of his better moments. At this point his films no longer represented him. This was the case with *Cuando levanta la niebla* (*When the Fog Lifts,* 1952), a psychological drama, and *Reportaje* (*Reportage,* 1953), a collage of various stories.

'El Indio' built his model and applied it. He was a man of one piece, including contradictions and ambiguities. This did not seem to concern him too much and he made his style a fixture. His intention was not to move forward, but to sink, identifying with his cinema until he merged with it. It is as if when faced with changes in the world, the cinema and life, his only response was affirmation and reaffirmation; another turn around the same axis that brought him fame. As he used to say, 'the individual with personality will always be the same'.

Characteristics of a Film Style

What are the characteristics of Emilio Fernández's passionately frozen style? His personal obsession allowed him to mix classic and contemporary

María Félix in ***Río Escondido*** (Emilio Fernández, 1947)

nationalist traditions; Eisenstein's ethical and aesthetic lessons with elements of the classic Hollywood cinema (he often acknowledged the influence of John Ford). From this base he developed a personal style made possible by his team. Gabriel Figueroa recalled that he shared with 'el Indio' 'the same sensibility towards the work … we spoke the same language and had the same objectives'.[24] This model, beginning with the scrupulous attention paid to beauty, attempted to represent a national essence, something stable that could not be changed or betrayed and that embodied the greatness of inflexibility. To this essence derived from contemporary popular traditions they added social messages referring to the need for education and the value of land for peasants. His basic concern was to produce a Mexican cinema: 'I dreamt and am still dreaming of a different cinema, of course, but Mexican, pure. Now I have this great desire to mexicanise the Mexicans, for we are becoming americanised.'[25] To achieve this goal, he aestheticised his vision.

Fernández clearly voiced the filmic aspirations of

his era, especially the desire to transform the cinema into an art form. Towards this end, he conceived of the cinema as the integration of all the arts: the fundamental concern was to 'make films as painting, photography, or photography in movement'.[26] This required aesthetic pulchritude, the composition of a painting in each image. He did not aspire to 'the pretty', but to 'the sublime' and 'the profound'. Like the muralists he imitated, he tried to unleash profound feelings: 'These are the things that Diego [Rivera] created in painting and I in the cinema'.[27] The image is fundamental to his cinema: 'I am more of a photographer than a director'.[28] Thus he subordinated narrative and music to the image. For example, in *María Candelaria* we do not hear the villagers discussions while they prepare to stone her, we only see their lips moving, and the dramatic weight of the scene is carried by the images and the music. Later he would insist on the aesthetics of the visual, to the degree that *La red* received a Cannes prize (1953) as the best still-image film.

Fernández's images often resembled still images or mural painting. In his drive to highlight beauty, he sometimes paralysed his figures and played with volume. In *La perla*, for example, the women are so still that only the fluttering of their clothes in the wind reminds us that this is a moving image. The same occurs in *Bugambilia* when a group of women carrying jugs descend a staircase with such magnificent slowness and impassive faces that they remind us of sculptures rather than properly moving cinematic subjects. Like baroque artists, he also played with shadows and tones: in *La perla*, the women wear white shawls, in *Río Escondido* they are dressed in black. Figueroa's filters highlighted the clouds in long shots that gave them volume and depth. A chiaroscuro effect was produced by oblique and Dutch canted angles. In sum, each image was a painting. His best films were made in black and white; colour became popular when he was already in decline.

Fernández's aesthetic drive encouraged his tendency to photograph objects that were already works of art: churches, altars, monuments, statues. These objects functioned as metaphors for the national essence. How can we forget the Cholula temples in *Enamorada*, the Ocotlán temples in *La malquerida*, the pre-Hispanic pieces in *María Candelaria* and *Salón México*? In *Río Escondido*, the murals of the Secretaría de Educación Pública have a voice of their own: they tell Rosaura (the schoolteacher who is late for her interview with the president) the history of Mexico and reproach her for

her tardiness. The grandiloquent, tense music adds power to these images.

La malquerida also provides a good example of the power of monuments for Emilio Fernández. As Raymunda leaves the Ocotlán temple her figure begins to disappear into the shadows of the nave. Slowly we see her body outlined in the space of the doorway, until it is suddenly inundated by light as she steps outside. The camera follows her with a travelling shot that matches the rhythm of her walk; it is a perfect pretext to highlight the dimensions of the building and the density of the light, which, apart from Raymunda, is the only thing that moves. The cinematography emphasises the doorways and windows and their chiaroscuro contrasts; the play of shadows and light is a dramatic resource. Gabriel Figueroa's talent behind the camera is evident. And the words of the director are also eloquent: 'The cinema is life and death, it is darkness and light. In life, the most dramatic moments take place at night. Sadness is produced with grays and with rain, happiness with the sun and with brightness.'[29]

The landscape was central to Fernández's images: the trees, nopals and magueys that remind us of Eisenstein. Sometimes so much emphasis was placed on nature that we lose sight of the faces. For example, in *Pueblerina*, during the final duel between the local caciques and Aurelio and his subsequent escape with wife and child, so much emphasis was placed on the clouds and countryside that man seems to be only a small dynamic element in this overwhelmingly beautiful world. Fernández tended to use either long shots or close-ups, but rarely medium shots. He especially liked close-ups, as in *La red*, when he observed Rossana Podestà's face minutely in order to highlight her beauty. In *La perla* 'el Indio' played with audience expectations:

> When the girl is about to throw the pearl into the sea and he is following her, I shot them from a distance. They are small figures lost in the immensity of the sea, the beach and the waves. There, at the Pie de la Cuesta, she raises her hand and, suddenly, we see him hit her from a distance and audiences jump … because I am breaking with conventions.[30]

Fernández's observation leads us to another characteristic of his filmic style: rhythm. He explained that 'The cinema is rhythm, everything in life is rhythmic, life is rhythm. … Its heart is rhythm, has a determined rhythm … when the heart stops it is dead, stasis is death.'[34] However, the rhythm of each of his sequences is autonomous. Slow rhythms were linked to the beauty he wanted to valorise: they gave the spectator the time to enjoy it, but he also liked to surprise audiences with sudden rhythmic shifts. For example, in *La malquerida:* Acacia is walking through the countryside, slowly but determined because she is running away from home, and the camera follows her rhythm, when suddenly Esteban's horse interrupts with another speed and power, exhibiting the violence with which he will prevent the kidnapping. This is a contrapuntal rhythm that alternates the slowness associated with peace with the speed and violence of the crime scenes.

Rhythm combined the already mentioned hieraticism with the slow night-time gliding of the canoe in Xochimilco in *María Candelaria*. This was also at work in *Pueblerina* in the scene of the preparations for the wedding feast that no one will attend because of the townspeople's fear of the enmity of the cacique. Also, in *Flor silvestre*, José Luis's morbid walk through the paternal hacienda destroyed by so-called Revolutionary bandits, gives him the time to accept his pain and the spectator an opportunity to perceive its brutality.

On the other hand, there were also moments of agitation. In *Flor silvestre*, for example, when Esperanza flees after being rejected by José Luis's parents, the desperation with which she rides her horse is contrasted with the impassive landscape in which she is the only moving element. Or in *Bugambilia,* when Amelia takes off one of her many crinolines, a scene copied from *Gone With the Wind* (Victor Fleming, 1939). Songs, dance music and the banter of secondary characters played an important role in this context, for they offered a respite between scenes of crisis and conflict, an element that Fernández adopted from the Mexican *género chico*.

In the face of such visual power, dialogues were only of secondary importance. They were generally meagre and communicated only well-thought out ideas. For example, in *Pueblerina*, Aurelio asks Amelia to marry him (she was raped by the local cacique and has had his child). He says little, but it is obvious that during the six years spent in prison for attacking the cacique he has thought of little else. Paloma's response is also spare, but forceful: she feels unclean and refuses him. Later, when she silently takes the clothes that he has just washed in the river, the gesture is a sign of her acceptance of his suit. No words are exchanged: there are only gestures and music.

Fernández's cinema reconciles aestheticism, the beauty of his shots, the splendour of the images and the care with which they are produced (Gabriel Figueroa's work is essential here) with speeches, ideas and propositions. He believed that films should have ideological goals and fundamental theses: 'A work is as important as its thesis. ... A narrative without a thesis has no meaning to me. ... If a film does not have social and moral content, a message or an expression that reveals suffering or another condition of the people it means nothing to me.'[31]

'El Indio's' theses were evident in all his films: nationalism, *indigenismo* and the need for education; these are all themes linked to the history of the country and ones which he developed according to his own obsessions. One must note that his films had no realist or naturalist aspirations. Despite his penchant for landscapes, he produced a personal universe with particular value systems: 'All of us see ourselves in what we would have liked to have been.'[32] Good films must establish an equilibrium between dialogue and image, although 'good films are more imagistic'.[33] Despite his meagre use of dialogue, his films often included speeches. In *Río Escondido,* for example, the schoolteacher Rosaura, while in charge of the school in a town that has been impoverished by the abusive local cacique, is given to long, emphatic monologues that curtail the power of the image. Fernández's speeches were often put in the mouths of bartenders, relatives, priests and teachers: men of a certain age who represent common sense in comparison with the delirium of the central characters. As Jorge Ayala Blanco has said, 'none of Fernández's characters speak like normal and simple creatures ... what speaks [through them] is the voice of the race ... the social forces and the convictions of the film-maker'.[34] In his later films, Fernández used speeches even more, as if he felt the need to emphasise his theses even further.

Mauricio Magdaleno collaborated closely with him in script writing and recalled that

the effects and all those sensational things were his [Fernández's]; in Hollywood he had developed a great visual sense ... and he left the dialogues to me. ... I was really bothered by the speeches, but he loved them: I would take them out, but he would start to improvise them while shooting, and when I realised how bad they were, I would write them back into the script.[35]

In *La red*, he did the opposite: the film has almost no dialogue and privileges the image. Without abandoning his model, 'el Indio' tested its limits.

Marga López in *Salón México* (Emilio Fernández, 1948)

Generally, his theses were coupled with tales of persecuted and unhappy loves. The speeches were the thread with which he embroidered the proposals that cut across all his films: education, peasants and Indians, marginalisation, injustice, and so on. *Indigenismo* was central to his cinematic practice. He proposed to establish a continuity between the idols of pre-Hispanic cultures and the nobility of contemporary Indians. Fernández himself acknowledged the influence of Robert Flaherty and of Friedrich W. Murnau's *Tabu* (1931). Fernández created a romantic image of Indians. His concern for their customs and rituals was filtered through an outsider's gaze, the marginalised whose look fluctuated between the anthropologist's scientific spirit and the emotion of appearing to give in to the forbidden (the remote world of nature and the 'noble savage'). Through this prism, Fernández inevitably produced uniform Indians. According to his films, to

be Indian meant simply not being white or civilised. They were all the same and part of the landscape called Mexico. He proposed his Indian world as the basis for nationalism, but what kind of nationalism can be based upon a marginalised group? He confused the concepts of fatherland, nation, state and race; he used them as synonyms and therefore weakened his own thesis.

This also helps to explain his peculiar folklore and blend of regionalisms. Fernández made the various natural zones of Mexico and their popular types uniform: differences disappeared into an inscrutable Mexican essence. Thus, the nation became something abstract, akin to the statement 'all Mexicans are very macho'. Of course, these abstractions could only lead to stereotypes, many of which he himself created.

Education, science and progress also made an appearance as tools for the universalisation of this eternal Mexico. These sequences often featured doctors, teachers and engineers. For example, *Río Escondido* makes demands for 'water, roads, neighbourhood streets, literacy and official morality'; *Maclovia* declares that 'the school is the sanctuary of Mexico', and associates the nation with religion; *Pueblito* mentions that 'to learn to read is to learn to be free'. However, the contradictions are not far off. On the one side, we are confronted with demands for knowledge and change, but on the other, left over at the end of most of his films, we find that conventional inertia triumphs. That is to say, despite his constant valorisation of knowledge, it hardly ever seems to have an impact upon the fate of men. Fernández's emphasis upon these elements was inscribed into one of his constant preoccupations: apparently convinced that his messages would not be easily understood, he determined to increase their voltage. He was not satisfied to express his emotions, but evaluated their potential effect and was himself moved when he imagined it. He could reiterate, but was unable to change: he did not admit any setbacks. He believed, was convinced, that this was the only way to avoid defeat.

Fernández has often been criticised. His cinema has been described as naive, rhetorical, demagogical, aestheticist, hieratic, repetitive. The most common criticism is that 'he has given in too often to the formal beauty of the images, to folklore, and to exoticism while sacrificing content'.[36] Notwithstanding this assessment, his work has retained its polemical value, though many would later credit his production team for this. Often this value is limited to individual scenes, but outside of the context that gives them meaning, these scenes cease to be moving. It is clear that the violent beauty of his images do more than tell stories or exercise a style; despite everything, it gives his films life and emotion.

The Sacred Substance of his Cinema

What is the central axis of the theme that Emilio Fernández tirelessly repeated through his persecuted loves and marginalised Indians? Beyond his stories and what they tell there is a human dimension. The visuals and theses are only but a path that leads to the central drama: to the encounter between man and his world. This was the basic foundation of his cinema.

Despite all appearances, Fernández's films were not critical. He was concerned with another sphere, that of deeply held beliefs and the rituals that represent them, and alluded to sacred worlds. For example, in his films the land had two values.

Explicitly, land was linked to social demands and to a social thesis: the need for agrarian reform. But the land also carried a more obscure, atavistic and ritualistic connotation: it was the basis for life, matter from and for the dead, what sustained life and provoked a sense of stability. *María Candelaria,* for example, is too afraid to seek a new life away from her people's threats because of a principle: 'We were born here and here we shall always remain … those who leave are worse off.' Thus the land becomes atavistic and an obstacle to progress. On this land, part of the landscape, live men who cannot leave. In *La malquerida,* Raymunda tells the faithful servant Juliana: 'The trees and the stones never leave, even when tortured by the wind, and you are much more than a tree or a stone.' More, but clearly made of the same substance.

The Revolution fought battles and proclaimed the well-being of the people, but the people are insensitive, like a homogeneous block that marches with torches or, at an individual level, like traitors who betray their heroes, the select members of the group, out of envy. In *Pueblerina,* Aurelio's friends want to help him with the corn harvest, but they refuse out of fear of the cacique. Because society is not a group of individuals but their sum, the protagonists' independent projects are subversive. This is an unjust but vigilant society that always maintains its equilibrium. Within this stable system, the conflicts of the films are accidental and ultimately do not alter the system itself.

'El Indio' used to say:

You can't halt progress; this unfortunate progress has ruined us. It has stripped us of our way of being, even our national spirit. … This is why I am old-fashioned. And I can afford to be because I am based in rural dramas and rural things have always been the same, always, always.[37]

Fernández favoured rural dramas because the countryside demonstrated the conflict between new generations and traditions: the conflict derived from change and the disorder that breaks established norms; the conflict that ruptures the idyll of the island (taken as a metaphor, the site of a self-sufficient world and a comfortable life). When he portrayed other situations, this fragile equilibrium broke down. Magdaleno remembered that Fernández shied away from urban themes and that he was only able to break down his resistance to shoot *Salón México.* This reluctance was apparently derived from a recognition that urban codes of honour lack precision: violations do not rupture a cosmic order as they do in rural areas, and even more so in the ones he created. In *Salón México* we meet Mercedes, a prostitute who steals the wallet of a villain. Lupe López, the policeman who watches over the dancehall where she works, witnesses the event. The next sequence shows Mercedes visiting the rich girls' boarding school where she is paying for her sister to receive an expensive education. In the foreground we see a dark uniformed back as it approaches the women and, expecting the worst, we register the fear and confusion in Mercedes's face. However, Lupe understands the situation immediately and lends her his support; in fact, he becomes her guardian angel. The policeman covers up her crime, and her prostitution is justified because it is financing her sister's education and social future. As long as Mercedes is able to keep her secret, the film has no great dramatic crises: in the city, private life constitutes its own moral codes and conflicts arise only when they become public. In his rural dramas, on the other hand, everyone already knows, the conflicts are always public. The protagonists' conflicts begin when, much to their sorrow, they are forced to subvert social norms. Their subversion is not a matter of choice, but of destiny.

In his films, Fernández unconsciously represented the problem of the transition from a traditional communitarian social model to an individualistic modern world. This has been a slow and painful process that began in the sixteenth century and has yet to resolve all its contradictions or to polish its rough edges. *María Candelaria* posits the kindness of the people and the Indians, and attempts to convince us of the authenticity of its characters. But they were dressed by Armando Valdés Peza, the most fashionable fashion designer of the period: 'Look here Lolita, you are playing a little indian, not Cleopatra, OK?',[38] but she continued to act more like Dolores del Río than the Xochimilco native *María Candelaria*. The glamour of the stars, the formalism of his style and the idealisation of the Indians explicitly contradicted the kind of film that the director wanted to make. Fernández declared that he wanted to film the suffering of the people, as he had learned from Eisenstein, the pain of the collective, but he seemed more sympathetic to the pain of those who break social norms to defend the fundamental and exclusive ideals of a couple in love.

It is important to note that it was difficult to escape from the influence of Hollywood in this period: the theme of romantic love was this cinema's biggest draw, and many firmly believed that movies should offer a world of fantasy to distract spectators from their daily woes. In addition to the desire for social redemption, the struggle to produce a personal cinema, and Eisenstein's legacy, Fernández had to drink from the fount of the Hollywood cinema which inundated Mexico. Despite their incoherences, his films are moving because aside from their specific stories, they share a common theme, a backdrop linked to a universal human conflict: the conflict between shelter and the inclement outdoors, between the desire to be safe and the desire to be free. Fernández's rural films demonstrated over and over again this tension between isolation and fusion, between the individual and society.

His films told love stories because love was the most vulnerable element in the crisis of the original order that is fundamental to all his narratives. The love between men and women appears as an ideal: two beings are irresistibly and unavoidably joined as if by an act of nature. In Fernández's films, the man-woman relation is idyllic: nourished by tenderness, without any visible eroticism, absolutely harmonious, and subject only to external conflicts. The required unconditional submission of the woman makes the couple seem like a single person with two faces. Despite the fact that these were naive innocent relationships, Fernández did not allow his couples to live together or to gain substance: 'Fernández is, therefore, a true romantic: happiness causes him anguish. It is only in unhappiness and the painful endings that he reestablishes his equilibrium.'[39] His protagonists do not have psychological or emotional complexity; they exist merely to serve the narrative conflict. The fallen women, like Margarita in *Las abandonadas* or Paloma in *Pueblerina*, allow men to redeem them and to fight for a better world. Their characters are stereotypes with only those characteristics required by the narrative. Sometimes they are more widely symbolic, like Rosaura, the schoolteacher of *Río Escondido*, who represents the nation. She is not in control of her life, but simply a narrative stratagem used to illustrate a deeper conflict and a more insidious battle.

Behind the tender love stories a multiple tension develops among men, nature and time. This tension has more to do with myth than with the stories, and it forms the framework, the backbone that sustains the thesis as well as the aesthetic principles of his films. We are dealing here with myth in its original sense: a tale that demonstrates and explains some aspect of human nature. Myth is inscribed in destiny, not in the individual will or in history. Fernández's characters do not understand what happens to them very clearly, but it doesn't matter: their pain is made out of a different substance and they accept it as such, for it alludes to the inexorable. It cannot be explained and is indifferent to time and place. Fernández, so given to speeches and apparently so sure of his opinions about good and evil, was unable to render judgment of his own theme.

The films that concern us refer to a ritualistic reality, and their central tension is that between nature and civilisation. This tension is represented in the conflicts faced by his men-landscape, who appear to doubt the appropriateness of their fusion with nature when they aspire to something as apparently simple as the fulfilment of love. At the centre of his stories is the expulsion from paradise, the moment that separates men from their origins and projects them into history, from shelter to the outdoors. This drama motivates his stories and structures his narratives. *Las abandonadas* conscientiously recounts the love between Margarita and General Juan Gómez until the crucial moment of the break: Gómez is a fake military man and Margarita a prostitute redeemed by love. When justice intervenes he is imprisoned and she returns to an apparently fixed destiny. María Candelaria and Lorenzo Rafael struggle to escape from the reality of an expulsion that has been envisioned since the beginning of the film: they do not succeed. Esperanza and Amelia, in *Flor silvestre* and *Bugambilia*, live in nostalgia. In *Pueblerina*, Aurelio and Paloma, aided by their exacerbated humility, can be ambitious or attempt to renovate their idyll, for they have done their penitence in advance. The original conflict is produced because this is a world where individual actions have social effects. Big and small are governed by similar rules, and peace lies in their fusion.

Fernández's heroes do not want to make choices, but they are forced to. Love subverts all of nature, including society, because it individualises the characters and sets them out as separate. This is an ambiguous solution that attracts, repels and connotes the tragic. The love of two individuals is an attempt to regain paradise, but it is always thwarted by a third element, be it the past of María Candelaria's mother, Nieves's illness (*La bien amada, The Well-Loved One*, 1951), family traditions (*Flor silvestre, Bugambilia*), justice (*Las abandonadas*) or ambition (*La perla*). This triangular structure is particularly obvious in *La red*. Three runaways from justice, two men and a woman, seek refuge on a remote beach: soon both men are in love with the woman and tragedy ensues. 'Where there is a female and two males soon there will be trouble,' warns one of the secondary characters of the film.

His heroes are part of this enslaving natural universe and are not very affected by the delirium of culture. The villains, however, have perversely refined ideas. The US doctor in *La perla* likes to swallow pearls with his drinks, and Rufino in *El mar y tú* (*The Sea and You,* 1951) grows orchids and keeps exotic birds. Without any manifest bad intentions, the refined artist who paints María Candelaria's face on top of another model's naked body unwittingly unleashes a tragedy.

Ricardo Muñoz Suay has said that 'nature is the most important character in Emilio Fernández's work. It is there that his visual style emerges.'[40] The narratives of his films unroll over the backdrop of nature. What he posits, undoubtedly, is how to reconcile the individual with civilisation. 'El Indio' does not render judgment or resolve the dilemma; he exhibits the options without offering any logical resolution. Contradictions exist, as in the baroque art he liked so much, out of the association of diverse stylistic elements.

We are faced precisely with the myth of the marginalised who longs for a lost world, who believes it can be glimpsed 'through the bars' of the fence, and who questions his expulsion and endless pain. When he presents this topic Fernández returns to an archetypal universal conflict. His characters are often Indian because they are the ones who suffer the most evident consequences of this debate, even though, beyond the surface of race, their human condition is what determines their tragedies. Yet a second aspect of this tension between nature and civilisation affects his aesthetics. We are in between order and delirium, between the harshness of the drama and a beautiful and dignified style of representation. In the same way that Fernández's personality concealed a great violence that often overflowed from behind a gentle and discreet exterior, his images attempted to control the indomitable force of the conflict. Thus, in this case, visual beauty constituted an indispensable limit.

Fernández established an equilibrium between excessive passion and the impassive faces and calm attitudes of his characters. The reasons for the suffering of María Candelaria, or Aurelio and Paloma in *Pueblerina*, were well known, but the characters behave with dignity and integrity. In a rather different type of film, such as *Cuando levanta la niebla* for example, the director got carried away. This film is a psychological drama about a personality exchange that leads to a murder in a mental hospital. Fernández developed the drama through excessively grandiloquent gestures, camera movements and dry-ice fog. The details were separated from their context – a doorknob, the feet and hands of a body – and Antonio Díaz Conde's music is so excessively dramatic that it precludes all reflection. In the films that were closer to him, the serenity of his heroes is one of their virtues.

His aesthetic style had as much to do with the underlying theme of a fractured cosmic order as with the stories in which he presented it. We have already seen, for example, that the rhythm of his films refers to a double time: the time of myth and the time of man, to which the narrative must be adapted. Mythic time is eternal: in the beginning there was immobility. Fernández repeated this over and over again in interviews: 'I have always lived in a sort of fourth dimension. Time does not exist for me. For me everything is the same: yesterday, today, tomorrow. Everything is in the present, no?'[41] This is a circular time turned onto itself, and very different from the time that is future-driven and the subject of history. This absolute time coincides with his huge long shots of solemn landscapes beyond man, with the rhythm that reflects the slowness of nature and participates in the fundamental essence of origins. The time of history, however, acquires a faster rhythm when things happen, when exterior forces invade or the interior escapes. This is the time of filmic narrative.

His films evidence a multifaceted, complex system. They show us the rhetorical face of his theses, the beautiful face of his images, the face of complacency and inertia, the rebel face of the struggle for love. These varied faces are sustained by an internal force: the conflict of the man who perceives that he is more than a product of nature. In only a few years, Fernández gathered traditions and innovations; gave voice to and promulgated the Mexican cinema; became successful, troubled and paralysed. Beyond the beauty of his images, the banality of his discourse, and the archaic voice that we find in his films today, there was a time when Fernández represented Mexico, when he in large part created the idea that the world had of Mexico, and even perhaps that Mexicans had of themselves (which must be further analysed).

'El Indio' was always a marginal: his spite was evident in all his films. Marginalised, he searched for a space that would welcome his characters. He unsuccessfully searched for harmony among man, time and nature. Like his characters, he pursued a lost idyll. This is where he attempted to work out a universal human problem, the myth, the sacred substance. And precisely where he overcame his own

limitations. His films are moving because they refer to something more profound than the theses and speeches which are today obsolete; they are moving because they address the difficulties of finding a place, and they are sincere because that struggle is the director's own. We must understand the man to understand his films. We have to understand that Emilio Fernández constructed his life with the same passion as he developed the characters of his films. In sum, we have to understand that he was a character worthy of his own films.

Notes

1. This conception of painting and sculpture was common among nineteenth-century art critics such as Ignacio Manuel Altamirano.
2. Aurelio de los Reyes, *Medio siglo de cine mexicano (1896–1947)* (Mexico City: Trillas, 1987), pp. 142 ff.
3. Ibid., p. 99.
4. Ibid.
5. Julia Tuñón, *En su propio espejo (Entrevista con Emilio 'el Indio' Fernández)* (Mexico City: Universidad Autónoma/Iztapalapa Metropolitana, 1988), pp. 24–5.
6. 'To a certain degree, the Mexican cinema was a Hollywood subsidiary even though a form of national expression.' De los Reyes, *Cine méxicano*, p. 126.
7. Tuñón, *En su propio espejo*, p. 24.
8. Ibid. Adolfo de la Huerta had been a Revolutionary, interim president, and a candidate for the presidency. In 1923 he headed a failed rebellion and subsequently sought refuge in the USA.
9. The Kikapú Indians belong to the Algonquin family and were established in the 1850s in El Nacimiento (Coahuila) in northern Mexico. They are more like the US 'red skins' than the typical indigenous peoples of meso-America.
10. Tuñón, *En su propio espejo*, p. 25.
11. Ibid., p. 27.
12. Ibid., p. 28.
13. 'This is a wonderful film! Marvellous! … This is the Mexican cinema, just like Eisenstein, a product of Eisenstein's. … Magnificent! With a wonderful conflict between workers and owners and a fishermen's story. Magnificent! What cinematography! Zinnemann was a great photographer!' Ibid., p. 30.
14. Ibid., p. 50.
15. Raymond Borde, 'Emilio Fernández', *Positif* (Paris), May 1954, p. 16.
16. Emilio García Riera claims that because this was the first Cannes festival after the end of the war, it had a celebratory rather than a competitive spirit: *María Candelaria* shared the award with eleven other films. Emilio García Riera, *Emilio Fernández (1904–1986)* (Guadalajara: CIEC, 1987), p. 55.
17. *El Cine Gráfico*, no. 686 (Mexico City), 11 August

1946, p. 2.

18. Juan León, 'El cine sigue su marcha', in *El Cine Gráfico* (Mexico City), no. 694, 6 October 1946, pp. 4–14.

19. This quote, and the previous one, are from Cagliostro, 'De lunes a domingo', in *El Cine Gráfico,* (Mexico City), no. 697, 27 October 1946, p. 7.

20. 'Triunfo legítimo de nuestro cine', in *Cinema Reporter* (Mexico City), no. 429, 5 October 1946, p. 27.

21. Carlos Monsiváis, 'Se fue el remolino y nos adecentó: la nostalgia en el cine', in *Siempre* (Mexico City), no. 1625, 15 August 1984, pp. 6–7.

22. They are: *Un día de vida* (1950), *Víctimas del pecado* (1950), *Islas Marías* (1950), *Siempre tuya* (1950), *La bien amada* (1951), *Acapulco* (1951), *El mar y tú* (1951), *Cuando levanta la niebla* (1952), *La red* (1953), *Reportaje* (1953), *El rapto* (1953), *La rosa blanca* (1953), *La rebelión de los colgados* (1954), *Nosotros dos* (1954), *La Tierra del Fuego se apaga* (1955), *Una cita de amor* (1956), *El impostor* (1956).

23. They are: *El impostor* (1956), *Un dorado de Pancho Villa* (1966), *El crepúsculo de un dios* (1968).

24. 'Gabriel Figueroa' in 'Testimonios para la historia del cine mexicano', *Cuadernos de la Cineteca Nacional,* vol. 3 (Mexico City: Cineteca Nacional, 1976), p. 55.

25. [Trans. note] Emilio Fernández used the words *nos apochamos,* suggesting that Mexicans were becoming too much like *pochos,* the derogative term used for Mexicans who live in the USA.

26. Tuñón, *En su propio espejo,* p. 65.

27. Ibid.

28. Ibid., p. 25.

29. García Riera, *Emilio Fernández,* p. 207.

30. Tuñón, *En su propio espejo,* p. 79.

31 Ibid., pp. 69–70; 'The cinema is like a magnifying glass, you can focus in and magnify whatever you want, but what matters is what you want to say and, later, how you say it.'

32. Ibid., p. 42.

33. Ibid., p. 67.

34. Jorge Ayala Blanco, *La aventura del cine mexicano* (Mexico City: Era, 1968), p. 93.

35. 'Mauricio Magdaleno' in 'Testimonios', p. 30.

36. Borde, 'Emilio Fernández', p. 20.

37. Tuñón, *En su propio espejo,* p. 77.

38. Julia Tuñón, 'Interview with Emilio Fernández', mimeo.

39. Borde, 'Emilio Fernández', p. 17.

40. Ricardo Muñoz Suay, 'La obra de Emilio Fernández', *El Sobre Literario* (Valencia), no. 3, September 1950.

41. Tuñón, *En su propio espejo,* p. 56.

Roberto Gavaldón

Ariel Zúñiga

Roberto Gavaldón, undoubtedly one of the most important directors of the Mexican cinema, was born in Ciudad Jiménez (Chihuahua) a year before the 1910 outbreak of the Revolution. He was born in the region that gave birth to the Revolutionary movement that shaped contemporary Mexico, and into a comfortable middle-class family that was divided and torn apart by the conflict.

Gavaldón went to the capital with the intention of studying either architecture or engineering. Mexico City was a national magnet where changes of major significance for the country were taking place. Gavaldón became part of the intellectual and artistic circles of the capital via his friendship with well-known personalities such as Salvador Novo, a poet from his region. But Gavaldón was neither a poet nor a bohemian and he pragmatically decided to go to the USA in search of better economic opportunities. He worked at various jobs in California and made connections with the film world indirectly, taking advantage of his sturdy physique while working as a nightclub bouncer. He worked as an extra in a number of US films and met other Mexicans in the film world who would also become important directors of Mexican cinema: Emilio 'el Indio' Fernández and Chano Urueta.

His stay in the USA was brief: Gavaldón was always in a hurry. Upon his return to Mexico he entered the nascent film industry via the most diverse jobs, ranging from small parts in films by the Mexican pioneers Sevilla and de Fuentes to prop man and assistant editor. He assisted most of the directors of the period: Portas, Benavides, Gout, Galindo, Orol, Urueta and Gabriel Soria. This last director would play a decisive role in Gavaldón's cinematic formation because of his patience, his Hollywood-acquired knowledge of the craft, his great sense of rhythm and his respect for pre-production script planning. Indeed, Gabriel Soria is one of the Mexican directors of the period who has still to be properly re-evaluated. Later, it is likely that Gavaldón

also assisted Joaquín Pardavé, a comic actor of the late 1930s who also directed several of the films in which he starred. Working with an actor-director allowed him to refine skills that would serve him well as a director.

He also co-directed, with Celestino Gorostiza, *Naná,* a 30s Hollywood success starring Lupe Vélez. Gavaldón had a strong personality and was good at getting the best out of any negotiation. His work coincided with the most productive period of Mexican cinema. A nationalist and a conciliatory man of order, Gavaldón produced his most significant body of work during the period when Mexico struggled to become an industrial nation, within which the film industry was an essential sector.

In 1944, Roberto Gavaldón made *La barraca (The Shack),* the first of the forty-seven features he directed throughout his career. That for this debut he chose to adapt a story by the Spanish writer Vicente Blasco Ibáñez is quite telling and provides a key to understanding his work as a whole. This was a story set in Spain towards the very end of the last century, but filmed entirely in Mexico. Many still believe that the film was shot in Spain because of its careful reconstruction and the detailed naturalism of its narrative development. This first film clearly marks the path that Gavaldón would follow throughout his career.

Gavaldón's films span the most diverse genres and social groups. Urban classes: *La otra (The Other,* 1946), *La diosa arrodillada (The Kneeling Goddess,* 1947) and *En la palma de tu mano (In the Palm of Your Hand,* 1950); rural classes: *La barraca* (1944), *Rosauro Castro* (1950), *El siete de copas (The Seven of Spades,* 1960) and *El gallo de oro (The Golden Cock,* 1964); the liberal professions: *La casa chica (The Small House,* 1949) and *El rebozo de Soledad (Soledad's Shawl,* 1952). He also made romantic melodramas like *Las tres perfectas casadas (The Three Perfect Wives,* 1952), *Camelia* (1953) and many others. Gavaldón produced some extraordinary box-office successes and was one of the most productive directors of Mexican cinema for over two decades. This was his most prolific period and the phase in which he developed an efficient narrative style.

It is not necessary to invoke the auteur theory to say that certain elements reappear in all his films. These are not formal or stylistic elements, but rather a personal approach to genres and themes linked to his own well-defined views of the world and the Mexican nation that surrounded him. Gavaldón worked for producers and accepted all types of

Stella Inda in *El rebozo de Soledad* (Roberto Gavaldón, 1952)

assignments; this was not unusual in this period, although other important directors like Emilio Fernández were quite selective. When conditions allowed, Gavaldón managed high-budget productions well, but his skill also allowed him to adapt to low budgets. In all instances, his films had the same ambition: to be successful and to communicate his personal views of the world and Mexico.

Given that the national and Latin American markets guaranteed financing, a return on investment and sizeable profits, few producers bothered to expand their markets. They always claimed that any expansion beyond these natural markets would require significantly larger investments. Thus the expressive power and formal richness of Mexican, and therefore of Gavaldón's, cinema were almost unknown throughout the world. The producers' lack of foresight benefited Hollywood and, some years later, was responsible for transforming Mexican cinema into an excellent provider of inexpensive, well-trained labour in beautiful and varied locales.

Without resorting to local colour or regionalisms,

a film like *Camelia* (1953), one of Gavaldón's least-known films, would have strengthened the position of Mexican cinema in markets other than its natural ones. The film adapts *La Dame aux camélias,* turning the female protagonist into an actress who plays Camille in a theatrical production as well as in her daily life. The parallel between the lives of the actress and her theatrical role, together with the film's solid formal structure, combine to produce an excellent atmospheric melodrama. *Camelia* has aged well and even today it is well received by audiences.

Another important aspect of his work is his choice of collaborators: the cinematographers Victor Herrera, Alex Phillips and Gabriel Figueroa; the script writers José Revueltas, Edmundo Baez, Mauricio Magdaleno and Hugo Argüelles. In each case he made the best possible choices. His close collaboration with Revueltas, one of the most important contemporary Mexican writers, and with Alex Phillips, a Russian-born cinematographer who had been in Hollywood and had been part of the German Expressionist movement, were of special significance. Together, the three men produced the most refined Mexican cinema of the 40s and early 50s, marked, above all, by the social concerns of their projects.

With few exceptions, such as *La vida íntima de Marco Antonio y Cleopatra* (*The Intimate Life of Mark Anthony and Cleopatra,* 1946) and *The Adventures of Casanova* (1947, a US production), Gavaldón worked with only three recurring themes. The first was the lost era of youth, manifested in the labyrinthine and obsessive geography of the family homes of most of his films. The second was the growing curiosity about the phenomenon of otherness, be it in the form of doubles or twins or as the search for identity common to the formation of nationalisms. Finally, the third theme was a marked obsession with death, as an individual preoc-cupation and as part of this same search for national identity that in Mexico has become a national mythic cult, functioning as an excuse for complacency. We could say that Roberto Gavaldón was an obsessive film-maker who repeated himself, always travelling on the same path while searching for new traces of his own self.

Attempting to establish a chronological hierarchy of Gavaldón's films would be unproductive, but if we begin with the premise that each of his films is as valuable as his entire oeuvre, it becomes possible to generate some interesting categories. First of all, there are the box-office successes that were also well received by critics; these are actually his best known

films: *La barraca* (1944), *La otra* (1946), *La diosa arrodillada* (1947), *En la palma de tu mano* (1950), *Rosauro Castro* (1950), *El rebozo de Soledad* (1950), *Macario* (1959) and *El gallo de oro* (1964).

The second category consists of films that were less popular or less appreciated critically, but which exhibit similarities to the rest of his oeuvre: *El socio* (*The Partner,* 1945), *Rayando el sol* (*The Dawn,* 1945), *Han matado a Tongolele* (*They Have Killed Tongolele,* 1948), *La casa chica* (1949), *Las tres perfectas casadas* (1952), *Sombra verde* (*Green Shadow,* 1954), *La escondida* (*The Hidden One,* 1955) and the greater part of his later films.

In third place, there is the exception: *Rosa Blanca* (*White Rose,* 1961). In the space between the reality and the myths of Mexican cinema's history, banned films have played a significant role and the two most relevant cases were those of *Rosa Blanca* and Julio Bracho's *La sombra del caudillo* (*The Shadow of the Leader,* 1960). It is impossible to separate Roberto Gavaldón's work from politics. No one in Mexico who achieves an important position can ignore the political dimension of social life, and Gavaldón was no exception. Therefore, breaking ranks with those in power implied an inevitable loss of creative and practical options. As is the case in every other national cinema, the Mexican cinema has certain themes that are considered taboo when seriously and critically developed. Anything dealing with the military, the figure of the president or national heroes is considered a sensitive topic. Bracho's *La sombra del caudillo* was based on an important Martín Luis Guzmán novel set in the immediate post-Revolutionary period. Since many of the political figures who participated in the events of the novel were still politically active and quite powerful when the film was made, the most expedient solution was to silence the film. The case of *Rosa Blanca* was similar. Even today, both films are still semi-clandestine: they are exhibited surreptitiously and in obscure locations and have not, therefore, received the attention they deserve. Nevertheless, there are video copies in private circulation.

Like *Macario* (1959), *Rosa Blanca* is based on a Bruno Traven story. The title refers to the name of a prosperous agricultural hacienda in the oil-rich Gulf of Mexico coastal region. A US company wants to put oil wells on the hacienda, which can easily be read as a metaphor for the nation, politically divided by the desire to promote agricultural development and industrialisation. Jacinto Yáñez, the proud owner of the hacienda and representative of the promoters of agricultural development is not impressed by the

Ignacio López Tarso in *Macario* (Roberto Gavaldón, 1959)

money he is offered and refuses to sell out. Through a series of clever ruses he is invited to travel to the USA to experience otherness, difference and alternative ways of understanding the world. Jacinto agrees to the trip, seduced by magazine reproductions of the marvellous animals bred in the farm owned by Abner, his North American host, without realising that Abner works for the oil company and wants to buy the hacienda. With the naivety of the underdeveloped, Jacinto goes to the USA and admires everything he is shown, but remains proudly inflexible when it comes to selling his hacienda. When Jacinto eventually loses patience and decides to return to Mexico, he is abducted. Back in Mexico, his defenceless family, ignorant and utterly dependent upon the patriarch, loses the property. Rosa Blanca becomes an oil field where the former farm workers now have to apply daily for work. Accompanying the credits, the image of a white rose

slowly covered by a shower of oil eloquently summarises the film.

A rigorous work, *Rosa Blanca* is a good example of the director's talents. It contains many powerful narrative moments: the meeting between Jacinto Yáñez and the first oil-company representative, in which Jacinto sings the praises of the land; the farm workers' march in a torrential downpour typical of the region, protesting the installation of the oil wells; the shacks where the dispossessed and evicted workers crowd together, and where the birth of a child coincides with the arrival of bulldozers preparing the land for the engineers' houses. However, the film skirts the edges of the permissible: the painful repression of railway workers had taken place only three years earlier. *Rosa Blanca* caused Gavaldón's fall from grace, and he was abandoned to his own devices in a country where film production was fundamentally linked to the state and where to oppose

La escondida (Roberto Gavaldón, 1955)

the government was synonymous to an *auto-da-fé*.

At this point it is important to mention Roberto Gavaldón's significant off-screen political work. He was an active participant in the various labour struggles of film workers, and one of the founders of the STPC (Sindicato de Trabajadores de la Producción Cinematográfica). The social achievements of this union and its ability to protect its members played an important role in the nation's labour history. As one of the directors of this union, Gavaldón became a national deputy and participated directly in the legislation affecting the film industry. Although Gavaldón was a liberal rather than a leftist, we cannot ignore the consequences of his work, his close relationship to well-known leftists such as José Revueltas and the fact that his sister, the actress Rosaura Revueltas (who appears in *El rebozo de Soledad*), starred in Herbert J. Biberman's *Salt of the Earth* (1954), a film more talked about than seen,

especially in the USA, and an amazing example of the courage of some of the victims of McCarthyism and the blacklist.

We have always been surprised by how little the victims of US intolerance who moved to Mexico actually contributed to Mexican cinema. There were some exceptions: Hugo Butler, who collaborated directly and indirectly in a number of Mexican films; the Biberman–Wilson team and their great film about Mexican immigration to the USA; Dalton Trumbo's Oscar-winning screenplay (under the pseudonym of Robert Rich) set in Mexico, for *The Brave One*, directed by Irving Rapper (1956). However, most of the excellent blacklisted screenwriters who lived among us for two or three years, even the most radical ones like Albert Maltz, Alvah Bessie and John Bright, never made any attempts to understand their new surroundings. Not even their novels refer to their stay in this country, except for Bright's script for Robert Rossen's uninspiring film *The Brave Bulls* (1951).

El rebozo de Soledad is a vigorous film with great dramatic power. In a letter sent to a proud doctor who decided to return to the city, a village priest reminisces about their first meeting, the doctor's eventful arrival and the great service he rendered to the God-forsaken little town. The doctor reads the letter while waiting for an interview with the pompous doctors of a rich city hospital, where the practice of medicine has an altogether different meaning. Towards the end, in open rebellion, the doctor decides to return to the village. A story of love, jealousy and battles for power and control over land serves as the backdrop for the drama. Several scenes, such as the emergency operation performed on a suffocating child under the eyes of its suffering mother (Rosaura Revueltas), accompanied by the noise of a railway engine which dominates the soundtrack, or the stand-off between the doctor and his male rival Roque, are so dramatically intense that they are still able to move audiences after all these years. The film was made during Gavaldón's most militant union period and it is interesting to see that the credits include the union initials after the names of all the participants: proof of his political commitment since no such identification was actually required by the union.

Another example of Gavaldón's growing cinematic radicalism was *Rosauro Castro* (1950), which many regard as his best film. Today, *Rosauro Castro* is a rarity because the negative was lost in the fire that destroyed the film archive in the early 80s. It is a film about individual honour besieged by the exterior world in the form of an intense study of the power relations between a cacique, that is to say, a rural potentate, and the townspeople. In my view, it is one of Mexican cinema's ten best films.

Returning to the films in the first category, it is important to point to *La otra* (1946) which, together with *La diosa arrodillada* (1947) and *En la palma de tu mano* (1950), can be seen as so many studies of the same female character. *La otra* tells of twins whose lives have led them to opposite social positions. María, the poor sister, murders her rich sister Magdalena to assume her social position and wealth, but she ends up paying for Magdalena's sins and the film thus concludes on a sceptical note: love is impossible. The truth which eventually triumphs is ambiguous and meaningless. The film's formal richness and complexity is evidenced in the treatment of the two female characters, both played by Dolores del Río, the Mexican actress who began her career in

Hollywood and had a famous romance with Orson Welles at the time of *Citizen Kane* (1941). Examples of this complexity can be seen in the way Gavaldón uses mirrors as symbolic rhetorical devices standing in for the duplicity of the image itself; in the sensuality of the scene where María disrobes her dead sister to don her clothes as she becomes 'the other one'; and even in the vicissitudes of a character who, faced with the impossibility of becoming 'other', resorts to auto-mutilation only to end up, ultimately, being buried in a way that stresses what they have in common.

La otra is an important film, especially if we take into account the typical characteristics of Mexican cinema at this time. It is worth mentioning the film's thematic similarity to *The Dark Mirror* (Robert Siodmak, 1946), a film released in Mexico only two months before *La otra*.[1] Both films were in production almost at the same time, one in Hollywood starring Olivia de Havilland, the other in Mexico. If we remember how strongly Mexican directors felt about competing with Hollywood, Gavaldón's state of mind may be readily understood, especially since at this time, immediately after the war, Hollywood was only beginning to conquer the markets previously dominated by Mexican cinema. Contrary to the situation today, US films then rarely did better than Mexican productions in the enormous Latin American market, even if the principal reason for this success was linguistic. However, linguistic arguments do not adequately explain this success of Mexican films in Latin America in this period. A comparison between *The Dark Mirror* and *La otra* tells us why.

The Dark Mirror is the more timid and puritan of the two films, it is a simply structured and much less formally ambitious work. If we recall Siodmak's previous films, especially *Phantom Lady* (1944) or *The Spiral Staircase* (1945), there was every reason to expect the director to show greater formal daring when dealing with such a topic which lent itself to stylistic ambition. However, in the end, the spectator is left disappointed and *The Dark Mirror* is less resistant to the ravages of time than *La otra*, despite the latter's melodramatic baggage. One lesson of such a comparison is that Mexican cinema cannot simply be regarded as a regional phenomenon, but that it deserves a complete reappraisal in an international context.

Even though *La diosa arrodillada* (1947) and *En la palma de tu mano* (1950) tackle different topics, they maintain a certain continuity with *La otra* regarding character development and the use of

Arturo de Córdova and Leticia Palma in *En la palma de tu mano* (Roberto Gavaldón, 1950)

mirrors, especially in the way they reflect the ineluctable process of dying. These films also insist upon the importance of a baroque conception of death: the decrepitude that afflicts biological man and proclaims the death of his flesh and his spirit, the decay that afflicts social man and renders him classless, the decomposition that overtakes man sociologically and entails the disintegration of the social itself.[2]

Gavaldón's use of this baroque figure dispenses with all the mythological overtones someone like Emilio 'el Indio' Fernández bestows upon death, dwelling instead on physical evidence rather than indulging in a more nostalgic and romanticised vision. *La noche avanza* (*The Night Advances,* 1951) is a typical film noir, following the story of the male protagonist of *La diosa arrodillada.* The character of Marcos (Pedro Armendáriz) is meticulously and convincingly developed as that of a highly strung, ambitious, yet cynically carefree, jai alai player, a ladies man who frequents gambling establishments. In the first part of the film, Marcos is discovered, holding a gun, beside the corpse of a woman who loved him. His gambling enemies begin to blackmail him and he becomes dependent upon a rich woman who could rescue him through marriage. Instead, however, the woman discovers his infidelities and kills him. The brutal depiction of the Mexico City setting and the detailed description of the gambling world add considerably to the film's power.

In 1953 Gavaldón directed *The Littlest Outlaw* for Walt Disney, a minor film rendered important mainly by the fact that it signalled Hollywood's recognition of a Mexican director, an aspect that remains relevant to this day and is part of the inescapable and determining logic of the national cinema, especially in the light of the evidence proving that the domestic US market is the most difficult to crack. Two years later, he directed *Historia de un amor (Love Story)* in Argentina, following the pattern established in 1950 when he filmed *Mi vida por la tuya (My Life for Yours)* in Argentina and which would continue later, in Spain, with *Don Quijote cabalga de nuevo (Don Quijote Rides Again,* 1972), *Un amor perverso (A Perverse Love,* 1974) and *La playa vacía (The Empty Beach,* 1976). Thus Gavaldón became one of the Mexican directors most closely affiliated with those other national cinemas which have aspects in common with Mexico's own industry.

Macario (1959), which received an Oscar nomination, is based on an original story by Bruno Traven. It is one of the purest cinematic examples of what has been called magical realism, which helps to explain why Gavaldón later collaborated with Gabriel García Márquez on the adaptation of Juan Rulfo's *El gallo de oro* (1964). Set in the colonial period, *Macario* tells of a poor lumberjack, who, despite his self-sacrificing wife and his extreme poverty, manages to fulfil his lifelong ambition to eat an entire turkey. He dies as a result. In the last scene, the lumberjack dreams that he has made a pact with Death, become rich, achieved control over the lives of others and earned his own perdition. Gavaldón establishes such a strong link between the mythical history of ancient and contemporary Mexico that, some years later, an anthropologist researching the legends of southern Mexico discovered that the plot of the film had been totally assimilated into the mythology of the region (where the film was widely distributed) as an ancient myth. *Deseada* (1950) was the first attempt to rework a theme similar to *Macario's* in the Yucatán region.

Among the least important or the less well-liked films, *Han matado a Tongolele* (1948) and *Sombra verde* (1954) deserve a mention. The first film stars Tongolele, a popular personality who still performs occasionally in variety shows. The detective story is set in a theatre with a complicated floor plan and labyrinthine corridors which play a key role in the drama. It is a competent film which foreshadows the importance of inner spatial labyrinths in later films such as *Doña Macabra* (1971). *Sombra verde* features a crucial scene in which the dramatic power and the narrative effect derive from the clever treatment of a closed space (a tropical forest) and two characters. A white hunter (Ricardo Montalbán, who later joined the Hollywood industry as an insufferable 'latin lover') and the local guide (Jorge Martínez de Hoyas, undoubtedly one of the greatest actors of contemporary Mexican cinema) get lost in the forest after being bitten by a snake. While filming on

location, a horse fell from a hanging bridge over a waterfall and Gavaldón decided to include the event in the film, throwing an old horse into the abyss. This anecdote, together with his strong, demanding temperament and his perfectionism, earned him the nickname 'the ogre'. Even today, those who knew him either respect and admire him or prefer not to talk about him at all.

We should also note the rhythm and the formal richness of *Las tres perfectas casadas* (1952), as well as the sensuality of its female characters and the apotheosis of its conclusion. *El siete de copas* (1960) is set in a rural environment where an orphan child becomes addicted to gambling and risks all in search of a lucky streak. *La escondida* (1955) offers an impoverished image of the 1910 Revolution: the colour cinematography, an accommodation to industrial demands, imbues it with an unreal and unconvincing atmosphere, which may help explain why Gabriel Figueroa demurred when Gavaldón wanted to shoot *Macario* in colour. Thankfully, Don Gabriel's view prevailed since a good part of *Macario's* power stems from its black and white cinematography. María Felix, already the 'Doña' of Mexican cinema, was no longer the Rebecca of *La diosa arrodillada* (1947), but she nevertheless produced an excellent performance under Gavaldón's direction in *Flor de mayo (May Flower,* 1957).

Having enjoyed a reputation as Mexico's film director *par excellence,* the winner of awards, the darling of producers and a guaranteed box-office success, what happened with *Rosa Blanca* and Gavaldón's subsequent withdrawal from politics generated much bitterness and blocked his development as a director, but there is one more important work that must be mentioned: *El gallo de oro* (1954), his last great film and a personal favourite of his. *El gallo de oro* offers a synthesis of Roberto Gavaldón's work as an auteur, summing up the consistency and coherent personal vision manifest throughout his career and evident even in his less important films as well as in the frankly decadent films he made towards the end of his Spanish sojourn and after his return to Mexico. His disorganised notes, unrealised scripts, 16mm film experiments and conversational statements seem to indicate that he was haunted throughout his life by a project he was never able to produce: a great film about the Mexican Revolution for which *La escondida* was only a sketch. *El gallo de oro* resumes and describes Gavaldón's vision of our national identity, what we might call Mexicanness or, more generally, Latin Americanness (although there will always be those who deny that there is such a thing). Here we find personal obsessions such as the home, the privileged object of his personal search. In this film, it is reconquered with the same ease with which it is lost in a card game. There is also the character of Bernarda, an earthy woman with telluric power, who represents the continuity of a pre-Hispanic culture unadulterated by the Conquest.

El gallo de oro begins with the death of the mother, without whom our culture is confused and incomprehensible. The death of Dionisio's mother opens up his world and affirms his sexuality. The beginning and the end of the film take place in the very heart of the home, its central patio: in the cock-fighting arena, the *palenque* installed there, only luck determines which cock, which masculinity will triumph. After winning the battle and recovering the space over which the vanquished Reglita used to hold sway (in one of the most beautiful shots of the film), he can lose the home again and even permanently, because what was important was not to have it, but to prove his ability to win and to lose. Once that feat has been accomplished, everything returns to the beginning as if nothing had happened. The hero bears a few more scars, but they are inflicted by life itself and are unavoidable. The eloquence of the song lyrics adds to the meaning of the film's action and, willingly or not, words and actions bring Rulfo's ideas closer to those of Gavaldón's. The written text and the filmic text narrate, with a single voice, in an appropriate tone and with the right distance, what we are.

Notes

1. Jorge Ayala Blanco, *Cartelera cinematográfica* (Mexico City: UNAM, 1982).
2. Pierre Petiot, *Cinéma de mort: esquisse d'un baroque cinématographique* (Fribourg: Éditions du Signe, 1972).

Luis Buñuel in Mexico

Tomás Pérez Turrent

Luis Buñuel liked to say that he learned how to make films in Mexico. Although he had already made three films before arriving in Mexico (*Un chien andalou,* 1928; *L'Age d'or,* 1930; *Las hurdes* aka *Land Without Bread,* 1932), he was a dilettante film-maker, a Spanish *señorito* with the luxury to make films as he pleased. However, the war and his exile in New York forced him into odd jobs on the fringes of the cinema world. His professional cinematic career really began in Mexico.

One prior experience was crucial to his subsequent Mexican career: his work as executive producer at the company Filmófono in Republican Spain (1935–6). At Filmófono he oversaw the production of four films: *La hija de Juan Simón (The Daughter of Juan Simón,* José Luis Sáenz de Heredia, 1935); *Don Quintín el amargao (Don Quintín, the Bitter One,* Luis Marquina, 1935); *Centinela alerta (Alert Sentinel,* Jean Grémillon, 1936) and *Quién me quiere a mi? (Who loves me?,* José Luis Sáenz de Heredia, 1936). Any attempt to unearth Buñuel's imprint in these films, although Buñuel himself would have claimed some of their details as his, is clearly an exaggerated form of auteurism. In fact, his Filmófono work involved primarily script super-vision, some technical matters and, above all, ensuring that productions did not exceed their assigned budgets. It is precisely because of this that the Filmófono experience was extraordinarily useful in Mexico.

When Luis Buñuel lived in Los Angeles, he had almost resigned himself to never working in the cinema again. He arrived in Mexico in 1946 almost by accident, something which the surrealist in him, the great lover of chance, appreciated. He accompanied Denise Tual to discuss her project to produce a film based on Federico García Lorca in France.[1] The film was not produced but, through his friend the Mexican writer Fernando Benítez, Buñuel met Dr Hector Pérez Martínez, the Minister of the Interior, and he was invited to remain in Mexico.

When Buñuel returned to Hollywood to gather his household belongings and family, he had already signed a contract with Oscar Dancigers that would enable him to resume the cinema career put on hold since 1932. On 19 December 1946 he began shooting his first Mexican film: *Gran casino.* Thus chance allowed him to begin a professional film-making career: to make films for a living, accepting the imperatives and limitations of the industry, but honestly and, as he himself said on many occasions, doing 'nothing to contradict my moral or political principles, nothing that betrays my beliefs'.

Gran casino is a melodrama peppered with numerous performances by its stars, the very successful singers Jorge Negrete and Libertad Lamarque. The intransigent surrealist made a film that seemed to contain everything he detested. Buñuel said that when he read the final script it seemed very bad:

> but I didn't give it much importance. Years had passed, we had lost the war, and I said to myself 'So much the worse!' Besides, I was interested in a career in the cinema, working in the studio, the organisation. … I had already been a producer at Filmófono and I knew the various aspects of the industry at various levels, I could work fast, as was the norm in the Mexican cinema. … I told myself: 'This is a little adventure romance. Is there anything in it that betrays my conscience? No? Well, then, let's get going!'[2]

According to Buñuel, *Gran casino* fully met his objectives: 'I had not filmed in a long time and was interested in discovering the secrets of film techniques.'[3] Thus he renewed his interest in what had intrigued him as a producer at Filmófono. His second film, *El gran calavera (The Great Madcap,* 1949), an adaptation of a Spanish theatrical comedy that marked the beginning of his association with Luis Alcoriza, allowed him to practise these techniques further: 'I enjoyed myself with the editing, structure, and angles. All this interested me because I was still learning how to make normal movies.' Later he referred to a much-repeated myth: 'Some people have said that film technique doesn't interest me, but I remember at that time I was fascinated with it and wanted to take advantage of its narrative possibilites.'[4] Because of the complete failure of *Gran casino,* Buñuel had been forced to wait almost three years before he could begin work on *El gran calavera.*

Luckily for him, however, this second film (the

only one in his filmography in which he did not also collaborate on the script) was successful, and he was able to use this success to convince Dancigers to produce *Los olvidados* (*The Young and the Damned*, 1950), his first personal film and the one that really renewed the film-making career interrupted in 1932. *Los olvidados* was not a box-office success in Mexico and, in fact, it bothered certain sectors of the Mexican government and bourgeoisie, but its exhibition at the 1951 Cannes festival and the best director award he received there led to the critical rediscovery of Buñuel in Europe and Mexico.

Between 1946 and 1965, he made twenty films in Mexico, to which we should add *Viridiana*, which, although filmed in Spain, had significant Mexican participation and starred Silvia Pinal. Sixteen of these films were totally Mexican productions; two were filmed in Mexico but co-produced with France and released in French and Spanish versions, *La muerte en este jardín/La mort en ce jardin* (*Death in the Garden*, 1956) and *Los ambiciosos/La fièvre monte à El Pao* (*Republic of Sin*, 1959). The remaining two were produced in collaboration with the USA: *Robinson Crusoe* (1952) was filmed in Mexico in English, *The Young One* (1960) was also filmed in Mexico in English with US production and script collaboration. In other words, the bulk of the 32 films that constitute his life's work was Mexican.

Buñuel's Mexican films may be classified into three groups: the major works; the medium films, honestly professional and made for purely commercial ends, but filled with the aesthetic and moral elements typical of Buñuel's style and attitude; and lastly, the professionally honest films that never overcame their formulaic commercial genesis. The routinely made films of this last category allowed Buñuel the freedom needed to make his more personal films. The films of the first category include *Los olvidados* (1952), *Robinson Crusoe* (1952), *El* (*This Strange Passion*, 1952), *Ensayo de un crimen* (*The Criminal Life of Archibaldo de la Cruz*, 1955), *Nazarín* (1958), *The Young One* (1960), *El ángel exterminador* (*The Exterminating Angel*, 1962) and *Simón del desierto* (*Simon of the Desert*, 1964). In the medium category are *El gran calavera* (1950), *Susana, carne y demonio* (*Susana/The Devil and the Flesh*, 1950), *La hija del engaño* (*Daughter of Deceit*, 1951), *Subida al cielo* (*Mexican Bus Ride*, 1951), *El bruto* (*The Brute*, 1952), *Abismos de pasión* (*Wuthering Heights*, 1953), *La ilusión viaja en tranvía* (*Illusion Travels by Streetcar*, 1953) and *La muerte en este jardín* (1956). The commissioned and routinely made films were *Gran casino*, *Una mujer sin amor* (*A*

Woman Without Love, 1951), *El río y la muerte* (*The River and Death*, 1954) and *Los ambiciosos*.

Despite the degree to which the films in this last category were routinely produced, the film-maker from Calanda never betrayed himself: he was always true to his moral, social and political convictions and to his conception of the world. Those that I have perhaps arbitrarily called the medium films and the commissioned, formulaic films served Buñuel to perfect his technique and adapt it to his style. For example, in *El gran calavera* he experimented with the sequence shot, which became a fundamental element of his style, without ever making the camera work obtrusive. In several of the lesser films (*El gran calavera*, *La hija del engaño*, *Subida al cielo*, *Abismos de pasión*, and so on), Buñuel worked with the soundtrack, freeing it from its usual illustrative functions, and even resorting to asynchronicity. Of course, in several cases Buñuel barely skirted disaster: the horrible cast and music of *Abismos de pasión*; the simple psychology used to illustrate a thesis in *El río y la muerte*,[5] the demonstrative tone with which the verbal substitutes the visual in *Los ambiciosos*. This last political film was made against his better judgment:

> The truth is that it didn't interest me very much, and I accepted it because at that time I accepted everything offered me. ... I think my lack of interest is apparent. It turned out to be a very routine film, made to get out of my financial predicament.[6]

However, a number of these works also served to help Buñuel define and tighten his themes, obsessions, and visual and audiovisual techniques. Several of them are in many ways sketches for future films. Thus, for example, the protagonist of *El bruto* is an antecedent of *Nazarín* in so far as he is a pure man, even though others take advantage of his purity for economic gain. The most striking example is *Ensayo de un crimen* (a major film which according to its genesis and production could have ended up a lesser one) and *Belle de jour* (1967). The protagonists of both films struggle to follow their instincts, to live out their fantasies, and to satisfy their desires: '*Archibaldo* and *Belle de jour* imagine forbidden things that they try to live out in real life. A major part of their lives is mere imagination.'[7] In both films, sound (a music box in *Ensayo*, the little bells in the coach in *Belle*) frees the imagination of the protagonists. Moreover, *Ensayo* further develops the relationship between love and death set up in *Un*

El (Luis Buñuel, 1952)

Key Meersman and Zachary Scott in *La Joven* aka *The Young One* (Luis Buñuel, 1960)

chien andalou (in the latter, the woman makes her loved one appear; in *Ensayo,* Archibaldo makes the object of his desire appear as a mannequin) and also skilfully developed in *Los olvidados, Subida al cielo* and *Abismos de pasión.*

In Mexico, Buñuel constantly worked on one of his favourite themes and made an involuntary metaphorical reference to his own means of production: frustration. His characters flounder about in frustration to a degree that almost reflects the exasperation Buñuel himself experienced in the production of his films. *Abismos de pasión,* for example, a much-longed for project to film *Wuthering Heights,* marks the abyss between what he imagined could be achieved and the brutal reality of his actors' ineptitude. Similarly, in *El ángel exterminador* he was unable to get the right actors and was forced to do a balancing act to overcome their shortcomings. *Simón del desierto* is only 43 minutes long because economic difficulties prevented him from filming a third part:

> Almost all of my films have this theme: frustration. Bourgeois people who cannot leave a room, people that want to eat and everything impedes them, a man who wants to kill but his crimes fail. Frustration already appears in *Un chien andalou:* the man approaches the woman, but his advance is impeded by ropes and the objects attached to them. In the garden scene in *L'Age d'or,* the lovers cannot even kiss. It is the distance between desire and reality, intent and failure.[8]

This theme appears obsessively in Buñuel's Mexican films. *Ensayo de un crimen* is exemplary: Archibaldo de la Cruz wants to kill, but somebody or something always gets there first. The inability to satisfy his desire causes all kinds of frustrations, especially sexual ones, since Archibaldo links sexual pleasure with the satisfaction of his desire, that is, with death. One must say that he adores and derives pleasure from his frustration and this makes the happy ending improbable. Like the endings of *Susana* and *El,* it must be read in the context of Buñuel's always ambiguous endings. Like Archibaldo de la Cruz's detailed preparations for his failed murders, Francisco Galván in *El,* another major work and perhaps his best Mexican film, is haunted by the ghost of a desire that jealousy prevents him from fulfilling. Susana's ambitions fall apart via a sort of divine intervention, and an unconsummated love is what drives the characters of *Abismos de pasión.* Nazarín attempts to

model himself upon Christ, but reality stops him, and something similar obstructs Viridiana's analogous quest. A group of people in a worldly salon are unable to leave the room, although no physical obstacle bars their exit. In *Simón del desierto,* the protagonist's hopes for a pure and free life lead him to an infernal New York den, and so on.

This theme is not developed mechanistically or rhetorically, but is tightly linked to another theme: instinct's struggle with and subsequent repression by convention. This struggle questions the status of truth and lies, the rational and the irrational, the individual and society, freedom and its phantasms:

> In *Un Chien andalou* I was consistent to surrealist principles such as the belief that the automatic unconscious is able to restore the mind to its real functions, beyond the control exercised by moral reasoning or aesthetics. Although I used oneiric elements, I was not describing a dream. On the contrary, the environment and the characters are real. The difference is that the characters are driven by impulses that emerge in irrationality.[9]

This principle may be applied to almost all of his twenty Mexican films, including prestige productions such as *Los olvidados* and *El ángel exterminador,* and commercial films such as *Susana, El bruto* and *La hija del engaño.* The struggle between instinct and convention motivating the characters is the conflict at the heart of all human societies: on one side, feelings of love; on the other, those of a religious, patriotic or humanitarian nature. Love, a selfish uncontrollable emotion, sexual instinct, and drive towards death, conflict with social norms and serve as a revolutionary catalyst. And to say love is also to say sex: 'In an organised hierarchical society, sex respects neither barriers nor laws and at any moment may become the source of disorder and danger.'[10] Although love is always threatened by the social and human pettiness engendered by values, it can still become an agent for revolt. In his Mexican films, Buñuel registers events, records causes, explores individual and social motivations, makes us uncomfortable, and leaves us feeling as if we are not living in the best of worlds. This helps explain why none of his Mexican films were box-office successes in Mexico, even though some of them had reasonable returns.

The conflict between instinct and convention (and its repression) leading to impotence and frustration is often linked to class: *El, Robinson Crusoe, Ensayo de un crimen, El ángel exterminador* and, at the other extreme, *Los olvidados* and *El bruto*. The result may be religious sublimation (*Nazarín, Viridiana, Simón del desierto,* father Lizardi in *La muerte en este jardín* and even *Robinson Crusoe*), but the origin is always the same: the clash between instincts (desire, hunger, love) and conventions (social, religious and moral norms). Mexican reality offered Buñuel perfect raw materials for the development of this theme, even though he was never interested in sociological analysis and, as critics often complained, had no in-depth knowledge of this society and its people. Thus, for example, the blind man in *Los olvidados* is not Mexican but derived directly from the Spanish picaresque tradition. Pedro's mother in the same film refused him food and, not without reason, many critics argued that no Mexican mother would ever behave in such a fashion. Similarly, Mexicans would never accord a priest the treatment given to Buñuel and Pérez Galdos's *Nazarín*. However, although the external characteristics of his characters were not mimetically Mexican, deep down, in their essence, the characters were right. This is why his films were able to move and disconcert all spectators, regardless of their origin and status.

This theme also justifies the importance of dreams in Buñuel's Mexican films. From *Los olvidados* and *Subida al cielo* to *El ángel exterminador* and *Simón del desierto* by way of *La ilusión viaja en tranvía,* his Mexican films are full of dreams. Be they unhappy like Susana and El Jaibo, pure like Simón or Francisco Galván, innocent and immediate like the travellers of *Subida al cielo* or *La ilusión viaja en tranvía* (surrealist collages and really voyages through the unconscious), Buñuel's characters liberate their instincts in dreams and in the imagination in order to realise their desires. Dreams are an integral part of their reality and enable them to free themselves from habits and certainties.

Buñuel's attitude towards the cinema and its producers should serve as a lesson for Mexican and Latin American film-makers. He knew how to adapt to pre-existing material conditions (without betraying himself or his principles), was always able to generate viable projects, and was never led astray by whims, extravagance, or, after winning international recognition, his own star status. Despite Oscar Dancigers's misgivings over some of Buñuel's more unconventional ideas (for example, the symphony orchestra playing on the metal structure of a building in *Los olvidados,* or the top hat in the dirty kitchen of the same film), no producer can say that he wasted money beyond what was originally allotted in the budget.

The vast majority of his twenty Mexican films were tightly budgeted and produced in three to four weeks, often with inadequate actors. But none of this stopped Buñuel from making films (the routine films as well as those that were intensely Buñuelian) that were always faithful to his moral, social, political and aesthetic convictions. Perhaps two of his films ought to be forgotten: *Una mujer sin amor* (even Buñuel considered it his worst film), a literal transcription of André Cayatte's adaptation of a Maupassant story, *Pierre et Jean* (1943), and *Los ambiciosos,* an obvious and demonstrative work that solves everything via dialogues. In all the other films, even in *Gran casino* and *El río y la muerte,* there are moments, sequences and situations that clearly evidence the author's touch.

Buñuel does not indulge his avant-garde tendencies. Instead of breaking with the genres, narratives, and figurative and representational forms of the contemporary Mexican cinema (a producer's cinema; only Manuel Barbachano Ponce in *Nazarín* and later Gustavo Latriste were able to grant him authorial freedom), Buñuel assumed them. A film like *Susana, carne y demonio* is in principle identical to any of the Mexican melodramas of the period; simply another version of the typical turn-of-the-century bourgeois melodrama. However, Buñuel transcends and transfigures the form through antiphrasis, by making things signify the opposite of what they are or have been established to be. From a conservative perspective, *Susana* is a perfectly moral film. Good triumphs over evil; order is imposed upon disorder and upon the subversion of instinct and its desires; prudery, or better yet, hypocrisy, wins over eroticism. The fact is that the perverse Susana escapes from prison thanks to the Lord's infinite and unfathomable wisdom, arrives at a sort of Mexican Arcadia (very similar to the ideal vision of a harmonious and non-conflictual world that the Mexican cinema had offered in the melodrama and the *comedia ranchera*) as an exterminating angel or seductive devil provoking disaster upon disaster, forcing all the characters to change, and turning the hacienda and its rules upside down. By the end, everything is back in order and happily resolved; birds sing, father and son and father and mother are reconciled, even the mare is healed and gives birth to a little colt, and Susana has been arrested and taken to jail. The hacienda becomes a paradise again![11] However, things are not quite what they seem. This is one of those ambiguous endings that Buñuel excelled at (cf. *El, Ensayo de un crimen, Viridiana* or *La voie lactée,* 1968). When the mare breaks into a

206

Ernesto Alonso and Ariadna Welter in *Ensayo de un crimen* (Luis Buñuel, 1955)

Jorge Pérez and Miguel Inclán in *Los olvidados* (Luis Buñuel, 1950)

trot, she reintroduces life and with it disquiet and disorder into the equation. She contradicts the order represented by the previous image of turkeys walking together. The sense of antiphrasis,[12] the humour and the exaggerated melodramatic conventions leading to absurdities and contradictions indicate that the truly important work is taking place at a latent level beneath the surface of the story. When asked if he considered *Susana* to be a philosophical work, Buñuel replied: 'Philosophical, no. A story, yes.'[13]

We can see a similar operation in less conventional and more ambitious and personal films such as *El*. Francisco Galván, an extension of sorts of Gaston Modot's character in *L'Age d'or,* is a pure man searching for the normalcy of love, but he can be turned inside out: he is really struggling to love himself. Francisco is egocentric[14] and a narcissist: this leads him to ignore all logic and therefore he goes mad. *El* is also a bourgeois melodrama, but unlike Susana, Francisco Galván cannot rid himself of his prejudices and complexes. Thus his contempt for reality is transformed into an excessive imagination, megalomania and mythomania. The result is frustration and, as with Archibaldo de la Cruz, literal and metaphorical impotence. *El* is a perfectly sober film in which each shot fulfils an exact function (there are no extraneous shots or dialogues); it has a much more complex story than *Susana,* but, once again, what takes place below the surface is what is most significant. Antiphrasis is also at work in *El* and things signify the opposite of what they appear to be. In *El,* humour plays an important function and melodramatic conventions are taken to absurd heights. But Francisco Galván also possesses many of the characteristics of Buñuel's Mexican (and other) characters. He is individualistic like Robinson Crusoe, Archibaldo de la Cruz, El bruto, or Miller (Zachary Scott) in *The Young One*. He is pure like Nazarín, El bruto or Simón, and undoubtedly prefigures the bourgeoisie of *El ángel exterminador*. In *El* we find the summation of the clash between instincts (love, desire, the fullness of life, the appeal of freedom) and their repression (the church, police, bourgeois morality, society).

Already in retirement, Buñuel remembered several of his Mexican films fondly, but also wished he had had the opportunity to remake them under other circumstances and using his films from the later European period as models. Nevertheless, his Mexican films, albeit simple, functional, narratively economic, with unobtrusive yet mobile camera work, and without special effects, have grown in importance over time. The European films of his last period are better 'dressed', possibly better acted, and more technically perfect, but they are no longer bothersome, do not shake us up; they are almost decaffeinated. They do not have the power of his great Mexican films.

Notes

1. *La casa de Bernalda Alba* also played a role in Buñuel's later life. In 1976, the Mexican producer Gustavo Alatriste, the producer of *Viridiana, El ángel exterminador* and *Simón del desierto,* bought the rights for Buñuel, who worked on the script, but finally gave up on the project. Alatriste himself ended up making the film in 1980. The results were less than satisfying, but Buñuel was quite amused. This did not stop Mario Camus from making another version in Spain in 1987.

2. José de la Colina and Tomás Pérez Turrent, *Prohibido asomarse al interior: conversaciones con Luis Buñuel* (Mexico City: Joaquín Mortiz–Planeta, 1986), p. 49.

3. Ibid., p. 51.

4. Ibid., pp. 52–3.

5. Ibid., p. 105: 'For the first time in my life, I was directing a *thesis* film and had doubts. The thesis was quite debatable, something like: If all men went to University, there would be fewer films. Can you believe it!'

6. Ibid., p. 131.

7. Ibid., p. 108.

8. Ibid., p. 100.

9. Ibid., p. 28.

10. Luis Buñuel (Jean-Claude Carrière), *Mi último suspiro* (Barcelona/Mexico City: Plaza y Janes Editores, 1982), p. 118.; English translation: *My Last Breath* (London: Jonathan Cape, 1983).

11. De la Colina and Péréz Turrent, *Prohibido a asomarse al interior,* p. 66.

12. In reference to this theme, see the essays by Claude Gautier, 'Buñuel et l'antiphrase' and 'Humour et erotisme dans *Susana la perverse*' in *Études Cinématographiques* (Paris), nos. 22–3, 1973, pp. 79–96 and 175–9.

13. De la Colina and Péréz Turrent, *Prohibido a asomarse al interior,* p. 69.

14. Claude Baylie, '*El* ou le héros Buñuélien' in *Études Cinématographiques* (Paris), nos. 22–3, 1973, pp. 180–6.

One Generation – Four Film-makers: Cazals, Hermosillo, Leduc and Ripstein

Leonardo García Tsao

The Mexican cinema was revitalised in the mid-60s after a long period of artistic stagnation. Firstly, the organisation of the first experimental cinema competition in 1964 proved that there was cinematic talent and imagination outside the traditional commercial industry. Secondly, we began to see evidence of a new generation of Mexican film-makers, the first to have learned the craft in the university. Four film-makers of this generation have produced a significant body of work and have sustained their careers for over thirty years. They are, in alphabetical order, Felipe Cazals, Jaime Humberto Hermosillo, Paul Leduc and Arturo Ripstein.[1]

Cazals

Born in 1937, Felipe Cazals is the oldest of the group by about a decade. His career illustrates the highs and lows faced by cineastes in a situation as unstable as the Mexican film production system. While on a scholarship to study film-making at the Institut des Haute Études Cinématographiques (IDHEC) in Paris, Cazals worked as assistant to directors like Joshua Logan and Mauro Bolignini. He returned to Mexico when the results of the First Experimental Cinema Competition were being announced. After filming several shorts, *¡Que se callen! (Silence Them)*, *Leonora Carrington o el sortilegio irónico (Leonora Carrington or an Ironic Spell)*, *Cartas de Mariana Alcoforado (The Letters of Mariana Alcoforado)*, for the film department of Bellas Artes in 1965–6, Cazals directed his first feature, *La manzana de la discordia (The Apple of Discord)* independently in 1968. As is usually the case in an auteur cinema, this debut feature already contained the principal themes and obsessions of its author. In a very simple story, three thugs follow orders and murder a cacique, but spontaneously narrated in a style that broke generic conventions, *La manzana de la discordia* challenged the mainstream Mexican cinema of the period and established the parameters of the director's work: a proclivity for circular narratives that underline the

futility of the characters' actions, a flashy treatment of violence seen as sordid but normal; the verisimilar recreation of properly Mexican attitudes and behaviours.

Given the difficulties of breaking into the national film industry, in 1969 Cazals, Arturo Ripstein and Rafael Castanedo created the short-lived group Cine Independiente de México (Mexican Independent Cinema). The sale of paintings donated by friends allowed them to produce his second feature, *Familiaridades (Familiarities*, 1969), a clever and somewhat absurd three-character comedy set almost entirely in an apartment. The light tone and happy ending of this film are atypical of the rest of Cazals's filmography.

To gain an entry into the industry, Cazals agreed to direct the super-production *Emiliano Zapata* (1970), a project initiated and financed by Antonio Aguilar, the actor-singer of innumerable *ranchera comedies,* who also starred in the film. The technical abilities of the director are evident in some scenes, but the film does not overcome the solemn and monolithic presentation of its patriotic hero. Subsequently, Cazals made two high-budget period films with state funding. *El jardín de tía Isabel (Aunt Isabel's Garden,* 1971) follows the painful journey through American lands of a group of shipwrecked Spaniards in the sixteenth century. Ruined in the editing process, the second part of the film moves too quickly, but one senses the desire to tell an anti-epic story, one which contradicts the accepted image of the so-called discoverers of the New World. The other film, *Aquellos años (Those Years,* 1972), tells the story of Benito Juárez's triumph over conservatives and French interventionists in the mid-nineteenth century. This ambitious super-production was unable to overcome the rigidity of the historical film format, although Cazals's formal skills are always evident.

The film that followed marked a transition for the film-maker. *Los que viven donde sopla el viento suave (Those Who Live Where the Light Wind Blows,* 1973) is a feature-length documentary, the only one to date in his filmography, about the daily difficulties of the Seris Indians in northern Mexico. With an interesting presentation of the problems of a specific ethnic group, the film highlights the element of ideological confusion and the abyss that separates the various national social strata. This preoccupation was important for the development of *Canoa* (1975), a successful recreation of real events: in 1968, four University of Puebla employees were lynched by the inhabitants of the town of San Miguel de Canoa. The townspeople were incited by a local priest who

Canoa (Felipe Cazals, 1975)

was terrified by the perceived communist threat of the Mexico City student movement. Based upon a well-developed script by film critic Tomás Pérez Turrent, the film uses a 'false documentary' style to de-dramatise the events while contextualising them. Even when the spectator is perfectly aware of what is going to happen, the cinematic rendition of the events is spellbinding. The winner of a special jury prize at the Berlin Film Festival in 1976, *Canoa* is a classic of the national cinema and fundamentally important within Cazals's filmography.

Cazals directed another important film in 1975, *El apando (Solitary),* an adaptation of a José Revueltas novel dealing with the sordid life of common prisoners in the Mexican penitentiary system. With a convincing cast and atmosphere, the cineaste describes an oppressive world of cruelty and brutality that is still resonant. Both *Canoa* and *El apando* drew uncharacteristically large audiences for

this kind of Mexican cinema. In 1976, the last year of the Echeverría *sexenio,* during which quality cinema had been favoured, Cazals again collaborated with Pérez Turrent in the production of *Las poquianchis (Miserere),* like *Canoa* a film based on tabloid material. *Las poquianchis* reconstructs the crimes committed by three merciless sisters who went so far as to murder some of the prostitutes of their bordello in the mid-60s. The film does not quite develop all the themes it proposes, such as, for example, the condition of the Mexican peasant, and in this sense it sins by default. However, the representation of the prostitutes as one more link in an interminable chain of submission and exploitation is crudely realistic and the very antithesis of what the *cabaretera* melodramatic tradition offered.

The situation of the Mexican cinema changed radically in 1977. The newly arrived president, José López Portillo, put his sister Margarita in charge of

210

Los poquianchis (Felipe Cazals, 1976)

the national cinema and the results were disastrous. Felipe Cazals and the other film-makers of his generation were unable to sustain the continuity they desired. After a period film that had little to do with his interests, *La güera Rodríguez* (*The Blonde Rodríguez,* 1977), and a failed Daniel Defoe adaptation about the potential effects of a plague in contemporary Mexico, *El año de la peste* (*The Year of the Plague,* 1978), Cazals was forced to accept work on commission. *Rigo es amor* (*Rigo is love*) and *El gran triunfo* (*The Great Triumph*), both made in 1980, are routine melodramas structured around the tropical music singer Rigo Tovar, while *Las siete cucas* (*The Seven Cucas,* 1980) is a picaresque comedy in which we can barely perceive the personality of the director.

Cazals did not obtain state financing for *Bajo la metralla* (*Under the Gun*) until the very last days of the Echeverría administration. This was a personal project about a terrorist group that falls apart because of internal conflicts. Although the film wanders while attempting to present the various fragmentary positions of the left, it marked the director's return to truly dramatic film-making and reinvigorated his privileged cinematic intuition.

During the Miguel de la Madrid *sexenio,* Cazals was unable to find many film-making opportunities. But even under these adverse conditions, *Los motivos de Luz* (*Luz's Motives,* 1985) is one of his best films. Based on the real story of a poor woman who is accused of murdering her four children, the film addresses the central preoccupations of his oeuvre:

the realistic portrait of marginalised classes, cultural clashes within a society, the daily violence of exploitation and ignorance. Furthermore, Cazals tells his story from a neutral, distanced perspective that makes it even more convincing.

El tres de copas (*The Three of Spades*, 1986) is an ironic Western based, without acknowledgment, on Jorge Luis Borges's *La intrusa (The Intruder)* and set in Mexico after the war against France. Its allusions to destiny and luck are reminiscent of *La manzana de la discordia*. *Las inocentes (The Innocents)*, a video work carried out for the state television network in the same year, is a Pirandello adaptation about the punishment accorded to four nuns who were raped and became pregnant. Just as the protagonists of *Las poquianchis* are victims of vice, the protagonists of *Las inocentes* are victims of innocence, and the two films are complementary. With great dramatic intensity resulting from the sombre and economic narrative, this telefilm is as good as the best films of the director. Paradoxically, few have seen it: the state television network refused to air it because of its open anti-clericalism.

El imperio de la fortuna (Arturo Ripstein, 1985)

The next project, *La furia de un dios* (*The Fury of a God*; original title, *Lo del César, Caesar's,* 1987) was a poor contemporary version of Camus's *Caligula* set on the Yucatán coast. The film was also a financial disaster for Cazals's production company. As a result, after years of surviving by working on commercials, the director made a couple of pseudo-erotic comedies in 1990 (*Burbujas de amor (Love Bubbles)* and *Desvestidas y alborotadas (Undressed and Excited)*), which are indistinguishable from the cheap, privately produced films flooding the Mexican market.

Thus, in this latest stage, Cazals's career appears to have lost its focus. His visceral cinematographic sense seems to have been wasted in alienating projects, and a good part of his efforts have been devoted to procuring financing for ambitious period productions that have failed to get off the ground. Thus, for example, the productions of *El Tigre de Santa Julia (The Santa Julia Tiger)*, *Padre Kino (Father Kino)* and *El batallón de San Patricio (The San Patricio Battalion)* were cancelled because of insufficient

funding. It is odd that the film-maker has insisted upon making super-productions when his most important films are notable for their modest budgets. Nevertheless, in 1991 Cazals was able to take up the production of *Kino* again, and we expect that the results will put him back on a consistent course worthy of his talents.

Ripstein

Although Arturo Ripstein, born in Mexico City in 1943, studied film-making at the Universidad Nacional Autónoma de México (UNAM) before the creation of the Centro Universitario de Estudios Cinematográficos (CUEC), his training was more practical than academic. Given that his father, Alfredo Ripstein Jr, was a producer, the film-maker was in touch with the commercial film-making world since childhood. While still quite young, Ripstein assisted Buñuel on *El ángel exterminador* (1962), as well as other directors. In 1965, in what has proven to be the most precocious debut of the Mexican cinema, he directed *Tiempo de morir (A Time to Die)*. Based on a script by Gabriel García Márquez, the film is a sort of Western in which a man who has recently been released from prison is determined to remake his life, but must first face the revenge of the son of the man he had killed in a duel. With unusual skill for a first-time director, Ripstein made this drama about a man unable to escape his destiny believable. This has continued to be a central theme of his work.

The episode *HO* of the compilation film *Juego peligroso (Dangerous Game,* 1966) and the ambitious but not very successful film set during the Mexican Revolution, *Los recuerdos del porvenir (The Memories of the Future,* 1968), were such disappointing experiences that Ripstein decided to retire from commercial film-making for a while. It was at this time that Ripstein, Cazals and Castanedo formed the Cine Independiente de México group to produce experimental works. In the mid-length feature *La hora de los niños (The Children's Hour,* 1969), a disquieting story about a clown who takes care of a child, and the shorts *Crimen, La belleza, Exorcismos*

Roberto Cobo in *El lugar sin limites* (Arturo Ripstein, 1977)

(all three from 1970) and *Autorretrato* (1971), Ripstein experimented with narrative dead time, de-dramatisation and humour.

Ripstein returned to com-mercial film-making with *El castillo de la pureza* (*The Castle of Purity,* 1972), a film based upon the real-life story of a man who imprisoned his wife and children at home to protect them from the impurities of the world. Gabriel Lima, the severe paterfamilias, is a key character in Ripstein's films: a solipsistic man who builds a utopia, a private unreal universe, and who will inevitably suffer greatly when he encounters reality. The film also evidenced the author's penchant for confined environments.

State support for the cinema during the Echeverría regime in the early 70s allowed Ripstein to film two period films with the highest budgets he has managed to obtain to date. *El Santo Oficio* (*The Holy Office,* 1973) describes the persecution of a Jewish family during the inquisition in Nueva España at the end of the seventeenth century. Although somewhat rigid and distant, the film exemplifies the film-maker's concern with all kinds of intolerance. *Foxtrot* (1975), a Mexico–UK–Switzerland co-production, tells the story of a Romanian count and his wife who flee during the Second World War to a deserted island, only to encounter the very violence from which they had attempted to escape. Although elegantly formulated and filmed, the film lacks dramatic tension, especially at the end. Nevertheless, it is a satisfactory film that did not deserve the excessively negative critiques it received when it was released.

In 1974, Ripstein made short and mid-length documentaries for the Secretaría de Educación Pública; in 1976, the last year of the Echeverría *sexenio,* he directed his only feature-length documentary, *Lecumberri: El palacio negro*

(*Lecumberri: The Black Palace*), a fascinating analysis of the world of the Mexican penitentiary and its peculiar spaces, rituals and systems of corruption. As the director said: 'It is an observational documentary, like all the other films I have made. … When all is said and done, I would rather move potential spectators than convince them that something is good or bad, or teach them things.'[2]

Curiously, Ripstein was able to continue filming in the early years of the unfortunate López Portillo *sexenio,* when he made two of his best films. *El lugar sin límites* (*The Place Without Limits,* 1977), a wonderful adaptation of José Donoso's homonymous novel, revolves around the unusual triangle of a small-town macho, a homosexual who lives in a provincial bordello, and the homosexual's daughter, conceived and born as the result of a wager, who manages the bordello. With a second half loaded with sexual ambiguity, the film has a climactic scene of rare intensity: after dancing with the homosexual, the macho's latent desires are awakened and he beats the homosexual to death.

That same year, the state offered Ripstein the opportunity to direct *La viuda negra* (*The Black Widow*). The director originally assigned to the project, Felipe Cazals, had been dismissed for introducing political elements into the script. Ripstein also had difficulties with the poor quality of the script and improvised as he filmed. As a result, the supposedly serious story of the scandalous sexual relation-ship between a priest and his unbalanced house-keeper became a malicious comedy that was banned by the censors for seven years.

Cadena perpetua (*Life Imprisonment,* 1978) is Ripstein's masterpiece and one of the best films of the Mexican cinema. To narrate the dilemmas of 'Tarzán' Lira, a petty thief unable to reform because a corrupt policeman blackmails him to continue stealing, the film-maker adapted the conventions of the Hollywood film noir to a specifically national context. The film incisively questions the Mexican authorities and the judicial system while re-elaborating the themes characteristic of its director. 'Tarzán' is another Ripstein character inexorably doomed to fulfil his destiny, to endlessly repeat certain scenarios determined by forces he cannot control. Likewise, he is also a caged character even though he is free to move: the city is his prison.

Soon after, Ripstein directed *La tía Alejandra* (*Aunt Alexandra,* 1978), a successful horror film about an evil old woman who causes the disintegration of a middle-class family. Once again, he makes clear reference to a Hollywood genre and

relocates it in a verisimilar Mexican context, although not with the power of *Cadena perpetua.*

The cinema crisis of the López Portillo regime finally affected Ripstein towards the middle of the *sexenio.* This problematic stage of his career began with *La ilegal* (*The Illegal,* ·1979), a commissioned film featuring Lucía Méndez, the wooden starlet of the Televisa consortium. It was followed by *La seducción* (*The Seduction,* 1979), an unfortunate adaptation of Heinrich von Kleist's story about a mother who uses her daughter as bait to assassinate federal agents during the Cristero Rebellion. Nevertheless, both films are of some interest. The same cannot be said of *Rastro de muerte* (*Trace of Death,* 1981), a state production which is perhaps the worst film of Ripstein's filmography. This confused melodrama with political overtones evi-dences only the film-maker's resignation to con-tinue directing no matter what the cost.

After three years of cine-matic inactivity, and already during the de la Madrid sexenio, Ripstein directed *El otro* (*The Other,* 1984). Despite scant resources and a weak script, the film manages to produce a mysterious feeling centred on a young woman who commits suicide for love. However, Ripstein's definitive comeback was *El imperio de la fortuna* (*The Empire of Fortune,* 1985), the second adaptation of a Juan Rulfo script (the first was directed by Roberto Gavaldón in 1964 and entitled *El gallo de oro* (*The Golden Cock*)). *El imperio de la fortuna* is also the first part of what may be called the 'Trilogy of Fatality', produced by Ripstein in collaboration with his companion, the scriptwriter Paz Alicia Garcíadiego. Once again, the protagonist is a man who attempts to create his own controlled universe, only to lose it all because of his own obsessions. Luck plays a fundamental role in this story (the protagonist wins a fortune playing cards), and Ripstein establishes the gradual degradation of his characters through the clinical repetition of situations and with a characteristically claustrophobic atmosphere. With its desolate images of the contamination of the province by urban influences, *El imperio de la fortuna* is the film that most successfully reflects the Mexico of crisis, an impoverished and saddened Mexico.

Mentiras piadosas (*Pious Lies,* 1988) is another story of doomed love in which the characters repeat the same errors from relationship to relationship, caught up in a perpetual cycle of jealousy, blackmail and betrayal. Set in the centre of Mexico City, this reworking of the classical melodrama also suggests that according to Ripstein, illusion (the characters

Reed: México insurgente (Paul Leduc, 1970)

Reed: México insurgente (Paul Leduc, 1970)

build an absurd model of an Aztec city with the hope of escaping from their poverty) is a way of establishing, by contrast, the harsh brutality of reality.

The trilogy was completed with *La mujer del puerto* (*The Woman of the Port,* 1991), a new version of the Maupassant story that had also inspired the Arcady Boytler film (1933) of the same title. The film narrates the tragic love affair between two siblings from three points of view that are not so much different as complementary. Here Ripstein takes melodramatic conventions apart by inverting their mechanisms and making no concessions. Set in an implacably sordid environment, the film seems to take place at the very edge of the end of the world. The typically pes-simistic vision of the director had never before been this extreme.

Although in the last few years Ripstein has not been directing as much as he would like, he has managed to produce personal films consistently while

taking on advertising and television work to survive. In late 1991, he was working on a film about the life of the singer Lucha Reyes.

Leduc

Born in Mexico City in 1942, Paul Leduc studied architecture and theatre and worked as a film critic before winning a scholarship to study film-making at IDHEC in Paris in the mid-60s. Upon his return to Mexico in 1967, he directed seventeen documentary shorts for the Olympic Committee with the group Cine 70 (which also included Rafael Castanedo, Alexis Grivas, Bertha Navarro and others) and three shorts for the Consejo Nacional de Huelga (the National Strike Council).

Although he shares some experiences with the other film-makers of his generation (such as his studies at IDHEC and a collaboration with Ripstein on the documentary *Q.R.R.* (Gustavo

Ofelia Medina and Max Kerlow in *Frida, naturaleza viva* (Paul Leduc, 1984)

Alatriste, 1970)), Leduc's career has developed on the margins of the industry. Until now, he has never directed a state-funded project and has worked with independent financing, be it through private producers, universities, co-operatives or foreign investors. Thus his filmography is still comparatively short: he has only completed five feature-length fiction films, three documentaries and a television movie; moreover, he did not work in 35mm until 1988. Nevertheless, he is the film-maker with the most interesting political commitment of his generation, evidenced especially in his documentaries.

In 1970, Leduc directed *Reed: México insurgente (Reed: Insurgent Mexico)*, an independent production shot in 16mm. The film was based on the homonymous book by US journalist John Reed, and presents a demystified version of the events of the Mexican Revolution. Previously, this period had only been authentically represented in two films, both by

Fernando de Fuentes: *El compadre Mendoza* (1933) and *¡Vámonos con Pancho Villa!* (1935). With sepia-tinted black and white images and an inspired period reconstruction, the film adopts an almost documentary realism to describe Reed's growing involvement with the Revolution and his active participation in the conflict. Winner of the Georges Sadoul prize in 1972, *Reed: México insurgente* demonstrated that a historical film could evade the solemnity of school textbooks and have the immediacy of a contemporary political documentary, and with a low budget to boot.

In the following years, Leduc made documentaries like *Sur: Sureste 2604 (South: South-east 2604,* 1973) and *Extensión cultural (Cultural Extension)*, *El mar (The Sea)* and *Bach y sus intérpretes (Bach and his Interpreters),* all three in 1975 for the Secretaría de Educación Pública (SEP). In 1976 he directed his cond feature film, *Etnocidio: notas sobre el Mezquital* (*Ethnocide: Notes About the Mezquital*), a documentary co-produced by the SEP and the National Film Board of Canada. Divided into chapters identified by letters of the alphabet, from the A of 'antecedents' to the Z of 'Zimapán', the film is a detailed, rigorous testimony of the tragedy of the Otomi, an Indian tribe of fewer than half a million members that has been the victim of exploitation and pillaging. Without using voice-over narration, Leduc allows his subjects to speak of their limited options: tilling arid lands, emigrating to Mexico City and surviving underemployment, or looking for illegal work in the USA. *Etnocidio* is one of the most powerful documentaries ever made about the miserable life and desperate plight of Mexican indigenous groups and rural workers.

Of course, Leduc was not able to finish many of the projects he conceived in this period. Among the projects that were never made in the late 70s were an adaptation of David Viñas's novel *Los hombres de a caballo* (*Men on Horses*) and an adaptation of Malcolm Lowry's *Under the Volcano*, scripted collaboratively by the director, Gabriel García Márquez and José Agustín Blanco.[3]

In 1978, Leduc made three documentary shorts for the Universidad de Puebla, *Había una vez* (*Once Upon a Time*), *Enrique Cabrera* and *Puebla hoy* (*Puebla Today*). All three have been compiled into a single feature called *Puebla hoy*. In addition, he made two notable art shorts: *Monjas coronadas* (*Crowned Nuns*) and *Estudios para un retrato: Francis Bacon* (*Study for a Portrait: Francis Bacon*), the latter co-directed with cinematographer Angel Goded and editor Rafael Castanedo, his two more constant collaborators. In these shorts we can already see the visual style that he would develop in later works.

Probably Leduc's most conventional film is *Historias prohibidas de Pulgarcito* (*Pulgarcito's Forbidden Stories*, 1980), a little-seen documentary about the guerrillas in El Salvador. His next feature, *Complot petrolero: la cabeza de la hidra* (*Petroleum Complot: The Head of the Hydra*, 1981) received even worse distribution: it was only shown in private screenings the year of its production. Based on a Carlos Fuentes novel, the film was planned as a four-episode television mini-series. Historian Emilio García Riera commented that: 'Although the story is confusing because of the many references to international intrigues threatening the national oil industry, the action is very entertaining because of the many real locations ... excellent direction, and excellent acting.'[4] Given that the rights to

Fuentes's novel have expired, the future of this film is uncertain.

Leduc's next film marked his transition to a freer cinematic style based on images rather than words. *Frida, naturaleza viva* (*Frida*, 1984) is an original biographical film that manages to avoid the conventions of the genre. Through impressionistic vignettes shot with long, descriptive travelling shots, the film-maker presents the principal motifs of the life and work of the painter Frida Kahlo as freely associated memories: her painful physical ailments, turbulent but loving marriage to Diego Rivera, militancy for the Communist Party, and relationship with Leon Trotsky. With very little dialogue, most of it incidental, Leduc produced a vital and emotional portrait of a woman who has become an international cult figure. *Frida, naturaleza viva* was widely praised in international festivals and attracted a sizeable national audience.

Production problems prevented Leduc from completing the production of *¿Cómo ves?* (*How Are You?*, 1985). Missing approximately a quarter of the script written by the director and José Agustín Blanco, who also collaborated on *Frida* and on the director's next two films, the film is no more than an incoherent collage of scenes about the problems of marginal Mexico City youths and their musical preferences, especially rock music. Dissatisfied with the results, Leduc asked for his name to be removed from the credits.

The formal characteristics of *Frida* were further developed in *Barroco* (1988), a very free adaptation of Alejo Carpentier's *Concierto barroco*. This time Leduc eliminated all dialogue to present the musical and cultural influences among Spain, Cuba and Mexico as a reflex of a historical process. The film is uneven because of its episodic structure, but its achievements are greater and more significant than its flaws. In its best moments, *Barroco* is an imaginative and suggestive fusion of images and musical genres.

Unfortunately, this same tendency seems exhausted in *Latino Bar* (1990), a Spain–Venezuela–Cuba co-production (the Mexican state cinema institute, IMCINE, was not interested in the project) that derives its tenuous narrative from Federico Gamboa's novel *Santa*, the cornerstone of the Mexican cinema's prostitute genre. If the absence of dialogues worked in *Frida* and in *Barroco* because of the artificiality of both projects, here it fails to sustain the love affair between a young man and a prostitute in a sombre tropical bordello. The incessant use of music and lateral travelling shots have now become mannerisms. However, it would

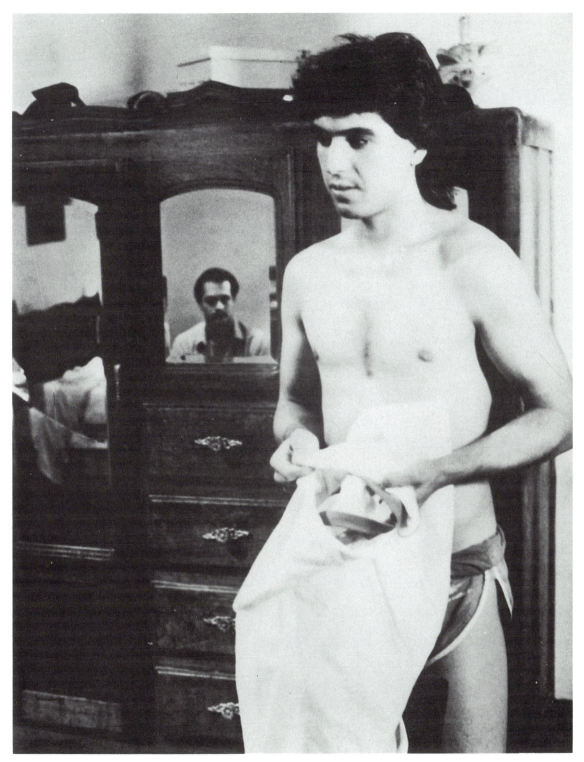

Gustavo Meza and Marco Antonio Treviño in *Doña Herlinda y su hijo* (Jaime Humberto Hermosillo, 1984)

Jorge Martínez de Hoyos and Héctor Bonilla in *El cumpleaños del perro* (Jaime Humberto Hermosillo, 1974)

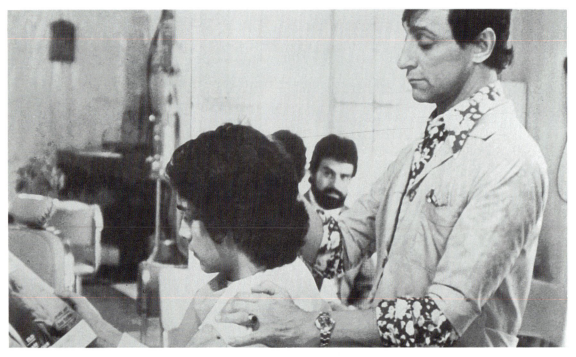

Las aparencias engañan (Jaime Humberto Hermosillo, 1977)

be premature to say that Leduc has reached an artistic impasse. Who could have predicted work of such quality? Thus we may expect a renovation at any moment.

Hermosillo

Born in Aguascalientes in 1942, Jaime Humberto Hermosillo has followed a different trajectory to the other film-makers of his generation. Confronted by similar practical film-making problems, Hermosillo has refused to direct any but his own personal projects. Amazingly, he has not had to direct commissioned films, commercials, documentaries or television programmes in order to survive. Thus his filmography is extraordinarily coherent thematically, although uneven in technical quality.

After working as an accountant in Mexico City, Hermosillo entered the Centro Universitarios de Estudios Cinematográficos (CUEC) in the mid-60s. Although he never got his degree, he did manage to direct two shorts: *Homesick* (1965) and *SS Glencairn* (1967). The first is significant because of its title: the literal meaning of the English word suggests both nostalgia for the home and being sick of the home, two emotions that will recur constantly throughout his films.

Hermosillo obtained his own financing for *Los nuestros* (*Ours*, 1969), a mid-length feature that clearly develops the director's basic themes. The film tells the story of a mother who is capable of planning a murder to protect the stability of her home. It credibly depicts a certain Mexican middle class and its fears and pettiness, as well as two fundamental character types: a dominating mother figure who controls all and an external figure who arrives to alter the established order.

His first feature film and commercial debut was *La verdadera vocación de Magdalena* (*Magdalena's True Vocation*, 1971), a lacklustre comedy that is interesting only because the browbeaten daughter who rebels against her mother's opposition to her marriage to a rock musician anticipates the themes of some of his later films. A year later, he made *El señor de Osanto* (*The Man from Osanto*, 1972), produced by the Churubusco studios and his only period film. Hermosillo used a Robert Louis Stevenson novel to recount the conflict that develops between two brothers when one of them leaves to fight in the war against the French intervention. The film demonstrates the director's technical devel-opment as well as the use of the sequence-shot that would become a characteristic of his style.

Hermosillo's first mature work is *El cumpleaños del perro* (*The Dog's Birthday*, 1974), a film that contrasts two marriages, one new and one old. In a moment of madness, the younger husband kills his wife and the older man covers up for him. With great simplicity, we watch the silent desperation of a middle class drowning in habits and social conventions from which the only escape is transgression, a solution with which the film-maker sympathises. This film also marks the first appearance of homosexuality in his work, although here it is suggested only as a latent possibility beneath the surface of male camaraderie.

1976 was a productive year in which Hermosillo directed his two most significant films. *La pasión según Berenice (The Passion According to Berenice)* is one of the Mexican cinema's most definitive portraits of feminine sexuality. The title character is a country woman who leads an ordinary life with her usurious godmother, until a city man appears and awakens her desire. The eruption of repressed emotions leads her to an incendiary act of final liberation. Hermosillo is a cinephile who has frequently mentioned his admiration for Hitchcock, Lang and Cukor; *La pasión según Berenice* demonstrates the combined influence of Sirk and Buñuel. The film-maker's love of classic Hollywood cinema is also evident in *Matinée*, an updated adventure film in which two boys from the provinces accidentally join a thieves' gang headed by a homosexual couple. Once again, Hermosillo positions himself on the side of those who break the law. This entertaining and well-filmed combination thriller-comedy culminates with an urgent call to anarchy: faced with a return to his boring school and family life, one of the boys unsuccessfully attempts to run away again.

Naufragio (Shipwreck) and *Las apariencias engañan (Looks Can Be Deceiving)*, both from 1977, are two variations on the theme of the disappeared relative who returns with unpredictable conse-quences. As in *El señor de Osanto*, Hermosillo collaborated with writer José de la Colina on the script for *Naufragio*. The film tells the story of an office worker who yearns for the return of her sailor son and of a co-worker who shares her fantasies. The result is a subtle film about the encounter between a grey reality and desire. With a memorable final image of the sea invading a Mexico City apartment, the film-maker once again lays odds on the power of desire. In *Las apariencias engañan,* a title that summarises another of the director's preoccupations, a man pretending to be the lost nephew of a wealthy old man who has returned to help him spend his last days in peace falls in love with a woman with a sexual secret. The description of the dissimulation and the hypocrisy of the provinces are on target, but the film proceeds towards a surprising climax too schematically. The risky topic of sexual ambiguity in this independent produc-tion was not well received by censors during the López Portillo *sexenio* and the film was banned for five years.

Produced by the state, *Amor libre* (*Free Love*, 1978) is a minor work, a light comedy about the rivalry of two friends who share the same name. The film is notable only because it demonstrates Hermosillo's formal fluidity, use of elegant sequence-shots, and good sense of space. Later, Hermosillo adapted a Maupassant story for the short *Idilio* (*Idyll*, 1978) and co-wrote with Gabriel García Márquez the script for *María de mi corazón* (*Maria of my Heart*, 1979), another independent production. In this film, a female magician meets up again with an old boyfriend, a thief, and their rekindled love seems to guarantee the happiness of both. However, she is acciden-tally locked up in a madhouse and presumed to be a patient, while he believes that she has abandoned him again. Perhaps influenced by *Sullivan's Travels* (Preston Sturges, 1941), the film shifts from comedy to tragedy, clearly illustrating how the difficulties of daily life can defeat the magic of love.

The 80s were a paradoxical decade for Hermosillo. On the one hand, his work was discovered by the international press and praised so highly that he developed a cult following. On the other, in Mexico most of his films of this period are considered to be among his weakest. *Confidencias* (*Confidences*, 1982) is an independent production that tackles the sexual, class and age differences between a servant and a bourgeois housewife, the only characters of the film. The acting is almost as obvious as the dialogue and the clever sequence-shot conclusion was ruined by photographic problems. *El corazón de la noche* (*The Heart of Night*, 1983), his last state-financed film, is a rare incursion into the fantasy genre: when he falls in love with a deaf mute, a young man becomes involved with a secret society of handicapped people. Here, the contrast between the ordinary and extraordinary is too obvious and, therefore, unbelievable. Nevertheless, New York critic Elliott Stein remarked: 'It is his most ambiguous film ... Freud, Tod Browning, Hitchcock, Buñuel, references abound, yet this fascinating, truly bizarre "botched" movie has a lifeblood all its own.'[5]

After making *El corazón de la noche*, Hermosillo moved to Guadalajara. This is where he set *Doña Herlinda y su hijo* (*Doña Herlinda and Her Son*, 1984), the first openly gay film in the history of the Mexican cinema. Whereas earlier he had dealt with homosexuality tangentially, in *El cumpleaños del perro, Matinée* and *Las apariencias engañan*, now it becomes the central theme of this comedy about a domineering mother who sustains the appearance of normality in her fiefdom by making her son's secret homosexual relationship possible. Despite the limitations of a non-professional cast and the forced humour of a demonstrative script, *Doña Herlinda y su hijo* inaugurated the Hermosillo cult abroad. The film travelled to many festivals and was an art-house hit in cities like London and New York.

Clandestino destino (*Clandestine Destiny*, 1987) did not have the same reception. Filmed twice (the first 16mm version was ruined), it is set in a near future where two couples explore their sexualities during a country outing. The film fails to convince at any level. This marked decline was not checked by his next film, *El verano de la señora Forbes* (*The Summer of Mrs Forbes*, 1988), part of the *Amores difíciles* (*Difficult Loves*) series of Gabriel García Márquez adaptations produced by Spanish television.[6] Filmed in Cuba, the film describes the double life of a German governess: by day a stern disciplinarian over her charges, by night, a voluptuously sensual being. Señora Forbes is similar to Berenice in *La pasión*, but her character is so obvious that one would not think it was by the same director. *El verano de la señora Forbes* found at least one admirer: the critic Donald Lyons was of the opinion that 'The movie is a deft and delicate visual poem of repression and passion. ... It takes Hermosillo's usual easy, urban, apartment-bound ironies down to a drowning depth where, paradoxically, they breathe and sigh as nowhere else in his work.'[7]

The production of *El verano de la señora Forbes* was so complicated and unsatisfactory for Hermosillo that he decided to experiment with 8mm video in search of a simple and inexpensive means of production. One of his exercises, entitled *El aprendiz de pornógrafo* (1989) for its commercial release, consisted of setting up an ostensible seduction from a single point of view: that of the camera itself hidden by one of the characters. This established the point of departure for his next two films, *Intimidades en un cuarto de baño* (*Intimacies in a Bathroom*, 1989) and *La tarea* (*Homework*, 1990). These mark the culmination of the director's interest in the sequence-shot: the films are shot in a single take and with no editing. In the first film, the spectator is positioned behind the bathroom mirror and witnesses the disintegration of a young middle-class couple pitted against an older one. In some ways, the situation is like *El cumpleaños del perro* fifteen years later, where the sickness of the family is made palpable through an eloquent script and an able cast, and is intensified by the execution of Hermosillo's singular formal choice (which is not at all like filmed theatre).

La tarea, on the other hand, is an erotic comedy, a revised and expanded version of *El aprendiz de pornógrafo.* Here we also have a seduction in front of a video camera, but the roles have been reversed: the woman takes the initiative. Once again, Hermosillo acutely observes the behaviour of the Mexican middle class. His recombination of sex, lies and videotape allows him to make incisive, and often very humorous, comments about the problems of casual sex in the age of AIDS, the hesitation of contemporary women's sexual initiatives, and the ubiquity of video, without forgetting to allude to cinema itself within what appears as a double representation. It is not surprising that *La tarea* was a great box-office hit in Mexico and one of the few national films of quality that has appealed to a mass audience.

Hermosillo has already finished *Encuentro inesperado* (*Unexpected Meeting,* 1991) and *La tarea prohibida* (*The Forbidden Task,* 1992), which means that he has directed a feature film every year since 1987, a production record that no other ambitious director of this last decade has matched, given the economic conditions of the Mexican cinema. This demonstrates his willingness to find alternative production modes which, together with his tendency to take formal and thematic risks, allows us to predict that he will continue a prolific career in the future.

Notes

1. If he hadn't been inactive for over a decade, the fifth film-maker to be included here would have been Jorge Fons, the director of notable films like the episode *Caridad (Charity)* of *Fe, esperanza y caridad* (*Faith, Hope and Charity;* the first two episodes were by Alberto Bojórquez and Luis Alcoriza, 1972) and *Los albañiles* (*The Bricklayers,* 1976). Recently, Fons returned to the cinema with *Rojo amanecer* (*Red Dawn,* 1989), an important film which broke the censorship taboo over the events of the 1968 student movement and its violent repression by the government, and which brought back a mass audience to the Mexican cinema of quality.

2. Emilio García Riera, *Arturo Ripstein habla de su cine* (Guadalajara: CIEC/Universidad de Guadalajara, 1988).

3. This is a project that, of course, did not have anything to do with the Hollywood version directed by John Huston (1984) and scripted by Guy Gallo.

4. Emilio García Riera and Fernando Macotela, *La guía del cine mexicano* (Mexico City: Patria, 1984).

5. Elliott Stein, 'Don Hermosillo and the sun' in *Film Comment,* vol. 22 no. 3, May–June 1986, p. 57.

6. *Clandestino destino* and *El verano de la señora Forbes* have never been exhibited commercially in Mexico. The films were shown only at special screenings and, later, on video.

7. Donald Lyons, 'Chambers of the sea' in *Film Comment,* vol. 27, no. 3 May–June 1991, p. 17.

Films

These notes were compiled by Carmen Elisa Gómez, Ulises Iñíguez, Rocío Pérez and Luz María Virgen (Centro de Investigación y Enseñanza Cinematográficas, Universidad de Guadalajara), with additional material from Chon A. Noriega and Steven Ricci (UCLA Film and Television Archive) and Paul Willemen. The films of Luis Buñuel, although among the finest films in Mexican cinema, have not been included because information about them is widely available.

El automóvil gris
aka *The Grey Automobile*
1919 117 mins. (30 episodes) b&w
d Enrique Rosas, Joaquín Coss, Juan Canals de Homes *p* Enrique Rosas y cia *sc* Enrique and Miguel Necoechea, Juan Manuel Cabrera *c* Enrique Rosas *ed* Manuel Vigueras supervised by Enrique Rosas
lp Juan Canals de Homes, Joaquín Coss, Juan Manuel Cabrera, Miguel Angel Ferriz, Enrique Cantalaúba, María Mercedes Ferriz, Dora Villa, María Tereza Montoya, Francisco Pesado, Carlos E. González

The interiors were filmed at the locations where the real events took place. Re-edited and with an added soundtrack, the serial was released as a conventional feature film in 1933 and 1937. The soundtrack for the 1933 version was produced by José Marino, using recordings made by the brothers Joselito and Roberto Rodríguez. This version has been lost. The 1937 version is well preserved and runs for 111 mins. In 1915, at the height of the Mexican Revolution, a gang of villains used their army connections, army uniforms and a grey automobile to hold up wealthy mansions. The assailants were captured and executed, with the exception of the gang's leader. The film includes documentary footage of the actual execution shot by Rosas.

Santa
1931 81 mins. b&w
d Antonio Moreno *p* Compañía Nacional Productora de Películas (Juan de la Cruz Alarcón, José Castellot Jr) *sc* Carlos Noriega Hope from the novel by Federico Gamboa *c* Alex Phillips *art dir* Fernando A. Rivero *ed* Aniceto Ortega *sd* Roberto and Joselito Rodríguez *m* Miguel Lerdo de Tejada *lyr* Agustín Lara
lp Lupita Tovar, Carlos Orellana, Juan José Martínez Casado, Donald Reed (pseud. for Ernesto Guillén), Antonio R. Frausto, Mimí Derba, Rosita Arriaga, Joaquín Busquets, Feliciano Rueda, Jorge Peón

This second of six films (to date) based on the celebrated novel by Gamboa, who affiliated himself with the French naturalists and was greatly influenced by Émile Zola. It is the first Mexican film to use synchronised sound and one of the formative popular melodramas, ushering in the national film industry both technically and generically. *Santa* was the paradigm for the cinematic opposition that would permeate Mexican melodrama in the years to come: the contrast of a bucolic province and a city corrupted by vice. Santa (Tovar), a young country girl, is raped by Marcelino (Reed) and runs away from her village in shame. She finds work in a city brothel where she meets the bullfighter Jarameño (Casado). They become lovers. Sometime later Marcelino comes looking for her and Jarameño catches them together. Plunged into despair, Santa cannot be saved even by her faithful and loving protector, the blind pianist Hipólito (Orellana).

El compadre Mendoza
aka *Godfather Mendoza*
1933 (released in 1934) 86 mins. b&w
d/ed Fernando de Fuentes *p* Interamericana Films (Rafael Angel Frías, José Castellot Jr), Producciones Aguila (Antonio Prida Santacilia) *sc* Mauricio Magdaleno *dial* Juan Bustillo Oro, Fernando de Fuentes *c* Alex Phillips *art dir* Beleho *sd* B.J. Kroger *m* Manuel Castro Padilla
lp Alfredo del Diestro, Carmen Guerrero, Antonio R. Frausto, Luis G. Barreiro, Joaquín Busquets, Emma Roldán, José del Rio, Abraham Galán, José Ignacio Rocha, Ricardo Carti

During the Revolution, rich landowner Rosalío Mendoza (del Diestro) makes his peace with the Huerta government's troops as well as with Zapata's. While he is marrying Dolores (Guerrero), the hacienda is attacked by Zapata, but General Felipe Nieto (Frausto) saves his friend Mendoza. The friendship between the two men grows and Felipe becomes the godfather of the couple's first child. When the Revolution threatens to ruin Mendoza, he accepts an offer from Huerta's troops to lay an ambush for Felipe, who is subsequently assassinated. A pointed commentary on the self-interested ambivalence of the middle class during the Revolutionary years, this film received little recognition until its rediscovery by French critic Georges Sadoul in the 60s.

La mujer del puerto
aka *Woman of the Port*
1933 76 mins. b&w
d Arcady Boytler, Raphael J. Sevilla *p* Eurindia Films (Servando C. de la Garza) *sc* Guz Aguila, Raphael J. Sevilla from *Le Port* by Guy de Maupassant *dial* Guz Aguila, Carlos de Nájera *c* Alex Phillips *art dir* Fernando A. Rivero *ed* José Marino *sd* José B. Carles *m* Max Urban *songs* Manuel Esperón and Ricardo López Méndez
lp Andrea Palma, Domingo Soler, Joaquín Busquets, Arturo Manrique 'Panseco', Jorge Treviño 'Panqué', Francisco Zárraga, Roberto Cantú, Consuelo Segarra, Luisa Obregón

This classic melodrama tells of Rosario (Palma), a young country girl seduced by her boyfriend (Zárraga). Her father Don Antonio demands satisfaction from the boyfriend who pushes him down the stairs. Seeking a means to support her ailing father, Rosario first approaches his boss, Don Basilio, who demands sexual services from her. She turns instead to her lover, only to discover that he is unfaithful to her. Her father dies and Rosario, now the victim of local rumours, moves to the distant port of Veracruz where she finally becomes a prostitute in a cabaret. She sleeps with the sailor Alberto (Soler). While chatting, they discover that they are brother and sister. She commits suicide by throwing herself into the sea. The film's depiction of inadvertent incest shocked contemporary audiences. Escaping official censorship, it enjoyed great popularity largely due to the controversy.

El prisionero trece
aka *Prisoner No. 13*
1933 74 mins. b&w
d Fernando de Fuentes *p* Compañía Nacional Productora de Películas *sc* Fernando de Fuentes from a story by Miguel Ruiz *c* Ross Fisher *ed* Aniceto Ortega *sd* José B. Carles *art dir* Fernando A. Rivero *m* Guillermo A. Posadas
lp Alfredo del Diestro, Luis G. Barreiro, Adela

Sequeyro, Arturo Campoamor, Adela Jaloma, Emma Roldán, Antonio R. Frausto, Luis Sánchez Tello, Joaquín Coss, Alicia Bolaños

The first of de Fuentes's trilogy about the Revolution uses the historical events as a background for a moralistic tale. According to Federico Serrano, the film shows de Fuentes more as an inspired craftsman than as the intelligent and ironic observer he later became. The story deals with moral decadence and corruption, starring the obese Chilean actor del Diestro, a refugee from Hollywood's Hispanic cinema, as the drunken colonel Carrasco whose wife Marta (Sequeyro) leaves him taking their son Juan (Campoamor). The boy grows up and falls in love with Lola (Bolaños). When Carrasco jails some Revolutionaries, his friend Zertuche (Barreiro) persuades him to take a bribe to release one of them and to substitute another prisoner, who turns out to be Juan. Carrasco is unable to save his son from the firing squad but he wakes up and realises it was all a bad dream induced by alcohol. Except for the forced happy ending, the film's implacable rhythm and economic style make for a remarkable work.

El Tigre de Yautepec
aka *The Tiger of Yautepec*
1933 86 mins. b&w
d Fernando de Fuentes *p* Producciones FESA (Jorge Pezet), Juan F. Azcárate *sc* Fernando de Fuentes, Jorge Pezet from a story by J. Pezet *c* Alex Phillips *sd* Roberto and Joselito Rodríguez *ed* Fernando de Fuentes *art dir* Fernando A. Rivero *m* Guillermo Posadas
lp Pepe Ortiz, Lupita Gallardo, Adria Delhort, Consuelo Segarra, Antonio R. Frausto, Alberto Miguel, Dolores Camarillo, Joaquín Busquets, Enrique Cantalaúva

De Fuentes's Western-style tale of the outlaw El Tigre (Ortiz) begins with a flashback to 1846 and a dramatically shot hold-up, a kidnapping and lyrical scenes of menacing landscapes. After that, the film moves ahead twenty years and settles into the conventions of the action melodrama, including musical numbers, until the climactic attack on a stagecoach and a sensationalist rape scene. The hero also indulges in an incestuous relationship with his sister Dolores (Gallardo), although the film turns a blind eye to this dimension. In the end, both Dolores and the bandit's mother Lupita (Delhort) are left grieving over the criminal's corpse. Emilio García Riera noted that de Fuentes never seemed to have decided whether El Tigre was a romantic rebel or a vicious criminal, a confusion that may explain the nature of this strangely uneven film.

Dos monjes
aka *Two Monks*
1934 85 mins. b&w
d Juan Bustillo Oro *p* Proa Films (José and Manuel San Vicente) *sc* José Manuel Cordero, adaptation by Juan Bustillo Oro *c* Agustín Jiménez *art dir* Mariano Rodríguez Granada, Carlos Toussaint *ed* Juan Bustillo Oro *sd* B.J. Kroger *m* Max Urban *songs* Manuel M. Ponce, Raúl Lavista
lp Magda Haller, Victor Urruchúa, Carlos Villatoro, Emma Roldán, Manuel Noriega, Sofía Haller, Alberto Miguel, Conchita Gentil Arcos, José Cortes

Melodrama set in the nineteenth century: two versions of the same story are narrated in counterpoint. The monks Juan (Urruchúa) and Javier (Villatoro), once rivals in a love triangle, recount their individual versions of the story in the confessional. The woman they both loved, Ana (Haller), died when she was accidentally shot by the revolver Juan was pointing at Javier. Javier dies in a fit of madness.

Janitzio
1934 (released in 1935) 56 mins. b&w
d Carlos Navarro *p* Cinematográfica Mexicana (Antonio Manero and José Luis Bueno) *sc* Luis Márquez from a Michoacán legend, adaptation by Roberto O'Quigley *c* Lauron 'Jack' Draper *art dir* José Rodríguez Granada *ed* Carlos Navarro *sd* José B. Carles *m* Francisco Domínguez
lp Emilio Fernández, María Teresa Orozco, Gilberto González, Max Langler, Adela Valdés

On the island of Janitzio, the indigenous fisherman Zirahuén (Fernández) fights with the white merchant Manuel when the latter demands that Zirahuén sell him fish at an unfair price. Manuel unjustly throws him in jail. In order to free the fisherman, his fiancée Eréndira (Orozco) submits to the sexual demands of Manuel. When the villagers discover Eréndira's treason, they stone her to death in accordance with local traditions. Zirahuén leaves with his loved one's body in his canoe. The film was shot after, but released before, *Redes*.

Redes
aka *Nets*
1934 (released in 1936) 65 mins. b&w

d Fred Zinnemann, Emilio Gómez Muriel *p* Secretaría *de* Educación Pública *sc* Agustín Velázquez Chávez, Paul Strand, adaptation by Fred Zinnemann, Emilio Gómez Muriel, Henwar Rodakiewicz *c* Paul Strand *ed* Emilio Gómez Muriel, Günther von Fritsch *sd* Roberto and Joselito Rodríguez *m* Silvestre Revueltas
lp Silvio Hernández, David Valle González, Rafael Hinojosa, Antonio Lara, Miguel Figueroa and the fishermen of Veracruz

The first film produced with the co-operation of the Mexican government. With the exception of Valle González, all the actors are amateurs. In the early stages of shooting, on location in the small fishing village of Alvarado near Veracruz, Julio Bracho also participated as co-director, but health problems forced him to abandon the production. A group of fishermen rebel against their exploiters and the police suppress the demonstration. Taking advantage of the confusion, an agitator (Hinojosa) kills Miro (Hernández), the leader of the fishermen, but they remain united in their struggle.

La familia Dressel
1935 90 mins. b&w
d/sc/ed Fernando de Fuentes *p* Impulsora Cinematográfica, S. A. *c* Alex Phillips, Ross Fisher *sd* José B. Carles *art dir* Francisco Gómez Palacio *m* Juan S. Garrido
lp Consuelo Frank, Jorge Vélez, Rosita Arriaga, Julián Soler, Ramón Armengod, Manuel Tamés, Liere Wolf

An ironic but scrupulously realistic family melodrama about a German family trying to establish roots in Mexico City. The family is dominated by the matriarch Frau Dressel (Arriaga) who tries to separate her son from his Mexican wife. Apparently, de Fuentes was inspired by an actual German family setting up a hardware store which still exists in Mexico City. A print from this film presumed lost has recently been recovered.

¡Vámonos con Pancho Villa!
aka *Let's Go with Pancho Villa!*
1935 (released in 1936) 92 mins. b&w
d Fernando de Fuentes *p* Clasa Films (Alberto R. Pani) *sc* Fernando de Fuentes, Xavier Villaurrutia from Rafael F. Muñoz's novel *c* Lauron 'Jack' Draper, Gabriel Figueroa *art dir* Mariano Rodríguez Granada, Antonio Ruiz *ed* José Noriega *sd* Eduardo Fernández, Rafael Ruiz Esparza *m* Silvestre Revueltas

lp Antonio R. Frausto, Domingo Soler, Manuel Tamés, Ramón Vallarino, Carlos López 'Chaflán', Raúl de Anda, Rafael F. Muñoz, Alfonso Sánchez Tello, Paco Martínez, Dolores Camarillo, Consuelo Segarra, Silvestre Revueltas, David Valle González, Max Langler, Miguel M. Delgado

The final installment of de Fuentes's Revolutionary trilogy is a classic film about the Mexican Revolution set in 1914. A group of six rancheros join Pancho Villa's armies. Three of them die in successive battles. Villa (Soler) gives the other three positions in his personal guard to reward their courage. Another one (Tamés) dies in a bar game and the youngest (Vallarino) in a cholera epidemic, during which Villa betrays cowardice, thus valorising the ordinary soldier as the true hero of the Revolution. The last surviving ranchero, Tiburcio Maya (Frausto), abandons the Villista army and, disappointed, returns to his home town. In an ending that was not circulated for many years, Villa returns and kills Tiburcio Maya. The film's populist perspective was in keeping with the new administration of Lázaro Cárdenas and received funding from the state, which had begun to produce films as a means of promoting the nationalist social agendas of the new president's party. The financial failure of this film, the first great epic of the period, foreshadowed the decline of that political movement and, subsequently, the film remained in obscurity for years.

Allá en el Rancho Grande

aka *Over on the Big Ranch*
1936 100 mins. b&w
d/ed Fernando de Fuentes *p* Alfonso Rivas Bustamante, Fernando de Fuentes *sc* Guz Aguila, Luz Guzmán de Arellano, adaptation by Fernando de Fuentes, Guz Aguila (Antonio Guzmán Aguilera) *c* Gabriel Figueroa *art dir* Jorge Fernández *m* Lorenzo Barcelata *songs* Lorenzo Barcelata, José López Alavés and anonymous ('Allá en el Rancho Grande')
lp Tito Guízar, René Cardona, Esther Fernández, Lorenzo Barcelata, Emma Roldán, Carlos López 'Chaflán', Manuel Noriega, Dolores Camarillo, Alfonso Sánchez Tello, Trío Tariácuri

The first great commercial success of Mexican cinema in Latin America. Felipe (Cardona) inherits the Rancho Grande hacienda from his father and appoints as *caporal* his childhood friend José Francisco Ruellas (Guizar), who is also the beautiful, asthmatic Cruz's (Fernández) fiancé. Cruz's godmother offers her to Felipe in exchange for money, but Cruz faints when she

finds herself alone with the boss. When José Francisco learns what has happened, he tries to kill Felipe, but Felipe convinces him that nothing took place. Cruz and José Francisco wed. The film inaugurated the *comedia ranchera,* a distinctly Mexican genre that reflects the values and customs of a ranching economy. The popularity of this new form was a conservative reaction to the progressive rural reform of President Cárdenas, whose agricultural policies shifted land ownership away from the ranch-owners. Replete with traditional song and dance, the *comedia ranchera* was an idealised depiction of old plantation life.

Aguila o sol

1937 (released in 1938) 77 mins. b&w
d Arcady Boytler *p* Cinematográfica Internacional (CISA) (Pedro Maus, Felipe Mier) *sc* Guz Aguila (Antonio Guzmán Aguilera), Arcady Boytler, adaptation by Arcady Boytler *c* Victor Herrera *art dir* José Rodríguez Granada *ed* José M. Noriega *sd* José B. Carles *m* Manuel Castro Padilla *songs* Manuel Castro Padilla, Rafael Hernández
lp Mario Moreno 'Cantinflas', Manuel Medel, Margarita Mora, Marina Tamayo, Luis G. Barreiro, Manuel Arvide, Margarita Sodi, Jesús de la Mora, José Girón Torres, Dora Ceprano

In an orphanage, brother and sister Carmelo and Adriana Aguila befriend the child Polito Sol and accept him as a brother. The trio escapes from the orphanage when threatened by separation. In the city, the boys sell newspapers and the girl lottery tickets in the streets. As adults, they work in a tent-show and produce musical and comic sketches. Polito and Adriana love each other, Carmelo loves Teresa but she does not respond in kind. As fate would have it, Polito and his real father, who unexpectedly becomes wealthy, meet and recognise each other. They all live happily ever after.

La Zandunga

1937 (released in 1938) 107 mins. b&w
d Fernando de Fuentes *p* Films Selectos (Pedro A. Calderón) *sc* Rafael M. Saavedra, adaptation by Fernando de Fuentes *dial* R.M. Saavedra, F. de Fuentes, Salvador Novo *c* Ross Fisher *art dir* Jorge Fernández *ed* Charles L. Kimball *sd* B.J. Kroger, José B. Carles *m* Max Urban *songs* Lorenzo Barcelata
lp Lupe Vélez, Rafael Falcón, Arturo de Córdova, Joaquín Pardavé, Carlos López 'Chaflán', Manuel Noriega, Rafael Icardo, Carmen Cortés

The isthmus of Tehuantepec is celebrating the fruit

festival. Lupe (Vélez) is courted by three suitors: the sailor Juancho (Córdova), Ramón of Tehuantepec (Falcón) and Don Atanasio (Icardo). Lupe loves Juancho, but he must leave the village for a while. Don Eulogio (Noriega), Lupe's father, refuses to give his daughter's hand to Don Atanasio, who takes away his banana plantation in revenge. Ramón fights with Atanasio and both land in jail. Lupe agrees to marry Ramón, but when Juancho finally returns, Ramón realises that Lupe loves the sailor and gives her up.

En tiempos de don Porfirio

aka *Melodias de antaño*
1939 (released in 1940) 160 mins. b&w
d Juan Bustillo Oro *p* Producciones Grovas-Oro Films (Jesús Grovas) *sc* Juan Bustillo Oro, Humberto Gómez Landero *c* Lauron 'Jack' Draper *art dir* Carlos Toussaint *ed* Mario González *sd* Roberto Rodríguez, Rafael Ruiz Esparza *m* Max Urban *songs* F. Villanueva, M.M. Ponce, Roca, Campodónico, Ch. Martínez, Alvarado, Carrasco, Perches Enríquez
lp Fernando Soler, Marina Tamayo, Emilio Tuero, Joaquín Pardavé, Dolores Camarillo, Aurora Walker, Agustín Isunza, Manuel Noriega

The story is set in the late 19th century in Orizaba. Doña Carlota (Walker) and Don Francisco (Soler) had a daughter when they were young. Carlota married someone else but was widowed shortly after. Carmen (Tamayo), the daughter, grows up and her mother wants her to marry Don Rodrigo Rodríguez y Eje (Pardavé), but she is in love with the student Fernando Villanueva (Tuero). Since Francisco has grown to care for his daughter, although she doesn't know his identity, he helps the young couple with all sorts of subterfuges and succeeds in convincing Don Rodrigo to break off the engagement. Carmen learns that Don Francisco is her father. At the end, two weddings are being planned: Francisco's with Doña Carlota and the young couple.

Los de abajo

aka *Con la división del norte*
1939 (released in 1940) 85 mins. b&w
d Chano Urueta *p* Producción Nueva América or Producciones Amanecer, Luis Manrique (Enrique L. Morfín) *sc* Chano Urueta from the novel *Los de abajo* by Mariano Azuela *dial* Aurelio Manrique *c* Gabriel Figueroa *art dir* Jorge Fernández *ed* Emilio Gómez Muriel *sd* B.J. Kroger *m* Jorge Pérez H.
lp Miguel Angel Ferriz, Esther Fernández, Isabela Corona, Domingo Soler, Carlos López Moctezuma, Alfredo del Diestro, Beatriz Ramos, Emma Roldán,

Emilio Fernández, Raúl Guerrero

Demetrio Macías (Ferriz), an agricultural worker, joins the Revolution on the side of Pancho Villa, participates in the takeover of Zacatecas and is promoted to the rank of lieutenant colonel. His reputation as a ladies' man is confirmed when two women fight to the death over him. Later, Villa is defeated and Demetrio dies with his compatriots, fighting to the bitter end.

Ahí está el detalle

aka *This is the Point*
1940 120 mins. b&w
d Juan Bustillo Oro *p* Producciones Grovas-Oro Films (Jesús Grovas) *sc* Humberto Gómez Landero, Juan Bustillo Oro *c* Lauron 'Jack' Draper *art dir* Carlos Toussaint *ed* Mario González *sd* Rafael R. Esparza *m* Raúl Lavista
lp Mario Moreno 'Cantinflas', Sofía Alvarez, Joaquín Pardavé, Dolores Camarillo, Sara García, Antonio Noriega, Antonio R. Frausto, Antonio Bravo, Agustín Isunza, Francisco Jambrina

Comedy of errors in which the carefree Cantinflas obliges his fiancée, the servant Pacita (Camarillo), by getting rid of the dog Bobby. However, Bobby is also the name of a gangster (Bravo) who is blackmailing Dolores (Alvarez), the beautiful lady of the house and wife of the jealous Don Cayetano Lastre (Pardavé). When the gangster is killed, Cantinflas is charged with the crime and brought to trial. Finally, the real killer appears and Cantinflas is freed. Cantinflas's character is that of an urban vagabond or *peladito,* who ridicules the arrogance and hypocrisy of the Mexican middle class. His unique wordplay prompted the Spanish Royal Academy of Language to admit the word *cantinflada* to describe nonsensical chatter. This film illustrates Cantinflas's trademark humour, reliant on puns and miscommunication.

El jefe máximo

aka *The Supreme Leader* aka *The Big Boss*
1940 90 mins. b&w
d Fernando de Fuentes *p* Financiadora de Películas, Fernando de Fuentes *sc* Fernando de Fuentes, Rafael F. Muñoz from the play *Los caciques* by Carlos Arniches *c* Gabriel Figueroa *sd* Ismael Rodríguez *ed* Charles L. Kimball *art dir* Manuel Fontanals *m* Manuel Esperón
lp Leopoldo Ortín, Joaquín Pardavé, Gloria Marín, Manuel Tamés, Emma Roldán, Pedro Armendáriz, Alfredo del Diestro, Luis G. Barreiro, Manuel Noriega

A comedy in the vein of Chaplin's *Great Dictator* (1940) alluding to the reign of General Calles, popularly known as the Jefe Máximo (1928–34). The target is represented by Maximo Terroba (Ortín), the mayor of Ponteverde de Abajo, backed by a US stooge, Will B. Trenchmouth (Pardavé), and the film protests against the government party's contemporary practice of imposing its candidates on an unwilling electorate.

¡Ay, qué tiempos, señor don Simón!
1941 106 mins. b&w

d Julio Bracho *p* Films Mundiales (Agustín J. Fink) *sc* Julio Bracho *co-dial* Neftalí Beltrán *c* Gabriel Figueroa *art dir* Jorge Fernández *ed* Emilio Gómez Muriel *sd* Howard E. Randall *m* Raúl Lavista *lp* Joaquín Pardavé, Arturo de Córdova, Mapy Cortés, Anita Blanch, Agustín Isunza, Luis G. Barreiro, Miguel Montemayor, Consuelo Guerrero de Luna, Dolores Camarillo, Carlos Martínez Baena, Diana Bordes

Two respectable young women go to an all-male variety show in order for one of them, Inés (Cortés), to confirm that her fiancé Miguel (de Córdova) betrays her with a performer. As a result of their trip, however, Inés is expelled from the League in Defence of Good Manners, which is presided over by the flirtatious Don Simón de Lira (Pardavé). Josefina (Bordes) and Ramoncito (Montemayor), Don Simón's nephew, are in love, but her father wants her to marry someone else. Don Simón and Inés become engaged. A misunderstanding occurs in the theatre: Miguel challenges Don Simón to a duel. Finally, all is cleared up: the two couples, Josefina and Ramoncito and Inés and Miguel, will be married.

Así se quiere en Jalisco
aka *That's How They Love in Jalisco*
1942 128 mins. colour

d Fernando de Fuentes *p* Jesús Grovas (Fernando de Fuentes) *sc* Guz Aguila from a play by Carlos Arniches, adapted by Fernando de Fuentes *c* John W. Boyle, Agustín Martínez Solares *ed* Mario González *sd* José B. Carles, Howard E. Randall *art dir* Jorge Fernández *m* Manuel Esperón, Juan José Espinoza *lp* Jorge Negrete, María Elena Marqués, Carlos López Moctezuma, Florencio Castelló, Dolores Camarillo, Eduardo Arozamena, Antonio R. Frausto, Lupe Inclán, Trio Los Plateados, Mariachi Marmolejo, Roberto Cañedo

This variation on *Allá en el Rancho Grande* (1936)

was filmed in Technicolor, although the film survives only in b&w copies. A *ranchera* comedy featuring Negrete as the singing cowboy. The plot has a benevolent boss (Moctezuma) who wants to possess Lupe Rosales (Marqués), the girlfriend of his noble foreman Juan Ramón Mireles (Negrete). Emilio García Riera commented that contrary to its promotional hype, this was not Mexico's first colour film: 'That honour belongs really to *Novillero* (1936). The colour, administered according to the sinister recipes of Mrs Natalie Kalmus, gave *Así se quiere en Jalisco* an exceptional plastic ugliness. On the other hand, the care that Mr Boyle (brought from Hollywood) took in the photography forced de Fuentes to make a very static ranchera comedy, which is why he filmed the most unfortunate final fight imaginable. Everything was subordinated to the colour, and the colour was the worst part of the film.'

El peñón de las ánimas
1942 117 mins. b&w

d/sc Miguel Zacarías *p* Jesús Grovas *c* Victor Herrera *ed* José Bustos *sd* Howard E. Randall, Consuelo Rodríguez, José B. Carles *art dir* Carlos Toussaint, Manuel Fontanals *m* Tchaikovsky, Beethoven, Paganini, Chopin *lp* Jorge Negrete, María de los Angeles Félix, René Cardona, Carlos López Moctezuma, Miguel Angel Ferriz, Virginia Manzano, Conchita Gentil Arcos, Manuel Dondé

María Félix's debut feature sees her opposite her future husband and rehearses a *Romeo and Juliet* plot: Fernando (Negrete) and María (Félix) belonging to rival families fall in love and come to a sticky end. The first meeting between the fated lovers where he gives her a pistol, has become a classic scene in Mexican film history. Emilio García Riera commented that 'Zacarías here produced one of his best works, perhaps because he accepted the conventions without fearing ridicule.'

Distinto amanecer
aka *A Different Dawn*
1943 141 mins. b&w

d Julio Bracho *p* Films Mundiales (Emilio Gómez Muriel) *sc* Julio Bracho *co-dial* Xavier Villaurrutia *c* Gabriel Figueroa *art dir* Jorge Fernández *ed* Gloria Schoemann *sd* Howard E. Randall *m* Raúl Lavista songs Agustín Lara, Abelardo Valdés and others *lp* Andrea Palma, Pedro Armendáriz, Alberto Galán, Narciso Busquets, Paco Fuentes, Octavio Martínez,

Felipe Montoya, Manuel Arvide, Beatriz Ramos

This is one of the few films of its time to offer a visually realist depiction of the city. It also deals with issues rarely treated in Mexican film, such as union corruption and campus political activism. A labour leader is assassinated in the Mexico City post office. He loses a set of documents that compromise a corrupt governor. Octavio (Armendáriz), a friend of the dead man, must recover the documents, but he is followed by an agent of the corrupt official. By chance, Octavio runs into the cabaret dancer Julieta (Palma), his former girlfriend from their student days. She is now unhappily married to Ignacio (Galán), a disgruntled bureaucrat and frustrated writer, who helps Octavio recover the documents. Julieta and Octavio do away with the agent. Octavio realises how miserable Julieta's life is and invites her to leave with him, but she chooses to remain with her family.

Doña Bárbara
1943 138 mins. b&w
d Fernando de Fuentes *p* Jesús Grovas, Clasa Films (Fernando de Fuentes) *sc* Rómulo Gallegos, Fernando de Fuentes from Rómulo Gallegos's novel *c* Alex Phillips *art dir* Jesús Bracho *ed* Charles L. Kimball *sd* Jesús González Gancy, Howard E. Randall *m* Francisco Domínguez, Prudencio Essa
lp María Félix, Julián Soler, María Elena Marqués, Andrés Soler, Charles Rooner, Agustín Isunza, Miguel Inclán, Eduardo Arozamena, Antonio R. Frausto, Pedro Galindo, Felipe Montoya

An adaptation of Gallegos's novel about the settlement of the Venezuelan savannas. In the role that established her as a formidable actress in Mexican film, María Félix plays Doña Bárbara, a tyrannical rancher. Having been raped as a young woman, her despotic control of the territory serves as a means of self-mastery. There is a savagery to Doña Bárbara's resistance to male authority, but the neatly polarised categories of nature and culture are undermined when she falls in love with Santos Luzardo (J. Soler) who arrives from Caracas to take charge of his cattle ranch. He confronts Doña Bárbara, who has a daughter, Marisela (Marqués), with Lorenzo Barquero (A. Soler), a cousin of Santos's who has become an alcoholic because of the Doña's spells. Santos rescues Marisela from her wild and almost uncivilised state, causing both mother and daughter to fall in love with him. The *peóns* get into a violent fight over valuable heron feathers and

Doña Bárbara is abandoned by her workers. Much to the happiness of the young Santos and Marisela, la Doña decides to disappear into the plains.

Flor silvestre
aka *Wild Flower*
1943 94 mins. b&w
d Emilio Fernández *p* Films Mundiales (Agustín J. Fink) *sc* Emilio Fernández, Mauricio Magdaleno from the novel *Sucedió ayer* by Fernando Robles *c* Gabriel Figueroa *art dir* Jorge Fernández *ed* Jorge Bustos *sd* Howard E. Randall, Fernando Barrera, Manuel Esperón *m* Francisco Domínguez *songs* Pedro Galindo, Los Cuates Castilla
lp Dolores del Río, Pedro Armendáriz, Miguel Angel Ferriz, Mimí Derba, Eduardo Arozamena, Agustín Isunza, Armando Soto La Marina, Carlos Riquelme, Tito Novaro, Margarita Cortés, Emilio Fernández

This film is the first product of the long and fruitful collaboration between director Fernández, cinematographer Figueroa, screenwriter Magdaleno, actress del Río and actor Armendáriz. This period piece presents a microcosm of Mexican society during the Revolution. The protagonist, José Luis Castro (Armendáriz), confronts the social and political complexities of the time. Esperanza (del Río) tells her military cadet son (Novaro) the family history: José Luis, the boy's father, was a rich *hacendado* in the Bajío region who was disinherited by his family when he secretly married Esperanza, a poor peasant. José Luis sympathises with the Revolution's egalitarian ideals and when it succeeds, they live happily for some time until Esperanza and her son are kidnapped by false Revolutionaries. José Luis must confront the outlaws to free his wife and child, but he dies in the process. Fernández makes an appearance himself as Rogelio Torres, one of the outlaws.

María Candelaria
1943 (released in 1944) 101 mins. b&w
d Emilio Fernández *p* Film Mundiales (Agustín J. Fink) *sc* Emilio Fernández, Mauricio Magdaleno from an idea by Emilio Fernández *c* Gabriel Figueroa *art dir* Jorge Fernández *ed* Gloria Schoemann *sd* Howard E. Randall, Jesús González Gancy, Manuel Esperón *m* Francisco Domínguez
lp Dolores del Río, Pedro Armendáriz, Alberto Galán, Margarita Cortés, Miguel Inclán, Beatriz Ramos, Rafael Icardo, Arturo Soto Rangel, Lupe del Castillo, Lupe Inclán, Salvador Quiroz

The collaboration between Fernández and Figueroa received international attention for the first time with this film epitomising the idyllic provincial settings and veneration of indigenous Mexican peoples, which became the signature of their work together. In Xochimilco, before the Revolution, two poor Indians, María Candelaria (del Río) and Lorenzo Rafael (Armendáriz), want to marry. But María, the daughter of a 'fallen women', contracts malaria and Lorenzo is arrested and jailed when he attempts to steal quinine for her. A painter (Galán) comes to the village and, believing the beauty and purity of the Mexican 'race' to be embodied in María, asks her to be his model. The painting, representing the intrusion of civilisation, ultimately causes chaos. María's face is superimposed onto a nude portrait for which another Indian woman posed. The villagers mistakenly believe that María posed 'indecently' and they stone her to death. The tragic story is told in flashback by the painter to a journalist (Ramos).

La mujer sin alma
aka *The Woman Without a Soul*
1943 129 mins. b&w
d Fernando de Fuentes *p* Compañía Cinematográfica de Guadalajara (Luis Enrique Galindo) *sc* Alfonso Lapena, Fernando de Fuentes from the novel *La Raison sociale* by Alphonse Daudet *c* Victor Herrera *ed* Rafael Ceballos *sd* Rafael Ruiz Esparza *art dir* Jesús Bracho *m* Francisco Domínguez, María Alma
lp María Félix, Fernando Soler, Carlos Martínez Baena, Carlos Villatoro, Mimí Derba, Luis G. Barreiro, Chela Campos, Antonio Badú, Emma Roldán, Andrés Soler, Virginia Serret, Rafael Icardo, María Gentil Arcos, José Arratia

A lurid melodrama warning against the evils of female ambition and sexuality. The beautiful Teresa (Félix), daughter of a lazy textile worker, seduces her way up the social ladder via the boss's nephew Enrique (Badú). She eventually winds up a prostitute and cabaret singer. The film confirmed the *femme fatale* image Félix had established with *Doña Barbara* (1943).

La vida inútil de Pito Pérez
aka *The Useless Life of Pito Pérez*
1943 110 mins. b&w
d Miguel Contreras Torres *p* Hispano Continental Films *sc* Miguel Contreras Torres from a novel by José Rubén Moreno *c* Ignacio Torres *sd* Fernando Barrera, Howard E. Randall *art dir* Ramón Rodríguez *ed* Fernando Martínez *m* José Sabre Marroquín *songs* José Sabre Marroquín, Alfonso

Esparza Oteo
lp Manuel Medel, Elvia Salcedo, Katy Jurado, Eduardo Arozamena, Dolores Tinoco, Manuel Arvide, Salvador Quiroz, Conchita Gentil Arcos, Lauro Benítez, Elías Haber, Lupita Torrentera

Contreras Torres drew the character of Pito Pérez from a 1938 José Rubén Moreno novel. This colourful provincial vagabond became such a popular character that two other films were made about Pito's bizarre and comical adventures. In this version, Pito Pérez is played by Manuel Medel who was for many years the straight man for the comic actor Cantinflas. Pérez returns to his home town, vagrant and drunk. He starts tolling the bells of the church and, when he will not stop, he is thrown into prison. After his release, Pito is compelled to relate the story of his life to his lawyer, the poet (Arvide). Pito's narrative weaves his random and fragmented experiences into an ingenious philosophy of life.

Las abandonadas
1944 (released in 1945) 103 mins. b&w
d Emilio Fernández *p* Films Mundiales (Felipe Subervielle) *sc* Mauricio Magdaleno, Emilio Fernández *c* Gabriel Figueroa *art dir* Manuel Fontanals *ed* Gloria Schoemann *sd* Howard E. Randall, Jesús González Gancy, Manuel Esperón *m* Manuel Esperón
lp Dolores del Río, Pedro Armendáriz, Victor Junco, Paco Fuentes, Arturo Soto Rangel, Lupe Inclán, Fanny Schiller, Alfonso Bedoya, Armando Soto La Marina

In 1911, somewhere in the Mexican provinces, Margarita Peréz (del Río) is abandoned pregnant by a man she believed to be her legitimate husband. Rejected by her family, she emigrates to the capital. She gives birth to a son, Margarito (Junco), but unable to find respectable employment is forced into prostitution. General Juan Gómez (Armendáriz) takes her out of the brothel, promises to marry her and to accept her son, but Juan is arrested and killed while trying to escape from the police. He is accused of being an impostor and a member of the grey automobile gang. Margarita is sent to prison as an accomplice and her son is placed in an orphanage. When she gets out of jail, Margarita anonymously sends her son money to pay for his legal studies. He becomes a brilliant attorney dedicated to helping the poor.

La barraca
1944 (released in 1945) 118 mins. b&w

d Roberto Gavaldón p Inter América Films (Alfonso Sánchez Tello) sc Tito Davison from Vicente Blasco Ibáñez's novel, adapted by Libertad Blasco Ibáñez, Paulino Masip c Victor Herrera art dir Vicente Petit, Francisco Marco Chillet ed Carlos Savage sd Eduardo Fernández, B.J. Kroger m Félix Baltasar Samper
lp Domingo Soler, Anita Blanch, Amparo Morillo, José Baviera, Luana Alcañíz, Manolo Fábregas, Narciso Busquets, Rafael Icardo, Felipe Montoya

Peculiar film set in Valencia (Spain) in 1880. It is even said that an alternative soundtrack in Valencian dialect was also produced. Riddled by debts, the Barret family emigrate in search of a better life. Their neighbours decide not to occupy the Barret land. Sometime later the even poorer Batiste family arrives and decides to live in the abandoned farm. The neighbours are hostile and Pimentó (Baviera), a loyal friend of the Barret family, encourages them. After much suffering, Batiste (Soler) kills Pimentó. The people set fire to Batiste's house and he and his family leave, as poor as when they arrived.

Bugambilia
1944 (released in 1945) 105 mins. b&w
d Emilio Fernández p Films Mundiales (Felipe Subervielle) sc Emilio Fernández, Mauricio Magdaleno c Gabriel Figueroa art dir Manuel Fontanals, Estrella Boissevain ed Gloria Schoemann sd Howard E. Randall, Jesús González Gancy, Manuel Esperón m Raúl Lavista from themes by Schubert, Chopin and Liszt
lp Dolores del Río, Pedro Armendáriz, Julio Villarreal, Alberto Galán, Stella Inda, Paco Fuentes, Arturo Soto Rangel, Elba Alvarez

In Guanajuato, towards the middle of the last century, Amalia de los Robles (del Río), the daughter of the rich miner Don Fernando (Villarreal), falls in love with the supervisor Ricardo Rojas (Armendáriz). In a duel to defend the honour of the young woman, Ricardo kills a man and must flee. While travelling he discovers a silver mine, becomes wealthy, and returns for Amalia. When Ricardo asks him for his daughter's hand, Don Fernando is insulted by his daring and kills him. Don Fernando commits suicide during the subsequent trial. Amalia shuts herself in the house, never to leave again.

Campeón sin corona
aka *Champion without a Crown*
1945 (released in 1946) 117 mins. b&w
d Alejandro Galindo p Raúl de Anda sc Alejandro Galindo from a story by Alvaro Custodio, adapted by Gabriel Ramírez Osante and Alejandro Galindo c Domingo Carrillo art dir Gunther Gerszo ed Carlos Savage sd B.J. Kroger m Rosalio Ramírez
lp David Silva, Amanda del Llano, Fernando Soto 'Mantequilla', Carlos López Moctezuma, Nelly Montiel, Victor Parra, María Gentil Arcos, José del Río, Félix Medel, Aurora Cortés

Director Galindo uses the familiar story of the rise and fall of a boxer to render a politically progressive film, acclaimed for its accurate depiction of urban slums. Roberto (Silva), an ice-cream vendor, gets into a street fight which leads him to professional boxing. He becomes a great boxer and assumes the name Kid Terranova. Roberto earns money and wins over Lupita (del Llano), the owner of the neighbourhood taco restaurant. Nevertheless, Joe Ronda (Parra), another boxer who speaks English, makes him feel very insecure. When Roberto suffers a knockout and wants to retire, Lupita dissuades him. Roberto goes on to triumph in the USA, but he lands in jail because of Susana (Montiel), a society girl who seduced him. Released, Roberto knocks out Ronda. However, he is unable to overcome his insecurities, abandons boxing and becomes a drunk. Eventually, his mother and Lupita convince him to go back to selling ice cream.

La perla
aka *The Pearl*
1945 (released in 1947) 87 mins. b&w
d Emilio Fernández p Aguila Films (Oscar Dancigers) sc Emilio Fernández, John Steinbeck, Jackson Wagner from John Steinbeck's story c Gabriel Figueroa art dir Javier Torres Torija ed Gloria Schoemann sd James L. Fields, Nicolás de la Rosa, Galdino Samperio m Antonio Díaz Conde
lp Pedro Armendáriz, María Elena Marqués, Fernando Wagner, Gilberto González, Charles Rooner, Alfonso Bedoya, Juan García, Raúl Lechuga

With the author's active support, John Steinbeck's *The Pearl* was filmed prior to the novel's publication in the USA. Co-produced by RKO, both Spanish and English versions were made of the film. In this traditional legend of western Mexico, Quino (Armendáriz) is a poor fisherman who lives with his wife Juana (Marqués) and their newborn son. While diving one day, he finds an enormous pearl. The news spreads quickly throughout the village and reaches two foreign brothers (González and García), a doctor (Rooner) who collects pearls and hates

Indians, and a merchant (Lechuga). After attempting to obtain the pearl by all sorts of subterfuges, the two brothers individually hound Quino and his family, following them into the desert, where the merchant kills the doctor and the baby. After killing him, Quino returns to the village and throws the pearl back into the sea.

La selva de fuego
aka *Jungle Fire*
1945 103 mins. b&w
d Fernando de Fuentes *p* Jesús Grovas, Producciones Diana (Mauricio de la Serna) *sc* Antonio Médiz Bolio, adapted by Paulino Masip, Tito Davison, Fernando de Fuentes *c* Agustín Martínez Solares *ed* Jorge Bustos *sd* Francisco Alcayde *art dir* Edward Fitzgerald *m* Max Urban
lp Dolores del Río, Arturo de Córdova, Miguel Inclán, Gilberto González, Luis Beristáin, José Torvay, Manuel Dondé, Daniel 'Chino' Herrera, Felipe Montoya, Juan José Laboriel

Emilio García Riera commented about this adventure melodrama featuring two prestigious actors: 'The author of *La Noche de los Mayas,* Antonio Médiz Bolio, imagined a story where the presence of a beautiful woman, Estrella (del Río), awakened enormous passions among the dirty, long-haired *chicleros* (gum pickers) struggling in the tropical jungle of the Quintana Roo. The woman had to face the smiling, lascivious and menacing assaults of a congenial group of villains but found refuge, love and understanding with the much less congenial Luciano (de Córdova).'

Enamorada
aka *A Woman in Love*
1946 99 mins. b&w
d Emilio Fernández *p* Panamerican Films (Benito Alazraki) *sc* Iñigo de Martino, Benito Alazraki, Emilio Fernández *c* Gabriel Figueroa *art dir* Manuel Fontanals *ed* Gloria Schoemann *sd* José B. Carles *m* Eduardo Hernández Moncada
lp María Félix, Pedro Armendáriz, Fernando Fernández, José Morcillo, Eduardo Arozamena, Miguel Inclán, Manuel Dondé, Eugenio Rossi, Norma Hill, Juan García

Loosely based on *The Taming of the Shrew* and Juan Manuel's *The Count Lucanor,* this is one of Emilio Fernández's rare forays into comedy. It nonetheless bears Fernandez's mark in the political idealism evident in the portrayal of the Mexican Revolution.

The film's focus on local monuments and landscapes is consistent with the director's desire to forge a unified cultural identity for Mexico. Set during the Juarez Revolution, the film opens in the town of Cholula, which has been seized by the Revolutionary general Juan José Reyes (Armendáriz). There he falls in love with the beautiful and headstrong Beatriz (Félix), the daughter of Don Carlos Peñafiel (Morcillo), a powerful landowner. Beatriz is engaged to Roberts (Rossi), a North American, and is disdainful towards the general and his attempts to win her favours. Nevertheless, when the general and his troops leave town, she abandons Roberts at the altar and accompanies the general's troops as a *soldadera.*

La otra
1946 104 mins. b&w
d Roberto Gavaldón *p* Producciones Mercurio (Mauricio de la Serna) *sc* José Revueltas, Roberto Gavaldón from a Rian James story *c* Alex Phillips *art dir* Gunther Gerszo *ed* Charles L. Kimball *sd* James L. Fields *m* Raúl Lavista
lp Dolores del Río, Agustín Irusta, Victor Junco, José Baviera, Manuel Dondé, Conchita Carracedo, Carlos Villarías, Rafael Icardo, the child Daniel Pastor

A melodrama about the poor servant María (del Río) who asks her twin sister Magdalena to come to her rooms because she is going to commit suicide. Magdalena has just been widowed by a millionaire, and María kills her when she arrives. María then fixes things to make it appear that she has committed suicide, dresses in her sister's clothes and goes to her house to assume her place. Shortly, María discovers that her sister had a young lover Fernando (Junco), with whom she had plotted to kill her husband. The crime is discovered by Roberto (Irusta), a policeman and María's boyfriend, who thinks she really died. Eventually, María is discovered and condemned to thirty years in jail.

Nosotros los pobres
aka *We, the Poor*
1947 (released in 1948) 128 mins. b&w
d Ismael Rodríguez *p* Rodríguez Hermanos (Armando Espinosa) *sc* Ismael Rodríguez, Pedro de Urdimalas adapted by Pedro de Urdimalas *c* José Ortiz Ramos *art dir* Carlos Toussaint *ed* Fernando Martínez *sd* Manuel Topete, Jesús González Gancy *m* Manuel Esperón
lp Pedro Infante, Blanca Estela Pavón, Evita Muñoz, Carmen Montejo, Miguel Inclán, Katy Jurado,

Rafael Alcayde, Delia Magaña, Amelia Wilhelmy, Pedro de Aguillón, Pedro de Urdimalas

A classic popular melodrama of the urban underclass, this film became the cinematic source material for virtually an entire genre of films set in the outlying quarters of the city. These marginal urban zones were typified as the place where the degradation of poverty mingles with the dignity of humble workers who, in true melodramatic fashion, can laugh through their tears because they believe in a merciful God. Screen legend Pedro Infante plays Pepe el Toro, a humble, widowed carpenter who takes care of his daughter Chachita (Muñoz). His life is complicated: he is engaged to Celia (Pavón), his mother is blind and paralysed, and his aunt is consumptive. Montes (Alcayde), a wealthy man, accuses Pepe of murdering a usurer. Pepe is arrested and his carpentry shop confiscated, but he escapes from prison and reveals to Chachita that his consumptive aunt is really his mother. Both his aunt and mother die in the hospital, where Pepe is caught by the police. In the penitentiary he identifies the real killer, makes him confess, and goes free. Finally he marries Celia and they have a child.

Río Escondido
aka *Hidden River*
1947 (released in 1948) 96 mins. b&w
d Emilio Fernández *p* Raúl de Anda *sc* Emilio Fernández *c* Gabriel Figueroa *art dir* Manuel Fontanals *ed* Gloria Schoemann *sd* Eduardo Fernández *m* Francisco Domínguez
lp María Félix, Domingo Soler, Carlos López Moctezuma, Fernando Fernández, Arturo Soto Rangel, Eduardo Arozamena, Columba Domínguez, Juan García, Miguel Dondé

The steely rural schoolteacher Rosaura (Félix in one of her strongest roles) is sent to the town of Río Escondido by presidential mandate. Felipe Navarro (Fernández), a medical aide, accompanies her. Río Escondido is suffering under the yoke of the cacique Regino Sandoval (Moctezuma) who refuses water to the peasants during a drought, giving it to his horses instead. Regino attempts to win over Rosaura, asking her first to be his lover, then his wife, and, when drunk, he rapes her. Rosaura shoots him while the peasants rebel and finish off the cacique's henchmen. Rosaura has a heart attack and is taken care of by Felipe, who confesses his love. She dies at the end, after receiving a letter of congratulations from the president. The film uses a powerful female

character as an effective indictment of machismo, suggesting that the need for public involvement in the development of the nation is also an issue of gender. The film is a notable example of Figueroa's cinematography, with its unusual camera angles and lighting.

Soledad
1947 103 mins. b&w
d Miguel Zacarías *p* Aguila Films (Oscar Dancigers) *sc* Miguel Zacarías, Edmundo Báez from the story by Silvia Guerrico *c* Ignacio Torres *ed* José Luis Busto *sd* José de Pérez, Fernando Barrera *art dir* Javier Torres Torija *m* Manuel Esperón
lp Libertad Lamarque, René Cardona, Marga López, Rubén Rojo, Consuelo Guerrero de Luna, Rafael Alcayde, Prudencia Grifell, Elena Contla, Armida Bracho

A young Argentinian servant girl, Soledad Somellera (Lamarque), is seduced by her master, Roberto (Cardona). He reluctantly marries her in secret, after which he abandons her for Elena (Bracho). Ashamed, Soledad raises her surly daughter, Evangelina (López), without telling her she is her mother until Roberto's mother claims the child. The wayward husband later marries an heiress and the heroine becomes a famous cabaret singer under the name Cristina Palermo. When her beloved daughter is betrayed by Roberto and threatened with rape, Soledad saves her by shooting the attacker. Daughter and mother tearfully fall into each other's arms.

Angelitos negros
aka *Little Black Angels*
1948 100 mins. b&w
d Joselito Rodríguez *p* Rodríguez Hermanos *sc* Rogelio A. González from a story by Joselito Rodríguez *c* José Ortiz Ramos *ed* Fernando Martínez *sd* Luis Fernández, Jesús González Gancy *art dir* Carlos Toussaint *m* Raúl Lavista, Nacho García
lp Pedro Infante, Emilia Guiú, Rita Montaner, Titina Romay, Chela Castro, Nicolás Rodríguez, María Douglas, Antonio R. Frausto

A rare Mexican melodrama addressing racial prejudice. The singer José Carlos Ruiz (Infante) falls in love with Ana Luisa (Guiú), an orphan raised by the black nursemaid Mercé (Montaner). They marry, but Ana Luisa behaves like a racist towards the black musicians who work with her husband. Tragedy strikes when she gives birth to a black daughter, whom she rejects believing her husband to be responsible. In fact, Ana Luisa was the child of the black nursemaid who looked after her all her life. Mother and daughter will be reconciled only on Mercé's deathbed.

Calabacitas tiernas
aka *Tender Litte Pumpkins*
1948 101 mins. b&w
d Gilberto Martínez Solares *p* Clasa Films Mundiales (Salvador Elizondo) *sc* Eduardo Ugarte, Gilberto Martínez Solares, Juan García from a story by Eduardo Ugarte *c* Agustín Martínez Solares *art dir* Jesús Bracho *sd* Rafael Ruiz Esparza, José de Pérez *ed* Jorge Bustos *m* Rosalío Ramírez, Federico Ruiz
lp Germán Valdés 'Tin Tan', Rosita Quintana, Amalia Aguilar, Marcelo Chávez, Rosina Pagán, Nelly Montiel, Jorge Reyes, Gloria Alonso, Nicolás Rodríguez, Francisco Reiguera, Juan Orraca, Julien de Meriche, Armando Velasco

One of the great comic actors of Mexican film, Valdés became famous for his character Tin Tan, a *pachuco* or a 'zoot-suiter'. Valdés began his career as a radio announcer in Tijuana and worked his way up touring vaudeville shows known as *carpas*. The unique combination of English and Spanish slang in Tin Tan's humour was picked up by Mexican-Americans in the 40s and can still be heard in contemporary slang on both sides of the border, particularly in east Los Angeles. 'Tender Little Pumpkins' is a reference to *rumberas,* dancers from Argentina, Cuba, Brazil and Mexico who perform with Tin Tan. A good guy trying desperately to be bad, the upwardly mobile huckster played by Tin Tan here is exemplary of the subtlety he brought to this form of satire.

La dama del velo
aka *The Veiled Lady*
1948 104 mins. b&w
d Alfredo B. Crevenna *p* Fama Films, Rodolfo Lowenthal *sc* Egon Eis, Edmundo Báez from a story by Eis *c* Lauron 'Jack' Draper *sd* James L. Fields, Rodolfo Solís, Galdino Samperio *ed* Rafael Portillo *art dir* Jesús Bracho *m* Raúl Lavista
lp Libertad Lamarque, Armando Calvo, Ernesto Alonso, Miguel Córcega, José Baviera, Bárbara Gill, Tana Lynn, Juan Pulido, María Gentil Arcos

While singing in her luxurious house, flashbacks show Andrea del Monte (Lamarque) recalling her past life from the moment she fell in love with a drunken clown, Esteban (Calvo). She overhears a telephone conversation revealing that he is a widower who murdered his wife. Defended by his childhood friend, the lawyer Cristobal (Alonso), Esteban is nevertheless sent to prison for twenty years. When Andrea bids him farewell, Esteban curtly informs her he will be marrying Teresa (Lynn) and Cristobal offers to marry Andrea, who now lives with the wealthy lawyer and his son Victor (Córcega).

¡Esquina ... bajan!
1948 115 mins. b&w
d Alejandro Galindo *p* Rodríguez Hermanos (Alvaro Bielsa) *sc* Alejandro Galindo (technical adviser: Rafael Cataño) *c* José Ortiz Ramos *art dir* Gunther Gerszo *ed* Fernando Martínez *sd* Jesús González Gancy, Javier Mateos *m* Raúl Lavista
lp David Silva, Fernando Soto 'Mantequilla', Olga Jiménez, Victor Parra, Delia Magaña, Salvador Quiroz, Miguel Manzano

Gregorio del Prado (Silva), a bus driver with a problematic personality, works with Regalito ('Mantequilla'), the conductor. Gregorio courts one of his passengers, Cholita (Jiménez), without knowing that she works for Langarica (Parra), the owner of a rival bus company. After a skirmish with the police, the driver and the conductor are fired, but Gregorio is given a secret assignment. The romance between Gregorio and Cholita begins when he defends her in a market. Meanwhile, Gregorio ends up in jail after being provoked by the rival company's bus drivers. When he gets out, Cholita helps him to uncover Langarica's crooked deals. Everything is cleared up in a meeting, Gregorio and Cholita get married and the bus company puts Gregorio back on his old route.

Una familia de tantas
1948 (released in 1949) 130 mins. b&w
d Alejandro Galindo *p* Producciones Azteca (Cesar Santos Galindo) *sc* Alejandro Galindo *c* José Ortiz Ramos *art dir* Gunther Gerszo *ed* Carlos Savage *sd* Luis Fernández *m* Raúl Lavista
lp Fernando Soler, Martha Roth, David Silva, Eugenia Galindo, Felipe de Alba, Isabel del Puerto, Alma Delia Fuentes, Manuel de la Vega

The calm home of Don Rodrigo Castaño (Soler) is upset when his daughter Maru (Roth) opens the door to a vacuum-cleaner salesman. The meticulous Roberto (Silva) not only sells his wares but also wins the heart of fifteen-year-old Maru, who has the courage to communicate the news to her father. The older siblings also have problems, but they are afraid of their father's wrath. Roberto asks Maru to marry him. She accepts, knowing that he has no money and in spite of her father's opposition. She leaves home with her mother's blessing, whom she pities for not being happily married. In the end, even the long-suffering mother of the family stands up to the patriarch, defending her children's right to live their own lives.

Maclovia

1948 100 mins. b&w
d Emilio Fernández *p* Filmex (Gregorio Wallerstein) *sc* Mauricio Magdaleno *c* Gabriel Figueroa *art dir* Manuel Fontanals *ed* Gloria Schoemann *sd* José B. Carles *m* Antonio Díaz Conde
lp María Félix, Pedro Armendáriz, Carlos López Moctezuma, Columba Domínguez, Arturo Soto Rangel, Miguel Inclán, José Morcillo

Following on from the 1934 film *Janitzio,* Emilio Fernández extends his portrayal of Mexican Indians struggling to maintain their traditions in the face of the tensions caused by encroaching westernisation. In 1914, José María (Armendáriz), a poor fisherman from Janitzio, and Maclovia (Félix), the daughter of local Indian chief Macario (Inclán), want to marry. Macario is completely opposed to the relationship and must also protect Maclovia against the advances of the evil sergeant of a neighbouring military base, Genovevo (Moctezuma), who represents all that is corrupt about civilised society. While on a canoe trip, José María and Maclovia are attacked by Genovevo. He sinks the canoe and wounds and imprisons José María, charging him with drunkenness. José María is sentenced to twenty-four years in prison. Village custom demands that Maclovia and José María be killed as it is assumed that Genovevo possessed her. However, on the night of the Day of the Dead, José María breaks out of prison, finds Maclovia and they escape across the lake. This ending represents a departure from *María Candelaria* (1943) by offering a critique of the traditional as well as modern culture.

Pueblerina

1948 (released in 1949) 111 mins. b&w
d Emilio Fernández *p* Ultramar Films-Producciones Reforma (Oscar Dancigers, Jaime A. Menasce) *sc* Emilio Fernández *c* Gabriel Figueroa *art dir* Manuel Fontanals *ed* Jorge Bustos *sd* James L. Fields, José B. Carles, Galdino Samperio *m* Antonio Díaz Conde
lp Columba Domínguez, Roberto Cañedo, Ismael

Pérez, Luis Aceves Castañeda, Guillermo Cramer, Manuel Dondé, Arturo Soto Rangel, Rogelio Fernández, Agustín Fernández

Fernández's last great film about provincial life focuses on the romantic struggles of the agrarian underclass. The peasant Aurelio Rodríguez (Cañedo) is released from prison and returns to his village. He learns that his mother has died and that his beloved Paloma (Domínguez) has been raped by his former friend, the evil Julio (Cramer), who was also responsible for his incarceration. Paloma now lives with her son Felipe (Pérez). Aurelio eventually overcomes Paloma's mistrust of men and they marry. However, the family is continuously besieged by Julio and his brother Ramiro (Castañeda). Aurelio kills them both in self-defence and goes on to enjoy a peaceful life with Paloma and Felipe. The film did not have pretensions beyond an aesthetic and musical depiction of a simple story and, though it did not receive great notoriety at home, it won an award at Cannes.

Salón México

1948 (released in 1949) 95 mins. b&w
d Emilio Fernández *p* Clasa Films Mundiales (Salvador Elizondo) *sc* Mauricio Magdaleno, Emilio Fernández *c* Gabriel Figueroa *art dir* Jesús Bracho *ed* Gloria Schoemann *sd* Rodolfo Solis, José de Pérez *m* Antonio Díaz Conde
lp Marga López, Miguel Inclán, Rodolfo Acosta, Roberto Cañedo, Mimí Derba, Carlos Músquiz, Fanny Schiller, Estela Matute, Silvia Derbez, José Torvay

Set in Mexico City, this film represents a thematic departure for Emilio Fernández, a director who had previously concentrated on pastoral, provincial settings. Amidst prospects of new prosperity, the story offers a bleak view of urban migration. Mercedes (López) is a *cabaretera* working in the Salón México. She lives with her pimp, the abusive Paco (Acosta), and works to pay for her younger sister Beatriz's (Derbez) studies in an elegant boarding school. Caught while committing a robbery, Paco hides out in Mercedes's room and she is arrested as an accomplice. While she is in jail, her policeman friend Lupe López (Inclán) visits Beatriz at school so that the girl won't suspect her sister's profession. Mercedes is eventually released and agrees to allow Beatriz and Roberto, a pilot of squadron 201 and son of the school principal, to marry. In the middle of a terrible fight, Mercedes and Paco shoot each other and die. Nightclub culture provides the focal point for Fernández's depiction of urban life, and popular music is featured throughout the film, including a spectacular performance by the Afro-Cuban group El Son Clave de Oro. The title of the film, as was that of an Aaron Copland suite, was taken from the original Mexico Saloon.

Aventurera

1949 (released in 1950) 111 mins. b&w
d Alberto Gout *p* Producciones Calderón (Pedro A. and Guillermo Calderón) *sc* Alvaro Custodio, adapted by Alvaro Custodio, Carlos Sampelayo *c* Alex Phillips *art dir* Manuel Fontanals *ed* Alfredo Rosas Priego *sd* Javier Mateos *m* Antonio Díaz Conde *songs* Agustín Lara, Alberto Domínguez
lp Ninón Sevilla, Tito Junco, Andrea Palma, Rubén Rojo, Miguel Inclán, Jorge Mondragón

Aventurera illustrates the shift in representations of women that took place at this time in Mexican cinema. Melodrama had traditionally held motherhood aloft as the unassailable symbol of family and morality, while the fallen woman was the figure of pathos. This film breaks with both conventions by portraying imperfect mothers alongside a woman whose strength lies in her street-smartness. The young Elena (played by the famous Cuban dancer Sevilla) discovers her mother with a lover. Her father commits suicide as a result. Elena looks for work, but in decent jobs the men try to take advantage of her. Working as a *cabaretera,* she is made drunk by a friend (Junco) and taken to a brothel owned by the hateful Rosaura (Palma) who also owns the cabaret. Elena manages to escape from the brothel and, although she runs into serious difficulties, it seems that she will finally be happy when the wealthy Mario (Rojo) proposes to her. When she meets Mario's mother, however, she turns out to be none other than Rosaura. Nevertheless, Elena and Mario marry, even after he learns of his mother's unsavoury activities. In the end, the couple leaves in an attempt to find happiness. The film features the noted Mexican singers Pedro Vargas and Los Panchos. The dance scenes were meant to be the film's biggest attraction even though *cabareteras* were socially condemned both off and on the screen.

El rey del barrio

1949 (released in 1950) 103 mins. b&w
d Gilberto Martínez Solares *p* As Films (Felipe Mier) *sc* Gilberto Martínez Solares, Juan García *c* Agustín Martínez Solares *art dir* Javier Torres Torija *ed* Jorge

Bustos *sd* Luis Fernández *m* Luis Hernández Bretón *lp* Germán Valdés 'Tin Tan', Silvia Pinal, Marcelo Chávez, Ismael Pérez, Juan García, Joaquín García 'Borolas', Ramón Valdés, Fanny Kaufman 'Vitola', Oscar Pulido

Although he is really the head of a band of pickpockets, Tin Tan pretends to be a railroad worker to his son and neighbours, helping his neighbours with the fruits of the gang's thievery. However, the young Carmelita (Pinal) refuses his help and goes to work in a cabaret. Tin Tan takes her away and asks her to help his son Pepito (Pérez) with schoolwork. Things get difficult when Tin Tan's 'business' begins to go awry, but in the end, he decides to go straight and becomes Carmelita's fiancé.

Crimen y castigo

aka *Crime and Punishment*
1950 120 mins. b&w
d Fernando de Fuentes *p* Filmes de Fuentes (Fernando de Fuentes) *sc* Paulino Masip from Dostoyevsky's novel *c* Jorge Stahl Jr *ed* Jorge Bustos *sd* Javier Mateos *art dir* Javier Torres Torija *m* Raúl Lavista
lp Roberto Cañedo, Lilia Prado, Carlos López Moctezuma, Luis Beristáin, Elda Peralta, Fanny Schiller, Lupe del Castillo, José Escanero

The ailing de Fuentes immediately followed his intense *Por la puerta falsa* with this atmospheric but fairly straight adaptation of the famous novel transposed to a Mexican setting. Raskolnokov has become Ramón Bernal (Cañedo) and the prostitute Sonia who eventually betrays him to the police is played by Prado. The victim is the greedy old woman and moneylender Lorenza (del Castillo).

Doña Perfecta

1950 (released in 1951) 120 mins. b&w
d Alejandro Galindo *p* Cabrera Films (Francisco de P. Cabrera) *sc* Alejandro Galindo, Iñigo de Martino, Francisco de P. Cabrera, Gunther Gerszo from Benito Pérez Galdós's novel *c* José Ortiz Ramos *art dir* Gunther Gerszo *ed* Fernando Martínez *sd* Manuel Topete, Galindo Samperio *m* Gustavo César Carrión
lp Dolores del Río, Esther Fernández, Carlos Navarro, Julio Villarreal, José Elías Moreno, Natalia Ortiz

In the late 19th century, the young engineer Pepe Rey (Navarro) arrives in Santa Fe to conduct some studies commissioned by the government. He lives in his Aunt Perfecta's (del Río) home, where he falls in love with his cousin Rosario (Fernández) who is afraid to speak to her mother about him. When Doña Perfecta discovers the relationship she misinterprets its nature and expels Pepe from her house. One night, Pepe goes back to the house to convince Rosario to elope, but he is killed by orders of Perfecta. Rosario curses her mother and leaves with the soldiers who remove Pepe's body.

En la palma de tu mano
1950 (released in 1951) 119 mins. b&w
d Roberto Gavaldón *p* Producciones Mier y Brooks (Felipe Mier, Oscar J. Brooks) *sc* Luis Spota, adapted by José Revueltas, Roberto Gavaldón *c* Alex Phillips *art dir* Francisco Marco Chillet *ed* Charles J. Kimball *sd* Rodolfo Benítez, Galdino Samperio *m* Raúl Lavista *songs* Juan Bruno Tarraza, Osvaldo Farrés *lp* Arturo de Córdova, Leticia Palma, Carmen Montejo, Ramón Gay, Consuelo Guerrero de Luna, Pascual García Peña, Manuel Arvide

The charlatan Jaime Karín (de Córdova) passes himself off as an astrologer to take advantage of the ladies who frequent the beauty salon where his wife works. The widow Ada (Palma) falls into his trap and confesses to 'professor' Karín that she and León (Gay), her nephew by marriage, poisoned her husband. Karín actually kills León and separates from his wife. Ada and Karín become allies, but they feel persecuted. The police question Karín, who confesses to his crime.

Por la puerta falsa
aka *The False Door*
1950 104 mins. b&w
d Fernando de Fuentes *p* Producciones Diana, Fernando de Fuentes *sc* Mauricio Magdaleno, Fernando de Fuentes from Mauricio Magdaleno's novel *Campo Celis c* Jorge Stahl Jr *ed* José W. Bustos *sd* Javier Mateos *art dir* Javier Torres Torija *m* Raúl Lavista
lp Pedro Armendáriz, Rita Macedo, Andrea Palma, Luis Beristáin, Ramón Gay, Antonio R. Frausto, José Muñoz, Pepe del Río, Enrique Díaz Indiano, Eduardo Vivas

Returning to the countryside for the best film of his later career, de Fuentes relied again on Mauricio Magdaleno, his trusted collaborator on *El compadre Mendoza* (1933). Emilio García Riera noted: 'The action is set just before the Revolution, since Porfirio

Díaz and General Bernardo Reyes were both said to be admirers of the pigs raised by staunchly independent rustics. The successful rustic in question, Bernardo Celis (Armendáriz), was known as brusque, even grotesque (at his engagement party, he horrifies his future wife and mother-in-law by imitating the pigs that made him rich). This character could be identified with other literary models where the man from humble beginnings, thanks to hard work and a strong will, becomes the hero of the rising bourgeoisie and can afford the luxury of buying even love. Nevertheless, Magdaleno and de Fuentes tend to see the main character as a lucky upstart of the same breed as *El compadre Mendoza,* and seem to share the same contempt for him shown by Adela (Macedo) and Abigaíl (Palma) in the film. ... Unfxortunately, one couldn't use Pedro Armendáriz in a film without giving some nobility to his character.'

Sensualidad
1950 (released in 1951) 101 mins. b&w
d Alberto Gout *p* Producciones Calderón (Pedro A. and Guillermo Calderón) *sc* Alvaro Custodio *c* Alex Phillips *art dir* Manuel Fontanals *ed* Alfredo Rosas Priego *sd* Enrique Rodríguez *m* Antonio Díaz Conde *lp* Fernando Soler, Ninón Sevilla, Domingo Soler, Rodolfo Acosta, Andrea Palma, Rubén Rojo, Andres Soler

A morality tale about the dangers represented by women to the guardians of the moral order. A prostitute, Aurora Ruiz (Sevilla), is sent to jail by judge Alejandro Luque (F. Soler). When she gets out, she takes revenge by seducing the judge. The judge falls in love with Aurora and even steals to please her. 'El Rizos' (Acosta), her accomplice, takes the judge's money and wounds him. Luque's son Raúl (Rojo) becomes involved in the affair to redeem his father, and courts Aurora in revenge. Luque asks his wife Eulalia for a divorce, but she dies unexpectedly. The judge kills 'El Rizos' only to discover that Aurora, the *cabaretera,* is about to elope with Raúl, and he strangles her, after which he is arrested.

El Suavecito
1950 (released in 1951) 89 mins. b&w
d Fernando Méndez *p* Cinematográfica Intercontinental (Raúl de Anda) *sc* Gabriel Ramírez Osante *c* Manuel Gómez Urquiza *ed* Carlos Savage *sd* Francisco Alcayde *art dir* Jorge Fernández *m* Gustavo César Carrión
lp Victor Parra, Aurora Segura, Dagoberto

Rodríguez, Enrique del Castillo, Gilberto González, Manuel Dondé, Eduardo Arozamena, Federico Curiel

The veteran Méndez, better known for his stylish horror films *Ladrón de cadáveres* (1956) and *El vampiro* (1957), turned his attention to gangsters with this melodrama in which the pimp Roberto, known as El Suavecito (Parra), and a taxi driver (Rodríguez) vie for the attentions of young Lupita (Segura) who looks after her disabled father. The ruthless Roberto, who lives with his mother while exploiting prostitutes in Acapulco and working for the gang boss El Nene (del Castillo), arranges for the taxi driver to lose his car during a gambling session and then frames him for a crime. In the end, however, the poor taxi driver and Lupita are united.

Víctimas del pecado
1950 (released in 1951) 85 mins. b&w
d Emilio Fernández *p* Producciones Calderón (Pedro A. Calderón) *sc* Emilio Fernández, Mauricio Magdaleno *c* Gabriel Figueroa *art dir* Manuel Fontanals *ed* Gloria Schoemann *sd* Enrique Rodríguez *m* Antonio Díaz Conde
lp Ninón Sevilla, Tito Junco, Rodolfo Acosta, Ismael Pérez, Rita Montaner, Margarita Ceballos, Francisco Reiguera, Carlos Riquelme

Rodolfo (Acosta), a pachuco, takes back the *cabaretera* Rosa on the condition that she leave her newborn son in a dustbin. Violeta (Sevilla), a friend from the cabaret, picks up the baby from the garbage, names him Juanito (Pérez) and brings him up as her own even though she is fired from the cabaret and must work on the street. There she meets Santiago (Junco), who takes her to his cabaret to work as a dancer and helps her to find a boarding school for her child. Rodolfo kills Santiago. Violeta kills Rodolfo when he tries to hit the child and she goes to jail. Meanwhile, Juanito sells newspapers and shines shoes. The prison warden is moved by Violeta's plight and arranges a presidential pardon. Violeta is freed and reunited with Juanito.

Cárcel de mujeres
aka *Women's Prison*
1951 98 mins. b&w
d Miguel M. Delgado *p* Internacional Cinematográfica *sc* Rogelio Barriga Rivas, adapted by Mauricio Magdaleno, Max Aub *c* Raúl Martínez Solares *ed* Jorge Bustos *sd* Rodolfo Benítez *art dir* Gunther Gerszo *m* Raúl Lavista
lp Miroslava, Sara Montiel, Luis Beristáin, María

Douglas, Tito Junco, Katy Jurado, Emma Roldán, Mercedes Soler, Elda Peralta

Delgado's contribution to the murky 'women in prison' exploitation genre starts with a pre-credit sequence in the best film noir tradition: the gloved hand of a woman shoots a gun and a man falls dead as the credits appear. The rest of the story is a voyeuristic and moralising melodrama featuring the blonde Evangelina (Miroslava), a respectable and much-loved wife imprisoned for killing the boyfriend of Dora (Montiel), who also happens to be an inmate. Dora later gives birth and all the jailed women are shown giving free reign to their maternal instincts. The drama culminates during a jailbreak involving both women.

Dos tipos de cuidado
1952 (released in 1953) 123 mins. b&w
d Ismael Rodríguez *p* Tele Voz (Miguel Alemán Jr, David Negrete) *sc* Ismael Rodríguez, Carlos Orellana *c* Gabriel Figueroa *art dir* José Rodríguez Granada *ed* Gloria Schoemann *sd* José B. Carles *m* Manuel Esperón
lp Jorge Negrete, Pedro Infante, José Elías Moreno, Carmen González, Yolanda Varela, Mimí Derba, Carlos Orellana, Queta Lavat

Rural *(ranchera)* comedy about Pedro (Infante) and Jorge (Negrete) who are in love with two girls. Pedro is rejected by María (Varela) but Rosario (González) welcomes Jorge's attentions. Jorge leaves town; when he returns a year later, he finds Pedro married to Rosario and with a daughter. Jorge feels betrayed and, out of spite, courts another girl. In the end, Jorge learns the truth: Pedro married Rosario out of kindness after she was raped during a trip to Mexico City and became pregnant. Pedro and Jorge are reconciled and each remains with their partner.

El rebozo de Soledad
1952 123 mins. b&w
d Roberto Gavaldón *p* STPC/Cinematográfica Tele-Voz (Miguel Alemán Jr) *sc* Javier Ferrer, adapted by José Revueltas, Roberto Gavaldón *c* Gabriel Figueroa *art dir* Salvador Lozano Mena *ed* Charles L. Kimball *sd* José B. Carles *m* Francisco Domínguez
lp Arturo de Córdova, Pedro Armendáriz, Stella Inda, Domingo Soler, Carlos López Moctezuma, Rosaura Revueltas, José Baviera, Gilberto González, Jaime Fernández

Alberto (de Córdova), a doctor, arrives in the city for

an interview at a hospital where there is a good job opening. He receives a package from his village that includes a letter from the local priest telling him about Soledad (Inda), a young girl who was in love with him, but who came to an unhappy end. The doctor goes to the interview where his future will be decided, but refuses the job he is offered, considering it superfluous and unimportant. Knowing that his presence is vital in the village, he decides to return.

Un rincón cerca del cielo
aka *A Corner Close to Heaven*
1952 120 mins. b&w
d Rogelio A. González *p* Filmex (Gregorio Wallerstein, Antonio Matouk) *sc* Rogelio A. González from a story by Rogelio A. González and Mauricio Wall (Gregorio Wallerstein) *c* Agustín Martínez Solares *ed* Rafael Ceballos *sd* Rodolfo Benítez, Jesús González Gancy *art dir* Jorge Fernández *m* Manuel Esperón
lp Pedro Infante, Marga López, Silvia Pinal, Andrés Soler, Tony Aguilar, Luis Aceves Castañeda, Juan Orraca, Arturo Martínez, Julio Ahuet, María Gentil Arcos

A relentless melodrama about the poor Pedro González (Infante) who lives with his wife (López) and son in a small room in the urban jungle. Refusing dishonest employment, he eventually finds work as a street clown. But when his son falls ill, he is reduced to beggary. Failing to obtain the required medicine in time, the son dies. Pedro tries to commit suicide, but his hopes are revived by the announcement that his wife is expecting another son. The film was made at the same time as *Ahora soy rico* by the same director and crew.

Espaldas mojadas
aka *Wetbacks*
1953 (released in 1955) 116 mins. b&w
d Alejandro Galindo *p* ATA Films (José Elvira), Atlas Films (Manuel Jasso Rojas) *sc* Alejandro Galindo *c* Rosalío Solano *art dir* Edward Fitzgerald *ed* Carlos Savage *sd* Rodolfo Solís, Jesús González Gancy *m* Jorge Pérez, popular songs
lp David Silva, Victor Parra, Martha Valdés, Oscar Pulido, José Elías Moreno, Pedro Vargas, Carolina Barret, Alicia Malvido, Eulalio González 'Piporro', Lola Beltrán

Made to discourage prospective immigrants from going north, *Wetbacks* depicts the inhumane working and living conditions of Mexicans who illegally entered the USA after the Second World War. In the border town of Ciudad Juárez, Rafael (Silva) does not have the necessary papers to cross into the USA as a *bracero*, so he crosses the Río Bravo with a group of 'wetbacks'. Always running from the police, Rafael works one job after another. When he stands up for a compatriot, he gets into a fight with Sterling (Parra), his North American boss. He runs away, meets the *pocha* (Mexican-American) María Consuelo (Valdés) and proposes to her. Rafael crosses the river and meets up with Sterling in Ciudad Juárez. He fights him and, with the aid of some Mexican friends, throws him into the river. The US border guards mistake Sterling for a wetback, and kill him. Rafael and María go off together into the Mexican countryside, returning to their roots to overcome their marginal status and to regain a sense of identity.

Raíces
(four episodes: Las vacas, Nuestra señora, El tuerto and La potranca)
1953 (released in 1955) 103 mins. b&w
d Benito Alazraki *p* Teleproducciones (Manuel Barbachano Ponce) *sc* Carlos Velo, Benito Alazraki, Manuel Barbachano Ponce, María Elena Lazo, Jomí García Ascot, Fernando Espejo from the stories of Francisco Rojas González *c* Ramón Muñoz *(Prologue)*, Walter Reuter *(Las vacas, El tuerto, La potranca)*, Hans Beimler *(Nuestra señora)* *ed* Luis Sobreyra, Miguel Campos *sd* Adolfo de la Riva, Galdino Samperio *m* Silvestre Revueltas *(Prologue)*, Guillermo Noriega *(Las vacas)*, Rodolfo Halffter *(Nuestra señora)* Blas Galindo *(El tuerto)*, Pablo L. Moncayo *(La potranca)*
lp Las vacas: Beatríz Flores, Juan de la Cruz, Conchita Montes, Eduardo Urruchúa; *Nuestra señora*: Olimpia Alazraki, Dr González, Juan Hernández; *El tuerto*: Miguel Angel Negrón, Antonia Hernández, Mario Herrera; *La potranca*: Alicia del Lago, Carlos Robles Gil, Teódulo González, Laura Holt

Filmed in Mezquital (Hidalgo), in the archaeological area of Tajín (Veracruz), and in Chiapas and Yucatán, with amateur actors from these regions. Four stories that in different ways attempt to explain the indigenous way of life and its problems of hunger, dignity, faith and honesty.

La red
1953 83 mins. b&w
d Emilio Fernández *p* Reforma Films (Salvador

Elizondo) *sc* Emilio Fernández, Neftalí Beltrán
c Alex Phillips *art dir* Jesús Bracho *ed* Jorge Bustos
sd Luis Fernández, Rafael Ruiz Esparza *m* Antonio
Díaz Conde
lp Rossana Podestá, Crox Alvarado, Armando
Silvestre, Guillermo Cramer, Carlos Riquelme,
Margarito Luna, Armando Velasco

José Luis (Silvestre), a sailor, holds up a customs post
with Antonio (Alvarado). He is wounded and asks
his accomplice to take care of Rossana (Podestá).
Antonio and Rossana become lovers on a deserted
beach. Later, José Luis joins them and the three of
them live by gathering sponges. Rossana's
charms cause problems between the men and
Antonio, feeling betrayed, kills her before he is killed
by the police. José Luis walks into the sea carrying
Rossana's corpse.

Después de la tormenta
aka *After the Storm*
1955 95 mins. b&w
d Roberto Gavaldón *p* PYDASA, Filmadora Argel
(Emilio Tuero) *sc* Roberto Gavaldón, Julio Alejandro
from Alejandro's story *El otro hermano* *c* Raúl
Martínez Solares *ed* Carlos Savage *sd* Manuel Topete
art dir Edward Fitzgerald *m* Gonzalo Curiel
lp Marga López, Lilia Prado, Ramón Gay, José Luis
Jiménez, Prudencia Grifell, Pepito Romay

Melodrama set on the Isla de Lobos, Wolf Island,
where the twin brothers Melchor and Rafael (both
played by Gay) man the lighthouse. Melchor is
married to Rosa (López) and his brother to María
(Prado), but the latter is attracted to her brother-in-
law. When the twins get caught in a storm on the
high seas, only one of them survives, but nobody
except the man's wife can tell which one it is.
Nevertheless, that night he goes to bed with the
'other wife'. When the second twin reappears the next
day, having survived after all, the fraught passions
eventually burst into the open, and the rapidly
deteriorating Melchor is shot by his wife. Rosa
spends the rest of her days atoning for her deed by
looking after children suffering from leprosy. The
film is told in flashback.

La escondida
1955 (released in 1956) 100 mins. colour
d Roberto Gavaldón *p* Alfa Films (Samuel Alazraki)
sc Miguel N. Lira, adapted by José Revueltas,
Gunther Gerszo, Roberto Gavaldón *c* Gabriel
Figueroa *art dir* Gunther Gerszo *ed* Jorge Bustos *sd*

Javier Mateos, Galdino Samperio *m* Raúl Lavista
songs Cuco Sánchez, M. Hoyos, Ramiro Hernández
lp María Félix, Pedro Armendáriz, Andrés Soler,
Arturo Martínez, Domingo Soler, Jorge Martínez de
Hoyos, Carlos Agosti, Sara Guash, Miguel Manzano,
Carlos Riquelme

The peasant woman Gabriela (Félix) becomes the
lover of General Garza (A. Soler) even though she has
always loved Felipe (Armendáriz), a Maderista soldier
who used to be a peasant. Later Gabriela meets up
with him and asks his forgiveness. At first, he rejects
her, but eventually forgives her and they go off to live
together. Later Felipe and Gabriela must separate for
a few days and on his return, he finds her dead.

¡Torero!
1956 (released in 1957) 80 mins. b&w
d Carlos Velo *p* Producciones Barbachano Ponce
(Manuel Barbachano Ponce) *sc* Hugo Mozo (Hugo
Butler), Carlos Velo *c* Ramón Muñoz *ed* Miguel
Campos, Luis Sobreyra *sd* Adolfo de la Riva
m Rodolfo Halffter *songs* Pepe Guízar,
Lorenzo Barcelata
lp Luis Procuna, his brother Angel, his wife Consuelo
and his children Luis, Carmen, Aurora, Flor and
Angel; Antonio Fayat, Paco Malgesto, Antonio
Sevilla, Ponciano Díaz, the bullfighters Manuel
Rodríguez 'Manolete', Alfonso Ramírez 'el Calesero',
Lorenzo Garza, Carlos Arruza

Drama-documentary recounting one day in the life of
the bullfighter Luis Procuna. The interludes about the
early life of the bullfighter are historical reconstructions.

El vampiro
1957 96 mins. b&w
d Fernando Méndez *p* Cinematográfica ABSA (Abel
Salazar) *sc* Ramón Obón *c* Rosalío Solano *art dir*
Gunther Gerszo *ed* José Bustos *sd* Rafael Ruiz Esparza
m Gustavo César Carrión
lp Abel Salazar, Ariadna Welter, Carmen Montejo, José
Luis Jiménez, Germán Robles, Mercedes Soler, Alicia
Montoya, José Chávez, Julio Daneri, Armando Zumaya

Made a year before Terence Fisher's *Dracula* (1958),
Méndez's film refers more to Tod Browning's 1931
version. The Hungarian Count Karol de Lavud
(Robles) buys a property called Sicomoros in the
Sierra Negra. It is inhabited by the lugubrious Eloisa
(Montejo), Emilio (Jiménez) and María Teresa
(Montoya). The latter is being buried when her niece
Marta (Welter) and Dr Enrique (Salazar) arrive. That

same day, Mr Duval aka Lavud receives a coffin. Mr Duval appears in Marta's room and manages to suck her blood. One more bite and she will become a vampire. In the morning, the girl seems to be dead, but Enrique gives her an injection and revives her. María Teresa, who is 'undead', at various moments intervenes to save the young couple and she finishes off Eloisa. Duval kidnaps Marta, but Enrique pursues them through subterranean crypts and saves her, burying a stake in Lavud's chest. The film achieves a funereal lyricism with expertly choreographed camerawork and suitably atmospheric sets. The transformation of vampires into bats is done by way of straight, but well-timed, cuts: in one scene, two vampires continue their dialogue uninterrupted as the transformation takes place. Montejo is excellent as the passionate spinster for whom vampirism represents sensual liberation. In 1968, an American version of the film was released, lacking c.20 mins. of the original and adding 9 mins. of new material.

El esqueleto de la señora Morales
1959 (released in 1960) 92 mins. b&w
d Rogelio A. González *p* Alfa Films (Sergio Kogan) *sc* Luis Alcoriza from Arthur Machen's novel *The Mystery of Islington c* Victor Herrera *art dir* Edward Fitzgerald *ed* Jorge Bustos *sd* Luis Fernández, Galdino Samperio *m* Raúl Lavista
lp Arturo de Córdova, Amparo Rivelles, Elda Peralta, Guillermo Orea, Rosenda Monteros, Luis Aragón, Mercedes Pascual

A black comedy about a repressed taxidermist Pablo (de Córdova) who is married to Gloria (Rivelles), a castrating invalid. He makes fun of her religious beliefs while she impedes and criticises everything he does. Pablo gets tired of the asphyxiating relationship with his wife and decides to murder her. The deed accomplished, he masterfully disposes of the body to make it appear that she went away, but everyone suspects that he killed her although no one can prove it. He is tried and found not guilty, but fate plays a cruel joke on Pablo when he accidentally drinks the same poison that killed Gloria.

Macario
1959 (released in 1960) 91 mins. b&w
d Roberto Gavaldón *p* Clasa Films Mundiales (Armando Orive Alva) *sc* Bruno Traven from the Brothers Grimm, adapted by Emilio Carballido and Roberto Gavaldón *c* Gabriel Figueroa *art dir* Manuel Fontanals *ed* Gloria Schoemann *sd* Jesús González

Gancy, Galdino Samperio *m* Raúl Lavista
lp Ignacio López Tarso, Pina Pellicer, Enrique Lucero, Mario Alberto Rodríguez, Enrique García Alvarez, Eduardo Fajardo

This film was so effective in its cinematic rendering of magical realism that the story was often mistaken for an ancient Mexican folktale. In 18th century colonial Mexico, the poor woodsman Macario (López Tarso) decides not to eat until he has a turkey all for himself. He finally gets one and goes off to the forest with the bird, refusing to share with either God or the Devil, but not with Death (Lucero). He makes a pact with Death that brings him luck via a miraculous liquid. Nevertheless, he falls into the hands of the Inquisition and is condemned to burn at the stake. He can only be saved if he heals the son of the viceroy, but the child dies. Macario escapes. His wife (Pellicer) discovers his body next to the untouched cadaver of the turkey. Figueroa's dramatic cinematography hauntingly visualises the world of the dead, so prevalent in the imagery of Mexico.

El pecado de una madre
aka *A Mother's Sin*
1960 90 mins. b&w
d Alfonso Corona Blake *p* Producciones Brooks (Oscar J. Brooks) *sc* Julio Alejandro from a story by Fernando Galiana *c* Lauron 'Jack' Draper *ed* Gloria Schoemann *sd* Rodolfo Solís *art dir* Jorge Fernández *m* Manuel Esperón
lp Libertad Lamarque, Dolores del Río, Pedro Geraldo, Enrique Rambal, Teresa Velázquez, Alejandro Ciangherotti, Eduardo Alcaraz, Luis Manuel Pelayo, Antonio Brillas, Javier Gómez

Corona Blake is best known for horror films, often featuring masked wrestlers, and melodramas. The successful singer Ana Maria Alvear (Lamarque) and her beloved Gustavo (Rambal) have a baby although Gustavo is still married to another woman, Gabriela (del Río). While driving to Acapulco, the couple's car crashes killing Gustavo and paralysing Ana Maria. Gustavo's legitimate wife, Gabriela, comes and claims her husband's son. When twenty years later the boy, also called Gustavo (Geraldo) has become a famous singer and Ana Maria has recovered, she takes a job in the spoiled youngster's theatrical company in order to be near him. The drama erupts when, unaware that he is addressing his real mother, the boy fires her from the company. Gabriela offers to tell all, but Ana María refuses. Years later, now fully informed, the boy finds his mother in the streets and she dies in his arms.

La sombra del caudillo

1960 (released in 1990) 129 mins. b&w
d Julio Bracho *p* STPC *sc* Julio Bracho, Jesús
Cárdenas from Martín Luis Guzmán's novel *c*
Agustín Jiménez *art dir* Jorge Fernández, Roberto
Silva *ed* Jorge Bustos *sd* Ernesto Caballero
m Raúl Lavista
lp Tito Junco, Tomás Perrín, Bárbara Gil, Miguel
Ángel Ferriz, Ignacio López Tarso, Carlos López
Moctezuma, Victor Manuel Mendoza, Kitty de
Hoyos, José Elías Moreno

A 'damned' film in Mexican cinema, it was not
released until thirty years after its production. It was
administratively censored, but its flaming political
content was the cause of its prohibition. The film
deals with the corrupt relations among a group of
military men, ex-Revolutionaries who occupy high
government posts and betray each other while
attempting to win the presidency. What scandalised
those in power was that the film was based on fact.

Yanco

1960 95 mins. b&w
d Servando González *p* Producciones Yanco
(Servando González, Miguel González) *sc* Jesús
Marín from a story by Servando González *c*
Alex Phillips Jr *ed* Fernando Martínez *m* Gustavo
César Carrión
lp Ricardo Ancona, Jesús Medina, María Bustamente

Independently produced, González's first feature film
is a mythic tale. Yanco (Ancona), a boy whose father
died in the Revolution, lives in Xochimilco with his
ailing mother (Bustamente). Mocked by other
children for his attempts to play a makeshift violin,
Yanco learns to play from an old man (Medina).
When the old man dies, his violin is placed in a store
window. Every night Yanco steals the violin from the
window to play it, returning it each morning to the
store. The townspeople believe the night music to be
a kind of magic. On the Night of the Dead, they go
in search of the music's source and find only the
violin floating in a whirlpool.

En el balcón vacío

1961 (released in 1962) 70 mins. (16mm) b&w
d Jomí García Ascot *p* Ascot/Torre N.C. *sc* María
Luisa Elío, adapted by María Luisa Elío, Jomí
García Ascot, Emilio García Riera *c* José María
Torre *ed* Jomí García Ascot, Jorge Espejel *sd*

Rodolfo Quintero *m* Bach, Tomás Bretón, popular
Spanish music
lp Nuri Pereña, María Luisa Elío, Conchita Genovés,
Jaime Muñoz de Baena, Belina García, Fernando
Lipkau, José Luis González de León, Esteban
Martínez, José de la Colina, Alicia Bergua

Independent production filmed on weekends
throughout a year. Gabriela Elizondo, a Spanish
refugee in Mexico, remembers her childhood
beginning with her father's disappearance during the
Spanish Civil War, her escape to France and her
arrival in Mexico. Time has passed, her mother
(Genovés) has died, and she has become a woman.
She returns to her childhood home and cries over her
solitude. The lead is played by Pereña as a girl and
María Luisa Elío as an adult.

Los hermanos del Hierro

1961 101 mins. b&w
d Ismael Rodríguez *p* Filmex (Gregorio Wallerstein)
sc Ricardo Garibay, adapted by Ismael Rodríguez *c*
Rosalío Solano *art dir* Jorge Fernández *ed* Rafael
Ceballos *sd* Rodolfo Benítez, Enrique Rodríguez *m*
Raúl Lavista *songs* Jesús Gaytán, Rubén Fuentes,
Eduviges Sánchez, Felipe Valdés
lp Antonio Aguilar, Julio Alemán, Columba
Domínguez, Patricia Conde, Pedro Armendáriz,
Emilio Fernández, David Silva, José Elías Moreno,
Ignacio López Tarso, David Reynoso,
Eduardo Noriega

Reynaldo del Hierro (Aguilar) and his brother
Martín (Alemán) ride with their father (Noriega) in
the countryside, where he is wounded by an
anonymous bullet and dies. Their mother
(Domínguez) teaches the children how to use
firearms with the hope that they will seek revenge.
When Reynaldo and Martín grow up, they meet their
father's killer and Martín, the youngest, kills him.
Afterwards he becomes a well-known hired killer,
which causes the family many problems. Because
they have many enemies, both brothers
are persecuted and die at the hands of a group
of soldiers.

Rosa Blanca

aka *The White Rose*
1961 (released in 1972) 100 mins. b&w
d Roberto Galvaldón *p* Clasa Films Mundiales
(Felipe Subervielle) *sc* Phil Stevenson, Emilio
Carballido, Roberto Gavaldón from a novel by
Bruno Traven *c* Gabriel Figueroa *art dir* Edward

Fitzgerald *sd* José B. Carles, Galdino Samperio *ed* Gloria Schoemann *m* Raúl Lavista

lp Ignacio López Tarso, Christiane Martel, Reinhold Olszewski, Rita Macedo, Begoña Palacios, Carlos Fernández, Luis Beristáin, John Kelly

Certain topics in Mexican history have not tolerated criticism and consequently have been considered taboo by film-makers. Among them is the period in the 30s when vast tracts of agricultural land were appropriated by powerful oil interests. This film broached that issue and was banned in Mexico until 1972. It remains one of the most notable cases of censorship in Mexico, in part because of Gavaldón's status as an established commercial director. The film is based on a story by Bruno Traven about Jacinto Yáñez (López Tarso), the proud owner of a rich farm. Despite offers he receives from multinational companies, he is a firm proponent of agricultural development and refuses to sell his land. The oil companies devise a duplicitous plan to obtain the land anyway by inviting Yáñez to the USA. When Yáñez proves recalcitrant, he disappears. Without him, the man's family is vulnerable to the companies and they lose their land.

Tlayucan
1961 (released in 1962) 103 mins. b&w
d Luis Alcoriza *p* Producciones Matouk (Antonio Matouk) *sc* Luis Alcoriza from a story by Jesús 'Murciélago' Velázquez *c* Rosalío Solano *art dir* Jesús Bracho *ed* Carlos Savage *sd* Javier Mateos, Enrique Rodríguez *m* Sergio Guerrero

lp Julio Aldama, Norma Angélica, Jorge Martínez de Hoyos, Andrés Soler, Anita Blanch, Noé Murayama, Dolores Camarillo, Pancho Córdova, Juan Carlos Ortiz, José Gálvez

In Tlayucan, Chabela (Angélica) and her husband Eufemio Zárate (Aldama), a humble peasant, are happy until their son Nicolás (Ortiz) falls ill and they have no money for medicines. In desperation, Chabela asks the dirty old man Tomás (Soler) for money. In return, Tomás demands that she sleep with him, which she refuses. To obtain money, Eufemio steals a pearl from a statue in a church, but loses it. The townspeople suspect him of the theft and he is imprisoned. They force Tomás to pay for Nicolás's treatments and Eufemio is freed for lack of proof. He finds the pearl and puts it back on the statue. The priest (de Hoyos) announces a miracle.

Días de otoño
aka *Days of Autumn*

1962 98 mins. b&w
d Roberto Gavaldón *p* Clasa Films Mundiales (Felipe Subervielle) *sc* Julio Alejandro, Emilio Carballido based on Bruno Traven's story *Frustration c* Gabriel Figueroa *art dir* Manuel Fontanals *sd* Jesús González Gancy *ed* Gloria Schoemann *m* Raúl Lavista

lp Pina Pellicer, Ignacio López Tarso, Evangelina Elizondo, Adriana Roel, Luis Lomelí, Graciela Doring

Following on from *Macario* (1959) and the controversial *Rosa Blanca* (1961), this is the last of Gavaldón's Bruno Traven trilogy. A provincial young woman, Luisa (Pellicer), comes to the big city to look for work. She gets a job as a cake decorator, which is appropriate enough since she also has a talent for embellishing the truth. When her boyfriend (Lomelí) walks out, her imagination takes flight as she invents a new boyfriend, then a marriage, a honeymoon and even a false pregnancy. When her world of delusions comes crashing down, at least her co-workers still love her, or so she thinks.

Tiburoneros
aka *Shark Hunters*
1962 (released in 1963) 94 mins. b&w
d Luis Alcoriza *p* Producciones Matouk (Antonio Matouk) *sc* Luis Alcoriza *c* Raúl Martínez Solares *art dir* Jesús Bracho *ed* Carlos Savage *sd* Luis Fernández, Enrique Rodríguez *m* Sergio Guerrero

lp Julio Aldama, Dacia González, David del Carpio, Tito Junco, Amanda del Llano, Eric del Castillo, Alfredo Varela Jr, Noé Murayama, Enrique Lucero, Conchita Gentil Arcos, Irma Serrano

This film challenged the prevailing cinematic stereotype that the city is sinful and the province virtuous. Director Alcoriza, who wrote screenplays for Buñuel, made this realistic film about a fisherman trying to juggle his divided loyalties between two polarised locales. Contrary to typical melodramas, Aurelio is not bolstered by sacrifice, but by pleasure. Neither the labour relations in the province, nor the ethics of its inhabitants are idealised. The story tells of the hard-working shark hunter Aurelio Gómez (Aldama) living off the coast of Tabasco. He is well regarded by the other fishermen, earns the money he needs and is happy with his young lover Manuela (González). His children and legitimate wife (Serrano) live in the city and ask him to return, since they haven't seen him in several years. He goes back, leaving behind an angry Manuela and 'Pigua' (del Carpio), her small friend. However, Aurelio has a hard time adjusting to the city and to his family. He tires of the passivity of the city and decides to return to the sea and his former friends.

En este pueblo no hay ladrones
aka *In This Town, There Are No Thieves*
1964 (released in 1965) 90 mins. b&w
d Alberto Isaac *p* Grupo Claudio (Alberto Isaac) *sc* Alberto Isaac, Emilio García Riera from a story by Gabriel García Márquez *c* Carlos Carbajal *art dir* Guadalupe Jara *ed* Carlos Savage *sd* Luis Fernández *m* Nacho Méndez
lp Julián Pastor, Rocío Sagaón, Graciela Enríquez, Luis Vicens, Antonio Alcalá, Alfonso Arau, Luis Buñuel, Héctor Ortega, Juan Rulfo, Abel Quezada, Leonora Carrington, José Luis Cuevas, Carlos Monsiváis, María Luisa Mendoza, Ernesto García Cabral, Arturo Ripstein, Elda Peralta, Gabriel García Márquez, Emilio García Riera, Alberto Isaac

Dámaso (Pastor), a loafer kept by his wife Ana (Sagaón), steals the balls of a quiet town's only billiards table. His theft causes chaos within the community and does not benefit him. Disillusioned, Dámaso returns the balls to the table. Gabriel García Márquez's story explores the effects of provincialism at its most extreme. Critically acclaimed as a crossroads in the formation of a new Mexican cinema, this experimental film is also notable for cameo appearances by a long list of prestigious artists and intellectuals.

La fórmula secreta
aka *The Secret Formula*
1964 (released in 1965) 45 mins. b&w
d Rubén Gámez *p* Salvador López O. *sc* Rubén Gámez, with texts by Juan Rulfo read by Jaime Sabines *c* Rubén Gámez *ed* Rubén Gámez *sd* Galdino Samperio *m* Vivaldi, Stravinsky, Leobardo Velázquez
lp Pilar Islas, José Castillo, José Tirado, Pablo Balderas, José González, Fernando Rosales, Leonor Islas, Francisco Corona, Guadalupe Arriaga, José M. Delgado

Metaphorical images of Mexican society organised into a poetic essay. The collage combines allegories of religious traditions, the *caciquismo* imposed upon peasants, national identity, and workers' exploitation. These reflections are presented with a macabre sense of humour, the result of the fusion of modern and ancient Mexico and the alienating presence of transnationals. Along with *En este pueblo no hay ladrones,* this experimental work signalled a new

course for independent film-making in the 60s.

El gallo de oro
aka *The Golden Cock*
1964 108 mins. colour
d Roberto Gavaldón *p* Clasa Films Mundiales (Manuel Barbachano Ponce) *sc* Juan Rulfo, adapted by Carlos Fuentes, Gabriel García Márquez and Roberto Gavaldón *c* Gabriel Figueroa *art dir* Manuel Fontanals *ed* Gloria Schoemann *sd* Luis Fernández *m* Chucho Zarzosa
lp Ignacio López Tarso, Lucha Villa, Narciso Busquets, Carlos Jordán, Agustín Isunza, Enrique Lucero, Agustín Fernández, Lina Marín

Luck alone determines destiny in this film based on Juan Rulfo's magical-realist story. Director Gavaldón uses the cock fights, spatially and thematically, as a metaphor for Mexico's social organisation, assertions of authority and virility masking a world that actually operates by chance. Dionisio Pinzón (López Tarso) is a poor town crier in a village. He rescues a dying golden rooster at a feast and nurses him back to health. The rooster goes on to win many cock-fights. Afterwards, Dionisio meets the powerful *gallero* Don Lorenzo (Busquets) and his lover, the singer Bernarda (Villa), alias 'La Caponera'. Don Lorenzo and Dionisio become partners and both profit from the relationship. 'La Caponera' feels neglected by Don Lorenzo and seduces Dionisio, but she continues to despise him. Don Lorenzo loses both his talismans, 'La Caponera' and Dionisio, the latter returning to his town, alone and poor.

Tiempo de morir
aka *Time to Die*
1965 (released in 1966) 90 mins. b&w
d Arturo Ripstein *p* Alameda Films (Cesar Santos Galindo, Alfredo Ripstein Jr) *sc* Gabriel García Márquez, adapted by Gabriel García Márquez, Carlos Fuentes *c* Alex Phillips *art dir* Salvador Lozano Mena *ed* Carlos Savage *sd* Jesus González, Galdino Samperio, Reinaldo Portillo *m* Carlos Jiménez Mabarak
lp Marga López, Jorge Martínez de Hoyos, Enrique Rocha, Blanca Sánchez, Tito Junco, Quintín Bulnes, Miguel Macía, Hortensia Santoreña, Carlos Jordán, Carolina Barret

Ripstein's first feature is in the tradition of the Western and concentrates on a middle-aged man, according to the director, in order to distinguish himself from his colleagues in the 'new wave' who focused on youth culture. Juan Sáyago (de Hoyos) returns to his village after eighteen years in prison, ready to begin a new life with Mariana Sampedro (López), his now-widowed former fiancée, but he cannot achieve his goal because the sons of the man he killed seek revenge. First, Juan opts to ignore their taunts. Later, realising that he has no future since they will not leave him alone, he decides to duel with them.

Los caifanes

(Five episodes: *Los caifanes, Las variedades de los caifanes, Quien escoje su suerte y el tiempo para exprimirla, Las camas del amor eterno* and *Se le perdió la paloma al marrascapache*)
1966 (released in 1967) 95 mins. colour
d Juan Ibáñez *p* Estudios América, Cinematográfica Marte (J. Fernando Pérez Gavilán, Mauricio Wallerstein) *sc* Carlos Fuentes, Juan Ibáñez *c* Fernando Alvarez Garcés 'Colín' *ed* J.J. Mungía *sd* Heinrich Henkel, Ricardo Saldívar *m* Mariano Ballesté, Fernando Vilches
lp Julissa, Enrique Alvarez Félix, Sergio Jiménez, Oscar Chávez, Ernesto Gómez Cruz, Eduardo López Rojas, Tamara Garina, Carlos Monsiváis, Ignacio Vallarta, Julien de Meriche

The grotesque nocturnal activities of a group of lower-class youngsters who accidentally join ranks with an upper-middle class couple. They joyride through the city together without paying attention to social conventions. Ultimately, however, social prejudices end the friendship among rich and poor and cause the breakup of the couple.

Pedro Páramo

1966 108 mins. b&w
d Carlos Velo *p* Clasa Films Mundiales, Producciones Barbachano Ponce (Manuel Barbachano Ponce, Federico Amérigo) *sc* Carlos Fuentes, Carlos Velo, Manuel Barbachano Ponce from a novel by Juan Rulfo *c* Gabriel Figueroa *art dir* Manuel Fontanals, Julio Alejandro *sd* José B. Carles, Galdino Samperio *ed* Gloria Schoemann *m* Joaquín Gutiérrez Heras
lp John Gavin, Ignacio López Tarso, Pilar Pellicer, Julissa, Graciela Doring, Carlos Fernández, Alfonso Arau, Roberto Cañedo, Jorge Rivero, Narciso Busquets, Augusto Benedico

Juan Rulfo's novel *Pedro Páramo* precipitated the Latin American literary boom of the 60s and was tremendously influential on that movement's articulation of a continental cultural identity. Inspired

by his recently deceased mother, Juan (Fernández) returns to Comala to seek out his estranged father, Pedro Páramo (Gavin). Juan finds Comala deserted, but his family history is spun by ghosts of women who emerge from the shadows of this abandoned town. Juan learns that his father was a notorious scoundrel and a ruthless landowner whose insatiable greed ravaged the region. Pedro Páramo even evaded the Revolution. In a gesture that fuses Juan's magical narrative with the realistic, historical narrative of his father, Pedro is killed by one of his many illegitimate sons and the only character who appears, unchanged, in both narrative realms. Páramo's death signals both revenge for those he wronged and the triumph of a new nation. However, Juan has already been swallowed up by the earth in Comala's graveyard. Myth and history no longer exist in pure form but have been forged into an idealistic realism which is haunted by the tyrannical patrimony of its past.

La soldadera

1966 (released in 1967) 85 mins. b&w
d José Bolaños *p* Producciones Marte, Técnicos Mexicanos, Jorge Durán Chávez *sc* José Bolaños *c* Alex Phillips *art dir* Roberto Silva *ed* Carlos Savage *sd* Nicolás de la Rosa, Galdino Samperio *m* Raúl Lavista
lp Silvia Pinal, Narciso Busquets, Jaime Fernández, Sonia Infante, Pedro Armendáriz Jr, Victor Manuel Mendoza, Chabela Vargas, Aurora Clavel, Alicia del Lago, Pancho Córdova

The story of a young village girl, Lázara (Pinal) whose husband (Fernández) is arbitrarily recruited by Revolutionaries on their wedding day and subsequently killed in battle. General Nicolás (Busquets) forces the beautiful Lázara to become his lover and *soldadera*. In spite of the fact that Lázara bears him a daughter, he neither cares for nor respects her. Every time they reach a town, she wishes she could abandon the Revolution to lead a normal life. Nicolás dies in battle and Lázara goes off with a soldier from the winning side.

Los adelantados

aka *Living on Credit*
1969 87 mins. (16mm) b&w
d/p Gustavo Alatriste *c* Genaro Hurtado, Felipe Mariscal, Gaby Goldman *sd* Rodolfo Solís *ed* Fernando Belina
lp Alva Sosa Soberanes and villagers from Yucatán

Alatriste's feature debut is a story set among the

hemp planters of Citikabchen in Yucatán. The first part of the film comprises interviews with the planters who find they are unable to redeem their debts from the local stores. The second half tells, via the character of a concerned politician (Soberanes) who acts as the viewer's guide, of the peasants' daily life. Although hailed as an attempt to find a new cinematic rhetoric suited to the topic, the film owes more to television reportage than to cinema direct.

El Águila Descalza
aka *The Barefoot Eagle*
1969 97 mins. colour
d Alfonso Arau *p* Producciones Jaguar *sc* Alfonso Arau, Héctor Ortega *c* Alex Phillips *m* Gustavo César Carrión
lp Alfonso Arau, Ofelia Medina, Christa Linder, José Gálvez, Virma González, Eva Müller, Roberto Cobo, Tamara Garina, Victor Ekberg, Héctor Ortega, Pancho Córdova

Arau's first feature is a Tashlinesque comedy starring himself in the three lead parts. Poncho is a working-class youth obsessed with comics, who inhabits a fantasy world. He identifies with the Barefoot Eagle, a superhero who cannot afford to add shoes to his costume and for whom nails are as dangerous as kryptonite is for Superman. The Eagle fights injustice in the shape of greedy entrepreneurs and assorted masked villains. The plot is complicated by the return of the Sicilian-American gangster Johnny Eaglepass who finds that all his rackets have been taken over by businessmen and bankers.

Familiaridades
1969 (released in 1979) 99 mins. b&w
d/p/sc Felipe Cazals *c* Alexis Grivas *ed* Giovanni Korporaal *sd* Salvador Topete *m* Joaquín Gutiérrez Heras
lp Betty Catania, Farnesio de Bernal, Ostro Reyes, Yola Alatorre Jr, Tomás Pérez Turrent, Juan Luis Buñuel, Arturo Ripstein

Betty (Catania), a young independent woman, breaks off with her lover. Alone and restless, she gets drunk. Despite her protests, a persistent salesman gets inside her apartment to demonstrate his cleaning products. Another salesman shows up and offers Betty train tickets to Acapulco. By the end of the afternoon, the three have become strangely familiar and they dine and dance together. The first salesman makes the second one leave the house. A wheelchair-bound woman from across the street tells Betty she has to go

to hospital. Betty and the salesman make love, quarrel, and he leaves. She goes to the hospital to visit her neighbour and then to the railway station, where she sees the first salesman. Without saying a word they board the train to Acapulco.

Las puertas del paraíso
aka *The Gates of Paradise*
1970 89 mins. colour
d Salomón Láiter *p* Cinematográfica Marte (J. Fernando Pérez Gavilán, Mauricio Wallerstein) *sc* Eduardo Lizalde, Salomón Láiter from a story by Elena Garro *c* Fernando Alvarez Garcés *ed* Sergio Soto *m* Rubén Fuentes
lp Jacqueline Andere, Jorge Luke, Milton Rodrígues, Ofelia Medina, Bárbara Angely, Arsenio Campos, Ernesto Gómez Cruz, Martín Lasalle, Jorge Mistral, Guillermo Murray, Isela Vega

A claustrophobic story featuring middle-class playboys and their girlfriends who, unable to understand or relate to the realities around them, seek refuge in crime, drugs and sexual experimentation, eventually finding their way to a lakeside populated by hippies. The film has been described as an action film set in an imaginary space, refusing any sense of psychology or identification, a pure cinematic mechanism designed to move the viewer. In this respect, the film's form is said to be analogous to its theme: the blockage experienced by a sector of the Mexican bourgeoisie when it attempts to anchor itself in reality.

El cambio
aka *The Change*
1971 87 mins. colour
d Alfredo Joskowicz *p* CUEC *sc* Alfredo Joskowicz, Luis Carrión, Leobardo López Aretche *c* Toni Kuhn *ed* Ramón Aupart *m* Julio Estrada
lp Sergio Jiménez, Héctor Bonilla, Ofelia Medina, Sofia Joskowicz, Héctor Andremar

A low-budget drama about the futility of hippy escapism. Two alienated urban youths, a painter (Jiménez) and his friend (Bonilla) leave the city to go and live in a hut by a lake. But the lake is poisoned by a factory's effluent. When they throw the dirty water over some factory managers, the local police shoot the two youths. The moral of the story is that one cannot escape from the real industrial and political problems by turning to nature.

Historia de un documento
1971 47 mins. (16mm) b&w

d/c Oscar Menéndez *p* Cine Independiente de México *sc* Rodolfo Alcaraz *ed* Janine Martin *m* Edgardo Cantón

This independent, militant film presents the history of the footage shot on super-8 by political prisoners at the Lecumberri prison in 1968. Menéndez first showed some of that material in his documentary *2 de octubre: aqui México* (1970). With the present documentary, the director catalogues the difficulties involved in obtaining the prisoners' footage and gives his reasons for showing it. In so doing, he provides a history not only of the film's images and sounds, but also of political detention in Mexico, during the period 1959–71, which culminated in the Tlatelolco massacre of 1968 and of a despotic political system which was generally regarded as 'liberal'.

El jardín de tía Isabel
aka *Aunt Isobel's Garden*
1971 (released in 1972) 112 mins. colour
d Felipe Cazals *p* Alpha Centauri (Guillermo Aguilar, Victor José Mora Jr) *sc* Jaime Casillas, adapted by Julio Alejandro and Jaime Casillas *c* Jorge Stahl Jr *art dir* Fernando Ramírez, Manuel Fontanals *ed* Rafael Ceballos, Peter Parashelles *sd* Javier Mateos *m* Bernardo Segall, Joaquín Gutiérrez Heras
lp Jorge Martínez de Hoyos, Claudio Brook, Ofelia Guilmain, Gregorio Casal, Jorge Luke, Javier Esponda, Augusto Benedico, Julián Pastor, Germán Robles, Alfonso Arau, Lilia Aragón, Martha Navarro, Héctor Ortega

In the late 16th century, an expedition containing friars, prostitutes, soldiers and liberated prisoners sets out from Sevilla for America. After a shipwreck off the American coast, the survivors elect a leader and, filled with wonderment, travel through the forests. Decimated and frightened by an earthquake, the castaways confess their anxieties and fears and get into fights. The women change their ways and the men, in need of tenderness, make them their wives. Their pilgrimage ends on the Pacific coast, by which time the intruders have adapted and become part of America.

Mecánica nacional
aka *The Mexican Way*
1971 (released in 1972) 105 mins. colour
d Luis Alcoriza *p* Producciones Escorpión (Ramiro Meléndez) *sc* Luis Alcoriza *c* Alex Phillips Jr *art dir* Manuel Fontanals *ed* Carlos Savage, Juan José Marino *sd* José B. Carles, Ramón Moreno

m Rubén Fuentes
lp Manolo Fábregas, Lucha Villa, Héctor Suárez, Sara García, Pancho Córdova, Fabiola Falcón, Gloria Marín, Fernando Casanova, Alma Muriel, Alejandro Ciangherotti Jr, Carlos Piñar, Federico Curiel

Eufemio (Fábregas), the owner of a car-repair shop, goes with friends and family to a car race. After the event, a traffic jam keeps Eufemio, his wife Chabela (Villa) and the rest of their group trapped in the middle of a milling crowd. Each of the family members behaves wildly in the face of such unforeseen circumstances as unlimited access to food, sex and drink. Their unexpected condition also highlights their bitterness and other difficulties within the family. The day in the country ends in tragedy.

Reed: México insurgente
aka *Reed: Insurgent Mexico*
1971 (released in 1972) 111 mins. (16mm)
b&w/colour/sepia
d Paul Leduc *p* Ollín y asociados (Rafael López) *sc* Paul Leduc, Juan Tovar from John Reed's Insurgent Mexico *c* Alexis Grivas, Ariel Zúñiga *art dir* Luis Jasso, Yolanda Melo *ed* Rafael Castanedo, Giovanni Korporaal *sd* Ernesto Higuera, Max López, Miguel Ramírez, Antonio Bermúdez, Salvador Topete
lp Claudio Obregón, Eduardo López Rojas, Ernesto Gómez Cruz, Juan Angel Martínez, Carlos Castañón, Hugo Velázquez, Eraclio Zepeda, Enrique Alatorre, Carlos Fernández del Real, Victor Fosado, Lynn Tillet

Paul Leduc's first feature tells the story of John Reed's 1913 sojourn in Mexico to report on the events of the Revolution. Reed (Obregón) attempts to analyse the nature of the Mexican national character and the complexity of the movement. Following the troops of General Tomás Urbina (López Rojas), he becomes involved in the fighting. In Nogales, he interviews Carranza (Alatorre). He also meets Francisco Villa (Zepeda) preparing to move to Torreon. The British release print ran for only 106 mins.

La verdadera vocación de Magdalena
aka *The True Vocation of Magdalena*
1971 94 mins. colour
d/sc Jaime Humberto Hermosillo *p* Cinematográfica Marco Polo *c* Rosalío Solano *ed* Rafael Ceballos *sd* Eduardo Arjonas *art dir* Salvador Lozano *m* Sigfrido García
lp Angelica María, Carmen Montejo, Javier Martín

del Campo, Farnesio de Bernal, Leticia Robles, Ricardo Fuentes, Emma Roldán, Mario Casillas, María Guadelupe, Rafael Balédon

After his independently made featurette *Los nuestros* (1969), Hermosillo further developed his basic theme of a suffocating matriarchy being disrupted by an arrival from the outside in this comedy which also marked his commercial debut. The plot revolves around a browbeaten daughter's (María) rebellion against her mother's (Montejo) opposition to her marrying a rock musician (del Campo). Hermosillo commented: 'My lack of experience with the film industry's system and the three weeks and three days I was given to film resulted in a regrettable product.'

El castillo de la pureza
aka *The Castle of Purity*
1972 (released in 1973) 116 mins. colour
d Arturo Ripstein *p* Estudios Churubusco-Azteca (Angélica Ortiz) *sc* Arturo Ripstein, José Emilio Pacheco *c* Alex Phillips *ed* Rafael Castanedo, Eufemio Rivera *sd* Jesús González Gancy *m* Joaquín Gutiérrez Heras
lp Claudio Brook, Rita Macedo, Arturo Beristáin, Diana Bracho, Gladys Bermejo, David Silva, María Barber, María Rojo, Inés Murillo, Cecilia Leger

Based on a true story, Gabriel (Brook), a strict paterfamilias, decides to protect his family from the perversions of the world and keeps them locked up in the family house for eighteen years. Only he is allowed to leave the house: he sells the rat poison produced by the family and breaks all his own rules. The situation gets out of control when the adolescent children tire of being locked up in the cell the father uses to punish them for every minor infraction of his obsolete rules. The police arrest Gabriel when a young woman accuses him of producing rat poison without the proper official documentation. His wife and children are freed, but they are at a loss in the world.

El principio
aka *The Beginning*
1972 (released in 1973) 148 mins. colour
d Gonzalo Martínez Ortega *p* Estudios Churubusco-Azteca (José Luis Bueno) *sc* Gonzalo Martínez Ortega *c* Rosalío Solano *art dir* Raúl Serrano *ed* Carlos Savage *sd* José B. Carles *m* Rubén Fuentes
lp Lucha Villa, Narciso Busquets, Fernando Balzaretti, Andrés García, Sergio Bustamante, Lina Montes, Patricia Aspíllaga, Patricia Luke, Bruno Rey,

Pilar Souza, Ernesto López Rojas, Rogelio Flores

Mexico is in the midst of the Revolution when David (Balzaretti) returns after studying in Paris for several years. His native town in the state of Chihuahua has been taken by Villista Revolutionaries. David visits his now uninhabited home and remembers people and events of his adolescence: his uncle Francisco, the chief of police; his sister Francisca's affiliation with a liberal club; taking baths in the river with girls from La Coquena's brothel. He also remembers the labour strike that ended in a massacre. David returns to the present and learns that his father was assassinated by La Coquena. In the company of his father's former butler, David joins the Revolutionary movement.

El rincón de las vírgenes
aka *The Virgin's Corner* aka *Nest of Virgins*
1972 99 mins. colour
d Alberto Isaac *p* Estudios Churubusco-Azteca (Angélica Ortiz) *sc* Alberto Isaac from Juan Rulfo's *Anacleto Morones* and *El día del temblor* *c* Raúl Martínez Solares, Daniel López *art dir* Lucero Isaac *ed* Carlos Savage Jr *sd* Javier Mateos *m* Joaquín Gutiérrez Heras
lp Alfonso Arau, Emilio 'el Indio' Fernández, Rosalba Brambila, Carmen Salinas, Pancho Córdova, Lilia Prado, Héctor Ortega, Graciela Doring, Marcela López Rey

A group of fanatically religious women search for the boorish Lucas Lucatero (Arau) to convince him to give testimony for the canonisation of the crooked faith-healer Anacleto Morones (Fernández). Lucas, his former 'partner' and brother-in-law, refuses to be Morones's character witness. He tells the women how he met Morones in the 20s and became his partner, how Morones began to perform 'miracles', and how he was imprisoned. The women begin to leave, but he continues his story, omitting the fact that he killed Anacleto when he escaped from jail. One of the pious women ends up spending the night in Lucas's arms.

El señor de Osanto
aka *The Lord of Osanto*
1972 108 mins. colour
d Jaime Humberto Hermosillo *p* Conacine, DASA Films *sc* José de la Colina, Jaime Humberto Hermosillo from Robert Louis Stevenson's *The Master of Ballantrae* *c* Gabriel Figueroa *ed* Rafael Ceballos *art dir* Lucero Isaac *m* Eduardo Mata
lp Daniela Rosen, Hugo Stiglitz, Mario Castillón

Bracho, Farnesio de Bernal, Fernando Soler, Rogelio Guerra, Patricia Reyes Spíndola, Salvador Sánchez

Hermosillo's only costume movie transposes Scotland to nineteenth-century Mexico for the story of the conflict that ensues between two brothers when one of them leaves to fight in the war against the French intervention. The film demonstrates the director's technical development as well as the use of the sequence-shot that would become a characteristic of his style. The scenarist de la Colina explained that 'we tried to make an anti-romantic melodrama, standing some of the conventional moral standards of the melodrama on their head. For instance, the "good" brother suddenly turns bad and vice versa, the scenes that seemed to be love scenes ended with characters talking about an inheritance, money or property.'

Juan Pérez Jolote
aka *Juan, the Chamula*
1973 (released in 1975) 120 mins. colour
d Archibaldo Burns *p* Victor Fuentes *sc* Archibaldo Burns from the anthropological book by Ricardo Pozas *c* Eric Sanen *sd* Robert Muñoz, Manuela García, Elías Martel *ed* Rafael Castanedo *m* Richard Alderson
lp Cándido Cueto

This film was based on an anthropological text written by Ricardo Pozas, who called the film 'a small monograph on the culture of the Chamulas', one of the few surviving Mayan tribes. The film intersperses fiction with documentary to explore current social conflicts encountered by this indigenous community when faced with nationalism and the economic imperatives of modern industrial society. Both Tzotzil, a contemporary Mayan dialect, and Spanish languages are spoken in the film. This bilingual track appropriately underscores the duality of Mexican society, in which the tribal traditions that predate the Spanish conquest are juxtaposed with the western attitudes that followed in its wake.

El Santo Oficio
aka *The Holy Office*
1973 (released in 1974) 130 mins. colour
d Arturo Ripstein *p* Conacine, Cinematográfica Marco Polo (Leopoldo Silva and Marco Silva) *sc* José Emilio Pacheco, Arturo Ripstein *c* Jorge Stahl Jr *art dir* José Rodríguez Granada *ed* Rafael Castanedo, Eufemio Rivera *sd* Jesús González Gancy, David Dockendorff, Bud Grenzbach *m* Joaquín

Gutiérrez Heras
lp Jorge Luke, Diana Bracho, Claudio Brook, Ana Mérida, Silvia Mariscal, Martha Navarro, Arturo Beristáin, Antonio Bravo, Peter González, Mario Castillón Bracho

The story takes place in the capital of Nueva España in 1593. The head of the Carvajal family dies. During the burial, a priest warns the congregation that the family is Jewish. The dead man's relations are all imprisoned and suffer a catalogue of ill-treatment including rape and torture. Luis (Luke), one of the children, escapes, and seeks refuge with a rabbi. However, someone informs on him and he is captured and tortured until he reveals the names of other Jews, who are subsequently tortured to death. On the brink of death, Luis prays in Hebrew. A title at the beginning of the film states that it is a work of 'fiction inspired by authentic documents and reality. It aspires not to the certainty of history but to the verisimilitude of a legend.'

La casa del sur
1974 104 mins. colour
d Sergio Olhovich *p* Conacine, DASA Films *sc* Sergio Olhovich, Eduardo Luján *c* Rosalío Solano *ed* Alberto Valenzuela *sd* José B. Carles *art dir* José Rodríguez Granada *m* Gustavo César Carrión
lp David Reynoso, Helena Rojo, Salvador Sánchez, Rodrigo Puebla, Patricia Reyes Spíndola, Manuel Ojeda

A group of very poor desert dwellers is taken by train to a luscious terrain by a lake. Unfortunately, the place is also infested by demagogues and priests. They are given useless farm machinery and they marvel at the wonders of technology. As the group begins to develop into a society, the boss (Reynoso) of the nearby ranch tries to drive them away with torture and brutality. The group's leader, Genaro (Sánchez) takes revenge by raping the rancher's daughter. Eventually, the peasants rebel and the ending finds them on a boat contemplating their 'promised land', now reduced to a wasteland.

El cumpleaños del perro
aka *The Dog's Birthday*
1974 (released in 1975) 86 mins. colour
d Jaime Humberto Hermosillo *p* Conacine, DASA Films (Enrique L. Morfín) *sc* Jaime Humberto Hermosillo *c* Alex Phillips Jr *art dir* Jorge Fernández *ed* Rafael Ceballos *sd* Eduardo Arjona *m* Joaquín Gutiérrez Heras

lp Jorge Martínez de Hoyos, Héctor Bonilla, Diana Bracho, Lina Montes, Marcelo Villamil, María Guadalupe Delgado, Delia Casanova

Hermosillo's third feature scrutinises sexual repression and misogyny in the Mexican middle class, and indirectly addresses homosexuality with its depiction of a homosocial bond between two married men. Two newlyweds, Gustavo (Bonilla) and Silvia (Bracho), dine with their best man and maid of honour: Don Jorge (de Hoyos) and Doña Gloria (Montes), a middle-aged couple without children. Although the couples generally get along well, there are various misunderstandings during dinner and they stop seeing each other. Months later, Gustavo kills Silvia. The other couple learns the news and Don Jorge decides to seek out his young friend and help him evade prison. Doña Gloria, on the other hand, is determined to inform the police against Gustavo. Don Jorge is opposed and kills his wife. The two male friends escape in the direction of Michoacán.

Presagio
1974 123 mins. colour
d Luis Alcoriza *p* Conacine and Producciones Escorpión (Ramiro Meléndez) *sc* Gabriel García Márquez, Luis Alcoriza *c* Gabriel Figueroa *art dir* Fernando Ramírez, Roberto Silva *ed* Carlos Savage *sd* Francisco Alcayde
lp David Reynoso, Fabiola Falcón, Lucha Villa, Pancho Córdova, Eric del Castillo, Enrique Lucero, Carmen Montejo, Gloria Marín, Amparo Rivelles, Silvia Mariscal, Gabriel Retes

In an anonymous village with an inhospitable ambience, Mamá Santos, the local midwife, helps with the labour of Felipe's wife (both Felipe and his wife are foreigners). During the birth, Mamá Santos breaks a bottle used during labour and predicts that bad luck will befall the village. Believing her to have miraculous powers, the villagers take her prediction seriously. They stop working and begin to go hungry. Strange events occur and everyone becomes aggressive. The villagers' superstitions lead them to think that the end is near, and one by one the families begin to abandon the village.

El apando
aka *Solitary* aka *The Heist* aka *Solitary Confinement*
1975 88 mins. colour
d Felipe Cazals *p* Conacite Uno, STPC (Roberto Lozoya) *sc* José Revueltas, José Agustín from the

novel by José Revueltas *c* Alex Phillips Jr *art dir* Salvador Lozano *ed* Rafael Castanedo *sd* Manuel Topete *song* 'Calla tristeza' by Gonzalo Curiel
lp Salvador Sánchez, José Carlos Ruiz, Manuel Ojeda, Delia Casanova, María Rojo, Ana Ofelia Murguía, Luz Cortázar, Max Kerlow, Alvaro Carcaño, Sergio Calderón, Roberto Rivero, Tomás Pérez Turrent, Gerardo del Castillo

In the ancient prison of Lucumberri, three prisoners, Albino (Ojeda), Polonio (Sánchez) and 'el Carajo' (Ruiz), connive to get drugs to satisfy their habits. Their visitors have the opportunity to bring them drugs and are eagerly awaited. Albino and Polonio suggest that el Carajo's mother do the same, since their respective lovers are in danger of being discovered. The mother agrees and brings in a cache, but the drugs are found and the guards inflict a horrible punishment on the prisoners. In the hope of provoking a scandal, the son denounces his own mother, who is arrested. The film is based on the novel written by José Revueltas while he was serving a prison sentence at Lecumberri on charges of organising student demonstrations in 1968. The film provoked a scandal of its own: the public outcry over its representation of torture was in large part responsible for the closing of the prison.

Canoa
1975 (released in 1976) 115 mins. colour
d Felipe Cazals *p* Conacine, STPC *sc* Tomás Pérez Turrent *c* Alex Phillips Jr *art dir* Salvador Lozano *ed* Rafael Ceballos *sd* Manuel Topete
lp Enrique Lucero, Salvador Sánchez, Rodrigo Puebla, Ernesto Gómez Cruz, Roberto Sosa, Arturo Alegro, Jaime Garza, Malena Doria

A man from the country narrates events that took place in the town of San Miguel Canoa in the state of Puebla on the night of 14 September 1968. Five employees of the Universidad de Puebla take a trip to visit the volcano of La Malinche. Bad weather forces them to spend the night in town, where a farm labourer Lucas García (Cruz) offers them shelter. Influenced by the priest Enrique Meza (Lucero), the townspeople believe that the visitors are communist agents, atheists and child kidnappers. At midnight, carrying torches, they attack Lucas's house with machetes and farm implements, killing him and two of his guests. The Puebla police find the survivors wounded and mutilated.

De todos modos Juan te llamas
aka *The General's Daughter*

1975 (released in 1976) 108 mins. colour
d Marcela Fernández Violante p Dirección General
de Difusión Cultural, UNAM sc Marcela Fernández
Violante, Mitl Valdez, Adrián Palomeque c Arturo de
la Rosa ed Marcelino Aupart, Giovanni Korporaal m
Marcela Fernández Violante
lp Jorge Russek, Juan Ferrara, Rocío Brambila,
Patricia Aspíllaga, José Martí, Pilar Souza

The film centres on the Cristero movement (a
Catholic fundamentalist uprising) of the late 20s.
The protagonists are a family, comprising a
Revolutionary general (Russek) who obeys his bosses'
contradictory orders; his wife, who will be killed by a
group of believers; and their three children. One of
these is a girl with a marked critical attitude and
feminist beliefs. Another official represents dissidence
within the military and offers the first signs of what
will later become Cardenismo, the movement that
brought General Cárdenas to power.

¡Maten al león!
aka *Kill the Lion!*
1975 129 mins. colour
d José Estrada p CONACINE, DASA Films,
Héctor López sc José Estrada from a story by Jorge
Ibargüengoitia c Gabriel Figueroa art dir Jorge
Fernández, Enrique Estévez, Adalberto López ed
Juan José Marino, Abraham Cruz m Joaquín
Gutiérrez Heras
lp David Reynoso, Jorge Rivero, Lucy Gallardo,
Ernesto Gómez Cruz, Guillermo Orea, Marta
Zamora, Enrique Lucero, Julián Pastor, Manuel
Medel, Ana Ofelia Murguía

President Echeverría's efforts to reconcile intellectuals
to the state gave young film-makers the means to
bring about a revival of Mexican cinematic comedy in
the 70s. This is a political satire set on the fictitious
Caribbean island of Arepa, ruled by the irrational and
bloody dictator, Manuel Balaunzaran (Reynoso) who
is subject to the film's ridicule, as is its bourgeoisie,
whose attempts to overthrow the regime only result in
bizarre tragedies. The absurd plans and exaggerated
behaviour of the opposition are charted over the fall
of one dictator and the rise of his equally tyrannical
successor (Lucero), which demonstrates their inability
even to manage a coup during a period of political
transition. After all the killing and the intrigues, the
situation returns to square one.

La pasión según Berenice
aka *The Passion According to Berenice*

1975 (released in 1976) 102 mins. colour
d/sc Jaime Humberto Hermosillo p Conacine and
DASA Films (Roberto Lozaya) c Rosalío Solano art
dir José González Camarena ed Rafael Ceballos sd
José B. Carles m Joaquín Gutiérrez Heras, with
fragments from Gustav Mahler's *Symphony No. 2*
lp Pedro Armendáriz Jr, Martha Navarro, Blanca
Torres, Emma Roldán, Magnolia Rivas, Manuel
Ojeda, Alejandro Rodríguez, Mario Oropeza, María
Guadalupe Delgado, Evangelina Martínez

In the small town of Aguascalientes, Berenice
(Navarro) is a seductive and enigmatic widowed
schoolteacher who lives with her godmother Josefina
(Roldán), an avaricious old woman. Berenice lives
according to middle-class provincial conventions.
However, she is socially stigmatised by the rumour
that she murdered her husband: a scar on her face is
taken as a sign of her guilt and reinforces the gossip.
Berenice falls madly in love with Rodrigo
(Armendáriz), a city dweller travelling through
Aguascalientes. She kills her godmother to run away
with him and escape her monotonous life, but
Rodrigo leaves without her.

La vida cambia
aka *Life Changes*
1975 104 mins. colour
d/sc Juan Manuel Torres p Conacine, STPC c Gabriel
Figueroa ed Alberto Valenzuela art dir Jorge
Fernández m Gustavo César Carrión
lp Mercedes Carreño, Arturo Beristáin, Maritza
Olivares, Pancho Córdova, Gloria Mestre,
Claudio Obregón

Melodrama about an unhappy *ménage à trois*
featuring Miguel (Beristáin), an out-of-work actor
who lives with his girlfriend Teresa (Carreño), a
beautician, and her sister Marta (Olivares), a nurse.
When Teresa discovers that Miguel and Marta are
having an affair, she takes an overdose of
tranquillizers. The sisters are eventually reconciled,
but in their struggle to make some money, Teresa is
forced into prostitution. In the end, after another
suicide attempt by Teresa, the situation returns to
'normal' as the three wait for the circumstances of
their lives to change.

Los albañiles
aka *The Bricklayers*
1976 120 mins. colour
d Jorge Fons p Conacine, Cinematográfica Marco
Polo (Luis García de León) sc Jorge Fons, Vicente

Leñero, Luis Carrión from the novel by Vicente Leñero *c* Alex Phillips Jr *art dir* Xavier Rodríguez González *ed* Eufemio Rivera *sd* Jesús González Gancy *m* Gustavo César Carrión
lp Ignacio López Tarso, Jaime Fernández, José Alonso, Salvador Sánchez, José Carlos Ruiz, Katy Jurado, Adalberto Martínez 'Resortes', David Silva, Leonor Llausás

Don Jesús, the night-watchman of a building under construction, is killed and his death is investigated. The police torture the suspected bricklayers during their interrogations. In the process, we learn about their work relations and problems and that the night-watchman had raped a young girl. Also uncovered are the suspicious deals between a foreman and a young architect (the son of the company's boss) and the architect's troubled family life.

Caminando pasos caminando
aka *Step by Step*
1976 103 mins. (16mm) colour
d/c Federico Weingartshofer *p* Patricia Weingartshofer *sc* Federico Weingartshofer, Mitl Valdez *ed* Ramón Aupart
lp Ernesto Gómez Cruz, Salvador Sánchez, Patricia Reyes Spíndola, Socorro Avelar, Roberto Sosa

The cinematographer Weingartshofer, a graduate from the CUEC, directed his second feature (after *Quizá siempre sí me muera,* 1971) in the isolated village of San Francisco Oxtotilpan. The story revolves around a teacher, Eulalio Guardado (Cruz), who, exasperated by the village's poverty and the feudal despotism blighting the community, initiates the building of a road to the nearest urban centre in spite of the opposition of his friend, the villager Rosendo, who warns that roads not only bring things, they also take things away. In the end, Rosendo is proved right and the teacher perishes in the attempt to stop the construction of the road as the bulldozers inexorably move forward.

Chin Chin el teporocho
aka *Chin Chin the Drunkard*
1976 100 mins. colour
d Gabriel Retes *p* Conacine, STPC *sc* Pilar Retes from a novel by Armando Ramírez Rodríguez *c* Daniel López *ed* Eufemio Rivera *sd* Javier Mateds *art dir* Jorge Fernández *m* Manuel Esperón
lp Carlos Chávez, Jorge Santoyo, Jorge Balzaretti, Abel Woolrich, Tina Romero, Mily Eurlong

A melodrama about four youngsters fighting for survival in a poor quarter of Mexico City. Rogelio (Chávez) marries Miguela (Romero), but finds that her father is a homosexual preying on children. Rogelio's cousin Victor (Balzaretti) wants to go and work in the USA but is killed in a fight with Rubén (Woolrich). Gilberto (Santoyo), one of their neighbours, seeks refuge in alcohol and Rubén, the toughest of the lot, is with Agnes (Eurlong), Miguela's sister, but he drifts into crime. In the end, Rogelio is overcome by the corruption and the misery surrounding him and turns into Chin Chin the Drunkard, the narrator of the story.

Etnocidio: notas sobre el Mezquital
aka *Ethnocide: Notes on Mezquital*
1976 127 mins. (16mm) colour
d Paul Leduc *p* Cine Difusión SEP (Carlos Resendi, Mexico), National Film Board (Canada) *sc* Roger Bartra, Paul Leduc *c* Georges Dufaux, Angel Goded *ed* Rafael Castanedo, Paul Leduc *sd* Serge Bauchemain *m* Rafael Castanedo

Documentary organised by chapters (from A to Z) consisting of interviews with Otomi Indians from the impoverished region of the Valle del Mezquital. Some members of this small indigenous group bear witness to the economic and cultural exploitation and pillaging they have suffered for centuries. In a Spanish that seems foreign to them (the original version was in both Otomi and Spanish), they cite *caciquismo* and the aridity of their lands as just two of the causes of their marginalisation. These problems have led to famine and to forced emigration, either to cities or to the USA.

Matinée
1976 (released in 1977) 96 mins. colour
d/sc Jaime Humberto Hermosillo *p* Conacite Uno, DASA Films (Eduardo de la Barra) *c* Jorge Stahl Jr *art dir* Agustín Ituarte *ed* Rafael Ceballos *sd* Agustín Topete *m* Joaquín Gutiérrez Heras
lp Héctor Bonilla, Manuel Ojeda, Armando Martín Martínez, Rodolfo Chávez Martínez, Narciso Busquets, Farnesio de Bernal, Emma Roldán

Hermosillo has drawn from action-adventure and thriller genres to create this humorous work about two schoolboys, Jorge (A.M. Martínez) and Aarón (R.C. Martínez) whose imagination has been over-stimulated by their shared passion for the cinema. During their school vacation, Jorge accompanies his truck-driver father and Aarón runs away with them. The truck is attacked by robbers who kill the father and hold the children hostage. Two of the assailants, Aquiles (Bonilla) and Francisco (Ojeda), have a homosexual relationship and commit various hold-ups with the children. The relations among the four deteriorate and during a hold-up of the Basílica de Guadalupe, Jorge warns the police and Aquiles and Francisco are killed. The children return home as heroes. Jorge accepts the tribute, but the disenchanted Aarón runs away again, this time by train. The one boy has found a formulaic hero's ending, while the other discovers that escape is the only solution to a personal crisis in a hostile and repressive society.

Las poquianchis
aka *Miserere*
1976 110 mins. colour
d Felipe Cazals *p* Alpha Centauri (Victor José Moya) *sc* Tomás Pérez Turrent and Xavier Robles *c* Alex Phillips Jr *ed* Rafael Castanedo *m* Dámaso Pérez Prado, Luis Arcaraz, Agustín Lara
lp Diana Bracho, Jorge Martínez de Hoyos, Salvador Sánchez, Pilar Pellicer, Leonor Llausás, Malena Doria, Ana Ofelia Murguía, Gonzalo Vega, Tina Romero, María Rojo, Alejandro Parodi, Enrique Lucero, Manuel Ojeda, Arturo Beristáin, Gina Moret

In 1964, in the state of Guanajuato, the crimes committed for more than a decade by Delfa, Chuy and Evá (Llausás, Doria and Murguía), three sisters nicknamed 'Las poquianchis', are discovered. The sisters managed a brothel with girls purchased and/or kidnapped from peasants. The victims were tortured and starved to break their will. When they were no longer useful, they were killed. All this was facilitated by hired gunfighters and police protection. The crimes were uncovered thanks to journalists and uncorrupt politicians.

Raíces de sangre
aka *Roots of Blood*
1976 (released in 1979) 100 mins. colour
d/sc Jesús Salvador Treviño *p* CONACINE *c* Rosalío Solano *ed* Joaquín Ceballos *sd* Sigfrido García *m* Sergio Guerrero
lp Richard Iñiguez, Ernesto Gómez Cruz, Malena Doria, Pepe Serna, Adriana Rojo, Roxana Bonilla–Gianini

The El Paso-born Chicano film-maker Treviño's low-budget debut feature is set in a *maquiladora,* a company town near the US border serving the US economy, and tells of the joint struggle by Mexicans and Chicanos to form a union to protect themselves against the slave-like working conditions in a garment factory. The situation also involves gun and drug trafficking as well as divide-and-rule tactics that pit Mexicans and Chicanos against each other. The focus of the story is a Harvard-trained lawyer, Carlos Rivera (Iñiguez) and his syndicalist girlfriend Lupe Carrillo (Bonilla-Gianini). The dialogue combines English and Spanish.

Las apariencias engañan
aka *Looks Can be Deceiving* aka *Deceptive Appearances*
1977 (released in 1979) 100 mins. (16mm) colour
d/sc/p Jaime Humberto Hermosillo *c* Angel Goded *art dir* Lucero Isaac *ed* Rafael Ceballos *sd* Fernando Cámara *m* songs performed by Son Clave de Oro, Hermanos Martínez Gil and others
lp Isela Vega, Gonzalo Vega, Manuel Ojeda, Margarita Isabel, Ignacio Retes, Roberto Cobo, María Rojo, Farnesio de Bernal

This convoluted plot parodies the constructions of sexuality that enforce social roles within the middle class. Rogelio (G. Vega), a young actor, pretends to be Adrián, an old man's nephew, in order to get his consent to the marriage of his niece, the beautiful Adriana Bejarano (I. Vega), to Sergio (Ojeda). Adriana takes care of her ancient uncle. Rogelio is perturbed by Adriana's beauty, especially after she fellates him in the bathroom. After a tennis match, Sergio impulsively kisses Rogelio. Meanwhile, Rogelio declares his love to Adriana and tells her that Sergio is a homosexual who will never make her happy. Sergio leaves and Rogelio desperately looks for Adriana, who is avoiding him. Finally, they meet in a beauty salon. When they take off their clothes, Rogelio discovers that she has a penis. They make love, she penetrates him. The couple is married in a church ceremony.

Los indolentes
aka *The Indolent*
1977 (released in 1979) 115 mins. colour
d José Estrada *p* Conacite Dos *sc* Rubén Torres, José Estrada from an idea by Rubén Torres *c* Miguel Garzón *art dir* Kleómedes Stomatiades *ed* Francisco Chiu *m* Joaquín Gutiérrez Heras
lp Rita Macedo, Isabela Corona, Miguel Angel Ferriz, Raquel Olmedo, Ana Martín, Anais de Melo, Rafael Banquells

The aristocratic Alday family, despite their lack of money, refuse to give up their social position and airs. In their half-ruined house live the grandmother who is lost in her memories, the unbalanced mother and the helpless, confused adolescent son. All three refuse to recognise the social changes that have taken place and to adapt their lives to the new circumstances. A young and industrious seamstress appears among them, sexually initiating the boy and offering the possibility of change for the whole family. However, this opportunity is rejected and the family disintegrates as the grandmother dies, the mother goes completely mad and the son simply gives up.

El lugar sin límites

aka *The Place Without Limits* aka *No End*
1977 (released in 1978) 110 mins. colour
d Arturo Ripstein *p* Conacite Dos (Francisco del Villar) *sc* Arturo Ripstein from the novel by José Donoso *c* Miguel Garzón *art dir* Kleómedes Staomatiades *ed* Fransisco Chiu *sd* Guillermo Carrasco *m* poplular Mexican songs
lp Roberto Cobo, Lucha Villa, Ana Martín, Gonzalo Vega, Julián Pastor, Carmen Salinas, Fernando Soler, Blanca Torres, Emma Roldán, Hortensia Santoveña

A decrepit brothel in a small town is the setting for an exploration of social boundaries and sexual stereotypes. It is run by an extravagant homosexual, 'La Mnauela' (Cobo), and his daughter 'La Japonesita'. 'La Manuela' anxiously awaits the return of the boastful Pancho (Vega), who has promised to give her/him a beating. Pancho returns and, days later, goes to the brothel with his brother Octavio. He mistreats 'La Japonesita' and the indignant 'La Manuela' comes out of hiding, dances with Pancho and kisses him. Octavio reproaches Pancho, who starts beating up 'La Manuela'. She/he escapes into the street, but the two men give chase and beat her/him to death. While indicting homophobia, the film implies that macho culture, as represented by Pancho, is founded on latent homoeroticism.

Naufragio

aka *Shipwreck*
1977 (released in 1978) 101 mins. colour
d Jaime Humberto Hermosillo *p* Conacite Uno, DASA Films (Roberto Gerhard) *sc* Jaime Humberto Hermosillo, José de la Colina *c* Rosalío Solano *art dir* Salvador Lozano *ed* Rafael Ceballos *sd* Javier Mateos *m* Joaquín Gutiérrez Heras *songs* Alberto Domínguez, Armando Orefiche, Gonzalo Curiel
lp José Alonso, María Rojo, Ana Ofelia Murguía, Carlos Castañón, Manuel Ojeda

Doña Amparito (Murguía) is obsessed by the memory of her son Miguel Angel who left home several years earlier to see the world. She still takes care of his room and personal effects. Amparito shares her apartment with Leticia (Rojo), a young co-worker, who colludes with her sick obsession over her son. Amparito is hospitalised and Miguel (Alonso) suddenly returns. He and Leticia spend a night together, but the mother does not believe her son has really returned. Back in the apartment, a fight breaks out between Miguel and a group of sailors and he suddenly decides to leave again. Leticia tells the mother everything. She dies and a wave destroys the apartment and carries all its contents into the sea.

La viuda negra

1977 (released in 1978) 94 mins. colour
d Arturo Ripstein *p* Conacine *sc* Vicente Armendáriz, Ramón Obón and Francisco del Villar from the play *Debiera haber obispas* by Rafael Solana *c* Jorge Stahl Jr *art dir* Salvador Lozano Mena *ed* Rafael Ceballos *sd* Alfredo Solís *m* Miguel Pous *songs* Luis Arcaraz
lp Isela Vega, Mario Almada, Sergio Jiménez, Hilda Aguirre, René Casados, Gerardo del Castillo, Leonor Llausás, Ana Ofelia Murguía

An orphan Matea (Vega), who spent her childhood in a religious environment, now works as Father Feliciano's housekeeper. Leonardo, the town doctor, seeks sexual favours from Matea. After she rejects him, he spreads the rumour that Matea and the priest (Almada) are having sex, and the community pressures him to fire her. Finally, the priest and the housekeeper become lovers, which caused censorship trouble for the film. Feliciano becomes ill and no one in town comes to his aid. Matea takes care of him on his deathbed, buries him and ultimately takes his place in the church as the priest had revealed everyone's confessional secrets to her.

Amor libre

aka *Free Love*
1978 92 mins. colour
d Jaime Humberto Hermosillo *p* Conacine *sc* Francisco Sánchez from his own story *c* Jorge Stahl Jr *ed* Rafael Ceballos *sd* Jorge Mateos *art dir* José Rodríguez Granada *m* Nacho Méndez *songs* Agustín Lara, Luis Arcaraz, Alvaro Dalmar
lp Julissa, Alma Muriel, Jorge Balzaretti, Manuel Ojeda, José Alonso, Roberto Cobo, Blanca Torres, Farnesio de Bernal, Ana Ofelia Murguía, Emma Roldán

An erotic comedy about two 'liberated' young women who liberally indulge their sexual appetites.

Whereas Hermosillo usually presents his fantasy of suffocating and hypocritical family life in Mexico City, here he shows the corresponding fantasy of a life free from the social and moral codes the family so oppressively embodies in his work. Significantly, while the family's oppressiveness is mostly depicted in terms of a despotic matriarch, freedom from oppression takes the form of showing promiscuous women embodying what a macho society assumes to be female sexuality.

Anacrusa o de cómo la música viene después del silencio

1978 102 mins. (16mm) colour
d/sc/ed Ariel Zúñiga *p* Sinc *c* Toni Kuhn, Antonio Ruiz, Santiago Navarrete, Jesús Zavala *sd* Bernardine Ligthart, José Luis Pérez R. *m* Alicia Urreta, J.S. Bach, F. Schubert
lp Adriana Roel, Carlos Castañón, Juan Angel Martínez, Eduardo López Rojas, Sergio Calderón, Alma Levi, Pedro Damián, Francisco Ibarra, René García, Ricardo Fritz, Felicitas Vásquez

Zúñiga's feature debut is a low-budget, independently made film about Victoria (Roel), a separated, self-absorbed lecturer in art history who suddenly learns that her daughter has been kidnapped. The search, with the help of a friendly, music-loving journalist (Castañón), confronts her with the social realities she had tried hard to ignore. She first encounters bureaucratic obstruction and indifference, then she descends into a nightmarish daily reality, shared by an increasing number of people, of terror and disappearances. The story was inspired by the case of a woman in Mexico City who, while looking for her 'disappeared' daughter, also disappears.

Cadena perpetua

aka *In For Life* aka *Vicious Circle*
1978 (released in 1979) 95 mins. colour
d Arturo Ripstein *p* Conacine (Francisco del Villar) *sc* Vicente Leñero, Arturo Ripstein from the novel *Lo de antes* by Luis Spota *c* Jorge Stahl Jr *art dir* Jorge Fernández *ed* Rafael Ceballos *sd* Rodolfo Solís, Jesús González Gancy *m* Miguel Pous *songs* J. Rodríguez, A. Domínguez, M. Matamoros
lp Pedro Armendáriz Jr, Narciso Busquets, Ernesto Gómez Cruz, Angélica Chaín, Ana Ofelia Murguía, Roberto Cobo, Yolande Rigel, Socorro de la Campa, Salvador Garcini, Pilar Pellicer

Ripstein transposed the conventions of Hollywood film noir into a specifically Mexican context with this story of an ex-convict who, though supposedly free, will remain a prisoner in urban life. After a botched hold-up, the thief 'el Tarzán' Lira (Armendáriz) decides to give up his criminal ways, marries and gets an honest job. However, he runs into Prieto (Busquets), a corrupt policeman, who blackmails him. This meeting makes him remember his delinquent life and his imprisonment in the Islas Marías prison. Lira desperately looks for his boss for support and to demonstrate his honesty, however he is unable to talk to him and, utterly demoralised, begins to commit robberies again.

María Sabina, mujer espíritu

1978 80 mins. colour
d Nicolás Echevarría *p* Centro de Producción de Cortometraje (Estudios Churubusco) *sc* Nicolás Echevarría with texts by Alvaro Estrada *c* Gonzalo Infante *ed* Saúl Aupart *m* Mario Lavista

Fascinating documentary of a ritual with hallucinogenic mushrooms conducted by María Sabina, a famous *curandera* (quack) from Oaxaca.

Bajo el mismo sol y sobre la misma tierra

aka *Under the Same Sun and on the Same Earth*
1979 90 mins. colour
d/ed Federico Weingartshofer *p* Patricia Weingartshofer *sc* Federico Weingartshofer, Heiner Hoffman, Eduardo Maldonado, Victoria Novelo, Mitl Valdez, Patricia Weingartshofer *c* Heiner Hoffman *m* Julio Estrada
lp Ana Ofelia Murguía, Guillermo Gil, Carlos Aguilar, César Arias de la Cantolla, Arturo Beristáin, Héctor Bonilla, Ernesto Gómez Cruz, Delia Casanova, José Domingo Carrillo, Fernando Coronado, Eduardo López Rojas, Juan Angel Martínez, Silvia Mariscal, Roberto Sosa, Salvador Sánchez

After chronicling the dangers of linking peasant villages to cities by building roads in *Caminando pasos caminando* (1976), Weingartshofer tells the story of Angela (Murguía), a peasant woman who tries to escape from rural oppression by migrating to the city and joining her brother in an industrial shanty town. The film also shows the lives of various other characters: the workers who live in fear of eviction when the factory boss decides to build luxury houses on the land they occupy, the loneliness of a truckdriver (Gil) who belongs neither to the city nor to the suburbs, and so on.

María de mi corazón
aka *Mary My Dearest*
1979 (released in 1981) 120 mins. colour
d Jaime Humberto Hermosillo *p* Universidad
Veracruzana (Hernán Littín) *sc* Gabriel García
Márquez, Jaime Humberto Hermosillo *c* Angel
Goded *art dir* Lucero Isaac *ed* Rafael Ceballos *sd*
Fernando Cámara
lp Héctor Bonilla, María Rojo, Armando Martín,
Salvador Sánchez, Tomás Mojarro, Evangelina
Martínez, Roberto Sosa, Dolores Beristáin, Martha
Navarro, Margarita Isabel

The love story of Héctor (Bonilla), a house robber,
and María (Rojo), a magician. He gives up robberies,
she teaches him magic and they stage a show
together. They marry and everything goes well until
they have to separate. María's car breaks down and
she hitches a ride on a truck that is transporting
women to an insane asylum. When they arrive, the
caretakers assume María is one of the crazy women
and refuse to let her go. Héctor thinks that she has
abandoned him. Later he finds María in the insane
asylum. They see each other, but he believes she is
really crazy and leaves her there. The mingling of
comic and tragic genres renders the film an
exemplary work of magical realism.

El niño Fidencio, taumaturgo de Espinazo
aka *Niño Fidencio, the Healer from Espinazo*
1980 (released in 1981) 75 mins. colour
d/c Nicolás Echevarría *p* Centro de Producción de
Cortometraje (Estudios Churubusco) *sc* Nicolás
Echevarría, Guillermo Sheridan *sd* Sibille Hayem *m*
Mario Lavista

Documentary about the ceremonies in honour of
Niño Fidencio, a famous *curandero* (quack) of the 20s,
in the town of Espinazo, in the state of Nuevo León.
The film combines archival material with testimonies
and interviews about the contempo-rary cult.

Confidencias
1982 90 mins. colour
d Jaime Humberto Hermosillo *p* Clasa Films
Mundiales (Manuel Barbachano Ponce) *sc* Jaime
Humberto Hermosillo from Luis Zapata's *De pétalos
perennes c* Heiner Hoffman *ed/m* Rafael Castanedo *sd*
Fernando Cámara
lp Beatriz Sheridan, María Rojo

An independent production shot in a house in
Cuernavaca tackling the sex, class and age differences

between a dark-haired servant (Rojo) and a blonde
bourgeois housewife (Sheridan), the only characters
of the film. The housewife, afraid of growing old and
losing her looks, tries to live through her servant
whom she dominates and manipulates. Gradually,
the servant rebels and she finally leaves. The original
intention of making the whole film in about fifteen
sequence-shots was defeated by the shoestring budget
and shooting conditions.

El diablo y la dama o El itinerario del odio
aka *The Devil and the Lady* aka *The Itinerary of Hate*
1983 98 mins. colour
d Ariel Zúñiga *p* Sinc, Conacite Dos, Estudios
América (Mexico), Les Films du Passage (Paris) *sc*
Ariel Zúñiga, Carlos Castañón *c* Tony Kuhn *ed*
Claire Painchault *m* Agustín Lara, Beto Méndez
lp Catherine Jourdan, Carlos Castañón, Richard
Bohringer, América Cisneros, Patricia Meyer, Juan
Manuel González

On a hot summer night, América (Jourdan), a young
French woman, is in a Paris hotel with her lover
(Bohringer). While he goes out to get cigarettes, she
imagines a trip to Mexico. In her dream, she stages a
cabaret number dancing with a doll dressed like a
devil. The routine is very successful, she gets mixed
up with Jimmy (Castañón), a Mexican gigolo, and
has many adventures with gangsters. The lover
returns from the tobacconist; she pulls out a pistol
and kills him.

Eréndira
aka *The Incredible and Sad Story of Innocent Eréndira
and the Artless Grandmother*
1983 103 mins. colour
d Ruy Guerra *p* Alain Queffelean, Films du Triangle,
Films A2, Cine Qua Non, Atlas Saskia Film, Austra
sc Gabriel García Márquez *c* Denys Clerval, Roberto
Tivera *art dir* Pierre Cadiou, Rainer Chaper *sd*
Claude Villand, Roberto Martínez *ed* Kenout Peltier,
Jeanne Kef *m* Maurice Lecoeur
lp Irene Papas, Claudia Ohana, Michel Lonsdale,
Oliver Wehe, Rufus, Blanca Guerra, Ernesto Goméz
Cruz, Pierre Vaneck, Carlos Cardan, Humberto
Elizondo, Jorge Fegan, Francisco Mauri, Sergio
Calderón, Martín Palomares

Eréndira is a Mexican-French-German co-production
that tells the story of an adolescent girl Eréndira
(Ohana) exploited as a prostitute by her eccentric and
domineering grandmother (Papas). The
grandmother's house is destroyed by a fire that

started in Eréndira's room and she holds Eréndira responsible, demanding payment. They travel around the desert, setting up camp wherever the grandmother can solicit clients. The vacancy and impermanence of the desert are evoked by the ceaseless wind. This unremitting climate is home to smugglers and an occasional politician who creates false images of change and abundance. Eréndira's grandmother is the consummate entrepreneur in this lawless region. Between her ruthlessness and Eréndira's mysterious beauty, Eréndira quickly becomes legendary throughout the desert. Eréndira, as enigmatic as her grandmother is flamboyant, is prone to falling asleep on her feet. In contrast, her grandmother tends to rave in her sleep. As long as the grandmother is alive, Eréndira is bound to her. The subtle black comedy of the film becomes hilarious when Ulysses (Wehe), a young man who has fallen in love with Eréndira, tries to kill the virtually immortal granny. He finally succeeds, but this also means that Eréndira vanishes without a trace. The British release print ran for only 97 mins.

Nocaut
aka *Knockout*
1983 90 mins. b&w
d/sc José Luis García Agraz *p* Cooperativa KINAM (Jorge Díaz Moreno) *c* Angel Goded *sd* Nerio Barberis *ed* Carlos García Agraz *art dir* Elizabeth Menz *m* Gerardo Suárez
lp Gonzalo Vega, Blanca Guerra, Guillermo Orea, Alejandro Parodi, Wolf Ruvinskis, Roberto Cobo, Ignacio Retes, Blanca Torres, Carlos East, Agustín Silva, Jaime Ramos, Dolores Beristáin

Agraz's first feature, shot on 16mm blown up to 35mm, starts with a murder committed by the hero, Rodrigo Saracho (Vega), and recounts in a series of abrupt flashbacks and staccato sequences the circumstances that led to the killing. Rodrigo is a boxer who fought his way into a professional Mexico City boxing milieu which is intertwined with the criminal underworld. Soon, he is involved in 'taking dives' and money from the mafia boss (Ruvinskis). Sickened by his life, Rodrigo wants to regain his innocence but finds that he is trapped. Even his family has turned against him. In the end, having killed the mafia boss, Rodrigo runs for his life through the city streets, pursued by gangsters, as past and present fuse into a world of paranoia.

Doña Herlinda y su hijo
aka *Doña Herlinda and Her Son*

1984 (released in 1986) 90 mins. colour
d Jaime Humberto Hermosillo *p* Clasa Films Mundiales (Manuel Barbachano Ponce) *sc* Jaime Humberto Hermosillo from a story by Jorge López Páez *c* Miguel Ehrenberg *art dir* Daniel Varela *ed* Luis Kelly *sd* Fernando Cámara *songs* Lauro D. Uranga, Pepe Guízar, Juan Gabriel, José Alfredo Jiménez
lp Guadalupe del Toro, Arturo Meza, Marco Antonio Treviño, Leticia Lupercio, Angélica Guerrero, Arturo Villaseñor, Lucha Villa

Rodolfo (Treviño), a homosexual doctor, is discreetly involved with Ramón (Meza), a music student. Rodolfo's mother, Doña Herlinda (del Toro), wants him to formalise his relationship with Olga (Lupercio). Ramón gets jealous, but Rodolfo tries to calm him and Doña Herlinda agrees to let him move into their house. That night, the two men make love. Given that the relationship between Rodolfo and Olga is progressing smoothly, the friendship between Doña Herlinda and Ramón also grows. The wedding takes place and when he returns from his honeymoon, Rodolfo assures Ramón that their relationship will continue. Doña Herlinda decides that they can all live together. During a party celebrating his first son's baptism, Rodolfo reads a poem that is, in part, an homage to his mother.

Frida, naturaleza viva
1984 (released in 1985) 108 mins. colour
d Paul Leduc *p* Clasa Films Mundiales (Manuel Barbachano Ponce), Cooperativa Buten *sc* José Joaquín Blanco, Paul Leduc *c* Angel Goded *art dir* Alejandro Luna *ed* Rafael Castanedo *sd* Ernesto Estrada, Penélope Simpson
lp Ofelia Medina, Juan José Gurrola, Salvador Sánchez, Max Kerlow, Claudio Brook, Cecilia Toussaint, Valentina Leduc, Margarita Sanz, Juan A. Martínez

Appropriately enough, this cinematic biography of Frida Kahlo places a greater emphasis on images than on sound. Leduc departs from traditional narrative continuity to create a biography which is not structured as a linear account of the artist's development. Instead, the film associates images and memories according to the prevailing themes and concerns of Frida's (Medina) life and work. The film explores her tempestuous relationship with Diego Rivera (Gurrola), her commitment to the Communist Party, her affair with Leon Trotsky (Sánchez) and her struggles with physical and emotional illness. Above all the film reflects the intensity of this artist who maintained a strong alliance with the Mexican left and devoted her unique vision to the people and traditions of Mexico.

Tlacuilo

1984 60 mins. colour
d/sc Enrique Escalona *p* Estudios Churubusco-Azteca, CIESAS, IMCINE, Enrique Escalona *animators* Rodolfo Segura, Abdías, Rosa María Torres, Carolina Herrera Zamarrón *ed* Jorge Vargas *m* Grupo Huehuecuicatl

Independently produced film using animation to offer a new interpretation of one of the few surviving pre-Columbian manuscripts, the Mendocino Codex. In a didactic documentary format, the film summarises previous readings of the pre-Hispanic codices derived for the most part from European perspectives on textual production. The makers of *Tlacuilo* have used careful historical and anthropological research to offer a reading of the codices which is more sensitive to the cultures in which they originated. The film is based on a single page of the codex in order to keep the task manageable, and the aesthetic style establishes a continuity with the indigenous past it salutes.

Vidas errantes

aka *Wandering Lives* aka *Errant Lives*
1984 90 mins. colour
d Juan Antonio de la Riva *p* Conacine, Estudios Churubusco (Juan Antonio de la Riva) *sc* Juan Antonio de la Riva, Tomás Pérez Turrent from a story by Juan Antonio de la Riva *c* Leoncio 'Cuco' Villarías *art dir* Josefina González de la Riva *sd* Oscar Mateos *ed* Luis Kelly *m* Antonio Avitia, Grupo Me Caí
lp José Carlos Ruiz, Ignacio Guadalupe, Josefina González, Eduardo Sigler, Juan Manuel Luevanos, José Manuel García, Gabriela Olivo de Alba, Javier Gómez, Pedro Armendáriz Jr

De la Riva's first film is a tribute to Mexican cinema of the 'golden age'. It has also been interpreted as an allegory of Mexican film history since its tale of a search for roots is interrupted by a fire, recalling the tragic fire which destroyed the Cineteca film archive in 1982. Francisco (Ruiz) and Guillermo (Guadalupe), two travelling projectionists, make their way though the towns of the Durango sierra showing classic Mexican films from a van equipped with a projector and white sheets. These screenings permit

the insertion of clips from the classic films and the excerpts become part of the meandering narrative. On their travels they make friends, have love affairs, and participate in town festivities. At one point, they are joined by Josefina (González), a farm girl in love with Guillermo. Finally, Francisco, the elder of the two brothers, saves enough money to fulfil his lifelong dream: to own a movie theatre on the outskirts of town. Built out of wood, the building material typical of the region, the theatre accidentally burns down and Francisco must return to the life of a travelling projectionist.

Amor a la vuelta de la esquina

aka *Love Around the Corner*
1985 (released in 1986) 90 mins. colour
d Alberto Cortés Calderón *p* Producciones Emyll (Miguel Camacho) *sc* Alberto Cortés Calderón, José Agustín *c* Guillermo Navarro *art dir* Alejandra Liceaga *ed* Juan Manuel Vargas *sd* Sergio Zenteno *m* José G. Elorza
lp Gabriela Roel, Alonso Echánove, Leonor Llausás, Martha Papadimitriou, Juan Carlos Colombo, Emilio Cortés, Pilar Pellicer

While escaping from prison, María (Roel) breaks her foot and is picked up by Julián (Echánove), the driver of a contraband truck. After setting her foot, they hide in a guesthouse, but María escapes when Julián leaves her alone for a few days. She leads an erratic life in nightclubs and flea-ridden hotels until she meets her friend Marta. Together they work the streets as prostitutes and petty thieves. They waste their money on useless purchases until María runs into Julián. With the loot from a robbery, she continues her dissolute life in Acapulco. Apparently betrayed by Julián, María is captured and returned to prison.

El imperio de la fortuna

aka *The Realm of Fortune*
1985 (released in 1987) 135 mins.
(155 mins.) colour
d Arturo Ripstein *p* IMCINE (Héctor López) *sc* Paz Alicia Garcíadiego from *El gallo de oro* by Juan Rulfo *c* Angel Goded *art dir* Anna Sánchez *ed* Carlos Savage *sd* Daniel García *m* Lucía Alvarez
lp Ernesto Gómez Cruz, Blanca Guerra, Alejandro Parodi, Zaide Silvia Gutiérrez, Margarita Sanz, Ernesto Yáñez, Socorro Avelar

The dismantling of the state production companies under the administration of López Portillo hit Ripstein, and the early 80s were a period of relative inactivity for him. This film marked his comeback and also inaugurated a sequence of films written by Paz Alicia Garcíadiego. This remake of Gavaldón's *El gallo de oro* (1964) adapted from a Juan Rulfo story tells of Dionisio Pinzón (Gómez Cruz), a miserable town-crier, who rescues and takes care of a golden cock that was about to be killed. Once healed, the cock goes on to win many cock-fights. Soon Dionisio rivals Don Lorenzo (Parodi), a powerful cock-fighting cacique. Don Lorenzo's lover, 'La Caponera' (Guerra), goes off with Dionisio and becomes his good-luck charm. Time passes and Dionisio becomes an inveterate gambler. 'La Caponera' dies in the middle of a game and Dionisio loses everything. Realising that she is dead, he commits suicide. Following in her mother's footsteps, her adolescent daughter, 'La Pinzona', makes the rounds of *palenques* (cock-fight arenas), singing.

Los motivos de Luz
aka *Luz's Motives* aka *Luz's Reasons*
1985 94 mins. (117 mins.) colour
d Felipe Cazals *p* Chimalistac (Hugo Scherer)
sc Xavier Robles *c* Angel Goded *ed* Sigfrido García
sd Roberto Camacho
lp Patricia Reyes Spíndola, Delia Casanova, Martha Aura, Ana Ofelia Murguía, Alonso Echánove, Carlota Villagrán, Carlos Cardán

The bodies of four murdered children are discovered in a very poor house in a Mexico City suburb. The prime suspect is their mother Luz (Aura), who only remembers getting into a fight with her lover Sebastián before the crimes were committed. During the investigation, Luz insists that her mother-in-law gave her a doctored drink to push her to murder. Luz remembers various aspects of her life: after being fired from a job as a maid, she became Sebastián's lover. Luz's case arouses special interest because of her mental unbalance: a female lawyer and a psychologist take up her defence in an attempt to discover her real motivations.

Ulama
aka *Ulama, el juego de la vida y de la muerte*
1986 60 mins. colour
d Roberto Rochín *p* Roberto Rochín, Filmographics
sc Roberto Rochín, Tomás Pérez Turrent, José Manuel Pintado *narration* Jorge Martínez de Hoyos *c* Arturo de la Rosa *ed* Ramón Aupart, Manuel Rodríguez *m* Antonio Zepeda

Like *Tlacuilo* (1984), this film about pre-Hispanic Meso-America is one of the most successful Mexican drama-documentaries. It describes the rubber-ball games of the Mayan peoples through a mixture of animation, dramatic re-enactment and documentary. Rubber was unknown in Europe before colonial contact, and the film looks at the way social organisation was structured around this resource which would later become a major commodity in global trade. The film offers insights into the unwritten history of indigenous Americans, alternating secondary accounts with fragments from the *Popol Vuh,* one of the only surviving Mayan manuscripts.

Mentiras piadosas
aka *White Lies*
1988 (released in 1989) 111 mins. colour
d Arturo Ripstein *p* Producciones Fílmicas Internacionales, Universidad de Guadalajara (DICSA-CIEC), STPC, ANDA, Kuikali, Fondo de Fomento a la Calidad Cinematográfica (J. Feldman and M. Salame) *sc* Paz Alicia Garcíadiego *c* Angel Goded, *colour art dir* Juan José Urbini *ed* Carlos Puente *m* Lucía Alvarez
lp Alonso Echánove, Delia Casanova, Ernesto Yáñez, Luisa Huertas, Fernando Palavicini, Leonor Llausás, Mario de Jesús Villers, César Arias, Osami Kawano, Justo Martínez, Jaime Casillas, Itzel Tapia

Israel Ordóñez (Echánove) is a herb merchant in downtown Mexico City. With his friend Matilde (Yáñez), an old pederast, he has built an enormous model of the ancient city of Tenochtitlán with the hope that its sale will solve his financial problems. Israel meets Clara Zamudio (Casanova), a health inspector, and seduces her. After some months they decide to leave their respective partners and live together, but jealousy and guilt take over their relationship and make it suffocating. Finally, Israel violently assaults Clara and she sets fire to the model. The model's destruction marks the end of their relationship. Clara leaves Israel for another lover.

El secreto de Romelia
aka *Romelia's Secret*
1988 100 mins. colour
d Busi Cortés *p* Centro de Capacitación Cinematográfica, IMCINE (Eduardo Maldonado, Gustavo Montiel) *sc* Busi Cortés from Rosario Castellanos's novel *El viudo Román c* Francisco Bojórquez *sd* Miguel Sandoval *ed* Federico Landeros *art dir* Leticia Venzor *m* José Amozurrutia
lp Diana Bracho, Pedro Armendáriz Jr, Dolores Beristáin, Arcelia Ramírez, Alejandro Parodi, Josefina

Echánove, Nuria Montiel, Mari Carmen Cárdenas, Alina Amozurrutia, José Angel García, Lumi Cavazos, Lisa Owen

Based on the novel by the noted poet and writer Rosario Castellanos, this is a foray into the memories and desires of three generations of women. Romelia Orantes (Beristáin) travels to her home town with her daughter and granddaughters to claim the inheritance left by her estranged husband, but the trip is also a journey into her past. Hints about Romelia's secret and her tormented history are gradually revealed. As the women integrate these snippets of information into their current relationship, the secrets come to symbolise the diverging social and moral imperatives of the three generations these women represent. Romelia does finally unveil the skeleton in her closet. Busi Cortés's first film employs family history as social history: Roselia's story and those of her younger relatives detail the cultural changes in Mexico since the Revolutionary years.

Goitia: Un dios para si mismo
aka *Goitia: A God for Himself*
1989 112 mins. colour
d Diego López *p* Imaginaria, IMCINE, Fondo de Fomento a la Calidad Cinematográfica, Gobierno del Estado de Zacatecas, Cooperativa José Revueltas, Diego López, Gonzalo Infante, Hugo Scherer *sc* Diego López with Enrique Vargas, Jorge González de León, Javier Sicilia, José Carlos Ruiz, Raúl Zermeño based on the life of Francisco Goitia *c* Arturo de la Rosa, Jorge Suárez *ed* Sigfrido García *art dir* Teresa Pecanins *m* Amparo Rubín
lp Patricia Reyes Spíndola, Alejandro Parodi, Ana Ofelia Murguía, Angélica Aragón, Alonso Echánove, Fernando Balzaretti, Martha Navarro, Aurora Clavel

Feeling death approaching, Francisco Goitia, an outstanding but little-known twentieth-century Mexican painter, begs God for the strength to paint his last picture. In an autobiographical monologue, the painter remembers returning from artistic training in Europe to find his native country shattered by the Revolution, an experience that shocked him into adopting a realist style with indigenist qualities, blending pain and misery with the sublime. Reflecting on his struggles with mental illness and its relation to his religious conversion, the film draws a picture of a painter torn between insanity and lucidity in a lifelong quest for identity. Still seeking some essential truth about humanity, the film ends with the gaunt and world-weary image of Goitia's face as he paints a self-portrait.

Intimidades en un cuarto de baño
aka *Bathroom Intimacies*
1989 (released in 1991) 75 mins. colour
d/sc Jaime Humberto Hermosillo *p* Profesionales and Sociedad Cooperativa de Producción Cinematográfica José Revueltas (Lourdes Rivera) *c* Guillermo Navarro *art dir* Leticia Venzor *sd* Salvador de la Fuente *m* Rockdrigo
lp Gabriela Roel, Martha Navarro, María Rojo, Alvaro Guerrero, Emilio Echeverría

At dawn, the young woman Gabriela (Roel) seeks refuge in the bathroom, where all the action of the film will take place. Her husband Roberto (Guerrero) arrives; he has been drinking and they get into a fight. When she refuses to make love to him, he rapes her. The couple lives in her parents' apartment because of their precarious economic position. Berta (Navarro), the mother, is a successful career woman who advises her daughter to leave Roberto. Juan (Echeverría), the father, is a frustrated writer and an avid reader of pornographic magazines. Overwhelmed by his problems and his relationship with Gabriela, Roberto commits suicide. Under the influence of her mother, Gabriela agrees to change her life.

La leyenda de una máscara
aka *The Legend of a Mask*
1989 95 mins. colour
d José Buil *p* CONACINE, IMCINE *sc* José Buil from his own story *c* Henner Hofmann *sd* Fernando Cámara, René Ruiz Cerón *ed* Sigfrido García Case *art dir* Patricia Eguía, Alfonso Morales *m* Oscar Reynoso
lp Héctor Bonilla, Héctor Ortega, María Rojo, Gina Morett, Pedro Armendáriz Jr, Martha Papadimitriou, Roberto Cobo, Damián Alcázar, Fernando Rubio, Gabriel Pingarrón

The masked wrestler is a phenomenon of Mexican popular culture witnessed not only in the ring but in comics, magazines, radio and film ever since Fernando Méndez's *Ladrón de cadáveres* (1956). A humorous tribute to this icon of the mass media, the film is presented as episode twenty-seven of a serial story and quotes film noir clichés as well as *Citizen Kane* (1941). When the Masked Angel (Bonilla) is found dead on the floor of his luxurious house, Olmo Robles (Alcázar), an obscure sports reporter, goes on assignment to investigate the true personality of the man behind the mask. In his search, Robles descends into Mexico City's underworld, gathers testimony from the Masked Angel's wives, his chauffeur, comic writers (including animated scenes) and film producers, and discovers that the legendary Masked Angel's secret identity is actually rather prosaic but kept shrouded in mystery by his partners and associates. Buil had made a short film paying homage to the masked wrestler Santo in 1981, *Adiós, adiós, ídolo mio.*

Lola

1989 92 mins. colour
d María Novaro *p* Cooperativa José Revueltas, Conacite Dos, Macondo Cine Video, Televisión Española (Dulce Kuri, Jorge Sánchez) *sc* María and Beatriz Novaro *c* Rodrigo García *sd* Carlos Aguilar *ed* Sigfrido Barjau *art dir* Marisa Pecanins *m* Gabriel Romo
lp Leticia Huijara, Alejandro Vargas, Martha Navarro, Roberto Sosa, Mauricio Rivera, Javier Zaragosa, Chell Godinez, Gerardo Martínez, Laura Ruiz

Awarded Best First Feature prizes at two Latin American film festivals, *Lola* is a personal and polemical consideration of the status of Mexican women. The film's central character, Lola (Huijara), is a young woman who, disoriented after her breakup with a rock musician, supports herself and her five-year-old daughter (Vargas) by selling clothes on the streets of Mexico City. The disarray of the city left by the 1985 earthquake provides a chaotic atmosphere for her daily life. The pressures of this urban existence overwhelm her and she abandons her daughter, escaping to the seaside. There, however, she is forced to confront reality and forge her identity in a world which has continuously limited her choices. Lola's uncertainty about her role as a mother is a marked contrast from the glorification of motherhood that pervades Mexican cinema. The summation of Lola's story confirms that this film has brought a unique perspective to Mexican feminism.

Maten a Chinto

aka *Kill Chinto*
1989 90 mins. colour
d/sc Alberto Isaac *p* Conacine, Estudios Churubusco *c* Jorge Stahl Jr *ed* Carlos Savage *sd* Daniel García, René Ruiz Cerón *art dir* Enrique Bernal *m* Lucía Alvarez
lp Pedro Armendáriz Jr, Gerardo Quiroz, Héctor Ortega, Eduardo López Rojas, Patricia Páramo,

Javier Masse, Alfredo Dávila

Inspired by an actual incident in Colima around Christmas 1944, Isaac's black comedy features the hotelier Chinto (Armendáriz), who terrorises the city when he suddenly goes mad and starts shooting at people. Police, the army and the navy (Colima is a port) are too disorganised and bureaucratic to cope with the psychotic hero's lethal outburst.

Una moneda en el aire

aka *A Coin in the Air*
1989 90 mins. colour
d Ariel Zúñiga *p* SINC, Cooperativa José Revueltas *sc* Hugo Bonaldi *c* Guillermo Navarro *ed* Gilberto Macedo *sd* Alejandro Aguilar
lp Arturo Beristáin, Isabel Benet, Andrea Ferrari, Jorge Martínez de Hoyos, Delia Casanova, Carmen Delgado, Rafael Cruz

An exploration of the conventions of film noir and the pleasures of the B-movie genre. A thriller plot with all the usual scenes of violence, suspense, *femmes fatales,* and so on, functions as the framework for this stylish experiment in semi-narrative cinema relying almost exclusively on the concatenation of familiar generic imagery presented in garish colour, allowing the suggestion of a story to emerge from the imagery itself.

Morir en el Golfo

aka *To Die in the Gulf*
1989 93 mins. colour
d Alejandro Pelayo Rangel *p* Compañía Tabasco Films, Sociedad Cooperativa de Producción de Cinematografía José Revueltas, IMCINE, Alejandro Pelayo *sc* Victor Hugo Rascón, Alejandro Pelayo from a novel by Héctor Aguilar Camín *c* Guillermo Navarro *sd* Miguel Sandoval López *ed* Oscar Figueroa Jara *art dir* Teresa Uribe *m* José Elorza, Marcial Alejandro
lp Blanca Guerra, Enrique Rocha, Alejandro Parodi, Carlos Cardán, Emilio Echeverría, María Rojo, Ana Ofelia Murguía, Luis Manuel Pelayo, Martín Lasalle

Loyalty and animosity are close cousins in this film about corruption within the ruling classes of society. Enemies are those you love to hate, good friends are the reverse. Raymundo Herrera is a seasoned journalist who takes pride in his honesty. At a press conference about developing the tourist industry in the Gulf state of Tabasco, he runs into a former schoolmate, Santana. Their good-natured political rivalry had grown bitter over a woman, Leonora, who ultimately chose to marry Santana. Now a local politician, Santana enlists Herrera's support to undermine the regional control of a mafioso landowner, Uscanga, but Santana is no angel himself and soon Herrera is embroiled in a vicious struggle for power. Herrera seals his involvement in the conflict when he and Leonora begin an affair. Herrera's character is similar to the lonesome detective in old gangster movies, but Herrera's unyielding principles get a dose of reality as he learns that right and wrong are not so easily separated in the real world.

Intimidad

1989 100 mins. colour
d Dana Rotberg *p* Producciones Metropolis (León Constantiner) *sc* Leonardo García Tsao from the play by Hugo Hiriart *c* Carlos Markovich *ed* Oscar Figueroa *sd* José Antonio García *art dir* Carlos Herrera *m* Gerardo Bátiz, Raúl Rojo and his orchestra
lp Emilio Echeverría, Lisa Owen, Angeles González, Acuaro Guerrero, Juan José Nebreda, Ana Ofelia Murguía, Agustín Silva

Rotberg's feature debut is a wry comedy about an ineffective, henpecked middle-aged teacher Julio (Echeverría) who falls in love with his neighbour, Tere (Owen). However, financial and marital constraints eventually get the better of him and he sinks back into his humdrum life. Rotberg commented that Constantiner had suggested that she make a film about love, or more precisely, about the couple. Although she did not think this a particularly interesting subject, it did allow her to make her first feature.

Cabeza de Vaca

aka *Shipwrecks*
1990 (released in 1991) 112 mins. colour
d Nicolás Echevarría *p* Instituto Mexicano de Cinematografía, Producciones Iguana with Televisión Española, Sociedad Estatal del Quinto Centenario, Channel Four Television (London), American Playhouse (Bertha Navarro) *sc* Guillermo Sheridan, Nicolás Echevarría from the autobiographical memoirs *Naufragios* by Alvar Núñez Cabeza de Vaca *c* Guillermo Navarro *art dir* José Luis Aguilar *ed* Rafael Castanedo *sd* Carlos Aguilar *m* Mario Lavista
lp Juan Diego, Daniel Giménez Cacho, Roberto Sosa, Carlos Castañón, Gerardo Villarreal, Roberto Cobo, José Flores, Farnesio de Bernal

After a shipwreck, Pánfilo Narváez's expedition arrives in Florida in 1527. The treasurer is Alvar Núñez Cabeza de Vaca (Diego) who recorded the fate of the expedition in a collection of writings which is the source of the film. The Spanish are exterminated by the aborigines. Cabeza de Vaca survives and is enslaved by a sorcerer who teaches him the craft of the shaman. Once free, he walks from what is now Florida to Sinaloa, performing miraculous cures and getting to know the various indigenous tribes. Eight years later, he finally rejoins the Spanish troops. The film combines ethnography and autobiography in a tale portraying the conflict between Spanish and American populations, while appreciating the mystical reality of the native peoples.

Latino Bar

1990 100 mins. colour
d Paul Leduc *p* Opalo Films (Barcelona), Universidad de los Andes (Venezuela), ICAIC (Cuba), Television Española (Madrid), Channel Four Television (London), José Antonio Pérez Giner *sc* Paul Leduc, José Joaquín Blanco from the novel *Santa* by Federico Gamboa *c* José María Civit *ed* Marisa Aguiñaga *sd* Victor Luckert *art dir* Haydée Pino *m* Joan Albert Amargos, Consejo Valiente, J. Antonio Mendez, Beny Moré, Gerardo Batiz, Tabu Ley Rocherau
lp Dolores Pedro, Roberto Sosa, Ernesto Gómez Cruz, Antonieta Colón, Norma Prieto, Cecilia Bellarin, Milagros Carias, Lisette Solorzano, Dianina Vargas, Janet Thode

A dialogue-free allegory about poverty, exploitation, violence and sensuality set in a dingy, waterfront bar-cum-brothel in the Caribbean. While a thunderstorm threatens, a man who stole some food is pursued by the police and hidden by the dock workers; a woman seeks employment in a bar. The man and the woman eventually meet and, each recognising a smouldering anger in the other, they get together. Then, the thunderstorm erupts. The film is the most recent adaptation of Gamboa's popular and often-filmed melodrama (cf. Antonio Moreno's *Santa,* 1931, Mexico's first sound feature).

Pueblo de Madero

aka *Timber Town* aka *Wooden Town*
1990 138 mins. colour
d Juan Antonio de la Riva *p* Conacite Dos, Televisión Española *sc* Juan Antonio de la Riva and Francisco Sánchez based on their own story *c* Leoncio Villarías

sd Miguel Sandoval *ed* Oscar Figueroa *art dir* Patricia Eguía *m* Antonio Avitia, Grupo Tránsito, Grupo Los Broncos de Reynosa
lp Alonso Echánove, Gabriela Roel, Ignacio Guadalupe, Jahir de Rubín, Ernesto Jesús, Angélica Aragón, José Carlos Ruiz, Mario Almada

Whereas de la Riva's first feature, *Wandering Lives* (1984), compared the cinema to a search for roots, *Timber Town* understands movies as a means of escape. Movies are the only thing to relieve the backwoods tedium of a lumber town in Durango, Mexico. More a portrait of the town than of any specific character, the film unfolds from the perspective of two vacationing schoolboys. The older people in the town avoid outsiders and anything else that might disturb their sense of peace. The two youngsters, inspired by the movies, try to break the monotony by getting into trouble. The films serve as a rite of passage for the boys. In the end, one goes off to the city for his education and the other stays to follow in his father's footsteps. *Timber Town* achieves a bittersweet nostalgia with its impressionistic depiction of this quiescent environment.

Retorno a Aztlán
aka *Return to Aztlán* aka *In Necuepalitzli in Aztlán*
1990 92 mins. colour
d Juan Mora Catlett *p* Producciones Volcán, Cooperativa José Revueltas, Dirección de Actividades Cinematográficas de la UNAM *sc* Juan Mora Catlett from an Aztec legend *c* Toni Kuhn *sd* Ernesto Estrada *ed* Jorge Vargas *art dir* Gabriel Pascal *m* Antonio Zepeda
lp Rodrigo Puebla, Rafael Cortés, Amado Sumaya, Socorro Avelar, Soledad Ruiz, José Chávez Trowe, María Catlett

This is the first feature film to devote itself entirely to the legends of pre-Columbian Aztec Mexico. Set in the 15th century before the Spanish conquest, the film incorporates Nahuatl, a native Mexican language. Moctezuma (Puebla) sends his envoys and a peasant (Cortés) on a magical journey to Aztlán, the Aztecs' mythical land of origin. The voyage is undertaken to seek the remedy for a four-year drought. The film portrays this ancient civilisation with respect and appreciation, understanding the violence of that culture as a part of the complex social fabric rather than as savagery. Shot in archaeological sites, the film authenticates its narrative with the exquisite art and gigantic pyramids of the Aztecs. All of the music in the film was made with pre-Columbian instruments.

La tarea
aka *Homework*
1990 (released in 1991) 85 mins. colour
d/sc Jaime Humberto Hermosillo *p* Clasa Films Mundiales (Pablo and Francisco Barbachano) *c* Toni Kuhn *art dir* Laura Santa Cruz *sd* Nerio Barberis *m* Luis Arcaraz, Hermanos Martínez Gil, Rosendo Ruiz Jr
lp María Rojo, José Alonso

This erotic comedy, a revised and expanded version of *El aprendiz de pornógrafo* (1989) shot to resemble video, reflects on the changing relations between the public and the private brought about by video. Shot in a single take from a fixed point of view, the film broaches a matter as private as a woman's tentative assumption of a sexual initiative. At the same time, the camera, in its constant allusions to cinema, remains, even in the private sphere, inextricably linked to voyeurism and the concept of public spectacle. Virginia (Rojo), a communications student, has made a date with her ex-lover Marcelo (Alonso), and sets up a hidden camera to tape the event. Marcelo is quite loving toward Virginia until he discovers that he is being taped. Though angry, he eventually agrees to help Virginia finish her homework and they make love. In the end, their children arrive and we discover the couple staged the making of the tape to supplement the family's income.

Ciudad de ciegos
aka *City of the Blind*
1991 93 mins. colour
d Alberto Cortés *p* IMCINE, Fondo de Fomento a la Calidad Cinematográfica, Tabasco Films, Bataclan Cinematográfica *sc* Hermann Bellinhausen, Alberto Cortés *c* Carlos Matcovich *sd* Sergio Zenteno *ed* Rafael Castanedo *art dir* Homero Espinoza *m* José Elorza
lp Gabriela Roel, Juan Ibarra, Carmen Salinas, Fernando Balzaretti, Silvia Mariscal, Claudia Fernández, Arcelia Ramírez, Verónica Merchant, Roberto Sosa, Zaide Silvia Gutiérrez, Silvana Orsatti, Blanca Guerra, Elpidio Carrillo, Benny Ibarra

One apartment in Mexico City is the common setting for ten different vignettes spread over thirty years, including the 1985 earthquake. Each of the vignettes depicts a completely private, and mostly sexual, anecdote located within the Mexican middle class. The outside world is glimpsed only through the objects contained in the apartment: the television, a phone, withered flowers, garbage. Dawn and nightfall are witnessed through the windows as the protagonists pass one another in the corridors like shadows.

Como agua para chocolate
aka *Like Water for Chocolate*
1991 116 mins. colour
d Alfonso Arau *p* Arau Films International, Cinevista Inc., Aviacsa, National Council for Cinema and the Arts, IMCINE *sc* Laura Esquivel from her own novel *c* Emmanuel Lubezki, Steve Bernstein *ed* Carlos Bolado, Francisco Chiu *sd* Marcos Welch *art dir* Marco Antonio Arteaga, Mauricio de Aguinaco, Denise Pizzini *m* Leo Brower
lp Marco Leonardi, Lumi Cavazos, Regina Torne, Mario Ivan Martínez, Ada Carrasco, Yareli Arizmendi, Claudette Maille, Pilar Aranda, Farnesio de Bernal, Rodolfo Arias, Sandra Arau, Joaquín Garrido, Margarita Isabel

Based on his wife's best-selling debut novel written in 1989, Arau's story about forbidden love is set on an isolated ranch near the Texas border in 1910, during the Revolution. The authoritarian, tradition-minded Mama Élena (Torne) offers Pedro Muzquiz (Leonardi) the hand of her second daughter Rosaura (Arizmendi) because the eldest daughter Tita (Cavazos) is supposed to look after her although Tita and Pedro are passionately in love. Pedro and Tita agree to the arrangement as it is the only way they can be near each other. For the rest of her life, Tita, who runs the kitchen staffed by Nacha (Carrasco) and Chencha (Aranda), will express her love for Pedro through her cooking. Another sister, Gertrudis (Maille), joins the Revolution. The film, partly funded by the Mexican Tourist Board, follows the book's device of starting every chapter with a recipe, associating food and sex but also introducing class as an issue, since the recipes actually are provided by the kitchen servants. The film is told in flashback from Pedro's daughter's point of view, incorporating lots of soft focus and warm colours. The title refers to a sense of boiling anger as well as passion.

Danzón
1991 104 mins. colour
d María Novaro *p* IMCINE, Macondo Cine Video, Fondo de Fomento a la Calidad Cinematográfica, Televisión Española, Tabasco Films, Gobierno del Estado de Veracruz (Jorge Sánchez, Dulce Kuri) *sc*

María and Beatríz Novaro *c* Rodrigo García *art dir* Marisa Pecanins, Norberto Sánchez-Mejorada *ed* Nelson Rodríguez, María Novaro *sd* Nerio Barberis *m* Luis Arcaraz, Agustín Lara and danzones performed by Danzonera Dimas, Pepe Luis and Orquesta Universitaria, Danzonera Alma de Sotavento, Manzanita and Son 4
lp María Rojo, Margarita Isabel, Tito Vasconcelos, Carmen Salinas, Blanca Guerra, Victor Carpinteiro, Cheli Godinez, Martha Novaro, Daniel Rergis

Julia Solórzano (Rojo), a Mexico City telephone operator, has an adolescent daughter and one passion: dancing. Carmelo (Rergis) has been her *danzón* partner for six years, but they meet only at the dancehall on Wednesdays and Sundays. When Carmelo disappears for two weeks without any notice or explanation, Julia begins to look for him. Not finding him in Mexico City, she goes to his home town of Veracruz. There she befriends Suzy (Vasconcelos), a transvestite, and has a love affair with the young Rubén (Carpinteiro). She returns to Mexico City without finding Carmelo. The director appears in the film as a witch.

Lolo
1991 88 mins. colour
d/sc Francisco Athié *p* Centro de Capacitación Cinematográfica, IMCINE (Gustavo Montiel) *c* Jorge Medina *ed* Tlacatéotl Mata *sd* Miguel Sandoval, Salvador de la Fuente *art dir* Marisa Pecanins *m* Juan Cristóbal Pérez Grobert
lp Roberto Sosa, Lucha Villa, Damián Alcazar, Alonso Echánove, Esperanza Mozo, Artemisa Flores, Alicia Montoya

Athié's debut feature set on the outskirts of Mexico City tells of betrayal and guilt. A factory worker, Dolores Chimal aka Lolo (Sosa), is mugged and hospitalised, and so loses his job. In the ensuing chaos, as he tries to redeem his girlfriend's watch, he kills an old woman and a local gang viciously try to force him to confess. Lolo invokes the help of his girlfriend, Sonia (Mozo), who is forced to prostitute herself to help him.

Mi querido Tom Mix
aka *My Dear Tom Mix*
1991 120 mins. colour
d Carlos García Agraz *p* Producciones Amaranta, IMCINE, Fondo de Fomento a la Calidad Cinematográfica, Gobierno del Estado de Zacatecas *sc* Consuelo Garrido from a story developed in

Gabriel García Márquez's screenwriters' workshop *c* Rodrigo García *sd* Nerio Barberis *ed* Tlacateotl Mata *art dir* Teresa Pecanins *m* Alberto Núñez Palacios *lp* Ana Ofelia Murguía, Federico Luppi, Manuela Ojeda, Damián García Vásquez, Zan Zhi Guo, Mercedes Olea, Jorge Fegan, Carlos Chávez, Eduardo Casab, René Pereira, Angelina Peláez, Eduardo Palomo

The action takes place in Ocotito, a Mexican border town, in the early 30s. Sixty-year-old Joaquina (Murguía) lives with her nephew Evaristo (Ojeda) and his wife Antonia (Olea). Joaquina is obsessed with the legendary cowboy, Tom Mix, but Antonia dismisses this as the delusions of an old crackpot. Consequently, Joaquina is forced to sneak out in order to watch the movies, secretly writing fan mail to Tom Mix in which she proclaims her adoration and offers him advice on his adventures. Antonia pressures her husband to send Joaquina to a larger town, thinking that the move will keep the elderly relative safe from the post-Revolutionary bandits who are raiding the countryside. The couple's nephew, Felipe (Vásquez), arrives for a vacation and is intrigued by the fantasies of his older relative. When Big Pancho's (Casab) gang hits town, Joaquina and Felipe write for Tom Mix's assistance. In the meantime, Domingo (Luppi), a sixty-year-old horse-breaker, cowboy and wanderer, has arrived in town and taken a job as the projectionist in the local movie theatre. He offers to help the men as they organise the town's defence, but they consider him too old. When Joaquina, Domingo and Felipe are trapped in the cinema surrounded by the gang, their fantasies of adventure become reality.

La mujer de Benjamín

aka *Benjamin's Woman* aka *Benjamin's Wife*
1991 90 mins. colour
d Carlos Carrera *p* Centro de Capacitación Cinematográfica, Estudios Churubusco-Azteca, IMCINE *sc* Carlos Carrera, Ignacio Ortiz *c* Javier Pérez Grobet *sd* Fernando Cámara *ed* Sigfrido Barjau, Oscar Figueroa *art dir* Gloria Carrasco *m* José Amozurrutia, Alejandro Giacomán
lp Eduardo López Rojas, Malena Doria, Arcelia Ramírez, Eduardo Palomo, Ana Bertha Espín, Juan Carlos Colombo, Farnesio de Bernal, Rubén Márquez, Enrique Gardiel, Luis Ignacio Erazo

Echoing Nelly Kaplan's crazy comedy *Papa les petits bateaux* (1971), routine harmony masks the frustration and disenchantment of banal everyday life in a small community. Seventeen-year-old Natividad (Doria) is tired of life in her village and dreams of travelling the world. She spends her time flirting with Leandro, the only other lively inhabitant. The others, bored and sexually repressed, work to drain the vitality from Natividad and Leandro. The tone shifts when Benjamín (Rojas), a middle-aged boxer, falls in love with Natividad and his friends arrange her kidnapping. Benjamín, considered the village fool, lives with his domineering sister Micaela (Ramírez). Natividad adapts to the situation and cunningly plays with the power she has over the devoted Benjamín, and before long she controls the household. Leandro's sudden interference instigates a violent episode which determines the fate of Natividad and restores Benjamín's reputation among the villagers.

La mujer del puerto

aka *The Woman of the Port*
1991 110 mins. colour
d Arturo Ripstein *p* Dos Producciones (Hugo Scherer, Mexico), Chariot 7 Production (Allen Persselin, Michael Donnely, Los Angeles) *sc* Paz Alicia Garcíadiego based on Guy de Maupassant's story *c* Angel Goded *art dir* Juan José Urbini *ed* Carlos Puente *m* Lucía Alvarez
lp Patricia Reyes Spíndola, Alejandro Parodi, Evangelina Sosa, Damián Alcázar, Ernesto Yáñez, Julián Pastor, Jorge Fegan, Alejandra Montoya, Fernando Soler Palavicini

Perla (Sosa) is the young star of a tacky port cabaret. Tomasa (Spíndola), her mother, has no qualms about prostituting her daughter. Perla does everything possible to get away from 'el Marro' (Alcázar), a feverish young sailor who has escaped from a quarantined ship. The three characters' stories are interwoven, completing and contradicting each other, around abortion, incest and suicide. Carmelo (Parodi), an old singer, is the fourth character: he dreams of a utopian brothel.

Solo con tu pareja

aka *Love in the Time of Hysteria*
1991 94 mins. colour
d Alfonso Cuarón *p* IMCINE, Fondo de Fomento a la Calidad Cinematográfica, Sólo Películas (Rosalía Salazar, Alfonso Cuarón) *sc* Alfonso Cuarón, Carlos Cuarón *c* Emmanuel Lubezki *sd* José Antonio García, Carlos Aguilar *ed* Alfonso Cuarón, Luis Patlán *art dir* Brigitte Broch *m* Wolfgang Amadeus Mozart, Carlos Warman
lp Daniel Giménez Cacho, Claudia Ramírez, Luis de Icaza, Astrid Hadad, Dobrina Liubomirova, Isabel

Benet, Ricardo Dalmacci, Claudia Fernández, Luz María Jerez, Toshiro Alberto Hisaki, Carlos Nakasone

A farce about a callously compulsive womaniser, presented as an endearing character, in the age of AIDS. Tomás Tomás (Giménez Cacho) is an advertising copy editor prepared to endanger anybody's life, including his own, by refusing to wear condoms. He is ridiculed when he reveals his fear of needles at an AIDS test. The film derives its satiric edge from first soliciting and then subverting the identification with the characters.

Angel de fuego
aka *Angel of Fire*
1992 90 mins. colour
d Dana Rotberg *p* Producciones Metrópolis, IMCINE *sc* Omar Aláin Rodrigo, Dana Rotberg *c* Toni Kuhn *sd* Nerio Barberis *ed* Sigfrido Barjau, Dana Rotberg *art dir* Anna Sánchez *m* Ariel Guzik, Ana Ruiz
lp Evangelina Sosa, Lilia Aragón, Roberto Sosa, Noé Montealegre, Alejandro Parodi, Salvador Sánchez, Mercedes Pascual, Gina Morett, Farnesio de Bernal, Martha Aura

A comment on religious fanaticism and moral hypocrisy touching on questions of incest and the oppression of women in the chaotic and cynical world of Mexico City. Thirteen-year-old Alma (Sosa) works as a trapeze artist and a fire-eater in a dilapidated circus on the outskirts of Mexico City. She becomes pregnant by her father, Renato (Parodi), the circus's sick old clown. When Renato dies, Alma is ostracised from the troupe for refusing to give up her baby, and lives alone on the streets until she meets a group of itinerant, evangelical puppeteers led by the fanatic and domineering Refugio (Aragón). Their message offers her a glimmer of hope and she eventually agrees to submit to a vicious purification rite of deprivation and pain, believing that God will protect her and her baby.

El bulto
aka *Lump* aka *Excess Baggage*
1992 114 mins. colour
d Gabriel Retes *p* Cooperativa Rio Mixcoac, Conexion, SCL *sc* Gabriel Retes, Mar del Pozo, Gabriela Retes *c* Chuy *sd* Antonio Diego *ed* Saul Aupart *art dir* Tomás Guevara, Francesca Appentzeller *m* Pedro Plascencia Salinas
lp Héctor Bonilla, José Alonso, Juan Claudio Retes, Lourdes Elizarrás, Delia Casanova, Cecilia Camacho, Gabriel Retes, Lucia Balzaretti, Luis Felipe Tovar

Opening with b&w documentary-type footage of riot police beating a journalist unconscious during the uprising in Mexico City in 1971, the uncompromising realism of the film's first images sets the tone for the story. After a twenty-year coma, the journalist revives, disabled. The world he awakens to has radically changed. His children have grown up, his wife has remarried, and his progressive tastes and opinions are now outdated. The film resists the melodrama of a disabled person's struggle, opting instead to portray 'the lump' as an intolerant man whose mind is stuck in the past. He finally accepts that global politics, popular culture and his own personal relations have shifted. Throughout all this, humour and an attention to the mundane steer the film clear of emotional histrionics.

Cronos
1992 92 mins. colour
d/sc Guillermo del Toro *p* Producciones Iguana (Bertha Navarro, Alejandro Springall, Bernard Nussbaumer) *c* Guillermo Navarro *ed* Raúl Davalos, Paul O'Brien *sd* Fernando Cámara *art dir* Tolita Figueroa, Brigitte Broch *m* Javier Alvarez
lp Federico Luppi, Ron Perlman, Claudio Brook, Margarita Isabel, Tamara Shanath, Daniel Giménez Cacho, Mario Iván Martínez, Juan Carlos Colombo, Farnesio de Bernal, Jorge Martínez de Hoyos

The feature debut of del Toro is an innovative vampire movie revolving around the Cronos device, the fountain of eternal life made by the alchemist Fulcanelli in the 16th century and found in old Jesús Gris's (Luppi) Mexico City junk shop. The problem with the device is that it must be fed with blood. A rich American businessman also covets the device and sends his brutal son to get it. The film lovingly and stylishly runs through the whole range of Mexican popular cinema, from its particular tradition of horror films to the masked wrestler genre and the thriller. In the end, the unkillable old man destroys the American tycoon, the symbol of absolute wealth and the brutality required to obtain it, as well as the Cronos device and its mortiferous associations with misguided European attempts to dominate nature.

Novia que te vea
aka *Like a Bride*
1992 115 mins. colour
d Guita Schyfter *p* Producciones Artes, IMCINE

(Tita Lombardo) *sc* Hugo Hiriart from Rosa Nissan's story *c* Toni Kuhn *ed* Carlos Bolado *sd* Salvador de la Fuente *art dir* Teresa Pecanins
m Joaquín Gutiérrez Heras
lp Claudette Maille, Angélica Aragón, Ernesto Laguardia, Mercedes Pascual, Maya Michalska, Veronica Langer, Pedro Armendáriz Jr

Focusing on two young Jewish Mexican girls in the 60s, the film charts the complexities of Jewish life in contemporary urban Mexico. Oshinica Mataraso (Maille) is from a Sefardic family whose archaic culture derives from medieval Spain whence Jewish families were expelled by the Catholic monarchy. Her friend Rifka Groman (Michalska) grew up in a family scarred by their experiences in Europe and the holocaust.

La vida conyugal
aka *Married Life*
1992 100 mins. colour
d Carlos Carrera *p* Fernando Sariñana, IMCINE, Fondo de Fomento a la Calidad Cinematográfica, Vida Films, Universidad de Guadalajara, Tabasco Films, Oxicem *sc* Carlos Carrera, Ignacio Ortiz from the novel by Sergio Pitol *c* Javier Pérez Grobet *ed* Carlos Bolado *sd* Fernando Cámara *art dir* Brigitte Broch *m* Enrique Quezada Luna
lp Socorro Bonilla, Alonso Echánove, Patricio Castillo, Isabel Benet, Damián Bichir, Margarita Sanz, Alvaro Guerrero, Nora Velázquez, Eduardo López Rojas, Regina Orozco

A black comedy about a petty-bourgeois couple, Jacqueline (Bonilla) and Nicolás (Echánove), whose marriage goes sour. Nicolás starts an affair with his secretary at his flourishing hardware store. He becomes a greedy real-estate developer and as they grow wealthier, Jacqueline uses her lovers in repeated attempts to kill her husband. The story spans forty years of married life and, according to the director, depicts love and hate carried to its fullest extremes.

Dollar Mambo
1993 80 mins. colour
d Paul Leduc *p* Arturo Whaley *co-p* Bertha Navarro, Angel Amigo *exec p* Alejandro Springall, Alejandra Liceaga *pc* Sindicato Nacional de Trabajadores de la Educacion, Tabasco Films, Instituto Mexicano del Seguro Social, Gecisa, Universidad de Guadalajara, Estudios Churubusco Azteca (Mexico), Euzkal Media (Spain), Channel Four Television (Britain), Swiss Development Corporation (Switzerland),

Ministère de la Culture, Ministère des Affaires Etrangères, Arion Productions (France) *sc* Paul Leduc with Jaime Avilés, José Joaquín Blanco, Héctor Ortega, Juan Tovar, Pedro Rivera *c* Guillermo Navarro *ed* Guillermo S. Maldonado *art dir* Arturo Nava *sd* Juan Carlos Cid, Andrés Franco, David Baksht *m* Eugenio Toussaint
lp Roberto Sosa, Dolores Pedro, Raúl Medina, Litico Rodriguez, Tito Vasconcelos, Kandido Uranga, Eduardo López Rojas, Silvestre Mendez, Olga de la Caridad Díaz, Gerardo Martínez 'Pichicuas', Gabriel Pingarron, Ana Silvia Valencia, Mónica Castillo, Gabino Diego

Continuing in the style of his *Latino Bar* (1990), Leduc's musical involves musicians, magicians and comedians. The story is based on an American newspaper item of 5 April 1990, which reported how a number of US soldiers participating in the Panama invasion had murdered a woman while on a drunken spree. The soldiers were charged with minor offences such as the unauthorised discharging of weapons, and allowed to return to active duty after a week. Leduc stages the 'everyday' life in Panama, including its gangsterism, in the form of various musical and dance numbers. When an American invasion disrupts the proceedings, Leduc transforms the film into a carnivalesque allegory of oppression, resistance and the irrepressible popular energy conveyed through the rhythms of the mambo and other contemporary musical genres. The climax comes when three GIs wearing gasmasks terrorise a woman in a bar and cause her gruesome suicide. The ending, repeating the beginning, ironically confirms that this whole story has been about 'nothing', since the events evoked were treated as a trifle in the USA by both the media and the army.

Principio y fin
aka *The Beginning and the End*
1993 188 mins. colour
d Arturo Ripstein *p* Alameda Films (Alfredo Ripstein), IMCINE, Fondo de Fomento a la Calidad Cinematográfica *sc* Paz Alicia Garcíadiego from Naguib Mafouz's novel *c* Claudio Rocha *ed* Rafael Castanedo *sd* Antonio Diego, David Baksht *m* Lucía Alvarez
lp Ernesto Laguardia, Julieta Egurrola, Bruno Bichir, Lucía Muñoz, Alberto Estrella, Blanca Guerra, Alonso Echánove, Verónica Merchant, Ernesto Yáñez, Luis Felipe Tovar, Luisa Hertas

After the death of the father, the Botero family is left destitute. The widow Ignacia (Egurrola) takes charge, placing her hopes in the brightest of her four children, Gabriel (Laguardia). They all make sacrifices to enable Gabriel to finish his studies, but none of the family's members will follow the path planned by Ignacia.

La reina de la noche
aka *Queen of the Night*
1994 118 mins. colour
d Arturo Ripstein *p* IMCINE, Ultra Films, Artist Entertainment-El Tenampa Film Works (Jeremiah Chechick, USA), Les Films du Nopal (Jean-Michel Lacor, France) *sc* Paz Alicia Garcíadiego *c* Bruno De Keyzer *ed* Rafael Castañedo *art dir* José-Luis Aguilar *sd* Carlos Aguilar *m* Lucía Alvarez
lp Patricia Reyes Spíndola, Alberto Estrella, Blanca Guerra, Ana Ofelia Murguía, Alex Cox, Arturo Alegro, Alejandra Montoya, Marta Aura, Roberto Sosa, Juan Carlos Colombo, Guillermo Gil

Invoking John Ford's famous injunction to 'print the legend', Ripstein's haunting evocation of Mexico in the 30s and 40s, from a script by his regular scenarist, provides the background for this intense 'imaginary biography' filmed in sequence-shots about Mexico's most famous popular singer, Lucha Reyes (Reyes Spíndola). The film concentrates on the star's fraught relationship with her mother (the madam of a brothel) and her equally troubled search for love from admirers. Starting as a child performer, she married while on a US tour aged fifteen; an abortion a year later left her sterile. Eventually, aged twenty-eight, she tried to settle down with the impressario Pedro Calderón (Estrella) and adopted (bought) the daughter of a beggar woman. While her career flourishes, including film roles in Hollywood and in Mexico, Lucha's inner torment and insecurities, her husband's insensitivity and the unresolved, violent relationship with her mother drives Lucha to alcohol, solitude and, in the end, suicide at the age of only thirty-eight. Betsy Pecanins provides the star's singing voice.

El jardín del Edén
aka *The Garden of Eden*
1994 (released in 1995) 104 mins. colour
d/co-sc/co-ed María Novaro *p* Jorge Sánchez, Lyse Lafontaine *pc* Macondo Cine Video, IMCINE, Verseau International (France), Universidad de Guadalajara, Fondo de Fomento a la Calidad Cinematográfica, Téléfilm Canada, Sogic (Québec), Ministères des Affaires Etrangères et de la Culture (France) *co-sc* Beatriz Novaro *c* Eric A. Edwards *co-ed* Sigfrido Barjau *art dir* Brigitte Broch *sd* Yvon Benoit *m* Pepe Stephens
lp Renée Coleman, Bruno Bichir, Gabriela Roel, Rosario Sagrav, Alan Ciangherotti, Ana Ofelia Murguía, Joseph Culp

With the help of (at last) adequate financial resources, María Novaro's feature is set and shot (mostly) in Tijuana, the legendary border-crossing between Mexico and the USA, where a 20km steel wall separates the two countries and where people from two cultures meet, each looking for something in the country the others want to leave. The episodic narrative weaves together a number of different stories: the thirty-year-old widow, Serena (Roel), and her three children who settle in the town; the American Jane (Coleman) looking for her Chicana friend Elisabeth (Sagrav) and her brother Frank (Culp), a writer who now passes his time watching whales; the young peasant Felipe (Bichir) who wants to emigrate to the USA and befriends Serena's son Julian (Ciangherotti). The focus of the film is Tijuana itself, simultaneously a characteristic Mexican microcosm and a mythical place 'on the edge' which used to be Hollywood's brothel and a cosmopolitan crossroads. Novaro described the town as 'an open wound and a refuge for the individual as well as the social salvation of a poor people, a prostitute town, very American in some ways, and terribly Mexican in others. There is an Indian community which lives on either side of the border, as if trying to articulate the two worlds which are stubbornly tending to separate.'

Film-makers

Nelson Carro

Benito ALAZRAKI

Born in Mexico City, 27 October 1923. Alazraki began his film career in films such as *Entre hermanos* (Ramón Peón, 1944) and *Enamorada* (Emilio Fernández, 1946). *Raíces,* his directorial debut, was produced outside the established industry and achieved a surprising international notoriety. He went to Spain in the early 60s, where he directed many television programmes and two co-productions. Upon returning to Mexico in 1972, he worked for the state television and cinema institutes before returning to film directing in 1987.

Filmography 1953: *Raíces;* **1956:** *Los amantes; A dónde van nuestros hijos;* **1957:** *Ladrones de niños; Rebelde sin casa;* **1958:** *El vestido de novia; Café Colón; Infierno de almas; La tijera de oro; Poker de reinas;* **1959:** *Tin Tan y las modelos; Pistolas invencibles; El toro negro; La ley de las pistolas; Peligros de juventud; Las hermanas Karambazo;* **1960:** *Muñecos infernales; Con quién andan nuestros locos; De hombre a hombre; Amor a balazo limpio;* **1961:** *Santo contra los zombies; El tigre negro; Espiritismo; Frankenstein; El vampiro y Cía; Los pistoleros;* **1962:** *A ritmo de twist; The Time and the Touch* (in the USA under the pseudonym Carlos Arconti); *1970: Los jóvenes amantes* (in Spain); **1971:** *Las tres perfectas casadas* (in Spain); **1976:** *Balún Canán;* **1978:** *El fantasma del lago;* **1987:** *El rey de los taxistas; Alicia en el país del dólar* (video); **1989:** *Objetos sexuales.*

Luis ALCORIZA

Born in Badajoz (Spain) 5 September 1921. Died in Cuernavaca, 3 December 1992. Grew up in a theatrical family and began acting as a boy. Left Spain during the civil war and moved to Mexico, where he began a long career as an actor (including the role of Christ in *María Magdalena* and *Reina de reinas,* both by Miguel Contreras Torres in 1945). He scripted eight films with Luis Buñuel, including *El gran calavera* (1949), *Los olvidados* (1950) and *El*

(1952). His independent films of the 60s were well received by critics.

Filmography 1960: *Los jóvenes;* **1961:** *Tlayucan;* **1962:** *Tiburoneros;* **1963:** *Amor y sexo;* **1964:** *El gángster; Tarahumara;* **1966:** *Divertimento* (sketch in *Juego peligroso,* Brazilian co-p; co-d Arturo Ripstein); **1968:** *La puerta; El oficio más antiguo del mundo;* **1969:** *Paraíso;* **1971:** *Mecánica nacional; El muro del silencio* (Colombian co-p); **1972:** *Esperanza* (sketch in *Fe, esperanza y caridad,* co-d Alberto Bojórquez and Jorge Fons); **1974:** *Presagio;* **1975:** *Las fuerzas vivas;* **1978:** *A paso de cojo;* **1979:** *Semana Santa en Acapulco;* **1981:** *Han violado a una mujer* (in Spain); **1983:** *El amor es un juego extraño;* **1984:** *Terror y encajes negros;* **1985:** *Lo que importa es vivir;* **1987:** *Día de difuntos;* **1989:** *La sombra del ciprés es alargada* (in Spain).

Brothers ALVA

(Salvador, Guillermo, Eduardo and Carlos) Without doubt the Alva brothers were among the principal documentary film-makers of the early Mexican cinema. They began projecting films in 1905, opened a movie house in 1906 and shortly after became associated with another film pioneer, Enrique Rosas. They were extraordinary chroniclers of the Mexican scene, first of daily life under Porfirio Díaz (*Concurso de niños, Combate de flores,* etc.) and later of the early days of the Revolution under Madero. With few exceptions, most of their films were short documentaries.

Filmography 1906: *Concurso de niños; Kermesse del Carmen;* **1907:** *La nevada del 11 de febrero; Kermesse en la Alameda de Santa Maria; Inauguración del tráfico internacional por el Istmo de Tehuantepec; Calle del empedradillo; Plaza de la Constitución; Estatua de Colón en la Reforma;* **1909:** *Viernes de Dolores; Combate de flores; La entrevista de los presidentes Díaz–Taft en El Paso, Texas, el 16 de octubre de 1909; Fiesta de toros;* **1910:** *Fiestas del Centenario de la Independencia; Gaona y Lagartijillo en el Toreo; Maniobras militares; La corrida de Covadonga; Corrida de Segura y Gaona en El Toreo; Corrida de toros organizada por la Unión Universal de Estudiantes; El Derby de México; Presentación de Rodolfo Gaona en la plaza El Toreo;* **1911:** *Novillada de la Sociedad de Artistas Españoles y Mexicanos; Llegada de la familia del primer mártir de la Revolución Aquiles Serdán; Banquete en Chapultepec; Triunfal arribo del jefe de la Revolución don Francisco I. Madero; Últimos sucesos de Ciudad Juárez; Aviadores* en el campo de Balboena; *Insurrección de México; Manifestaciones en la capital; Entrada triunfal en México de don Francisco I. Madero; Entrega de la bandera del 32 batallón; Viaje del señor Madero de Ciudad Juárez a la Ciudad de México; Sismo en México el 7 de junio; Solemne entrega del cañón por las fuerzas insurgentes; Viaje del señor Madero al sur; Carrera de autos Imparcial-Puebla;* **1912:** *Simulacro de guerra por los voluntarios del Colegio Militar; Revolución orozquista o La Revolución en Chihuahua;* **1913** *El aniversario del fallecimiento de la suegra de Enhart* (fiction); *Decena trágica; La explotación del maguey;* **1914:** *El incendio de El Palacio de Hierro; Sangre hermana.*

Raúl de ANDA

Born in Mexico City, 1 July 1908. The son of a *charro* (traditional cowboy) from the state of Jalisco, de Anda began to appear in folkloric shows at a young age and travelled throughout Mexico, to various South and Central American countries and throughout the south-western USA. His acting career began in the USA and continued in Mexico with Santa. He made his debut as producer in 1935, becoming well known with films like Alejandro Galindo's *Campeón sin corona* (1945), Emilio Fernández's *Rio Escondido* (1947) and Fernando Méndez's *El suavecito* (1950), and the following year as director.

Filmography 1938: *La tierra del mariachi;* **1939:** *Con los dorados de Villa;* **1940:** *El Charro Negro;* **1941:** *La vuelta del Charro Negro; Del rancho a la capital; La venganza del Charro Negro;* **1942:** *Amanecer ranchero;* **1943:** *Toros, amor y gloria;* **1945:** *Guadalajara pues; La reina del trópico;* **1946:** *Los cristeros; Yo maté a Rosita Alvirez;* **1947:** *El último chinaco;* **1948:** *Comisario en turno;* **1949:** *El Charro Negro en el norte; Angeles del arrabal; Dos gallos de pelea; La fe en Dios;* **1950:** *Una mujer decente;* **1951:** *Sígueme corazón; Cuatro noches contigo;* **1954:** *Con el diablo en el cuerpo; La gaviota;* **1955:** *El siete leguas; Enemigos; Bataclán mexicano;* **1956:** *Las manzanas de Dorotea; La máscara de carne; 1958: Estampida;* **1964:** *El pozo;* **1965:** *Sí quiero;* **1970:** *Sucedió en Jalisco;* **1974:** *El padrino … es mi compadre;* **1978:** *Guerra de sexos;* **1979:** *Amor a la mejicana.*

Alfonso ARAU

Born in Mexico City in 1932. After acting and dancing studies, Arau and Sergio Corona created a dancing team that made its first cinematic appearance in 1955. Later, Arau hosted a television programme in Havana and spent two years in Paris

studying pantomime. Back in Mexico, he returned to the stage to appear in *Locuras felices,* a play directed by Alejandro Jodorowsky. His first feature was the critical comedy *El águila descalza* (1969).

Filmography 1960: *Alfredo va a la playa* (Short; in Cuba); **1969:** *El Águila Descalza;* **1973:** *Calzonzín inspector;* **1976:** *Caribe, estrella y águila* (doc; in Cuba); **1979:** *Mojado Power* (in the USA); **1986:** *Chido Guan: el tacos de oro;* **1991:** *Como agua para chocolate;* **1994:** *A Walk in the Clouds* (in the USA).

Pedro ARMENDÁRIZ

Born in Mexico City, 9 May 1912; committed suicide in Los Angeles, 18 June 1963. After studying in the USA, Armendáriz returned to Mexico in the early 30s. He worked in the theatre and, after 1935, in the cinema, both in Hollywood and in Europe, but made his reputation in the films of Emilio Fernández. His son, Pedro Armendáriz Jr, is also a prolific actor.

Filmography 1935: *María Elena* (Raphael J. Sevilla); *Rosario* (Miguel Zacarías); **1937:** *Las cuatro milpas* (Ramón Pereda); *Amapola del camino* (Juan Bustillo Oro); *Jalisco nunca pierde* (Chano Urueta); *La Adelita* (Guillermo Hernández Gómez); *Mi candidato* (Chano Urueta); **1938:** *Los millones de Chaflán* (Rolando Aguilar); *El indio* (Armando Vargas de la Maza); *Canto a mi tierra* (José Bohr); *La reina del río* (René Cardona); *La China Hilaria* (Roberto Curwood); *Una luz en mi camino* (José Bohr); **1939:** *Con los dorados de Villa* (Raúl de Anda); *Los olvidados de Dios* (Ramón Pereda); *Borrasca humana* (José Bohr); **1940:** *El Charro Negro* (Raúl de Anda); *Pobre diablo* (José Benavides Jr); *Mala yerba* (Gabriel Soria); *El jefe máximo* (Fernando de Fuentes); *El Zorro de Jalisco* (José Benavides Jr); *El secreto del sacerdote* (Joselito Rodríguez); **1941:** *Ni sangre ni arena* (Alejandro Galindo); *La epopeya del camino* (Francisco Elías); *Simón Bolívar* (Miguel Contreras Torres); *Del rancho a la capital* (Raúl de Anda); *Allá en el Bajío* (Fernando Méndez); *La isla de la pasión* (Emilio Fernández); **1942:** *Soy puro mexicano* (Emilio Fernández); *Tierra de pasiones* (José Benavides Jr); **1943:** *Las calaveras del terror* (Fernando Méndez); *Flor silvestre* (Emilio Fernández); *Konga Roja* (Alejandro Galindo); *Distinto amanecer* (Julio Bracho); *María Candelaria* (Emilio Fernández); *La guerra de los pasteles* (Emilio Gómez Muriel); **1944:** *El corsario negro* (Chano Urueta); *Alma de bronce* (Dudley Murphy); *Las abandonadas* (Emilio Fernández); *El capitán*

Malacara (Carlos Orellana); *Entre hermanos* (Ramón Peón); *Bugambilia* (Emilio Fernández); **1945:** *Rayando el sol* (Roberto Gavaldón); *La perla* (Emilio Fernández); **1946:** *Enamorada* (Emilio Fernández); **1947:** *Albur de amor* (Alfonso Patiño Gómez); *La casa colorada* (Miguel Morayta); *Juan Charrasqueado* (Ernesto Cortázar); *The Fugitive* (John Ford); **1948:** *Fort Apache* (John Ford); *Maclovia* (Emilio Fernández); *En la hacienda de la Flor* (Ernesto Cortázar); *Al caer la tarde* (Rafael E. Portas); *Three Godfathers* (John Ford); **1949:** *La malquerida* (Emilio Fernández); *Pancho Villa vuelve* (Miguel Contreras Torres); *El abandonado* (Chano Urueta); *El charro y la dama* (Fernando Cortés); *Bodas de fuego* (Marco Aurelio Galindo); *Tulsa* (Stuart Heisler); *We Were Strangers* (John Huston); **1950:** *Rosauro Castro* (Roberto Gavaldón); *Tierra baja* (Miguel Zacarías); *La loca de la casa* (Juan Bustillo Oro); *Por la puerta falsa* (Fernando de Fuentes); *Camino del infierno* (Miguel Morayta); *The Torch* (Del odio nació el amor; English version of Enamorada) (Emilio Fernández); **1951:** *Por querer a una mujer* (Ernesto Cortázar); *Ella y yo* (Miguel M. Delgado); *La noche avanza* (Roberto Gavaldón); *Carne de presidio* (Emilio Gómez Muriel); *Los tres alegres compadres* (Julián Soler); **1952:** *El rebozo de Soledad* (Roberto Gavaldón); *El bruto* (Luis Buñuel); *Les Amants de Tolède* (Henri Decoin); **1953:** *Reportaje* (Emilio Fernández); *Reto a la vida* (Julio Bracho); *Mulata* (Gilberto Martínez Solares); *Lucrèce Borgia* (Christian-Jaque); *Border River* (George Sherman); **1954:** *Dos maridos y un amor* (Alfredo B. Crevenna); *La rebelión de los colgados* (Emilio Fernández and Alfredo B. Crevenna); *Fortune carrée* (Bernard Borderie); **1955:** *La escondida* (Roberto Gavaldón); *Canasta de cuentos mexicanos* (Julio Bracho); *Tam-tam mayumbe* (Gian Gaspare Napolitano); *The Littlest Outlaw* (Roberto Gavaldón); *Diane* (David Miller); *The Conqueror* (Dick Powell); *The Big Boodle* (Richard Wilson); *Uomini e lupi* (Giuseppe De Santis); **1956:** *El impostor* (Emilio Fernández); **1957:** *La mujer que no tuvo infancia* (Tito Davison); *Los salvajes* (Rafael Baledón); *Flor de mayo* (Roberto Gavaldón); *El zarco* (Miguel M. Delgado); *Ando volando bajo* (Rogelio A. González); *Así era Pancho Villa* (Ismael Rodríguez); *Stowaway Girl* (Guy Hamilton); *Yo quiero ser artista* (Tito Davison); **1958:** *Cuando ¡Viva Villa! es la muerte* (Ismael Rodríguez); *Café Colón* (Benito Alazraki); *Los desarraigados* (Gilberto Gazcón); *Dos hijos desobedientes* (Jaime Salvador); *La Cucaracha* (Ismael Rodríguez); *Sed de amor* (Alfonso Corona Blake); *Las señoritas Vivanco* (Mauricio de la Serna); *Pancho Villa y la Valentina* (Ismael Rodríguez); *The Little Savage* (Byron Haskin); **1959:** *Yo pecador* (Alfonso Corona Blake); *El hambre nuestra de cada día* (Rogelio A. González); *Calibre 44* (Julián Soler); *The Wonderful Country* (Robert Parrish); **1960:** *La cárcel de Cananea* (Gilberto Gazcón); *Los hermanos del Hierro* (Ismael Rodríguez); *El indulto* (José Luis Saenz de Heredia); **1961:** *Los valientes no mueren* (Gilberto Martínez Solares); *El tejedor de milagros* (Francisco del Villar); *Francis of Assisi* (Michael Curtiz); *I titani* (Duccio Tessari); **1962:** *La bandida* (Roberto Rodríguez); **1963:** *Captain Sinbad* (Byron Haskin); *From Russia With Love* (Terence Young).

Manuel BARBACHANO PONCE

Born in Yucatán in 1924. Died in Mexico, 21 April 1994. Barbachano Ponce began to produce the newsreel *Tele-Revista* directed by Carlos Velo in 1950, and started *Cine-Verdad*, a monthly newsreel about cultural events, in 1953. That same year he began independent feature-film production with *Raíces*. Soon after he produced *¡Torero!, Nazarín* and various newsreels *(EMA, Cámara Deportiva)*. In the late 60s, he moved over to television and started the *Tele-Cadena Mexicana*. Early in the following decade Barbachano Ponce acquired the almost mythical production company Clasa Films Mundiales and was able to support and provide opportunities for many young cineastes and independent film-makers.

Filmography 1953: *Raíces* (Benito Alazraki); **1956:** *¡Torero!* (Carlos Velo); **1958:** *El brazo fuerte* (Giovanni Korporaal); *Nazarín* (Luis Buñuel); *Chistelandia; Nueva Chistelandia; ¡Vuelve Chistelandia!* (Manuel Barbachano Ponce, Carlos Velo, Jomí García Ascot and Fernando Marcos) **1959:** *Sonatas* (Juan Antonio Bardem); *Cuba baila* (Julio García Espinosa); **1964:** *El gallo de oro* (Roberto Gavaldón); **1965:** *Amor, amor, amor* (José Luis Ibáñez, Miguel Barbachano Ponce and Héctor Mendoza); *Los bienamados* (Juan José Gurrola and Juan Ibáñez); **1966:** *Pedro Páramo* (Carlos Velo); **1971:** *María* (Tito Davison); **1978:** *Cuentos de principes y princesas* (Rafael Castanedo); **1979:** *María de mi corazón* (Jaime Humberto Hermosillo); **1982:** *Confidencias* (Jaime Humberto Hermosillo); **1983:** *De veras me atrapaste* (Gerardo Pardo); **1984:** *Doña Herlinda y su hijo* (Jaime Humberto Hermosillo); *Frida, naturaleza viva* (Paul Leduc); **1987:** *Clandestino destino* (Jaime Humberto Hermosillo); **1990:** *La tarea* (Jaime Humberto Hermosillo; co-p Pablo Barbachano Ponce); **1991:** *Anoche soñé contigo* (Marysa Sistach); *Encuentro inesperado*

(Jaime Humberto Hermosillo); **1992:** *Tequila* (Rubén Gámez); *La tarea prohibida* (Jaime Humberto Hermosillo).

José BOHR

Born in Bonn (Germany), 3 September 1901. Spent his youth in Argentina and Chile. In the latter country, he directed *Actualidades Magallánicas* (1918–19) and the comedies *Morvello, como un tubo* (1919) and *Mi noche alegre o Los parafinas* (1921). He became a successful radio singer and composer, a radio and variety theatre star and went on to appear in a number of US films, among them *Sombras de gloria* (Andrew L. Stone, 1929), one of the first Spanish-language US productions. In Mexico (after 1931) Bohr produced and directed a number of films (with his wife Eva Limiñana, 'La Duquesa Olga'), several of which he also scored, edited and acted in. At the end of the decade, he returned to Chile where he continued his film career. By 1969 he had directed over fifteen films (among them *El renegado de Pichitún* (1945), *Amor que pasa* (1946), *La dama de las camelias* (1947), *Si mis campos hablaran* (1947), *Veintisiete millones* (1947) and *Un chileno en España* (1962). He now lives in Denmark.

Mexican Filmography 1933: *La sangre manda* (co-d Raphael J. Sevilla); **1934:** *¿Quién mató a Eva?;* *Tu hijo;* **1935:** *Sueño de amor; Luponini de Chicago;* **1936:** *Así es la mujer; Marihuana (El monstruo verde);* **1938:** *El rosario de Amozoc; Por mis pistolas; El látigo; Una luz en mi camino; Canto a mi tierra;* **1939:** *Borrasca humana; Traicionera (Herencia macabra).*

Alberto BOJÓRQUEZ

Born in Motul (Yucatán) in 1938. He arrived in Mexico City in 1961 and studied film production at the Centro Universitario de Estudios Cinematográficos (CUEC) from 1964 to 1969.

Filmography 1967: *Sociología* (short doc); *Escuela Nacional de Ontología* (short doc); **1969:** *A la busca;* **1970:** *Los meses y los días;* **1972:** *Fe* (episode in *Fe, esperanza y caridad,* co-d Luis Alcoriza and Jorge Fons); **1974:** *La lucha con la pantera; Cuando llego al jardín* (short doc); **1975:** *Los hermanos del viento; 20 de noviembre* (short doc); **1976:** *Lo mejor de Teresa;* **1978:** *Cosas de Yucatán* (doc); *Adriana del Río, actriz;* **1979:** *Retrato de una mujer casada;* **1985:** *Robachicos;* **1991:** *Los años de Greta.*

Arcady BOYTLER

Born in Moscow, 31 August 1895, from an Irish father and a Russian mother; died in Mexico City, 24 November 1965. Boytler began theatrical, ballet, mime and film work while very young, collaborating with the likes of Stanislavski and Meyerhold, and directing and acting in many short films just before the 1917 Revolution (for example, *Da zdravstvujut … mysli; Mecta kuziny; Muzh, shansonetka, zhena i bankir; Muzhestvennaya devushka zhenstvennyj muzhchina; Nedorazumenie; Nescastnyj drug; Semejnyj treugol'nik; Spiriticeskij seans; Trizhdy muzh; Sud'ba gornicnoj; Arkady kontroler spal'nych vagonov; Arkady zenitsija; Arkady Sportsman ili Dlja ljubvi pregrady net; Komnata N. 13 ili Arkashke ne vezhet; Konkurs krasoty,* etc.). He emigrated to Germany, where he starred in two Russian-produced comedies between 1920 and 1922: *Boytler gegen Chaplin* (playing both roles) and *Boytler tötet Lange Weil.* Boytler went to Paris and toured Europe with the theatre company Le Coq d'Or (1923–4). He then worked in Argentina before emigrating to Chile (where he shot his first feature film, *El buscador de fortuna o No hay que desanimarse* in 1927), and moving to Peru and then to New York (where he participated in the production of many Spanish-language shorts at the Metropolitan Studio in New Jersey). In 1930 he came to Mexico to make films for the Casa Empire, where he befriended Eisenstein, appearing in a scene of *¡Que Viva México!* He directed eight features between 1932 and 1944. Afterwards, he abandoned directing to manage his two movie theatres in Mexico City.

Filmography 1931: *Un espectador impertinente* (short; co-d Raphael J. Sevilla); **1932:** *Mano a mano;* **1933:** *La mujer del puerto; Joyas de México* (short doc); **1934:** *Revista musical* (short doc); **1935:** *El tesoro de Pancho Villa; Celos;* **1937:** *¡Así es mi tierra!; Aguila o sol;* **1938:** *El capitán aventurero;* **1944:** *Amor prohibido.*

Julio BRACHO

Born in Durango, 17 July 1909; died in Mexico City, 26 April 1978. Part of a famous artistic family: cousin of Ramón Novarro and Dolores del Río, brother of Andrea Palma and Jesús Bracho, and father of the actress Diana Bracho. He became interested in experimental theatre while very young, organising several theatrical troupes such as the Escolares del Teatro and the Teatro de los Trabajadores. He also directed at the Teatro Orientación de Bellas Artes and founded the first university theatre. His film career began in the 30s as a scenarist. Health problems prevented him from directing *Redes.* In the early 40s, he became the most prestigious and best-paid director of Mexican cinema.

Filmography 1941: *¡Ay, qué tiempos, señor don Simón!;* **1942:** *Historia de un gran amor; La virgen que forjó una patria;* **1943:** *Distinto amanecer; La corte de Faraón;* **1944:** *Crepúsculo;* **1945:** *El monje blanco; Cantaclaro;* **1946:** *La mujer de todos; Don Simón de Lira;* **1947:** *El ladrón;* **1948:** *Rosenda;* **1949:** *San Felipe de Jesús; La posesión;* **1950:** *lnmaculada; Historia de un corazón,* **1951:** *Paraíso robado; La ausente;* **1952:** *Rostros olvidados; La cobarde; Mujeres que trabajan;* **1953:** *Llévame en tus brazos; Reto a la vida;* **1954:** *María la voz;* **1954:** *Señora ama* (in Spain); **1955:** *Canasta de cuentos mexicanos;* **1957:** *La mafia del crimen;* **1958:** *México lindo y querido; Una canción para recordar;* **1959:** *Cada quien su vida; ¡Yo sabia demasiado!;* **1960:** *La sombra del caudillo;* **1962:** *Corazón de niño;* **1963:** *Historia de un canalla; He matado a un hombre; Amor de adolescente;* **1964:** *Guadalajara en verano; Cada voz lleva su angustia* (in Colombia); **1965:** *El proceso de Cristo; Cuernavaca en primavera; Morelos siervo de la nación* (Short); **1966:** *Damiana y los hombres;* **1967:** *Andante;* **1973:** *En busca de un muro;* **1975:** *Espejismo de la ciudad;* **1977:** *El difunto al pozo y la viuda al gozo* (episode of *Los amantes fríos,* co-d Julián Soler and Miguel Morayta).

Luis BUÑUEL

Born in Calanda (Spain), 22 February 1900; died in Mexico City, 29 July 1983. As a student, Buñuel was friends with Federico García Lorca, Salvador Dalí, José Ortega y Gasset, Ramón Gómez de la Serna and Rafael Alberti. He also founded the first Spanish film society in the early 20s. He went to Paris in 1925 and worked as Jean Epstein's assistant. In 1928, based on a script written with Salvador Dalí, he made his debut with *Un chien andalou.* Returned to Spain to direct *Las Hurdes* (1932). He emigrated and worked as dubbing supervisor at Paramount and Warner Bros., and was a producer at Filmofono in 1935 (*Don Quintín el amargao* by Luis Marquina, *La hija de Juan Simón* and *¿Quién me quiere a mi?,* both by José Luis Sáenz de Heredia, and Jean Grémillon's *¡Centinela alerta!*). In 1937, he supervised *España leal en armas* in Paris. Returning to the USA in 1939, he worked at the Museum of Modern Art (New York). Almost by accident, he returned to Mexico in 1946 and began directing again with *Gran casino.*

Mexican Filmography 1946: *Gran casino;* **1949:** *El gran calavera;* **1950:** *Los olvidados; Susana (Carne y*

demonio); **1951:** *La hija del engaño; Una mujer sin amor; Subida al cielo;* **1952:** *El bruto; Robinson Crusoe* (US co-p); *El;* **1953:** *Abismos de pasión; La ilusión viaja en tranvía;* **1954:** *El río y la muerte;* **1955:** *Ensayo de un crimen;* **1956:** *La Mort en ce jardin/La muerte en este jardín* (French co-p); **1958:** *Nazarín;* **1959:** *La fièvre monte à El Pao/Los ambiciosos* (French co-p); **1960:** *La joven* (*The Young One;* US co-p); **1961:** *Viridiana* (Spanish co-p); **1962:** *El ángel exterminador;* **1964:** *Simón del desierto.*

Juan BUSTILLO ORO

Born in Mexico City, 2 June 1904; died in 1989. After abandoning his law studies, he debuted as a director with *Yo soy tu padre.* In the early 30s, he founded the avant-garde theatre group Teatro Ahora with Mauricio Magdaleno. Shortly after he wrote screenplays and screen adaptations for Ramón Peón (*Tiburón,* 1933) and Fernando de Fuentes (*El compadre Mendoza,* 1933; *El fantasma del convento,* 1934). He became his own producer in 1937 and made some of the most successful films of the period 1938–41. He published a book of memoirs, *Vida cinematográfica* (1984).

Filmography 1927: *Yo soy tu padre;* **1934:** *Dos monjes;* **1935:** *Monja y casada, virgen y mártir; El misterio del rostro pálido;* **1936:** *Malditas sean las mujeres; El rosal bendito; Nostradamus;* **1937:** *Amapola del camino; La honradez es un estorbo; Huapango;* **1938:** *La tía de las muchachas; Cada loco con su tema;* **1939:** *Caballo a caballo; En tiempos de don Porfirio;* **1940:** *Ahí está el detalle; Al son de la marimba;* **1941:** *Cuando los hijos se van; Mil estudiantes y una muchacha;* **1942:** *El ángel negro;* **1943:** *El sombrero de tres picos; México de mis recuerdos;* **1944:** *Cuando quiere un mexicano;* **1945:** *Canaima; Lo que va de ayer a hoy; No basta ser charro;* **1946:** *En tiempos de la Inquisición; Los maderos de San Juan;* **1947:** *Dos de la vida airada; Fíjate que suave;* **1948:** *Las mañanitas; Sólo Veracruz es bello; Cuando los padres se quedan solos;* **1949:** *El colmillo de Buda; Las tandas del Principal; Vino el remolino y nos alevantó;* **1950:** *El hombre sin rostro; La loca de la casa; Casa de vecindad;* **1951:** *Acá las tortas; La huella de unos labios;* **1952:** *Por ellas aunque mal paguen; Esos de Pénjamo;* **1953:** *Retorno a la juventud; Siete mujeres;* **1954:** *La sobrina del señor cura; La mujer ajena; Las engañadas; Padre contra hijo; El asesino X; El medallón del crimen;* **1955:** *Del brazo y por la calle;* **1956:** *Las aventuras de Pito Pérez; Los hijos de Rancho Grande;* **1957:** *Cada hijo una cruz; Donde las dan las* *toman;* **1959:** *El último mexicano;* **1963:** *México de mis recuerdos;* **1964:** *Así amaron nuestros padres;* **1965:** *Los valses venían de Viena y los niños de Paris.*

Mario Moreno, CANTINFLAS

Born in Mexico City, 12 August 1911. Died in Mexico 21 April 1993. He began his career in travelling shows and became well known in variety theatre. In 1936 he transferred his *peladito* character to the cinema, initiating a long career that made him Mexico's most popular comedian.

Filmography 1936: *No te engañes corazón* (Miguel Contreras Torres); **1937:** *¡Así es mi tierra!* (Arcady Boytler); *Aguila o sol* (Arcady Boytler); **1939:** *El signo de la muerte* (Chano Urueta); *Siempre listo en las tinieblas* (Fernando A. Rivero; Short); *Jengibre contra dinamita* (Fernando A. Rivero; Short); **1940:** *Cantinflas y su prima* (Carlos Toussaint; Short); *Cantinflas boxeador* (Fernando A. Rivero; Short); *Cantinflas ruletero* (Fernando A. Rivero; Short); *Ahí está el detalle* (Juan Bustillo Oro); *Recordar es vivir* (Fernando A. Rivero; compilation film); **1941:** *Ni sangre ni arena* (Alejandro Galindo); *El gendarme desconocido* (Miguel M. Delgado), *Carnaval en el trópico* (Carlos Villatoro); **1942:** *Los tres mosqueteros* (Miguel M. Delgado); *El circo* (Miguel M. Delgado); **1943:** *Romeo y Julieta* (Miguel M. Delgado); **1944:** *Gran Hotel* (Miguel M. Delgado); **1945:** *Un día con el diablo* (Miguel M. Delgado); **1946:** *Soy un prófugo* (Miguel M. Delgado); **1947:** *A volar joven* (Miguel M. Delgado); **1948:** *El supersabio* (Miguel M. Delgado); *El mago* (Miguel M. Delgado); **1949:** *Puerta ... joven* (Miguel M. Delgado); **1950:** *El Siete Machos* (Miguel M. Delgado); *El bombero atómico* (Miguel M. Delgado); **1951:** *Si yo fuera diputado* (Miguel M. Delgado); **1952:** *El señor fotógrafo* (Miguel M. Delgado); **1953:** *Caballero a la medida* (Miguel M. Delgado); **1954:** *Abajo el telón* (Miguel M. Delgado); **1956:** *Around the World in 80 Days* (Michael Anderson, USA); *El bolero de Raquel* (Miguel M. Delgado); **1958:** *Sube y baja* (Miguel M. Delgado); *Ama a tu prójimo* (Tulio Demicheli); **1960:** *Pepe* (George Sidney, USA); *El analfabeto* (Miguel M. Delgado); **1962:** *El extra* (Miguel M. Delgado); **1963:** *Entrega inmediata* (Miguel M. Delgado); **1964:** *El padrecito* (Miguel M. Delgado); **1965:** *El señor doctor* (Miguel M. Delgado); **1966:** *Su excelencia* (Miguel M. Delgado); **1968:** *Por mis pistolas* (Miguel M. Delgado); **1969:** *Un Quijote sin mancha* (Miguel M. Delgado); **1970:** *El profe* (Miguel M. Delgado); **1971:** *Don Quijote cabalga de nuevo* (Roberto Gavaldón; Spanish co-p); **1973:**

Conserje en condominio (Miguel M. Delgado); **1975:** *El ministro y yo* (Miguel M. Delgado); **1977:** *El patrullero 777* (Miguel M. Delgado); **1981:** *El barrendero* (Miguel M. Delgado).

Felipe CAZALS

Born in Guéthary (France), 27 June 1937, but has lived in Mexico since his childhood. In the early 60s, Cazals won a scholarship to study at IDHEC (Paris). Upon his return to Mexico, he collaborated on the television programme *La hora de Bellas Artes,* co-ordinated by Manuel Michel, where he made his first short films. With Arturo Ripstein, Rafael Castanedo and Pedro F. Miret, he created the group Cine Independiente in the late 60s, producing films such as Ripstein's *La hora de los niños* and his own *Familiaridades.*

Filmography 1965: *¡Qué se callen!* (short doc); *Leonora Carrington o el sortilegio irónico* (short doc); *Alfonso Reyes* (short doc); **1966:** *Cartas de Mariana Alcoforado* (short doc); *La otra guerra* (short doc); **1968:** *Trabajos olímpicos* (short doc); *Testimonios y documentos: paro agrario* (short doc); *La manzana de la discordia;* **1969:** *Familiaridades;* **1970:** *Emiliano Zapata;* **1971:** *El jardín de la tía Isabel;* **1972:** *Aquellos años;* **1973:** *Los que viven donde sopla el viento suave* (doc); **1975:** *Canoa; El apando;* **1976:** *Las poquianchis;* **1977:** *La güera Rodríguez;* **1978:** *El año de la peste;* **1980:** *Las siete cucas; El gran triunfo; Rigo es amor;* **1982:** *Bajo la metralla;* **1985:** *Los motivos de Luz;* **1986:** *Cuentos de madrugada* (TV); *El tres de copas; Las inocentes* (video); **1987:** *La furia de un dios;* **1990:** *Burbujas de amor; Desvestidas y alborotadas;* **1992:** *Kino.*

Miguel CONTRERAS TORRES

Born in Ciudad Hidalgo, state of Michoacán, 16 September 1899; died in Mexico City, 5 June 1981. Born into a comfortable Porfirian family, he nevertheless joined the Revolution in the ranks of Carranza. Afterwards he (and others such as Guillermo Calles, Rafael Bermúdez Zatarain and José Manuel Ramos) developed a nationalist folkloric Mexican cinema, continuing this project for over forty years. He produced all his own films and was the only Mexican film-maker whose career was not interrupted by the transition to sound. He also wrote a number of books, such as *El libro negro del cine mexicano,* in which he recounts his battles with William Jenkins, owner of the dominant theatrical exhibition monopoly.

Filmography 1921: *El caporal* (co-d Rafael Bermúdez Zatarain and Juan Canals de Homes);

1922: *El hombre sin patria; El sueño del caporal* (Short); **1923:** *Almas tropicales* (co-d Manuel R. Ojeda); **1924:** *Aguiluchos mexicanos* (co-d Gustavo Sáenz de Sicilia); **1925:** *Oro, sangre y sol;* **1926:** *El relicario* (Mexico/Spain/USA); **1926–8:** *Ejército mexicano* (doc); *Ejército cubano* (doc; Cuba); **1927:** *El león de la Sierra Morena* (Spain/France); **1929:** *El águila y el nopal;* **1930:** *Soñadores de la gloria* (Spain/Morocco/USA); **1931:** *La sombra de Pancho Villa; Zitari;* **1932:** *Revolución;* **1933:** *Juárez y Maximiliano; La noche del pecado;* **1934:** *No matarás* (USA); *¡Viva México!; Tribu;* **1936:** *No te engañes corazón;* **1937:** *La paloma;* **1938:** *La golondrina;* **1939:** *The Mad Empress* (USA); **1940:** *Hombre o demonio; Hasta que llovió en Sayula;* **1941:** *Simón Bolívar;* **1942:** *Caballería del imperio; El padre Morelos;* **1943:** *El rayo del sur; La vida inútil de Pito Pérez;* **1944:** *Bartolo toca la flauta; Rancho de mis recuerdos;* **1945:** *El hijo de nadie; María Magdalena; Reina de reinas;* **1948:** *Bamba;* **1949:** *Pancho Villa vuelve;* **1950:** *El amor a la vida;* **1951:** *Soy mexicano de acá de este lado;* **1952:** *Sangre en el ruedo* (Spanish co-p); **1953:** *Tehuantepec;* **1956:** *El último rebelde;* **1958:** *Pueblo en armas; ¡Viva la soldadera!;* **1964:** *El hermano Pedro* (Guatemalan co-p).

Arturo de CÓRDOVA

Born in Mérida (Yucatán), 7 May 1908; died in Mexico City in 1973. He studied journalism in Lausanne (Switzerland) and spent some time as assistant director of United Press in Santiago (Chile). His popularity as a radio personality in the 30s was a prelude to his long international career as an actor.

Filmography 1935: *Celos* (Arcady Boytler); **1936:** *Cielito lindo* (Roberto O'Quigley); *¡Esos hombres!* (Rolando Aguilar); **1937:** *Ave sin rumbo* (Roberto O'Quigley); *La paloma* (Miguel Contreras Torres); *La Zandunga* (Fernando de Fuentes); **1938:** *Hombres de mar* (Chano Urueta); *Refugiados en Madrid* (Alejandro Galindo); *La casa del ogro* (Fernando de Fuentes); *Mientras México duerme* (Alejandro Galindo); *La bestia negra* (Gabriel Soria); **1939:** *La noche de los mayas* (Chano Urueta); *Odio* (William Rowland and Fernando Soler); *¡Qué viene mi marido!* (Chano Urueta); *Miracle on Main Street* (Steve Sekely); *Los hijos mandan* (Gabriel Soria); **1940:** *Hombre o demonio* (Miguel Contreras Torres); *Mala yerba* (Gabriel Soria); *¡Cuando la tierra tembló!* (Antonio Helú); *Recordar es vivir* (Fernando A. Rivero, compilation film); *El milagro de Cristo* (Francisco Elías); *El secreto del sacerdote* (Joselito Rodríguez); **1941:** *Cinco minutos de amor* (Alfonso Patiño Gómez); *¡Ay, qué tiempos, señor don Simón!* (Julio Bracho); *¿Quién te quiere a ti?* (Rolando Aguilar); *El conde de Montecristo* (Chano Urueta); *Alejandra* (José Benavides Jr); *Incendiary Blonde* (George Marshall); *For Whom the Bells Toll* (Sam Wood); *Hostages* (Frank Tuttle); **1944:** *Crepúsculo* (Julio Bracho); *The Frenchman's Creek* (Mitchell Leisen); *A Medal for Benny* (Irving Pichel); **1945:** *La selva de fuego* (Fernando de Fuentes); *Masquerade in Mexico* (Mitchell Leisen); **1946:** *Su última aventura* (Gilberto Martínez Solares); *Cinco rostros de mujer* (Gilberto Martínez Solares); **1947:** *La diosa arrodillada* (Roberto Gavaldón); *Algo flota sobre el agua* (Alfredo B. Crevenna); *New Orleans* (Arthur Lubin); *Dios se lo pague* (Luis César Amadori); *Adventures of Casanova* (Roberto Gavaldón); **1948:** *Medianoche* (Tito Davison); *Pasaporte a Río* (Daniel Tinayre); **1949:** *Yo no elegí mi vida* (Antonio Momplet); *Fascinación* (Carlos Schlieper); *La balandra Isabel llegó esta tarde* (Carlos Hugo Christensen); **1950:** *El hombre sin rostro* (Juan Bustillo Oro); *Furia roja* (Steve Sekely); *María Montecristo* (Luis César Amadori); *En la palma de tu mano* (Roberto Gavaldón); *Nacha Regules* (Luis César Amadori); **1951:** *Paraíso robado* (Julio Bracho); *Mi esposa y la otra* (Alfredo B. Crevenna); *Te sigo esperando* (Tito Davison); *La ausente* (Julio Bracho); **1952:** *El rebozo de Soledad* (Roberto Gavaldón); *Cuando levanta la niebla* (Emilio Fernández); *Las tres perfectas casadas* (Roberto Gavaldón); *Fruto prohibido* (Alfredo B. Crevenna); *El* (Luis Buñuel); **1953:** *Reportaje* (Emilio Fernández); *El valor de vivir* (Tito Davison); **1954:** *La entrega* (Julián Soler); *Un extraño en la escalera* (Tulio Demicheli); *Amor en cuatro tiempos* (Luis Spota); *Mãos sangrentas* (Carlos Hugo Christensen); **1955:** *Bodas de oro* (Tito Davison); *Feliz año, amor mío* (Tulio Demicheli); *Canasta de cuentos mexicanos* (Julio Bracho); *Los peces rojos* (José Antonio Nieves Conde); *Leonora dos sete mares* (Carlos Hugo Christensen); **1956:** *La ciudad de los niños* (Gilberto Martínez Solares); *El arzobispo no ha muerto* (Rafael A. Portas); *La herida luminosa* (Tulio Demicheli); **1957:** *A media luz los tres* (Julián Soler); *Mi esposa me comprende* (Julián Soler); *Mis padres se divorcian* (Julián Soler); **1958:** *El hombre que logró ser invisible* (Alfredo B. Crevenna); *Miércoles de ceniza* (Roberto Gavaldón); *El hombre que me gusta* (Tulio Demicheli); *Isla para dos* (Tito Davison); *La cigüeña dijo sí* (Rafael Baledón); *Ama a tu prójimo* (Tulio Demicheli); **1959:** *El esqueleto de la señora Morales* (Rogelio A. González); *El amor que yo te di* (Tulio Demicheli); **1960:** *Hay alguien detrás de la puerta* (Tulio Demicheli); **1961:** *Pecado de juventud*

(Mauricio de la Serna); *El amor de los amores* (Juan de Orduña); **1962:** *Cena de matrimonios* (Alfonso Balcázar); **1963:** *Así era Pedro Infante* (narrator); **1964:** *El gángster* (Luis Alcoriza); *El amor no es pecado* (Rafael Baledón); *El pecador* (Rafael Baledón); *La recta final* (Carlos Enrique Taboada); *Cuando acaba la noche* (Julián Soler); **1965:** *Despedida de soltera* (Julián Soler); *¿Qué haremos con papá?* (Rafael Baledón); *Juventud sin ley* (Gilberto Martínez Solares); *Los perversos (a go go)* (Gilberto Martínez Solares); **1966:** *Matar no es fácil* (Sergio Vejar); **1969:** *La agonía de ser madre* (Rogelio A. González); **1970:** *El profe* (Miguel M. Delgado).

Oscar DANCIGERS

French producer of Russian origin who settled in Paris after the First World War and then sought refuge from Nazism in Mexico in 1940. In the 40s and 50s he produced many of Buñuel's Mexican films (*Los olvidados* and *La muerte en este jardín*) and some classics by Emilio Fernández and Gabriel Figueroa (*La perla, Pueblerina*).

Filmography 1943: *El jorobado* (Jaime Salvador); *El rebelde* (Jaime Salvador); **1944:** *La hija del regimiento* (Jaime Salvador); **1945:** *Pepita Jiménez* (Emilio Fernández); *La perla* (Emilio Fernández); **1946:** *El ahijado de la muerte* (Norman Foster); *Gran casino* (Luis Buñuel); **1947:** *Soledad* (Miguel Zacarías); **1948:** *Pueblerina* (Emilio Fernández); **1949:** *La hija del penal* (Fernando Soler); *La liga de las muchachas* (Fernando Soler); *El gran calavera* (Luis Buñuel); *Otra primavera* (Alfredo B. Crevenna); *Yo quiero ser hombre* (René Cardona); **1950:** *Los olvidados* (Luis Buñuel); *Huellas del pasado* (Alfredo B. Crevenna); *Si usted no puede yo sí* (Julián Soler); **1951:** *La hija del engaño* (Luis Buñuel); *La mujer sin lágrimas* (Alfredo B. Crevenna); *Los enredos de una gallega* (Fernando Soler); *La miel se fue de la luna* (Julián Soler); *Angélica* (Alfredo B. Crevenna); **1952:** *Robinson Crusoe* (Luis Buñuel); *No te ofendas, Beatriz* (Julián Soler); *El* (Luis Buñuel); *La extraña pasajera* (Fernando A. Rivero); **1953:** *Lágrimas robadas* (Julián Soler); *Abismos de pasión* (Luis Buñuel); **1954:** *La visita que no tocó el timbre* (Julián Soler); *Caín y Abel* (René Cardona); *Los margaritos* (René Cardona); *La vida no vale nada* (Rogelio A. González); **1955:** *El inocente* (Rogelio A. González); **1956:** *La mort en ce jardin/La muerte en este jardín* (Luis Buñuel); **1959:** *La fièvre monte à El Pao/Los ambiciosos* (Luis Buñuel); **1965:** *Viva Maria!* (Louis Malle).

Tito DAVISON

Born in Chillán (Chile) in 1912; died in Mexico City in 1986. In the late 20s, he worked as a journalist for various Chilean and Argentine publications. He went to the USA in 1927, where he acted in Spanish-language films and also did technical work. In Argentina he wrote screenplays, and assisted and worked on adaptations for Luis César Amadori. He made his directorial debut with *Murió el sargento Laprida*. Back in the USA, he became Latin American Affairs adviser for Fox before departing for Mexico (in 1944) to begin a long film career, first as scenarist and then, after 1947, as director.

Filmography 1937: *Murió el sargento Laprida* (in Argentina); **1938:** *Las de Barranco* (in Argentina); **1943:** *Casi un sueño* (in Argentina); **1947:** *La sin ventura; Que Dios me perdone;* **1948:** *Dueña y señora; Medianoche;* **1949:** *El baño de Afrodita; El embajador; Un cuerpo de mujer; Doña Diabla;* **1950:** *La mujer que yo amé; Curvas peligrosas; Negro es mi color;* **1951:** *Mujeres sin mañana; Enséñame a besar; Te sigo esperando;* **1952:** *Las tres alegres comadres; Sor Alegría; Nunca es tarde para amar;* **1953:** *El valor de vivir; Cuando me vaya;* **1954:** *Prisionera del pasado; El caso de la mujer asesinada; Para siempre, amor mío* (Spanish co-p); **1955:** *Cabo de Hornos* (Chilean co-p); *Música en la noche; Bodas de oro;* **1956:** *La dulce enemiga; La Diana cazadora; Música de siempre;* **1957:** *La mujer que no tuvo infancia; Quiero ser artista;* **1958:** *Sabras que te quiero; Impaciencia del corazón; Isla para dos; Mujeres de fuego* (Brazilain co-p); **1959:** *Amor en la sombra; Las canciones unidas* (co-d Alfonso Patiño Gómez and Chano Urueta); **1960:** *La hermana blanca;* **1961:** *La furia del ring; Gelaguetza* (Short); **1962:** *La edad de la inocencia;* **1963:** *Cri Cri el grillito cantor; Canción del alma;* **1964:** *El burócrata* (in Chile); *Más allá de Pipilco* (in Chile); **1965:** *El candidato González* (in Chile); *Si yo fuera intendente* (in Chile); **1966:** *El derecho de nacer;* **1967:** *Corazón salvaje* (USA/Argentina); **1968:** *El terrón de azúcar* (US co-p); **1970:** *Mamá Dolores;* **1971:** *María* (Colombian co-p); **1972:** *Natacha* (in Peru); **1973:** *El amor tiene cara de mujer;* **1974:** *Un amor extraño; Un mulato llamado Martín* (Peruvian co-p); **1978:** *Te quiero;* **1979:** *Amigo;* **1982:** *La guerra es un buen negocio.*

Mimí DERBA

Born in 1888; died in 1953 in Mexico City. She began her career as a theatrical actress and singer. In 1917 she teamed up with Enrique Rosas and Azteca Films, a company that produced numerous films in which Derba worked as producer, screenwriter and/or actress. She directed at least one film, *La tigresa* (1917), which makes her the first Mexican woman to direct a feature. Her acting career was interrupted between 1919 and 1931, and although she made a comeback with *Santa*, she played mainly secondary roles.

Filmography 1917: *En defensa propia* (Joaquín Coss); *Alma de sacrificio* (Joaquín Coss); *La soñadora* (Eduardo Arozamena and Enrique Rosas); *En la sombra* (Enrique Rosas?); *La tigresa;* **1919:** *Dos corazones* (Francisco de Lavillete); **1931:** *Santa* (Antonio Moreno); **1935:** *Martín Garatuza* (Gabriel Soria); *Sor Juana Inés de la Cruz* (Ramón Peón); **1936:** *Mujeres de hoy* (Ramón Peón) **1937:** *Abnegación* (Rafael E. Portas); **1938:** *Refugiados en Madrid* (Alejandro Galindo); *María* (Chano Urueta); **1939:** *Adiós mi chaparrita* (René Cardona); *Café Concordia* (Alberto Gout); *El secreto de la monja* (Raphael J. Sevilla); **1942:** *El baisano Jalil* (Joaquín Pardavé); *La razón de la culpa* (Juan J. Ortega); *María Eugenia* (Felipe Gregorio Castillo); **1943:** *Flor silvestre* (Emilio Fernández); *El espectro de la novia* (René Cardona); *La hija del cielo* (Juan J. Ortega); *Un herrero* (Ramón Pereda); *Una carta de amor* (Miguel Zacarías); *Balajú* (Rolando Aguilar); *Naná* (Celestino Gorostiza); *Una gitana en México* (José Díaz Morales); *La mujer sin alma* (Fernando de Fuentes); *México de mis recuerdos* (Juan Bustillo Oro); *Fantasia ranchera* (Juan José Segura); **1944:** *Porfirio Díaz* (Raphael J. Sevilla); *La trepadora* (Gilberto Martínez Solares); *El capitán Malacara* (Carlos Orellana); *Me he de comer esa tuna* (Miguel Zacarías); *Toda una vida* (Juan J. Ortega); *Por un amor* (José Díaz Morales); *Club verde* (Rolando Aguilar); *La hora de la verdad* (Norman Foster); *Su gran ilusión* (Mauricio Magdaleno); **1945:** *¡Qué verde era mi padre!* (Ismael Rodríguez); *Lo que va de ayer a hoy* (Juan Bustillo Oro); *Papá Lebonard* (Ramón Peón); *Las colegialas* (Miguel M. Delgado); *Cuando lloran los valientes* (Ismael Rodríguez); *La casa la zorra* (Juan J. Ortega); **1946:** *Rocambole* (Ramón Peón); *Cásate y verá* (Carlos Orellana); **1948:** *Ustedes los ricos* (Ismael Rodríguez); *Salón México* (Emilio Fernández); *Prisión de sueños* (Victor Urruchúa); **1949:** *Rondalla* (Victor Urruchúa); *La malquerida* (Emilio Fernández); *El abandonado* (Chano Urueta); *Un grito en la noche* (Miguel Morayta); *La hija del penal* (Fernando Soler); *El seminarista* (Roberto Rodríguez); *La vida en broma* (Jaime Salvador); **1950:** *Rosauro Castro* (Roberto Gavaldón); *Cabellera blanca* (José Díaz Morales); *Traicionera* (Ernesto Cortázar); *Nosotras las taquígrafas* (Emilio Gómez Muriel); *¡Ay amor, cómo me has puesto!* (Gilberto Martínez Solares); *Mi mujer no es mía* (Fernando Soler); *Inmaculada* (Julio Bracho); *La loca de la casa* (Juan Bustillo Oro); *Historia de un corazón* (Julio Bracho); **1951:** *Sangre en el barrio* (Adolfo Fernández Bustamante); *Acapulco* (Emilio Fernández); *La ausente* (Julio Bracho); **1952:** *Dos tipos de cuidado* (Ismael Rodríguez); *El plebeyo* (Miguel M. Delgado); *Cuatro horas antes de morir* (Emilio Gómez Muriel); **1953:** *Casa de muñecas* (Alfredo B. Crevenna).

Nicolás ECHEVARRÍA
Born in Tepic (Nayarit), 8 August 1947. He studied music in Carlos Chávez's studio (1969), and founded, with Mario Lavista, the composers group Quanta (1970). Subsequently, he studied film-making at the Millenium Film Workshop in New York (1972). All his films bear witness to the religious, artistic and cultural manifestations of indigenous Mexicans, although his most recent film, *Cabeza de Vaca*, is set on the North American continent during the early days of the conquest.

Filmography 1973: *Judea: Semana Santa entre los coras* (short doc); **1976:** *Los conventos franciscanos en el antiguo señorío* (doc); **1977:** *Hikure-Tame: La peregrinación del peyote entre los huicholes* (doc); *Hay hombres que respiran luz* (short doc); **1978:** *Flor y canto* (short doc); *María Sabina, mujer espíritu* (doc); **1979:** *Teshéinada: Semana Santa tarahumara* (doc); **1980:** *Poetas campesinos* (doc); **1981:** *El niño Fidencio, taumaturgo de Espinazo* (doc); **1985:** *San Cristobal* (short doc); **1987:** *Las trampas de la fe* (video); **1988:** *Los enemigos: La invención de América* (video); *De la calle* (video); *De película* (video); **1990:** *Cabeza de Vaca*.

José ESTRADA
Born in Mexico City, 11 October 1938; where he died, 23 August 1983. Estrada studied architecture, sociology, law and dramatic arts. In the 60s, he wrote several plays, which he produced alongside others by Beckett, Ionesco, Valle Inclán, etc. After working as assistant director to Jorge Fons in 1968, he made his directorial debut in one of the episodes of *Siempre hay una primera vez*. A professor at the Centro Universitario de Capacitación Cinematográfica (CCC) and at the Centro Universitario de Estudios Cinematográficos (CUEC), he was also very active with the film labour unions, and was general secretary of the Sindicato de Trabajadores de la Producción Cinematográfica (STPC).

Filmography 1969: *Rosa* (episode in *Siempre hay*

una primera vez; co-d Mauricio Wallerstein and Guillermo Murray); **1970:** *Para servir a usted;* **1971:** *Cayó de la gloria el diablo; Los cacos; Uno y medio contra el mundo; El primer paso … de la mujer;* **1972:** *El profeta Mimí;* **1973:** *Chabelo y Pepito contra los monstruos; Chabelo y Pepito detectives;* **1974:** *El albañil;* **1975:** *Recodo de purgatorio; ¡Maten al león!;* **1977:** *Los indolentes;* **1978:** *Angela Morante, ¿crimen o suicidio?;* **1979:** *¡Pum!; China* (Short); **1980:** *Angel del barrio;* **1981:** *La pachanga;* **1983:** *Mexicano, tú puedes.*

María FÉLIX

Born in Alamos (Sonora), 4 May 1914. Félix grew up in Guadalajara, where she was carnival queen. She arrived in Mexico City in the late 30s and was discovered by Fernando Palacios. Her first on-screen appearance in *El peñón de las ánimas* (1942) began a brilliant acting career: she worked with Emilio Fernández, Fernando de Fuentes, Julio Bracho, Luis Buñuel, Jean Renoir, etc., and became 'la Doña', a mythic and legendary cinematic figure.

Filmography 1942: *El peñón de las ánimas* (Miguel Zacarías); *María Eugenia* (Felipe Gregorio Castillo); **1943:** *Doña Bárbara* (Fernando de Fuentes); *La china poblana* (Fernando A. Palacios); *La mujer sin alma* (Fernando de Fuentes); **1944:** *La monja alférez* (Emilio Gómez Muriel); *Amok* (Antonio Momplet); **1945:** *El monje blanco* (Julio Bracho); *Vértigo* (Antonio Momplet); **1946:** *La devoradora* (Fernando de Fuentes); *La mujer de todos* (Julio Bracho); *Enamorada* (Emilio Fernández); **1947:** *La diosa arrodillada* (Roberto Gavaldón); *Río Escondido* (Emilio Fernández); *Que Dios me perdone* (Tito Davison); **1948:** *Maclovia* (Emilio Fernández); *Mare Nostrum* (Rafael Gil); **1949:** *Doña Diabla* (Tito Davison); *Una mujer cualquiera* (Rafael Gil); **1950:** *La noche del sábado* (Rafael Gil); *La corona negra* (Luis Saslavsky); **1951:** *Mesalina* (Carmine Gallone); *Incantésimo trágico* (Mario Sequi); **1952:** *La pasión desnuda* (Luis Cesar Amadori); **1953:** *Camelia* (Roberto Gavaldón); *Reportaje* (Emilio Fernández); *El rapto* (Emilio Fernández); **1954:** *La Belle Otéro* (Richard Pottier); *French Cancan* (Jean Renoir); *Les héros sont fatigués* (Yves Ciampi); **1955:** *La escondida* (Roberto Gavaldón); *Canasta de cuentos mexicanos* (Julio Bracho); 1956: *Tizoc* (Ismael Rodríguez); **1957:** *Flor de mayo* (Roberto Gavaldón); *Faustina* (José Luis Saénz de Heredia); **1958:** *Miércoles de ceniza* (Roberto Gavaldón); *Café Colón* (Benito Alazraki); *La estrella vacía* (Emilio Gómez Muriel); *La cucaracha* (Ismael Rodríguez); **1959:** *Sonatas* (Juan Antonio Bardem); *La Fièvre monte à El Pao/Los ambiciosos* (Luis Buñuel); **1960:** *Juana Gallo* (Miguel Zacarías); **1962:** *La bandida* (Roberto Rodríguez); *Si yo fuera millonario* (Julián Soler); **1963:** *Amor y sexo* (Luis Alcoriza); **1965:** *La Valentina* (Rogelio A. González); **1970:** *La generala* (Juan Ibáñez).

Emilio FERNÁNDEZ

Born in El Hondo (Coahuila) in 1904; died in Mexico City, 6 August 1986. In the 20s, Fernández went to the USA and played numerous small roles in English- and Spanish-language films. Upon his return to Mexico, he became a lead actor and landed two significant roles in *Janitzio* (Carlos Navarro, 1934) and *Adiós Nicanor* (Rafael E. Portas, 1937). He made his directing debut in 1941 with *La isla de la pasión.* When he teamed up with cinematographer Gabriel Figueroa, screenwriter Mauricio Magdaleno and the actors Dolores del Río and Pedro Armendáriz in 1943, his films began to win numerous film festival prizes and brought Mexican cinema to international attention.

Filmography 1941: *La isla de la pasión – Clipperton;* **1942:** *Soy puro mexicano;* **1943:** *Flor silvestre; María Candelaria;* **1944:** *Las abandonadas; Bugambilia;* **1945:** *Pepita Jiménez; La perla;* **1946:** *Enamorada; The Fugitive* (co-d John Ford); **1947:** *Río Escondido;* **1948:** *Maclovia; Salón México; Pueblerina;* **1949:** *La malquerida; Duelo en las montañas; The Torch* (*Del odio nació el amor;* English version of *Enamorada*); **1950:** *Un día de vida; Víctimas del pecado; Islas Marías; Siempre tuya;* **1951:** *La bien amada; Acapulco; El mar y tú;* **1952:** *Cuando levanta la niebla;* **1953:** *La red; Reportaje; El rapto; La rosa blanca* (Cuban co-p); **1954:** *La rebelión de los colgados* (co-d Alfredo B. Crevenna); *Nosotros dos* (Spanish co-p); **1955:** *La Tierra del Fuego se apaga* (in Argentina); **1956:** *Una cita de amor; El impostor;* **1961:** *Pueblito;* **1962:** *Paloma herida* (Guatemalan co-p); **1966:** *Un dorado de Pancho Villa;* **1968:** *El crepúsculo de un dios;* **1973:** *La choca;* **1975:** *Zona roja;* **1977:** *México norte;* **1978:** *Erótica.*

Marcela FERNÁNDEZ VIOLANTE

Born in Mexico City in 1941. Studied film-making at the Centro Universitario de Estudios Cinematográficos (CUEC), where she later taught directing and screenwriting before becoming technical secretary and director.

Filmography 1967: *Azul* (Short); **1971:** *Frida Kahlo* (short doc); **1974:** *De todos modos Juan te llamas;*

1976: *Cananea;* **1979:** *Misterio;* **1980:** *En el país de los pies ligeros;* **1987:** *Nocturno amor que te vas;* **1991:** *Golpe de suerte.*

Gabriel FIGUEROA

Born in Mexico City in 1908. Figueroa made his cinematic debut in 1932 as a still photographer in Miguel Contreras Torres's *Revolución* and Raphael J. Sevilla's *Almas encontradas.* Shortly after he went to Hollywood and trained with Gregg Toland. Returning to Mexico, he began a long career as cinematographer, notably for Emilio Fernández and Luis Buñuel. He also worked with a number of US directors, such as John Ford, John Huston and Don Siegel.

Filmography 1934: *El escándalo* (Chano Urueta); *El primo Basilio* (Carlos Najera); **1935:** *¡Vámonos con Pancho Villa!* (Fernando de Fuentes); *María Elena* (Raphael J. Sevilla); **1936:** *Las mujeres mandan* (Fernando de Fuentes); *Cielito lindo* (Roberto O'Quigley); *Allá en el Rancho Grande* (Fernando de Fuentes); **1937:** *Bajo el cielo de México* (Fernando de Fuentes); *Jalisco nunca pierde* (Chano Urueta); *Canción del alma* (Chano Urueta); *La Adelita* (Guillermo Hernández Gómez); *Mi candidato* (Chano Urueta); **1938:** *Refugiados en Madrid* (Alejandro Galindo); *Padre de más de cuatro* (Roberto O'Quigley); *La casa del ogro* (Fernando de Fuentes); *Los millones de Chaflán* (Rolando Aguilar); *Mientras México duerme* (Alejandro Galindo); *La bestia negra* (Gabriel Soria); **1939:** *La noche de los mayas* (Chano Urueta); *Papacito lindo* (Fernando de Fuentes); *Los de abajo* (Chano Urueta); *La canción del milagro* (Rolando Aguilar); *¡Que viene mi marido!* (Chano Urueta); **1940:** *Allá en el trópico* (Fernando de Fuentes); *El jefe máximo* (Fernando de Fuentes); *Con su amable permiso* (Fernando Soler); *El monje loco* (Alejandro Galindo); *Creo en Dios* (Fernando de Fuentes); **1941:** *Ni sangre ni arena* (Alejandro Galindo); *El rápido de las 9:15* (Alejandro Galindo); *¡Ay, qué tiempos, señor don Simón!* (Julio Bracho); *La casa del rencor* (Gilberto Martínez Solares); *El gendarme desconocido* (Miguel M. Delgado); *La gallina clueca* (Fernando de Fuentes); *Virgen de medianoche* (Alejandro Galindo); *Mi viuda alegre* (Miguel M. Delgado); **1942:** *Cuando viajan las estrellas* (Alberto Gout); *Historia de un gran amor* (Julio Bracho); *Los tres mosqueteros* (Miguel M. Delgado); *El verdugo de Sevilla* (Fernando Soler); *La Virgen que forjó una patria* (Julio Bracho); *El circo* (Miguel M. Delgado); **1943:** *Flor silvestre* (Emilio Fernández); *El espectro de la novia* (René Cardona);

El as negro (René Cardona); *La mujer sin cabeza* (René Cardona); *Distinto amanecer* (Julio Bracho); *María Candelaria* (Emilio Fernández); *La fuga* (Norman Foster); **1944:** *El corsario negro* (Chano Urueta); *El intruso* (Mauricio Magdaleno); *Adiós, Mariquita linda* (Alfonso Patiño Gómez); *Las abandonadas* (Emilio Fernández); *Más allá del amor* (Adolfo Fernández Bustamante); *Bugambilia* (Emilio Fernández); **1945:** *Un día con el diablo* (Miguel M. Delgado); *Cantaclaro* (Julio Bracho); *La perla* (Emilio Fernández); **1946:** *Su última aventura* (Gilberto Martínez Solares); *Enamorada* (Emilio Fernández); **1947:** *The Fugitive* (John Ford); *La casa colorada* (Miguel Morayta); *Río Escondido* (Emilio Fernández); *María la O* (Adolfo Fernández Bustamante); *Tarzan and the Mermaids* (Robert Florey); **1948:** *Maclovia* (Emilio Fernández); *Dueña y señora* (Tito Davison); *Medianoche* (Tito Davison); *Salón México* (Emilio Fernández); *Pueblerina* (Emilio Fernández); *Prisión de sueños* (Victor Urruchúa); **1949:** *El embajador* (Tito Davison); *Opio* (Ramón Peón); *La malquerida* (Emilio Fernández); *Un cuerpo de mujer* (Tito Davison); *Duelo en las montañas* (Emilio Fernández); *The Torch* (Emilio Fernández); *Nuestras vidas* (Ramón Peón); **1950:** *Un día de vida* (Emilio Fernández); *Los olvidados* (Luis Buñuel); *Víctimas del pecado* (Emilio Fernández); *Pecado* (Luis César Amadori); *Islas Marías* (Emilio Fernández); *El gavilán pollero* (Rogelio A. González); *El bombero atómico* (Miguel M. Delgado); *Siempre tuya* (Emilio Fernández); **1951:** *Los pobres van al cielo* (Jaime Salvador); *Un gallo en corral ajeno* (Julián Soler); *La bienamada* (Emilio Fernández); *Hay un niño en su futuro* (Fernando Cortés); *El mar y tú* (Emilio Fernández); *Ahí viene Martín Corona* (Miguel Zacarías); *El enamorado* (Miguel Zacarías); **1952:** *El rebozo de Soledad* (Roberto Gavaldón); *Ni pobres ni ricos* (Fernando Cortés); *Cuando levanta la niebla* (Emilio Fernández); *El señor fotógrafo* (Miguel M. Delgado); *Dos tipos de cuidado* (Ismael Rodríguez); *Ansiedad* (Miguel Zacarías); *El* (Luis Buñuel); **1953:** *Camelia* (Roberto Gavaldón); *Llévame en tus brazos* (Julio Bracho); *El niño y la niebla* (Roberto Gavaldón); *La rosa blanca* (Emilio Fernández); **1954:** *La rebelión de los colgados* (Emilio Fernández and Alfredo B. Crevenna); *La mujer X* (Julián Soler); *Pueblo, canto y esperanza* (Mexican episode by Rogelio A. González; co-d Julián Soler and Alfredo B. Crevenna); *Estafa de amor* (Miguel M. Delgado); *El monstruo en la sombra Zacarías* (Gómez Urquiza); **1955:** *La doncella de piedra* (Miguel M. Delgado); *Historia de un amor* (Roberto Gavaldón); *La escondida* (Roberto Gavaldón); *Canasta de cuentos* mexicanos (Julio Bracho); *La Tierra del Fuego se apaga* (Emilio Fernández); **1956:** *Una cita de amor* (Emilio Fernández); *Sueños de oro* (Miguel Zacarías); *El bolero de Raquel* (Miguel M. Delgado); *Mujer en condominio* (Rogelio A. González); **1957:** *Aquí esta Heraclio Bernal* (Roberto Gavaldón); *La venganza de Heraclio Bernal* (Roberto Gavaldón); *La rebelión de la sierra* (Roberto Gavaldón); *Flor de mayo* (Roberto Gavaldón); *Una golfa* (Tulio Demicheli); *La sonrisa de la Virgen* (Roberto Rodríguez); **1958:** *Carabina 30–30* (Miguel M. Delgado); *Impaciencia del corazón* (Tito Davison); *Café Colón* (Benito Alazraki); *Isla para dos* (Tito Davison); *Nazarín* (Luis Buñuel); *La cucaracha* (Ismael Rodríguez); *La estrella vacía* (Emilio Gómez Muriel); **1959:** *Sonatas* (Juan Antonio Bardem and Cecilio Paniagua); *La Fièvre monte à El Pao/Los ambiciosos* (Luis Buñuel); *Macario* (Roberto Gavaldón); **1960:** *La Joven/The Young One* (Luis Buñuel); *Juana Gallo* (Miguel Zacarías); **1961:** *Rosa Blanca* (Roberto Gavaldón); *Animas Trujano* (Ismael Rodríguez); *El tejedor de milagros* (Francisco del Villar); **1962:** *El ángel exterminador* (Luis Buñuel); *Días de otoño* (Roberto Gavaldón); **1963:** *El hombre de papel* (Ismael Rodríguez); *Entrega inmediata* (Miguel M. Delgado); *En la mitad del mundo* (Ramón Pereda); *The Night of the Iguana* (John Huston); **1964:** *Escuela para solteras* (Miguel Zacarías); *El gallo de oro* (Roberto Gavaldón); *Los tres calaveras* (Fernando Cortes); *Los cuatro Juanes* (Miguel Zacarías); *Simón del desierto* (Luis Buñuel); **1965:** *Un alma pura* (Juan Ibáñez); *Las dos Elenas* (José Luis Ibáñez); *Lola de mi vida* (Miguel Barbachano Ponce); *Cargamento prohibido* (Miguel M. Delgado); *¡Viva Benito Canales!* (Miguel M. Delgado); **1966:** *Pedro Páramo* (Carlos Velo); *El asesino se embarca* (Miguel M. Delgado); *El escapulario* (Servando González); *Domingo salvaje* (Francisco del Villar); *The Chinese Room* (Albert Zugsmith); *Su excelencia* (Miguel M. Delgado); *Los angeles de Puebla* (Francisco del Villar); **1967:** *El jinete fantasma* (Albert Zugsmith); *Mariana* (Juan Guerrero); *Corazón salvaje* (Tito Davison); *¿Pax?* (Wolf Rilla); **1968:** *El terrón de azúcar* (Tito Davison); *Narda o el verano* (Juan Guerrero); **1969:** *Two Mules for Sister Sara* (Don Siegel); **1970:** *La generala* (Juan Ibáñez); *El cielo y tú* (Gilberto Gazcón); *El profe* (Miguel M. Delgado); *Kelly's Heroes* (Brian C. Hutton); **1971:** *Los hijos de Satanás* (Rafael Baledón); *Hijazo de mi vidaza* (Rafael Baledón); *María* (Tito Davison); **1972:** *El monasterio de los buitres* (Francisco del Villar); *El señor de Osanto* (Jaime Humberto Hermosillo); *Once a Scoundrel* (George Schaefer); *Interval* (Daniel Mann); *El festín*

de la loba (Francisco del Villar); **1973:** *El amor tiene cara de mujer* (Tito Davison); *Los perros de Dios* (Francisco del Villar); **1974:** *El llanto de la tortuga* (Francisco del Villar); *Presagio* (Luis Alcoriza); **1975:** *Coronación* (Sergio Olhovich); *La vida cambia* (Juan Manuel Torres); *Maten al león* (José Estrada); **1976:** *Balún Canán* (Benito Alazraki); *Cananea* (Marcela Fernández Violante); *Los aztecas* (Marcel Boudou) (TV); **1977:** *Divinas palabras* (Juan Ibáñez); *La casa del pelícano* (Sergio Vejar); *The Children of Sanchez* (Hall Bartlett); **1978:** *DF* (Rogelio A. González); *Te quiero* (Tito Davison); *A paso de cojo* (Luis Alcoriza); **1980:** *El jugador de ajedrez* (Juan Luis Buñuel) (TV); *México mágico* (Alejandro Tavera, Raúl Zermeno and Luis Mandoki); **1981:** *México 2000* (Rogelio A. González); *El héroe desconocido* (Julián Pastor); **1983:** *El corazón de la noche* (Jaime Humberto Hermosillo); *Under the Volcano* (John Huston).

Jorge FONS

Born in Tuxpan (Veracruz) in 1939. Fons was part of the first graduation class of the Centro Universitario de Estudios Cinematográficos (CUEC). He became an actor and theatrical assistant, assistant-operator to José Luis Ibáñez and Juan Ibáñez, and assistant director to Arturo Ripstein. Fons distanced himself from the cinema for a decade (1979–89), but remained active as a director of *telenovelas*.

Filmography 1968: *La sorpresa* (episode of *Trampas de amor;* co-d Tito Novaro and Manuel Michel); **1969:** *El quelite; Nosotros* (episode of *Tú, yo, nosotros:* co-d Gonzalo Martínez and Juan Manuel Torres); **1971:** *Los cachorros, Jory* (US co-p; co-d Salomón Láiter); **1972:** *Cinco mil dólares de recompensa; Caridad* (episode of *Fe, esperanza y caridad;* co-d Alberto Bojórquez and Luis Alcoriza); **1974:** *La ETA* (short doc); **1976:** *Los albañiles;* **1979:** *Así es Vietnam* (doc); **1989:** *Rojo amanecer;* **1994:** *El callejón de los milagros.*

Fernando de FUENTES

Born in Veracruz, 13 December 1894; died in Mexico City, 4 July 1958. De Fuentes entered cinema as the manager of the Teatro Olimpia. In the early sound years he was second assistant to Antonio Moreno on *Santa* (1931) and dialogue coach and co-director of *Una vida por otra* (John H. Auer, 1932). He became the most important figure of Mexican cinema in the 30s, not only because of his trilogy about the Revolution (*El prisionero trece, El compadre Mendoza* and *¡Vámonos con Pancho Villa!*), but also because of other films in which he introduced and sustained genres as the basis of the national cinema. In the 40s, as producer and in association with Juan Bustillo Oro and Miguel Zacarías, he unsuccessfully attempted to challenge William Jenkins's exhibition monopoly.

Filmography 1932: *Una vida por otra* (co-d John H. Auer); *El anónimo;* **1933:** *El prisionero trece; La calandria; El Tigre de Yautepec; El compadre Mendoza;* **1934:** *El fantasma del convento; Cruz Diablo;* **1935:** *¡Vámonos con Pancho Villa!; La familia Dressel;* **1936:** *Las mujeres mandan; Allá en el Rancho Grande; Desfile deportivo* (short doc); *Petróleo* (short doc); **1937:** *Bajo el cielo de México; La Zandunga;* **1938:** *La casa del ogro;* **1939:** *Papacito lindo;* **1940:** *Allá en el trópico; El jefe máximo; Creo en Dios;* **1941:** *La gallina clueca;* **1942:** *Así se quiere en Jalisco;* **1943:** *Doña Bárbara; La mujer sin alma;* **1944:** *El rey se divierte;* **1945:** *Hasta que perdió Jalisco; La selva de fuego;* **1946:** *La devoradora;* **1948:** *Allá en el Rancho Grande; Jalisco canta en Sevilla* (Spanish co-p); **1949:** *Hipólito el de Santa;* **1950:** *Por la puerta falsa; Crimen y castigo;* **1952:** *Los hijos de María Morales; Canción de cuna;* **1953:** *Tres citas con el destino* (Spain/Argentina; co-d Florián Rey and León Klimovsky).

Alejandro GALINDO

Born in Monterrey (Nuevo León), 14 January 1906. Galindo abandoned school to go to Hollywood, where he made a living on the fringes of the industry and learned about cinematographic design, screenwriting, theatrical staging and acting. He returned to Mexico in 1930 and wrote for radio; later drafting dialogues and working on the scripts of *La isla maldita* (Boris Maicon, 1934), *El baúl macabro* (Miguel Zacarías, 1936) and *Ave sin nido* (Roberto O'Quigley, 1937). He made his directorial debut with *Almas rebeldes*. Set in contemporary urban locales, his films of the 40s and early 50s (*Campeón sin corona, ¡Esquina … bajan!, Una familia de tantas,* etc.) were commercially successful and still enjoy critical acclaim. Galindo was also a leader within the Sindicato de Trabajadores de la Producción Cinematográfica (STPC) and the author of many essays about Mexican cinema.

Filmography 1937: *Almas rebeldes;* **1938:** *Refugiados en Madrid; Mientras México duerme;* **1939:** *Corazón de niño; El muerto murió;* **1940:** *El monje loco;* **1941:** *Ni sangre ni arena; El rápido de las 9:15; Virgen de medianoche o El imperio del hampa;* **1943:** *Konga Roja; Divorciadas; Tribunal de justicia;* **1944:** *La*

sombra de Chucho el Roto; **1945:** *Tú eres la luz; Campeón sin corona;* **1946:** *Los que volvieron;* **1947:** *Hermoso ideal; El muchacho alegre;* **1948:** *¡Esquina … bajan!; Una familia de tantas; Hay lugar para dos;* **1949:** *Confidencias de un ruletero; Cuatro contra el mundo;* **1950:** *Capitán de rurales; Doña Perfecta;* **1951:** *Dicen que soy comunista;* **1952:** *El último round; Los dineros del diablo; Por el mismo camino; Sucedió en Acapulco; Crisol del pensamiento mexicano* (Short); **1953:** *Espaldas mojadas; Los Fernández de Peralvillo; La duda; Las infieles;* **1954:** *¡Y mañana serán mujeres!; Historia de un marido infiel;* **1955:** *Tres melodías de amor;* **1956:** *Hora y media de balazos; Policías y ladrones; Tu hijo debe nacer; Esposa te doy;* **1957:** *Piernas de oro; Te ví en TV; Manos arriba; Echenme al gato;* **1958:** *Raffles; La edad de la tentación; El super-macho; México nunca duerme; La vida de Agustín Lara;* **1959:** *Ni hablar del peluquín; Ellas también son rebeldes;* **1960:** *Mañana serán hombres;* **1961:** *La mente y el crimen;* **1967:** *Corona de lágrimas;* **1968:** *Remolino de pasiones;* **1969:** *Cristo 70;* **1970:** *Verano ardiente; Simplemente vivir;* **1971:** *Tacos al carbón; Triángulo; Pepito y la lámpara maravillosa;* **1972:** *San Simón de los magueyes;* **1973:** *Ante el cadáver de un líder; El juicio de Martín Cortés;* **1974:** *Y la mujer hizo al hombre;* **1977:** *Las del talón; Que te vaya bonito, Mojados;* **1978:** *Milagro en el circo;* **1979:** *Dimas de León; El giro, el pinto y el colorado;* **1981:** *El sexo de los pobres; Cruz de olvido;* **1982:** *El color de nuestra piel;* **1985:** *Cárdenas.*

Sara GARCÍA

Born in Orizaba (Veracruz), 8 September 1895; died in Mexico City, 21 November 1980. She abandoned a career as a governess in 1917 to work in films (first with Joaquín Coss and Azteca Films) and theatre (at the Teatro Virginia Fabregas). Throughout her more than sixty years in the business and in over 150 films she always played self-sacrificing and suffering mothers or grandmothers.

Filmography 1917: *En defensa propia* (Joaquín Coss); *Alma de sacrificio* (Joaquín Coss); *La soñadora* (Eduardo Arozamena and Enrique Rosas); **1933:** *El pulpo humano* (Jorge Bell and Guillermo Calles); *El vuelo de la muerte* (Guillermo Calles); *La sangre manda* (José Bohr and Raphael J. Sevilla); **1934:** *¡Viva México!* (Miguel Contreras Torres); **1936:** *Así es la mujer* (José Bohr); *Marihuana (El monstruo verde)* (José Bohr); *Las mujeres mandan* (Fernando de Fuentes); *Malditas sean las mujeres* (Juan Bustillo Oro); *No te engañes corazón* (Miguel Contreras Torres); **1937:** *No basta ser madre* (Ramón Peón); *La* *honradez es un estorbo* (Juan Bustillo Oro); **1938:** *Pescadores de perlas* (Guillermo Calles); *Por mis pistolas* (José Bohr); *Padre de más de cuatro* (Roberto O'Quigley); *Dos cadetes* (Jorge López Portillo and René Cardona); *Perjura* (Raphael J. Sevilla); *Su adorable majadero* (Alberto Gout); *El capitán aventurero* (Arcady Boytler); *Los enredos de papá* (Miguel Zacarías); **1939:** *La calumnia* (Francisco Elías); *Papacito lindo* (Fernando de Fuentes); *En un burro tres baturros* (José Benavides Jr); *Miente y serás feliz* (Raphael J. Sevilla); **1940:** *Allá en el trópico* (Fernando de Fuentes); *Mi madrecita* (Francisco Elías); *Ahí esta el detalle* (Juan Bustillo Oro); *Recordar es vivir* (Fernando A. Rivero; compilation film); *Papá se desenreda* (Miguel Zacarías); *Al son de la marimba* (Juan Bustillo Oro); *Papá se enreda otra vez* (Miguel Zacarías); *Las tres viudas de papá* (Miguel Zacarías); **1941:** *Cuando los hijos se van* (Juan Bustillo Oro); *¿Quién te quiere a ti?* (Rolando Aguilar); *Dos mexicanos en Sevilla* (Carlos Orellana); *La gallina clueca* (Fernando de Fuentes); *Alejandra* (José Benavides Jr); **1942:** *Regalo de reyes* (Mario del Río); *La abuelita* (Raphael J. Sevilla); *Historia de un gran amor* (Julio Bracho); *El Baisano Jalil* (Joaquín Pardavé); *El verdugo de Sevilla* (Fernando Soler); **1943:** *Resurrección* (Gilberto Martínez Solares); *No mataras* (Chano Urueta); *Caminito alegre* (Miguel Morayta); *Toros, amor y alegría* (Raúl de Anda); **1944:** *Mis hijos* (Ramiro Gómez Kemp); *La trepadora* (Gilberto Martínez Solares); *El secreto de la solterona* (Miguel M. Delgado); *Tuya en cuerpo y alma* (Alberto Gout); *El jagüey de las ruinas* (Gilberto Martínez Solares); *Como yo te quería* (Raphael J. Sevilla); **1945:** *Escuadrón 201* (Jaime Salvador); *La señora de enfrente* (Gilberto Martínez Solares); *¡Ay, qué rechulo es Puebla!* (René Cardona); *Mamá Inés* (Fernando Soler); *El barchante Neguib* (Joaquín Pardavé); **1946:** *Los cristeros* (Raúl de Anda); *Los que volvieron* (Alejandro Galindo); *El ropavejero* (Emilio Gómez Muriel); *Los tres García* (Ismael Rodríguez); *Vuelven los García* (Ismael Rodríguez); **1948:** *Madre adorada* (René Cardona); *Dueña y señora* (Tito Davison); *La familia Pérez* (Gilberto Martínez Solares); *Tía Candela* (Julián Soler); *Dicen que soy mujeriego* (Roberto Rodríguez); **1949:** *Eterna agonía* (Julián Soler); *Novia a la medida* (Gilberto Martínez Solares); *El diablo no es tan diablo* (Julián Soler); *Dos pesos dejada* (Joaquín Pardavé); *Yo quiero ser hombre* (René Cardona); **1950:** *Mi preferida* (Chano Urueta); *Si me viera don Porfirio* (Fernando Cortes); *Azahares para tu boda* (Julián Soler); *Mi querido capitán* (Gilberto Martínez Solares); *Yo quiero ser tonta* (Eduardo Ugarte); *La reina del mambo* (Ramón

Pereda); *El papelerito* (Agustín P. Delgado); *Doña Clarines* (Eduardo Ugarte); **1951:** *La duquesa del tepetate* (Juan José Segura); *Acá las tortas* (Juan Bustillo Oro); *La miel se fue de la luna* (Julián Soler); **1952:** *Misericordia* (Zacarías Gómez Urquiza); *Por el mismo camino* (Alejandro Galindo); *El lunar de la familia* (Fernando Méndez); *Sólo para maridos* (Fernando Soler); **1953:** *Los que no deben nacer* (Agustín P. Delgado); *Los Fernández de Peralvillo* (Alejandro Galindo); **1954:** *El hombre inquieto* (Rafael Baledón); *El crucifijo de piedra* (Carlos Toussaint); **1955:** *La tercera palabra* (Julián Soler); *El inocente* (Rogelio A. González); *The Living Idol* (Albert Lewin); **1956:** *La ciudad de los niños* (Gilberto Martínez Solares); **1957:** *Pobres millonarios* (Fernando Cortes); *El gran premio* (Carlos Orellana); **1958:** *Los santos reyes* (Rafael Baledón); *Las señoritas Vivanco* (Mauricio de la Serna); *Con el dedo en el gatillo* (Luis Spota; four-part series: *El anónimo*, *El vengador*, *El dinamitero* and *La tumba*); **1959:** *Yo pecador* (Alfonso Corona Blake); *El proceso de las señoritas Vivanco* (Mauricio de la Serna); *Mis abuelitas … nomás* (Mauricio de la Serna); **1960:** *El buena suerte* (Rogelio A. González); *Paloma brava* (Rogelio A. González); *El malvado Carabel* (Rafael Baledón); *El analfabeto* (Miguel M. Delgado); *Las hijas del Amapolo* (Gilberto Martínez Solares); **1961:** *El caballo blanco* (Rafael Baledón); *Bello recuerdo* (Antonio del Amo); **1962:** *Ruletero a toda marcha* (Rafael Baledón); *Las chivas rayadas* (Manuel Muñoz); *Los fenómenos del fútbol* (Manuel Muñoz); *Los dinamiteros* (Juan Atienza); **1963:** *Nos dicen las intocables* (Jaime Salvador); *Héroe a la fuerza* (Miguel M. Delgado); **1964:** *Canta mi corazón* (Emilio Gómez Muriel); *Escuela para solteras* (Miguel Zacarías); *Nos lleva la tristeza* (Jaime Salvador); *Los dos apóstoles* (Jaime Salvador); **1965:** *Joselito vagabundo* (Miguel Morayta); **1966:** *Un novio para dos hermanas* (Luis César Amadori); **1967:** *No se mande profe* (Alfredo B. Crevenna); *Sor Ye-yé* (Ramón Fernández); *Las amiguitas de los ricos* (José Díaz Morales); **1968:** *El día de las madres* (Alfredo B. Crevenna); *Flor marchita* (Rogelio A. González); *Por qué nací mujer* (Rogelio A. González); **1969:** *La hermana Dinamita* (Rafael Baledón); *La casa del farol rojo* (Agustín P. Delgado); **1970:** *La inocente* (Rogelio A. González); *Fin de fiesta* (Mauricio Wallerstein); *Nadie te querrá como yo* (Carlos Lozano Dana); *Mecánica nacional* (Luis Alcoriza); **1972:** *Entre monjas anda el diablo* (René Cardona); *Caridad* (Jorge Fons, sketch of *Fe, esperanza y caridad*; co-d Luis Alcoriza and Alberto Bojórquez); *Los leones del ring* (Chano Urueta); *Los leones del ring contra la cosa nostra (Chano Urueta); *Nosotros los feos* (Ismael Rodríguez); *Valente Quintero* (Mario Hernández); **1973:** *El hijo del pueblo* (René Cardona); **1975:** *Como gallos de pelea* (Arturo Martínez); *Nobleza ranchera* (Arturo Martínez); *La comadrita* (Fernando Cortés); **1977:** *La vida difícil de una mujer fácil* (José María Fernández Unsaín); **1980:** *Como México no hay dos* (Rafael Villaseñor Kuri).

Jomí GARCÍA ASCOT

Born in Tunisia in 1927; died in Mexico City, August 1986. García Ascot arrived in Mexico in 1936 fleeing from republican Spain. He was a poet, essayist, and one of the principal figures of the IFAL (Instituto Frances de América Latina) film society. He worked in newsreel production with the Manuel Barbachano Ponce group in the 50s, and was also one of the scenarists of *Raíces* (Benito Alazraki, 1953). In the early 60s, García Ascot, Emilio García Riera, José de la Colina and others founded the group Nuevo Cine, calling for a new cinema and new critical practices. He put those ideas to work in *En el balcón vacío*.

Filmography 1958: *Chistelandia; Nueva Chistelandia; ¡Vuelve Chistelandia!* (humorous anthologies of *Tele-Revista* newsreels; co-d Manuel Barbachano Ponce, Carlos Velo and Fernando Marcos); **1960:** *Un día de trabajo* and *Los novios* (episodes of *Cuba 58;* co-d Jorge Fraga; in Cuba); **1961:** *En el balcón vacío;* **1966:** *Remedios Varo* (short doc); **1976:** *El viaje.*

Roberto GAVALDÓN

Born in Chihuahua, 7 June 1909; died in Mexico City, 4 September 1986. After a stay in the USA, Gavaldón began to work in Mexican cinema as an actor and assistant director. *La barraca,* an adaptation of the Vicente Blasco Ibáñez novel, revealed the directorial skills of this exceptionally gifted technician. In the 40s and 50s, he gathered a working group which included, among others, the screenwriter José Revueltas, musician Rodolfo Halffter, set decorator Gunther Gerzso and cinematographers Gabriel Figueroa and Alex Phillips. Working with the latter, he directed many important films. He was also a film labour union leader and a federal deputy.

Filmography 1944: *La barraca;* **1945:** *Corazones de México; Rayando el sol; El socio;* **1946:** *La otra; La vida íntima de Marco Antonio y Cleopatra; A la sombra del puente;* **1947:** *La diosa arrodillada;*

Adventures of Casanova (in the USA); **1948:** *Han matado a Tongolele;* **1949:** *La casa chica;* **1950:** *Rosauro Castro; Deseada; Mi vida por la tuya; En la palma de tu mano;* **1951:** *La noche avanza;* **1952:** *El rebozo de Soledad; Acuérdate de vivir; Las tres perfectas casadas;* **1953:** *Camelia; El niño y la niebla; The Littlest Outlaw* (in the USA); **1954:** *Sombra verde; De carne somos;* **1955:** *Después de la tormenta; Historia de un amor; La escondida;* **1957:** *Aquí está Heraclio Bernal; La venganza de Heraclio Bernal; La rebelión de la sierra; Flor de mayo;* **1958:** *Miércoles de ceniza;* **1959:** *Macario;* **1960:** *El siete de copas;* **1961:** *Rosa Blanca;* **1962:** *Días de otoño;* **1964:** *Los hijos que yo soñé; El gallo de oro;* **1969:** *Las figuras de arena; La vida inútil de Pito Pérez;* **1971:** *Doña Macabra;* **1972:** *Don Quijote cabalga de nuevo* (Spanish co-p); **1974:** *Un amor perverso* (Spanish co-p); **1975:** *El hombre de los hongos;* **1976:** *Las cenizas de un diputado; La playa vacía* (Spanish co-p); **1977:** *Cuando tejen las arañas.*

Gunther GERSZO

Born in Mexico City in 1915. Gerszo lived in Switzerland until 1931. A designer of sets and costumes for ballet, in 1935–40 he studied decoration in Cleveland (USA) and began to paint. He then returned to Mexico and began his career as a film-set designer on the third version of *Santa*. He continued as a set designer until the early 60s; and also occasionally worked as a scenarist. He was an important and prolific artist.

Filmography 1943: *Santa* (Norman Foster); **1945:** *Corazones de México* (Roberto Gavaldón); *La morena de mi copla* (Fernando A. Rivero); *Campeón sin corona* (Alejandro Galindo); **1946:** *El ahijado de la muerte* (Norman Foster); *Su última aventura* (Gilberto Martínez Solares); *La otra* (Roberto Gavaldón); *Los que volvieron* (Alejandro Galindo); *Todo un caballero* (Miguel M. Delgado); *A la sombra del puente* (Roberto Gavaldón); **1947:** *Hermoso ideal* (Alejandro Galindo); *El casado casa quiere* (Gilberto Martínez Solares); *Mystery in Mexico* (Robert Wise); **1948:** *El supersabio* (Miguel M. Delgado); *¡Esquina … bajan!* (Alejandro Galindo); *El mago* (Miguel M. Delgado); *Una familia de tantas* (Alejandro Galindo); *Hay lugar para … dos* (Alejandro Galindo); **1949:** *Confidencias de un maletero* (Alejandro Galindo); *Puerta … joven* (Miguel M. Delgado); *La posesión* (Julio Bracho); *Cuatro contra el mundo* (Alejandro Galindo); *Tú, sólo tú* (Miguel M. Delgado); *Bodas de fuego* (Marco Aurelio Galindo); *Las joyas del pecado* (Alfredo B. Crevenna); **1950:** *Un día de vida* (Emilio Fernández); *Rosauro Castro* (Roberto Gavaldón);

Capitán de rurales (Alejandro Galindo); *El siete machos* (Miguel M. Delgado); *Susana* (Luis Buñuel); *Entre tu amor y el cielo* (Emilio Gómez Muriel); *Menores de edad* (Miguel M. Delgado); *El papelerito* (Miguel M. Delgado); *Camino del infierno* (Miguel Morayta); *Doña Perfecta* (Alejandro Galindo); *El bombero atómico* (Miguel M. Delgado); **1951:** *Una mujer sin amor* (Luis Buñuel); *Dicen que soy comunista* (Alejandro Galindo); *Cárcel de mujeres* (Miguel M. Delgado); *Ella y yo* (Miguel M. Delgado); *Si yo fuera diputado* (Miguel M. Delgado); *El cardenal* (Miguel M. Delgado); *La ausente* (Julio Bracho); **1952:** *La bestia magnífica* (Chano Urueta); *El bruto* (Luis Buñuel); *El último round* (Alejandro Galindo); *Sor Alegría* (Tito Davison); *El señor fotógrafo* (Miguel M. Delgado); **1953:** *El monstruo resucitado* (Chano Urueta); *Les Orgueilleux* (Yves Allegret); *La ladrona* (Emilio Gómez Muriel); *El valor de vivir* (Tito Davison); *Caballero a la medida* (Miguel M. Delgado); *Sombrero* (Norman Foster); *La duda* (Alejandro Galindo); **1954:** *La gitana blanca* (Miguel M. Delgado); *El río y la muerte* (Luis Buñuel); *La bruja* (Chano Urueta); *Al son del charleston* (Jaime Salvador); *Estoy tan enamorada* (Jaime Salvador); *… ¡Y mañana mujeres!* (Alejandro Galindo); *La sombra de Cruz Diablo* (Vicente Oroná); *Historia de un marido infiel* (Alejandro Galindo); *Abajo el telón* (Miguel M. Delgado); *A los cuatro vientos* (Adolfo Fernández Bustamante); *A Life in the Balance* (Harry Horner); **1955:** *El rey de México* (Rafael Baledón); *Tres melodías de amor* (Alejandro Galindo); *Historia de un amor* (Roberto Gavaldón); *Bailando cha cha cha* (Jaime Salvador); *La escondida* (Roberto Gavaldón); *Mi desconocida esposa* (Alberto Gout); *Pensión de artistas* (Adolfo Fernández Bustamante); *Hora y media de balazos* (Alejandro Galindo); *Bambalinas* (Tulio Demicheli); **1956:** *¡Qué seas feliz!* (Julián Soler); *Policías y ladrones* (Alejandro Galindo); *Tú y la mentira* (Alejandro Galindo); *El bolero de Raquel* (Miguel M. Delgado); *Ladrón de cadáveres* (Fernando Méndez); *El ratón* (Chano Urueta); *Cuando México canta* (Julián Soler); *Esposa te doy* (Alejandro Galindo); *Cielito lindo* (Miguel M. Delgado); **1957:** *La mafia del crimen* (Julio Bracho); *Tres desgraciados con suerte* (Jaime Salvador); *¡Ay … calypso no te rajes!* (Jaime Salvador); *Te vi en TV* (Alejandro Galindo); *Los mujeriegos* (Jaime Salvador); *Cuatro copas* (Tulio Demicheli); *El vampiro* (Fernando Méndez); *Manicomio* (José Díaz Morales); *Manos arriba* (Alejandro Galindo); *Desnúdate Lucrecia* (Tulio Demicheli); *El superflaco* (Miguel M. Delgado); *Pistolas de oro* (Miguel M. Delgado); *Una golfa* (Tulio Demicheli); *Misterios de la magia negra* (Miguel M. Delgado); *El ataúd del vampiro* (Fernando Méndez); *El castillo de los monstruos* (Julián Soler); **1958:** *Sabrás que te quiero* (Tito Davison); *Raffles* (Alejandro Galindo); *La edad de la tentación* (Alejandro Galindo); *Mi niño, mi caballo y yo* (Miguel M. Delgado); *El hombre que me gusta* (Tulio Demicheli); *Misterios de ultratumba* (Fernando Méndez); *Sube y baja* (Miguel M. Delgado); *Los diablos del terror* (Fernando Méndez); *El grito de la muerte* (Fernando Méndez); *Sábado negro* (Miguel M. Delgado); *México nunca duerme* (Alejandro Galindo); **1959:** *Sonata* (Juan Antonio Bardem); *Ellas también son rebeldes* (Alejandro Galindo); *Puños de roca* (Rafael Baledón); *El gato* (Miguel M. Delgado); *Los resbalosos* (Miguel M. Delgado); **1960:** *Cómicos y canciones* (Fernando Cortés); *Caperucita y sus tres amigos* (Roberto Rodríguez); *Pepe* (George Sidney); *El buena suerte* (Rogelio A. González); *Paloma brava* (Rogelio A. González); *Amorcito corazón* (Rogelio A. González); *El aviador fenómeno* (Fernando Cortés); *El bronco Reynosa* (Miguel M. Delgado); *En cada feria un amor* (Rogelio A. González); *El analfabeto* (Miguel M. Delgado); *El jinete negro* (Rogelio A. González); *La marca del muerto* (Fernando Cortés); **1961:** *Casi casados* (Miguel M. Delgado); *Se alquila marido* (Miguel M. Delgado); *Jóvenes y bellas* (Fernando Cortés); *La furia del ring* (Tito Davison); *Estoy casado ja … ja …* (Miguel M. Delgado); **1962:** *Los forajidos* (Fernando Cortés); *El extra* (Miguel M. Delgado); **1982:** *Under the Volcano* (John Huston).

Alberto GOUT

Born in Mexico City, 14 March 1913; where he died, 7 July 1966. Gout's Mexican film career began in the 30s as a make-up artist, a trade he learned at 20th Century-Fox in the USA. Most notable among his films are the cabaret melodramas of the late 40s and early 50s, with scripts by the Spaniard Alvaro Custodio, cinematography by Alex Phillips and featuring the most famous rumba dancers of the period (Ninón Sevilla, María Antonieta Pons and Meche Barba).

Filmography 1938: *Su adorable majadero;* **1939:** *Café Concordia;* **1942:** *Cuando viajan las estrellas;* **1943:** *San Francisco de Asís;* **1944:** *Tuya en cuerpo y alma; Una sombra en mi destino;* **1945:** *Los buitres sobre el tejado;* **1946:** *Humo en los ojos;* **1947:** *La bien pagada; Cortesana;* **1948:** *Revancha; El gallo giro;* **1949:** *Rincón brujo; Aventurera;* **1950:** *En carne viva; Sensualidad;* **1951:** *No niego mi pasado; Quiero vivir; Mujeres sacrificadas;* **1952:** *Aventura en Río;*

1954: *La sospechosa;* **1955:** *Mi desconocida esposa;* **1956:** *Adán y Eva;* **1960:** *El rapto de las sabinas;* **1966:** *Estrategia matrimonio.*

Jaime Humberto HERMOSILLO

Born in Aguascalientes in 1942. Hermosillo studied at the Centro Universitario de Estudios Cinematográficos (CUEC), where he directed two short student films, *Homesick* and *SS Glencairn,* already demonstrating the themes and obsessions that have been central throughout his career. He made his commercial film debut with *La verdadera vocación de Magdalena.* Since then, difficult conditions within the Mexican industry have forced him to alternate commercial films with independent productions and, most recently, work on video. He has lived in Guadalajara since 1984, where he has directed many films. He teaches at the CUEC, the Centro de Capacitación Cinematográfica (CCC) and the Centro de Investigación y Enseñanza Cinematográficas (CIEC).

Filmography 1965: *Homesick* (Short); **1967:** *SS Glencairn* (Short); **1969:** *Los nuestros;* **1971:** *La verdadera vocación de Magdalena;* **1972:** *El señor de Osanto;* **1974:** *El cumpleaños del perro;* **1975:** *La pasión según Berenice;* **1976:** *Matinée;* **1977:** *Naufragio; Las apariencias engañan;* **1978:** *Idilio* (Short); *Amor libre;* **1979:** *María de mi corazón;* **1982:** *Confidencias;* **1983:** *El corazón de la noche;* **1984:** *Doña Herlinda y su hijo;* **1987:** *Clandestino destino;* **1988:** *El verano de la señora Forbes* (in Cuba); **1989:** *Un momento de ira* (video); *El aprendiz de pornógrafo* (video); *Intimidades en un cuarto de baño;* **1990:** *La tarea;* **1991:** *Encuentro inesperado;* **1992:** *La tarea prohibida.*

Pedro INFANTE

Born in Guamúchil (Sinaloa) in 1917; died in a plane accident in Mérida (Yucatán), 15 April 1957. Infante became interested in popular Mexican music while very young and began to sing on radio in Mexico City (1938). He was to become a mythic figure in Mexican popular culture. The trilogy of films by Ismael Rodríguez starring Infante (*Nosotros los pobres, Ustedes los ricos* and *Pepe el Toro*) is a good example of suburban working-class cinema.

Filmography 1942: *La feria de las flores* (José Benavides Jr); *Jesusita en Chihuahua* (René Cardona); *La razón de la culpa* (Juan J. Ortega); **1943:** *Arriba las mujeres* (Carlos Orellana); *Cuando habla el corazón* (Juan José Segura); *El ametralladora* (Aurelio Robles Castillo); *Mexicanos al grito de guerra* (Alvaro Gálvez y Fuentes and Ismael Rodríguez); *Viva mi desgracia* (Roberto Rodríguez); **1944:** *Escándalo de estrellas* (Ismael Rodríguez); **1945:** *Cuando lloran los valientes* (Ismael Rodríguez); **1946:** *Si me han de matar mañana …* (Miguel Zacarías); *Los tres García* (Ismael Rodríguez); *Vuelven los García* (Ismael Rodríguez); **1947:** *La barca de oro* (Joaquín Pardavé); *Soy charro de Rancho Grande* (Joaquín Pardavé); *Nosotros los pobres* (Ismael Rodríguez); *Cartas marcadas* (René Cardona); **1948:** *Los tres huastecos* (Ismael Rodríguez); *Angelitos negros* (Joselito Rodríguez); *Ustedes los ricos* (Ismael Rodríguez); *Dicen que soy mujeriego* (Roberto Rodríguez); **1949:** *El seminarista* (Roberto Rodríguez); *La mujer que yo perdí* (Roberto Rodríguez); *La oveja negra* (Ismael Rodríguez); *No desearas la mujer de tu hijo* (Ismael Rodríguez); **1950:** *Sobre las olas* (Ismael Rodríguez); *También de dolor se canta* (René Cardona); *Islas Marías* (Emilio Fernández); *El gavilán pollero* (Rogelio A. González); *Las mujeres de mi general* (Ismael Rodríguez); **1951:** *Necesito dinero* (Miguel Zacarías); *ATM (A toda máquina)* (Ismael Rodríguez); *¿Qué te ha dado esa mujer?* (Ismael Rodríguez); *Ahí viene Martín Corona* (Miguel Zacarías); *El enamorado* (Miguel Zacarías); **1952:** *Un rincón cerca del cielo* (Rogelio A. González); *Ahora soy rico* (Rogelio A. González); *Había una vez un marido* (Fernando Méndez); *Por ellas aunque mal paguen* (Juan Bustillo Oro); *Los hijos de María Morales* (Fernando de Fuentes); *Dos tipos de cuidado* (Ismael Rodríguez); *Ansiedad* (Miguel Zacarías); *Pepe el Toro* (Ismael Rodríguez); **1953:** *Reportaje* (Emilio Fernández); *Gitana tenías que ser* (Rafael Baledón); **1954:** *Cuidado con el amor* (Miguel Zacarías); *El mil amores* (Rogelio A. González); *Escuela de vagabundos* (Rogelio A. González); *La vida no vale nada* (Rogelio A. González); *Pueblo, canto y esperanza* (Julián Soler and Alfredo B. Crevenna); *Los gavilanes* (Vicente Oroná); **1955:** *Escuela de música* (Miguel Zacarías); *La tercera palabra* (Julián Soler); *El inocente* (Rogelio A. González); *Pablo y Carolina* (Mauricio de la Serna); **1956:** *Tizoc* (Ismael Rodríguez); *Escuela de rateros* (Rogelio A. González).

Alberto ISAAC

Born in Colima in 1925. A prize-winning swimmer, a painter, caricaturist, film journalist and member of the Nuevo Cine group, Isaac also directed the entertainment section of the sports newspaper *Esto.* He won second prize in the first experimental cinema competition with *En este pueblo no hay ladrones,* based on a story by Gabriel García

Márquez, and directed the official documentaries of the nineteenth Olympic Games and the soccer World Cup. In the early 80s, he headed the Dirección de Cinematografía de RTC and was the first director of the Instituto Mexicano de Cinematografía (IMCINE).

Filmography 1964: *En este pueblo no hay ladrones;* **1967:** *Las visitaciones del diablo;* **1968:** *Olimpíada en México* (doc); **1970:** *Fútbol México 70* (doc); **1971:** *Los días del amor;* **1972:** *El rincón de las vírgenes;* **1974:** *Tívoli;* **1976:** *Cuartelazo;* **1977:** *Las noches de Paloma;* **1980:** *El pueblo del sol* (doc); **1981:** *Tiempo de lobos;* **1987:** *Mariana, Mariana;* **1989:** *Maten a Chinto;* **1994:** *En el aire.*

Katy JURADO

Born in Gaudalajara in 1927. She began her acting career aged fifteen, with *Internado para señoritas.* From the 50s on, her career developed primarily in the USA, where she worked with Budd Boetticher, Fred Zinnemann, Mark Robson, Carol Reed, Marlon Brando, John Huston, etc. Jurado consented to make sporadic appearances in Mexican cinema for certain exceptional roles (for example, *Los albañiles, La viuda de Montiel*).

Filmography 1943: *Internado para señoritas* (Gilberto Martínez Solares); *No matarás* (Chano Urueta); *Balajú* (Rolando Aguilar); *La vida inútil de Pito Pérez* (Miguel Contreras Torres); **1944:** *La sombra de Chucho el Roto* (Alejandro Galindo); *El museo del crimen* (René Cardona); *Bartolo toca la flauta* (Miguel Contreras Torres); *Rosa del Caribe* (José Benavides Jr); **1945:** *Soltera y con gemelos* (Jaime Salvador); *Guadalajara pues* (Raúl de Anda); *La viuda celosa* (Fernando Cortés); **1947:** *Nosotros los pobres* (Ismael Rodríguez); *El último chicano* (Raúl de Anda); **1948:** *Hay lugar para … dos* (Alejandro Galindo); **1949:** *El seminarista* (Roberto Rodríguez); *Mujer de medianoche* (Victor Urruchúa); *El sol sale para todos* (Victor Urruchúa); *The Bullfighter and the Lady* (Budd Boetticher); **1950:** *Cabellera blanca* (José Díaz Morales); **1951:** *Cárcel de mujeres* (Miguel M. Delgado); **1952:** *El bruto* (Luis Buñuel); *High Noon* (Fred Zinnemann); **1953:** *Tehuantepec* (Miguel Contreras Torres); *El corazón y la espada* (Carlos Vejar); *San Antone* (Joseph Kane); *Arrowhead* (Charles Marquis Warren); **1954:** *Broken Lance* (Edward Dmytryk); **1955:** *The Racers* (Henry Hathaway); *Trial* (Mark Robson); **1956:** *Trapeze* (Carol Reed); *Man From Del Rio* (Harry Horner); **1957:** *Dragoon Wells Massacre* (Harold Schuster); **1958:** *The Badlanders* (Delmer Daves); **1959:** *One-Eyed Jacks* (Marlon Brando); *Any Second Now* (Gene Levitt); **1960:** *Y Dios la llamó tierra* (Carlos Toussaint); **1961:** *Barabba* (Richard Fleischer); *I briganti italiani* (Mario Camerini); **1962:** *La bandida* (Roberto Rodríguez); **1963:** *Un hombre solo* (Harald Philip); **1966:** *Smoky* (George Sherman); *A Covenant With Death* (Lamont Johnson); **1969:** *Faltas a la moral* (Ismael Rodríguez); *El hacedor de miedo* (Anthony Carras); **1970:** *The Bridge in the Jungle* (Pancho Kohner); **1972:** *Caridad* (Jorge Fons, episode of *Fe, esperanza y caridad;* co-d Alberto Bojórquez and Luis Alcoriza); *Once a Scoundrel* (George Schaefer); *Pat Garrett and Billy the Kid* (Sam Peckinpah); **1975:** *El elegido* (Servando González); **1976:** *Los albañiles* (Jorge Fons); *Pantaleón y las visitadoras* (Mario Vargas Llosa and José María Gutiérrez); **1977:** *El recurso del método* (Miguel Littín); **1978:** *The Children of Sanchez* (Hall Bartlett); **1979:** *La viuda de Montiel* (Miguel Littín); *La seducción* (Arturo Ripstein); *DF* (Rogelio A. González); **1981:** *Barrio de campeones* (Fernando Vallejo); **1982:** *Under the Volcano* (John Huston).

Matilde LANDETA

Born in San Luis Potosí in 1910. Landeta entered Mexican cinema as a continuity girl in the 30s (her brother, Eduardo Landeta, was an actor), where she worked for a dozen years, alongside directors like Julio Bracho and Emilio Fernández. She made her directing debut in 1948, but the industry's bias against women directors forced her to give up her career. Estranged from feature films for forty years (she wrote various scripts and produced shorts for US television), Landeta has recently returned to directing with *Nocturno a Rosario.*

Filmography 1948: *Lola Casanova;* **1949:** *La Negra Angustias;* **1951:** *Trotacalles;* **1990:** *Islas Revillagigedo* (doc); **1991:** *Nocturno a Rosario.*

Paul LEDUC

Born in Mexico City, 11 March 1942. While studying architecture at the Universidad Autónoma de México, Leduc organised film societies, did theatre work and wrote film reviews. After receiving a scholarship to study film-making at IDHEC (Paris), Leduc returned to Mexico in 1967 and created the group Cine 70 with Rafael Castanedo, Alexis Grivas and Bertha Navarro. Together with Rafael Castanedo he made seventeen short films for the Olympic Committee (1967) and three shorts called *Comunicados del Consejo Nacional de Huelga* (1968). His entire career evolved on the margins of the commercial Mexican cinema. His most recent films were produced abroad.

Filmography 1970: *Parto psicoprofiláctico* (short doc); **1971:** *Reed: México insurgente;* **1973:** *Sur: Sureste 2604* (Short); **1975:** *Extensión cultural* (short doc); *El mar* (short doc); *Bach y sus intérpretes* (short doc); **1976:** *Etnocidio: notas sobre el Mezquital* (doc); **1978:** *Estudio para un retrato: Francis Bacon* (short doc; co-d Rafael Castanedo and Angel Goded); *Puebla hoy* (doc); *Monjas coronadas* (short doc); **1980:** *Historias prohibidas de Pulgarcito* (doc); **1981:** *Complot petrolero: La cabeza de la hidra* (TV); **1984:** *Frida, naturaleza viva;* **1985:** *¿Como ves?;* **1989:** *Barroco* (Cuba/Spain); **1990:** *Latino Bar* (Venezuela/Spain); **1993:** *Dollar Mambo.*

Ignacio LÓPEZ TARSO

Born in Mexico City, 15 January 1925. López Tarso enrolled in the dramatic arts academy of the INBA in 1949 and a year later began a career as stage actor, appearing in plays such as *La Celestina, Cyrano de Bergerac, El rey se muere, L'Avare, King Lear* and *El vestidor.* He made his film debut in 1954. He has been a labour leader at ANDI, ANDA (Asociación Nacional de Actores) and the STPC as well as a federal deputy.

Filmography 1954: *La desconocida* (Chano Urueta); **1955:** *Chilam Balam* (Iñigo de Martino); *Feliz año, amor mío* (Tulio Demicheli); **1956:** *Vainilla, bronce y morir* (Rogelio A. González); **1958:** *Nazarín* (Luis Buñuel); *La cucaracha* (Ismael Rodríguez); *La estrella vacía* (Emilio Gómez Muriel); **1959:** *Sonatas* (Juan Antonio Bardem); *El hambre nuestra de cada día* (Rogelio A. González); *Macario* (Roberto Gavaldón); *Ellas también son rebeldes* (Alejandro Galindo); **1960:** *La sombra del caudillo* (Julio Bracho); *Juana Gallo* (Miguel Zacarías); *Y Dios la llamó tierra* (Carlos Toussaint); **1961:** *Rosa Blanca* (Roberto Gavaldón); *Los hermanos del Hierro* (Ismael Rodríguez); **1962:** *La bandida* (Roberto Rodríguez); *Corazón de niño* (Julio Bracho); *Furia en el Edén* (Mauricio de la Serna); *Dias de otoño* (Roberto Gavaldón); **1963:** *El hombre de papel* (Ismael Rodríguez); *Cri Cri, el grillito cantor* (Tito Davison); *Un hombre en la trampa* (Rafael Baledón); **1964:** *El gallo de oro* (Roberto Gavaldón); *Tarahumara* (Luis Alcoriza); **1966:** *Pedro Páramo* (Carlos Velo); **1967:** *Las visitaciones del diablo* (Alberto Isaac); *Un largo viaje hacia la muerte* (José María Fernández Unsaín); **1968:** *La trinchera* (Carlos Enrique Taboada); *La mujer del carnicero* (Ismael Rodríguez and Chano

Urueta); **1969:** *La vida inútil de Pito Pérez* (Roberto Gavaldón); **1970:** *La generala* (Juan Ibáñez); **1971:** *Cayó de la gloria el diablo* (José Estrada); **1972:** *El profeta Mimí* (José Estrada); **1973:** *En busca de un muro* (Julio Bracho); *Rapiña* (Carlos Enrique Taboada); **1975:** *Renuncia por motivos de salud* (Rafael Baledón); **1976:** *La casta divina* (Julián Pastor); *Los albañiles* (Jorge Fons); **1977:** *El soplador de vidrio* (Julián Soler, episode of *Los amantes fríos;* co-d Julio Bracho and Miguel Morayta); **1978:** *The Children of Sanchez* (Hall Bartlett); **1982:** *Antonieta* (Carlos Saura); *Toña Machetes* (Raúl Araiza); **1984:** *El otro* (Arturo Ripstein); *Under the Volcano* (John Huston); **1985:** *Astucia* (Mario Hernández); **1987:** *Muelle rojo* (José Luis Urquieta); **1992:** *Tirano Banderas* (José Luis García Sánchez, Cuban–Spanish co-production).

Mauricio MAGDALENO

Born in Zacatecas in 1906; died in Mexico City in 1986. Magdaleno participated in the movement backing the candidacy of José Vasconcelos in 1929. He organised the avant-garde group Teatro Ahora with Bustillo Oro, and became a novelist and an exceptional screenwriter (the cornerstone of Emilio Fernández's team, alongside Gabriel Figueroa, Pedro Armendáriz and Dolores del Río). He directed four films (1944–6).

Filmography 1933: *El compadre Mendoza* (Fernando de Fuentes); **1943:** *Flor silvestre* (Emilio Fernández); *María Candelaria* (Emilio Fernández); *Tentación* (Fernando Soler); *Miguel Strogoff* (Miguel M. Delgado); **1944:** *El intruso* (Mauricio Magdaleno); *Las abandonadas* (Emilio Fernández); *Entre hermanos* (Ramón Peón); *Su gran ilusión* (Mauricio Magdaleno); *Bugambilia* (Emilio Fernández); **1945:** *Vertigo* (Antonio Momplet); *Bodas trágicas* (Gilberto Martínez Solares); *Pepita Jiménez* (Emilio Fernández); **1946:** *La fuerza de la sangre* (Mauricio Magdaleno); *La herencia de la Llorona* (Mauricio Magdaleno); *La mujer de todos* (Julio Bracho); *Gran casino* (Luis Buñuel); **1947:** *La sin ventura* (Tito Davison); *Río Escondido* (Emilio Fernández); **1948:** *Salón México* (Emilio Fernández); *Maclovia* (Emilio Fernández); *Ojos de juventud* (Emilio Gómez Muriel); *Pueblerina* (Emilio Fernández); **1949:** *Eterna agonía* (Julián Soler); *Coqueta* (Fernando A. Rivero); *La malquerida* (Emilio Fernández); *Duelo en las montañas* (Emilio Fernández); *Vino el remolino y nos alevantó* (Juan Bustillo Oro); *Lluvia roja* (René Cardona); *La casa chica* (Roberto Gavaldón); **1950:**

Un día de vida (Emilio Fernández); *Azahares para tu boda* (Julián Soler); *Víctimas del pecado* (Emilio Fernández); *Pata de palo* (Emilio Gómez Muriel); *Por la puerta falsa* (Fernando de Fuentes); *Islas Marías* (Emilio Fernández); *Historia de un corazón* (Julio Bracho); *Siempre tuya* (Emilio Fernández); *Entre tu amor y el cielo* (Emilio Gómez Muriel); **1951:** *La estatua de carne* (Chano Urueta); *Cárcel de mujeres* (Miguel M. Delgado); *La bien amada* (Emilio Fernández); *El mar y tú* (Emilio Fernández); *Cuando los hijos pecan* (Joselito Rodríguez); **1952:** *Acuérdate de vivir* (Roberto Gavaldón); *Las tres perfectas casadas* (Roberto Gavaldón); *La segunda mujer* (José Díaz Morales); *Ley fuga* (Emilio Gómez Muriel); **1953:** *Reportaje* (Emilio Fernández); *El rapto* (Emilio Fernández); *La rosa blanca* (Emilio Fernández); **1956:** *Una cita de amor* (Emilio Fernández); **1961:** *Pueblito* (Emilio Fernández).

Eduardo MALDONADO

Born in Mexico City, 14 November 1941. Studied film and television in England and Ireland, and was in charge of communication and cinema in the agricultural programme of the Centro Nacional de Productividad, where he produced his first films. In 1973 he created the Grupo Cine Testimonio with cinematographer Francisco Bojórquez and sound engineer Raúl Zaragoza. They specialised in documentaries analysing Mexico's social and political problems. Maldonado was director of the Centro de Capacitación Cinematográfica (CCC) from 1983 to 1989. All his films are documentaries.

Filmography 1966–9: *Gira educativa* (Short); *El mirasol* (Short); *Siembra y fertilización del medio rural* (Short); *Programa de altos rendimientos* (Short); **1970:** *Testimonio de un grupo*; **1971:** *Equilibrio y movimiento* (Short); *Sociedad Cooperativa Quechehueca* (Short); *Santo Domingo de los Reyes*; **1972:** *Reflexiones*; **1973:** *Atencingo, cacicazgo y corrupción*; **1975:** *Una y otra vez*; **1977:** *Jornaleros*; **1982:** *Laguna de dos tiempos*; **1987:** *Xochimilco*; **1990:** *Resplandores del alba*.

Gilberto MARTÍNEZ SOLARES

Born in Mexico City, 19 January 1906. In the late 20s, he attempted to set up a photographic studio with his friend and co-worker Gabriel Figueroa. Later he moved to Hollywood, where he continued his photographic career and worked on several films. After a stay in Paris, he returned to Mexico in the early days of sound cinema. In 1935 he worked as first camera operator with his brother Raúl on Miguel Zacarías's *Rosario*. After taking up direction in 1938, he shot and scripted a great many films. In the 40s he directed Tin Tan in some of his best comedies (with Juan García's scripts).

Filmography 1938: *El señor alcalde*; **1939:** *Hombres del aire*; *La locura de don Juan*; **1941:** *La casa del rencor*; **1942:** *Las cinco noches de Adán*; *Yo bailé con don Porfirio*; **1943:** *Resurrección*; *Internado para señoritas*; *El globo de Cantolla*; *Así son ellas*; **1944:** *La trepadora*; *Un beso en la noche*; *El jagüey de las ruinas*; **1945:** *La señora de enfrente*; **1946:** *Bodas trágicas*; *Su última aventura*; *Cinco rostros de mujer*; **1947:** *El casado casa quiere*; *Extraña cita*; *La novia del mar*; **1948:** *Conozco a los dos*; *Tuya para siempre*; *Calabacitas tiernas*; *La familia Pérez*; **1949:** *Yo soy charro de levita*; *No me defiendas compadre*; *El rey del barrio*; *Novia a la medida*; **1950:** *La marca del Zorrillo*; *Mi querido capitán*; *Simbad el mareado*; *¡Ay amor … cómo me has puesto!*; **1951:** *El revoltoso*; *El ceniciento*; *Chucho el Remendado*; *Las locuras de Tin Tan*; **1952:** *Rumba caliente*; *Ahí vienen los gorrones*; *El bello durmiente*; *Me traes de un ala*; **1953:** *Dios los cría …*; *El mariachi desconocido*; *Mulata*; **1954:** *Los líos de Barba Azul*; *Pobre huerfanita*; *Que lindo cha cha cha*; *Contigo a la distancia*; *Hijas casaderas*; *El sultán descalzo*; *El vizconde de Montecristo*; **1955:** *El chismoso de la ventana*; *Club de señoritas*; *Pura vida*; *El vividor*; *Vivir a todo dar*; *Lo que le pasó a Sansón*; **1956:** *La ciudad de los niños*; *El organillero*; *Los tres mosqueteros … y medio*; *Escuela para suegras*; **1957:** *La feria de San Marcos*; *El ciclón*; *Besos de arena*; *Paso a la juventud*; *La sombra del otro*; **1958:** *Escuela de verano*; *Mientras el cuerpo aguante*; *Kermesse*; **1959:** *Una estrella y dos estrellados*; *El tesoro de Chucho el Roto*; *Vuelta al paraíso*; *La casa del terror*; *Vivo o muerto*; **1960:** *El duende y yo*; *El violetero*; *Las Leandras*; *¡Suicídate mi amor!*; *Ojos tapatíos*; *Las hijas del Amapolo*; **1961:** *Los valientes no mueren*; *Viva Chihuahua*; **1962:** *Una joven de 16 años*; **1963:** *Torero por un día*; *Napoleoncito*; *La gitana y el charro*; *Alazán y enamorado*; *De color moreno*; **1964:** *Los tales por cuales*; *Mi héroe*; *Alma llanera*; *Me ha gustado un hombre*; *Marcelo y María*; *Tintansón Crusoe*; **1965:** *El camino de los espantos*; *Los Perversos (a go go)*; *Cada quien su lucha*; *Juventud sin ley*; *Los tres salvajes*; *Dos meseros majaderos*; *La criada malcriada*; **1966:** *El ángel y yo*; *Gregorio y su ángel*; **1968:** *Blue Demon contra las invasoras*; *Misión cumplida*; *El misterio de los hongos alucinantes*; *Las sicodélicas*; **1969:** *El médico módico*; *Santo y Blue Demon en el mundo de los muertos*; *Santo y Blue Demon contra los monstruos*; **1970:** *El bueno para nada*; *El metiche*; *El nano*; *El rey* de Acapulco; Chanoc en las garras de las fieras; **1971:** Cuna de valientes; Chanoc contra el tigre y el vampiro; Las tarántulas; **1972:** Las hijas de don Laureano; **1973:** El carita; El investigador Capulina; Satánico pandemonium; **1974:** Chanoc en el foso de las serpientes; El guía de las turistas; **1975:** Capulina chisme caliente; El compadre más padre; **1976:** En está primavera; **1977:** La banda del polvo maldito; Caballo prieto afamado; El circo de Capulina; Un cura de locura; De Cocula es el mariachi; Misterio en Las Bermudas; **1978:** Angel del silencio; Pasión por el peligro; El norteño enamorado; **1979:** Hijos de tigre; OK Mr Pancho; El contrabando del Paso; **1980:** El que no corre … vuela; **1981:** El vecindario; El vecindario II; El peleador del barrio; **1982:** El ratero de la vecindad; **1983:** Rosita Alvírez, destino sangriento; El día de los albañiles; **1984:** El ratero de la vecindad II; **1985:** El día de los albañiles 2; **1986:** Tres mexicanos ardientes; **1987:** El día de los albañiles 3; Los gatos de las azoteas; **1988:** Diario íntimo de una cabaretera; **1990:** Ondina.

Fernando MÉNDEZ

Born in Michoacán, 22 July 1908; died in Mexico City, 17 October 1966. The nephew of the pioneer Michoacán cineaste Francisco García Urbizu, Méndez began his Mexican career in the 30s after a stay in Hollywood. He began his directorial career with the religious melodrama *La Reina de México*. From then on he divided his time between directing and writing scripts for other directors.

Filmography 1940: *La Reina de México;* **1941:** *Allá en el Bajío;* **1942:** *La leyenda del bandido;* **1943:** *Las calaveras del terror;* **1944:** *El criollo;* **1948:** *Tres hombres malos;* **1949:** *Matrimonio y mortaja;* **1950:** *Barrio bajo; Los apuros de mi ahijada; El Suavecito; Fierecilla;* **1951:** *La hija del ministro; La mujer desnuda;* **1952:** *Había una vez un marido; Sí, mi vida; El lunar de la familia; Genio y figura;* **1953:** *As negro;* **1954:** *Los aventureros; Vaya tipos; Tres bribones; Los tres Villalobos; La venganza de los Villalobos;* **1955:** *Fugitivos; Hay ángeles con espuelas;* **1956:** *Rapto al sol; Ladrón de cadáveres;* **1957:** *La locura del rock and roll; La esquina de mi barrio; El vampiro; El ataúd del vampiro;* **1958:** *Señoritas; El cofre del pirata; Misterios de ultratumba; Los diablos del terror; El grito de la muerte;* **1959:** *Los hermanos Diablo* (co-d Chano Urueta); *El renegado blanco; Venganza apache;* **1960:** *Mujeres engañadas.*

Jorge NEGRETE

Born in Guanajuato in 1911; died in the USA in 1953. After studying at the Colegio Militar (1927–9), he became a singer on radio (1930) and acted in variety shows. His first film appearance was in 1927. He successfully played typical *machista* and melomaniac *charro* characters. Founder and the first general secretary of the Asociación Nacional de Actores (ANDA).

Filmography 1937: *La madrina del diablo* (Ramón Peón); **1938:** *La Valentina* (Martín de Lucenay); *Caminos de ayer* (Quirico Michelena); *Perjura* (Raphael J. Sevilla); *Aquí llegó el valiente* (Fernando A. Rivero); *Juan sin miedo* (Juan José Segura); *Juntos, pero no revueltos* (Fernando A. Rivero); *El cementerio de las águilas* (Luis Lezama); **1941:** *¡Ay Jalisco, no te rajes!* (Joselito Rodríguez); *Seda, sangre y sol* (Fernando A. Rivero); *Fiesta* (Le Roy Priz); **1942:** *Cuando viajan las estrellas* (Alberto Gout); *Historia de un gran amor* (Julio Bracho); *Así se quiere en Jalisco* (Fernando de Fuentes); *El peñón de las ánimas* (Miguel Zacarías); *Tierra de pasiones* (José Benavides Jr); **1943:** *El jorobado* (Jaime Salvador); *Una carta de amor* (Miguel Zacarías); *El rebelde* (Jaime Salvador); **1944:** *Cuando quiere un mexicano* (Juan Bustillo Oro); *Me he de comer esa tuna* (Miguel Zacarías); **1945:** *Canaima* (Juan Bustillo Oro); *Hasta que perdió Jalisco* (Fernando de Fuentes); *No basta ser charro* (Juan Bustillo Oro); *Camino de Sacramento* (Chano Urueta); **1946:** *En tiempos de la Inquisición* (Juan Bustillo Oro); *El ahijado de la muerte* (Norman Foster); *Gran casino* (Luis Buñuel); **1948:** *Allá en el Rancho Grande* (Fernando de Fuentes); *Si Adelita se fuera con otro* (Chano Urueta); *Jalisco canta en Sevilla* (Fernando de Fuentes); **1949:** *Lluvia roja* (René Cardona); *La posesión* (Julio Bracho); **1950:** *Siempre tuya* (Emilio Fernández); *Teatro Apolo* (Rafael Gil); **1951:** *Un gallo en corral ajeno* (Julián Soler); *Los tres alegres compadres* (Julián Soler); *Hay un niño en su futuro* (Fernando Cortés); **1952:** *Dos tipos de cuidado* (Ismael Rodríguez); *Tal para cual* (Rogelio A. González); **1953:** *Reportaje* (Emilio Fernández); *El rapto* (Emilio Fernández).

María NOVARO

Born in Mexico City, 11 September 1951. She studied sociology at the UNAM, and later filmmaking at the Centro Universitario de Estudios Cinematográficos (CUEC).

Filmography 1982: *Conmigo la pasas muy bien* (Short); **1983:** *Querida Carmen* (Short); *7 AM* (Short); **1984:** *Una isla rodeada de agua* (Short); **1985:** *La pervertida* (Short); **1988:** *Azul celeste*

(episode of *Historias de ciudad;* co-d Ramón
Cervantes, Rafael Montero and Gerardo Lara); **1989:**
Lola; **1990:** *Danzón;* **1992:** *Otoñal* (Short); **1994:** *El
jardín del Edén.*

Juan OROL GARCÍA

Born in El Ferrol (Spain), 4 August 1897; died in
Mexico City in 1988. He led an adventurous life as a
young man, travelling to numerous Latin American
countries and working at an assortment of jobs
(boxer, bullfighter, baseball pitcher, journalist, etc.).
After a trip to Hollywood, he moved to Mexico and
produced and acted in *Sagrario* (Ramón Peón, 1933).
The following year he directed his first film and
began a long and unique career.

Filmography 1934: *Mujeres sin alma* (co-d Ramón
Peón); **1935:** *Madre querida;* **1936:** *El calvario de
una esposa; Honrarás a tus padres;* **1937:** *El derecho y
el deber; Eterna mártir;* **1938:** *Siboney* (in Cuba);
1943: *Cruel destino;* **1944:** *Los misterios del hampa;*
1945: *Pasiones tormentosas; Embrujo antillano*
(Cuban co-p; co-d Geza P. Polaty) **1946:** *Una mujer
de Oriente; El amor de mi bohío* (Cuban co-p); **1947:**
*Tania, la bella salvaje; El reino de los gángsters;
Gángsters contra charros;* **1948:** *El charro del Arrabal;*
1949: *Amor salvaje;* **1950:** *Cabaret Shanghai; ¡Qué
idiotas son los hombres!; El infierno de los pobres;
Perdición de mujeres; Hombres sin alma; Madre
querida;* **1952:** *La diosa de Tahití; Sandra, la mujer de
fuego* (Cuban co-p); **1953:** *El sindicato del crimen*
(Cuban co-p); **1954:** *Bajo la influencia del miedo; La
mesera del café del puerto* (Cuban co-p); **1955:**
Secretaria peligrosa (Spanish co-p); *El farol en la
ventana* (Cuban co-p); **1956:** *Plazos traicioneros; Te
odio y te quiero;* **1957:** *Zonga, el ángel diabólico;*
1958: *Thaimi, la hija del pescador* (Cuban co-p);
1960: *La tórtola del Ajusco;* **1962:** *Bajo el manto de la
noche; Sangre en la barranca;* **1963:** *El crimen de la
hacienda* (Puerto Rican co-p); **1964:** *La maldición de
mi raza* (Puerto Rican co-p); **1965:** *La virgen de la
calle* (Puerto Rican co-p); **1966:** *Contrabandistas del
Caribe* (Puerto Rican co-p); *Antesala de la silla
eléctrica* (Puerto Rican co-p); *Pasiones infernales*
(Puerto Rican co-p); **1968:** *Organización criminal*
(Puerto Rican co-p); *Historia de un gángster* (Puerto
Rican co-p); **1970:** *El fantástico mundo de los hippies*
(US co-p); **1978:** *El tren de la muerte.*

Joaquín PARDAVÉ

Born in Guanajuato, 30 September 1900; died in
Mexico City, 20 July 1955. Pardavé's parents were
actors and he developed an interest in the variety

theatre at an early age. He acted in the cinema,
directed and scripted films. A well-known composer
of popular tunes such as 'Varita de nardo', 'La
Panchita', 'Negra consentida', and many others.

Filmography (* directed only) **1919:** *Viaje redondo*
(José Manuel Ramos); **1929:** *El águila y el nopal*
(Miguel Contreras Torres); **1932:** *Aguilas frente al sol*
(Antonio Moreno); **1937:** *Bajo el cielo de México*
(Fernando de Fuentes); *Jalisco nunca pierde* (Chano
Urueta); *Canción del alma* (Chano Urueta); *Mi
candidato* (Chano Urueta); *La Zandunga* (Fernando
de Fuentes); **1938:** *Tierra brava* (René Cardona); *Los
millones de Chaflán* (Rolando Aguilar); *La tía de las
muchachas* (Juan Bustillo Oro); *Luna criolla* (Raphael
J. Sevilla); *El señor alcalde* (Gilberto Martínez
Solares); *Cada loco con su tema* (Juan Bustillo Oro);
1939: *Hombres del aire* (Gilberto Martínez Solares);
Caballo a caballo (Juan Bustillo Oro); *Viviré otra vez*
(Vicente Oroná); *En un burro tres baturros* (José
Benavides Jr); *En tiempos de don Porfirio* (Juan
Bustillo Oro); *¡Qué viene mi marido!* (Chano
Urueta); **1940:** *Ahí está el detalle* (Juan Bustillo Oro);
El jefe máximo (Fernando de Fuentes); *Al son de la
marimba* (Juan Bustillo Oro); **1941:** *Cuando los hijos
se van* (Juan Bustillo Oro); *¡Ay, qué tiempos, señor don
Simón!* (Julio Bracho); *Mil estudiantes y una
muchacha* (Juan Bustillo Oro); *¿Quién te quiere a ti?*
(Rolando Aguilar); **1942:** *El que tenga un amor*
(Carlos Orellana); *Caballería del imperio* (Miguel
Contreras Torres); *Tu mujer es la mía* (Rafael E.
Portas); *El ángel negro* (Juan Bustillo Oro); *El baisano
Jalil* (Joaquín Pardavé); *Yo bailé con don Porfirio*
(Gilberto Martínez Solares); *Cinco fueron escogidos*
(Herbert Kline); **1943:** *Adiós juventud* (Joaquín
Pardavé); *El sombrero de tres picos* (Juan Bustillo
Oro); *México de mis recuerdos* (Juan Bustillo Oro);
1944: *Como todas las madres* (Fernando Soler); *Los
hijos de don Venancio* (Joaquín Pardavé); *El gran
Makakikus* (Humberto Gómez Landero); **1945:** *Una
virgen moderna*; *La reina de la opereta* (José
Benavides Jr); *Los nietos de don Venancio* (Joaquín
Pardavé); *El barchante Neguib* (Joaquín Pardavé);
1946: *Don Simón de Lira* (Julio Bracho); *El
ropavejero* (Emilio Gómez Muriel); *La niña de mis
ojos* (Raphael J. Sevilla); *Lágrimas de sangre*; **1947:**
La barca de oro; *Soy charro de Rancho Grande*;
1948: *Los viejos somos así* (Joaquín Pardavé); *Ojos de
juventud* (Emilio Gómez Muriel); *La familia Pérez*
(Gilberto Martínez Solares); *Arriba el norte* (Emilio
Gómez Muriel); **1949:** *Dos pesos dejada* (Joaquín
Pardavé); *Una gallega en México* (Julián Soler); *Sangre
torera*; **1950:** *Amor vendido*; *Arrabalera*;

Pasionaria*; Azahares para tu boda (Julián Soler); *Primero soy mexicano* (Joaquín Pardavé); *Una gallega baila mambo* (Emilio Gómez Muriel); *El gendarme de la esquina* (Joaquín Pardavé); **1951:** *Del can can al mambo* (Chano Urueta); *Mi campeón* (Chano Urueta); *Pompeyo el conquistador* (René Cardona); **1952:** *Esos de Penjamo* (Juan Bustillo Oro); *Doña Mariquita de mi corazón* (Joaquín Pardavé); *El casto Susano* (Joaquín Pardavé); **1953:** *Mi adorada Clementina* (Rafael Baledón); *Reportaje* (Emilio Fernández); **1954:** *La gitana blanca* (Miguel M. Delgado); *El hombre inquieto* (Rafael Baledón); *El mil amores* (Rogelio A. González); *Pueblo, canto y esperanza* (Julián Soler and Alfredo B. Crevenna); *A los cuatro vientos* (Adolfo Fernández Bustamante); *Magdalena*; Dios nos manda vivir*; Secreto profesional*;* **1955:** *Medias de seda* (Miguel Morayta); *Club de señoritas* (Gilberto Martínez Solares); *La virtud desnuda* (José Díaz Morales).

Alex PHILLIPS

Born in Canada in 1900; died in Mexico City in 1977. His career as a cinematographer began in Hollywood in the 20s, working with the best US camera operators. He came to Mexico to shoot the first sound film, *Santa,* and remained in the country until his death. In his forty-year career he collaborated with the most important directors of Mexican cinema and photographed more than 200 films. He also directed *Hoy comienza la vida* (1935).

Filmography 1931: *Santa* (Antonio Moreno); **1932:** *Aguilas frente al sol* (Antonio Moreno); *Revolución* (Miguel Contreras Torres); *Una vida por otra* (John H. Auer and Fernando de Fuentes); *Mano a mano* (Arcady Boytler); *Un espectador impertinente* (Arcady Boytler and Raphael J. Sevilla); **1933:** *Su última canción* (John H. Auer); *Juárez y Maximiliano* (Miguel Contreras Torres); *La noche del pecado* (Miguel Contreras Torres); *Sagrario* (Ramón Peón); *Profanación* (Chano Urueta); *El Tigre de Yautepec* (Fernando de Fuentes); *Enemigos* (Chano Urueta); *Aguilas de América* (Manuel R. Ojeda); *La mujer del puerto* (Arcady Boytler); *La sangre manda* (José Bohr and Raphael J Sevilla); *El compadre Mendoza* (Fernando de Fuentes); **1934:** *Chucho el Roto* (Gabriel Soria); *¿Quién mato a Eva?* (José Bohr); *Corazón bandolero* (Raphael J. Sevilla); *Mujeres sin alma* (Ramón Peón); *Cruz Diablo* (Fernando de Fuentes); *Tribu* (Miguel Contreras Torres); *Tu hijo* (José Bohr); **1935:** *Martín Garatuza* (Gabriel Soria); *El tesoro de Pancho Villa* (Arcady Boytler); *Sueños de amor* (José Bohr); *La familia Dressel* (Fernando de

Fuentes); *Sor Juana Inés de la Cruz* (Ramón Peón); *Hoy comienza la vida* (Alex Phillips and Juan José Segura); *Silencio sublime* (Ramón Peón); *Más allá de la muerte* (Ramón Peón); *Celos* (Arcady Boytler); **1936:** *¡Ora, Ponciano!* (Gabriel Soria); *Mater nostra* (Gabriel Soria); *El baúl macabro* (Miguel Zacarías); *Marihuana (El monstruo verde)* (José Bohr); *Judas* (Manuel R. Ojeda); *Irma la mala* (Raphael J. Sevilla); *Suprema ley* (Rafael E. Portas); *Cielito lindo* (Roberto O'Quigley); *Mujeres de hoy* (Ramón Peón); *No te engañes corazón* (Miguel Contreras Torres); **1937;** *Ave sin rumbo* (Roberto O'Quigley); *La madrina del diablo* (Ramón Peón); *La mujer de nadie* (Adela Sequeyro); *La paloma* (Miguel Contreras Torres); *Noches de gloria* (Rolando Aguilar); *Ojos tapatíos* (Boris Maicon); **1938:** *México lindo* (Ramón Pereda); *A lo macho* (Martín de Lucenay); *La golondrina* (Miguel Contreras Torres); *Un viejo amor* (Luis Lezama); *María* (Chano Urueta); *El capitán aventurero* (Arcady Boytler); *Los enredos de papá* (Miguel Zacarías); **1939:** *Perfidia* (William Rowland); *Mujeres y toros* (Juan José Segura); *Corazón de niño* (Alejandro Galindo); *Café Concordia* (Alberto Gout); *Viviré otra vez* (Roberto Rodríguez); *Los olvidados de Dios* (Ramón Pereda); *El gavilán* (Ramón Pereda); *Madre a la fuerza* (Roberto O'Quigley); **1940:** *Hombre o demonio* (Miguel Contreras Torres); *Viejo nido* (Vicente Oroná); *Papá se desenreda* (Miguel Zacarías); *Hasta que llovió en Sayula* (Miguel Contreras Torres); *El secreto del sacerdote* (Joselito Rodríguez); *Papá se enreda otra vez* (Miguel Zacarías); *Las tres viudas de papá* (Miguel Zacarías); **1941:** *¡Ay, Jalisco, no te rajes!* (Joselito Rodríguez); *Mi amigo Benito* (Norman Foster); **1942:** *Caballería del Imperio* (Miguel Contreras Torres); *Secreto eterno* (Carlos Orellana); *Yolanda* (Dudley Murphy); *El padre Morelos* (Miguel Contreras Torres); **1943:** *El jorobado* (Jaime Salvador); *Doña Bárbara* (Fernando de Fuentes); *El rayo del sur* (Miguel Contreras Torres); *San Francisco de Asís* (Alberto Gout); *Miguel Strogoff* (Miguel M. Delgado); *Naná* (Celestino Gorostiza); *Fantasía ranchera* (Juan José Segura); **1944:** *Gran hotel* (Miguel M. Delgado); *Amok* (Antonio Momplet); *Tuya en cuerpo y alma* (Alberto Gout); *Crepúsculo* (Julio Bracho); *Una sombra en mi destino* (Alberto Gout); **1945:** *El monje blanco* (Julio Bracho); *Pepita Jiménez* (Emilio Fernández); *La viuda celosa* (Fernando Cortes); *Vértigo* (Antonio Momplet); *María Magdalena* (Miguel Contreras Torres); *Reina de reinas* (Miguel Contreras Torres); **1946:** *La mujer de todos* (Julio Bracho); *La otra* (Roberto Gavaldón); *Los que volvieron* (Alejandro Galindo); *Bel Ami*

(Antonio Momplet); *A la sombra del puente* (Roberto Gavaldón); **1947:** *La diosa arrodillada* (Roberto Gavaldón); *La sin ventura* (Tito Davison); *La bien pagada* (Alberto Gout); *Cortesana* (Alberto Gout); *Que Dios me perdone* (Tito Davison); **1948:** *Los viejos somos así* (Joaquín Pardavé); *Revancha* (Alberto Gout); *El gallo giro* (Alberto Gout); *Flor de caña* (Carlos Orellana); *Bamba* (Miguel Contreras Torres); *Secreto entre mujeres* (Victor Urruchúa); *El dolor de los hijos* (Miguel Zacarías); **1949:** *Coqueta* (Fernando A. Rivero); *Novia a la medida* (Gilberto Martínez Solares); *Pancho Villa vuelve* (Miguel Contreras Torres); *La casa chica* (Roberto Gavaldón); *Doña Diabla* (Tito Davison); *Perdida* (Fernando A. Rivero); *Aventurera* (Alberto Gout); **1950:** *Pobre corazón* (José Díaz Morales); *El pecado de ser pobre* (Fernando A. Rivero); *Mi querido capitán* (Gilberto Martínez Solares); *Deseada* (Roberto Gavaldón); *Curvas peligrosas* (Tito Davison); *Sensualidad* (Alberto Gout); *En la palma de tu mano* (Roberto Gavaldón); **1951:** *Vuelva el sábado* (René Cardona); *Paraíso robado* (Julio Bracho); *Dancing* (Miguel Morayta); *Subida al cielo* (Luis Buñuel); *Quiero vivir* (Alberto Gout); *Mujeres sacrificadas* (Alberto Gout); *La ausente* (Julio Bracho); **1952:** *La mujer que tú quieres* (Emilio Gómez Muriel); *Rostros olvidados* (Julio Bracho); *Aventura en Río* (Alberto Gout); *Robinson Crusoe* (Luis Buñuel); *Mujeres que trabajan* (Julio Bracho); **1953:** *La red* (Emilio Fernández); *Reportaje* (Emilio Fernández); *Les Orgueilleux/Los orgullosos* (Yves Allegret); *Los Fernández de Peralvillo* (Alejandro Galindo); *The Littlest Outlaw* (Roberto Gavaldón); **1954:** *María la voz* (Julio Bracho); *Sombra verde* (Roberto Gavaldón); *Qué bravas son las costeñas* (Roberto Rodríguez); *Nosotros dos* (Emilio Fernández); **1955:** *Mi canción eres tú* (Roberto Rodríguez); *Las medias de seda* (Miguel Morayta); *Música en la noche* (Tito Davison); *Chilam Balam* (Iñigo de Martino); *Mi desconocida esposa* (Alberto Gout); *Plaza prohibida* (Julián Soler); **1956:** *Adán y Eva* (Alberto Gout); *Tizoc* (Ismael Rodríguez); *Música de siempre* (Tito Davison); *Escuela de rateros* (Rogelio A. González); *El diario de mi madre* (Roberto Rodríguez); **1957:** *Los salvajes* (Rafael Baledón); *Los legionarios* (Agustín P. Delgado); *La odalisca número 13* (Fernando Cortés); *The Western Story* (George Sherman); **1958:** *Sube y baja* (Miguel M. Delgado); *Los hijos ajenos* (Roberto Rodríguez); *Sierra Baron* (James B. Clark); *Villa!* (James B. Clark); *The Last of the Fast Guns* (George Sherman); *Ten Days to Tulara* (George Sherman); **1959:** *Caperucita roja* (Roberto Rodríguez); *Mi madre es culpable* (Julián Soler); *Aventuras de Joselito y

Pulgarcito (René Cardona and Antonio del Amo); **1960:** *Juan sin miedo* (Gilberto Gazcón); *El rapto de las sabinas* (Alberto Gout); *For the Love of Mike* (George Sherman); **1961:** *Los espadachines de la reina* (Roberto Rodríguez); *Pueblito* (Emilio Fernández); *Geronimo* (Arnold Laven); *The Last Sunset* (Robert Aldrich); **1962:** *La fierecilla del puerto* (Alfredo B. Crevenna); *La rabia por dentro* (Myron Gold); *Of Love and Desire* (Richard Rush); **1963:** *Alazán y enamorado* (Gilberto Martínez Solares); *Una cara para escapar* (Robert Gordon); **1964:** *Guadalajara en verano* (Julio Bracho); *Viento negro* (Servando González); *Cuando acaba la noche* (Julián Soler); **1965:** *La alegría de vivir* (Julián Soler); *Tiempo de morir* (Arturo Ripstein); *Juan Colorado* (Miguel Zacarías); *Los alegres Aguilares* (Miguel Zacarías); *Tres mil kilómetros de amor* (Agustín P. Delgado); **1966:** *La soldadera* (José Bolaños); *Estrategia matrimonio* (Alberto Gout); *Damiana y los hombres* (Julio Bracho); *Despedida de casada* (Juan de Orduña); **1967:** *No hay cruces en el mar* (Julián Soler); *La guerrillera de Villa* (Miguel Morayta); *El zángano* (Agustín P. Delgado); *Andante* (Julio Bracho); *Corazón salvaje* (Tito Davison); **1968:** *Los recuerdos del porvenir* (Arturo Ripstein); **1969:** *Los años vacíos* (Sergio Vejar); *Remolino de pasiones* (Alejandro Galindo); *El hacedor de miedo* (Anthony Carras); **1970:** *Arde, baby, arde* (José Bolaños); *Bang bang y al hoyo* (René Cardona Jr); *Santo contra la mafia del vicio* (Federico Curiel); *La noche de los mil gatos* (René Cardona Jr); **1972:** *El castillo de la pureza* (Arturo Ripstein).

Silvia PINAL

Born in Guaymas (Sonora) in 1931. Pinal appeared on radio while still a student. Afterwards, she moved on to experimental theatre: Alejandro Casona's *Nuestra Natacha* staged by Rafael Banquells. Almost at the same time, Contreras Torres hired her for her first film, *Bamba*. She subsequently alternated between theatre, television and cinema work (appearing in several of Luis Buñuel's most important films) in Mexico and Spain.

Filmography 1948: *Bamba* (Miguel Contreras Torres); *El pecado de Laura* (Julián Soler); **1949:** *Escuela para casadas* (Miguel Zacarías); *La mujer que yo perdí* (Roberto Rodríguez); *Puerta … joven* (Miguel M. Delgado); *Mujer de medianoche* (Victor Urruchúa); *El rey del barrio* (Gilberto Martínez Solares); **1950:** *La marca del Zorrillo* (Gilberto Martínez Solares); *El amor no es ciego* (Alfonso Patiño Gómez); *Recién casados, no molestar* (Fernando

Cortés); *Una gallega baila el mambo* (Emilio Gómez Muriel); *Azahares para tu boda* (Julián Soler); **1951:** *La estatua de carne* (Chano Urueta); **1952:** *Un rincón cerca del cielo* (Rogelio A. González); *Por ellas, aunque mal paguen* (Juan Bustillo Oro); *Me traes de un ala* (Gilberto Martínez Solares); *Doña Mariquita de mi corazón* (Joaquín Pardavé); *El casto Susano* (Joaquín Pardavé); *Cuando los hijos pecan* (Joselito Rodríguez); *Sí, mi vida* (Fernando Méndez); **1953:** *Reventa de esclavas* (José Díaz Morales); *Yo soy muy macho* (José Díaz Morales); *Las tres viudas alegres* (Fernando Cortés); *Las cariñosas* (Fernando Cortés); *Si volvieras a mí* (Alfredo B. Crevenna); **1954:** *Hijas casaderas* (Juan Bustillo Oro); *Un extraño en la escalera* (Tulio Demicheli); *Pecado mortal* (Miguel M. Delgado); *La vida tiene tres días* (Emilio Gómez Muriel); *Historia de un abrigo de mink* (Emilio Gómez Muriel); *El vendedor de muñecas* (Chano Urueta); *Amor en cuatro tiempos* (Luis Spota); *La sospechosa* (Alberto Gout); **1955:** *El inocente* (Rogelio A. González); *Locura pasional* (Tulio Demicheli); *Mi desconocida esposa* (Alberto Gout); *Cabo de Hornos* (Tito Davison); **1956:** *La adúltera* (Tulio Demicheli); *La dulce enemiga* (Tito Davison); *Una cita de amor* (Emilio Fernández); *Dios no lo quiera* (Tulio Demicheli); *El teatro del crimen* (Fernando Cortés); *Viva el amor* (Mauricio de la Serna); **1957:** *Préstame tu cuerpo* (Tulio Demicheli); *Desnúdate Lucrecia* (Tulio Demicheli); *Una golfa* (Tulio Demicheli); **1958:** *El hombre que me gusta* (Tulio Demicheli); *Las locuras de Bárbara* (Tulio Demicheli); **1959:** *Charleston* (Tulio Demicheli); *Uomini y nobiluomini* (Giorgio Bianchi); **1960:** *Adiós, Mimí Pompón* (Luis Marquina); *Maribel y la extraña familia* (José María Forqué); **1961:** *Viridiana* (Luis Buñuel); **1962:** *El ángel exterminador* (Luis Buñuel); **1964:** *Simón del desierto* (Luis Buñuel); *Buenas noches, año nuevo* (Julián Soler); **1965:** *Los cuervos están de luto* (Francisco del Villar); **1966:** *La soldadera* (José Bolaños); *Estrategia matrimonio* (Alberto Gout); *Divertimento* (Luis Alcoriza; episode in *Juego peligroso;* co-d Arturo Ripstein); *La güera Xochitl* (Rogelio A. González); **1967:** *Shark* (Samuel Fuller); *La Bataille de San Sebastian* (Henri Verneuil); *María Isabel* (Federico Curiel); **1968:** *El cuerpazo del delito* (René Cardona Jr, Rafael Baledón and Sergio Véjar); *El despertar del lobo* (René Cardona Jr); *Veinticuatro horas de placer* (René Cardona Jr); **1969:** *La mujer de oro* (René Cardona Jr); *Los novios* (Gilberto Gazcón); *La hermana Trinquete* (René Cardona Jr); **1970:** *Bang bang y al hoyo* (René Cardona Jr); *Secreto de confesión* (Julián Soler); **1971:** *Cómo hay gente sinvergüenza* (René Cardona Jr); *Los cacos* (José

Estrada); **1976:** *Divinas palabras* (Juan Ibáñez); **1977:** *Las mariposas disecadas* (Sergio Véjar); **1982:** *Pubis angelical* (Raúl de la Torre, in Argentina); **1991:** *Modelo antiguo* (Raúl Araiza).

José REVUELTAS

Born in Durango in 1914; died in Mexico City in 1976. A militant communist throughout his life, he was an important writer of short stories, novels, essays, journalism and screenplays. His first script was an adaptation of Jack London's *El Mexicano,* and shortly after, he published his second novel, *El luto humano* (1943), one of his most important works. His most significant contributions to the cinema were made in collaboration with Roberto Gavaldón *(La otra, La diosa arrodillada, En la palma de tu mano).*

Filmography 1944: *El mexicano* (Agustín P. Delgado); **1945:** *Cantaclaro* (Julio Bracho); *Amor de una vida* (Miguel Morayta); **1946:** *La otra* (Roberto Gavaldón); *A la sombra del puente* (Roberto Gavaldón); **1947:** *La diosa arrodillada* (Roberto Gavaldón); *Que Dios me perdone* (Tito Davison); **1948:** *Medianoche* (Tito Davison); **1949:** *La casa chica* (Roberto Gavaldón); *Perdida* (Fernando A. Rivero); **1950:** *Rosauro Castro* (Roberto Gavaldón); *Deseada* (Roberto Gavaldón); *En la palma de tu mano* (Roberto Gavaldón); **1951:** *La noche avanza* (Roberto Gavaldón); **1952:** *El rebozo de Soledad* (Roberto Gavaldón); *Las tres perfectas casadas* (Roberto Gavaldón); **1953:** *La ilusión viaja en tranvía* (Luis Buñuel); *Sombra verde* (Roberto Gavaldón); **1955:** *Amor y pecado* (Alfredo B. Crevenna); *Donde el círculo termina* (Alfredo B. Crevenna); *La escondida* (Roberto Gavaldón); **1959:** *Sonatas* (Juan Antonio Bardem); *Las hermanas Karambazo* (Benito Alazraki); **1960:** *Con quien andan nuestros locos* (Benito Alazraki); **1975:** *El apando* (Felipe Cazals).

Dolores del RÍO

Born in Durango, 3 August 1904; died in Newport Beach (California), 11 April 1983. While she was studying in Europe, the US director Edwin Carewe 'discovered' her and took her to Hollywood, where she enjoyed an important career that spanned the years from her cinematic debut in 1925 to her return to Mexico in 1942. In Mexico, she began a second career working primarily with Emilio Fernández *(Flor silvestre, María Candelaria, Bugambilia, etc.)* and Roberto Gavaldón *(La otra, La casa chica).*

Filmography 1925: *Joanna* (Edwin Carewe); **1926:** *High Steppers* (Edwin Carewe); *Pals First* (Edwin

Carewe); *The Whole Town's Talking* (Edward Laemmle); *What Price Glory?* (Raoul Walsh); **1927:** *Resurrection* (Edwin Carewe); *The Loves of Carmen* (Raoul Walsh); **1928:** *The Gateway of the Moon* (John G. Wray); *The Trail of '98* (Clarence Brown); *Ramona* (Edwin Carewe); *No Other Women* (Lou Tellegen); *The Red Dance* (Raoul Walsh); *Revenge* (Edwin Carewe); **1929:** *Evangeline* (Edwin Carewe); **1930:** *The Bad One* (George Fitzmaurice); **1932:** *The Girl of the Rio* (Herbert Brenon); *The Bird of Paradise* (King Vidor); **1933:** *Flying Down to Rio (Carioca)* (Thornton Freeland); **1934:** *Wonder Bar* (Lloyd Bacon); *Madame Dubarry* (William Dieterle); **1935:** *In Caliente* (Lloyd Bacon); *I Live For Love* (Busby Berkeley); *The Widow From Montecarlo* (Arthur Collins); **1936:** *Accused* (Thornton Freeland); **1937:** *The Devil's Playground* (Erle C. Kenton); *Lancer Spy* (Gregory Ratoff); **1938:** *International Settlement* (Eugene Forde); **1940:** *The Man From Dakota* (Leslie Fenton); **1942:** *Journey into Fear* (Norman Foster); **1943:** *Flor silvestre* (Emilio Fernández); *María Candelaria* (Emilio Fernández); **1944:** *Las abandonadas* (Emilio Fernández); *Bugambilia* (Emilio Fernández); **1945:** *La selva de fuego* (Fernando de Fuentes); **1946:** *La otra* (Roberto Gavaldón); **1947:** *The Fugitive* (John Ford); **1948:** *Historia de una mala mujer* (Luis Saslavsky); **1949:** *La malquerida* (Emilio Fernández); *La casa chica* (Roberto Gavaldón); *Deseada* (Roberto Gavaldón); **1950:** *Doña Perfecta* (Alejandro Galindo); **1953:** *Reportaje* (Emilio Fernández); *El niño y la niebla* (Roberto Gavaldón); **1954:** *Señora ama* (Julio Bracho); **1956:** *¿A dónde van nuestros hijos?* (Benito Alazraki); **1958:** *La cucaracha* (Ismael Rodríguez); **1960:** *El pecado de una madre* (Alfonso Corona Blake); *Flaming Star* (Don Siegel); **1964:** *Cheyenne Autumn* (John Ford); **1965:** *La dama del alba* (Francisco Rovira Beleta); *C'era una volta* (Francesco Rosi); **1966:** *Casa de mujeres* (Julián Soler); **1977:** *The Children of Sanchez* (Hall Bartlett).

Arturo RIPSTEIN

Born in Mexico City, 13 December 1943. The son of producer Alfredo Ripstein Jr, he has been involved in the film industry since childhood. He studied law at UNAM, history at the Colegio de México and art history at the Universidad Iberoamericana. In the early 60s, he appeared in supporting roles in a number of films and was Luis Buñuel's assistant director for *El ángel exterminador* (1962). Aged twenty-one he made his directorial debut with *Tiempo de morir,* an adaptation of a Gabriel García Márquez script.

Filmography 1965: *Tiempo de morir;* **1966:** *HO* (episode of *Juego peligroso;* co-d Luis Alcoriza); **1968:** *Los recuerdos del porvenir;* **1969:** *La hora de los niños;* **1970:** *Crimen* (Short); *La belleza* (Short); *Exorcismos* (Short); *Autorretrato* (Short); *El náufrago de la calle Providencia* (doc; co-d Rafael Castanedo); **1972:** *El castillo de la pureza;* **1973:** *El Santo Oficio;* **1974:** *Tiempo de correr* (short doc); *Los otros niños* (doc); **1975:** *Foxtrot* (UK–Swiss co-p); **1976:** *Lecumberri: El palacio negro* (doc); *El borracho* (short doc); *La causa* (short doc); **1977:** *El lugar sin límites; La viuda negra;* **1978:** *Cadena perpetua; La tía Alejandra;* **1979:** *La ilegal; La seducción;* **1981:** *Rastro de muerte;* **1984:** *El otro;* **1985:** *El imperio de la fortuna;* **1988:** *Mentiras piadosas;* **1991:** *La mujer del puerto;* **1993:** *Principio y fin;* **1994:** *La reina de la noche.*

Ismael RODRÍGUEZ

Born in Mexico City, 19 October 1917. The Rodríguez family emigrated to Los Angeles in 1926, where Ismael's elder brothers, Roberto and Joselito, experimented with a sound system of their own invention. They returned to Mexico in 1931, while Antonio Moreno's *Santa* was in production, and Ismael obtained a walk-on part. He acted in several films, did technical jobs (especially with sound crews), founded a production company with his brothers (Películas Rodríguez) and made his directorial debut in 1942. In the late 40s and early 50s, he contributed to the consecration of Pedro Infante's fame with his trilogy *Nosotros los pobres, Ustedes los ricos* and *Pepe el Toro.*

Filmography 1942: *¡Que lindo es Michoacán!;* **1943:** *Mexicanos al grito de guerra* (co-d Alvaro Gálvez y Fuentes); **1944:** *Amores de ayer; Escándalo de estrellas;* **1945:** *Cuando lloran los valientes; ¡Qué verde era mi padre!;* **1946:** *Ya tengo a mi hijo; Los tres García; Vuelven los García;* **1947:** *Chachita de la Triana; Nosotros los pobres;* **1948:** *Los tres huastecos; Ustedes los ricos;* **1949:** *La oveja negra; No desearas la mujer de tu hijo;* **1950:** *Sobre las olas; Las mujeres de mi general;* **1951:** *ATM (A toda máquina); ¿Qué te ha dado esa mujer?; ¡¡¡Mátenme porque me muero!!!;* **1952:** *Del rancho a la televisión; Dos tipos de cuidado; Pepe el Toro;* **1953:** *Romance de fieras; Borrasca en las almas;* **1954:** *Maldita ciudad; Los paquetes de Paquita; Cupido pierde a Paquita; El monstruo de la montaña hueca* (in the US, co-d Edward Nassour); **1955:** *Las aventuras de Daniel Boone* (in the US, co-d Albert Gannaway); **1956:** *Tizoc; Tierra de hombres;* **1957:** *Así era Pancho Villa;* **1958:** *Pancho Villa y la Valentina; Cuando ¡Viva Villa! es la muerte; La* cucaracha; **1959:** *La ciudad sagrada;* **1961:** *Los hermanos del Hierro; Animas Trujano;* **1963:** *El hombre de papel; Así era Pedro Infante;* **1964:** *El niño y el muro;* **1965:** *Autopsia de un fantasma;* **1968:** *La mujer del carnicero* (co-d Chano Urueta); *Cuernos debajo de la cama;* **1969:** *Faltas a la moral; Trampa para una niña; El ogro;* **1971:** *Mi niño Tizoc;* **1972:** *Nosotros los feos;* **1975:** *Somos del otro Laredo;* **1978:** *Ratero;* **1979:** *El secuestro de los cien millones;* **1980:** *Blanca Nieves y sus siete amantes;* **1981:** *Burdel;* **1983:** *Corrupción;* **1986:** *Yerba sangrienta;* **1987:** *Solicito marido para engañar;* **1988:** *Dos tipas de cuidado; Masacre en el Río Tula;* **1989:** *Ellos trajeron la violencia.*

María ROJO

Born in Mexico City in 1944. Rojo made her acting debut as a child in the play *La mala semilla* and in the weekly television programme *El teatro fantástico* directed by Ernesto Alonso. Her film debut came with Rafael Baledón's *Besos prohibidos* (1956). She studied dramatic arts at the university of Veracruz, and after her first starring role in *El apando,* she worked with the most important Mexican directors: Jaime Humberto Hermosillo, Arturo Ripstein, Paul Leduc, Jorge Fons, María Novaro, etc. Her career has been divided between cinema, theatre and television.

Filmography 1956: *Besos prohibidos* (Rafael Baledón); **1968:** *Los recuerdos del porvenir* (Arturo Ripstein); **1971:** *Los cachorros* (Jorge Fons); **1972:** *El castillo de la pureza* (Arturo Ripstein); **1975:** *El apando* (Felipe Cazals); **1976:** *Nuevo mundo* (Gabriel Retes); *Lo mejor de Teresa* (Alberto Bojórquez); *Las poquianchis* (Felipe Cazals); **1977:** *Naufragio* (Jaime Humberto Hermosillo); *Las apariencias engañan* (Jaime Humberto Hermosillo); **1978:** *Idilio* (Jaime Humberto Hermosillo); **1979:** *María de mi corazón* (Jaime Humberto Hermosillo); **1981:** *Complot petrolero: la cabeza de la hidra* (Paul Leduc); **1982:** *La víspera* (Alejandro Pelayo); *Confidencias* (Jaime Humberto Hermosillo); *Bajo la metralla* (Felipe Cazals); **1983:** *El corazón de la noche* (Jaime Humberto Hermosillo); **1985:** *Robachicos* (Alberto Bojórquez); *Viaje al paraíso* (Ignacio Retes); **1986:** *Las inocentes* (Felipe Cazals); *Lo que importa es vivir* (Luis Alcoriza); **1988:** *Los confines* (Mitl Valdés); *Día de difuntos* (Luis Alcoriza); *Me llaman la Chata Aguayo* (Manuel Bonilla); *Break of Dawn* (Isaac Artenstein); **1989:** *Morir en el Golfo* (Alejandro Pelayo); *El otro crimen* (Carlos González Morantes); *Rojo amanecer* (Jorge Fons); *Vai trabalhar vagabundo II* (Hugo Carvana); *La sombra del ciprés es alargada*

(Luis Alcoriza); **1990:** *La leyenda de una máscara* (José Buil); *Danzón* (María Novaro); *Intimidades en un cuarto de baño* (Jaime Humberto Hermosillo); *La tarea* (Jaime Humberto Hermosillo); **1991:** *Encuentro inesperado* (Jaime Humberto Hermosillo); **1992:** *Tequila* (Rubén Gámez); *Otoñal* (María Novaro); *La tarea prohibida* (Jaime Humberto Hermosillo); **1993:** *Los vuelcos del corazón* (Mitl Valdez).

Enrique ROSAS

Rosas was a pioneer of the Mexican cinema who worked as an exhibitor, director and producer during the first two decades of the century. His career began in 1899, when he opened a movie theatre in Mexico City, building it into an exhibition circuit (the Compañía Rosas–Aguilar) by 1950. He was also a travelling exhibitor who on his trips throughout the country would film the mores of Porfirian society. In association with the brothers Alva, he founded the production company Rosas, Alva and Co. (1908). Between 1910 and 1917, he directed several documentaries about Revolutionary activities. Afterwards, together with the actress Mimí Derba and General Pablo González, he organised Azteca Films and produced several fiction features *(En defensa propia, Alma de sacrificio, La soñadora).* His last job was the production and direction of *El automóvil gris,* a twelve-episode serial. He died in Mexico City on 9 August 1920. Unless otherwise indicated, all his films are documentary shorts.

Filmography 1903: *Aventuras del sexteto Uranga;* **1904:** *Vistas de Orizaba y sus alrededores* (co-d Agustín Jiménez); *La Cervecería Moctezuma de Orizaba* (co-d Agustín Jiménez); *Salida de la misa de 12 de la Parroquia de Orizaba* (co-d Agustín Jiménez); **1905:** *Vistas al día siguiente de la inundación de Guanajuato; Panorama de Guadalupe Hidalgo; Vapor mercante entrando al puerto de Veracruz; Comité patriótico en el parque Castillo de Orizaba; Buque velero frente al faro de San Juan de Ulúa; Puente de Río Grande; Toros en Saltillo; Vistas de León; Funerales del embajador Aspiroz en la ciudad de México; Jamaica escolar en Orizaba; Botes pescadores entrando en la bahía de Veracruz;* **1906:** *Fiestas presidenciales en Mérida* (feature); *Carnaval de Mérida;* **1908:** *Primera corrida de Gaona; Beneficio de Gaona; Beneficio de Gaona en México; Exposición de Coyoacán;* **1909:** *Incendio del Teatro Guerrero de Puebla; El Rosario de Amozoc* (fiction); *Don Juan Tenorio* (fiction); *Cogida de Rodolfo Gaona en Puebla; Arribo del nuevo arzobispo;* **1912:** *Revolución en*

Veracruz (feature); **1913:** *Decena trágica* (feature); **1916:** *Documentación histórica nacional, 1915–1916* (feature); **1917:** *La soñadora* (fiction; co-d Eduardo Arozamena); *Alma de sacrificio; En la sombra* (fiction); **1919:** *Emiliano Zapata en vida y muerte* (feature); *El automóvil gris* (fiction serial; co-d Joaquín Coss and Juan Canals de Homes).

Ninón SEVILLA

Born in Havana (Cuba), 10 November 1921. Studying classical dance as a child, Sevilla made her dancing debut in Havana (1942). She subsequently moved to Mexico in 1946 to work in cinema. Her career culminated with the *cabaretera* films (cabaret melodramas) directed by Alberto Gout and scripted by Alvaro Custodio *(Aventurera; Sensualidad)*.

Filmography 1946: *Carita de cielo* (José Díaz Morales); **1947:** *Pecadora* (José Díaz Morales); *La feria de Jalisco* (Chano Urueta); *Señora Tentación* (José Díaz Morales); **1948:** *Revancha* (Albert Gout); **1949:** *Coqueta* (Fernando A. Rivero); *Perdida* (Fernando A. Rivero); *Aventurera* (Alberto Gout); **1950:** *Víctimas del pecado* (Emilio Fernández); *Sensualidad* (Alberto Gout); **1951:** *No niego mi pasado* (Alberto Gout); *Mujeres sacrificadas* (Alberto Gout); **1952:** *Aventura en Río* (Alberto Gout); **1953:** *Llévame en tus brazos* (Julio Bracho); *Mulata* (Gilberto Martínez Solares); **1955:** *Amor y pecado* (Alfredo B. Crevenna); *Club de señoritas* (Gilberto Martínez Solares); **1956:** *Yambaó* (Alfredo B. Crevenna); **1957:** *Maratón de baile* (René Cardona); **1958:** *Mujeres de fuego* (Tito Davison); *Música de ayer* (Juan de Orduña, in Spain); **1981:** *Noche de carnaval* (Mario Hernández); *Las noches del Blanquita* (Mario Hernández); **1982:** *El mexicano feo* (Alfredo B. Crevenna); **1983:** *Viva el chubasco* (Mario Hernández); **1987:** *Hoy como ayer* (Sergio Véjar and Constante Diego).

Raphael J. SEVILLA

Born in Mexico City, 3 September 1905, where he died in 1975. Sevilla went to the USA as a boy and gained much experience in Hollywood, where he worked as a technical adviser at Warner Bros. In 1930 he became one of the pioneers of Mexican sound cinema by producing, writing and directing *Más fuerte que el deber,* a sound-on-disc melodrama.

Filmography 1930: *Más fuerte que el deber;* **1932:** *Un espectador impertinente* (co-d Arcady Boytler); **1933:** *La sangre manda* (co-d José Bohr); *Almas encontradas;* **1934:** *Corazón bandolero;* **1935:** *María*

Elena; Lola Triana; El 113 (in Spain); **1936:** *Irma la mala;* **1937:** *La gran cruz; Guadalupe la Chinaca; A la orilla de un palmar;* **1938:** *Luna criolla; Perjura;* **1939:** *Miente y serás feliz; El secreto de la monja; Fantasma de medianoche;* **1940:** *El insurgente; La torre de los suplicios;* **1941:** *Amor chinaco;* **1942:** *La abuelita; Maravilla del toreo;* **1944:** *Como yo te quería; Porfirio Díaz; Asesinato en los estudios;* **1946:** *La niña de mis ojos; El amor abrió los ojos;* **1948:** *Una mujer con pasado;* **1949:** *Canas al aire; El miedo llegó a Jalisco;* **1950:** *Quinto patio;* **1951:** *El billetero;* **1953:** *La calle de los amores;* **1954:** *Tu vida entre mis manos;* **1955:** *Encrucijada;* **1958:** *Paraíso escondido* (co-d Mauricio de la Serna).

Fernando SOLER

Born in Coahuila, 24 May 1896, according to some sources; died in Mexico City, 24 October 1979. Born into a family of actors and directors, Soler appeared in *The Spanish Jade* as an adolescent. He entered Mexican cinema in 1934, with the starring role in *Chucho el Roto* (Gabriel Soria), and subsequently never stopped acting, directing, producing and writing screenplays. His best-known acting persona was that of a harsh and tyrannical father, which reached perfection in *Una familia de tantas* (Alejandro Galindo, 1948).

Filmography (* only directed) **1915:** *The Spanish Jade* (Wilfred Lucas); **1925:** *La verdad de la vida* (Alejandro Peniche Sierra); **1931:** *¿Cuándo te suicidas?* (Manuel Romero); **1934:** *Chucho el Roto* (Gabriel Soria); **1935:** *Celos* (Arcady Boytler); **1937:** *Abnegación* (Rafael E. Portas); **1938:** *Refugiados en Madrid* (Alejandro Galindo); *Por mis pistolas* (José Bohr); *La casa del ogro* (Fernando de Fuentes); *Dos cadetes* (Jorge Lopez Portillo and René Cardona); *La bestia negra* (Gabriel Soria); *Verbena trágica* (Charles Lamont); **1939:** *Los hijos mandan* (Gabriel Soria); *Papacito lindo* (Fernando de Fuentes); *Odio* (Fernando Soler and William Rowland); *En tiempos de don Porfirio* (Juan Bustillo Oro); **1940:** *Pobre diablo* (José Benavides Jr); *Con su amable permiso* (Fernando Soler); *Al son de la marimba* (Juan Bustillo Oro); *Creo en Dios* (Fernando de Fuentes); **1941:** *Cuando los hijos se van* (Juan Bustillo Oro); *El barbero prodigioso* (Fernando Soler); **1942:** *El verdugo de Sevilla* (Fernando Soler); *¡Que hombre tan simpático!* (Fernando Soler); **1943:** *Tentación* (Fernando Soler); *Ojos negros* (Fernando Soler); *La mujer sin alma* (Fernando de Fuentes); *México de mis recuerdos* (Juan Bustillo Oro); **1944:** *Como todas las madres* (Fernando Soler); *La mujer que engañamos*

(Humberto Gómez Landero); *El rey se divierte* (Fernando de Fuentes); *Capullito de alelí* (Fernando Soler); **1945:** *Flor de durazno* (Miguel Zacarías); *La reina de la opereta* (José Benavides Jr); *Las cinco advertencias de Satanás* (Julián Soler); *Mamá Inés* (Fernando Soler); **1946:** *El conquistador*; Me persigue una mujer*; Los maderos San Juan* (Juan Bustillo Oro); *Todo un caballero* (Miguel M. Delgado); **1947:** *Que Dios me perdone* (Tito Davison); **1948:** *Rosenda* (Julio Bracho); *Una familia de tantas* (Alejandro Galindo); *Cuando los padres se quedan solos* (Juan Bustillo Oro); *El dolor de los hijos* (Miguel Zacarías); **1949:** *Las tandas del Principal* (Juan Bustillo Oro); *El gran calavera* (Luis Buñuel); *La oveja negra* (Ismael Rodríguez); *No desearás la mujer de tu hijo* (Ismael Rodríguez); *Cuide a su marido* (Fernando Soler); *Las joyas del pecado* (Alfredo B. Crevenna); *La hija del penal*; La liga de las muchachas*;* **1950:** *Mi mujer no es mía*; El grito de la carne* (Fernando Soler); *Azahares para tu boda* (Julián Soler); *Mi querido capitán* (Gilberto Martínez Solares); *Yo quiero ser tonta* (Ernesto Ugarte); *Susana* (Luis Buñuel); *El amor a la vida* (Miguel Contreras Torres); *Sensualidad* (Alberto Gout); **1951:** *Los enredos de una gallega*; María del Mar*; La hija del engaño* (Luis Buñuel); *Mamá nos quita los novios* (Roberto Rodríguez); **1952:** *Prefiero a tu papá* (Roberto Rodríguez); *Por ellas aunque mal paguen* (Juan Bustillo Oro); *El gran mentiroso* (Fernando Soler); *Solo para maridos* (Fernando Soler); **1953:** *Reportaje* (Emilio Fernández); **1954:** *Maldita ciudad* (Ismael Rodríguez); *Educando a papá* (Fernando Soler; Spanish co-p); *El indiano* (Fernando Soler; in Spain); **1956:** *Cuando México canta* (Julián Soler); **1960:** *Las memorias de mi general* (Mauricio de la Serna); **1961:** *El amor de los amores* (Juan de Orduña); *Sol en llamas* (Alfredo B. Crevenna); *Pueblito* (Emilio Fernández); **1962:** *María Pistolas* (René Cardona); *El corrido de María Pistolas* (René Cardona); **1963:** *Historia de un canalla* (Julio Bracho); *He matado a un hombre* (Julio Bracho); *Amor de adolescente* (Julio Bracho); *México de mis recuerdos* (Juan Bustillo Oro); *La edad de la violencia* (Julián Soler); **1964:** *Campeón del barrio* (José María Fernández Unsaín); *Los tales por cuales* (Gilberto Martínez Solares); *Así amaron nuestros padres* (Juan Bustillo Oro); *Los hermanos Muerte* (José María Fernández Unsaín); **1965:** *Los valses venían de Viena y los niños de Paris* (Juan Bustillo Oro); **1966:** *El derecho de nacer* (Tito Davison); *Casa de mujeres* (Julián Soler); *Siete días para morir* (Emilio Gómez Muriel); *Me quiero casar* (Julián Soler); *Amanecí en tus brazos* (Rafael Portillo); *Los ángeles de Puebla* (Francisco del Villar); **1967:** *No hay cruces en el mar*

(Julián Soler); **1968:** *Romeo contra Julieta* (Julián Soler); *Cuando los hijos se van* (Julián Soler); *El día de las madres* (Alfredo B. Crevenna); *Misión cumplida* (Gilberto Martínez Solares); *Muchachas, muchachas, muchachas* (José Díaz Morales); **1969:** *El hacedor de miedo* (Anthony Carras); *Anita de Montemar* (Manuel Zeceña Diegues); **1971:** *Hoy he soñado con Dios* (Julián Soler); *Yesenia* (Alfredo B. Crevenna); **1972:** *Pobre, pero … ¡honrada!* (Fernando Cortés); *El señor de Osanto* (Jaime Humberto Hermosillo); **1975:** *La comadrita* (Fernando Cortés); **1976:** *Pedro Páramo* (José Bolaños); **1977:** *El lugar sin límites* (Arturo Ripstein); **1978:** *El gran perro muerto* (Rogelio A. González).

Gabriel SORIA

Born in Michoacán in 1903; died in Mexico City, 30 June 1971. Soria won a competition sponsored by the newspaper *Excélsior* and obtained a scholarship to study in the USA. Upon returning to Mexico, he made a series of newsreels before directing *Chucho el Roto*. He abandoned his career in 1944 and moved to Europe, where he lived for a long time in Spain.

Filmography 1934: *Chucho el Roto;* **1935:** *Los muertos hablan; Martín Garatuza;* **1936:** *¡Ora Ponciano!; Mater nostra;* **1938:** *La bestia negra;* **1939:** *Los hijos mandan* (in the USA); **1940:** *Mala yerba;* **1942:** *Casa de mujeres; La virgen morena;* **1943:** *La dama de las camelias.*

Jorge STAHL

Born in Puebla in 1886; died in Mexico City in 1979. In the early 1900s he was a travelling film exhibitor, and later established a film distribution company. He founded the México Films studio in 1933, where he worked in the processing laboratory. In 1942 he became manager of the Clasa Studios and in 1945 he set up the San Angel Inn studios. He worked as a cinematographer between 1921 and 1946.

Filmography 1921: *El crimen del otro* (Carlos Stahl); *Malditas sean las mujeres* (Carlos Stahl); *La dama de las camelias* (Carlos Stahl); *Mitad y mitad* (Carlos Stahl); **1922:** *Bolcheviquismo* (Pedro J. Vázquez); **1924:** *Aguiluchos mexicanos* (Miguel Contreras Torres); **1925:** *La linterna de Diógenes* (Carlos Stahl); **1928:** *El secreto de la abuela* (Cándida Beltrán Rendón); **1929:** *La boda de Rosario* (Gustavo Sáenz de Sicilia); *Los hijos del destino* (Luis Lezama); **1933:** *Tiburón* (Ramón Peón); **1944:** *El capitán Malacara* (Carlos Orellana); *Como México no hay dos* (Carlos

Orellana); *Un corazón burlado* (José Benavides); *Su gran ilusión* (Mauricio Magdaleno); *Song of Mexico* (James A. Fitzpatrick); **1945:** *Cuando lloran los valientes* (Ismael Rodríguez); *Corazones de México* (Roberto Gavaldón); *Las cinco advertencias de Satanás* (Julián Soler); *La hija del payaso* (Joselito Rodríguez); **1946:** *El amor abrió los ojos* (Raphael J. Sevilla).

Germán Valdés, TIN TAN

Born in Mexico City in 1915, where he died in 1973. He grew up in Ciudad Juárez, working as a radio announcer until joining the theatre troupe of ventriloquist Pancho Miller. Valdés travelled with him to the capital, where he appeared in light comedies at the Iris and Follies theatres, and often shared the stage with Cantinflas and Palillo. He made his film debut in 1943 with a small role in *Hotel de verano*. His best films are the ones directed by Gilberto Martínez Solares and written by Juan García.

Filmography 1943: *Hotel de verano* (René Cardona); **1945:** *El hijo desobediente* (Humberto Gómez Landero); **1946:** *Hay muertos que no hacen ruido* (Humberto Gómez Landero); *Con la música por dentro* (Humberto Gómez Landero); **1947:** *El niño perdido* (Humberto Gómez Landero); *Músico, poeta y loco* (Humberto Gómez Landero); **1948:** *Calabacitas tiernas* (Gilberto Martínez Solares); **1949:** *Yo soy charro de levita* (Gilberto Martínez Solares); *No me defiendas compadre* (Gilberto Martínez Solares); *El rey del barrio* (Gilberto Martínez Solares); **1950:** *La marca del Zorrillo* (Gilberto Martínez Solares); *Simbad el mareado* (Gilberto Martínez Solares); *¡Ay amor, como me has puesto!* (Gilberto Martínez Solares); *También de dolor se canta* (René Cardona); *Cuando las mujeres mandan* (José González Prieto); **1951:** *El revoltoso* (Gilberto Martínez Solares); *¡¡¡Mátenme porque me muero!!!* (Ismael Rodríguez); *El ceniciento* (Gilberto Martínez Solares); *Chucho el remendado* (Gilberto Martínez Solares); *Mi campeón* (Chano Urueta); *Las locuras de Tin Tan* (Gilberto Martínez Solares); **1952:** *El bello durmiente* (Gilberto Martínez Solares); *Me traes de un ala* (Gilberto Martínez Solares); *Isla de mujeres* (Rafael Baledón); **1953:** *El vagabundo* (Rogelio A. González); *Dios los cría …* (Gilberto Martínez Solares); *Reportaje* (Emilio Fernández); *El mariachi desconocido* (Gilberto Martínez Solares); **1954:** *El hombre inquieto* (Rafael Baledón); *El vizconde de Montecristo* (Gilberto Martínez Solares); *Los líos de barba azul* (Gilberto Martínez Solares); *El sultán descalzo*

(Gilberto Martínez Solares); **1955:** *Lo que le pasó a Sansón* (Gilberto Martínez Solares); *El vividor* (Gilberto Martínez Solares); *El médico de las locas* (Miguel Morayta); **1956:** *Las aventuras de Pito Pérez* (Juan Bustillo Oro); *El gato sin botas* (Fernando Cortés); *Música de siempre* (Tito Davison); *Tres mosqueteros y medio* (Gilberto Martínez Solares); *El teatro del crimen* (Fernando Cortés); *Escuela para suegras* (Gilberto Martínez Solares); *El campeón ciclista* (Fernando Cortés); *Refifí entre las mujeres* (Fernando Cortés); **1957:** *Locos peligrosos* (Fernando Cortés); *Paso a la juventud* (Gilberto Martínez Solares); *Las mil y una noches* (Fernando Cortés); *El que con niño se acuesta* (Rogelio A. González); *Quiero ser artista* (Tito Davison); *Viaje a la luna* (Fernando Cortés); *Rebelde sin casa* (Benito Alazraki); *La odalisca número 13* (Fernando Cortés); **1958:** *El cofre del pirata* (Fernando Méndez); *Tres lecciones de amor* (Fernando Cortés); *Vagabundo y millonario* (Miguel Morayta); *Escuela de verano* (Gilberto Martínez Solares); *Vivir del cuento* (Rafael Baledón); *Ferias de México* (Rafael Portillo); *La tijera de oro* (Benito Alazraki); *Dos fantasmas y una muchacha* (Rogelio A. González); **1959:** *Tin Tan y las modelos* (Benito Alazraki); *El fantasma de la opereta* (Fernando Cortés); *El pandillero* (Rafael Baledón); *Una estrella y dos estrellados* (Gilberto Martínez Solares); *La casa del terror* (Gilberto Martínez Solares); *Variedades de medianoche* (Fernando Cortés); **1960:** *El duende y yo* (Gilberto Martínez Solares); *El violetero* (Gilberto Martínez Solares); *¡Suicídate mi amor!* (Gilberto Martínez Solares); *Locura de terror* (Julián Soler); **1961:** *Viva Chihuahua* (Gilberto Martínez Solares); **1962:** *Pilotos de la muerte* (Chano Urueta); *En peligro de muerte* (René Cardona); *Fuerte, audaz y valiente* (René Cardona); *El tesoro del Rey Salomón* (Federico Curiel); **1964:** *Los fantasmas burlones* (Rafael Baledón); *Tintansón Crusoe* (Gilberto Martínez Solares); **1965:** *Especialista en chamacas* (Chano Urueta); *Loco por ellas* (Manuel de la Pedrosa); **1966:** *El ángel y yo* (Gilberto Martínez Solares); *Seis días para morir* (Emilio Gómez Muriel); *Detectives o ladrones* (Miguel Morayta); *Gregorio y su ángel* (Gilberto Martínez Solares); **1968:** *Duelo en el Dorado* (René Cardona Jr); **1969:** *El capitán Mantarraya* (Germán Valdés); *El quelite* (Jorge Fons); *El ogro* (Ismael Rodríguez); *Trampa para una niña* (Ismael Rodríguez); **1970:** *Caín, Abel y el otro* (René Cardona Jr); *Chanoc en las garras de las fieras* (Gilberto Martínez Solares); *En estas camas nadie duerme* (Emilio Gómez Muriel); **1971:** *Acapulco 12–22* (Aldo Monti); *Los cacos* (José Estrada); *Chanoc contra el tigre y el vampiro* (Gilberto Martínez

Solares); *El increíble profesor Zovek* (René Cardona); *Las tarantulas* (Gilberto Martínez Solares); **1972:** *La disputa* (René Cardona Jr); *Noche de muerte* (René Cardona).

Salvador TOSCANO

Born in Jalisco, 24 March 1872; died in Mexico City, 10 April 1947. After training as an engineer at the Mining School, he opened Mexico City's first movie theatre in 1897. At the same time, he began to produce, film and archive documentary films, building an important collection dating from the end of the Porfiriato through the Revolution. His daughter, Carmen Toscano, included many of these in the feature-length *Memorias de un mexicano* (1950). Unless otherwise indicated, all his films are short documentaries.

Filmography 1898: *La Alameda; Corrida de toros por Guerrita; Escenas de la Alameda; Norte en Veracruz; Llegada del Tlacotalpan a Veracruz; Charros mexicanos lazando un potro; El Zócalo; Pelea de gallos; Corrida de toros en las plazas mexicanas;* **1899:** *Rancheros mexicanos domando caballos; Terrible percance a un enamorado en el cementerio de Dolores* (fiction); *Sevillanas* (fiction); *Don Juan Tenorio* (fiction); *Paseo en la Alameda de México; Charros mexicanos lazando caballos; Entrada de un vapor al puerto de Veracruz; Baño de caballos en la hacienda de Atequiza; Corrida de toros en Tacubaya; Canarios de café* (fiction); *Jarabe tapatío; Don Porfirio Díaz paseando a caballo en el bosque de Chapultepec;* **1900:** *Don Juan Tenorio* (fiction); *Saliendo de la catedral de Puebla;* **1904:** *Fiestas el 16 de septiembre en Tehuacán;* **1905:** *Guanajuato; La inundación de Guanajuato; Llegada a Veracruz de los restos del embajador Aspiroz;* **1906:** *Concurso y combate floral; Fiestas del 5 de mayo en Orizaba; Lago de Chapultepec; Incendio del cañón de ropa La Valenciana el 14 de abril; Gran corrida de toros en Guadalajara; Viaje a Yucatán; Los charros mexicanos; Fiestas de la Covadonga en el Tívoli del Eliseo; Un 16 de septiembre en México; Fiesta popular en los llanos de Anzures; Combate de flores;* **1907:** *Inauguración del tráfico internacional de Tehuantepec;* **1910:** *Fiestas del Centenario de la Independencia;* **1915:** *Historia completa de la revolución de 1910–1915;* **1916:** *Historia completa de la revolución mexicana de 1910–1916;* **1921:** *Fiesta del Centenario de la consumación de la Independencia.*

Lupe VÉLEZ

Born in San Luis Potosí, 18 July 1909; she committed suicide in the USA, 13 December 1944.

Vélez got started in variety theatre at an early age. She made her Hollywood debut in 1927 in the short, *What Women Did For Me*. She only appeared in two Mexican films: *La Zandunga* and *Naná.*

Filmography 1927: *What Women Did For Me* (James Parrott; Short); *Sailors, Beware!* (Hal Yates; Short); **1928:** *The Gaucho* (F. Richard Jones); *Stand and Deliver* (Donald Crisp); **1929:** *Lady of the Pavements* (David W. Griffith); *Wolf Song* (Victor Fleming); *Where East is East* (Tod Browning); *Tiger Rose* (George Fitzmaurice); **1930:** *Hell Harbor* (Henry King); *The Storm* (William Wyler); *East is West* (Monta Bell); *Oriente es occidente* (George Melford); **1931:** *Resurrection* (Edwin Carewe); *Resurrección* (David Selman); *The Squaw Man* (Cecil B. DeMille); *The Cuban Love Song* (W.S. Van Dyke); *Hombres en su vida* (David Selman); **1932:** *The Broken Wing* (Lloyd Corrigan); *Kongo* (William J. Cowen); *The Half–Naked Truth* (Gregory LaCava); **1933:** *Hot Pepper* (John G. Blystone); *Mister Broadway* (Johnnie Walker and Edgar G. Ulmer); **1934:** *Laughing Boy* (W.S. Van Dyke); *Palooka* (Benjamin Stoloff); *Hollywood Party* (Richard Boleslawsky); *Strictly Dynamite* (Elliott Nugent); **1935:** *The Morals of Marcus* (Miles Mander); *Stardust* (Melville Brown); **1936:** *Gypsy Melody* (Edmond T. Greville); **1937:** *High Flyers* (Edward F. Cline); *La Zandunga* (Fernando de Fuentes; in Mexico); **1939:** *The Girl From Mexico* (Leslie Goodwins); *Mexican Spitfire* (Leslie Goodwins); **1940:** *Mexican Spitfire Out West* (Leslie Goodwins); **1941:** *Six Lessons From Madame La Zonga* (John Rawlins); *Mexican Spitfire's Baby* (Leslie Goodwins); *Playmates* (David Butler); *Honolulu Lu* (Charles Barton); **1942:** *Mexican Spitfire at Sea* (Leslie Goodwins); *Mexican Spitfire Sees a Ghost* (Leslie Goodwins); *Mexican Spitfire's Elephant* (Leslie Goodwins); **1943:** *Ladie's Day* (Leslie Goodwins); *Redhead From Manhattan* (Lew Landers); *Mexican Spitfire's Blessed Event* (Leslie Goodwins); *Naná* (Celestino Gorostiza, in Mexico).

Carlos VELO

Born in Cartelle (Galicia, Spain), 15 November 1909; died in Mexico City, 10 March 1988. A biologist by training, Velo began to direct short documentaries with Fernando G. Mantilla in 1935. Forced into exile by the civil war, he arrived in Mexico in 1939. He directed the newsreel EMA (1941–51), and became an associate of Manuel Barbachano Ponce in Teleproducciones (1953), where he fulfilled various functions (director, editor, etc.)

for the newsreel series *Tele-Revista, Cine-Verdad, Cámara* and *Cine-Selecciones*. He also worked as an editor and technical adviser on *Raíces* (Benito Alazraki, 1953). In 1956 he directed the semi-documentary *¡Torero!* and made some forays into commercial film-making in the mid-60s. He was appointed director of short film production at the Churubusco studios in 1971, where he made several documentaries. In 1975, he became head of the newly created Centro de Capacitación Cinematográfica (CCC).

Filmography 1935–6: *Almadrabas; La ciudad y el campo; Infinitos; Felipe II y El Escorial; Santiago de Compostela; Castillos de Castilla; Yebala; Galicia Saudade* (short films directed in Spain with Fernando G. Mantilla); **1936:** *Romancero marroquí* (in Spain); **1956:** *¡Torero!;* **1958:** *Chistelandia; Nueva Chistelandia, ¡Vuelve Chistelandia!* (humorous compilations of *Tele-Revista* footage; co-d Manuel Barbachano Ponce, Jomí García Ascot and Fernando Marcos); **1966:** *Pedro Páramo; Don Juan 67;* **1967:** *Cinco de chocolate y uno de fresa;* **1969:** *Alguien nos quiere matar;* **1970:** *El medio pelo;* **1971:** *Los que sí y los que no* (doc); **1972:** *El rumbo que hemos elegido* (doc); *Cartas de Japón* (doc); **1973:** *A la mitad del camino* (doc); **1974:** *Baja California: último paraíso* (doc); **1975:** *Baja California, paralelo 28* (doc); **1983:** *El pueblo maya* (doc); **1984:** *Cambio* (TV series).

Ariel ZÚÑIGA

Born in Mexico City in 1947. The son of the sculptor and engraver Francisco Zúñiga, Ariel studied art history at the Sorbonne and film-making in workshops at IDHEC (Paris) and at the Centro Universitario de Estudios Cinematográficos (CUEC). He subsequently worked as an assistant or cameraman for independent productions such as Paul Leduc's *Reed: México insurgente* (1971).

Filmography 1973: *Fundición a la cera perdida* (short doc); **1974:** *Apuntes;* **1976:** *Con el sudor de tu frente no comerás* (Short); *Aquí y allá* (doc); *Juegos deportivos anuales del INPI* (short doc); **1977:** *Tentativa 1: de la escultura de Francisco Zúñiga* (short doc); **1978:** *Anacrusa o de cómo la música viene después del silencio;* **1981:** *Uno entre muchos o una anécdota subterránea* (co-d Alberto Cortés); **1983:** *El diablo y la dama o El itinerario del odio;* **1989:** *Una moneda en el aire.*

Mexican Feature Film Production: 1906–91

Eduardo de la Vega Alfaro

Year of Production	Films	Year of Production	Films	Year of Production	Films	Year of Production	Films
1906	1	1931	2	1952	98	1973	69
1909	2	1932	6	1953	83	1974	65
1910	1	1933	21	1954	118	1975	59
1911	1	1934	23	1955	89	1976	56
1914	2	1935	22	1956	99	1977	77
1915	1	1936	25	1957	102	1978	107
1916	3	1937	38	1958	136	1979	113
1917	17	1938	57	1959	114	1980	107
1918	6	1939	38	1960	114	1981	97
1919	14	1940	29	1961	71	1982	87
1920	7	1941	37	1962	81	1983	91
1921	22	1942	47	1963	83	1984	68
1922	15	1943	70	1964	109	1985	89
1923	7	1944	75	1965	107	1986	76
1924	4	1945	82	1966	100	1987	88
1925	13	1946	72	1967	91	1988	74
1926	10	1947	58	1968	110	1989	100
1927	9	1948	81	1969	89	1990	52
1928	7	1949	108	1970	93	1991	34
1929	7	1950	125	1971	87		
1930	5	1951	101	1972	89		

Sources

Emilio García Riera, *Filmografía mexicana de medio y largometrajes, 1906–1940* (Mexico City: Cineteca Nacional, 1985) and his *Historia del cine mexicano* (Mexico City: SEP/Foro 2000, 1986); Nelson Carro, 'El cine mexicano de los ochenta: ante el cadáver de un difunto' in *Dicine* (Mexico City), no. 33 (March 1990). Nevertheless, the figures for the periods 1906–30 and 1980–91 are only approximate.

Bibliography

Paulo Antonio Paranaguá

This bibliography does not claim to be exhaustive. It excludes all titles referring to Luis Buñuel, since these are readily available elsewhere. It also omits most ephemera and reviews as well as publications in periodicals, with the exception of some monographs and dossiers. We thank the archivists and librarians at the Filmoteca of the Universidad Nacional Autónoma de Mexico (UNAM), of the Cineteca Nacional and the Centro de Investigaciones y Enseñanza Cinematográficas (CIEC) of the University of Guadalajara.

Almoina, Helena, *Notas para la historia del cine en México* (Mexico City: Filmoteca UNAM, 1980).
– *Bibliografía del cine mexicano* (Mexico City: Filmoteca UNAM, 1985).
– *Hacia una bibliografía en castellano del cine* (Mexico City: SEP/INBA/UNAM, 1988).

Alvarez Bravo, Manuel, et al., *Paul Strand, Ned Scott: Redes, 32 fotocuprigrafías* (Mexico City: Filmoteca UNAM, 1982).

Amador, Maria Luisa and Jorge Ayala Blanco, *Cartelera cinematográfica 1930–1939* (Mexico City: Filmoteca UNAM, 1980); id., *1940–1949* (Mexico City: CUEC/UNAM, 1982); id., *1950–1959;* id., *1985;* id., *1960–1969;* id., 1986; id., *1970–1979;* id., *1988.*

Anduiza Valdelamar, Virgilio, *Legislación cinematográfica mexicana* (Mexico City: Filmoteca UNAM, 1983).

Anuario de la producción cinematográfica mexicana, 1970 (Mexico City: Procinemex, 1970); id., *1971, 1972, 1973, 1974, 1975, 1976, 1977.*

Anuario 1963 (Mexico City: Departamento de Actividades Cinematográficas, UNAM, 1963); id., *1964, 1965, 1966–1967.*

Arai, Alberto T., *Voluntad cinematográfica: Ensayo para una estética del cine* (Mexico City: Cultura, 1937).

Arau, Alfonso, Juan de la Cabada, Eduardo del Río (Rius) and Héctor Ortega, *Calzonzín inspector* (Mexico City: Dix, 1974).

Arguelles, Hugo and Francisco del Villar, *La primavera de los escorpiones* (Mexico City: Novaro, 1973).

Arieles, Los, *50 años del cine sonoro mexicano* (Mexico City: 1981).

Ayala Blanco, Jorge, Gustavo García and Carlos Monsiváis, *Dolores del Río* (Huelva: Festival de Cine Iberoamericano, 1983).
– *La aventura del cine mexicano* (Mexico City: Era, 1968); 3rd edition (Mexico City: Posada, 1985).
– *La búsqueda del cine mexicano* (Mexico City: UNAM, 1974); 2nd edition (Mexico City: Posada, 1986).
– *La condición del cine mexicano* (Mexico City: Posada, 1986).
– *La disolvencia del cine mexicano, entre lo popular y lo exquisito* (Mexico City: Grijalbo, 1991).

Balzaretti, Lucila and Jaime Valdés, *Album de estrellas* (Mexico City: Ediciones Cinematográficas, 1943).

Barbachano H., Francisco and Miguel Barbachano Ponce, *Epoca de oro del cine mexicano* (Mexico City: CLASA Films Mundiales, 1986).

Barbachano Ponce, Miguel, *Críticas* (Mexico City: Cineteca Nacional, 1988).

Bohr, José, *Desde el balcón de mi vida* (Buenos Aires: Sudamericana/Planeta, Aires, 1987).
– *¡Luz! ¡Cámara! ¡Acción!* (Santiago de Chile: Pacífico, 1976).

Burdin, Henry, *La Mexicaine: María Félix, le roman d'une vie* (Paris: Encre, 1982).

Bustillo Oro, Juan, *Vida cinematográfica* (Mexico City: Cineteca Nacional, 1984).

Cabada, Juan de la, *El brazo fuerte* (Xalapa: Universidad Veracruzana, 1963); id. (Culiacán: Universidad Autónoma de Sinaloa, 1980).
– *Raíces/Simitrio* (Culiacán: Universidad Autónoma de Sinaloa, 1981). Cámara Nacional de la Industria Cinematográfica, 1942–l976 (Mexico City, s.d.).

Cardero, Ana María, *Diccionario de términos cinematográficos usados en México* (Mexico City: UNAM, 1989).

Carro, Nelson, *El cine de luchadores* (Mexico City: Filmoteca UNAM, 1984).

Casas, Alfonso, Sergio Díaz González, Fernando Montes de Oca and Martha Vidrio, *Guiones 1987*

(Guadalajara: CIEC, 1989).

Castelazo, Javier, *Cantinflas: Apología de un humilde* (Mexico City: Paralelo, s.d.).
– *Los tres mosqueteros de la canción mexicana: Javier, Jorge y Pedro* (Mexico City: Liverpool, 1976).

Castro Leal, Antonio, *El libro de oro del cine mexicano* (Mexico City: Comisión Nacional de Cinematografía, 1949).

Catálogo de ejercicios fílmicos escolares (Mexico City: CUEC–UNAM, 1989).

Cazals, Felipe, Carlos Fuentes and Jose Iturriaga, *Aquellos años* (Mexico City: Comisión Nacional para la Conmemoración del Centenario del Fallecimiento de Don Benito Juárez, 1972).

Centro Universitario de Estudios Cinematográficos, *1974–1980* (Mexico City: UNAM, s.d.).

Cinema Messicano: Il 'Frente Nacional de Cinematografistas' (Pesaro: Mostra Internazionale del Nuovo Cinema, 1976).

'Cinéma mexicain, Le', *Positif* (Paris), no. 10, 1954.

'Cine mexicano, ayer y hoy', *Revista de la Universidad de México,* (Mexico City), vol. 26 no. 10, June 1972.

Cineteca Nacional, *Mexico 1974* (annually until 1982), then *Memoria 1982* until 1989.

'Cine y la Revolución mexicana, El', *Filmoteca,* (UNAM, Mexico City), no. 1, November 1979.

Colina, José de la, *Miradas al cine* (Mexico City: SEP, 1972).
– *Emilio Indio Fernández* (Huelva: Festival de Cine Iberoamericano, 1984).

Comisión de Estudio y Asesoría del Anteproyecto de la Nueva Ley Federal de Cinematografía, *Memoria de trabajos* (Mexico City: RTC, 1982).

Contreras Torres, Miguel, *El libro negro del cine mexicano* (Mexico City: Hispano-Continental Films, 1960).

Contreras Y Espinosa, Fernando, *La producción: Sector primario de la industria cinematográfica* (Mexico City: UNAM, 1973).

Cordero, Joaquín, *Anécdotas de un actor* (Mexico City: Diana, 1990).

Costa, Paola, *La 'apertura' cinematográfica, México 1970–1976* (Puebla: Universidad Autónoma de Puebla, 1983).

Custodio, Alvaro, *Notas sobre el cine* (Mexico City: Patria, 1952).

Davalos Orozco, Federico and Esperanza Vázquez Bernal, *Filmografía general del cine mexicano (1906–1931)* (Puebla: Universidad Autónoma de Puebla, 1985).

Delly, W., *Vida y amores de Ramón Novarro* (Buenos Aires: Liverpool, 1931).

Demicheli Tarpin, Humberto, *Guía mexicana del espectáculo* (Mexico City: Magic Films, 1982).

Domínguez Aragonés, Edmundo, *Tres extraordinarios: Spota, Jodorowsky, El Indio Fernández* (Mexico City: Juan Pablos, 1980).

Echeverría Alvarez, Rodolfo, *'72 informe general* (Mexico City: Banco Nacional Cinematográfico, 1973); *'73,* id., 1974; *'74* id., 1975; *'75* id., 1976; *1976 cineinforme general,* id., 1976.

Eder, Klaus, *Arturo Ripstein: Filmemacher aus Mexico* (Munich: Filmfest, 1989).

Eisenstein, S.M., *Dibujos mexicanos inéditos* (Mexico City: Cineteca Nacional, 1978).
– *¡Que Viva México!* (London: Vision Press, 1951); *¡Que viva Mexico!* (Mexico City: Era, 1964); id., 1971.

Espino, Fidel Angel, *Clavillazo: Cuando las manos hablaron* (Mexico City: Diana, 1989). *Estudios America, S.A.* (Mexico City, s.d.).

Félix Romandia, Cristina and Jorge Larson Guerra, *El cartel cinematográfico mexicano* (Mexico City: Cineteca Nacional, 1987).

Fernández, Adela, *El Indio Fernández, vida y mito* (Mexico City: Panorama, 1988).

Fernández Cuenca, Carlos, *Homenaje a Emilio Fernández* (San Sebastian: IX Festival Internacional del Cine, 1961).

Fernández Violante, Marcela, *La docencia y el fenómeno fílmico: Memoria de los XXV años del CUEC, 1963–88* (Mexico City: UNAM, 1988).

Figueroa Perea, Maricarmen and Ernesto Román, 'Premios y distinciones otorgados al cine mexicano: festivales internacionales, 1938–1984', *Documentos de investigación,* no. 3 (Mexico City: Cineteca Nacional, 1986).

Flores García, Alejandro, *Cinecompendio 1971–1972* (Mexico City: A. Posta, 1973); *1972–1973,* id., 1974; *1973–1974,* id., 1975; *1974–1975.* id., 1976.

Franco Sodja, Carlos, *Lo que me dijo Pedro Infante* (Mexico City: Edamex, 1977).

Fuente, María Isabel de la, *Indice bibliográfico del cine mexicano (1930–1965)* (Mexico City: Author's edition, 1967); id., *1966–1967,* id., *1968.*

Fuentes, Carlos, *Orquídeas a la luz de la luna: Comedia mexicana* (Barcelona: Seix Barral, 1982).

Fuentes Navarro, Raúl, *La investigación de comunicación en méxico: Sistematización documental 1956–1986* (Mexico City: Comunicación, 1988).

Fundación Mexicana de Cineastas, *Hojas de cine: Testimonios y documentos del nuevo cine latinoamericano,* vol. 2, *México* (Mexico City: SEP/Universidad Autónoma Metropolitana, 1988).

Galindo, Alejandro, *Una radiografía histórica del cine mexicano* (Mexico City: Fondo de Cultura Popular, 1968).
– *El cine, genocidio espiritual* (Mexico: Nuestro Tiempo, 1971).
– *Verdad y mentira del cine mexicano* (Mexico City: Aconcagua, 1978); id. (Mexico City: Katún, 1981).
– *El cine mexicano, un personal punto de vista* (Mexico City: Edamex, 1985).

Garcia Canclini, Nestor (ed.), *Los nuevos espectadores: Cine, televisión y video en México* (Mexico City: IMCINE, 1994).

García Riera, Emilio, *El cine mexicano* (Mexico City: Era, 1963).
– *El cine y su público* (Mexico City: Fondo de Cultura Económica, 1974).
– *Il Cinema Messicano nel 1936, Il Cinema Messicano di Oggi 1976* (Venice: La Biennale, 1976).
– *Historia documental del cine mexicano: Epoca sonora,* 9 vols. (Mexico City: Era, 1969–78).
– et al., 'Mexique', *Les cinémas de l'Amérique latine* (Paris: Pierre Lherminier, 1981).
– and Gustavo García, *El cine mexicano en documentos* (Mexico City: CCC/CUEC/CEC, 1981–2).
– and Gustavo García, *El cine mudo mexicano* (Mexico: SEP/Martín Casillas, 1982).
– and Fernando Macotela, *La guía del cine mexicano* (Mexico City: Patria, 1984).
– *Fernando de Fuentes* (Mexico City: Cineteca Nacional, 1984).
– *Filmografía mexicana de medio y largo metrajes, 1906–1940* (Mexico City: Cineteca Nacional, 1985).
– *Historia del cine mexicano* (Mexico City: SEP/Foro 2000, 1986).
– *Julio Bracho* (Guadalajara: CIEC, 1986).
– *Emilio Fernández* (Guadalajara/Mexico City: ClEC/Cineteca Nacional, 1987).
– and Gustavo García, *La década perdida: Imagen 24x1* (Mexico City: Universidad Autónoma Metropolitana/Azcapotzalco, 1987).
– *Arturo Ripstein habla de su cine* (Guadalajara: CIEC, 1988).
– *El cine es mejor que la vida* (Mexico: Cal y Arena, 1990).
– *México visto por el cine extranjero,* 6 vols. (Mexico City: Guadalajara: Era/ClEC, 1987–90).
– *Los hermanos Soler* (Guadalajara: CIEC/IMCINE, 1990).
– *Historia documental del cine mexicano* (Mexico City/Guadalajara: Cal y Arena/Universidad de Guadalajara, 1992–).

García, Sergio, *Hacia el 4º cine* (Zacatecas: Universitaria, 1973).

García Tsao, Leonardo, *Felipe Cazals habla de su cine* (Guadalajara: CIEC, 1994).

Garmabella, Jose Ramón, Pedro Vargas, *'Una vez nada mas'* (Mexico City: Comunicación, 1985).

Gasca, Luis, *Dolores del Río* (San Sebastian: XXIV Festival Internacional de Cine, 1976).

Gavaldón, Roberto and José Revueltas, *La otra* (Mexico City: Comisión Nacional de Cinematografía, 1949).

Geduld, Harry M. and Ronald Gottesman (eds.), *Sergei Eisenstein and Upton Sinclair: The Making and Unmaking of ¡Que Viva México!* (Bloomington, Indiana: Indiana University Press, 1970).

Giménez Caballero, Ernesto, *Amor a México (A través de su cine)* (Madrid: Seminario de Problemas Hispanoamericanos, 1948).

Godoy, Alberto L., *Directorio Cinematográfico Internacional de México, 1938–39* (Mexico City: Jack Starr-Hunt, 1939).

Gomezjara, Francisco A. and Raúl Martínez Merling, *Praxis Cinematográfica: Teoría y técnica* (Mexico City/Querétaro: Nueva Sociología/Universidad Autónoma de Queretaro, 1988).

González Casanova, Manuel, *Crónica del cine silente en México* (Mexico City: UNAM, 1989).

Guerrero Suárez, Jorge, *El cine sonoro mexicano: Sus inicios (1930–1937)* (Mexico City: Cuadernos de la Cineteca Nacional no. 8, 1978).

– *Dolores del Río: La vocación de la belleza* (Mexico City: Author's edition, 1979).

Guzmán, Martín Luis, Federico de Onis and Alfonso Reyes, *Frente a la pantalla* (Mexico City: UNAM, 1963).

Hennebelle-Martineau, Monique, *Aspects du cinéma mexicain, hier et aujourd'hui* (Paris: INRP/CNDP, 1989).

Hermosillo, Jaime Humberto, *La pasión según Berenice* (Mexico City: Katún, 1981).
– *La tarea* (Mexico City: Sitesa, 1991).

Heuer, Federico, *La industria cinematográfica mexicana* (Mexico City: Author's edition, 1964).

'Homenaje al cine mexicano', *Vogue* (Mexico) Year 8, no. 90, November 1987.

Homenaje a los iniciadores del cine en México (1896–1938) (Mexico City: Cuadernos de la Cineteca Nacional no. 9, 1979).

Iglesias, Norma, *La visión de la frontera a través del cine mexicano* (Tijuana: Centro de Estudios Fronterizos del Norte de México, 1985).

Isaac, Alberto, *Conversaciones con Gabriel Figueroa* (Guadalajara: CIEC, 1993).

Jablonska, Aleksandra and Juan Felipe Leal, *La revolución mexicana en el cine nacional: Filmografía 1911–1917* (Mexico City: Universidad Pedagógica Nacional, 1991).

Jiménez Cara, Roberto, *Bibliografía de tesis sobre cine* (Mexico City: Documentos de Investigación no. 1, Cineteca Nacional, 1985).

Jodorowsky, Alejandro, El Topo: *Fábula pánica con imágenes* (Mexico City: Novaro, 1970);
– El Topo: *A Book of the Film* (New York/London: Douglas Links, 1971).

Karetnikova, Inga, *Mexico According to Eisenstein* (Albuquerque: University of New Mexico Press, 1991).

King, John, Ana M. López and Manuel Alvarado, *Mediating Two Worlds: Cinematic Encounters in the Americas* (London: BFI, 1993).

Krohn, J.L., *La vida novelesca de Ramón Novarro* (Buenos Aires: Tor, s.d.).

Lamarque, Libertad, *Autobiografía* (Buenos Aires: Javier Vergara, 1986).

Lapena, Alfonso and Miguel Zacarías, *Me he de comer esa tuna* (Mexico City: Albatros, Mexico, s.d.).

Larson Guerra, Samuel, *Análisis de publicaciones periódicas sobre cine: Nuevo Cine, Cine Club, Otro Cine, Octubre* (Mexico City: Documentos de Investigación no. 2, Cineteca Nacional, 1986).

Leduc, Paul and José Joaquín Blanco, *Frida: naturaleza viva* (Puebla: Universidad Autónoma de Puebla, 1992).
– and Juan Tovar, *Reed: México insurgente* (Puebla: Universidad Autónoma de Puebla, 1992).

Leñero, Vicente, *Tres guiones cinematográficos:* Magnicidio, Los albañiles, Cadena perpetua (Mexico City: Marcha, 1982).
– and José Revueltas, Los albañiles: *Un guión rechazado* (Mexico City: Premiá, 1983).

Ley y reglamento de la industria cinematográfica (Mexico City: Secretaría de Gobernación, 1966).

Lillo, Gastón, 'El melodrama mexicano', *Archivos de la Filmoteca* (Valencia) no. 16, February 1994.

Lombardo Toledano, Vicente, *Cine, arte y sociedad* (Mexico City: UNAM, 1989).

López-Vallejo y García, Maria Luisa, 'Archivo del cine nacional', *Cine* (Mexico City), nos. 1–29, 1978–80.

Luna, Andrés de, *La batalla y su sombra: La Revolución en el cine mexicano* (Mexico City: Universidad Autónoma Metropolitana/Xochimilco, 1984).

María Félix [Preface by Octavio Paz], (Mexico City: Cineteca Nacional/RTC/Dirección General de Comunicación Social de la Presidencia de la Republica, 1992).

Martínez Gandia, Rafael, *Dolores del Río: La triunfadora* (Madrid/Barcelona/Buenos Aires: Compañía Iberoamericana de Publicaciones, 1930).

Martínez Tames, Héctor, *Breve historia del cine mexicano* (Mexico City: Delegación Venustiano Carranza, 1983).

Méndez Berman, León and Santos Mar, *El embrollo cinematográfico* (Mexico City: Cooperación, 1953).

Meyer, Eugenia, *Testimonios para la historia del cine mexicano* (Mexico City: Cuadernos de la Cineteca Nacional nos. 1–7, 1975–6).

Michel, Manuel, *El cine y el hombre contemporáneo* (Xalapa: Universidad Veracruzana, 1962).
– *Al pie de la imagen: Críticas y ensayos* (Mexico City: UNAM, 1968).

Miguel, Angel, *El nacimiento de una pasión: Luis G. Urbina, primer cronista mexicano de cine* (Mexico City: Universidad Pedagógica Nacional, 1991).
– *Los exaltados: Antología de escritos sobre cine en periódicos y revistas de la ciudad de México, 1896–1929* (Guadalajara: CIEC, 1992)

Millán Nava, Jesús, *Alma nacional: Treinta argumentos cinematográficos* (Mexico City: Botas, 1947).

Mojica, O.F.M., *Fray José Francisco de Guadalupe, yo pecador* (Mexico City: Jus, 1956).

Monsiváis, Carlos, *Escenas de pudor y liviandad* (Mexico City: Grijalbo, 1981).
– and Carlos Bonfil, *A través del espejo: El cine mexicano y su público* (Mexico City: El Milagro/IMCINE, 1994).

Monroy, Alberto, *Guía oficial del cine en méxico, 1943–44* (Mexico City, [1945]).

Mora, Carl J., *Mexican Cinema: Reflections of a Society, 1896–1980* (Berkeley: University of California Press, 1982).

Moral, Fernando Del and Federico Serrano, *Guiones clásicos del cine mexicano:* El automóvil gris (Mexico City: Cuadernos de la Cineteca Nacional no. 10, 1981).

Morales, Miguel Angel, *Cómicos de México* (Mexico City: Panorama, 1987).

Murillo, Alfonso and Antonio Suárez Guillén, *Anuario cinematográfico latinoamericano 1946–47* (Mexico City, 1947).

Negrete, Diana, *Jorge Negrete: Biografía autorizada* (Mexico City: Diana, 1987).

Noriega, Chon and Steve Ricci (eds.), *The Mexican Cinema Project* (Los Angeles: UCLA Film and Television Archives, 1994).

Noriega Hope, Carlos, *El mundo de las sombras: El cine por fuera y por dentro* (Mexico City: Andrés Botas e Hijo, s.d.).

Olea, Antonio J., *El cine gráfico: Anuario 1942–43* (Mexico City); *1944–45; 1945–1946 y 1947; 1950.*

Orellana, Margarita de, *La mirada circular: El cine norteamericano de la Revolución mexicana* (Mexico City: Joaquín Mortiz, 1991).

Ortega, Carmen Patricia and Jorge Prior, *Diagnóstico del cine mexicano* (Mexico City: Universidad Autónoma Metropolitana/Xochimilco, 1985).

Pacheco, José Emilio and Arturo Ripstein, *El castillo de la pureza* (Mexico City: Novaro, 1973).
– *El Santo Oficio* (Culiacán: Universidad Autónoma de Sinaloa, 1980).

Paez Varela, Alejandro, *Tin Tan: La historia de un genio sin lámpara* (Ciudad Juarez: Estado de Chihuahua, 1990).

Paranaguá, Paulo Antonio and Alberto Ruy Sánchez, *Semaine nationale du cinéma mexicain* (Locarno: Festival International du Film, 1982).
– *Cinema na América Latina: Longe de Deus e perto de Hollywood* (Porto Alegre: L&PM, 1985).
– *Le Cinéma mexicain* (Paris: Centre Georges Pompidou, 1992).
– 'Dossier: Le Mélo', *Cinémas d'Amérique Latine,* no. 1, Toulouse, 1993.

Pelayo, Alejandro, *La víspera* (Puebla: Universidad Autónoma de Puebla, 1984).

Peralta, Elda, *La epoca de oro sin nostalgia: Luis Spota en el cine* (Mexico City: Grijalbo, 1989).

Perea, Héctor, *La caricia de las formas: Alfonso Reyes y el cine* (Mexico City: Universidad Autónoma Metropolitana, 1988).

Pérez, Ismael Diego, *Cantinflas: Genio del humor y del absurdo* (Mexico City: Indo-Hispana, 1954).

Pérez Turrent, Tomás, *Luis Alcoriza* (Huelva: Semana de Cine Iberoamericano, 1977).
– et al., *Rafael Corkidi* (Mexico City: RTC, 1978).
– Canoa: *Memoria de un hecho vergonzoso, la historia, la filmación, el guión* (Puebla: Universidad Autónoma de Puebla, 1984).
– *Anuario cinematográfico '84* (Mexico City: Filmoteca UNAM, 1985).
– *La fabrica de sueños: Estudios Churubusco, 1945–1985* (Mexico City: IMCINE, 1985).

Pina, Francisco, *Praxinoscopio* (Mexico City: UNAM, 1970).

Pineda Alcalá, Francisco, *La verídica historia del cine mexicano* (Mexico City: Author's edition, 1965).

Poniatowska, Elena, *Todo México* (Mexico City: Diana, 1990).

[Portas, Rafael. E. and Ricardo Rangel], *Enciclopedia cinematográfica mexicana, 1897–1955* (Mexico City: Publicaciones Cinematográficas, 1957).

Pulido Islas, Alfonso, *La industria cinematográfica de México* (Mexico City: México Nuevo, 1939).

Quiroz, Alberto, *Nociones de estética cinematográfica*

(con ejemplos mexicanos) (Mexico City: 1942).

Ramírez, Gabriel, *El cine Yucateco* (Mexico City: Filmoteca UNAM, 1980).
– *Lupe Vélez:La mexicana que escupía fuego* (Mexico City: Cineteca Nacional, 1986).
– *Crónica del cine mudo mexicano* (Mexico City: Cineteca Nacional, 1989).
– *Miguel Contreras Torres* (Guadalajara: CIEC, 1994).

Ramírez Berg, Charles, *Cinema of Solitude: A Critical Study of Mexican Films, 1967–1983* (Austin: University of Texas Press, 1992).

Ramón, David, *La Santa de Orson Welles* (Mexico City: UNAM/Cineteca Nacional, 1991).
– *Sensualidad: Las películas de Ninón Sevilla* (Mexico City: UNAM, 1989).
– and María Luisa Amador, *80 años de cine en México* (Mexico City: UNAM, 1977).

Reachi, Santiago, *La Revolución, Cantinflas y Jolopo* (Mexico City: Edamex, 1982).

Reseña de las Reseñas, (Mexico City: Cineteca Nacional, 1987).

Revueltas, José, *El conocimiento cinematográfico y sus problemas* (Mexico City: UNAM, 1965); id. (Mexico City: Era, 1981).
– *Tierra y Libertad: Guión cinematográfico* (Mexico City: Era, 1981).

Revueltas, Rosaura, *Los Revueltas (Biografía de una familia)* (Mexico City: Grijalbo, 1980).

Reyes, Aurelio de los, *Cine y sociedad en México, 1896–1930,* vol.1, *Vivir de sueños (1896–1920)* (Mexico City: UNAM, 1980).
– *Los orígenes del cine en México* (1896–1900) (Mexico City: UNAM, 1973; also Mexico City: Fondo de Cultura Económica/SEP, 1984.
– *Con Villa en México: Testimonios de los camarógrafos norteamericanos en la Revolución* (Mexico City: UNAM, 1985).
– *Filmografía del cine mudo mexicano 1896–1920* (Mexico City: Filmoteca UNAM, 1986).
– *Medio siglo de cine mexicano (1986–1947)* (Mexico City: Trillas, 1987).
– *Manuel Gamio y el cine* (Mexico City: UNAM, 1991).

Reyes de la Maza, Luis, *Salón Rojo* (Mexico City: UNAM, 1973).

Reyes Nevares, Beatriz, *Trece directores del cine mexicano* (Mexico City: SEP, 1974); *The Mexican Cinema: Interviews with Thirteen Directors* (Albuquerque: University of New Mexico Press, 1976).

Rovirosa, José, *Miradas a la realidad: Ocho entrevistas a documentalistas mexicanos* (Mexico City: CUEC/UNAM, 1990).

Rozado, Alejandro, *Cine y realidad social en México: Una lectura de la obra de Emilio Fernández* (Gaudalajara: CIEC, 1991).

Rulfo, Juan, *El gallo de oro y otros textos para cine* (Mexico City: Era, 1980); id. (Madrid: Era/Alianza, Madrid, 1982).

Ruy Sánchez, Alberto, *Mitología de un cine en crisis* (Mexico City: Premiá, 1981).
– 'El arte de Gabriel Figueroa', *Artes de México,* no. 2, winter 1988.
– 'Revisión del cine mexicano', *Artes de México,* no. 10, winter 1990.
– *Gabriel Figueroa: Dueño de la luz* (Valladolid: 37 Semana de Cine, 1992).

Sánchez, Francisco, *Crónica antisolemne del cine mexicano* (Xalapa: Universidad Veracruzana, 1989).
– *Hermosillo: Pasión por la Libertad* (Mexico City: RTC, 1989).

Sánchez García, José María, *Maria Félix: Mujer y artista* (Mexico City: Netzahualcoyotl, 1949).

Sarriá Villegas, Efraín, *María Félix* (Huelva: VI Festival de Cine Iberoamericano, 1980).

Saucedo, María Elena, *María Félix en pantuflas* (Mexico City: Excélsior, 1948).

Segura, Alfonso, *El cine en México* (Mexico City: Barón de Segurola, 1938).

Taibo I, Paco Ignacio, *Siempre Dolores* (Mexico City: Planeta, 1984).
– *La música de Agustín Lara en el cine* (Mexico City: Filmoteca UNAM, 1984).
– *El Indio Fernández: El cine por mis pistolas* (Mexico City: Joaquín Mortiz/Planeta, 1986).
– *María Félix: 47 pasos por el cine* (Mexico City: Joaquín Mortiz/Planeta, 1985); id., 1986 and 1987.
– *Los toros en el cine mexicano* (Mexico City: Plaza y Valdés/NBA/Sociicultur, 1987).
– *Gloria y achaques del espectáculo en México* (Mexico City: Leega/Júcar, 1988).
– *El Indio Fernández* (Mexico City: Planeta, 1991).
– *La Doña* (Mexico City: Planeta, 1991 and 1992).

Tapia Campos, Martha Laura, *La dramática del mar en el cine mexicano* (Mexico City: Ciencias de la Comunicación no. 3, UNAM, 1989).

Toledo, Teresa, *10 años del nuevo cine latinoamericano* (Madrid: Verdoux/Quinto Centenario/CI, 1990).

Torres Bodet, Jaime, *La cinta de plata (Crónica cinematográfica)* (Mexico City: UNAM, 1986).

Torres San Martín, Patricia, *Crónicas tapatías del cine mexicano* (Guadalajara: Universidad de Guadalajara, 1993).
– and Eduardo de la Vega Alfaro, *Adela Sequeyro* (Guadalajara: CIEC, 1995).

Tuñón, Julia, *Historia de un sueño: El Hollywood tapatío* (Guadalajara: CIEC/UNAM, 1986).
– *En su propio espejo (Entrevista con Emilio 'el Indio' Fernández)* (Mexico City: Universidad Autónoma Metropolitana/Iztapalapa, 1988.

Vaidovits, Guillermo, *El cine mudo en Guadalajara* (Guadalajara: CIEC, 1989).

Vega Alfaro, Eduardo de la, *El cine de Juan Orol* (Mexico City: Filmoteca UNAM, 1985).
– *Juan Orol* (Guadalajara: CIEC, 1987).
– *Alberto Gout* (Mexico City: Cineteca Nacional, 1988).
– *El primer cine sonoro mexicano: Siete décadas de cine mexicano* (Mexico City: Filmoteca UNAM, s.d.).
– *Raúl de Anda* (Guadalajara: CIEC, 1989).
– *La industria cinematográfica mexicana: Perfil histórico social* (Guadalajara: Universidad de Guadalajara, 1991).
– *Arcady Boytler* (Guadalajara: CIEC/IMCINE, 1992).
– *Gabriel Soria* (Guadalajara: CIEC/IMCINE, 1992).
– *José Bohr* (Guadalajara: CIEC, 1992).
– *Fernando Méndez* (Guadalajara: CIEC, 1995).

Veronneau, Pierre, *Mexique: cinéma d'hier et d'aujourd'hui* (Montreal: La Cinémathèque Québecoise, 1974).

Villatoro, Angel, *Anuario cinematográfico latinoamericano* (Mexico City: ACLA, 1942).
– *Hablando con las estrellas* (Mexico City: ACLA, 1945).

Villaurrutia, Xavier, *Crítica cinematográfica* (Mexico City: UNAM, 1970).

Viñas, Moisés, *Historia del cine mexicano* (Mexico City: UNAM, 1987).

Zavala, Lauro, *Material inflamable: Reseñas y crítica cinematográfica* (Mexico City: Universidad Autónoma Metropolitana/Xochimilco, 1989).

Zúñiga, Ariel, *Vasos comunicantes en la obra de Roberto Gavaldón* (Mexico City: El Equilibrista, 1990).

Specialised publications, unless otherwise indicated, all published in Mexico City:

Cámara (1978–89), *Cartel* (1947–8), *Celulóide* (1946), *Cine* (1938–9), *Cine* (1978–80), *Cine Album* (1959–65), *Cine-Arte* (1986–91), *Cine Avance* (1963–70), *Cine Club* (1955), *Cine-Club* (Guadalajara, 1960), *Cine Club* (1970–1), *Cinecompendio* (1973), *Cine Continental* (1945), *Cine en Video* (1991–), *Cinéfilo* (1975–6), *El Cine Gráfico* (1932–54), *Cinelandia* (1956–76), *Cinema* (1978), *Cinema Reporter* (1938–65), *Cinema, Teatro, TV* (1984–8), *Cinemateca* (1972–3), *Cine Mex* (1959–62), *Cine Mexicano* (1943–55), *Cine Montaje* (1966), *Cine Mundial* (1953–), *Cine Novelas* (1959–64), *CinEstudio* (1965), *Cinerama* (Guadalajara, 1964–7), *Cineteca Nacional* (1984–), *Cine Universal* (1956–68), *Cinevoz* (1948–9), *Diario Fílmico Mexicano* (1943–4), *Dicine* (1983–), *Eco* (1947), *En Video* (1985–8), *Estrellas de Cinelandia* (1959–69), *Estrellita* (1947), *El Exhibidor* (1932–47), *Filmográfico* (1933–7), *Filmoteca* (1978), *Filmoteca* (1979–81), *Foto-Cine* (1961), *Foto-Film Cinemagazine* (1946), *Foto Guión* (1950–3), *Gaceta filmográfica de México* (1968–74), *Guía Cinematográfica* (1965–7), *Guía Cinematográfica* (Merida, 1956–90), *Imágenes* (1979–80), *Intolerancia* (1986–90), *México Cinema* (1942–59), *Mundo Cinematográfico* (1930–8), *Nitrato de Plata* (1990–), *Novelas de la Pantalla* (1940–62), *Novela Semanal Cinematográfica* (1939–57), *Nuestro Cine* (1971), *Nuevo Cine* (1961–2), *Octubre* (1974–80), *Otrocine* (1975–6), *La Pantalla* (1940–5), *Pantalla* (1985–), *Pantallas y Escenarios* (Guadalajara, 1936–45), *La Película* (1947), *Pel-Mex* [1977], *Primer Corte* [1979], *Primer Plano* (1981), *El Primer Plano* (1991), *Proyector* (1947), *El Reporte Cinematográfico* (Coahuila, 1989–90), *Revista Cinematográfica* (1964), *Saludos* (1948–58), *La Semana Cinematográfica* (1948–9), *La Semana en el Cine* (1962–6), *Séptimo Arte* (1957–62), *Set* (1942), *Set* (1973), *Sin aliento* (Morelia, 1984–5), *35mm* (1967–9), *VAM* (1947), *Vida Nueva*.

Contributors' Notes

Nelson Carro Rodríguez
(b. Montevideo, 1952) worked at the Uruguayan Cinémathèque and later at the Filmoteca of the Universidad Nacional Autónoma de México (UNAM). Has worked as a critic for *Unomásuno* (since 1977), *Imágenes* (1979–80) and *Tiempo Libre* (since 1980), and has been editor of the magazine *Dicine* since 1989. He is the author of *El cine de luchadores* (1984).

Gustavo García Gutiérrez
(b. Tuxtla-Gutiérrez, Chiapas, 1954) has worked as a critic for *Unomásuno* (1979–90), and taught at the school of Political and Social Sciences (UNAM), at the Universidad Autónoma Metropolitana/Xochimilco, and at the Centro Universitario de Estudios Cinematográficos (CUEC). He edits the cinema journal *Intolerancia* (1986), and is author of *El cine mudo mexicano* (1982) and *La década perdida* (1987).

Emilio García Riera
(b. Ibiza, Spain, 1931) has lived in Mexico since 1944 and was one of the founders of *Nuevo Cine* (1961–2). He pioneered and has continued to foster the historical study of the cinema. He edited *La Semana en el Cine* (1962–6), *Imágenes* (1979–80) and *Dicine* (1983). He teaches at CUEC, at the school of Political and Social Sciences (UNAM) and at the Centro de Capacitación Cinematográfica (CCC), and is director of the Centro de Investigación y Enseñanza Cinematográficas (CIEC) at Guadalajara. He has published many works, including *El cine checoslovaco* (UNAM, 1963), *El cine mexicano* (1963), *Historia documental del cine mexicano* (1969–78), *El cine y su público* (1974), *Fernando de Fuentes* (1984), *Historia del cine mexicano* (1986), *Julio Bracho* (1986), *México visto por el cine extranjero* (1987–90), *Emilio Fernández* (1987), *Erich von Stroheim* (CIEC, 1988), *Arturo Ripstein habla de su cine* (1988), *Howard Hawks* (CIEC, 1988), *Max Ophüls* (CIEC, 1988), *El cine es mejor que la vida* (1990, Xavier Villaurrutia award), *Los hermanos Soler* (1990), *Historia documental del cine mexicano* (1992). He is also the co-author of *La guía del cine mexicano* (1984).

Leonardo García Tsao
(b. Mexico City, 1954) is a critic for *Unomásuno, La Jornada* and *El Nacional,* and has written for *Film Comment, Cine, Imágenes* and *Dicine.* His published works include *Orson Welles* (CIEC, 1987), *François Truffaut* (CIEC, 1987), *Andrei Tarkovsky* (CIEC, 1988), *Como acercarse al cine* (Limusa, 1989), *Sam Peckinpah* (CIEC, 1990). He also wrote the screenplay for Dana Rotberg's *Intimidad* (1990).

Carmen Elisa Gómez Gómez
(b. Guadalajara, 1966) is a critic working at the CIEC.

Marco Ulises Iñiguez Mendoza
(b. Apatzingán, Michoacán, 1957) has worked at the CIEC since 1987.

Andrés de Luna
(b. Tampico, 1955) is a researcher at the Universidad Autónoma Metropolitana; he teaches at UNAM and is associated with the journal *Intolerancia.* Author of *La batalla y su sombra: la Revolución en el cine mexicano* (1984), *Martín Luis Guzmán* (1987), *Arnold Belkin* (1987), *Erótica: la otra orilla del deseo* (Grijalbo, 1992).

Rafael Medina de la Serna
(b. Mexico, 1953) is a critic for *Cine, Dicine, Epoca, El Nacional* and *El Universal.*

Carlos Monsiváis Aceves
(b. Mexico City, 1938) is an incisive polemicist and one of his generation's most important writers. A founder of *Nuevo Cine,* he has worked as the announcer on a specialised programme for *Radio Universidad* until 1972 and edited *La Cultura en México* (1972–87), an important cultural supplement published by the magazine *Siempre.* He has published extensively: *Antología de la poesía mexicana del siglo XX* (1966), *Principados y potestades* (1968), *Días de guardar* (1970), *Robert Lowell* (1975), *Amor perdido*

(1976), *A ustedes les consta* (1978), *Escenas de pudor y liviandad* (1981), *Nuevo catecismo para indios remisos* (1982), *Celia Montalván: Te brindas, voluptuosa e impudente* (1982), *De qué se ríe el licenciado* (1984), *Lo fugitivo permanece: Antología del cuento mexicano* (1985), *Confrontaciones* (1985), *Jorge Cuesta* (1986), *María Izquierdo* (1986), *Luis García Guerrero* (1987), *Entrada libre: Crónicas de la sociedad que se organiza* (1988), *José Chávez Morado* (1989), *El género epistolar* (1991).

Paulo Antonio Paranaguá

(b. Rio de Janeiro, 1948) worked as a journalist for *Journal do Brasil,* and later for Radio France Internationale (since 1982). A critic for *Positif* and *Framework* since 1977, he is the author of many works: *Cinema na América Latina* (1985), *Le Cinéma brésilien* (awarded the Prix littéraire de la critique de cinéma 1987), *Le Cinéma cubain* (1990), *A la découverte de l'Amérique Latine: Petite anthologie d'une école documentaire méconnue* (1992), the last three works all published by the Centre Georges Pompidou. He is the co-author of *Cinémas d'Amérique latine* (Lherminier, 1981), *La historia y el cine* (Fontamara, Barcelona, 1983), *Cinéma brésilien 1970–1980* (Festival de Locarno, 1983), *Dictionnaire du cinéma* (Larousse, 1986), *Cesare Zavattini* (Centre Pompidou, 1990); *Historia general del cine* (Madrid: Cátedra, 1995). He was awarded a Vitae Fellowship (Sao Paulo, 1990).

Rocío Pérez Solano

(b. Mexico City, 1964) has worked at the CIEC since 1988.

Tomás Pérez Turrent

(b. Mexico City, 1937) is associated with the group *Nuevo Cine,* and has worked at the Cinémathèque française. A collaborator and later correspondent for *Positif,* he has worked as a critic for *El Nacional* (1964–8), *El Día* (1968–73), *El Universal* (since 1973) and *El Semanario* (since 1982), as well as writing for *Cine, Imágenes, Dicine, Pantalla* and *International Film Guide* (since 1973). He has taught screenwriting at CUEC since 1968, and is a researcher at the Filmoteca of the UNAM (since 1982). He has written the screenplays for many films: *Canoa, Mina, viento de libertad* (Antonio Eceiza, 1976), *Las poquianchis, Lecumberri, El complot mongol, Benjamín Argumedo* (Mario Hernández, 1978), *Jubileo* (Rafael Castanedo, 1979), *Complot*

petrolero, Alsino y el condor (Miguel Littin, 1982), *Prometeo* (Walter de la Gala, 1983), *Vidas errantes, Las inocentes, Ulama, La furia de un Dios, El otro crimen* (Carlos González Morantes, 1988), *Sandino* (Littin, 1989), *Kino.* Author of *Luis Alcoriza* (1977), *El futuro nos visita* (Conacyt, 1981), *Canoa* (1984), *La fábrica de sueños* (1985), *Buster Keaton* (CIEC, 1991). He is the co-author of *Luis Buñuel: Prohibido asomarse al interior* (Joaquín Mortiz-Planeta, 1986).

Alexandra Pineda Buenaventura

(b. Cali, 1954) is a Colombian journalist who has worked for the daily *El Espectador* (Bogota, 1980–3) and Radio France Internationale (since 1984).

Aurelio de los Reyes

(b. Aguascalientes, 1942) works at the Institute for Aesthetic Research and at the Filmoteca of the UNAM. He won the Ariel award for best short film with *Cuando el cine llegó a México* (1991). Author of *Los orígenes del cine en México* (1973), *Cine y sociedad en México* (1983), *Medio siglo de cine mexicano* (1987), *Filmografía del cine mudo mexicano* (1986), *Con Villa en México* (1985), *Los caminos de la plata* (Universidad Iberoamericana, 1990), *Manuel Gamio y el cine* (1991). He is also the co-author of *80 años de cine mexicano* (1977).

Julia Tuñón Pablos

(b. Monterrey, 1948) works at the Directorate of Historical Research at the Instituto Nacional de Antropología e Historia (INAH), and is a teacher at the Universidad Autónoma Metropolitana/Iztapalapa (Mexico City). He is the author of *Historia de un sueño: El Hollywood tapatío* (1986) and *En su propio espejo (Entrevista con Emilio 'el Indio' Fernández)* (1988).

Eduardo de la Vega Alfaro

(b. Mexico City, 1954) is a researcher associated with CIEC, and has worked at the Filmoteca of the UNAM and at the Cineteca Nacional. A critic for various newspapers *(Unomásuno, La Jornada, El Nacional, El Universal, El Occidental),* he has also contributed to *Filmoteca, Cine, Imágenes, Pantalla* and *Dicine.* His published works include: *El cine de Juan Orol* (1985), *Juan Orol* (1987), *Alberto Gout* (1988), *Raúl de Anda* (1989), *La industria cinematográfica mexicana: Perfil histórico-social* (1991), *Gabriel Soria* (1992),

Arcady Boytler (1992).

Luz María Virgen Aguilar
(b. Colima, 1958) is a critic; she has also worked at the CIEC since 1986.

Ariel Zúñiga
is a film-maker and the author of *Vasos comunicantes en la obra de Roberto Gavaldón* (see the 'Film-makers' section in this volume for further details about his film career).

Index of Main Films Cited
(Parts 2 - 5 only)